THE

PAPERBOY

THE BEST ENTRY LEVEL JOB IN AMERICA

KERRY C. KACHEJIAN

F◌RTIS

TITLES DISTRIBUTED IN
North America
United Kingdom
Western Europe
South America
Australia
China
India

THE

PAPERBOY

THE BEST ENTRY LEVEL JOB IN AMERICA

KERRY C. KACHEJIAN

FORTIS

THE PAPERBOY

THE BEST ENTRY LEVEL JOB IN AMERICA

KERRY C. KACHEJIAN

ISBN 9781937592707 (HARDBACK) PRIVATE PUBLICATION (COLOR INTERIOR VERSION)

ISBN 9781937592714 (HARDBACK) COMMERCIAL PUBLICATION VERSION

PUBLISHED BY FORTIS, A NONFICTION IMPRINT FROM ADDUCENT

FORTIS

JACKSONVILLE, FLORIDA
WWW.ADDUCENTCREATIVE.COM
PRINTED IN THE UNITED STATES OF AMERICA

TABLE OF CONTENTS

ACKNOWLEDGMENTS

I had a lot of help from others while compiling all these stories. I needed to constantly check facts and make sure I was giving due credit to those who were involved in this awesome journey.

The Daily Local News (DLN)—The West Chester, Pennsylvania newspaper wrote many articles about our family after my brother Kevin's serious accident. The DLN, which I delivered six days a week, documented Kevin's long recovery, the miraculous lottery ticket that saved our house, and the unforgettable high school graduation day when he stepped out of his wheelchair and walked to get his diploma.

My family—My wife Alice and sisters Gina and Shelley helped to recount many of the family stories from the good old days. Our children, Kent, Kara, and Katie, assisted me with the editing. I'd like to particularly thank Uncle Haig Geovjian and his son, John Geovjian for illuminating much of the family's Armenian heritage. John researched much of our family's history and immigration records.

Mike Willover and Jim Gasho—My long-time friends from Henderson High School. Our teenage experience was like living in the movie *American Graffiti*. I'm glad we survived.

West Point colleagues—I spoke with a few dozen buddies to verify details of many Army stories from West Point, Airborne and Ranger training, Germany, Iraq, Afghanistan and our military service over a thirty-year period. Among them were Robert B. Abrams, Bob Carlson, John Naccarelli, Bo Dyess, Alex Gorsky, Ed Reynolds, Bob Scurlock, Rich York, Kevin Merrigan, Tim Gallagher, Margaret Williams Burcham, Joe Hajost, Jeff Irwin, Ben Bergfelt, John Proulx, Mike Bruhn, and Pete DeMarco.

Mike Hollingsworth—My long-time friend, a man of impeccable character and one of America's best kept secrets.

Walt Havenstein—Former Raytheon executive and later CEO of BAE and SAIC. I'm glad he had a sense of humor.

Mark and Carol Reynolds—Who hosted many Army-Navy games in their suite and showed deep respect to all those serving in the Armed Forces.

Honorable Paul McHale—Former Assistant Secretary of Defense for Homeland Defense who stepped out of a senior leadership position and into harm's way.

Marty Horowitz—Our former neighbor and U.S. Secret Service agent.

Gregg Zelkin—A family friend and accomplished sports photographer. Thank you for sharing your work with us.

Walter and Phebe Potthoff—The parents of high school friends Mark, Steven, Terri, and Debbie. They always treated me like another son. Thank you for visiting me during some lonely days as a Plebe at West Point.

Mikeal Staier—For his eagle eye and attention to detail, good traits he learned in the U.S. Coast Guard.

Bob Lott—A former paperboy from America's Greatest Generation. He provided great enthusiasm for this project and a detailed review of the draft version. He is a clear candidate for the Paperboy Hall of Fame.

Burke Community Church (BCC)—Pastors Marty Baker and Michael Coffey and the entire BCC Men's Ministry. They have helped me understand my faith and have been incredibly supportive of the stories I have shared.

Dennis Lowery—A great teammate who helped me edit and whose company published this book. He can do it all, and make it look easy. Thank you, my friend.

DEDICATION

To my parents, Karabed "Rocky" and Helen Kachejian. Thank you for dedicating your lives to your children. Please save us a nice spot in Heaven.

To my siblings, Gina, Shelley, and Kevin. Thanks for making my childhood such a fantastic time, and for convincing mom to spare my life on numerous occasions.

On that note...

Gina, I forgive you for spitting in my food. What else did you do to me? As for you, Shelley, I know how you really broke the rear window of our family car. It had nothing to do with playing softball. And, finally, Kevin—I can't believe we survived the homemade bomb that blew us up in our fort. My ears still hurt.

To my children, Kent, Kara, and Katie. This book is my gift to you. It contains part of your family heritage. After I am gone, you will be able to share some of these stories with future generations. I love you guys. But if you ever attempt to do any of the really dumb stunts that I did as a kid, you will be in for a whooping! ☺

To my future grandchildren, just because I got away with it doesn't mean you can too.

To my wife, Alice. I hope you enjoy these confessions. I am sure you wished I had written this book before you decided to marry me. Sorry. You can't change your mind—or me—now.

To my buddies from Henderson Senior High School. Don't tell my kids any other stories about me, or I'll hunt you down. Yeah, you too, Willover.

To anyone else, I failed to mention. Sorry. Writing a book is like making sausage. It was messy and I did the best I could.

ABOUT THE TITLE

When I was twelve years old, life was simple. Every day, I rode my bicycle to the nearby convenience store in West Chester, Pennsylvania and picked up my bundle of newspapers. Six times a week, I would deliver forty-four copies of The Daily Local News. Each paper sold for a dime, earning me three cents. Every week I collected sixty cents per house, and for my diligent efforts, I made $1.32 per day, $7.92 per week. The paper route was a cash business. And though I wasn't sure what taxes were, I proudly paid them. Dental and healthcare were benefits not afforded to me. The money I made was deposited into an old coffee can because that was what I was taught to do: put it in a safe place. Life was good, and in the years ahead I never imagined leaving my hometown to experience anything bigger or better. I didn't know that those years, in what seemed a far distant future, would become the beginning of an amazing journey.

This journey, at times, has been incredible, and it seems the decades have flown by. The role I played varied broadly and was analogous to a football game. Sometimes I was the quarterback, responsible for executing the play. Other times, I was the coach on the sidelines, helping to select the right play to be called. Often, I was simply a spectator in the stands, cheering on my family and friends.

I have lived in or traveled to 60 countries and 45 states. I've escorted American hostages returning home from Iran, served on a State Funeral detail for General of the Army, Omar Bradley, witnessed the 9/11 attack on the Pentagon, served in two wars, signed the steel at the top of the new World Trade Center, raced Porsches on the track and autobahn, explored underground bunkers in Iraq, met the President of the United States in China and once, even stood in as part of a murder lineup. I have parachuted from planes, passed the Army's grueling Ranger Course, become an expert in explosives, been trained to use small nuclear weapons, survived truck bombs and rocket attacks. I am honored to have served our nation in uniform for 34 years, while simultaneously serving in the defense and intelligence industries with great organizations like GE Aerospace, DARPA, Raytheon, and Harris. After graduating from college, I went on to receive two master's degrees, all the while never paying a cent for my education. In most cases, I was paid a salary to do all of it. In retrospect, I might have given Forrest Gump a run for his money (I ask my family reading this to please not chant, "Run Kerry, Run!"). I mean, I even learned how to distinguish red wine from the white stuff! How could life possibly be any better? How could all of these incredible experiences happen to a simple paperboy?

Most importantly, I discovered that God does exist. Through the years, I have been truly blessed in many ways. One of which is my family. I've seen much good and evil in the world and, as many people have, tragedy has touched my family. I saw my younger brother paralyzed in a horrible bicycle accident. To pay for medical bills, my family put our house up for sale. Miraculously, my father won the lottery just in time to save it. I can also say, with confidence, that no one has ever had more fun with a paralyzed kid. We played some of the best practical jokes that shocked the hell out of anyone nearby. Years later, in one of my proudest moments for my brother, I watched him stand from his wheelchair, and walk up to the stage to receive his high school diploma.

I can still remember being a determined twelve-year-old kid who would ride hard and fast—legs pumping—through the neighborhood, in spite of the large, heavy bag of newspapers that encumbered me. Often, I wore a muscle shirt in an attempt to catch the eyes of the girls in junior high. I steered my banana-seated bike with one hand and opened mailboxes with the other; this was, of course, before it was a federal crime to open a mailbox. I was the most respected twelve-year-old in the neighborhood. Adults would anxiously await my arrival to see what fantastic news I lugged around in that giant, loaded bag.

I was proud of my job and performed it well. I was more than just a paperboy. To my neighbors and friends, I was *the* paperboy.

IN THE BEGINNING
-FOREWORD-

Being a paperboy prepared me for a future career in the military and in industry. I learned both leadership and business skills and owned total profit or loss responsibility. It was my first big break in corporate America and a real resume builder, providing me early executive experience in some key corporate roles.

First of all, as the Chief Operating Officer, I was expected to run day-to-day operations. That meant delivering my product early, regardless of inclement weather and Little League football schedule conflicts. As a trained and dedicated professional, the mission always came first. I took pride in delivering the newspaper to every home on my route before the postman had arrived; yet another triumph of the private sector over government institutions. The mailman faced daily humiliation at the hands of a twelve-year-old paperboy.

I was also Corporate Lead for Business Development and Strategy; I sought new customers for my route. Each new client was worth three cents of additional, personal, revenue per day: three pieces of penny candy ripe for the taking. The stakes and rewards were high: Bazooka bubble gum, Caramel Cremes, jaw breakers and the like. Only limited by my available cash on hand, it was all within my grasp.

Additionally, I collected competitive intelligence about other paperboys that were operating in my territory. The competing newspaper, *The Philadelphia Inquirer*, also delivered in my neighborhood, posed a direct threat to my market share. I needed to protect my turf.

One of the most critical roles, Chief Finance Officer and Controller, required that I keep records of the accounts receivable. Collections happened door to door, and I spent four hours each Saturday visiting all the houses on my route so I could pay both the Daily Local News and myself. Many of the neighbors weren't home. Some didn't have any change and asked me to put it on their account. So, a 12-year old paperboy extended credit to adult customers on an honor policy. I wrestled with important questions: Did I really need to collect each week (one customer actually wrote me a sixty cent check every week requiring a special trip to the bank to cash it), or could I modify my payment terms to bi-weekly and better leverage my time?

As the Customer Relations Manager, I had to remain professional and not laugh at the adults that came to the door in their underwear and slippers. I pretended not to hear the family arguments that I interrupted by ringing the doorbell. I patiently stood at the front door for ten minutes, while my customer desperately searched in the sofa and the laundry basket for the sixty cents they owed me. I received a verbal reprimand for occasionally delivering papers late when my bicycle broke or after football practice. Occasionally, my family was on the front page of the newspaper, and I would politely answer questions about my paralyzed brother and our family situation.

I was also the Supply Chain VP responsible for logistics. The bag (its loading and unloading), the bike and the delivery of product all had to seamlessly come together to complete the mission.

Later, I stepped into the shoes of HR Director. After conducting an extensive interview process, my sister, Shelley, was recruited to deliver the papers when I was at football practice. She was a temporary hire, but I offered her full-time pay and benefits.

From a young age, I prided myself as a captain of industry and continued to learn about hard work and to feel the satisfaction of earning a paycheck. Experimenting with different jobs, I began to work my way up the corporate food chain. After completing a two-year tour as a paperboy, I set out on for new ventures. By the time I was 17, my resume was diversified with some memorable jobs.

My time spent networking as a paperboy led to an exciting new career mowing lawns. One of my best paper customers paid an incredible $8 per lawn cut. I wanted to cut that lawn every day, but his house was near the woods, in a shady area, and the grass grew too slowly. This particular business also taught me about working with partners and investors; when my dad learned I was using his lawnmower and gasoline, he wanted a cut of my revenues.

Speaking of lawn care, I quickly learned I could expand my services into new markets. I picked dandelion flowers and sold them by the bucket to my sixth-grade math teacher, Bob Reber. He would pay fifty cents for a half gallon (several hundred flowers were needed to fill each container). Upon being handed that pot chock-full of weeds, Mr. Reber would then disappear into his basement to brew his famous dandelion wine. Yes, there was good money in those weeds.

In addition to supplying the raw materials to brew moonshine, I ventured into the food preparation industry, in two different delicatessens making hoagie sandwiches. My first deli job was at "The Little Store" on Boot Road, a convenience store run by the Baldino family. A fast-paced environment with high-quality standards, working at the deli was demanding, but the people and the work were both fun. Paid two dollars an hour, I was also allowed to eat any sandwich I could make. Every day, I took full advantage of this benefit and consumed a massive Philly cheese steak and a pound of French fries. It was an awesome job for a high school football player who was always hungry.

The other deli job paid an additional twenty-five cents an hour. There I learned some valuable business management lessons: Where you work and who you work for are major factors in job satisfaction, and not all employers and employment are equal. At this deli job, I soon learned that the management and benefits were poor. I was charged for any food I ate and would work all day on the weekends, skipping meals. The guy that owned the store was a shady character. He was found collapsed in the parking lot one day while his store was burning. Local authorities suspected that he set the business on fire for the insurance money.

Speaking of heat, my former junior high school football coach, Mr. John Thompson, hired me to help him roof houses one summer. His younger brother, Bill, joined us. I was the rookie on the team, and I had to haul heavy stacks of shingles up a ladder and onto a blazing hot roof. There were no nail guns on the job; each nail had to be driven by hand. The heat, the sweat constantly stinging my eyes... it was hard work. I felt bad when I made some mistakes aligning the shingles, but Mr. Thompson quickly forgave me and fixed them. I will always appreciate that opportunity and respect him for teaching me how hard some men work to earn a living.

One of my most unique jobs was a one-time gig that paid ten dollars. I volunteered to stand in a murder line up. It was an interesting learning experience, and I will share more about this story in a later chapter. You don't want to miss that one.

Occasionally, I was hired by my neighbor, Mr. Horace Wright, who was a store manager at the local Shop-Rite. My job was to patrol the parking lot in search of any abandoned shopping carts. For capturing said wayward carts and returning them to the store, I made a whopping $3.25 an hour! I felt incredibly well paid, so much so that I felt compelled to give some of it back. Twenty years later, I was surprised and delighted to find that Mr. Wright's daughter, Rene, was a senior nurse at Fairfax Hospital in Virginia, and she helped to deliver our first daughter, Kara.

The summer before my senior year in high school, I had a full-time job cleaning up debris: scrap lumber, carpet remnants, nails, rocks, broken glass and electrical wiring, on a construction site for new homes. Provided with an old pickup truck and work gloves, I made $3.50 per hour, and my weekly paycheck came to about $140 before taxes. I felt a sense of gratification seeing the new houses go up, becoming more complete each day, as they were built and sold. One day a man approached me about another job in construction. He wanted to hire me to wire all the houses and offered to pay me $100 per house. I declined. I had no electrical training—not the faintest idea where the wires needed to run—and no tools. To top it off, he was not even going to supervise my work. It was a perfect recipe for disaster. Wiring was a serious job, requiring experience and qualifications. The guy simply did not care. He just wanted to dump the work on me, despite my inability to do it properly. He kept insisting, and I kept declining. I'm proud that I stuck to my guns.

Granted, work wasn't everything during this time. But it did fill the void between school and playing sports. This was long before time occupiers like mobile phones, cable TV or Facebook and the Internet were available. Fortunately, I found a good balance between being a student, an athlete, and a teenage worker. Despite my family's limited resources and special duties tending to the needs of my paralyzed brother, my parents still allowed me to wrestle as well as play baseball and football. Somewhere along the way, I also picked up a lacrosse stick and became a decent player.

These early experiences all came together my senior year of high school when I received an offer of admission to the United States Military Academy at West Point. My life was on the cusp of taking an incredible turn. It was an opportunity that transformed my life, revealing a future that this paperboy never thought was possible.

SECTION 1

DAD & MOM

CHAPTER 1
ARAM AND ROCKY (DAD)

My father, Karabed (Rocky), was born in the United States to Armenian immigrants, Aram and Regina Kachejian. Fleeing Armenia from a mass genocide, my grandparents' journey to America was remarkable. It would be a crime if no one took the time to preserve their stories.

Starting April 24, 1915, through 1917, the Ottoman Empire systematically murdered upwards of 1.5 million Armenians, wiping out entire villages and driving refugees to countries around the globe. Well-documented by American diplomats and newspapers at the time, the plight of the "starving Armenians" received significant public attention. I heard several brief accounts of events involving our family during this period, but much of the oral history has faded over the decades. Here's what I know:

In the midst of the conflict, Aram was conscripted into the Ottoman horse cavalry, where he was used as a translator. He would learn of imminent plans the Ottoman's had for destroying Armenian villages, and he secretly warned many of his fellow Armenians to escape before the next attack. When the Ottomans became suspicious of his actions, Aram fled the country and made his way to the United States.

Portrait of Aram and Regina Kachejian *(found this charcoal portrait of Aram and Regina in the attic and had it restored)*

According to records at Ellis Island, my grandfather, Aram Kachejian, and his sister, Shahanik Kachejian, arrived in New York City on 2 November 1920. He was 26, and she was 18 years old. Aram and Shahnik's last name was originally spelled Chyackejian but later changed to Kachejian. Parnag Geovjian, a friend of my grandfather, came to America three years earlier, and after settling in, sent a message back to Armenia to "send a wife." This was well before the era of social media and online dating services, so the word moved slowly. He wasted no time in marrying Shahanik soon after her arrival.

The actions and exploits of Aram before he came to the United States painted him as an Armenian mixture of Nathan Hale and Paul Revere. How our grandfather made his living in America, however, was not quite as gallant or celebrated. Aram's future wife, Regenti (Regina) Hagopian arrived in the United States on September 1, 1921, at the age of 20. With Parnag's help, Aram opened a shoe repair shop in Philadelphia and later opened another in Media, Pennsylvania.

Penniless yet hardworking, he and Regina had five children, the third of which they named Garabed, the Armenian equivalent of Charles. Unfortunately, their poor knowledge of English resulted in difficulty communicating with the hospital staff, and the birth record misspelled my father's name. Despite attempts to correct it, Regina and Aram became resigned to the fact that their son would live the rest of his life as "Karabed." However, my father's childhood friends called him Charlie. The other four Kachejian children were Elsie (Adrina), Alex, George and Edward (Eddie).

We knew Aram as "PopPop." He loved playing cards and would come home after a game and pull out $1 bills and iron them on the table with his hand. He once pulled out a silver dollar and gave it to one of the children. We thought he was a rich man.

English as a Second Language

Aram wasn't the only one struggling to learn English in their new country. Parnag had challenges too. He was in a horse and buggy and had an accident with a truck. When he went to court, the judge asked Parnag if he was an American citizen. A bit confused, Parnag replied, "No, but my horse is."

On another occasion, Parnag needed eggs from the local grocery store. He could not find them, and the owner asked him what he was looking for. Parnag picked up a small potato, held it behind his rear end and said, "Cluck,

Cluck Cluck." The storekeeper went to the back of the store and brought him out some fresh eggs.

Rocky & Haig

Dad's cousin (a bit of a misnomer since they were more like brothers), Haig Geovjian, Parnag's son, lived in Philly where his family had also started a shoe repair business on Willows Avenue. Haig was a city kid, but in the summers, he lived with his cousin Charlie on State Street in Media.

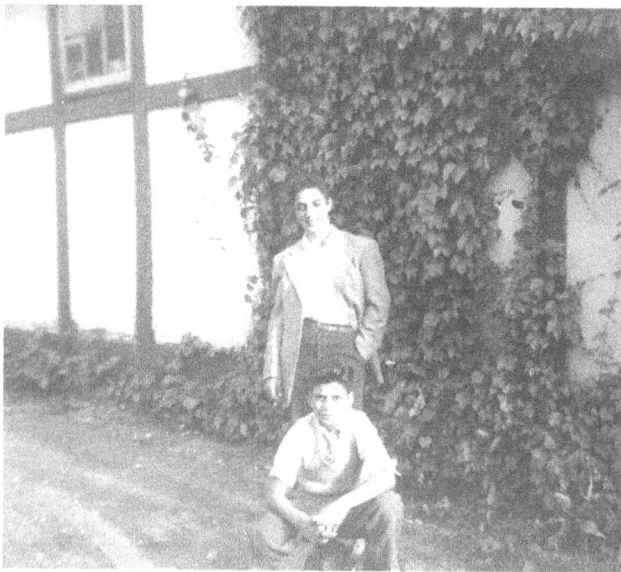

Rocky Kachejian (standing) and Haig Geovjian (kneeling)

As a boy, my father liked to fish, build gas-powered model airplanes and play in Lawrence Park. As a teenager, he reminded people of the famous professional boxer, Rocky Marciano. And that's why everyone began to call him 'Rocky.' Ironically, the real fighter in the family was Haig; an excellent amateur with a record of 13-1. His one boxing loss was to Frankie Sodano, who wound up representing the United States in the 1948 Olympics. Haig told me how he learned to fight as a young boy. The son of immigrants, with an olive complexion and funny sounding name, the bullies in the neighborhood would pick on him. It did not turn out well for them. Young Haig soon outfought his weight class in the neighborhood.

I remember visiting Grandfather Aram's shoe repair shop and the home where Rocky grew up. The smell of fresh leather permeated the store, and the workshop area always had a pile of rawhide shavings scattered across the floor. I would watch with curiosity as my grandparents re-soled shoes, carefully cutting and shaping the thick leather. Sadly, few of the neighborhood shoe repair shops from that era survive today, as it is more convenient to simply buy a new pair. After that generation passed away, I saved some of the old shop tools and leather pieces as part of the family heritage. As a product of "America's Greatest Generation," Rocky worked hard, sought little personal credit and, other than love and respect, expected little in return. He was slow to anger and rarely swore. Though we did not regularly attend church, he taught his kids many Bible stories. Dad was not only our mentor but also our Go-To-Guy to get us out of trouble. Whenever one of his children broke something, he would immediately drop everything and fix it before mom had the opportunity to discover the damage.

I had a great relationship with dad, and regret he died before I was able to spend a good portion of my adult years with him. Although I wish I had more time with him, I count myself fortunate. Dad was everything a son could ask for in his father, and he left me with quite a few memories. Here are some of my favorite ones:

Lamb Chops

When dad was a little boy, his father, "Pop," brought home a little lamb. The five Kachejian kids played all day with the little fellow and adopted him as their pet. But this was during the Great Depression, and Pop had a different plan in mind. A few days later, the lamb went missing. The kids were devastated. Pop tried to cheer them up by serving a rare treat for dinner that evening, Shish Kabob. It didn't work. Seeing the plate of prepared food, the kids then knew what fate befell the little lamb, and Pop ate alone.

Good Tread

My dad never talked much about his youth. Growing up in the depression, he learned at a young age how to make ends meet. He never threw anything away, a habit which persisted his entire life.

He and his cousin, Haig, would collect scrap metal and lumps of coal and re-sell them to make a little change. Old tires were a major find—they could be sold to a re-tread shop. Dad's attraction to old tires carried on for decades. When I was in high school, dad used to stop the car on a highway to run over and pick up old tires lying near the side of the road. You could always tell which route dad used to drive to work, as it was the only one picked clean of old tires. He'd always say, "It had good rubber" and act like he'd hit the lottery. Using them to trade with his colleagues, he stored scores of old tires in our backyard shed and in the crawl space under our house. Not one of them fit any of our cars, but they all had plenty of tread.

Car Collecting

Speaking of cars, dad could never get rid of them either. At one point, we owned seven, and they were all parked in the front yard. On any given day, about three of these cars would start. My family was the primary reason Homeowner Associations became popular in the United States. Despite being immobile, there is one good thing about having cars that won't start—they never get stolen either. All of them were at least ten years old. One—the queen of them all—was a twenty-five-year-old yellow car with a red roof which we called "Eloise." She looked like a taxi cab from the early 1950s. We thought she was pretty cool.

Old Eloise

We also had two convertibles, real status symbols. The flagship of the Kachejian fleet was a white 1967 Plymouth Fury convertible. We painted over the major rust stains, so from a distance, the car looked pretty good. The size of an Army tank, it was a gas guzzler, but back then fuel was cheap. The other luxury vehicle was a dilapidated black 1963 convertible with a ragtop roof that dad bought for one hundred dollars. He called it a "pervertible," later explaining that a pervertible is a car where "the top won't go down, but the driver will." Dad was a master of the one-liner jokes. He brought it home, painted it with a can of black spray paint, and then touched it up with a 4-inch paint brush. Despite the new paint job, the car looked awful, and the roof never opened properly. My sister, Shelley, broke the rear window glass one day when she was trying to put the top down with Amy Stapleford. She later lied to my parents and told them a neighbor broke it with a baseball. Sorry Shelley, but it's time to confess.

A master of getting his money's worth, dad never changed the oil in a car. He would just add more once it got a couple of quarts low. He felt he was saving a lot of money by never changing the oil or air filters. Another part of his rationale was that as the oil got thicker, it would have a harder time leaking out the seals. Logically, we never needed to change the seals in the engine either.

The Heisman

Rocky Kachejian - Philadelphia Armenian Football League

11

Rocky was an excellent athlete in high school. He did not mention much to his children about his achievements, but I learned about his skills from some of his friends, brothers, and cousins. Baseball and football were his two favorite sports. Back in the day, wearing a facemask in football was a luxury reserved for the wealthy, wimpy kids. Consequently, dad broke his nose several times. Gina and I found an old picture of him (#32) playing football for the Philadelphia Armenian Football League. The image captures a rare glimpse of Rocky Kachejian in his Heisman Trophy pose.

Once Rocky became a father, he coached teams for my brother and me in Little League baseball and the Little All-American Football Association. A big advocate of sportsmanship, he never failed to inspire his players to play honorably and never quit until the final whistle blew. During one football game, dad's team of 12-year-olds was winning 28-0 in the third quarter. Not wanting to run the score up any further, he told his team to punt on 1st down. Despite the loud objections of one parent, his decision was widely respected throughout the league.

Army Duty

After completing high school, Rocky served in the Merchant Marine for six years. To pass the time while cruising to and from South America, dad played cards, and he and won a bit of money. After he left the Merchant Marines, he saved enough money to pay cash for a new car, with thirty-two $100 bills, and to open a bar and restaurant, The Nu Studio Lounge located on Market Street in West Chester, Pennsylvania. Gradually, the place grew in popularity, and even some notable sports stars from the Philadelphia Eagles would frequent it. Things got a little out of hand, once, when some of the Eagles football players started driving a mini-bike through the bar.

Life was good for a year or so, but at the age of 26, dad unexpectedly received his draft notice. Reporting for duty in the Army, he was forced to leave his blossoming enterprise in the hands of his partner, who would get drunk and fall asleep at the bar. Patrons would then serve themselves without paying, which led to the death of his prosperous business.

When dad completed his military service in 1957, he returned home to find that he had lost his entire investment. A very bad thing. But something good did happen around that time: in the mid-1950s he had met Helen Browne, and they married about a year later.

After leaving the Army and settling down, he restarted his career in the restaurant business. Over the course of the next five years, Rocky and Helen had four children together: Gina, Shelley, me and Kevin.

That Ain't Coke

In the early 1960s, dad managed a restaurant, The Drummer's Table, and worked extended hours. Coming home from work late one evening, he brought a few steaks back with him - hoping for a nice, quiet dinner with mom.

Before starting the grill, he decided to make a couple of martinis for them both. Unable to find a suitable container to mix the cocktails in, he used two empty Coke bottles, shaking and placing them in the refrigerator to chill. After lighting the coals, he went upstairs to change out of his work clothes. After he was comfortable, he returned to the grill to start the steaks.

What dad didn't know is that while he was upstairs, Shelley, my four-year-old sister, strolled into the kitchen looking for a drink. In the refrigerator, she had spied something tantalizing—a Coke bottle (this was back when a Coca-Cola was a special treat)—and without asking, gulped down the contents. She emptied the bottle, not noticing that it tasted different.

When my parents found Shelley rolling around on the kitchen floor next to an empty Coke bottle, they figured out what happened. Immediately calling the doctor, my mother was advised to put Shelley in her bedroom where she would eventually sleep it off. And sleep she did. For two days.

For any shocked readers wanting to charge either Helen or Rocky Kachejian with child endangerment, let me put forth a few mitigating circumstances. First and foremost, this story is now over 50 years old. Not only are my parents dead, but surely the statute of limitations has long expired. Second, Shelley is not complaining. So just laugh about it. It could happen to your kid next.

Bowling for Fries

Some days during the summer, I would go to work with dad at The Drummer's Table and earn a small paycheck. My specialty was washing dishes and making the French fries. I made 25 cents an hour and got to eat all the fries I wanted. When I took my breaks, I went to the bowling alley next door with my earnings to play a game. At the end of the day, I almost never came home with any money, but I was always happily full of carbohydrates.

Busted

Although we lived in Pennsylvania, my dad's restaurant was in Price's Corner, Delaware. For nineteen years, he worked six days a week managing the business. Dad commuted an hour each way, and worked extended hours from open to close, without exception. Additionally, he spent an entire Sunday each month conducting an inventory of the restaurant supplies. Watching him work so much convinced me to stay away from the restaurant business.

Since my dad was responsible for the entire restaurant, each night he would take the restaurant receipts to deposit at the local bank. It was usually dark, and dad made the trip in his car alone—save for his 7.65cal CZ pistol.

One night in 1968, mom got a call from dad. He was being detained at a police station in Delaware. It all had started when dad closed his restaurant that evening. In the late 1960s, before credit cards were widely used, most of the daily receipts were cash. At closing, dad put the day's receipts into a bank bag and headed to the local bank drop box for a night deposit. He left the restaurant and before getting to the bank was pulled over by a police officer, who asked for his identification. His car was similar to one that was involved in a recent string of robberies.

When the police found a bag of money and a handgun in the car, they were fairly convinced that they had their man. Dad was then promptly hauled off to jail where he made his one phone call home. It took several hours to sort it all out—his long day made even longer—but dad's story eventually checked out. He did run a restaurant and was making a regular bank deposit; not an armed withdrawal. But I don't think dad ever took that gun with him again. It was more trouble than he bargained for.

WWII Stories

Dad was only fifteen years old when the war ended, so he was too young to serve. But he was the president of the Mills Creek Lion's Club in Delaware, and several of his colleagues were veterans of WWII. Two of his good buddies,

14

Jack Hager and Harry Cook, would tell many stories that got better every time we heard them.

One of them involved the island-hopping campaign in the Pacific where the U.S. was taking back islands from the Japanese. As the story goes, the island was mostly secure, so Harry Cook took a Patrol Torpedo (PT) boat out to catch some fresh fish. Unfortunately, fishing rods were in short supply in the Pacific. So instead, Harry, an innovator by nature, decided to use a more readily available device to catch breakfast. Hand grenades. The grenades going off too close the side, of course, severely damaged the PT boat, and it ended up sinking in shallow water.

When Harry's Commanding Officer learned about the incident, Harry was told he was going to be court-martialed. The Commander said the only way he could avoid punishment was to replace the boat. Taking the CO at his word, Harry snuck over to the Japanese-held side of the island and stole a boat. The CO kept his word, and Harry kept his fish. No one but Harry Cook knows if that story was really true, but he certainly told it with conviction.

Monday Night Football

Monday Night Football was a new phenomenon in America in the 1970s. Howard Cosell, Dandy Don Meredith, and Frank Gifford would be on live TV each week, covering the big game.

Some of the regular customers at dad's restaurant, The Drummer's Table, were real characters, and they created a new tradition. Each week, a different person in the group would host the Monday night game at their home and buy an old TV for the party.

The group loved watching the game, but Howard Cosell was a lawyer that had never actually played football—they hated hearing him comment on the game. That didn't stop Howard from talking big and boisterously about the players and the game itself. People either loved or hated him. Dad's restaurant patrons were in the latter group.

The highlight of these Monday night events was at the conclusion of the game when Howard would make some closing remarks. At this point, the weekly host would stand up in front of the TV and say, "Goodnight Howard." The host would then pull out a pistol and have the honor of shooting the TV while Cosell was jabbering away. The TV tube would implode, and Howard would finally shut up.

I am not sure how long the tradition lasted or whether my dad actually attended one of these Monday night events. I know that he didn't host one at our house—my mother would have taken the pistol and whipped those guys with it. I do think, however, that dad made money supplying the old TVs to them, which explained why my dad always kept seven old black & white TVs in our house.

Scam Artist

There were about a dozen, kind-hearted, blue collar patrons who gathered at The Drummer's Table each day at Happy Hour looking for a cold beer and some good stories. One day a new guy came into the bar. We'll call him "Bob." He ordered a beer and started chatting and getting to meet some of the regulars, who soon learned that Bob was a business traveler on the road. After about half an hour, the phone in the bar rang, and the barmaid picked it up. There was a panicked caller on the other line who urgently needed to talk to Bob, as his wife had just been killed in a car accident. The barmaid handed the phone to Bob and keeping her voice low, told the patrons at the bar about the call and terrible news he was receiving. The idle chatter between them stopped as they watched Bob. He hung up, and the shock and grief were visible on his face as he turned to them, "I need... I need to get home to my children! But I don't have money for the airfare." He looked at them, his face showing he was close to tears. "I don't know what to do!"

The response from the patrons was overwhelming. Everyone chipped in and gave Bob a pile of cash so he could quickly get back home. The man needed to be with his children. It was a sobering night. The following day, the regular patrons learned that Bob had pulled the same scam in several nearby bars and restaurants. They had all been duped, and Bob was now a marked man. About a decade later, "Bob" came back to The Drummer's Table and tried the same stunt. Some of the same patrons immediately recognized the scam and alerted the police, who later arrested the jerk.

Gravity

Every few years, the exterior of our house would need to be repainted. One year, after a particularly rough winter, the wooden siding was in pretty bad shape. Dad only had one week of vacation each year and did not have any paid sick days. So, he took his week of vacation in the summer and spent much of it on a ladder, working his way around the house with a paint brush and bucket. It didn't seem to bother him as he had served in the Merchant Marines, spending some of that time painting and maintaining the ships.

Dad liked to have a cold beer with him while painting to help pass the time. To facilitate that, he fashioned a small chain that hung around his neck with a metal clasp that could hold a beer, dangling on his chest, to keep his hands free.

Every few feet, dad would climb down the ladder and move it over to the next spot. Up, down and around the outside of the house, this routine went on for several days. Finally, dad was approaching the completion of the second coat and the end of the week-long job. From the top of the ladder, he saw a spot to his left that needed a bit more work. Too tired to climb down and move the ladder again, dad went for a long final stretch. Reaching as far as he could to put the final touch of paint on the house, the predictable happened. Suddenly, with no warning, the ladder kicked out from under him.

The next few seconds were like that classic scene from the Road Runner cartoons when the Coyote runs off the cliff. Dad defied gravity for a few milliseconds, but thinking quickly and using his lightning fast reflexes, dad stabbed his paintbrush into the wall of the house. In this last act of desperation, he somehow hoped that the paint would instantly dry, and the brush would stay glued to the second floor.

His best efforts failed, however, and dad came streaking down the front of the house leaving a white brush stroke on the brick face. History recorded the moment as that white paint streak plunged to the ground, and poor dad hit the concrete sidewalk with a loud cracking sound. "OUCH!" Dad was in pain. He hurt his leg badly, but he knew we had no money to pay for a hospital visit. He did the next best thing. Hopping into the house on his good leg, he got a cold beer out of the refrigerator to put out the fire of pain in his leg. As he sat in his recliner to watch a football game, the realization set in that his leg was undeniably broken. The swelling got progressively worse and, when the game was over, he did the unthinkable; dad actually went to the hospital emergency room. That's when we knew the injury was pretty serious.

We moved out of that house a few years later, and that white streak on the brick was visible for another decade. Although he might not have been particularly fond of its memory, it turned out to be his best stroke.

Picnics

During the summer, mostly on Sundays, mom and dad would host a picnic in the backyard. The biggest of these was on the 4th of July, which took days of preparation. An hour or so after noon, several cars would pull up to the curb outside our house. From them poured about a dozen people, claiming to be our relatives, who would then begin to eat our food and drink our beer.

The Bartley and Morgan families always joined us. Tab Bartley was my Little League coach. He and my brother Kevin shared the 4th of July as their birthday. Dave and LaRue Morgan, long-time friends of ours, often gave Kevin a great birthday gift; a day at a Philadelphia Phillies game. Dave always came to the picnic armed with new jokes that we called the "dirty dozen."

The adults would play cards and tell stories about the old country. Sometimes, Mr. Tancini would shock us kids by pulling out his dentures at the picnic table; he'd hold them in his hand and convince us that they could still bite. There was a rumor he might also pull out a fake eye.

To escape the heat, the kids would jump in the pool and play Marco Polo. Another favorite activity was running around the yard, spitting watermelon seeds at each other until we all collapsed. We played horseshoes (Tab Bartley was the King of the Horseshoe Pit), softball, started crab apple fights and usually capped it off with a game of Smear the Queer. I loved those days—long before cable TV and the Internet.

*Rocky Kachejian with Gina and Rocky "Batman" Kachejian
sends the Bat Signal with Kevin*

At one picnic on West Bernard Street, a swarm of bees was in the area and swooped past us. The bees zooming by reminded dad of his baseball days at Media High School; the swarm flew like some of the curve balls and sliders he had faced at the plate. Inspired, he jumped up and grabbed my plastic baseball bat. Creating a batter's box, he started to show off his batting skills in the backyard by knocking Bumble bees over the fence and into the Bartley's yard.

Haig Geovjian—Fast Forward

Haig was also once a paperboy. He and his brother John delivered Jewish newspapers once a week on the weekends. Later, Haig went on to serve in the Army during the Korean War. He scored well on aptitude tests and took full advantage of technical training related to setting up secure communications. One of his skills was teletype cryptologic repair. He left the Army in 1954 and went to work for Remington Rand. In 1970, he then set up his own business. He and his wife Barbara raised three children: John, Beth, and Patty.

Ironically, John was also a paperboy. There must be a genetic predisposition in our family to sling newspapers. John delivered the Philadelphia Evening and Sunday BULLETIN paper after school from 1974 to 1977. Beth and Patty filled in on the weekends when John had camping trips with the Boy Scouts. As evidence of his dedicated service, John offered this photo of his old paperboy bag.

I came to know my dad's cousin as "Uncle Haig." Along the way, he also became "Hollywood Haig" having served in several roles as an extra in the TV series Hack and the movie Jersey Girl. He had to re-cut a scene climbing a stairwell 23 times. His granddaughter, Faylyn, was an infant actress in the movie "Unbreakable." For decades, Uncle Haig was very involved in his church men's group. He has a prayer, which he adapted from an old (James Stewart) movie. I keep it in my wallet. Uncle Haig Geovjian's Prayer:

> Thank you, Father, for Thy care,
> For Thy bounty everywhere,
> For this and every other gift,
> Our grateful hearts to Thee we lift.
> And thank you, Lord, for giving us another day,
> Where we can say "Amen."

CHAPTER 2

MOM

While my father brought Armenian heritage to the family, my mother descended from a long line of English, Irish, and Scottish peoples. Even though these three groups spent several centuries killing each other, my maternal ancestors somehow managed to survive, intermarry and migrate to America in the mid-1800s.

My grandmother, Janet Kift, married Thomas Browne and my mother, Helen Kift Browne, was born and grew up in West Chester, Pennsylvania in the 1930s. The Depression was a tough time for many families in America, but the Kift's were better off than most, owning several houses and a prosperous floral business. The Kift family also had a connection to American history. Their main home, nicknamed "Rest Cottage," had been used as a stopping point for slaves escaping from the South and part of the Underground Railroad during the Civil War.

Although the family was more fortunate than many others, they were not left untouched by misfortune. Three members of the Browne family died in the worldwide influenza pandemic of 1918 that claimed up to fifty million lives. That outbreak killed far more people than the sixteen million lives lost during World War I. Decades later, when Thomas Browne, eventually succumbed to a lengthy and costly illness, the family lost their income and was forced to sell everything to pay for his medical bills. The people of that generation simply accepted their situation and made the best of it. They moved into a small townhouse and to make ends meet, mom worked in a deli as a young girl, while her mother worked in the Post Office.

Helen Browne (Kachejian)

In 1956, Helen met her hero, Rocky Kachejian, in the Aztec Lounge. They were soon married and raising four children. Despite all the chaos my sisters, brother and I created, she somehow managed to keep us all on a straight path.

Famous Relatives

When we were young, my mother told us about some of our famous relatives. And since our concept of fame was rather simple, we were easily impressed. If you were interviewed on the radio or were mentioned in the local newspaper, you were famous. But mom also told us of the real rock stars in our family. First, we were descendants of Nathan Kift, who worked at the Royal Botanic Gardens in Edinburgh, Scotland. His son, Joseph Kift, immigrated to New York in 1848-1849, where he started a family in West Chester and opened Kift's Flower shop. He imported lilies from Bermuda and marketed them as "Easter Lilies." They were a hit, and the flowers soon became an American tradition; the business at Kift's Flower Shop in West Chester boomed.

Joseph Kift (in the doorway) circa 1890

Joseph was also a leading advocate for establishing "Mother's Day" as a national holiday. I am sure he had two motives for supporting this new holiday: to honor his mother as well as to increase sales at his floral shop.

One of Joseph's decedents, Jane Leslie Kift, wrote daily gardening articles that were widely read in newspapers in the United States and Canada. She authored two books: A *Woman's Flower Garden, Indoor and Outdoor* (1928) and *Success with House Plants* (1932). She was our family's first publish author.

Another family rock star was William Browne, a.k.a. "Uncle Will" who was credited as being the third Caucasian man to cross the Florida Everglades on foot across the Tamiami Trail, a path originally blazed by Native Americans. In the early 1900s, the Everglades were the final frontier in South Florida. When mom told the story, the achievement sounded like the equivalent of climbing Mount Everest or rivaling Neil Armstrong's Apollo 11 moon walk. We clearly had a great explorer in our family. I never dared to raise the question, "Why did he attempt to cross the Everglades on foot? Was he lost?" Uncle Will eventually made his home in Tampa and opened a successful dog race track.

Mom also made us aware of family connections with Hollywood. Her second cousin once dated or was engaged to an actress on the TV show *Flipper*. Flipper was a popular bottlenose dolphin that starred in a television show in the mid-1960s. Sadly, the phone call inviting us to Hollywood never came. The couple split up, so my siblings and I were never given a chance to meet the actress or Flipper in person.

I did, however, get to meet one family rock star as a young boy: George Kachejian, my father's brother, was both a beer distributor and notary public in Conshohocken, Pennsylvania. At the time, I wasn't sure what a notary public was, but Uncle George could sign a bunch of official documents and buy a case of Ortlieb's beer (16-ounce cans) for only $1.65. All in a single day. That was a powerful man, both politically and economically.

Ouch (many times)

Mom was prone to accidents, but she rarely complained. As a teenager, working in the deli shop, she cut off the tip of her finger. Meat slicers work on all types of meat: chicken, beef, pork (the other white meat) and human fingers. Not wanting to miss work, mom quickly put the dime size piece of finger back in place and bandaged it. In her haste, the fingerprints were not aligned properly, and the severed tip healed crooked. It was after this incident that my mother abandoned any future prospects of a life of crime; she would have been an easy match in the FBI fingerprint database.

The unfortunate incident involving the meat slicer was not to be the last of the injuries my mother's hands would suffer. Years later, in 1970, our family cat, Ebenezer, was chased up a tree by a neighbor's dog. The tree was fairly tall and sat in a field across from our house. Mom dragged our metal extension ladder across the street and set it up. Our neighbor, Mr. Eichey, saw mom about to scale the ladder and offered to go up it instead. Gladly accepting his offer, she remained on the ground to steady the ladder while Mr. Eichey began the climb. They didn't know the ladder was not locked into the extended position; the safety latch was not proper engaged. Mr. Eichey had climbed about ten feet up when the top half of the ladder suddenly slid back down driven by the weight of a 170-pound man. Keeping hold of the ladder, mom was sliced across her left hand, causing severe damage. She spent about a year in physical therapy trying to get better use out of her hand. I remember she never complained while working one-handed for many months as the cashier at the Fern Hill Elementary School cafeteria.

The string of accidents which mom lived through is more storied than that, though. When she first started driving, she was in a severe head-on crash. The engine of her car was shoved back into the passenger compartment. Because she was not wearing a seatbelt, she was thrown aside and not crushed by the engine. She often cited this accident to explain to her children why she rarely wore seatbelts. "I have a better chance of being thrown clear of the crash."

About fifteen years later, dad was driving our Volkswagen minivan, and mom was in the passenger seat, not wearing a seatbelt. When dad made a left turn, they realized that mom's door was not properly latched closed. As the van proceeded through the turn, she flew out and hit the ground at about 20 mph. She was badly bruised and torn up from the loose gravel. The side of her face and body, on which mom landed, were bloodied. Shocked at how bad she looked; dad immediately took her to the Chester County Hospital Emergency Room. There the hospital nurse suspected that my mother's injuries were caused by domestic violence and immediately began to interrogate my dad. Although the situation was soon resolved, I can't imagine how offended my father was.

In the end, mom's theory about seatbelts was confirmed; she had been successfully thrown free of the vehicle. But the fact that she refused to wear a seatbelt caused both the accident and her injuries. On the ride home from the hospital, we all made a note of mom grudgingly putting on her seatbelt. From that day forward, we never caught her in a car without one.

There was another unfortunate, but memorable, accident involving mom. My sister, Shelley, was on her mini-bike doing a few laps around the house. She was having great fun, but when mom came out, joining me in the backyard to watch, I was unsure if she approved. Half-jokingly, I asked her if she would like to take a ride. I was totally floored when she said, "Yes."

After carefully showing mom how to sit on the mini-bike, how to use the throttle and the handbrake, we watched as she hopped on and took a slow lap around the house. During that first one, she looked confident and was enjoying the ride. As she started her second lap, she picked up a little speed. I noticed a bit of concern on her face, but she had good control. Tragically, that control was about to rapidly disappear. On the third lap, mom screamed around the corner of the house, mini-bike at full speed, like a cat set on fire. With a death grip on the throttle, in a full panic, mom could be seen desperately trying to step on a foot brake that did not exist. If there ever was a time for Superman to appear, this was it.

He must have been busy saving Lois or Jimmy—maybe off fighting Lex Luthor—because he no-showed, and mom kept accelerating until she smashed directly into the side of our metal tool shed. The echo of the resulting loud and horrible noise had barely stopped when we were at her side to see how she was. To our great relief, she got up and walked away under her own power. A little cut up and visibly shook, but okay. Our mother's resilience and toughness exceeded that of the other parties involved in the crash. The mini-bike was mangled, and the tool shed was crushed. Shelley and I immediately imposed a lifetime ban on mom riding mini-bikes. We were lucky that day, but we now had a good story to tell.

Silence was Golden

Our house was always noisy with four active children screaming for attention. Mom usually responded by kicking us out of the house to expend all that energy in our system, outdoors. There was never a shortage of things to do outside: baseball, football, street hockey, lacrosse, kick-the-can, manhunt, archery, BB gun fights, exploring in the woods and building forts were just a few activities which kept us entertained.

If the weather was bad, leaving us kids trapped inside the house—and mom with us—we (she) needed another strategy to keep the noise level down. That's when she fed us her world-famous "Peanut Butter and Bacon" sandwiches on toast. Man, those were good. She would put a nice thick layer of peanut butter in them. We'd be licking our gums for an hour after wolfing down those sandwiches. And it worked; it kept us quiet, and nobody had to call child protective services.

Lost in Space

Mom made Thursday evening our big "Family Night." Gina, Shelley, Kevin and I all had to be bathed and in our pajamas by 7:30 PM. Then mom would make popcorn, and we'd all watch *Lost in Space* on TV. This was before the Apollo moon landing, and when space exploration still captivated America and its children. We thought the robot was amazing, and I considered Judy Robinson my first girlfriend. Nobody wanted to miss an episode, and mom made it a special event for us.

Making Ends Meet

Although we did not have much money, my parents could always figure out how to make ends meet. Dad often brought home leftover food from his restaurant, and that saved mom both time and money. And our dog, Queenie, loved restaurant scraps too.

Mom was a talented seamstress, enjoyed sewing, and she made some of our clothes on an old Singer machine. She would buy all the fabric and materials on sale and make the patterns. My brother, Kevin, after he was paralyzed and confined to a wheelchair, always needed specially made clothes. And as with most families, we also handed clothes down. I was a bit nervous about this tradition, as my two older siblings were both girls. I flinched at the thought of being told, "it looks fine on you... no one will ever know it was your sister's." Fortunately, their clothes did not fit me, so I occasionally received new clothes or shoes, but they had to last me many years. When the knees in our pants wore out, we would simply iron on patches and wear them for a few more years. No one in our family wore the latest fashions, but mom always made sure the clothes were clean.

Mom also made our Halloween costumes by hand. For our first big Halloween, we were dressed as four Pilgrims in a neighborhood parade float. The next year we were Raggedy Anns and Andys. We competed in many local parades in West Chester, usually won a small cash prize and had our photo in the local newspaper. One year, mom and dad drove us to be in parades in Coatesville and Downingtown, where her costumes won awards in each city.

Halloween Costumes

Over forty years later, I dug out my old Raggedy Andy costume. My young son, Kent, wore it for Halloween that year. I think he really wanted to be something a little cooler, like Batman. The Raggedy Andy costume showed its age, but that night brought back old memories. I was proud of him for giving new life to my Mother's creation.

Eating Out

Once a week, mom would take us out to a local fast food burger restaurant called "Gino's," a competitor to McDonald's. The founder, Gino Marchetti, was a legendary defensive end with the Baltimore Colts. My dad loved the Colts, so we did too. Gino was now making hamburgers for us. That was our big night out; we would get all pumped up and race to get in the car. Three miles later we'd then pull into Gino's parking lot.

Eating out was pure luxury for our family. Mom took pride in the fact that she could feed four kids for under a dollar. We each got one hamburger and a small order of French fries that cost 24 cents for each child. We were not allowed to order sodas, as we couldn't afford them. We couldn't get cheese on the burger either. I always wanted to trade my pickle slice for some cheese, but I could never make that happen. And it didn't bother me much. I was just thrilled to be going out to eat.

There was one strange part of our tradition. Something that my sister Gina and I always wondered about. Only mom would go inside Gino's to order while my sisters, brother and I sat in the car and waited. When she came out a few minutes later, we would all eat as a family—in winter cold or summer heat—in the car. The car had no air conditioning, but we were used to that. We went to Gino's for several years, but as children, Shelley, Gina, Kevin and I never set foot in that restaurant. Maybe it cost more to go inside.

When I was a teenager, I heard Gino's was scheduled to be torn down. I rode my bike there and went inside to take a look. I saw that there were other things on the menu like desserts and milkshakes. I think mom had not wanted us to see the menu and would have been embarrassed if we saw other kids eating food that she could not buy for us. If we stayed in the parking lot, we wouldn't know what we were missing and would be happy with what we had. She was right. We didn't, and we were.

Mom in Action

Whatever her children were doing, mom got involved. She was an active member of the Fern Hill Elementary School PTA, worked in the concession stand at Little League football, served as a teacher's aide, and was the secretary of the local West Point Parent's Club. Mom also worked as a cashier in the Fern Hill School cafeteria, and, to our dismay, her kids could never buy the nickel ice cream when she was on duty.

At home, she had no time to rest and was constantly busy with cleaning, always cleaning, sewing or making lists of errands to do (or things to clean). I wouldn't have been surprised if I had caught her vacuuming the sidewalk.

Whenever mom had a few spare moments, she would break out a crossword puzzle or write a list of all the states and their capitals. With this, she inspired my interest in geography. As she grew older, if there was one thing she disliked, it was working on a computer. They never seemed to work when she needed them. Her attitude softened a bit once she learned the CD tray was not intended to be a coffee cup holder.

Mom also helped me get my first big break in the corporate world and arranged an interview with a manager at our local newspaper, the Daily Local News. Because of her, I became *the* paperboy that all my future route customers came to rely on and respect.

Mom's greatest achievement, however, was her total devotion to caring for my brother Kevin. After he broke his neck in a horrific bicycle accident in 1974—you'll read more about that and Kevin in the next section—mom took charge and moved the family forward. You name it, mom did it: doctor visits, rehabilitation, medication, bathing, feeding, clothing, personal hygiene, wound care, laundry, and much more. She got a lot of help from Gina, Shelley and me, but ultimately, she took full responsibility.

Christmas Traditions

Santa knew we didn't have a lot of money, but he still hit our house hard. Mom's Christmas shopping was usually done three months ahead of the holidays. Since one of my chores was taking out the trash, I would secretly check all the store receipts in the garbage can to see what gifts had been purchased, checking those applicable off my list and adding new ones.

The Kachejian crew—Christmas 1962

On Christmas morning, mom would have us open our stockings as a family. She then made breakfast and afterward we would go into the living room to open our gifts under the tree. We'd take turns and see what each other got. I had already figured out most of my gifts, but there were always a few surprises. After Christmas dinner, we'd sit back out in the living room, and mom would appear with one more mystery gift left by Santa. Mom also bought gifts for our cat, Ebenezer, and our dog, Scrooge (later on, Queenie). She would always wrap several catnip toys and store them in a bedroom with a pile of other presents. One day, she failed to close the bedroom door. Old Ebenezer snuck in and ripped through about a dozen gifts until she found the catnip. We found her later, lying on her back in a pile of shredded wrapping paper, looking like a drunk who had fallen off his barstool.

In retrospect, I realize that Christmas was largely a secular cultural event at our house and primarily about Santa. It was my dad who introduced his children to the theological foundation upon which Christmas was built. It took me a few years to figure out that it was really about the birth of Christ. Thanks, dad—I understand now.

For many years, dad's brother, Alex, came from Baltimore to spend Christmas with us. Uncle Alex was a Navy veteran who served in World War II. He never married, kept to himself, and it was obvious he led a very sad life. Our only real chance to talk to him every year was on Christmas morning. As he came down the stairs, he would stop and call over the four the Kachejian kids. He would give us each a quarter, and wish us a Merry Christmas. He would then apologize, saying it was all he could afford. We were sincerely grateful for his gift and gave him a hug. After breakfast, Uncle Alex would retreat back to the guest bedroom and disappear from our house a couple of days later. Mom and dad never told us any more about him. Alex died alone in a Veterans Hospital a few years later, and we wished we knew him better.

Frequent Flier

In 1985, Mom and Kevin decided to visit me while I was in the Army stationed in Germany. My father had passed away the previous year, so the trip was a good way for us to be together as a family. Mom was 53 years old and had never flown before. She was a heavy smoker, and I was concerned if she could make it for seven hours on an airplane without trying to roll down the window. I was also concerned that Kevin, a quadriplegic, could have a medical problem during the long journey.

It was their first major trip anywhere, and they had never been outside the United States. I anxiously waited for them at the Frankfurt Airport. They arrived without any problems, and we spent almost three weeks together, seeing sites in Germany, France, and Austria. Mom especially enjoyed the village I lived in, Bad Wimpfen, as well as Paris, Salzburg, and Heidelberg.

On our city tour of Paris, the bus stopped every ten minutes so that the passengers could get off and see the city: Notre Dame, Eiffel Tower, Place de la Concorde, and many other locations.

Each time, I would jump off and pull Kevin's wheelchair out of the luggage storage area. I would then put the brakes on the chair, go back into the bus, and carry Kevin down the stairs and buckle him into his chair. This gave us a few minutes to see the local attraction.

The driver would signal when it was time to go, and I would carry Kevin back into the bus, fold up and store the chair back underneath the bus. And on we would go to the next destination. We probably made a dozen stops, and I got a good workout. It felt fantastic that Mom and Kevin could see Paris. I mainly wanted my mother to enjoy the experience, and, to my pleasure, she was soaking it up.

Mom and Kevin in Paris

31

My mother dedicated her entire life to others. In addition to raising her children and a nephew, she cared for my brother from the time he was paralyzed and also took care of my father, who had terminal cancer, until he passed away. Everything in mom's life centered on what others needed, and with little thinking about herself, she did her best to provide for them.

I once asked her if she won the lottery, what would she do—where would she want to go. Being of Irish decent, she without any hesitation said, "Ireland." She had always talked about going to the Emerald Island and kissing the Blarney stone, which was the #1 spot on her list of places she wanted to visit. So, on her 60th birthday, in 1992, we had a surprise party with her friends. At the restaurant, we set up the room like the TV show *Let's Make a Deal*, and mom became a contestant. Of course, we rigged the script so she would win the trip. After pressure from the audience, she reluctantly traded a trip to Florida (Door #2) and behind Door #3 was the trip to Ireland.

Mom spent nine days in Ireland in June of that year. The first eight days it did not rain, and the Irish called it a drought. The tour bus barely fit on the narrow Irish roads, and our stops included Bunratty Castle. Limerick, the Ring of Kerry, Lakes of Killarney, and Killorglin. At Blarney Castle, mom climbed straight to the top of the castle and wasted no time in kissing the famous stone. She didn't even stop for a cigarette on the way up.

32

Kerry & Mom—Ring of Kerry

My sister, Gina, made mom's dream possible by caring for Kevin during the trip. She gave mom an opportunity to see the Emerald Isle. However, there is more to this story. Mom had serious reservations about leaving her home in West Chester for such a long trip to Ireland. Refusing to let her give up such an opportunity, we insisted that she go and assured her that everything would be okay. Mom didn't know it, but her house was struck by lightning moments after she left for the airport. The lightning blew a hole in the roof, flames leaped from the electrical sockets, the carpets were burned, and all the appliances were fried. Gina and Kevin worked feverishly to repair the damage so mom couldn't come home and say, "I knew I shouldn't have left."

A few years later in 1995, mom, Kevin and I jumped on another airplane and spent a week in Orlando touring all the attractions. This was her first domestic flight as well as her first trip to Florida in sixty years. The three of us rented a wheelchair van and toured Disney, Universal Studios, and Sea World; another great trip which was long overdue.

For her 70th birthday, my siblings gave mom another fabulous trip. This time to Scotland. In Edinburgh, mom and I stopped at the Royal Botanic Gardens, where her great, great, great, great grandfather Nathan Kift had worked and whose son immigrated to the United States, where he started the

33

family I am blessed to have today. Once again, it was Gina's support at home that made this trip for mom possible.

Sterling Castle (Glasgow)

Mom at St Andrews

Mom & Kerry at Royal Botanic Gardens

I am very thankful we were able to send mom to Scotland, as she died the following year. Decades of heavy of smoking finally caught up with her. When diagnosed with both lung cancer and emphysema, she didn't seek medical treatment until the last month of her life—fairly typical of her generation. A woman who dedicated the last 30 years of her life to caring for our paralyzed brother, her devotion to her children was incredible. I am so glad we were able to show mom, in her later years, just how much we appreciated her.

She is, and always will be, my role model for selfless service and love.

SECTION 2
KEVIN

CHAPTER 3
BEFORE THE ACCIDENT

Kevin was my younger brother and the baby of the family. Once Kevin was born, that made the Kachejian family—with two parents and four children—a complete 6-pack. My siblings and I were surprised to learn, many years later when we overheard my mother make a passing remark to a friend, that we almost had another brother or sister, but mom had miscarried.

Born on the 4th of July, Kevin was a real fireball during his early years. Each year, in the evening after Kevin's birthday party, our family would walk down the block to watch the local fireworks. We convinced young Kevin the entire country was celebrating his birthday.

As a toddler, he could find plenty of ways to get into trouble, but sometimes he had help. My sister, Gina, once filled his bottle with chocolate milk. Instead of drinking it, Kevin proceeded to shake the bottle and spray chocolate milk all over the wallpaper. He did a particularly nice job covering the walls along the stairwell going up to the second floor. Later that night, he didn't quite understand mom's lack of appreciation for his masterpiece when she discovered his artwork.

Kevin occasionally got mad too. Prone to releasing his frustration by head butting the small glass panels in our basement door, this curious behavior lasted about a year. During this time, he managed to smash about a dozen panes of glass with his forehead, and when he ran out of glass panels at home, he went to the next-door neighbor's house. Incredibly, Kevin never got a scratch, but my parents always got the neighbor's repair bill.

On this sixth birthday, Kevin got a new Whirly-Bird ride. All the neighborhood kids would visit and ride with him for hours. Sitting together in its four seats, they would push and pull on hand and foot bars to rapidly spin in a circle. Each summer, while my parents held their annual yard sale, the kids would hold a fair with games and prizes. The fish pond, the haunted house, horseshoes, and the Whirly-Bird were the big attractions. In fact, the Whirly-Bird became so popular that Kevin started charging five cents per ride. The same kids who used to ride for free all year round were now lined up to pay Kevin. Fortunately for my sisters and me, Kevin gave family members a discount.

Kevin and the McKannan sisters on the Whirly-Bird

The kids in our neighborhood, along Morstein Road, played outdoor games all summer long. Kick-the-Can was nothing short of a community pastime. It was epic. We had about ten kids on each side, and the game was played over several families' yards—a great aerobic workout. Covering about four acres, we had excellent terrain for the game: hills, trees, rock walls, houses, and open fields. The hardest part was finding an old can. Capture the flag was also quite popular. Kevin was gifted with natural speed and agility, so whenever we picked teams, he was always selected early.

We filled our summer days with games like baseball, football, street hockey, tetherball, volleyball, and croquet that were balanced with other adventures like exploring in the nearby quarry and fishing at Turtle Pond.

Kevin and I loved playing in the neighborhood football games. I was so proud when Don Delaney picked me to be on his team, "The Packers." I remember catching my first pass and feeling like I had just won the Super Bowl. And being on Don's team had an added benefit. He lived next door to a pretty girl named Lori Ridington, the future Henderson High School

Homecoming Queen. I was always hoping she would come out and play for the Packers too.

When Kevin and I played baseball in the yard, we would take the worst player on the team and make them stand in the street next to the sewer. Their only responsibility was to keep the baseball from rolling into the open sewer. This new position on the baseball team was located deep in right-center field. We called it the "Sewey Hole Patrol."

Special Operations

Kevin and I planned all of our secret operations in our central command post, by "The Big Rock and The Big Tree." Both were located in the extreme corner of our yard and a good spot because no one could hear what we were talking about.

WARNING: Children, do not attempt any of the following reckless actions. We were just dumb kids trying to have fun. Read at your own risk.

One of our big ops was building a series of forts in the field across the street (establishing early-on my combat engineering skills). We dug five forts and covered them with camouflage. Having watched a lot of *Hogan's Heroes* on TV, we decided to build an extensive tunnel network to connect the forts. Digging the tunnels was both time-consuming and arduous, as we had to move a lot of clay and rock.

After several weeks of hard work, our efforts finally paid off when we completed the network of tunnels. Man, did we smell when we came home each night. We were also loaded with ticks. I found over twenty on me one day. Once we were operational, Kevin volunteered as our tunnel rat. He'd run important messages through the tunnels to the different forts.

A few weeks later, I was shocked to discover all of the tunnels had collapsed. Our neighbor, Mr. Wright, had heard about them from someone— a mole or somebody with loose lips—and went to the site. He realized the tunnels were structurally unsupported. If one of them collapsed, a child could have easily become buried inside, and no one would have known. Using hand tools, Mr. Wright caved in all of the tunnels. We never rebuilt them as there were too many other fun things to do.

The Most Dangerous Game

BB guns were quite the rage in the 1960s and 70s, and one day, my dad brought one home. Nothing special, it was used and had a single pump and limited power. But it was an immediate hit. Kevin and I set up targets in the backyard: cans, balloons, eggs and cereal boxes soon felt our deadly accuracy. We grew quickly tired of hitting stationary targets and moved on to more challenging quarry: flies and bees. We would set up baited ambushes on the picnic table. Whenever an unsuspecting fly or bee landed, we'd draw a bead and spank him. Mom did not appreciate all the carcasses strewn about and BB nicks in her picnic table.

We decided to raise the stakes and hunt the big game. We convinced a couple of neighborhood kids to hide in the field. We suggested they wear a winter coat so the BBs would not hurt as much. We gave them a five-minute head start and then the hunt was on. Fortunately, nobody we played with got seriously injured. Today's generation is doing the same thing, it's just much safer with paintball guns, airsoft rifles, and eye protection. Still, I couldn't believe my friends volunteered to be human targets; I'd never let them hunt me. Ironically, the next year in school, I read a short story entitled *The Most Dangerous Game*, where things did not turn out so well for the hunter.

Pro Wrestling

Another special operation with Kevin and our neighbor Mark Wright was called "Fake Fights." We all watched pro wrestling on TV Channels 29 and 48 and were big fans, so we created our own version of that theatrical entertainment. We would position ourselves near the edge of Morstein Road and wait for cars turning off Boot Road. As the car began its 200-yard drive toward us, we would start a major—simulated—fist fight. We had practiced some really slick head locks, body kicks, karate chops and flying elbows, but we pulled our punches. Nobody was hurt, but to the driver coming toward us, it appeared incredibly real.

Once the car was about 30 yards away, we'd look up at them trying to make eye contact with the driver—deer in the headlight's startled—and then take off running into the nearby field as if we were guilty of something. It was great watching the shocked looks on the faces of people in the car. This was twenty years before the invention of the cell phone, so the cops were never called. After hiding for a few minutes until the car was out of sight, we'd then go back to the road and rehearse for the next car. Many of these cars were just driving through, heading for the much nicer neighborhood in Chart Chase. They were probably glad they arrived home safely. We loved to mess with those rich people, and I am sure we gave them a good story to tell their friends.

The Battle(s) of Morstein Road

In the winter, we would have neighborhood-wide snowball fights. We'd build a small snow fort and stockpile a few dozen snowballs. With our armaments and fortifications completed, we'd then jump over the wall and charge the enemy line with reckless abandon. There were no rules, just run and gun. A hailstorm of snowballs would come flying at us, and we'd dodge the incoming rounds. The fight usually ended when our fingers were frost bitten, and mom came out the front door and yelled, "Hot Cocoa." It's possibly the most effective cease fire tactic I've ever seen employed; it always worked.

Military mayhem was not reserved solely for winter. The big one of the year—the Mother of all Battles—was on the Fourth of July. Mr. Wright would make a fireworks run to South Carolina and drive back with an arsenal: firecrackers, bottle rockets, Roman candles, and sparklers. He bought the stuff by the case and openly shared it with his neighbors.

The battlefield had the Kachejian family on one side: Gina, Shelley, Kerry, and Kevin, along with three or four other friends. One the other side was the Wright family: Mark, Rene, Michael and Roseann and usually a few cousins to round out their team.

In between our two houses was considered "No Man's Land," (NML) or maybe better said, it was the suburban equivalent of pre-WWII Poland, caught between Nazi Germany and the Soviet Union. And there stood the house where the Bruce family lived.

The Bruce's were new to the neighborhood, recently moving in after the Hauck family (Charlie, Liz, and Claudia) left. The Bruce's were non-

41

combatants, trapped between warring factions, and their property almost always suffered collateral damage. Fortunately, the Bruce family was usually out of town for the Fourth of July.

The Kachejians and Wrights would plan the annual battle together and distribute munitions that morning. Horace Wright's son, Mark, always kept a big stash of the best fireworks for himself. Mark held onto the entire supply of Roman candles, and occasionally had a few M-80 firecrackers that were powerful enough to blow off part of your hand. These were the big weapons, providing the Wrights with superior firepower. If Mark hurled an M-80 at us, we would break ranks and run for cover.

The Kachejian's, forced to do battle with whatever was left, were usually allotted about 300 bottle rockets, a thousand firecrackers and a few dozen boxes of sparklers. With significantly less firepower, we needed to be accurate with our fire and conserve ammo whenever possible. What we did have going for us, however, was better tactics, team speed, and agility.

The day of the battle, the Wright family would have a big BBQ party at their house, and the Kachejian's were always invited to join the daytime celebration and sometimes this merged with our own holiday backyard picnic. Mrs. Louise Wright would lead the entertainment. Dozens of Italian relatives were all over the house and yard. Without fail, a keg of beer was on tap, and there was never a lack of food. We played all the usual outdoor summer games like horseshoes and wiffle ball. They loosened us up for what was to come.

The battle typically started shortly after sunset. In the lull before the storm, the Kachejian team would return home where we would finalize our plans. Our battle strategy was munitions attrition; we would start on the defense and make the Wrights attack first—drawing them in—to expend much of their ammo.

If we survived their initial onslaught, we would counterattack fast and hard, a merciless mixture of shock and awe. In the ensuing chaos, using speed and agility to our advantage, we'd trap them in the kill zone on their back patio. This allowed us to capture more ammo, and to continue the battle until their eventual defeat. It was the same plan every year, but it worked.

Just as dusk set in, a barrage of—about two dozen—bottle rockets launched from the Wright's house, across No Man's Land, and with barely an arc to their trajectory, hit near our defensive positions. It was at this moment that Mark Wright bolted from a concealed position in the bushes and flew across the Bruce's front yard, screaming like a madman and carrying a lit Roman candle in each hand. The one-man kamikaze attack was meant to rattle us and make us lose faith. Every few seconds, a flaming ball flew toward us. Knowing that a moment's hesitation meant possible death, we dove for cover, returning fire with a combination of bottle rockets and flying sparklers. Once his Roman candles were spent, Mark retreated to the Wright's house as Kevin continued to fire bottle rockets ensuring his exodus was not a feint for an end-around attack.

The exchange of fire raged across the NML for another half an hour then ebbed as the Wright's pulled back to their home to refit and resupply. I immediately conducted reconnaissance on their far-left flank.

Sneaking over a hill through the Herndon's yard, I hugged the line of bushes behind the Bruce's home. It was now significantly darker outside as I followed the line of bushes to a concealed position overlooking the Wright's patio.

I was excited and emboldened upon discovering they had not put out any sentries and were standing in the open discussing what to do next. My stealthy infiltration to gather intel proved, instead, to be an opportunity to strike at the soft underbelly of my enemy.

Having the element of surprise, I needed to boldly take action. Lighting off two packets of firecrackers, a total of 64 rounds, I surged through the bushes to deliver a fiery barrage that landed all around them. Bracketed by the sudden explosions, they broke and ran.

The Wright's German Shepard, Suzie, began to freak out, and I thought I may have a vicious hand-to-paw canine fight next. She backed down, and I retreated to my egress point, grabbing a bunch of additional bottle rockets and a treasured Roman candle along the way.

These battles typically lasted about two hours, until we ran out of fireworks or some neighbor called the cops. The following morning there was widespread debris, the detritus of war, and scars visible everywhere. Bottle rocket sticks were scattered across rooftops and yards and could also be found polluting the Bruce's swimming pool. After the battle, the fumes of war lingered. The neighborhood smelled like exploded gunpowder for several days.

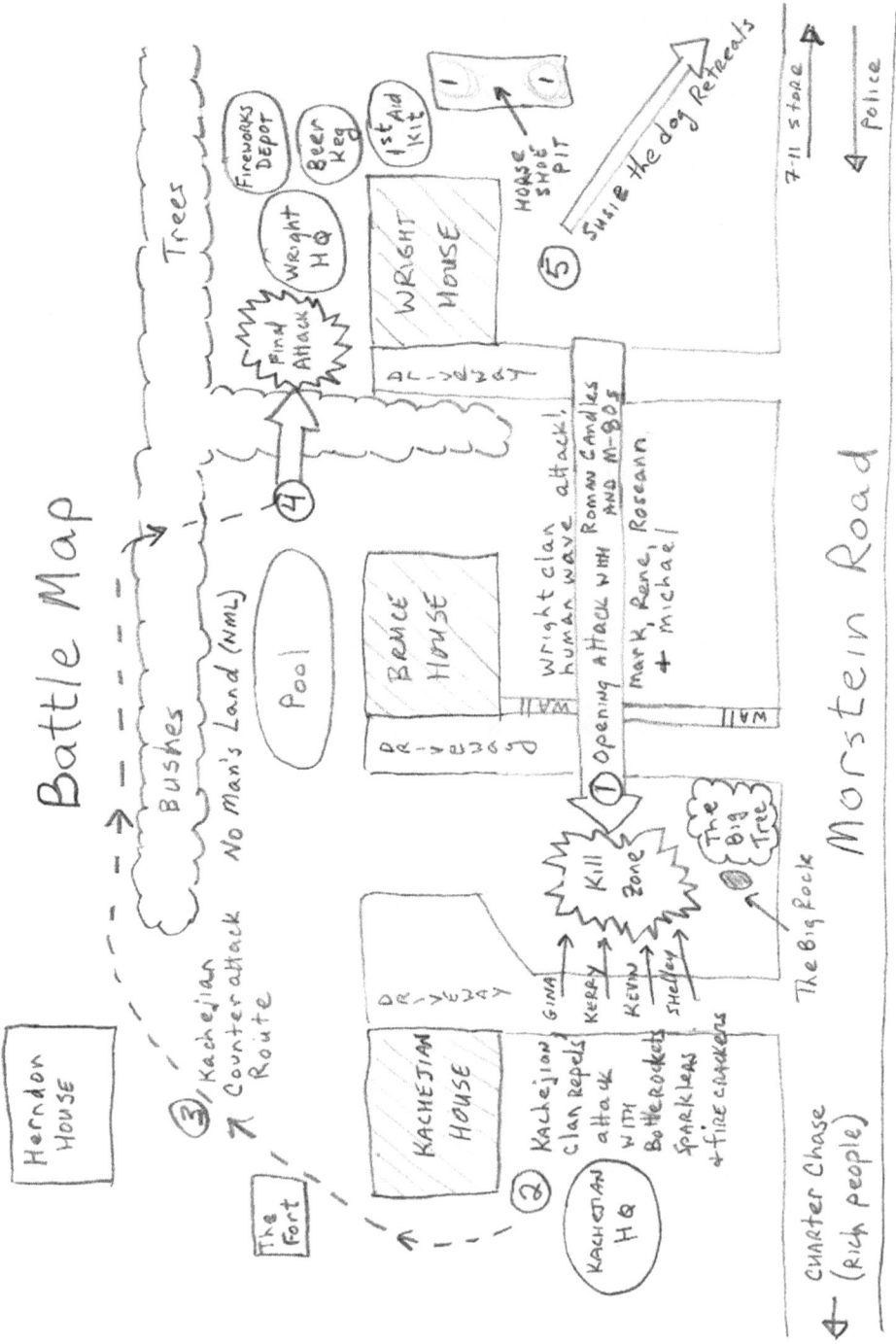

Battle Map

The Bomb

What Kevin and I lacked in common sense, we made up for in boldness. We once made a small bomb; the thing was about the size of a golf ball. Scraping the gunpowder out of a couple of thousand caps and some .22 caliber bullets, we wrapped it in a piece of paper bag from the grocery store and inserted a short fuse from an old firecracker. All we needed now was a place to detonate it, somewhere mom could not see us.

Suddenly, we realized we had the ideal location. The year before, Kevin and I had built a backyard fort out of old shipping pallets. It was a one-room square shack, measuring about five feet on each side and four feet high with a corrugated fiberglass roof. The wood from the pallets was well-seasoned and extremely hard. In constructing the fort, we drove hundreds of nails into the walls; many were bent or had the sharp ends protruding out inside the fort.

Yes, I know what you're thinking. Just wait for it.

We discovered mom was running an errand, and that made it even better timing. It was a perfect opportunity to let it rip. Taking the bomb inside the fort, we lit the fuse. Instead of running, we stayed inside the tiny fort to get a closer look at the explosion. We eagerly awaited the spectacle as the fuse shortened until BOOOOOM!

Kevin and I were instantly skewered on the nails protruding inside the walls of the fort—hoisted on our own petard, literally, some might say. We couldn't see; grains of explosive powder burned our eyes. We couldn't hear, the blast wave left our ears ringing. We couldn't even breathe, as the fort was now full of smoke and still-settling airborne debris.

What we could do was hurt as we finally, blindly, crawled out of the fort. We both flopped all over the yard, choking, like deaf and dumb fish out of water, for a few minutes until we regained our senses.

But there was one sense we never regained—our common sense. That was gone forever. Arguably, it was never there, to begin with.

As an adult, I now realize how dumb and dangerous that stunt was. I still maintain, however, that my parents are to blame for not supervising us properly.

If my kids ever try to do the same stuff Kevin and I did as kids, they will be in for a whooping.

Dance Lessons

My two sisters, Gina, and Shelley, took dancing lessons when they were little. My mother and the dance instructor, Carolyn Stahl, conspired to recruit Kevin and me in similar dance classes. Kevin and I were about 4-5 years old and had not yet started to play sports. I didn't like dancing but had no alternative. My dad worked all the time, so he did not get a vote. When my sisters went to dancing lessons, my brother and I were forced to go with them. Kevin and I suffered through two years of tap dancing and ballet lessons, not realizing there was an alternative for aspiring young men.

Finally, my father came to the rescue by enrolling us in Little League baseball and football. At last, Kevin and I could hang out with our buddies and be led by male role models. Several years later, dad got us some weights and a bench press. We began body building, and our program of self-improvement enabled our sports careers to take off. But, decades later, I still can't dance.

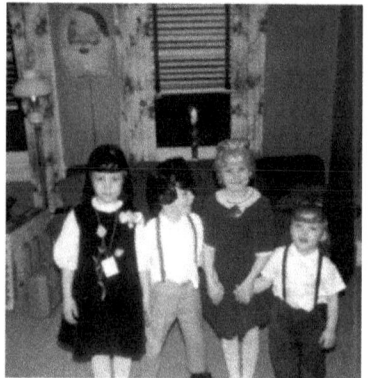

Kevin

CHAPTER 4
THE ACCIDENT

March 6, 1974, was a tragic day that cast a dark mark on the Kachejian family. On this day, Kevin's life was completely and irreversibly changed, as well as the lives of all members of our family. Decades later, my memory of that day is vivid and stark, permanently burned into my mind like the harsh glare of an old-style photographic flash used to illuminate the scene.

Society was very different then. There were no cell phones or helicopter Moms. There was no fear of kidnappers and pedophiles. Kids were mostly free to play outdoors throughout the neighborhood. Broken arms and scrapped skin were part of the life. Kids only stayed inside during thunderstorms and on Saturday mornings to watch cartoons. Life as a child was an outdoor sport.

In the 1970s, Evel Knievel was a popular motorcycle daredevil who used a ramp to jump over dozens of cars, buses, and even the Snake River Canyon. He was a national figure always pushing the envelope with new death-defying jumps. Anytime Evel was jumping, the nation was watching on TV.

Inspired by him, the kids in our neighborhood built a small jump ramp out of scrap lumber. We started small. Low jumps and short distances, nothing too daring.

I jumped the ramp a few times but preferred other stunts. My specialty was riding my banana-seat bike fast and hitting the curb hard, and launching myself over the handle bars. I tumbled at high speed onto the grass, and to most observers, it looked like a serious wreck. Optimally timing the fake wreck when a car or a pedestrian was nearby, I would lie in the grass motionless for a few minutes to see who would come running to the scene. At thirteen-years-old, I considered myself an aspiring professional stunt kid. I got a few scratches and bruises, but nothing worse.

But the jumpers, having mastered the small jumps, began to stage bigger ones. The neighborhood jump ramp was placed at the top of a small hill entering a field, effectively giving the ramp four feet of elevation at the point of takeoff. The kids—legs pumping like pistons—zoomed across the

47

neighbor's lawn, across Morstein Road and hit the ramp. Once airborne, they held onto their bike as best they could, until they crashed in the field. Some of the kids would try the jump with no hands or no feet. Not one of the jumpers had an ounce of common sense. When mom learned Kevin was part of that crowd, she immediately grounded him.

On March 6, 1974, eleven-year-old Kevin did not follow mom's orders. He snuck out of the house and joined his friends. On one of his jumps, Kevin tried to pull a wheelie while in the air and rocked back too far on his bike. He landed on the back of his head and did not get up. He had broken two vertebrae in his neck. At Kevin's urging, the other kids tried to pick him up, and this may have caused additional damage to his spine.

The kids ran to our house and alerted my mother and my sister, Gina, who immediately called the ambulance. The Good Fellowship Ambulance crew arrived quickly. Fortunately, they had neck braces and a stretcher. They took Kevin to Chester County Hospital where a medical team was waiting for him. One of the police officers at the scene of the accident destroyed the jump ramp.

At the time, I was at junior high school wrestling practice. Our neighbor, Mrs. Louise Wright, rushed there to pick me up. I was confused as to why my mother was not picking me up. Mrs. Wright told me my brother had a terrible accident and was in the hospital. He could not move, and my parents were with him. Although I had a sense of the seriousness, I did not yet understand the permanence of Kevin's paralysis.

My parents spent the next few days camped at the hospital. Mrs. Stapleford, a neighbor, and registered nurse, stayed with Shelley, Gina and me that evening. She told us what happened to Kevin and what his expected outcome was. The sharpness of those first days after the accident faded. I felt overwhelmed as the gravity of the situation sank in. The following week was mostly a blur. I recall much of it was spent at Chester County Hospital.

I was shocked when I first saw Kevin in his hospital bed. He had been put in a Stryker frame, a halo-like traction unit that bolted into his skull. Its purpose was to pull on his neck and spine to remove stress on the damaged vertebrae. It looked like a medieval torture apparatus. Kevin's head was shaved, and holes were drilled in his skull to hold the frame. A cable, pulley and a sandbag weight were used to keep Kevin's neck extended. Every two hours, twelve times a day, nurses would strap a second gurney on top of

Kevin, making him look like a sandwich. Once secured, they would spin him from face down to face up to reduce the chances of getting bedsores.

Over the course of the six grim weeks Kevin spent in Chester County Hospital, several professional athletes came to visit. We were grateful they came to lift our hearts and spirits. The list included Jon Matlack from the NY Mets, LeRoy Ellis from the 76ers, Al Nelson from the Philadelphia Eagles, and Carl Gersbach from the San Diego Chargers. As Kevin's rehabilitation continued over the next year, he was presented with an autographed baseball from Mike Schmidt of the Philadelphia Phillies, as well as a hockey stick autographed by the 1974-1975 Flyers, who had just won the Stanley Cup, sending Philadelphia into a frenzy of pride. Letters and prayers also flooded in. Senator Ted Kennedy wrote Kevin a letter of

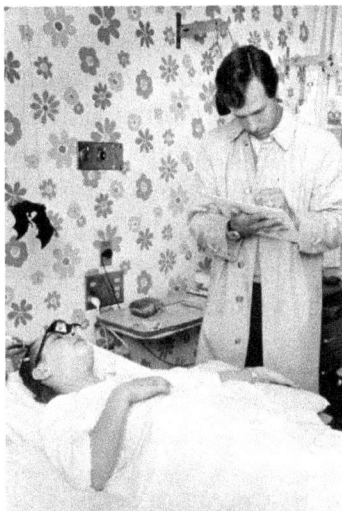

Jon Matlack visits Kevin in Stryker traction

encouragement, sharing how he had also spent time in a Stryker unit following a plane crash.

The teachers and administrators from Fern Hill Elementary School were inspired by Kevin's desire to keep up with his studies. He had been an A student before the accident, and his teachers came to his bedside and tutored him. Sometimes Kevin, in the Stryker frame, would be lying face down, and nurses would come in to find Mr. John Bullock or Mr. Dave Morgan sitting on the floor with a textbook, looking up at Kevin, giving him the latest lesson. The Fern Hill PTO held bake sales, car washes and book sales to raise money to help us pay the huge medical bills our family faced. Despite the tragic accident, the Kachejian's had gained something we never imagined possible— the entire Fern Hill School community had become our extended family.

Gina stepped up to take on many of the duties, which my parents could not attend to; they needed to be with Kevin. Having recently received her driver's license, she ran most of the family errands. Most days, mom just gave her the car keys and a list of chores. But Gina didn't just run errands, she ran the house.

The story of my brother's accident made the headlines of the Daily Local News, the newspaper that I delivered each day. In the initial article, written by Jane Sebold, my father was very grateful and complimentary to all the people who responded to the accident and cared for Kevin in the hospital.

Over the next twenty years, Kevin's remarkable story of progress continued to be covered by the Daily Local, providing hope and serving as an inspiration to readers all throughout Chester County.

After some time, Kevin was transferred to the Nemours / Alfred I DuPont Institute in Delaware. He needed major surgery to fuse his spine, followed by six more weeks in a Stryker traction unit and months of rehabilitation. Ironically, my father drove past the institution every day on the way to his restaurant. Although this was a bleak time, our hope grew each time a small muscle movement came back to Kevin.

Fern Hill Fundraiser

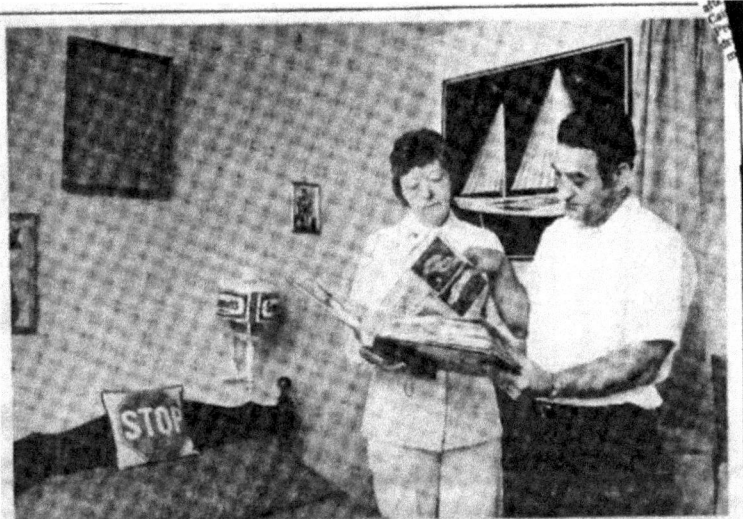

The Kachejians look at Kevin's get-well cards *May 30, 1974*

Kachejians wait, hope...

By JANE SEBOLD
(Local News Correspondent)

Eleven-year-old Kevin Kachejian of Morstein road in West Goshen township has a framed copy of the Declaration of Independence hanging above his bed at home.

It is appropriate because Kevin is a pretty independent sort of fellow: he was born on the Fourth of July. But right now March 6 is the date Kevin and his family can't forget because that's the day that "the course of human events" caught up with them and delivered one of those devastating blows most families experience only in nightmares.

That's the day three of Kevin's friends came running into the Kachejian house yelling for his mother because Kevin was lying in the field across the street and "couldn't move."

"He had taken his bike, a regular high-rise, over a ramp they had built," Mr. Kachejian says. "The ramp was just a foot high, but it was on a four-and-a-half foot embankment and Kevin flew about 20 feet before he landed."

Paralyzed

"He broke two vertebra in his neck and is about 90 per cent paralyzed," Mrs. Kachejian continues. "There's no way the doctors can tell how much might be permanent, but they know the spinal cord is not severed. It can take up to two years before we really know about the damage. Just last week Kevin started to move the toes on his left foot, then he could

pull up from the knee again. It's a matter of learning all over; he has to retrain the muscles.

"The doctors had to fuse the neck in order to stabilize it. They have explained to us that 90 per cent of the cure from here on is mental. If a patient has the desire it is miraculous how he can recover, and a child has a better chance than an adult," Mrs. Kachejian says.

Kevin never lost consciousness after the accident. "He had asked the boys to lift him up and when they couldn't they came and got me. I had my oldest daughter call the ambulance. The Good Fellowship ambulance was here almost immediately from the time we called, and two West Goshen po-

(Continued on Page 2, Column 1)

KEVIN KACHEJIAN

Kachejians wait, hope

(Continued From Page 1)

lice cars arrived instantly.
Praise Ambulance, Police
The Kachejians speak of the ambulance service and the police almost reverently. "Good Fellowship had the proper stretchers and proper neck braces which they had stopped to grab at the last minute. One of the police officers immediately dismantled the ramp and the police stayed until the ambulance had taken Kevin right to Chester County Hospital."

Enter the third group of local miracle workers, according to Mr. and Mrs. Kachejian. "There

were hordes of doctors right there to meet us at the door of the hospital. Their timing was beautiful."

A neighbor who is a registered nurse stayed with the Kachejians that night to fill them in on what was happening to their son in the intensive care unit. "At first they thought the spinal cord was severed. It took 24 hours of constant probing to be sure.

"Our neighbors, friends and associates were just beautiful," Mr. Kachejian says. "They fed our family, took care of everything. This whole accident started a chain of events that I think could only happen in this country.

I wouldn't want people to have to get into this position to find out how wonderful it is."

'Unbelievable'

After Kevin was removed from the intensive care unit, he was put into the pediatrics wing at Chester County Hospital. "The nurses there are just unbelievable. I'll just never forget the head nurse, Miss Alexander. She even used to stay after her hours to read to Kevin. Two of the nurses have driven all the way to Wilmington to visit him. All I can say is 'Support your local hospital,'" says Mr. Kachejian.

Kevin remained at Chester County in a Stryker frame for six weeks, and on April 22 he was

moved to the Alfred I. Dupont Institute in Wilmington which has the kind of rehabilitation facilities he needs. After the transfer the doctors decided another fusion was needed, so Kevin must spend six more weeks on a Stryker unit while that heals.

The Stryker unit came into the public eye after Senator Ted Kennedy's nearly fatal plane crash in 1964 when pictures were released of the Senator spread eagle on the apparatus. Kevin has to be turned every two hours, and now that he is in a wide collar which throws his head back, he can only look at things upside down.

"While he was at Chester County my husband's Lions Club,

51

for paralyzed son

the Millcreek one in Delaware, bought Kevin a pair of prism lenses so he could read and look at TV. We fix mirrors for him and everything and he gets along pretty well."

Athletes Visit

Kevin had lots of visitors at Chester County, too. A few were pretty special for a guy who likes sports and has played both little league football and baseball. ? l Nelson of the Eagles came by; LeRoy Ellis of the 76ers dropped in, and Carl Gersbach from the San Diego Chargers who was graduated from West Chester State and had been a student teacher at North Junior High School when the Kachejian girls

were there, paid a call.

Until Kevin gets out of the Stryker frame, his rehabilitation is limited to arm and leg physical therapy every day. Mrs. Kachejian goes to Wilmington each afternoon and stays to give Kevin his dinner in the hospital. His father, who runs a restaurant nearby, slips in for a visit when he can.

Meanwhile, the other Kachejian children, Regina, 16, Rochelle, 15, and Kerry, 14, keep things moving at home. "Our oldest daughter drives. She got her license in November and we hardly let her go more than a hundred miles," says Mrs. Kach-

ejian. "Now she does all the grocery shopping, takes the others where they need to go after school, and runs all our errands for us."

Philosophical

The Kachejians are philosophical about the Evel Knievel aspects of Kevin's accident. "There is just no way you can protect your kids from everything," Mr. Kachejian says. "None of us even knew the ramp was there; all the kids did it, but usually they didn't go quite so high. Kevin just went outside to ride his bike. For about three weeks after this happened you didn't see one bike around here."

Kevin was an "A" student at Fern Hill Elementary School before this accident happened, and he is an "A" student now. "While he was at Chester County Hospital, Fern Hill set up a home instruction program for him. He had his own homeroom teacher, Mr. Reber, and he was all caught up with his class when he went to Wilmington. Now he gets his instruction through the state of Delaware. We've already made put his seventh grade class list at

North Junior High for September.

Add Fern Hill Elementary School to the Kachejian's list of miracles. "That's some place," Mr. Kachejian says. "All our children went there. We've gotten to know the teachers. My wife's always been active in the PTO, our main concern has been doing things with the children. Fern Hill has a real family type atmosphere."

Fern Hill thinks a lot of the Kachejians too. The PTO has already held a bake sale to help with the astronomical medical bills even insured families face after a catastrophic illness, and the week of June 3 through June 7 has been named Kevin Kachejian week at the school. Every class has planned a special project, from car washes to book sales.

Meanwhile, Kevin doesn't get as much company since he was transferred to Wilmington, so he really enjoys getting mail. If you'd like to drop him a line just address it to Kevin Kachejian, c/o Alfred I. Dupont Institute, Box 269, Wilmington, Del., 19899.

Phillip

During his time at AI DuPont, Kevin met a new friend. Phillip was a 19-year old patient with severe multiple sclerosis. Despite not being able to get out of bed, Phillip was always upbeat and had kind things to say. Although Phillip did not complain, it sometimes felt like he was treated like a zoo animal. People came to look at him and feed him. He was a great person that was dealt a difficult hand in life. Every day, a team of doctors would make the rounds and check on Kevin and then Phillip. Phillip wanted to have some fun with the doctors and asked us to pick him up a "whoopee cushion." That's a small rubber bladder you blew up with air, and when you sat on it, the cushion emitted a loud gaseous noise. In laymen's terms, it made a big farting sound. The comedian George Carlin called it a "bilabial fricative." We brought Phillip several whoopee cushions, filled with air, and set them up before the doctors made the rounds. Phillip waited until the doctors surrounded his bed and then, managing to sit on the cushions, blasted a thunderous and realistic sounding, though fake, barrage of farts. Phillip howled with laughter, and even the serious looking doctors got a good laugh out of it.

Summer Adoption

That summer of 1974, I was invited to live with the Reber family. Bob Reber was my former math teacher and Kevin's homeroom teacher. His wife, Kathleen, had her hands full raising five sons: Bob Jr., Chris, Mark, Matt, and Chet. Yet Bob and Kathleen generously opened their home to take on a sixth boy. There were a lot of bunk beds in that house, and I was given a top bunk. Since I was now with the Rebers, my parents could spend more time focusing on Kevin. Shelley picked up my responsibilities delivering the newspaper.

Coming Home

In the Fall of 1974, Kevin returned home from AI DuPont, and started seventh grade at North Middle School, attending several days each week. He eventually came back to school full-time and caught up on all his studies. He had an electric wheelchair now and was gaining some independence.

Hot Wheels

My parents drove Kevin to rehabilitation in Delaware several times each week. One of those trips was almost catastrophic. Mom was driving southbound on Route 202. Kevin was strapped into his electric wheelchair which was belted into our modified Volkswagen (VW) bus. Suddenly the wheelchair battery caught on fire. The VW immediately filled with toxic fumes from the burning plastic and acid. Mom hit the brakes and stopped on the shoulder of the road. Kevin was trapped inside the vehicle and could not get out of the burning wheelchair. Incredibly, a police officer following behind mom was able to pull Kevin out of the van before he suffocated. I don't know the officer's name, but he was yet another unsung hero there in our family's time of need.

Financial Impact

The medical bills piled up, reaching several hundred thousand dollars. Our health insurance paid for much of it, but my father could never afford to pay off the tens of thousands we still owed. While my parents were in the midst of discussing whether or not they would have to sell the house, a small miracle happened.

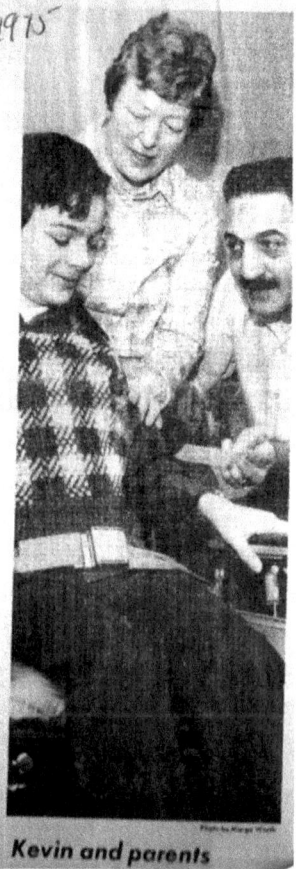

A story of luck long overdue...

march 8, 1975

By ROBERT H. LUDWICK JR.
(Of the Local News Staff)

On March 6, 1974 eleven-year-old Kevin Kachejian of Morstein road, West Goshen, was seriously injured in a bicycle accident in a field near his home.

Kevin, a student at Fern Hill Elementary School, broke two vertebrae in his neck and was about 90 per cent paralyzed. He was trying to impersonate motorcycle daredevil Evel Knievel on a ramp on a four and a half foot embankment.

It was an agonizing tragedy for the other five members of the Kachejian family. Fortunately, the boy's spinal cord was not severed and, after many tense moments, the youngster began the slow, tedious recovery process.

The past year has been a hectic one for the Kachejians. Kevin's mother, Helen, remained at his side nearly every day during his long hospital stay. When he was transferred from Chester County Hospital to the Alfred I. Dupont Institute, Wilmington, Del., a rehabilitation center, his mother visited Kevin every afternoon and stayed to give him his dinner.

Kevin, in the initial recovery, was on a Stryker frame for 12 weeks. He couldn't move. As a result of the attention focused on Kevin by his parents, sisters Regina and Rochelle and brother Kerry took on added responsibilities.

That was a year ago.

Today, things are looking better. Kevin, now 12, confined to a wheelchair, began classes recently at North Junior High School where he is in the seventh grade. Prior to his accident, Kevin was an "A" student. This week Kevin attended school two full days and two half days. Next week, his mother said, Kevin will try three full days.

"He's much better than we ever anticipated he'd be," said Mrs. Kachejian. "There's a long way to go yet. He still goes to therapy once a week."

Kevin's improving condition, however, isn't the only good news to come the Kachejian's way this week. On Thursday, one year to the day Ke-

vin had his accident, the Kachejians won $20,000 in the state's Bakers Dozen lottery. The magic digits were 460919.

It started Thursday at Thrifty Beverage, Rt. 202, Concord Township, Delaware County. That's where Kevin's father, Karabed, proprietor of a Wilmington, Del., restaurant, stopped to buy a lottery ticket. However, Mrs. Kachejian said, her husband stopped to buy a ticket for next week's lottery. He usually buys one weekly, she added, but hadn't gotten one this week.

"He thought it was too late to get one for this week," said Mrs. Kachejian. "The lady (at the beer mart) said she had a couple left. He decided to get one."

Mrs. Kachejian said the family was out Thursday night — Kevin was taking swimming lessons at West Chester State College — and they did not realize they were winners until yesterday morning.

"We read it in the Daily Local this morning," she said yesterday. "We couldn't believe it."

Mrs. Kachejian said she kept very calm. She did admit, however, she took Kevin's cereal bowl from his tray and put it in the washer. She said the money would be deposited in the bank temporarily "until we recuperate from the shock."

Although Kevin's accident resulted in expensive medical bills, she said the family is "fairly well caught up" on the payments. Blue Cross took care of most of the bills, she said, and a Kevin Kachejian Fund at Fern Hill School contributed $5,000 and a fund by the Little League Football Association of West Chester added $1,600. Mrs. Kachejian called the funds a "Godsend."

She said some bills for Kevin have not been received, "although the worst is over." The money will help pay them. The money will also help send daughter Regina, who graduated from high school in June, to college, Mrs. Kachejian said.

Asked if a portion of the windfall might be used for a "good time for all the family," Mrs. Kachejian responded: "We could stand that for a change."

Kevin and parents

A story of luck long overdue

On March 6, 1975, exactly one year to the day after Kevin's accident, dad was driving Kevin to physical therapy when he stopped at a convenience store to get his weekly Pennsylvania "Bakers Dozen" Lottery ticket. Later, after I delivered the Daily Local News, dad opened it and read the winning lottery numbers. He discovered that we had won $20,000. The For Sale sign came down, and we were able to keep our house. If you want to play the winning number again, try 460919. Later, Kevin became a beneficiary of "Brian's Run," a ten-kilometer race for the benefit of the handicapped. Without Brian's Run, Kevin would not have had the opportunity to achieve as much as he did. The money donated to Kevin paid for his electric wheelchair and handicapped van, as well as his education from West Chester University, and Law School at Villanova. Once again, supporting Kevin in his hour of need, my Mother was always the MVP on the team. She drove Kevin 80 miles every day, for three years so, he could complete his law studies. Gina and Shelley were there to back her up.

Moving

In the late 1970s, our family moved to a single-floor ranch house on Ashbridge Road, a few miles away. The house was much more suitable for a wheelchair, but it required modifications. Several teachers from Henderson Senior High School came to help. They built a large concrete driveway and entrance ramp for the home. We could now easily offload Kevin and his wheelchair from our handicapped van and roll him into the house. The men who built this handicapped accessible parking had volunteered their time, and so Kevin insisted they sign their good work so we could always remember them. Here's a big "Thank You" almost 40 years later from the Kachejian's to the men who signed their creation: Hancock, Bowen, Smida, Wray, Nicols, Swope, Walker, Reichert, MacIver, Pryor, Walsh, Lammey, and Von.

Standing

Concerned friends and neighbors continued to generously support our family for years in various ways. When Kevin needed a unique rehabilitation device to practice standing, a local man built the hardwood standing table by hand. It was of incredibly high quality, and Kevin used it for several hours each day to lock himself into an upright position. The standing table was good for both his morale and his circulation. Eventually, Kevin gained the ability to walk short distances using parallel bars under direct supervision.

The Walk

By his senior year at Henderson High School, Kevin had spent six years in physical rehabilitation. As graduation neared, one of Kevin's friends asked him what he wanted to do at the ceremony.

Kevin replied, "I want to walk up to get my diploma." He was serious but did not intend it to be the big event that it soon became. News of Kevin's intent spread through the local community like wildfire, and it wasn't long before someone alerted the news media.

On graduation day, June 6, 1980, a TV news helicopter flew in to cover the story. The stadium was packed to capacity. When Kevin's name was called, several thousand spectators let out a deafening roar.

I was standing on a small hill overlooking the field and watched as, with the help of two close friends, Kevin unbuckled his seatbelt and stood from his wheelchair. At that moment, he seemed taller than anyone else. Kevin then walked several dozen steps and received his diploma.

My knees buckled at the sight of my brother walking. The noise was unbelievable. It was an awesome, inspiring and unforgettable moment that was captured in the newspapers and on television. Everyone in the stadium was crying. I felt the hand of God was with our family, and it was absolutely one of the greatest days of my life.

My only regret is that the poor student who received his diploma immediately after Kevin was lost in the commotion. His graduation moment was completely overwhelmed by Kevin's walk. But he had the best seat in the house that day, and I'm sure he was just fine.

A teacher shares thoughts inspired by Kevin's walk

Editor News: For 11 years I have worked with the youth of this community; as a teacher, I have shared with these young people many moments of victory, of defeat, of joy, of sadness. As memorable as each of these moments has become, one recent moment will always remain foremost in my mind — the courage, the determination, and the sheer beauty of watching Kevin Kachejian walk to the dais to receive his diploma.

For some the rain on graduation evening was a blessing for it concealed a steady flow of tears, for others the rain was immaterial, for nothing could dampen the unabashed joy every graduate, faculty member, and citizen in attendance shared as Kevin stepped forward to accept his diploma.

Few who attended the graduation ceremony will ever forget the inexplicable sense of overwhelming joy and pride we as a community shared in Kevin's walk. As one privileged to have Kevin in class, I speak for the entire faculty in saying Kevin has taught each of us a lesson in sharing, in caring, in believing, in living.

Each of us left the stadium enriched by a renewed ability to accept upcoming challenges; each of us felt the growth of a mustard seed within us. And indeed each of us is indebted not only to Kevin but also to the entire Kachejian family for the opportunity to witness a miraculous accomplishment and to learn a profound lesson in life.

RICHARD I. MULLER
Henderson Faculty

Kevin's Graduation Walk

VOL. CVIII, NO. 167

WEST CHESTER—PAOLI—COATESVILL

'I never gave up the hope of walking'

By GAIL O. GUTERL
(Of the Local News Staff)

On Friday Kevin Kachejian will walk up and get his diploma at Henderson High School commencement exercises.

So big deal, you may say.

But it will be no small matter for this 17-year-old to stand up in front of a packed audience of family, friends, and classmates and accept a diploma for four years of hard work.

With the aid of two junior ushers for balance, Kevin will do just what the doctors said he would never do: walk.

Kevin, who lives in West Goshen, broke two vertebra in his neck March 6, 1974 — "I will always remember that date," — when as an 11-year-old he tried to maneuver his bicycle over a small ramp near his home.

"I was riding a bicycle and trying to jump a ramp and I didn't land right," Kevin said yesterday. "My mother believes I was trying to imitate Evil Knievel."

Kevin was paralyzed from the neck down and doctors told his parents, Helen and Karabed, that the most he would ever be able to do was move his head and eyes.

After six hard years of exercises, swimming, and physical therapy with the aid of volunteers, Kevin is modest about his accomplishment.

Got better each year

"I never gave up the hope of walking again," he said. "I told myself whatever (mobility) I didn't have I would try for and whatever I did have I would try to improve. Each year I got better and better. According to the doctors, I'm not supposed to be able to do anything."

Kevin sports more than determination: he has a penchant for puns, a quiet, bright sense of humor, and parents and a family who really care.

"Besides my family and Mr. (Hank) Goodwin, (associate professor of physical education at West Chester State College, where Kevin swims regularly): the volunteers at school have done so much," he said.

When he entered junior high school, local physical therapist Carolyn Thomas trained adult volunteers to work with Kevin at developing his muscles. He had physical therapy several times a week during his scheduled gym period at East Junior High School, now Fugett Middle School. Thomas was aided by Sally

(Continued on Page 2, Column 5)

Kevin Kachejian at an assembly rehearsal

58

'I never gave up hope'

(Continued from Page 1)

Ginther and "other mothers who were trained to transfer me from my chair to a special bench and to help me to walk."

"Therapy wasn't painful. I took it and gradually worked up. I wanted to go full speed and the volunteers didn't believe I should rush, so we hit a good middle road."

Kevin said he always set goals for himself.

"As soon as I met one goal, I'd set another one. I might break a record one day in physical therapy and tell the volunteers that I'm not tired. But when I'd get home I'd be so tired, I'd never realize it during gym."

He took his first steps in the West Chester State College swimming pool with the aid of Goodwin, who runs a Thursday night swim program for the handicappped.

"I walked backwards," Kevin said, laughing. "But I walked."

Mrs. Kachejian said her son was excited about his first steps and couldn't wait to tell his doctors.

"When he told them their response was, 'Well, what are you going to do? Flood the halls of the school?'"

Measured tiles

Kevin measured his progress in walking by the number of tiles on the floor in the hallway outside the gym.

"We'd put the parallel bars in the hallway and each day we'd move them one tile down, so I would have to walk further."

Kevin is so used to goals that he forgot he had decided he would walk to receive his high school diploma. Mrs. Kachejian reminded him.

"Well," she said. "Mrs. Thomas called me and said, 'Guess what Kevin intends to do? He wants to walk to get his diploma.'"

"I really said it half jokingly," Kevin remembered.

Besides his rigorous physical training, Kevin has found the time to serve as treasurer of his senior class. He intends to enter West Chester State College in the fall, "partly because of Mr. Goodwin and partly because they have the facilities for handicapped students."

He will live in one of the handi-capped-equipped dormitories at the college, will major in political science, and hopes to go into law or politics.

"Another Franklin Roosevelt," his older brother Kerry predicted.

Kevin's next goal is "to finish college, but I would like to get my license and drive." That will have to wait because specially-equipped vans cost about $20,000, Mrs. Kachejian said.

Biofeedback

"Now I don't have conventional physical therapy," Kevin explained. "I go to Wilmington twice a week for biofeedback."

And although the Kachejians say their doctors don't approve of biofeedback, Kevin said he is making progress.

Mrs. Kachejian said Kevin has been invited to speak and demonstrate his skills to groups of paraplegics. One group paid for their transportation and hotel.

"At that visit he got into the hotel pool and showed them how he could swim," she said. "People were amazed. One young man who was a quadriplegic just sat there. He had been that way for six years and the doctors said he would never be able to do more than that. Well, Kevin lent him his pen-holder and the young man wrote his name. You would have thought he had given him the world."

Mrs. Kachejian said she is very thankful "we didn't listen to (some of) the doctors and physical therapists," or Kevin may never have walked.

"I'm working on the grip on my right hand now," Kevin said. "Three electrodes are attached to my hand that measure the electrical impulses of my muscles. I have to keep concentrating on my arm and although I may not be moving it, the increased impulses in the muscles show on the monitor. I know then that I'm moving the muscles even though you can't see it with your eyes."

Kevin, who must now use a special pen-holding device to write, is working on his grip because he wants to be able to hold crutches.

"Ultimately my goal is to walk into my biofeedback session on crutches someday."

Something That Never Changed

My relationship with Kevin never changed after he became paralyzed. Instead, we just found new ways to have fun.

CHAPTER 5
HAVING FUN WITH A PARALYZED KID

When Kevin came home from his long rehabilitation, our family needed to adjust to "the new normal." We all had to assume new responsibilities and change our schedules. Every day was a character-building experience. Kevin needed help with everything: feeding, bathing, dressing, medicating, hygiene, wound care, lifting, driving, shopping and school work. Being with him made us all more grateful for the simple pleasures we have in life.

After his accident, Kevin did not stop having fun. He made the best of every moment. His paralysis might have limited him physically, but there was no way he'd let it hinder his ability to have a great time. He and I were always cracking jokes and looking for fun, wherever we might find it. Having BB gun fights and making small bombs were no longer on the agenda, so we came up with some creative ideas to continue our fraternal shenanigans. We started out slowly, testing the waters to determine what we could get away with.

Pool Pranks

Speaking of water, Mr. Hank Goodwin, a coach and faculty member at West Chester State College, volunteered to give Kevin swimming lessons at the college pool. The water was a perfect rehabilitation medium as it provided Kevin some buoyancy. Continuing to make physical progress, Kevin soon learned to slowly walk backward while in the pool. Kevin also liked to practice floating face down in the water. As a quadriplegic, he used little oxygen and could hold his breath for up to two minutes. Slowly moving his arm like a flipper, he could turn his head to catch a mouthful of air. If he needed help, he would signal us by wiggling his hand. For safety, we always stayed within an arm's reach of him.

Kevin's sense of humor was re-emerging as well. He would use his newly discovered breath-holding ability to mess with anyone nearby. He liked to act as if he was drowning, and he was quite convincing. Unfortunately, for those that weren't in on the joke, it was very distressing to see a motionless paralyzed youth floating face down in the pool.

The prank began when Kevin and I would see someone nearby, and float over toward them. Then Kevin would start his motionless dead-man-in-the-pool routine. Mom hated when we did this, but she would not get in the pool. Mr. Goodwin would sit back and chuckle. After thirty seconds of lifeless floating, the eyes of everyone nearby would be on Kevin. At about a minute's worth of staring, people were open-mouthed, transfixed and becoming visibly nervous. I would just calmly stand next to Kevin and watch him, which wigged them out even further. At a minute and a half, old women, except for mom, were ready to jump into the pool to save the poor kid. At about two minutes, Kevin would slowly roll over on his side, face the gaping-eyed crowd, and squirt a jet of water out of his mouth right at them. Like a whale clearing his blow hole. Mission complete! Kevin and I would smile and then float along to seek new victims.

Home Recon

Our house on Morstein Road was a split-level home with five floors. It was a crazy layout, with a couple of rooms on each floor. Each level was separated by five or six steps. The ground floor became Kevin's new bedroom. One day, Gina realized that Kevin hadn't seen any of the top three floors in a long time. When our parents weren't home, Gina helped Kevin out of his wheelchair and dragged him, one step at a time, up each flight of stairs. At each landing, Kevin got to lie on floor and peak in each of the rooms of the house and see how the rest of the family lived. Kevin enjoyed the ride, and Gina got a great workout.

Baja Rides

Another day, Gina loaded Kevin in our VW and went Baja-ing in the field across the street to have some fun. Of course, our parents had no idea that the minivan was being used for a cross-country ride. Gina and Kevin would take it down trails barely wide enough for a mini-bike, then come home minutes before mom returned. If caught, Kevin could always claim he was kidnapped. Careful to avoid arousing suspicion, Gina would always remember to scrape the mud and sticks out of the fenders, leaving mom in perpetual bewilderment as to what was wrong with the front-end suspension on her van. Sorry, Gina, mom's passed away, and it's high time the truth came out.

Trading Places

During Kevin's first year home from rehab, mom would constantly hover over him. And Kevin and I loved to play tricks on her.

One day, while he and I were watching TV in the ground floor family room, we decided to have some fun. Mom was in the second-floor kitchen and would look down the stairwell every five minutes to make sure Kevin was okay. Immediately after one of mom's inspections, Kevin and I executed "Operation Trading Places," a carefully conceived plan designed to shock and confuse the victim. We sprang into action. I took the blanket off Kevin and lifted him out of his wheelchair, placing him on a nearby sofa that was out of view from the kitchen. With precisely orchestrated timing, I then flipped the wheelchair on its side with a loud crashing noise and jumped into the seat. With a flourish, as a finishing touch, I pulled the blanket over my body, spun the top wheel of the chair, and wiggled my upper arm to appear as if I was struggling. To heighten the drama, Kevin yelled, "Help, mom, Help!" Like a streak of lightning, mom was down the stairs. Shocked at the sight of her son's overturned wheelchair, she quickly righted the chair and began to lift him back into it. As she looked into my face, I could see her total confusion. At the sound of Kevin laughing hysterically on the sofa across the room, mom turned to look at him and realized she had been duped. Kevin and I were in tears laughing, but mom was not happy about our little stunt. I feared she would commence retaliatory actions but got off with only a stern verbal reprimand as mom, still shaking, retreated to the kitchen. After she was out of sight, Kevin and I exchanged a few high fives and began planning our next stunt.

Wheelchair Boxing

For many years, during the day, Kevin wore a removable body cast called an orthoplast jacket. This brace conformed to his body, prevented him from slumping in his chair, which would have resulted in scoliosis. The jacket was made of sturdy plastic, and it kept him sitting upright in this chair.

When he wore a baggy shirt, no one would know Kevin was wearing it underneath. We used to kid about him being bullet-proof; an early version of Iron Man. When he first started wearing it, I tapped on his chest a few times and asked if it hurt. Kevin indicated he could feel pressure, but no pain.

Soon Kevin and I began to play boxing against each other. I'd jab at him in the jacket and dance around, and Kevin would juke his electric wheelchair left and right and slap back at me. When I hit him in the chest, the jacket would make a loud snapping noise, and Kevin would theatrically jerk his body back and let out a loud moan. The drama was well-choreographed, we spent a few weeks rehearsing our lines, staging and practicing our moves. Once we were good enough, Kevin and I headed off to the Exton Shopping Mall, seeking the busiest area we could find. Escalators were always a great spot, where dozens of shoppers could easily watch the commotion we were about to start. We'd kick it off by pretending to be arguing, and then gradually get louder to draw the spotlight.

"Take it back!".

"I ain't taking it back!"

At this point, I'd get up close in Kevin's face. "You'd better take it back!"

"I AIN'T TAKING IT BACK!"

Nearby shoppers began to watch what was going on. And those riding the escalators down, bringing them closer to the action, would watch us the whole way. Those going up would turn their heads, craning, to see what was happening. Once we had a sizeable turnout for our performance, I'd initiate the physical part of the altercation.

POW! I hit him in the chest.

Timing it perfectly, Kevin violently rocked back in his chair with a convincing moan before retaliating with a furious swing. When he began to juke me out with his wheelchair, we struggled to avoid busting out into laughter.

We loved seeing the shocked faces of all the shoppers. Making sure to never stay in one place for too long, we'd then race off and find another crowd for an encore performance. We kept an eye out for "Mall Cops" that might spoil our fun. Kevin and I would also pull this stunt in hospitals, parking lots and anytime we were bored and wanted to spice things up.

One time, however, it went too far. I had a party at our house, and about a dozen of my football teammates from the Henderson High School were there. Kevin was always a hit at social events. Everyone on the team was his big brother, and nobody messed with him. About an hour into the event, Kevin and I started our usual stunt—we'd never done it in front of our friends. Once our yelling had gotten everyone's attention, I hit him in the jacket. Kevin made sure to play his part and began to fight back. We must have put on a pretty good show, because, in the middle of our act, several of my teammates were about to drag me out in the yard and murder me. Thankfully, Kevin immediately spoke up and told them it was all a joke. Thinking he was just covering for my angry outburst, still intent on taking my life—and very protective of Kevin—my teammates remained unconvinced. Fearful of a merciless beating, I provided further proof of my innocence by lifting up Kevin's shirt and showing them his orthoplast jacket. I rapped the jacket hard with my knuckles, my teammates could hear the cracking sound, and my life was spared. After that close call, Kevin and I were a lot more cautious about pulling that stunt.

Faking Seizures

Kevin was a naturally gifted actor with a unique set of skills, such as rolling his eyes back in his head and convulsing. He could make a pretty convincing gurgling noise too. He would showcase these talents as part of another stunt he liked to pull.

He was on about eight different medications and took up to 28 pills a day. Some of them were big horse pills. Mom was highly organized and kept a daily log of everything he was to take and when. She was superb about making sure his meds were taken in the right dosages and promptly.

My best friend in high school was Mike "Willie" Willover. He and I hung out together all the time, and he always looked out for Kevin. If Kevin asked for a favor, Mike would jump and do it.

One night, Mike, Kevin and I were at a party, having a good old time. Confession, there was a keg of beer at this party, and we were all still in high school. Keg parties were a frequent weekend event back in the 1970s, and parents often looked the other way. In other words, there was a complete lack of adult supervision. But speaking of beer, these parents were part of "America's Greatest Generation." They had served in WWII or the Korean

War and fought for the right to drink beer. That hard-won gift, in their eyes, was transferred to their children. In fact, my generation of high school students was honoring the service and sacrifice of our parents by drinking beer. This was an act of patriotism, and it would have been disrespectful to do otherwise. [Are any of you buying any of this crap?]

Back to Kevin. Mike knew Kevin took many different medications and that he didn't drink alcohol. As part of yet another stunt, Kevin made a show of repeatedly asking Willie if he could have a cup of beer. Not in on the joke, Mike thought it wasn't a good idea. Kevin, persistent as ever, reassured Mike it would be okay. After all, it was just one beer. Not wanting to deny Kevin so humble a request, Mike poured him a small glass. After taking a few gulps, when Kevin knew the spotlight was on him, it was show time. First, he began to convulse. Next, his eyes rolled back in his head, and he started gurgling. It did not take long to send Mike into a full-blown panic, thinking he had just poisoned my paralyzed kid brother. Seeing this was my cue to further escalate Mike's distress, I immediately rushed to Kevin and knelt beside him. Looking scared I stared up at Mike—building the tension, watching panic grow in his eyes—and wailed, "Oh no! You didn't give him a beer, did you?" By this point, I was having a pretty hard time keeping a straight face. After letting Mike sweat for a few more moments, the scene concluded when Kevin miraculously recovered with a big smile.

Adult Years

Eventually, Kevin and I realized we needed to become responsible adults and find other ways to entertain ourselves. In time, Kevin finished his undergraduate degree at West Chester University, earned his law degree at Villanova University and became a Judicial Clerk at Chester County Courthouse for Judge Larry Wood. He took great pride in his profession as well as the great friends he knew and worked with.

Kevin would often host game nights at the house, and his friends from the Court House would come over to play Trivial Pursuit, among other games. On game night, he would serve only the finest gourmet meals: Benny's Pizza, Red Twizzler sticks, and Diet Cherry Coke were the staple delicacies at these gatherings.

But game night was not the only way Kevin knew to have fun. One time, at a wedding, Kevin scooted his electric wheelchair out onto the dance floor with Mrs. LaRue Morgan. Really getting into it, Kevin started doing 360-degree spins and zipping all over the dance floor. In the midst of a quick spin, the foot rests on his wheelchair hit Mrs. Morgan's ankles and cut her legs out from under her. She hit the floor hard but amazed us all when she sprang up and kept dancing as if it didn't happen.

Kevin wasn't just all play, though. He had a knack for business as well as a good sense of humor. Back when Gina had her own personal training business, Kevin helped his big sister by designing her business cards. The slogan read, "If you have the guts, I'll help you lose them."

Wheelchair Drag Racing

As my sisters and I grew up and had children of our own, Kevin loved to let his nieces and nephews climb on his electric wheelchair and ride around with him. The kids would sit on his lap or hang onto his handlebars while Uncle Kevin would burn down the driveway like a scene out of a Mad Max movie. Kevin was a master at wheelchair drag racing, executing precision turns, both on and off-road. As the founding father of wheelchair motocross, I am surprised he did not try to build a wheelchair jump ramp.

Travel

After dad passed away, Mom and Kevin came to visit me for three weeks while I was stationed in Germany. Kevin made such an impression on my landlords, the Schimmel family, that they named their newborn son after him. They also asked my brother to be their child's godfather even though he lived across the Atlantic Ocean. My brother made sure to send Kevin Schimmel birthday and Christmas gifts every year, and they had a special relationship. I often wondered whether my brother would eventually become the next U.S. Ambassador to Germany.

On another trip, with Mom and Kevin, in 1995—this time to Orlando— we hit nearly all the sights. Disney World and Universal Studios were great as we were granted early park access with their handicapped-friendly policies. Knowing Kevin was a huge Trekkie, he and I made a short Star Trek movie during our visit to Universal Studios. He dressed as Captain Kirk, and I was Mr. Spock. It was a lot of fun and later that night, we returned home to await our call from a major Hollywood producer. More than two decades later, we are still looking forward to the day we can resume our film careers.

A Man of Character

Make no mistake, my brother, Kevin, was a man of great character and has been a tremendous source of inspiration to our family, the community and everyone who met and knew him. Kevin was determined to live an active and independent life. As a Christian, Kevin's source of strength was his faith in God. Gina took Kevin to a full immersion baptism, where it took four men to help accomplish it. When he could, Kevin would leave the house and ride in his electric chair down the road to the local church. When he was too ill to attend, Gina would pick up the audio tapes of the sermon and bring them home.

Being paralyzed for 32 years took an enormous toll on Kevin's body, but not his mind. No one faced adversity better. No matter how ill he was, his mission was to cheer others up. He spent most of the last two years of his life in the hospital and in rehabilitation. During this time, mom passed away, and I received orders to deploy to Baghdad. As always, my sister Gina was the rock, keeping things moving during this very trying time.

When I called Kevin from Baghdad in late March 2004, he had been hospitalized and bedridden for two months. He had just come off his respirator. It was so typical of his character that Kevin did not complain about his situation, and his only concern was for my safety. The privilege of having him for a brother lifted my spirits and made every day in Iraq a little bit easier. And I still—to this day—miss you, buddy.

SECTION 3

GROWING UP IN PENNSYLVANIA

CHAPTER 6

YARD & HOUSE FIRES, BUTCHIE, DOGS & CRABS

All generations in human history had to learn how to entertain themselves. Growing up in Pennsylvania in the 1960s and 1970s was no different. Sadly, today's generation of kids live in an increasingly fearful society, one which often discourages physical activity that might skin their knees or taking pride in their faith by wearing a t-shirt that might hurt someone else's feelings. And God forbid if someone chips a tooth or feels offended. It's no wonder that a good number of modern kids limit themselves to an unimaginative, introverted existence within video games.

My siblings and friends grew up before the internet, and social media were born. We had to make do. As kids, we did not have many material things, so we improvised and adapted. We had fun despite wearing hand-me-down clothes and frequently scraped knees. Most of us survived our journey to adulthood, gaining some common sense along the way. Although many of the witnesses are now old, senile or gone, I want to pass these stories on to my children and grandchildren.

As I've grown older, I've come to realize that retirement is a period in your life in which you have increasingly vivid memories of events that never occurred. So, I am documenting these events during the lucid period in my life before I retire, and the facts become blurred, and all the good stories are over-embellished. Having recounted some childhood stories about tunnels, bombs, epic neighborhood firework battles, BB gun fights, ticks, sewey hole patrol, staged bike wrecks, and Baja riding, I can undisputedly claim I had a lot of fun while running around outside with my buddies. But there was much more mischief that I will soon reveal.

And if my kids or their children ever try to do half the stuff I did as a kid, I'll whoop 'em. Maybe it's a double standard, but I learned some hard lessons that my children won't have to that I'm sharing in this section of the book.

OK, let's light this candle.

Cooking the Yard

Speaking of lighting, Kevin and I liked to watch my dad light the charcoals in the BBQ grill every Sunday. He'd use lighter fluid, and it was exciting to see the flames leap a couple of feet high. Kevin and I tried to do this one morning without any parental supervision, and it turned out to be a very dangerous adventure.

We put the charcoals on the grill. Unable to find the lighter fluid, we grabbed a five-gallon gas can that dad used for the lawn mower. The can was half-full, and I used a good portion of it to soak the coals. Putting down the can, I threw a match on the grill, and the flames shot up several feet. Kevin and I were impressed with our work. Just like dad did it.

The flames began to ebb as the coals started a slow burn. I picked the gas can back up and poured more fuel on. That's when the hard lesson—that lighter fluid burns very differently from gasoline—started. The flames from the grill leaped into the air—following the stream of fuel—and the gas can I was holding over my head ignited. I immediately threw the burning can away from my body. While the can was in flight, burning fuel poured out of the spout. The can hit the ground and tumbled, spitting out more blazing fuel. Afraid it was going to explode next to the house, I ran up and kicked the can as hard as I could toward the street sewer. More gas came spraying out as it took three more kicks to get the can out of the yard and into the street. I turned back toward the house to see there were a couple of dozen burning patches of grass in the yard. Kevin and I madly tried to stomp out the flames. I got some of the gas on my feet and was doing an Irish jig trying to stomp out burning grass with fiery shoes. We finally got all the yard fires out, but the can continued to burn in the street for a while.

Unbelievably, no one in the neighborhood saw any of this. No one called the fire department or came to assist. Thankful for that, Kevin and I began to cover up the evidence. We poured water on the coals and killed the grill fire. We then cleaned the mushy coals out of the grill and returned it where we found it. When the five-gallon-can cooled down, it was a bit dented and singed. We returned it to the shed and hid it behind another gas can.

Looking out into the yard, I noticed several dozen brown patches of burned grass. A clear sign to my parents that something that happened! I searched for some green spray paint, but could only find the can of black we had used to paint the old convertible. I had no way to cover up the yard damage. I needed a plausible story to tell my dad when he discovered the torched grass. Perhaps I could blame it on a UFO landing in the neighborhood; at second thought, I knew I had to come up with something better.

Then my feet started to hurt. I looked down and saw my blue jeans were scorched, and my Keds sneakers were partially melted. They were old, though, so I dug a hole in the nearby field and buried them. Maybe mom would not notice their absence. I threw my old, tattered jeans in the washing machine, hoping mom would not look too hard at them.

My dad came home that night after dusk, so he did not see the damage until the next morning. When he called me, I came running. The yard burns were still visible, but now there were also big grass patches killed by unburned gasoline. I played dumb, and, for once, it paid off. Not pressing the matter any further, dad cut the grass that day, and it eventually grew back. My parents never learned the truth. I was thankful I had dodged the wrath of Mom.

A month later, we were sitting at the dinner table when mom told a tragic story about the father of one of Kevin's friends from elementary school. The man was lighting an outdoor grill using a gasoline can; it ignited, and the father was severely burned. He died after suffering in a hospital for several weeks. Kevin and I sat silently through the meal realizing how lucky we had been.

Flaming Bees

Another close encounter with fire almost consumed our home. Our house on Morstein Road had two thick evergreen trees located on either side of the front door. At the time of this incident, these trees were about eight feet tall and nearly touched the roofline. We never paid much attention to them until some aggressive bees built a large hive inside them. Entering or exiting the house without being stung became a challenge.

Our house on Morstein Road

Mom complained several times while unlocking the front door, and I decided to take some decisive action to get rid of the nest. I recruited my sister, Shelley, to help. We did not have any wasp spray, so I was forced to improvise. My plan was to smoke out the bees.

I took a six-foot-long metal clothes pole from the back yard and wrapped a couple of old t-shirts around the end. I doused the rags in lighter fluid, and we marched around to the front of the house. As Shelley lit the rags, I told her to stay back. I knew the bees would be really pissed off when I lit them up.

I moved up to the tree and thrust the lit end of the pole into the center, just below the bee's nest. Within seconds, the nest caught on fire. The bees were caught off-guard, but a few dozen came flying out. While I was focused on burning the nest and beating off bees, the entire tree suddenly burst into flames. Although the outside of this tree was green, inside was a dense mesh of dead pine needles. Fueled by that dry tinder, flames climbed the tree quickly, and within seconds, were touching the roofline of the house.

Holy smokes! Literally.

I had not considered this a possibility, nor did I have any sort of contingency plan. I needed to take immediate action, or the roof was going to be set ablaze. I screamed at Shelley, "Get an ax! Get an ax!"

Yes, my plan was to cut down a burning tree while flaming bees ran kamikaze missions against me. I know. Brave, but stupid.

Shelley started to go for the ax, but she hesitated, and turned to shout, "What about the hose?" I wasn't listening, what with burning bees and all that. I screamed again for the ax. Shelley didn't move and pointed to the hose, lying about ten feet away. The lightbulb in my head went on. That was a much better plan. The tree was now completely engulfed in flames, and the eaves of the roof had started to smolder. Within fifteen seconds I was attacking the fire with water, as Shelley ran into the house to call the fire department.

About three minutes into this drama, neighbors started to assemble in the street to watch. I was a bit surprised none of them offered to help. Shortly after that, the fire trucks came screaming up to the house. At this point, I had the situation under control. The bee's nest was toast. I thought, OK, mission complete. Then I realized there was collateral damage. Although the fire had been extinguished, the front of the house was a bit blackened, and the tree was still smoking. After loitering a couple of minutes, the fire trucks left surprisingly quickly. Perhaps they were returning to their annual "Fire

Fighters" Picnic. As our neighbors started to disperse, some seemed disappointed that the tacky Kachejian family wasn't burned out of their home.

By the time this misadventure had come to a conclusion, two things were certain. First, Shelley was the real hero that day, alerting me to the nearby hose and saving the house from further damage. Second, I had learned a valuable lesson: invest in wasp spray, it's well worth the money.

Butchie

Mom had a nephew, our cousin, named William Peters. For some reason, he got the nickname "Butchie." He lived with us for a few years and was like a big brother to me. Butchie would sometimes take me hunting or fishing. I always enjoyed our time together.

Early in life, the Kachejian kids learned that we didn't want to get in trouble with mom. If we did something wrong, mom held us responsible. We all lived in fear of her wrath, which struck like a Category 3 hurricane. Fortunately, when Butchie lived with us, we'd blame everything on him. Now he was not a perfect child (which helped when throwing fault on him). He was capable of mischief. My dad once caught him shooting at moving cars, with a BB gun, from the first-

William "Butchie" Peters

floor window of our house. Dad told him it was wrong to shoot at cars, but also that if he wanted to improve his marksmanship, he should lead any moving target by a few feet.

Once he had been caught with the BB gun, the Kachejian kids could then blame him for everything. It was open season: broken vase, missing keys, mud on the carpet, it didn't matter. "Butchie did it." When I was three years old, I even tried to blame him for wetting my pants. No matter how convincing we thought we were, my mother just didn't buy it. Concerning the wet pants, I'd like to finally issue a public apology to Butchie, and just come clean. My brother Kevin did it.

Sibling Rivalry

The four Kachejian kids had their internal feuds. I once bought a big bag of popcorn at the grocery store and was accused of not sharing enough of it with Gina. She got me back that evening when she set the dinner plates. Gina licked my plate and spit in my food before I arrived. She let me eat it and asked me how the meal was. Then she dropped the bomb and told me what she had done. I gave chase, but she was quick—a nimble gymnast—and escaped to her bedroom and locked the door. I camped outside her door for an hour waiting to pounce. She would not come out.

Gina went through a phase of hit and run attacks against me—a punch, a pinch, a slap—and would always manage to escape my retaliation. But, one day—I had become smarter than the average bear—I anticipated her attack and caught her by the ankle before she fled upstairs to her room. Dragging her down the stairs, I beat the crap out of her. Fifteen-year-old Gina never again messed with her twelve-year-old brother. I finally had her respect.

Many years later, I had one last act of retaliation in store for Gina. When she and Peter Curley announced their engagement, I sent my future brother-in-law a Deepest Sympathies card. It was meant to be humorous. I quickly learned that women do not appreciate men's—or at least my—humor. I was in the dog house with her for quite a while.

On Gina's wedding day, we had a photographer at our house before the ceremony. Most of us left early to get a good place to park near the church. The wedding was to begin at noon. Her soon-to-be husband, Peter, was there, but Gina was missing. This was before cell phones were available, so no one knew the reason for the delay. We became very concerned after 30 minutes passed. Gina and her friends had simply lost track of time while taking photos. About an hour after the planned start, the bridal party arrived to everyone's relief. Ironically, many of the bridal photos taken at our house had a grandfather clock in the background documenting the time as the pictures were taken. The happy bride-to-be was clearly unaware she was missing her

74

own wedding. But the wedding eventually worked out fine, it just started an hour later than originally scheduled.

Scrooge and Queenie

My first dog was named Scrooge. What a great friend. We had him for several years, but he suddenly disappeared.

Years later I learned why. Some kid in our neighborhood had a coonskin hat just like Daniel Boone wore. It was a cool looking furry hat with a raccoon tail dangling off the back. The kid often ran through our yard. When Scrooge saw the raccoon on this kid's head, he chased it and jumped up to grab it. Scrooge scared the kid, and the neighbor complained. My parents probably over reacted but got rid of my dog—gave him away. Man, that hurt.

My second dog was a girl named Queenie. She was another great mutt. I'd ride my bike with her running behind me, and we'd wrestle and play Frisbee in the yard. With Queenie around, I always had someone to play with. When I was about ten, I received my first cassette tape recorder as a birthday gift. It was cool to be able to record people's voices on a shoebox-sized device. I put it to work by recording my voice calling the dog. "Here Queenie! Here Queenie! Come here, girl!" She was very loyal and came to me instantly.

Always the prankster, I recorded my calls to the dog every minute on a 30-minute tape. The next day, I put the tape recorder in the living room closet, turned it on, and ran upstairs to another closet. I waited for the recorder to make its first call. Seconds later came the sound: "Here Queenie! Here Queenie"! My dog ran to the living room and did not see me. She sniffed around the closet. Then I called her from upstairs. Queenie sprinted up the stairs looking for me. A few seconds later, the tape recorder called the dog again, and she ran back to the living room. After about 15 minutes of running the stairs, that dog was worn out, and I was quite proud of the results of my Pavlovian experiment.

Happiest Dog in Pennsylvania

Queenie was one of the best-fed dogs in America. Once a week, dad would bring home a five-gallon bucket of scraps from the restaurant. It was full of half-eaten burgers, pieces of steak, chicken, fish and other goodies.

She would come running to the door each night, hoping dad brought home the bacon (sometimes literally). She would be the happiest dog in Pennsylvania. When we ran out of restaurant scraps, we fed Queenie the cheapest dog food mom could find (a brand called Cadillac). That stuff smelled awful, and Queenie would never touch it. She had been permanently spoiled by dad.

Happiest Crabs in Maryland

Our family took two vacations to the Elk River in Maryland, near the town of Elkton. It was located at the northern end of the Chesapeake Bay. We spent a week in a small house that had a dock on the river.

Queenie came with us, and dad brought two five-gallon buckets of restaurant scraps. Gina, Shelley, Kevin and I spent time fishing off the end of the dock. We had dug up some worms for bait and were having luck, catching a small fish every half hour or so. Then, dad brought out some crab traps and tied some scrap meat in them. We dropped them in the water. Queenie stood on the dock and watched as we pulled up crabs every 20 minutes.

We were quick studies and changed the bait on our fish hooks from worms to restaurant scraps. We also threw some scraps in the river as chum. Holy Smokes! The four of us reeled in over 60 fish in an hour. Sometimes the fish had a crab attached to it. Every crab and fish within five miles were now churning around our dock.

Queenie got so excited she jumped off the dock toward the water. This was a near catastrophe as she was chained to a piling at the time. When she jumped, she hung herself and was dangling above the water by her neck. Choking and struggling, we thought she was going to die. The water was full of hundreds of crabs, and I hesitated to jump in. But I couldn't lose my dog, so in I went. I got to Queenie just as my siblings were pulling her back up by the chain. Queenie survived, and we didn't chain her to the dock again (ever). Once the rescue was over, the Kachejian kids went back to fishing.

CHAPTER 7
BARTLEY'S, BIKE RIDE & HAROLD

Tip and Tab Bartley

In the early 1960s, my family lived in a row house on West Barnard Street in West Chester. The Bartley family lived next door. Mr. William "Tab" Bartley and his wife Laura "Tip" Bartley, had three children: Greg, Patricia "Pat" and Mike.

No one in this part of town had a lot of money, but they made do though it was often very hard when raising children. Unfortunately, one holiday season, Tab Bartley was temporarily laid off from his job at Lukens Steel. My dad gave Tab $100 to help pay for Christmas. That act cemented a friendship which lasted the rest of their lives.

For decades, the Kachejian and Bartley families shared many birthdays and holidays. Tab became my Little League football coach and was like a second father. Greg later served in the Army in Vietnam. Pat became an honor graduate of Cheney State College and was inducted into their Athletic Hall of Fame for Tennis and Basketball. Mike was an All-American gymnast at Odessa Jr. College and later competed nationally for the LSU Tigers. He went on to start Bartley Gymnastics, a business that helped hundreds of young men develop into outstanding athletes. It was incredible how the lives of two families could be so closely tied together all from a single act of kindness several decades earlier.

Eating Right

Kevin and I each had a sweet tooth and loved eating white sugar; taking turns pouring it straight into our mouths, like a couple of drug addicts. We even liked going to our dentist, Dr. Gentile, because he gave us a Tootsie Pop after he filled in our cavities. That's called business development.

Onto us, mom started hiding the sugar pourer, but we'd dig through the kitchen cabinets and find it. We'd then put the near empty pourer back before mom caught us. But she outsmarted us. One time she filled the sugar pourer with salt. As the older brother, I always worked things to get the first mouthful. Kevin, seeing my reaction and discovering how we'd been ambushed—by our own mother—didn't take his turn that day. Not caring if we suffered from sucrose withdrawal, mom, in one fell swoop, broke our sugar addiction.

Like most kids, I liked to eat chocolate. There was usually some in the house after Easter. We had no air conditioning, so it wasn't unusual to put the chocolate in the freezer for storage. I started digging in the fridge one day, looking for something to eat, when I discovered a motherlode; well wrapped and hidden from us kids. I thought it was my lucky day until I took a big chomp of the frozen chocolate and realized it was really liver. Thanks, mom.

One Saturday morning, I woke up and went downstairs to breakfast. No one else was awake. I looked in the kitchen cabinet and found only one box of cereal, Corn Flakes. I was hoping to find something with a little more kick to it like Corn Pops, Frosted Flakes or Sugar Smacks, but I was happy that we had something to eat. After pouring a big bowl, I turned to the refrigerator to get some milk. I discovered there wasn't any in the house.

I knew I could eat Sugar Smacks and Corn Pops dry, but Corn Flakes... those needed to be washed down. I thought about eating them with water, but then I saw a half-empty can of Blatz Beer sitting on the refrigerator shelf. Feeling both hungry and adventurous—and necessity being the mother of invention—I thought to myself, "OK, let's give this a try." I poured Blatz Beer on the Corn Flakes. The beer was flat, so there was not much foam. I scooped a spoonful of cereal—gave it a taste—and immediately realized it was a bad idea. It was against all my principles, but I threw out the bowl of cereal. I stayed hungry until mom got up and made lunch.

Rich Kid

When I was four years old, my family took a trip to Hershey Park. It was one of my first travel memories. The park was busy, and I was too young for many of the rides. I also was not tall enough to see over all the adults and enjoy the sights. I remember holding my mother's hand for hours and walking around as I looked at people's legs.

We crossed a bridge, and I saw the largest goldfish, a Koi, that my young mind could have fathomed. I threw a small pebble into the water, and the fish immediately ate it. Clearly, these were carnivorous fish, so I stayed back from the water. I was kind of bored, constantly looking at the ground, until I saw a one-dollar bill lying in front of me. I grabbed it and thought I was the richest kid in the world. I could buy a lot of penny candy when I got home. My attitude changed immediately. Hershey Park was a great place. Fortunes could be found there.

The Smoking 60s

In the 1960s, most adults in America were smokers and so were many teenagers. The health effects weren't a big concern. Smoking was promoted in society, not suppressed. My dad had a crew cut, and that allowed him to stick a lit cigarette behind his ear—just like a pencil. Some people would consider that hazardous, but to dad, ears were designed to hold a burning smoke. As long as the gel in his hair was non-flammable, everything was fine.

My dad gave me the best lesson about smoking I ever received. I was four years old and sitting on his lap when he gave me a puff of his cigarette. I immediately turned green and coughed and hacked for about fifteen minutes. It was disgusting, and I had no idea why anyone would smoke. That experience permanently stopped any interest I had in picking up the habit. Today, a parent would be arrested for giving their kid a cigarette. I'm telling you, it saved me from ever having the temptation to light up.

We lived in a row house on West Washington Street from 1961-65. There was a corner store at the end of the block where I would buy penny candy. When I was five, mom would occasionally send me to the store to pick up groceries (something no sane parent would do today). She could not always make the trip, as my little brother, Kevin, required constant care. Mom would call the store owner with the order first and let him know I was coming. That way, I came home with the right groceries.

And on some of these store runs, mom had me pick up a pack of cigarettes with the grocery order.

There was one thing about smoking that I found exciting. I liked watching people throw their cigarette butts on the ground and smoosh them with their shoe. To a little kid, crushing cigarettes in the street looked fun and cool. I really wanted to take a pack of my mom's cigarettes into the alley behind our house and smoosh them. But mom would know if her Pall Mall cigarettes went missing. So, I convinced Kevin to give me a dollar of his birthday money, and I went to the corner store. Five-year-old Kerry walked into the store and ordered a pack of Paul Mall cigarettes from the owner. He asked if my mother sent me, and I deceitfully nodded yes.

I marched out the store with my purchase, went home, and took Kevin into the alley. After all, he had funded the venture. I broke open the pack of cigarettes and threw a couple of cancer sticks on the ground. Kevin and I went at it with our shoes. I dumped a couple more out just as mom showed up at the scene. I was holding the pack in my hand, crushed cigarettes at my feet. Things looked really bad for the future paperboy. There was no way I could blame this on my cousin Butchie. Mom began her interrogation, and it didn't take long for us to crack. Satisfied with our confession, mom never let me go to the store again for cigarettes.

First Bike Ride

When Shelley got a bicycle for her sixth birthday and was learning how to ride, I was only four but also eager to learn. One night not long after, I dreamed—it was vivid and highly motivational—that I could ride that bicycle.

The next morning, I woke up, headed downstairs, took Shelley's bike and went out to the sidewalk. Without any permission or supervision, I got on the bike, rode a couple of feet and fell over.

I repeated this two or three more times. Finally, I learned how to pedal fast enough to stay upright. Weaving all over the sidewalk, working hard to keep the bike going, I passed several row houses. I was struggling, but the thrill of the ride was incredible.

As I approached the store at the end of the block, only about 200 feet from me, I noticed a police car parked on the corner. The cop sitting inside looked up as I closed in on his cruiser. And while I now knew how to keep my balance while moving forward, I had no idea how to turn or how to apply the brakes. My dream had taught me nothing about turning and braking.

I had the full attention of the donut-eating cop as I crashed Shelley's teetering bike into the side of his vehicle. I fell to the sidewalk, terrified that the cop was going to arrest me for stealing Shelley's bike or damaging government property.

I scrambled to my feet just as the cop got out of his cruiser. He walked toward me—I was going to be a four-year-old with a rap sheet—and I wet my pants. He asked me where I lived, and I pointed down the block. He turned me around and suggested that I walk the bike home.

Relieved that I would be spared prosecution, I went straight home and put Shelley's bike back where I found it. Wanting to lie low after the incident, I didn't ride a bike again for months. Years later, I would hone my bike riding skills as a paperboy.

Harold

When I was a youth, my dad told me, "Son, nobody gets out of life alive."

That humorous statement about our mortality was thought provoking. I knew God was always watching us, and I wanted to get into Heaven. Was I on the right path? How would I know? It was a weighty question.

As the years passed, I found my behavior and actions were often tempered by knowing I would be judged at the end of my life. I wanted to enjoy my life, but not be too tempted by evil. That was a tough proposition for a young man.

When I first started to learn about God, I was somewhat confused. We rarely attended church as children, but dad would occasionally tell us stories from the Bible. I picked up information a little bit at a time. During this period, I was convinced that God's name was Harold. All the evidence supported it. The Lord's Prayer was quite clear. "Our Father, who art in Heaven, Harold be Thy name." My belief was further reinforced in December listening to Christmas carols about Harold's angels singing. On the record player and radio, every day during the holiday season, I would hear that song *Hark the Harold Angels Sing* (and wonder what "hark" meant). For several years, I wondered why God wanted to be called Harold. I am glad that's cleared up now.

CHAPTER 8
ARCHERY, MILK, NAPKINS, TV & CLUNKER CARS

Archery

I took archery lessons at North Junior High School when I was in 7th grade and really enjoyed them. I asked for a bow and arrow for my thirteenth birthday, and it was an immediate hit. Kevin and I set up targets in the yard and started developing our skill, spending many hours trying trick shots. We shot at cans, cereal boxes and dummies. I tried riding my bike with no hands and firing an arrow on the move. That took dexterity. My accuracy began to improve, but I could not find any volunteers to practice my William Tell shot. We started firing our arrows straight up in the air to see how high they would travel. We did not appreciate just how dangerous this was, often running for cover when the arrows began their deadly plunge back to earth.

I couldn't afford to buy many new arrows on a paperboy's salary, so I kept repairing the ones I had. Sometimes I'd glue the feathers back on. When the metal tips broke off, I would just use a knife and sharpen the wood to make the arrow into a long flying pencil.

Several of my friends, Kurt LaMarch, Scott Boyd and Al Money, had their own bows. They hunted bullfrogs in a nearby pond and invited me to join them. Once I saw what they were doing, I could not draw my bow. It was senseless and cruel. I could kill animals for food, but I did not enjoy killing them for sport. Many years later, as an Army Ranger, I killed animals for survival; I was hungry, and those critters were chow. And I had no moral difficulty engaging enemy insurgents in the Iraq War; it was part of the mission.

My cousin Butchie once invited me to go deer hunting in Snow Shoe, Pennsylvania. He took a shotgun, and I brought my bow and arrow. It was winter and freezing cold. We arrived in the evening and slept in an old farmhouse with a wood burning stove. Roughing it, there was no electricity, running water or indoor facilities. I went to use the outhouse, behind the farmhouse, at about 2:00 AM and was startled by a large animal when I opened the door. We both ran in opposite directions. In my mind, it must have been a vicious wolverine. But Pennsylvania wasn't a wolverine habitat, so I probably stumbled on an opossum or raccoon.

Three hours later, at 5:00 AM we began the deer hunt. After a few hours, a deer ran within 30 feet of us. Butchie raised his shotgun and fired. It was a deafening noise. The deer kept running. We looked for any evidence that he had wounded the deer, but there was no blood. It was as if he fired a blank round. It was incredible that he had missed the deer at such a short range. He called it "Buck Fever," a kind of anxious anticipation to shoot something. A few minutes later, I took a shot at a chipmunk from a short distance with my bow and arrow thinking I would miss. The arrow had bad feathers, and the metal tip was broken. Unfortunately, I hit the little fellow.

Spilled Milk

After Kevin's accident, Gina, Shelley and I were called on to perform many family chores. She was a new driver and was constantly going to the store or running her siblings to school sports.

One time, she made a milk run to the local market in our VW bus, and as she merged back onto Airport Road, the milk bottle tipped over on the floor. Gina immediately leaned over to the passenger side to pick the leaking bottle up. In doing so, she veered into a guardrail. This was before airbags, and Gina was injured when her torso hit the steering wheel. She brought the damaged van home and then went to the hospital to get checked out. Fortunately, she only suffered some bruising. Gina was upset more that she had damaged the only reliable vehicle we had to transport our paralyzed brother. When dad came home and got the word of the accident, he pulled Gina aside. In his typical supportive style, dad told Gina, "Don't cry over spilled milk."

Napkins

When I turned ten years old, my mother gave me permission to ride my bicycle on Boot Road. That road was relatively busy with traffic and led to the local 7-11 convenience store and a small family-owned grocery store. I could now go anytime I wanted to buy some penny candy.

Mom had her own motives for granting me this new privilege. She needed me to make runs to pick up supplies. She gave me a list and a few dollars, and I would accept the mission and move out.

One Saturday, mom was preparing for a BBQ picnic and realized we were out of supplies needed for the event. She called me into action. My mission: to pick up a package of paper plates and plenty of napkins. I took the money, repeated my instructions to confirm I understood them and promised to be home in 30 minutes. Roger that.

Mounting my bike, I zipped down Boot Road. I was peddling hard, and the breeze was blowing through my hair. There were no bike helmets required. Life was good. I parked my bike in front of the little grocery store and went inside. I felt important; I had money and was a paying customer. I found the paper plates right away but was disappointed I could not find any napkins. Not wanting to disappoint my mother—understanding even as a young boy that men don't ask for help to find things in a store—I searched the aisles and shelves several times. I finally found napkins; a high-quality brand that was super absorbent (it must be so since it said it right on the wrapper). But they were a bit more expensive than I expected. I grabbed the package and went to the counter to pay.

The guy on register hesitated and gave me a strange look. He rang it up, and I barely had enough money. I jumped back on my bike and got home in less than thirty minutes. I put the bag and change on the kitchen table and turned to mom. Mission completed! She usually thanked me when I ran errands, but this time mom was unusually quiet. Something seemed unsaid about my store run, but I just shrugged and went about the doings of that day.

After my 18th birthday, my mother told me the rest of the Story of the Napkins. What I bought at the market that day were feminine napkins. That explained why they weren't located with the paper supplies and why they were so pricey. And the funny look from the cashier. And why they weren't used at the picnic the following day.

TV

We didn't watch much TV as kids, except for Saturday morning cartoons, which were the weekly highlight. Four hours of pure animated joy: *Pink*

Panther, Space Ghost, Scooby Doo, Rocky & Bullwinkle. And every day after school, I'd watch Speed Racer.

One day, dad brought home a color TV, our first, and put it in the living room. As we got older, Channels 17, 29 and 48 in the Philly area always had something good. I just had to adjust the UHF loop antenna to reduce the snowy static on the screen. I soon got hooked on professional wrestling; after all, it was real—they, more or less, said so during the matches. Bruno Sammartino was the long-time reigning champion. I felt robbed when he lost his championship.

On Tuesday nights, dad would watch the bull fights from Mexico or Spain, and the rest of us would join him. We kids were convinced that dad was once a matador. He would show us his bull horns and poster featuring him as the lead matador. Packing in close around the TV—this was long before big screens, you had to jockey for a good viewing angle—we would listen as dad described the action.

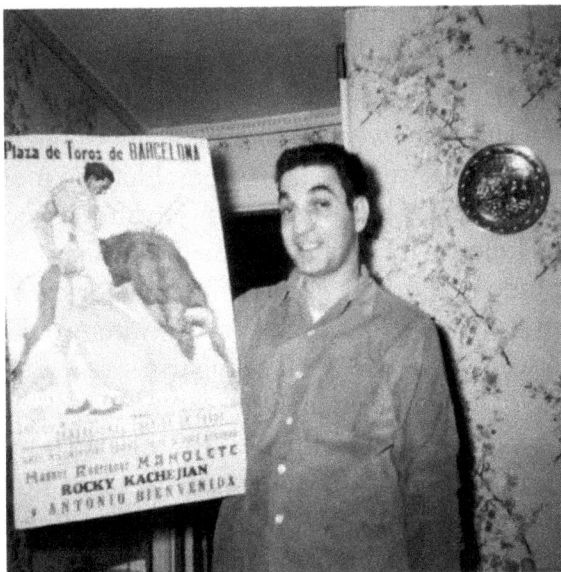

Rocky Kachejian's Bullfight Poster

Ironically, our cat, Ebenezer, would join us. I would lie on the floor watching the TV, and Ebby would sit on the top of the sofa. At the height of the bout—*the corrida de toro*—the tensest moment, the cat would spring, claws extended, and land on my back like a *picador* spearing the bull. That was one crazy cat.

Clunker Cars

The Kachejian clan had a fleet of old clunker cars, but we did little auto maintenance. When Kevin had his accident, we had to convert the VW bus into a wheelchair van. It started to get a lot of rust on it, so we improvised an inexpensive solution. We simply hid the new rust spot by covering it with a bumper sticker. We didn't care what the bumper sticker was for. If it was the right size to cover the rust, we slapped it on; an effective cosmetic, if not a structurally sound solution.

I drove a 1967 Chevy Nova or a 1969 white Plymouth Fury convertible in high school. The Fury had less rust than any other car in the family fleet. It was a gas guzzling tank, but gas was relatively cheap, and I could drive several other teammates to football or lacrosse practice. One winter, we had a severe snowstorm—with temperatures well below freezing—for several days. All our cars were buried deep. When the Fury was finally dug out of the snow, I got it started and drove to the deli where I worked. It began overheating, but thankfully, I made it back to our house. When my dad came home from his job, he crawled under the car and announced that the freeze plugs had blown out. Until they were repaired, coolant would continue to leak from the vehicle.

This was a real problem. I had no money to fix the car or pay for new coolant, and I had to get to my job after school. Dad planned to repair the car the following weekend. In the meantime, I would have to settle on a simpler solution; pouring water in the radiator each way to ride a few miles to and from my job. When I did this, the water would immediately begin leaking out; the car would barely make the trip.

I did not want to get stranded, so I started taking an emergency six-pack of Blatz Beer with me... for the car (it was dad's beer, but he had a lot of it in the fridge). Uncle George, my dad's brother, was a beer distributor for several companies: Ortleib's, Blatz and Rolling Rock. He used to get dad an entire case of 16-ouncers for only a $1.65. Beer did not freeze as quickly as water, so I decided to use it as an improvised coolant. The leaks worsened, and the Fury would overheat after a mile or so. At that point, I would jump out and pour a couple of 16-ouncers in the radiator and continue my, thankfully, short ride each way to work. My strategy worked out that week, and while Blatz Beer was not suitable for Corn Flakes, it proved to be a cost-effective emergency coolant in easy open containers. Everybody was a winner. I was able to get to work and get paid. My employer was happy I showed up on time. Dad was glad the engine block did not crack, and he was able to fix the car as promised. And Uncle George was able to sell more beer.

Every once in a while, I would put the convertible top down on the Fury. It had a finicky rag top, so getting it up and down was not easy. There was a lot of wind noise when the top was down, but that was easy to compensate for. I just turned the radio up. One hot day, I was driving to play in a summer league lacrosse game about 15 miles away. I was on Ship Road and was approaching an unguarded railroad crossing. The sun was shining, and Lynyrd Skynyrd was blasting on the radio. Life was good, but at that moment, mine almost came to an abrupt end. The train track was not visible from a distance due to a small hill and some trees—it created a blind spot as you came onto the tracks. As I crossed them that day, I looked to the right, and a train was closing in on me. It narrowly missed me (or better said, I barely got clear). Had I been there a few seconds later, I would have been T-boned. The Fury and its driver would have lost that battle.

CHAPTER 9
TOOLS, MOON, ARCHIE, COLLECTIONS, AMBUSH & CHICKEN

Tools

Kevin and I had plenty of free time during the summer. The activities we undertook to fill that time often—well, sometimes—taught us valuable lessons. We once stumbled into a dozen wooden shipping pallets and decided to use them to build a fort in our back yard.

Pulling the pallets apart was hard work, and we needed to save the nails in the process so we could re-use them. We spent many hours straightening out bent nails by hammering them on a concrete pad.

When it came time to build the fort, we had no real plan or training, and our only tools were a hammer and a rusty saw. We went to work without any adult supervision, each of us taking turns with the hammer. Every dozen nails or so, one of us would miss and smash his fingers—soon there was as much of that as driving nails. Man, that hurt. Finally, Kevin set the ultimate standard for how not to hammer a nail. Instead of holding it between his thumb and forefinger, somehow, he got his left thumb over the head of the nail. He swung the hammer and smashed his thumb onto the head of the nail. Man was that a gruesome sight. It was so bad we sought out Mrs. Stapleford, our neighbor nurse, to bandage it up. Kevin took the rest of the day off. We couldn't figure out how to blame the accident on my cousin Butchie, but we did learn it pays to have the right carpentry tools and to be trained on how to use them.

Speaking of tools and wounded appendages, fast forward about twenty years. I was in the garage trying to build a wooden shelf about eight feet off the ground. Armed with a screw gun, I was on a step ladder that was too short, on my toes stretching to hold a screw and drive a 2x4 piece of lumber in the wall. The screws were long, unwieldy—evil and possibly possessed by a demon—and I was pressing hard to force it into the wall. I had already bent several screws because of the odd angle of my body. I was bound and determined to get the one I was leaning into aligned and straight through the board. Then it happened.

I gave another big push, and suddenly the screw bent. The screw gun was still spinning, and I drilled a hole in my left hand just below the knuckle of my index finger. At the same time, the ladder kicked out from under me, and I crashed onto the garage floor. I did not stick the landing; it was a flailing flop kind of impact. I laid there, my back and ribs stinging. Then I looked at my hand. The flesh was still smoking from the new circular hole in it. I screamed for Alice, who was inside the house watching TV. I finally got her attention during a commercial break. We made a trip to the emergency room. Amazingly, there was little blood. The screw gun cauterized the wound, and the drill just missed the joint and connective tissues. No permanent damage.

I have sometimes embellished this story, describing how I drilled the screw through my left hand and into the wall; centrifugal force of the screw gun splattering blood. When the ladder kicked out, I was hanging from the wall with my left hand pinned to the garage wall and pounding for help with my right. Alice did not answer, and I knew I had to take my rescue into my own hands—no pun intended. Disregarding the blood and the pain, I reversed the drill and backed the screw out of my left hand. That's when I fell to the floor and busted my ass. I liked the way that version of the story really shocked people, but I would confess the less dramatic truth after I had them convinced. Storytelling is an art form, and you must practice daily to get good at it.

Lunar Landing

I grew up when the breaking news included the JFK and MLK assassinations, the Vietnam War and the Watergate scandal. Tucked in between these headlines were the Apollo lunar missions. I had my own four-foot-tall Saturn V rocket model. I could separate the three rocket stages, the lunar module, and the command module. It was cool.

The Apollo moon missions fostered national interest in science, and the lunar exploration captivated and inspired my generation. It began my interest in aerospace engineering. The program culminated on July 20, 1969, when Neil Armstrong and Buzz Aldrin landed on the moon's surface as Mike Collins orbited the moon in the Command Module. My family watched it live on TV in our living room. It was a great day for our nation, and it put America ahead in the space race against the Soviet Union. Two of these men were graduates of West Point, a mysterious place on the Hudson River that I knew nothing about at the time. It was an academy where a young paperboy from Pennsylvania would eventually be fortunate enough to attend.

Archie Kift

My maternal great grandfather was Archibald Kift, and he liked to stay active. He was 60 years old when the United States entered WWII, and he joined the Military Police Auxiliary.

After the war, he lived in Bridgeport, New Jersey and applied to be the captain of a ferry boat that ran across the Delaware River to Chester, Pennsylvania. During the job interview, Archie was told he needed to inform his supervisor when he was approaching his 65th birthday, that was the mandatory retirement age. Archie agreed and took the job. At the time of the offer, Archie was nearly 70. He had no concern that his 65th birthday was on the horizon, so his boss never needed notification. As Archie

Archie Kift

was approaching his 80th birthday, he was finally asked how old he was. He finally let his company know, and they told him it was time to retire. Archie went back to his little house in Bridgeport where he raised vegetables and chickens. I remember riding the Chester-Bridgeport Ferry boat to visit him. Eventually, a bridge was built, and the ferry ceased operations.

Collections

When you grow up with modest means, you try to find innovative ways to accumulate wealth. I thought having a valuable collection was a smart way to accomplish that. Wealth is a relative term, and—when it comes to collections—as the expression goes, "one man's junk is another man's treasure."

I started collecting coins at age five when I was ripped off by Mark Stahl. He traded me a new penny for an old wheat penny. I thought newer was better, so I took the deal. After I handed him my wheat penny, he told me it was rare and more valuable than the new one. It was an expensive lesson, and I was never going to let that happen again. I started hoarding every wheat penny I could find. My collection eventually expanded to Buffalo nickels, Mercury dimes, Silver Certificates and even foreign currency. I felt coins did have some intrinsic value as they were a combination of bullion, art, and history all in one little package.

As I got older, my portfolio of collectibles began to diversify. My beer can collection included Billy Beer. I saved old film negatives, as they contained silver that could be recycled and sold. I kept all my baby teeth and wisdom teeth in a baggie—you never know when you may need a spare tooth. I found old medicine bottles in the woods. They had to be worth something.

My collections also included records, cassette tapes, and a few prized GI Joe action figures. I had an extra GI Joe that I used for experiments. He was one tough dude. I would bury him waist deep in the yard and run over him with the lawn mower. The mower blades would send GI Joe flying across the yard. Man, that guy could take some punishment and kept his cool. He never lost his head.

I tended to hang onto things. At the end of every school year, Fern Hill had a Field Day with relay races, sack races, etc. My class won the games, and we each got a gift certificate for a "Free Mr. Misty at Thomas's Dairy Queen in West Chester," a place I rarely got to go. And I had never had the famous Mr. Misty drink, but I wanted to save the certificate for a special day. There was no expiration date on the gift card. Thirty-five years later, I rolled back through West Chester and presented my gift card. The staff would not accept it. They no longer made the Mr. Misty. I felt robbed. I should have hired an attorney. My effort on that Field Day was wasted. My bubble was busted. Saving these—those—things doesn't pay. Translation: use your frequent flier miles now, before they go away.

My grandmother, Janet Browne, worked for the Post Office, much of her adult life. Every Christmas she would give me a block of new stamps for my collection. I had hundreds, and every year Nana gave me dozens more. I acted excited, but that just encouraged Nana to keep giving me more. Sorry Nana, but stamps were not my thing. They were just stickers with numbers on them. I did, however, appreciate every other gift you got me, including the bow and arrow set.

I believe collecting stuff was a genetic trait. My brother Kevin also collected coins and liked to buy commemorative ceramic plates and comic books. Gina and Shelley collected dolls. Kevin and Shelley collected baseball cards.

But our dad was the true king of collectors. At his bar and restaurant in Delaware, he collected commemorative Jim Beam whiskey bottles. Back then, we had scores of them at home, and after 40 years, they are still hard to sell. The restaurant had a revolutionary war theme, so he also had a collection of antique rifles on the walls. Another of his collections was a bit odd. Instead of saving money, dad bought a lottery ticket each week and over the years kept all his losers. He planned on wallpapering a bathroom with them. Dad liked bullfighting, so he had artifacts like horns and matador tapestries. He couldn't turn down a good deal so he would pick up old TVs if they were cheap or free. We had eleven TVs at one point, and all but one was black and white. We felt rich because we kept a small black and white TV in the bathroom so we could watch football games while on the throne. Dad's car collection included seven clunkers that sat on our lawn and undoubtedly drove down the property values in the neighborhood.

Outside the coin collection and the antique rifles, not much of what my family collected had value, but it made us feel like we were getting ahead financially. We would have been much better off buying some tech stocks.

My wife's side of the family was a lot more investment savvy. Alice's dad, Jim Bush, collected presidential autographs, rare Pony Express postage, and antiques. He had every president except Jefferson. Many autographs from Truman on were personal to him. That was a better long-term strategy but required a larger upfront capital investment, one which the Kachejian clan could not make.

Ambush on Route 202

OK. I actually debated about whether I should include this story. I decided that confession would cleanse my soul. It was over forty years ago, and fortunately, no one was hurt. I'm glad my kids never tried this because I'd whoop 'em good.

There were a handful of kids my age running around our neighborhood. Among them were Paul Sheehan, Mark Wright, and two brothers: Mike and Paul Mahoney. We were about 12 years old and looking for the next exciting thing to do.

It was the Mahoney boys who led the way. Yes, I am throwing them under the bus. They lived in a house that backed up to the new Route 202 bypass that carved around West Chester. That fortunate geographic location created an opportunity for mischief. The nearby Morstein Road bridge crossed over the four-lane Route 202, and there were no ramps for traffic to get on or off. Recognizing an opportunity — a bridge with a strategic location and maximum visibility—Mike and Paul decided to take a Playboy centerfold photo and tape it to the bridge overpass so the northbound traffic on Route 202 could get a good look. Numerous cars honked their horns in appreciation. Mike and Paul felt like local heroes. Of course, some Moms driving their kids were much less appreciative.

That successful stunt raised the question, what can we do next with this great location? The answer: water balloons. The Mahoney boys broke out the garden hose and started filling balloons. They positioned themselves on the bridge and started dropping them on the highway. It was summertime, and an occasional convertible would be cruising up Route 202 with the top down. Bad luck for the rich guy—only they could afford a convertible with a working top and not held together by bumper stickers. Mike and Paul would brazenly stand on the bridge and hold the water balloon in full view of the oncoming cars. Let it not be said the Mahoney boys did not give fair warning. These cars would honk their horns and try to change lanes to avoid the incoming water bombs. This all culminated, and the apex of water-based munitions was reached, when Mike ran out of balloons and filled a Wonder Bread bag: he watched, probably prayed, for a big truck. The bread bag was the Mother of all water bombs.

When supplies got low, the boys would raid a neighbor's garden and get tomatoes. I am sure they picked that garden clean and Mrs. Mahoney had to wonder where all her tomatoes went.

The bridge brigade expanded one day when the rest of the neighborhood gang joined the Mahoney boys. Somebody brought spare fireworks from the 4th of July: bottle rockets and a Roman candle. That's when several adult neighbors snuck up and counterattacked the squad of young rascals—retaking the high ground. Kids ran for their lives. One of them was captured, detained in a private home and interrogated. Fortunately, the captors did not know how to waterboard the young man. The youth was later force marched to his home and was presented to his mother. For that young man, it was a fate worse than death. And he could not blame it on Butchie. He was grounded for a full month, but he was paroled after a week.

That was the last time Route 202 was threatened by youthful insurgents. The highway was now secure for all Americans to travel. Once again, liberty defeated tyranny.

Human Shield

Speaking of interrogation and punishment for youthful indiscretions, my dad shielded us from the wrath of Mom. If we broke something, dad would repair it before mom discovered the damage. He knew accidents happened, particularly when Kachejian kids were nearby.

One day, Kevin and I were playing catch with a baseball - *in the dining room*. I made a bad throw that hit the shelf which held mom's antique set of demitasse cups and saucers, and they came crashing to the ground. We felt awful; it was a family heirloom. More importantly, we knew that mom had brought us into this world, and this was as good a reason as any for her to take us out. Dad came home, learned about the accident, and glued the cups and saucers together. Once repaired, they looked fine from a distance. The deception worked well for a few weeks, that is until mom started cleaning the china. She saw the repairs and blew a gasket. To drive the message home, she told us she had planned to sell the china set to help pay for our education. "That mistake just cost you your college." I wasn't completely sure what college or tuition was but knew it was a long way off. I was still working on getting out of elementary school. Alive.

The Price for Winning a Game of Chicken

We often played street hockey on Morstein Road, yielding to cars when they approached, but only as soon as there was a break in the action. One of the drivers, probably one of the rich people in the nearby new neighborhood of

Charter Chase, called the police on us. Many of them drove new cars and looked down on us as if we were 12-year old street urchins waiting to steal their hubcaps.

The squad car pulled up, and we immediately stepped off the road and tried to play it cool. The friendly cop rolled down his window and asked us to get in the back of his patrol car. We acted surprised but immediately complied. No one in my neighborhood was screaming, "Hands up! Don't shoot!" or resisting the cops.

Officer Friendly understood our desire to play sports and explained how we must clear the way more promptly; cars needed to use the road. He was a nice guy and did not break out the handcuffs. After a few minutes of a pep talk, he told us we could go back to being kids. Since he was nice to us, we didn't leave any bubble gum stuck on his back seat.

Half an hour later, my sister, Gina, turned off Boot Road and onto Morstein. She was driving a 1967 white Plymouth Fury; a convertible about the size of an aircraft carrier. I was on the street, and we were 150 yards apart when we saw each other. I defiantly held out my hockey stick like I was going to cross check her car if she came toward our game.

Gina responded to the challenge by hitting the gas and accelerating toward me. The game had changed. We were now playing chicken. She was driving almost two tons of steel at about 35 miles per hour. I held my ground in the middle of the road with my 26-ounce street hockey stick. Both genetically predisposed to have stubborn Armenian pride, neither of us yielded. I was confident she would hit the brakes. She was sure I would step aside. She hit the point of no return—realized it—and jammed on the old, worn brakes.

I stood frozen on the road like a squirrel stuck in tar and instantly knew this was going to end badly for me—there was going to be one less 12-year-old street urchin for the Charter Chase dwellers to worry about. Gina stood on the brakes, and the car skidded to a stop, but about three feet behind me.

The car hit me with the hardest hip check I ever felt. I toppled on the hood and rolled off to the side. Holy smokes that hurt my body. But at least not my pride. I hobbled off to the side of the road and declared victory. Although I won the chicken contest, I also knew I lost. My hip hurt like hell for weeks.

95

Charter Chase

When the new Charter Chase development was being built, and after people moved in, we used to ride our bicycles through the neighborhood and gawk at the houses. Trash day was best. The rich people would through away some pretty good toys, old bicycles, and other stuff. One man's trash was another man's treasure.

I snuck into their community pool one day. I did not own a proper pair of swimming trunks and was wearing some cut-off jeans. The lifeguard told me I could stay, but I could not get in the pool, or the filter might get clogged. After a while, I forgot what she said and jumped in. The rich people promptly evicted me from the pool area.

As I entered my teenage years, I met several really nice people who lived in Charter Chase and realized that being rich wasn't their fault. They were just born with a wealth handicap, and I needed to be more tolerant.

Since the kids there had more money, they could also get into bigger trouble and much faster. One of my new buddies from Charter Chase built a small waterproof pipe bomb and stuck it in a five-gallon bucket of water on his front lawn. He lit it, and we ran. The bucket exploded, and so did the front picture window of his house. I stayed out of the neighborhood for a few weeks after that caper.

There were a bunch of pretty girls that lived in Charter Chase. I would ride my bike around the neighborhood in my muscle shirt, hoping some princess would be looking for an ugly frog. Unfortunately, that frog never got kissed. But the neighborhood did produce a future brother-in-law, Billy Martyn.

CHAPTER 10
FERN HILL, TURTLE POND, LAFA & ROCKETS

Mr. Morgan

Kerry Kacheji...   English
June 10, 196?
            Our Principal

Fern Hill School principal name is Mr. Morgan
He works in the office with Mrs. McCarter.
He is about 5 feet 3 inches tall. He is very very
nice. He has black hair and brown eyes. When
it is time to leave, he calls the buses over the
speaker. He calls bus 17 bus 8 bus 29 bus 4 and bus 53
He is just right for me. When I grow up I want to
be a principal.

Essay on Mr. Morgan

97

My siblings and I attended Grade 1-6 at Fern Hill Elementary School, and the principal was Mr. Dave Morgan. He ran a tight ship. The kids feared getting in trouble with him. His booming voice ran shivers down our spines. When he walked into our classroom unexpectedly, all the kids stopped slouching and sat up straight. We wouldn't blink as he walked around and observed the class.

There was a rumor that Mr. Morgan had a paddle in his office, and nobody wanted to meet "The Paddle." This weighed on my mind when I was sent—once—to the office for wrestling with Richie Stapleford during recess. Rich had tried to hijack the ball from me while we were playing dodgeball. He was fairly big, and most kids did not resist when he took their ball. I wasn't going to be a victim that day, so Rich and I rolled on the ground as he tried to rip the ball from me.

Next thing I knew, I was on my feet and ordered to report to Mr. Morgan's office. I knew I was likely going to meet "The Paddle." I reluctantly moved toward the principal's office, but I made a quick stop at the boy's room and stuffed toilet paper in my back pockets to cushion the blow. Fortunately, I had written a flattering essay about Mr. Morgan earlier, which bought me some good will. I ratted out Rich and threw him under the bus (metaphorically speaking). It worked, and I never got spanked.

Mr. Leiser

Our Physical Education teacher at Fern Hill was Mr. LeRoy "Lee" Leiser. He loved all the school kids, and we always had fun in his class. We loved his corny jokes and his great belly laugh. He knew all four of the Kachejian kids, particularly my sister, Gina, who was one of his star gymnasts. But he never could correctly pronounce our last name.

One day in 3rd grade, my class sat on the gym floor and did stretching exercises during his class. He began to ask questions about what we wanted to do when we grew up. He turned to me and asked," Mr. Ka-Chee-Gee-Inn, what college do you want to go to?"

I paused. My parents never went to one, and I knew little about colleges. I felt like I needed to offer an answer and blurted out the name of the only college I knew of, about two miles from my house. "I want to go to Immaculata."

Mr. Leiser let out one of those belly laughs. "Mr. Ka-Chee-Gee-Inn, that's a nun's college... for women."

I was quite embarrassed, but it did make me pay more attention to colleges. Ironically, my father worked for Immaculata College 15 years later, after he left managing The Drummer's Table restaurant in Delaware. So, one of the Ka-Chee-Gee-Inn males eventually got in there.

Turtle Pond

During the summers, Kevin and I would ride our bikes a mile down Morstein Road and cut into a wooded area to go fishing in Turtle Pond. Our dog, Queenie, would run behind our bikes, and she was completely gassed by the time we arrived.

Turtle Pond was our secret place where my neighborhood friends would go to spend a hot summer day. We would dig up earthworms and catch sunfish and perch. We caught a snapping turtle one time, but he looked pretty mean, so we let him go. The pond was privately-owned, but no one ever asked us to get off their property. They appeared to be kind people who just wanted kids to have fun.

On the way to the pond, we slowed down as we passed by the Hurley's house. Mr. Bill Hurley was a pilot on Air Force One, sometimes transporting then President Ford and the press corps. He had four sons, and we occasionally talked to Chip. I hoped that we might run into the president, who might be visiting the Hurley family. It never happened.

Buzzed

I played in the Little All-American Football Association (LAFA) league for five years, until I was twelve years old. My father was a coach and mom worked at the snack bar to raise money.

I played quarterback and was a much better runner than a passer. Fortunately, at that age, running was 90% of the game.

Football has some well-known hazards: broken bones, twisted knees, chipped teeth, and concussions (AKA, "getting your bell rung"). Bloody noses, bruises, and scraped hands were among the most common injuries we endured.

However, I had the distinction of pioneering a new form of football trauma. It happened during a scrimmage when I was eleven-years-old. I faked a hand-off to our fullback on the left side of the line and reversed field to sweep around the right end. The play was working great; I'd faked the defenders out of their jock straps. I turned the corner and accelerated up the right sideline.

It was the beginning a great run; if only the pro scouts had been there.

Suddenly, something strange and painful happened. Somehow, half a dozen bees were inside my helmet stinging my eyes, face, and ears. The attack increased; those bees were furious. I threw the football down, tore off my helmet and started beating and slapping myself in the head to get the buzzing bastards off of me. Players and coaches were initially confused as to why I was running erratically and beating myself in the head. Perhaps it was a celebratory dance, but the puzzler was that I hadn't made it to the end zone and scored. The whistle blew, and the play was over. I was escorted off the field to a nearby water hose, where the coach rinsed out my helmet. The lesson I learned here was not to spill soda pop in my helmet during a sideline break.

Big Bertha and Insect Astronauts

Model rocketry became popular in our neighborhood, and Kevin and I often asked for model rockets for birthday gifts. I would even spend the precious money I earned on my paper route to get spare rocket engines and fuses.

We always wanted to re-use our rockets, so we made sure the parachutes were packed with wadding and would deploy properly and not burn up when falling back to the ground. One of the other significant risks was having the parachutes snag in the tops of tall trees during descent, and we would not be able to recover the rocket. Some of the rockets had multiple stages, and one of the most popular models was called the "Big Bertha," that required a more powerful engine. Big Bertha came with a clear plastic compartment that we used to put an insect inside. Our first "manned" flight featured a live cricket. An insectonaut. The launch was perfect, but we never found the rocket and payload. If the cricket survived the high-G forces of the launch and the searing heat of the engine, it most likely could not get out of the capsule after it landed. It was a bad day for Jiminy Cricket.

100

CHAPTER 11

HENDERSON HIGH - RIVALRY, ACADEMICS, PPP, MURDER LINE UP

The Rivalry

I went to Henderson Senior High School in West Chester. A few years earlier, the new East High School opened and split the student population. Some of my junior high friends went to East. After the split, Henderson got the reputation as the school for the "townies" and had students generally from working class families. East was considered more affluent and had more of the preppy rich kids. At least that was how the reputation started. The two schools became immediate rivals.

I would call one of my long-time friends, Mark Morgan, who went to East, the morning of the big rivalry football game each Thanksgiving weekend, and boldly predict that Henderson was going to crush his team. Fortunately, we did. So now I can remind him of that for the rest of his life. The Henderson-East football game was a big event for my dad too. Before my first game, he took me out to a local diner for a steak and egg breakfast. This was a first for me. That day, I felt like a kid who came from a rich family.

Academics

My 10th-grade geometry teacher, Mr. Dallin, liked to crack one-liners in class. He once advised our class, "Don't enter a battle of brains without a weapon." Some of the students understood the joke. The others were apparently unarmed.

As one of the students who got the meaning of Mr. Dallin's advice, I got good grades in high school. I took some honors classes, some were serious math and science classes, including calculus and seminar level classes. I could have studied more, but my schedule was quite full. I played on the Henderson football and lacrosse teams, after school I had practices and worked at various jobs. Saturdays were preserved for football games. Henderson kids believed most of the kids at East were from wealthy families and did not have to hold a job. I don't know if anyone conducted an authoritative study.

Wood Shop

I wanted to have some balance at school, so I took a wood shop class. It was a good experience to learn about tools and practical skills. We built some wooden lamps and other simple creations.

I liked the fact that we could pick our own projects, and one of mine was making a replica flintlock pistol. I turned the barrel on a metal lathe and fashioned the stock out of mahogany. It looked nice, but it was completely non-functional. My teacher approved the project, and I received an A when it was completed. Today, a school would call the police and suspend a student— or the teacher—for making a gun on school property.

For another wood shop project, I built a bar for my basement. I designed it and bought the materials. Again, my teacher approved the project, and I received an A. The bar was in my parent's home for over 35 years and was used at many parties. I topped it off by making a mahogany mount for six beer taps. After finishing the bar, I built a shuffleboard for the basement bar room—you need to have some entertainment while you drink.

That wood shop class was great, and although the teacher emphasized safety, some of us still screwed up. I can recall one student who failed to remove the chuck key when he powered up a drill. The chuck key was attached to a chain, which wrapped around his finger when the drill bit began to spin. The result: it ripped off one of his fingers. Albeit less severe, I also had an accident in shop class. I attempted to extract a nail by prying it up with a chisel in each hand. I knew these were the wrong tools to use, but I was young and dumb. I was convinced I could use brute force to pry the nail out of a board. When the chisel in my right hand inevitably slipped off the nail head, I drove it into my left index finger. The wound was deep, almost to the bone, and bled profusely. Wrapping my hand in a rag and applying pressure, I sped off from the basement wood shop, across the school, to the nurse's office. Along the way, some administrator stopped me and reprimanded me for running in school. When I handed the guy the bloody rag and apologized, he wouldn't touch it and immediately shut up. I kept running. After being stitched up at the hospital, I returned to school later that day. Fortunately, the accident happened between football and lacrosse seasons, and I had a few weeks to heal.

We all liked to have fun, but a few kids in the wood shop class were excessive. To these class clowns, life was just one big joke. One day, they pulled a prank on a 70-year-old man who was a last-minute substitute teacher. The poor guy moved very slowly. Unfortunately, not slowly enough for some, as a couple of kids halted his movement entirely when they glued him to his seat. I had missed class that day and later heard about the incident. I thought it was incredibly disrespectful.

Underground Society

We had a secret group at Henderson called the Assassin Gang. Thanks to the efforts of a dozen innovative students, they published an underground comic strip which later expanded into an equally underground newsletter called the Push, Pull Press (PPP).

New issues each month featured satirical articles about other students as well as administrators. Always a bit edgy and zany, the PPP gave students a chance to be heard, as well as demonstrate their creativity.

The official response was predictable. School administrators wanted to restrict and edit the articles. Their efforts to censor the students, however, only led a string of increasingly outrageous articles and stunts.

One of them included nominating the Senior Prom theme song to be "White Punks on Dope." This was immediately rejected by school officials. To complement the school's annual blood drive, the PPP gang sponsored a high school sperm drive. Administrators rejected this idea also. As a senior class prank, the gang proposed the mass sterilization of the sophomore class. That was strike three with the principal. Silently, I think the administration enjoyed the sophomoric behavior, but they had to portray an outward sense of morality authority.

Teenage—journalistic—rebellion was alive and well in my generation and made our high school experience more memorable. After four decades, I will reveal their real identities. Among the gang's members were Walter Morton [who had a longstanding rivalry with a female classmate and ended the battle by leaving a dead cow on the girl's front lawn], Andy Parke, Jim Thompson, Gary Krause, Kevin McGlinchey, Nat Whitten, Jeff Smith and Aaron Bram [Aaron Bram took flying lessons at the local airport and crashed because the fuel in the aircraft was contaminated. He spent weeks in the hospital. Everyone was shocked when they wheeled him into our physics class after a couple of months. All four of his limbs were in casts, and his jaw was wired shut, but the guy was happy because he had eaten mostly ice cream since the accident.]

Some of these guys are now probably doctors, lawyers, and PhDs. I am sure they are still quietly proud of their high school achievements, but any political aspirations would be at risk if the full details of their activities in high school were made known. However, a bottle of nice red wine, shipped to this author, might silence him for another decade.

Murder Line Up

One of my most unique jobs, as a youth, was standing in a murder line up; an interesting experience. It happened one day when our Henderson High School football team had just finished practice, and we were cleaning up in the locker room. Two police detectives came in and introduced themselves. They said they needed "reasonable facsimiles." I was confused and had no idea what that meant. The detectives went on to explain that they needed volunteers to be in a murder line up. The locker room went completely silent. We had been at practice all day, a rock-solid alibi.

The detectives continued to explain they had a suspect but needed to form a lineup so their witness could identify—hopefully—the suspect. The room was still silent as my teammates all looked at each other. Then the detectives announced, "We'll pay ten dollars to anyone who volunteers to be in the lineup." That closed the deal. I said, "I'll do it." A few other teammates also agreed.

The next day, I rode my bicycle six miles to stand in that murder lineup. The detectives had us gather in a room and began collecting names and addresses. We were interrupted when a loud-mouthed lawyer came in with the real suspect. The suspect looked like he had a rough life and appeared to have been cleaned up to look like a non-threatening citizen. His long biker hair had been combed and washed. He was wearing a suit and tie like he was a respectable businessman. Most of the "reasonable facsimiles" with me wore what I did, a t-shirt and blue jeans. He looked uncomfortable in the suit and was out of place with the rest of us. He apparently ran with a different crowd.

Then the bucket-mouth lawyer demanded to see the other men in the lineup. We lined up for him to inspect us. He stood in front of the first "reasonable facsimile" and shouted, "This man looks nothing like my client!" Alarm bells went off in my head. The first guy is getting thrown out of the lineup, and he probably won't get paid. This lawyer is trying to make the lineup look unfair to his client. The gas bag then walked up to the second guy. "Are you kidding me? This man looks nothing like my client." The lawyer made another derogatory comment about the third guy in the lineup. Now I'm thinking, "Holy smokes, we're all getting thrown out." As I was next, I studied his client and tried to look more like him. I really needed that ten bucks. I put on my best killer look and slightly flexed my arms and neck muscles. I stared that pencil-pushing geek in the eye. He stood in front of me, and neither of us blinked. I was in a semi-attack position. He paused, said not a word, and then moved on to the fifth guy. My initial reaction was relief. I had made it and was sure to collect. After a few seconds, a different feeling washed over me. I found myself offended that the lawyer thought I was as ugly and nasty as his client. But I stayed silent. Just take the money and run.

The next phase was to finish gathering names and addresses. The suspect, now with us, included. That wasn't part of the deal. When they asked me for my information, I hesitated, not wanting some killer knowing who I was and where I lived. If he was to break out of jail, we might be his next victims. I wanted to enter the witness protection program, but my protests were to no avail. I had to bark out my full name and home address and watch my back for the next 50 years.

The authorities were now ready to bring in the witness. We were directed to line up against the wall. Nobody wanted to be next to the killer, so we jockeyed for a spot, trying to be the farthest from the alleged bad guy. Standing shoulder to shoulder, each of us was leaning away from the only man in a business suit. The officers brought in the witness behind a two-way mirror so that none of us could see or hear their identity. All we could do was stand there silently like we were facing a firing squad.

Suddenly, it was over. A cop handed me ten bucks and made me sign for it. Relieved that the witness did not pick me, I left the station without a criminal record. I jumped on my bicycle and raced home. Along the way, I thought that our family might need to relocate for our own safety. I appreciated the easy ten bucks, but I wondered how much the police would pay me if they needed a confession.

Fortunately, the witness picked the right guy. I later read about the trial in the Daily Local News, the same paper I had delivered for several years. I recall the suspect's name was Daniel Gentry. He had robbed a store, and his crime partner had shot the clerk. But Gentry had jumped over the counter and stabbed the clerk another 28 times to make sure the victim was dead. He was convicted, and I never heard any further details.

CHAPTER 12

HENDERSON HIGH - SENIOR CLASS PRANK

Caution: Do not attempt these immature stunts at home. Please take a selfie instead, or if you are an amateur idiot, find something else dumb to do.

There were several separate groups of students planning class pranks my senior year at Henderson High School. Since we did not have email, Facebook or Twitter, these were not coordinated efforts, which led to more chaos and confusion.

Our senior prank team had three guys on it, including me and my best friend, Mike Willover. Mike and I played football and lacrosse together, so teaming up on the class prank was natural for us. We also recruited Rick Chew. Rick was a standout athlete in four sports: gymnastics, soccer, ice hockey and baseball. He was "The Daredevil" at Henderson High School. Several students had dared Rick Chew to jump off the back of the football stadium onto a mattress - a drop of about 30 feet. He did it. It was hard for anyone to beat fearless Rick at anything requiring physical skill.

Mike and I conducted our initial planning at Diane Dusinberre's house. Her parents liked us and would never have believed we were plotting a prank against the school. Diane's neighbor, Jeff Wolfe, wanted to help with the effort. He was a high school junior and the varsity quarterback. Since Jeff was not part of our class, he had plausible deniability (something I learned more about later in my career).

Our team wanted to pull a funny stunt, but not one that caused monetary damage. If a student caused financial harm, the administration would hunt them down and keep them from graduating - ruining any hope of an adult life before it began. In short, we did not want our careers to peak in high school.

First, we reviewed the school pranks from prior years. Someone had pulled a car into the school auditorium and put it on the stage. Other pranksters super glued all the door locks. That was a good stunt, but it cost the school significant money to get the locks changed. Those kids were hunted down.

Another group from East High School made small waterproof "cherry bombs" out of empty CO_2 cartridges and match heads. They inserted a waterproof fuse and sealed the cartridge with wax and tested their design in a bucket of water in the front yard of a house in Charter Chase. The device exploded, metal shrapnel shredded the bucket and took out the picture window in the front of the house. [I mentioned, in a previous story, I was there when that one went off.] Once they had perfected the design, they dropped a couple in the school toilets, flushed and blew the commodes off the walls. It was an innovative idea, but it caused extensive flooding, and I considered it a criminal act. Rick, Mike and I weren't going to do anything that stupid. We still wanted to graduate from high school in case we were caught in the act.

We planned several pranks over the course of a week. The first was hanging a dummy from the flag pole in the school courtyard. We decided to dress it in some Class of 1978 spirit wear. I had just the right outfit in mind. My Uncle George was a sales representative for Rolling Rock beer. He always gave us Rolling Rock t-shirts, stickers, hats and other trinkets. We dressed our dummy in a Rolling Rock t-shirt and put an empty 6-pack of Rolling Rock beer in his hand. Jeff Wolfe had an extra Henderson Warrior football helmet, which we updated with Rolling Rock stickers. We put some old blue jeans on it and stuffed him with newspapers (I provided the *Daily Local News*). The Henderson Rolling Rock Warrior dummy was now ready, and he looked pretty good. It was now time to execute phase two of the operation.

At about 11:00 PM, we arrived at Henderson High School in Mike's 1967 Plymouth Belvedere. Under cover of darkness, we pulled the dummy out of the car and snuck across the campus toward the courtyard. I was worried that some nosey neighbor might see us and call the police to report two men carrying a dead body. We had to act quickly. We arrived at the flag pole and tied the dummy to the cable. We disconnected the ends of the cable, so it no longer formed a loop. That way we could hoist the dummy, but there was no way to easily lower it back down. The plan worked. We raised the dummy, and it was flying at the top of the flagpole. Mike and I proudly saluted the Rolling Rock Warrior and ran back to the car.

The next morning, Mike and I wore Rolling Rock t-shirts to school. We wanted our fellow students to know who the proud masterminds were. Upon arriving at campus, we immediately went to the courtyard and found some workers standing on scaffolding and beating the dummy down with a long pole. This wasn't right. The Rolling Rock Warrior was gone before most students had even arrived at school. Few students knew of our legendary deed; our 15 minutes of fame went all but unnoticed. The administration would need to pay for disrespecting our masterful creation.

We needed a new prank; something more daring and difficult to undo. Our attention stayed focused on the flag pole. But what to do with it? There was an old car repair shop near the school with a pile of old tires lying in the front. That was our inspiration. For this operation, we unleashed our secret weapon: Rick Chew. The plan was to hoist Rick to the top, supply him with old tires—rolling them from the repair shop yard and lifting them to him—and he'd drop a few dozen over the pole, which would disappear inside a 25-foot tall pile of tires. It was a great plan.

Once again, at about 11:00 PM, Mike and I arrived at Henderson in the Belvedere to sneak across campus toward the courtyard. This part of the plan worked well. We created a loop in the flag pole cable for Rick to put his foot in. We asked Rick if he still wanted to climb the pole. He was rock steady. Mike and I pulled on the cable and lifted Spiderman skyward.

As we were raising Rick, I thought about the pulley at the top of the pole. The pulley usually handled a 3-pound flag which was at most 10 pounds if dripping wet. We were now hoisting a 160-pound human up using that same pulley which we could not see or inspect. If the pulley broke and Rick fell, there wasn't any mattress for Rick to hit. There was no safety plan, and we didn't make Rick sign a liability waiver before undertaking this dangerous stunt.

When Rick was at half mast, he reported everything was going well. Mike and I kept hoisting, and Rick made it to the top. That's when Rick grabbed the brass ball "truck" at the head of the flag pole. The brass ball was rusted and bent when Rick grabbed it. Rick lost his balance but fortunately was able to grab the pole before falling. When he told us about the incident, we decided to bring him back down and waive off the prank. There was no way we could safely haul him up the pole a few dozen times while balancing on one foot and carrying a tire. Rick was amazing but not immortal.

We looked around the school grounds for a ladder—maybe we could make our plan work with it if it was long enough—but no luck. We didn't find a ladder but did discover several rolls of wooden fencing and thought we could fence in the school. That idea lasted about two minutes, and we dropped it too. We wrapped up our tactical operations for the night and headed home—mission aborted—unsatisfied.

In retrospect, Mike and I could have just left Rick at the top of the flag pole all night. When Rick was found the next morning, he could claim he was mugged and hoisted to the top. But we liked Rick too much, so lowering him back to terra firma was the right thing to do. A better idea would have been to snatch a student from our rival East High School and hoist him up the flag pole. Now *that* would have been epic.

CHAPTER 13
HENDERSON HIGH - SPORTS AND FRIENDS

Sports

My siblings and I were athletes. Gina was a gymnast, played field hockey and lacrosse. Shelley competed in softball and was a fearless field hockey goalie. Until his bicycle accident, Kevin played football, baseball and wrestled. Early-on I shared these same sports but later dropped baseball and wrestling, picking up lacrosse instead.

The Kachejians were a short and powerfully-built clan. On occasion, I would tell new friends a fabricated story about my heritage: that I had come from a long line of professional midget wrestlers. With a straight face, I would explain that my mother and father were pioneering tag team wrestlers on TV Channel 29. At five feet seven inches, I was the giant in the family. I always enjoyed watching the initial look of shock on my new friend's face, and then transition into gut-busting laughter once they had caught on to my false claim to fame.

Football

Kevin and I played Little League football in addition to plenty of pick-up games with the neighborhood kids. The Brunner family lived right down the street, and they had two sons, Scott and Jack. Although Kevin and I were several years younger, Scott and Jack were kind enough to have an occasional catch with us. Scott was a star quarterback at Henderson High School but then moved when his dad was offered a coaching position at Rutgers. Scott went on to play for the University of Delaware Fighting Blue Hens. He became an All-American, set several passing records and led Delaware to the national title (he was later inducted into the NCAA Division II Hall of Fame). His football career wasn't over with college. Scott was drafted into the National Football League and played for the New York Giants, the Denver

Broncos, and the St. Louis Cardinals. I'd like to think the extra practice Scott had passing a football with the young Kachejian boys helped him sharpen his skills and compete in the NFL.

Now, as with many stories, there is a sad part. The Brunner's had a big dog named Smokey. Like most dogs, Smokey loved to chase balls. One day, Smokey disappeared. We later heard that some kids drove through the neighborhood and had thrown a cherry bomb out the window. Smokey chased it and picked it up. It exploded, and Smokey was injured so badly that the only thing anyone could do was to put him out of his pain. The loss of Smokey shook all the neighborhood kids.

Three years after Scott Brunner played Henderson football, I was on the same high school team. Mike Hancock was our coach, a former Navy officer who had served during the early '60s and was on duty during the Bay of Pigs invasion. Our assistant coaches were Paul Stankewicz, Joe Walsh, and Skip Bowen. We had a tight group of guys on the team who all worked and played hard. I played positions on offense, defense and on special teams - almost the entire game. I was exhausted by the time the clock ran out. I was a quarterback for some years, but given my short, stocky build, I was better suited to fullback on the varsity team. However, our wingback, Mike Willover broke his leg in the first game, putting him out for most of the season. Since I also knew the wingback position, the coach moved me there. On defense, I played cornerback. I was on the kickoff return team, the punt team, and was the holder for extra points and field goals. The only time I was not on the field was for the kickoff.

Early in the season, we faced the Coatesville Red Raiders. They had a running back named Sherman "Tank" Myers. The guy's nickname fit him. He was one of the star running backs of the ChesMont League. Myers later played football for Temple where he set the single-game scoring record. During that Henderson-Coatesville game, Myers took a pitch and swept around the right end, flying up the sideline. I came across the field from the far side cornerback position. We were both accelerating at the moment of impact and knocked the snot out of each other. He was knocked out of bounds, and I crashed behind him. Unfortunately, I landed on my own wrist–hard–and it hurt. I thought it was just a sprain, so I taped it up and played the rest of the game.

That night I laid awake with a throbbing left wrist. The next day, mom took me to Chester County Hospital for X-rays, but the images were inconclusive. Leaving the hospital without any explicit medical restrictions, I

112

continued to wrap my wrist with an Ace bandage before each practice and played six more games. Something wasn't right. It still hurt, and I thought it might be broken. I did not want to miss my senior year of football, so I just kept playing. I heard the wrist re-break during practice while trying to catch a ball in the end zone. Coach Hancock chewed me out for dropping a pass I should have caught. He had no idea my wrist was broken, and I did not tell him. I felt I would be giving him some feeble excuse.

In mid-November, I had to take a physical fitness test in Philadelphia to apply to West Point. One of the events was a pull-up test. I was able to do 14 pull-ups while trying to protect my left wrist. At the end of the test, all the candidates were asked if we had any physical limitations that prevented us from performing at our full potential. I told the officer that my left wrist might be broken, but the initial X-rays were inconclusive. He directed me to get additional X-rays. Mom took me back to the hospital radiology lab. We waited for the results for about 40 minutes. A technician came into the busy waiting room and asked for me. I stood to identify myself. He blurted out, "Do you know your wrist has been broken for six weeks?" I knew it hurt and wasn't surprised.

I did not anticipate my mother's reaction; she went totally protective. She told the football coach about the injury and insisted that I not play in the final game of the season against arch-rival East High School. She did not want me to aggravate the injury and ruin an opportunity to go to West Point. When mom told me what she had done, I was livid. This was the last football game of my career. I had just played six games with the injury, and I could play one more. After some heated debate, Skip Bowen, the Henderson trainer, borrowed a soft cast from the West Chester State football team, and my mother allowed me to play with it. The only caveat was that I could not carry the football, so I was moved to defensive end. Mike Willover's broken leg had finally healed, and he was back playing in the East game. Unfortunately, he broke his arm during that final game. Willie couldn't get a lucky break that season, but he literally got two unlucky ones: one leg and one arm. I was glad I could play in the final game, and we won 24-14.

Afterward, I went to the orthopedist and had a hard cast put on the wrist. I wore the cast for six weeks through the Christmas holiday. My wrist constantly itched. It finally was removed in January. Although my wrist had suffered some atrophy, I was pleased to find a new pencil and about 70 cents in change inside the cast.

There were many other memorable moments during my high school football career. Here are a few. Back then, helmets weren't that protective. During my junior year, our linebacker, Randy Burridge, and I hit hard helmet-to-helmet, and we dropped to our knees. I felt like I was on the deck of a ship, in rough seas, and the world was moving all around me.

Kevin & Kerry (with cast) – Christmas 1977

When someone got a concussion, we would simply say, "He got his bell rung." I sat out a couple of plays. Then, Randy and I collided—just as hard—a second time. We looked at each other and had no interest in doing it a third time. I wound up staying at Chester County Hospital for observation. I had to sit out the next game.

Our coaches consistently emphasized that we should always wear our protective equipment. Kevin McDonald had decided not wear a cup at football practice. One day he was knocked out cold when he got hit in the family jewels. I guess overwhelming pain can make the body shut down.

During a JV game, our 4th string running back had his football pants pulled to the ground while being tackled. He did not know he should wear a girdle pad under the pants. The referees had to stop the game because both teams were in tears laughing as the poor guy was laying on the ground in only a jockstrap. His pasty-white butt mooned the entire stadium. I will withhold his name to spare him further embarrassment.

I also remember a varsity game where nothing went right. The low point of the game was when our punter, Matt Stasny, kicked the football straight up into a strong headwind. It landed just beyond the line of scrimmage and started a 30-yard backward bounce behind us. The other team jumped on the ball in the end zone and scored. I had never seen anything like it; a punt for negative 30 yards resulting in a touchdown.

Lacrosse

I decided to try lacrosse in 10th grade and was given a used stick and some old equipment. Lacrosse felt like a modern-day gladiator sport. We wore helmets and arm pads and got to beat each other with sticks. The lacrosse locker room always played our theme song, Hotel California, before each game, which was cool. And I learned a lot under coaches Bob Britton and Paul "Stank" Stankewicz, and eventually, I picked up some decent stick skills.

Metal lacrosse sticks were the new technology being used by attack and midfielders. Metal shafts weighed less and enabled faster shots. Many of the defensemen, however, still used older wooden sticks. It was considered a badge of honor to have a wooden stick broken over your body. If you were practicing against defenseman Rick Petrondi, there was a good chance you could earn a badge of honor.

A lacrosse ball is made of dense rubber, and it can hurt when it hits you. One time, while I was taking a water break during practice, I had my helmet off, and somebody yelled, "heads up!" While turning toward the field and looking up, I was nailed square in the forehead with a long pass thrown by a defenseman. The ball bounced about 10 yards after hitting me. I am very thankful it did not hit my eye. Ironically, I would not have been hit if they hadn't yelled: "heads up."

During a scrimmage, Doug Heald took a shot at the goal. I was standing between him and the net. I had my chin up, and the ball flew directly under my helmet and hit me square in the throat. My airway collapsed, and I could not breathe. I fell to my knees and tried to inhale. I felt my life was in imminent danger. The team circled around me, and I was concerned someone might administer my last rites. After about forty seconds (which felt like an hour), I managed to get my first gasp of air into my lungs. After a few more breaths, Coach Stank stood over me and said, "Hey Kachejian. It feels pretty good, doesn't it? To breathe again!" I walked around with a big contusion on my throat for a week.

Henderson High School hosted a lacrosse tournament each year, and a couple of top rated teams from Long Island came to play. Later in the season, we traveled to Long Island to play a few local schools, including Lynbrook. Those teams were good. Some of their kids must have been born with lacrosse sticks in their hands. The great advantage of having a tournament in New York was that, at the time, the drinking age in that state was only 18. As seniors, many of us were of legal age. So, we tried to keep the Lynbrook players out all night before the tournament to degrade their playing skills. It worked. Lynbrook only scored nine goals on us. Unfortunately, our sleep-deprived Henderson team scored zero. During the Spring season of my senior year, I was contacted by the lacrosse coach at West Point, Dick Edell. He told me my application at West Point looked good, and there was a chance I would be playing lacrosse for Army that summer. This was the first indication of what my future might hold. During his career, Dick became a legendary coach with one of the best winning records in the country, and he was inducted into the U.S. Lacrosse Hall of Fame.

Wrestling

Wrestling is a tough sport, and it is an individual event. You cannot hide on a team. Each match is a one-on-one event where you will win, lose or draw. Because I had been lifting weights since the age of 12, I had unusual strength that helped me in my early wrestling years. And while wrestling was my best sport, I did not have the desire to learn new skills, and I did not want to go on crash diets to make the weight class. In my final year, my record was 28-2-1, including matches, scrimmages, and tournaments. I lost to the eventual Pennsylvania State Champion in a tight 2-1 match. Although I was physically stronger, that kid was clearly a better wrestler.

One of my signature wrestling moves was what my teammates called the "Armenian cross face," a punishing maneuver that often weakened an opponent's will to resist. It was legal, simple and effective. On several occasions, opponents bled on the mat, and one kid had a severely broken nose that required surgery. I was a bit embarrassed that my teammate, Brad Donnelly, used to yell "Make him bleed Cheech!" during my matches. I did not seek to draw blood, but it sometimes happened. I later learned that some students were placing bets in the stands that I would make my next opponent bleed. This theater and cheering made me feel like a hired gun, and it diminished the sport. Both skill and passion are needed to succeed in any sport, and I did not have enough of either for wrestling. I dropped it and focused on football and lacrosse.

Service Academies

Several student-athletes from our high school went to the service academies. The Henderson class ahead of me, 1977, sent three of its members to the U.S. Naval Academy. Lex Lauletta was our high school quarterback and later played Navy football. He married his high school sweetheart, Lisa Arabia. Jay Zurlo was a standout soccer player, and his little sister, Dina was Kevin's classmate. Paul Ricutti was a gifted lacrosse player, and his siblings Drew, Chris and Anne were also talented athletes. The following year, I was the lone wolf who went to the rival academy.

Gina's Friends

My sister, Gina, had several interesting friends in her high school class and from the local West Chester area. I would occasionally meet them at our home.

Her 9th-grade football team included standout athletes like Pete Latta, Bob Brewer, Scott Brunner and others who were unstoppable. Their football team was undefeated, untied, unscored on, and no other team got a first down against the varsity players. It was a dream team that would have dominated the state had the student body not been split up between Henderson and East High Schools for grades 10 through 12.

Bob and Joe Senser were brothers who went to West Chester State College. Bob was 6' 6" and weighed 260. Joe was 6'4" and weighed 240. When they came to our house, they would have to duck under the doorways. Joe was a college basketball star and led the NCAA in field goal shooting percentage. He also played football as a tight end and was drafted by the Minnesota Vikings in the NFL, going on to play in the Pro Bowl.

Gina also met "Jungle Jim" Liberman, who was from the local area and became a nationally renowned drag racer. His name used to be all over the radio in the Philadelphia area. I thought I would have a chance to meet Jungle Jim, but he was killed in his Corvette when he hit a SEPTA bus near our house in West Goshen Township.

CHAPTER 14

HENDERSON HIGH - HAIRCUTS, FASHION, TREE FROG BEER, OCEAN CITY & DEATHS

Cousin It

I had bushy hair in high school, and at times it would get out of control. Sometimes I looked like Cousin It from the Adams Family. When people had to look down at my feet to see which way I was facing, I knew it was time to get a haircut. That meant mom showed up with the scissors and an electric razor. She did not want to pay for a bad haircut when I could get the same at home, no charge.

Fashion Statement

I didn't have a lot of new clothes, so my wardrobe included hand-me-downs from other families. I would wear clothes until they were worn out, and mom constantly sewed and patched my shirts and jeans, extending their functional life. I had to buy a new suit, however, to attend an important interview with a board appointed by Congressman Dick Schultz as part of my application to West Point.

In the Fall of 1977, mom took me shopping. I came home as the proud owner of a green polyester, bell-bottom leisure suit. And the salesman made sure I also had a pair of 2–inch platform shoes. When I wore my fashionable threads, I felt like the new Armenian John Travolta. I wore the suit to the Homecoming dance first. Everyone at my dinner table was chuckling for a few minutes. Finally, my lacrosse buddy, Randy Waters, let me know the price tag for my suit was still dangling from the armpit of the jacket. I was even more embarrassed at the low price on the tag. Thankfully the tag was long gone when I wore the suit for my senior class picture.

After I was accepted to West Point in the Spring of 1978, I no longer needed it. I wore military uniforms for the next decade. But I kept my lucky, green, polyester, bell-bottom leisure suit and platform shoes in the closet for the next 20 years. After I had met my wife, Alice, she kept trying to throw my suit out. I did not own many civilian clothes, and I noticed when it was missing from my closet. I dug it out of the Good Will donation pile several times. I knew she hated it, but I was hoping the style would eventually come back. Alice permanently ditched it when I went off on a week-long business trip. I felt betrayed and wounded, but she promised to get me a more currently stylish replacement.

Tree Frog Beer

One of the more entertaining commercials I heard on the radio, growing up in southeastern Pennsylvania, was for a then new product called "Tree Frog Beer." The ads were clearly appealing to inquisitive young men in their high school years. The short, catchy advertising jingle went something like this:

> *Tree Frog Beer!... It's Green!*
> *Tree Frog Beer!... It don't taste too good, but it gets you there!*
> *Faster!*

Too bad Uncle George never worked for that beer company.

Beach Trips to Ocean City

My high school buddies made frequent trips to the nearest beach in Ocean City, New Jersey, a two-hour ride from West Chester. We'd pack several guys in a car and split the cost of gas and tolls, traveling to the south Jersey beach for the weekend when the weather got warm. Some of these friends used to spend their entire summers in Ocean City.

During the ride to the beach, we would come up with creative ways to entertain ourselves; immature stunts reminiscent of the popular George Lucas directed, Ron Howard film, *American Graffiti*. On one trip, Mike Willover and I were in the car. I was driving, and Mike had fallen asleep in the front seat. We were on a deserted section of road—no other cars around—and I decided to scare the living crap out of him. While moving at about 50 mph, I slammed on the brakes, hit the horn and let loose a panicked bloodcurdling scream at the top of my lungs. Mike was instantly startled out of his deep sleep and started screaming too, thinking we were about to have a horrible collision. His eyes were the size of golf balls, and he was hyperventilating. I was in tears laughing and had to pull over to the shoulder of the road. I wish I had a video camera back then. Man, was Mike pissed off. I told him to relax, as I had just saved his life. Despite my best efforts to console him after our "near death experience," Mike insisted on taking over the driving for the rest of the trip. After that day, he never fell asleep on another road trip.

Another stunt feigned a kidnapping. We needed at least three guys in the car and would designate one to be the victim tied up in the back seat. For extra effect, we might rope his hands and gag him with a sock or some duct tape. We'd have our victim lay down in the back seat on the passenger side. The biggest guy in the car would play the thug and sat next to them. We would drive in the left lane of the highway and roll down the windows on the passenger side. The stunt would commence when we pulled up to a red light. The unsuspecting car next to us would soon be in for a shock. We'd time the action to start just as the light is turning green. The victim would quickly sit up and stick their gagged face out the window and try to scream for help. He'd raise his hands to show they were tied, and he'd make terrified eye contact with the driver in the nearby car. The thug would them grab the victim by the back of the neck and shove him to the floor. Our driver would then peel out and flee from the traffic light. Meanwhile, the people in the car next to us would drop their jaws and try to figure out what the heck had just happened. No one had cell phones back then, so there was no risk of a Good Samaritan calling the police or issuing an Amber Alert. After each successful stunt, we would be laughing hard for a good ten minutes. Today that act would get us quickly arrested and possibly shot.

Sometimes our car would get stuck behind a school bus. One of our favorite maneuvers was to rotate the windshield wiper sprayers, so they both sprayed to the right. A good sprayer would squirt fluid about ten feet. After the kids were off the bus, our car would slowly troll behind the school bus and hose them down. The stunt worked better if we rolled down the window and asked the young pedestrians for directions. As they approached our stopped car to help, we'd soak them with both wiper barrels.

Some of my buddies pulled stunts that demonstrated no fear and little regard for public safety. Fortunately, I missed some of the crazier antics, but

I heard their stories several times. Two of the most notorious automotive pranksters were Jim Gasho and Jeff Wolf. In this case, Jim was the driver, while Jeff sat in the back seat. Jeff's job was to cover Jim's eyes with his hands. Jeff would tell Jim if the car was drifting into another lane and how he needed to correct his steering. Jeff also gave Jim instructions on accelerating or braking. If driving blind wasn't daring enough, these guys bragged about how they did it while trying to pass other cars on the bridge spanning the Delaware River from Pennsylvania to New Jersey. That was nuts, and I am thankful they survived and did not hurt anyone. Decades later, Jim commented, "What were we thinking? ... Oh, we weren't."

Ocean City and Somers Point

Once the Henderson High students made it to their destination, the fun would begin. But we had to make a penultimate stop because Ocean City was a family-oriented town, a dry town where no alcohol could be served. The drinking age in New Jersey at the time was 18 years old, and many high school seniors were already of age. Just across the bridge from Ocean City was the town of Somers Point with the Circle Liquor store and two bars that catered to young beachgoers: Tony Marts and The Anchorage.

Upon arrival in Somers Point, we would go shopping in the Circle Liquor store and take our legally purchased beer and spirits to Ocean City. We'd usually start the evening playing "Tops," a game of skill that we had created the prior year. A forerunner of the game beer pong, the objective was to throw a bottle top into the glass of your seated opponent. Whoever got a score of ten first was the winner.

In Ocean City, we'd sleep on floors and eat cheap food—keeping costs down. Every few days, we'd go back to Somers Point to experience some of the nightlife.

Tony Marts had good Rock-n-Roll music and lots of girls. One evening, I was standing outside the main entrance to Tony Marts in a t-shirt, waiting for Willie to arrive. I had my arms crossed over my chest. I had lifted weights for years, and people thought I was a bouncer. At first, I told them I was just standing there waiting for a friend. After being shown several IDs by other youths, I started to play the part of the bouncer. Any guy that approached me got grilled. "What's your date of birth? What's your middle name? This photo doesn't look like you. Are you sure this isn't a fake ID?"

121

Any pretty girl who showed me her ID would get a different set of questions. "What's your phone number? Where's your boyfriend?" I would also tell the girls I was waiving the cover charge. That made me pretty popular with the ladies.

The Anchorage served seven beers for a dollar. No kidding. Seven beers at seven ounces each. It was Ortlieb's beer, another beverage company where my Uncle George served as a Regional Sales Representative. Most of the high school males started their evening at The Anchorage, and after spending two bucks there, they'd head over to Tony Marts. At the end of the night, we would go back to Ocean City and sleep it all off.

Momma's Boy

One evening, Mike "Willie" Willover and I drove a few miles from Ocean City to look for something different to do. Phil Swingle joined us. It didn't take long to find a new pub. Willie had packed a baloney sandwich and left it sitting half-eaten on the dashboard when we went in to check it out. We quickly decided it wasn't a good fit for us and too expensive for our high school budget.

We jumped back into Willie's car, a green Opel. The first thing I did was put my seat belt on. Willie and Phil heard me click the belt, and they began to give me crap, calling me "Momma's boy," and other less than flattering names connoting a lack of courage. I told them I wasn't planning on hitting the windshield if we had a wreck.

Willie pulled out of the parking lot and onto the highway. Within 30 seconds the Opel hit a pole at about 40 mph. Both Willie and Phil launched from their front seats and smashed head first into the windshield. Both were bleeding, and their skulls had made two big circular impact craters in the windshield. I was perfectly fine and had a great view of the entire incident while safely buckled in the back seat. My immediate concern was that a big tractor trailer might be following behind us and could run us over after we survived the initial collision.

We got out of the car to see what we hit. Sure enough, the third lane that we were driving in abruptly ended at the intersection, and the highway immediately reduced to two lanes. The pole we hit was in the middle of the 3rd lane that had just ended. It was dusk, and none of us had seen it coming, and we were all completely sober.

Within minutes, the police and an ambulance arrived at the scene. The cop noticed that Willie was wearing a University of West Chester t-shirt, a school where he was an alumnus. The cop immediately liked Willie, and since we were his passengers, Phil and I also passed his good guy test. The cop noted that there was a serious accident at that intersection every week and something needed to be done about it.

At this point, Willie and Phil needed to go to the emergency room for X-rays. I reassured them there was nothing to worry about. They both had thick skulls with a commensurate lack of brain tissue and probably just needed some stitches and may have only suffered some facial scarring. "Don't worry guys, Momma's boy will be there when you get released from the hospital," I taunted. Willie and Phil then got into the ambulance and sped off with the siren blaring. The cop knew I did not have a ride, so he gave me a lift to the police station in his cruiser.

After I arrived at the police station, I sat in a wooden chair for about four hours. It was about 1:30 AM, and I was falling asleep. The desk sergeant saw my head bobbing and told me to go into the empty jail cell and lay down to get some rest. Alarm bells were now going off in my head. My brain was racing with questions:

- "What if the cop goes off duty and the next shift doesn't know who I am? Will they think I am a suspect? Will I be detained for a few days?
- Did the West Chester police still have my name and address from the murder lineup?"
- "What if a drunken madman serial killer is arrested and thrown in my cell while I am sleeping in there?"
- "Do people really get raped in prison?"
- "Will the cops serve me breakfast?"

The desk sergeant was insistent—I think he was concerned about liability if I nodded off and fell from the chair and hurt myself—so I finally went in there and tried to get some shut eye, but I kept one eye open the entire night. Every time someone came into the station, I sat up to see if I was getting a felon for a roommate. Bottom line: I don't recommend jail cells for anyone seeking rest and relaxation.

The next morning, Willie and Phil were released from the hospital and were transported back to Ocean City. The police kindly offered to drive me back as I did not have a vehicle. I rode in three different squad cars, as I was transferred by cops from one jurisdiction to the next. Eventually, I made it back and let Willie and Phil sleep in. When they awoke, I asked them about their injuries. Eventually, the Opel was repaired, and Mike got his wheels back, along with the half-eaten baloney sandwich.

Lost Souls

During my senior year in high school, six fellow students died in tragic accidents. It was a terrible time for the entire school. Four of the students were quite close to me.

My friend, Joey Devereaux was the first student we lost. He had been on our football team and was elected as the class president. I also wrestled with Joey. He was in a multi-car crash, and three other friends were very seriously injured. I found out about the accident when I arrived at football practice one Saturday morning. Coach Walsh told me Joey was killed the night before; following our football game. I felt like I had been punched in the stomach. It was such a shock. I had never lost a friend before.

Three more friends died in another accident over the Christmas holiday season. Jim Jennings sat in front of me in my homeroom class. He was a good guy and always polite. In the same car were Jeff Payne and Greg Deaver. They were fellow midfielders on my high school lacrosse line. I was the center midfielder. Jeff and Greg played on the wings. When I ran out on the field at the first lacrosse practice that spring season, Jeff and Greg were absent, leaving me as the only surviving member of our line. It was a sad and eerie experience.

SECTION 4
WEST POINT

CHAPTER 15

APPLICATION AND ADMISSION TO THE U.S. MILITARY ACADEMY

During high school, I took the SAT exam. I scored reasonably well and began to receive mail from dozens of colleges. My parents never had an opportunity to attend college and had no idea which one might be right for me. The bigger issue that loomed was how to pay the tuition. Our family almost lost our home paying the extraordinary medical bills associated with Kevin's paralysis. The odd jobs I held working in a deli, pushing shopping carts, cleaning construction sites and delivering newspapers were insufficient to cover the cost of a college education. My parents and I didn't know what we didn't know.

Then I received a postcard from the United States Military Academy. I wasn't completely sure what it was or where West Point was located, but I could read my parent's body language when they handed me the card. Printed on a cheap piece of card stock and clearly produced by the lowest cost government contractor, it was undoubtedly genuine. Somehow that made it distinct. All the other colleges had a better marketing budget and sent me an attractive, glossy color brochure.

It's a trite—often overused—cliché, but in that instance, it was entirely accurate. I held my future in my hands. Not that I fully understood that at the time, but I could sense that it was a game-changing opportunity.

After a brief discussion with my parents, I told them I wanted to apply and ignored every other college letter I received. West Point was the only college I applied to. If I did not get admitted, I had no backup plan. It was a high-risk strategy, a gamble really. In hindsight, I would never advise a young person to follow this all-or-nothing approach.

The application process was arduous and required almost two years. I credit my Mother for much of the effort. She was caring for Kevin's physical needs and working in the school cafeteria, yet she was able to drive me to all the interviews, physical fitness tests, psychological screenings, receptions and other events. It paid off. I was one of the several candidates to eventually receive a nomination from Congressman Dick Schultz. It was now up to West Point to pick from the final list.

In early spring of 1978, I received an unexpected phone call at home from Mr. Dick Edell, the legendary coach of the Army Lacrosse team. He told me my application looked good. This was the first indication that I might be selected for admission. My morale improved, but I asked myself, "Why me?" Sure, I was a good lacrosse player, but the really great players were from New York. Mr. Edell called me again in early April and gave me more reason for optimism. Still, I wondered how a paperboy would be considered for such an opportunity. I tempered my expectations.

On April 21, 1978, I was in Mr. Pederson's Physics class. My high school guidance counselor, Mr. Collier, walked in and interrupted. "Kerry..." Surprised to be singled out, I looked up at him. "I want to be the first to congratulate you. You've been offered admission to West Point." He motioned for me to stand so he could shake my hand. As I stood an electric shock shot through my body that turned my knees to rubber. It was the greatest opportunity I could have ever asked for.

That day changed the entire course of my life. I absolutely know that God had his hand in it and on me. He was telling me I had a mission much greater than being a paperboy.

Beast Barracks

I entered the United States Military Academy (USMA) at West Point in July 1978. The first two months of training were called Cadet Basic Training (CBT), also referred to as "Beast Barracks."

During this period, new students were officially called "New Cadets." As one, my peers and I were subjected to a highly regimented and disciplined environment that involved continuous stress. It started the first day, the first moment, once we were separated from our parents. Seemingly, perhaps actually, pissed off upperclassmen (senior and junior cadets) started screaming and ordered us to board a bus. These mean guys were called "The Cadre," and the pressure they applied continued for the rest of summer.

That first day as a New Cadet was perhaps the longest day of my life. It was called "R-Day," short for Reception Day. To this day, I've never been to a reception quite like that one. We were immediately taught the proper position of attention, to crank our necks back, pop out our chests and straighten our arms in ways I thought were anatomically impossible. We learned how to march, salute, stand, eat and sleep at the position of attention. We were in-processed, measured by tailors and issued uniforms. Our heads were shaved, and the pasty-white skin on our ears and necks was soon torched by the hot summer sun.

Our first amendment rights were redefined. We were authorized to have only four responses to any upper-class cadet:

- "Yes, Sir!"
- "No, Sir!"
- "No excuse, Sir."
- "Sir, I do not understand!"

Any other response unleashed their full fury. If you absolutely needed to make a statement, you could not do so without explicit permission. A New Cadet could ask, "Sir, may I make a statement?" Making this request was ill-advised and at your own peril. It was usually much smarter to just answer, "No Excuse Sir" and stop drawing attention to yourself. They smelled blood and would tear into you if you made undisciplined or bogus statements.

R-Day was a fast-paced blur. By the end of the first day at West Point, New Cadets were clean-shaven, dressed in new tailored uniforms and marched in a parade to take the Oath of Office in front of their parents. It is an unbelievably rapid transformation from high school to the premier training institution of the U.S. military.

After several hours, my squad leader directed me to my room on the sixth floor of Central Barracks. I entered the Spartan room and looked around. My roommate's new uniforms and military gear were sitting on his bed. His last name was Mills, but I never met him. I was told he quit in the first couple of hours. My second roommate lasted about a week. He was an All-American swimmer and left the academy for a full scholarship to the University of Florida. After that, nobody wanted to room with New Cadet Kachejian. I must have been bad luck.

* * *

For a New Cadet, anybody in a position of authority— even the mailman— was to be called "Sir" or "Ma'am," and should be given a crisp salute. During Beast Barracks, all upperclassmen were saluted, as were officers. "Good Morning, Sir!" "Good Afternoon, Sir!" and "Beat Navy, Sir!" could be heard every day during CBT. The unofficial policy on saluting was, "If in doubt, whip it out!" Being new to the military, I was still learning the different ranks and uniforms. I saluted several enlisted guys near the parade field, and they told me I shouldn't do that. Now I was even more confused and decided it was just easier for me to salute everyone.

I was assigned to the 8th Cadet Basic Training Company along with 160 other New Cadets. My company commander was a senior named Cadet Rock. The guy's name sounded like someone who ate nails for breakfast, so I planned to avoid him at all costs.

My platoon started Beast Barracks with about forty New Cadets. There were ten in my squad, and we had to immediately work as a team to have any chance of success. Our squad included Jim North, Ed Reynolds, Thomas Murphy, Keith Fink, Paul Wood, Mark Swanson, Barry Dominick and the two other men we lost early. Jim North and Thomas Murphy drew the short straws and became my new roommates. Jim was a smart guy who later studied Russian and became a surgeon. Thomas was a walking encyclopedia of knowledge who hailed from Dallas, Texas. I did not tell him I was a Philadelphia Eagles fan.

Barry Dominick was a former enlisted soldier that spent a year at the USMA Prep School. He was several years older and was a rare breed of cadet that entered West Point already wearing the Army's coveted Ranger tab. Barry reminded me of a younger version of my father: his haircut, mannerisms, and even his dry sense of humor. He had the experience, perspective, and confidence needed to survive the stress-filled, challenging environment of Beast Barracks. He introduced me to some his crazy "Prepster" buddies that were also New Cadets.

During the first week of CBT, we were marched to an auditorium and given a briefing on our training and the standards of excellence required for everything we did. The briefer then told us to look at the New Cadet to our immediate left and right. At the end of our time at West Point, one of the three of us would not graduate from the academy. Man, was I relieved. I had already lost two roommates and had exceeded my quota. Perhaps I could coast through the next four years.

First-year cadets are referred to by several names. Officially, we were New Cadets during the summer. When it was over, freshmen joined the Corps of Cadets and were then officially called cadets. As freshmen, we were fourth-class cadets, the lowest in the caste system. Sophomores were called third class cadets, or Yearlings. Juniors were second class cadets or Cows. Seniors were first class cadets or Firsties.

Fourth-class cadets had some other less flattering names: Plebe, Beanhead, Smack, and the all-purpose, "Mister." Upperclassmen often did not know the names of individual Plebes. There were over a thousand of us pinging around the academy grounds. Firsties would often bark commands like, "Mister, halt!" or "Hey Smack, stop gazing around in my mess hall!" Or one of our favorites "Beanhead, stick out your tiny bird-like chest!"

If the Firstie knew the last name of a Plebe, the order would be something along the lines of, "Mr. Smith, post over here," or "Mr. Jones, how many days are there until Army beats Navy in football?"

All New Cadets were issued a book of West Point and Army history and trivia called "Bugle Notes." Plebes had to memorize much of the content verbatim and recite it upon demand by an upperclassman. To not know the answer to a question was grounds for demerits which often lead to punishment tours. Some examples:

Q: "What is the definition of leather?"
A: "Sir, if the fresh skin of an animal, cleaned and divested of all hair, fat, and other extraneous matter, be immersed in a dilute solution of tannic acid, a chemical combination ensues; the gelatinous tissue of the skin is converted into a nonputrescible substance, impervious to and insoluble in water; this Sir is leather."

Q: What is the significance of the Cadet Colors?
A: Sir, the components of gunpowder are charcoal, saltpeter (potassium nitrate) and sulfur, which are black, gray, and gold in color.

Q: With what is Abner Doubleday, Class of 1842, credited?
A: Sir, he is credited with having invented the sport of baseball.

New Cadets stood in formation near the parade field three times each day: before breakfast, lunch, and dinner. During the evening formation, a

130

bugler would play "Retreat," and then a resounding boom would echo across the campus as a cannon fired. Black powder only, for obvious safety reasons there was no projectile, and aimed across the river, toward Constitution Island and the town of Cold Spring. The noise rocked the nearby Hudson Valley. While we stood at attention, we enjoyed watching civilians, unprepared for the cannon shot, jump or gasp in a moment of shock and panic.

After a few weeks of observing, all New Cadets knew exactly when and where the blast would occur. One of the Plebes in my platoon dared to ask a Firstie a question about it. "Sir, every night I see that cannon go off, but I never see where the cannonball lands." The Firstie and rest of the Plebes all burst into a moment of authorized laughter. The guy seriously thought we were firing cannon balls across the Hudson River every evening.

Contact with relatives and friends during CBT was limited to U.S. mail. Packages sent to New Cadets were inspected, and any food was confiscated during the first month. New Cadets were on a strict diet. We ate at the position of attention and often only got a few bites of food. One upperclassman made his Plebes cut their peas in half before eating them individually. After a few days of near starvation, toothpaste became a potential source of food. There were rumors Crest had more calories than Colgate and included vitamins, too.

After a month, Plebes were permitted to receive and open mail packages that contained food. By that time, the food was often stale. Barry Dominick opened his box, to find petrified cookies—they were hard as concrete.

That night, we decided to get even with the Firsties for confiscating our chow. It was a dark evening, and Barry quietly opened a window in our room and looked out. He grasped a big cookie like a hand grenade, pulled out an imaginary pin, and tossed it from our 6th floor window at some Firsties walking across the courtyard, which was called "Central Area." When the ossified cookie hit the asphalt, it shattered into a dozen pieces sending shrapnel flying in all directions. We could hear the Firsties yapping about something being thrown at them, but they could not figure out which one of a hundred windows it came from. A new group of Firsties would walk by every few minutes, and Barry and I tossed a half dozen "fragmentation cookies" at them and then ducked to prevent detection. Every Firstie that crossed Central

Area that night was bombarded. Barry and I owned the night. Beast Barracks was getting better.

Tragically, my friend Barry Dominick died a few weeks after our class graduated while training at Airborne School. I will always remember his exceptional qualities and the memories we shared as Plebes.

* * *

During my first summer, I had permission to make two short phone calls to my parents and scraped together enough quarters to feed the basement pay phone. The waiting lines for the pay phones were an hour long, but the call was essential to coordinate a brief parent visit halfway into the summer training.

New Cadets could not leave the academy grounds, so I enjoyed a family picnic along the Hudson River with real food from home. My parents brought Kevin with them. I was pushing him around the academy grounds in his wheelchair and saluting upper-class cadets and officers every couple of minutes. I'd pop off, "Good Morning, Sir!" or I'd belt out, "Beat Navy, Sir!" It turned out that returning a salute to a Plebe pushing his wheelchair-bound brother made the upper-class cadets *very* uncomfortable. In fact, some crossed the street a block away to avoid meeting us. Kevin and I turned the tables on them. I'd push faster, so we were in hot pursuit and head right into a pack of cadre members to make them squirm and scatter. I used Kevin as a human bowling ball, and he was knocking over mean Firsties and doing a masterful job staring them down.

Spending a few hours with my parents and brother was good therapy. While I had often thought that Beast Barracks was tough, having Kevin there that day was humbling and put things in perspective. He always had a much harder day than me.

Training

Our schedule was highly programmed and packed full of classes on the Code of Conduct, uniforms, drill and ceremony (parades), ethics, the honor code, safety and first aid, and Army Regulations. We also had a daily inspection of our rooms and uniforms, ate square meals (at the position of attention), walked fast (120 steps per minute was the absolute minimum) and endured a lot of physical training.

We learned how to fire the M-16 rifle, and bayonet training taught us how to beat and impale the godless communist soldiers we would be fighting in the next big war. We always ran to bayonet training in a military formation, singing the cadence, "Blood, Blood, Blood makes the grass grow!" We later included the bayonet in the design of our class crest.

In the afternoon, cadets competed in intramural or intercollegiate sports. That's when I went to the lacrosse field and met the coaches and other New Cadets that had been recruited. I met and made new friends like Ken Dahl, Kyle MacGibbon, Mark Albe, Rich Kubu, Bill Hargraves, John "Mick" Nicholson, Stuart Harrison and two dozen others. Lacrosse practice was tough, but the military atmosphere on the team was more relaxed. The academy realized it would be hard to play NCAA sports at the position of attention.

At the end of summer training, our class spent several days living in small tents alongside Lake Frederick. Over a thousand New Cadets then marched back, about 12 miles, to West Point and were officially accepted into the Corps of Cadets. Plebes then joined their academic company where they would stay for the remainder of their cadet career.

By the end of August 1978, I had plenty of material to write an essay on "What I Did During my Summer Vacation."

CHAPTER 16
PLEBE YEAR

The Gators

When Cadet Basic Training ended, Plebes were integrated into the thirty-six companies that comprise the United States Corp of Cadets (USCC). The Corps had four regiments with nine companies (A-I). I was assigned to Company G2. That meant I was in G Company of the 2nd Regiment. Amazingly, my new company was in the same building and on the same sixth floor where I spent Beast Barracks. I wasn't moving far, and that's where I lived for the next four years.

Although it was the highest floor in the building, cadets were not permitted to use the elevator. The elevator was a luxury reserved for maintenance personnel and the tactical officers who supervised each cadet company.

As Plebes, we walked fast and squared corners at the position of attention, ran up and down the stairwells a dozen times a day to go to classes, meal formations, parades, and athletics. We sometimes joked about having leg muscles like the famous NFL running back, Earl Campbell.

Every company had a mascot, and the members of Company G2 were known as the Gators. Several of my fellow lacrosse players were also assigned to G2: Mark "Albs" Albe, Kyle "Mac" MacGibbon, and Bill "Sweet Willie" Hargraves. The Gator men also included Robert Bruce "Abe" Abrams, Bob "Bosco" Scurlock, Rich York, Kevin Merrigan, Torin Bussey, Rod "Junior" Mateo, Billy Ward, "Two Dash" Tey Wiseman, John Madrid, Rick Hayden, Steve Eden, Mike Roemer and a dozen others.

The Firsties in the Class of 1979 were the last all-male class at West Point. The Class of 1982 was only the third class with women. Women cadets were still relatively new to the culture of USMA. Not all companies had them. G2 had four female cadets. These lady classmates included Sue Sowers, April Hughlett, Barb Grofic and Ellen Groschelle.

G2 Gators before their graduation in 1982

USMA Class of 1982

I met many other cadets from the eight other companies of the 2nd Regiment (and the other regiments) at athletic events and social functions that became friends and colleagues. The full list is too long, but it includes: Steve Salazaar, Bo Dyess, Rick Waddell, John "Mick" Nicholson, Alex Gorsky, Jim Sharman, Ed Cardon, Paul Mooradian, Brent Willis, Pete Mansoor, Ed Olivares, Bill Mayville, Margaret Williams (Burcham), Randy Fofi, Casey Haskins, Jay Jennings, Bob Carlson, John Garrison, Brian Allgood, Jim Brown, Nadja (Grammer) West, Ole Knudson, Everett McDaniel, Tom Muir, Mark Palzer, Rob Baker, Doug Strock, Dominick Baragona, Bill Sardella, Paul Mooradian, Bryan Watson, Kevin Mangum, Tom Lynch, Tim O'Rourke, Steve Croskery, John Naccarelli, and Craig Fox.

Fast forward thirty years: many of these classmates have served our nation with distinction as General Officers and Colonels, Special Operators, National Security Council members, Senior Executives, CEOs and Industry leaders, University Professors, Surgeons, Lawyers, Federal Judges, and Chaplains. Hundreds served in military operations in Iraq, Afghanistan, Bosnia, Panama, and Grenada. Several died in training accidents or were killed or wounded in combat. Regardless of which path each of us took, we will always be brothers/sisters for life because of the bonds we formed in the Class of 1982. After our graduation, I would not see many of these classmates again for over 20 years. But when I arrived in Iraq in 2004, I discovered scores of my academy colleagues still serving the nation, battling a raging insurgency in a hostile country.

Fourth-Class System

Living under the rigors of the Fourth-Class System instilled confidence and taught self-discipline, teamwork, selfless service and time management. But it was the longest year of my life. All Plebes had special duties to perform to include delivering mail and laundry to upperclassmen, pulling guard duty, marching in parades and calling minutes (this is when a Plebe is assigned to stand at attention next to a clock and call out the time remaining before a formation or inspection). Attending classes and meals was mandatory. Missing one event, being late to a single class or formation or not memorizing required information (known as, "Plebe poop") was inexcusable and resulted in demerits or punishment tours. But, all my classmates had to endure the same environment, and that shared burden made it seem lighter. The Fourth-Class system was not lifted until the Firsties completed their graduation parade the following June.

* * *

We had academic classes seven days a week. Saturday classes went until noon. That was often followed by a mandatory parade and a football game. On Sunday evenings, we had foreign language training. Each of us carried an academic load of 18 to 21 credit hours every semester. After four years, a graduate of West Point had completed about 160 credits, thirty percent more than required to graduate from a civilian university. The academics were challenging and Ivy League caliber. Plebe English required writing two papers per week. Failure of this single course led to the loss of 10% of our class.

The Honor Code

The honor code is clear and straightforward: "A cadet will not lie, cheat, steal, or tolerate those who do." Any cadet accused of violating it is investigated, and it may lead to a formal hearing by a board of their peers. If found guilty, the only punishment authorized at the time was separation from the academy.

Ethics classes were pounded into cadets, particularly the Plebes. Case studies were presented and discussed. Some were obvious honor violations, but others were quite sobering. A cadet who wanted to study late one night after lights out put a towel under his door to prevent light from being seen in the hallway. An honor board found the cadet guilty of deceiving an inspecting officer. In another case, a cadet filled a Listerine bottle with whiskey and put the bottle in his medicine cabinet. This was also considered deceit, and he was found guilty of an honor violation. A more common violation involved cadets that snuck off post but declared they were "on limits" such as in the library or in a study hall.

Walking the Area

There was a very formal and structured system of rewards and punishments at USMA. The near-term rewards were few: oxygen, food, a bed, and a few extra hours of sleep on Sunday mornings. As a Plebe, we were permitted one "short" weekend off post during the second semester, if we were in good academic standing. That weekend started at noon on Saturday and ended at 8:00 PM on Sunday. Thirty-two hours of freedom. It was a big incentive for a lonely Plebe.

The long-term reward for enduring this strict lifestyle was far better: A West Point education and diploma, a commission as an Army officer, a guaranteed job with no college debt, the ability to serve your country and opportunities for international travel and adventure. And you didn't have to worry about buying business suits.

Violations of the strict standards of personal conduct and appearance provided endless opportunities for punishment. Minor infractions were recorded, and cadets received bad points called demerits. Plebes were often cited, but they were permitted up to 26 demerits each month. As cadets progressed each year, fewer demerits were allowed. Yearlings were alloted 18, Cows had approximately 14, and Firsties only had about ten.

A cadet could get two demerits for improperly leaving a pencil laying on their desk. Other common infractions included: having improperly folded underwear, textbooks on the shelf that were not aligned in height order, not

137

sweeping the room or cleaning the sink daily, having a dusty rifle, leaving a wallet unsecured, shoes not properly shined, having a smudge on your belt buckle, not making the bed properly, failure to turn in a homework assignment on time, or being a minute late to a class or formation. The list of potential regulation violations seemed unlimited.

Every demerit over the monthly limit resulted in an hour of punishment, known as "Walking the Area." During a punishment tour (a.k.a. an area tour), offenders put on their uniform, were inspected (potentially leading to more demerits) and walked, with a rifle, up to three hours back and forth in Central Area. There was no talking or smiling, just hours of solitary marching with an M-14 rifle (only 9.2 lbs. without a loaded magazine, 2 lbs. heavier than an unloaded M16, but still became tiring after carrying it for a while).

Forget any free time you may have had on Saturday or Sunday. Up to five punishment tours could be served each weekend. Cadets walking off the punishment tours were called "Area Birds." Walking the Area was even more miserable when there was a freezing rain or snow.

If the U.S. president or a foreign leader visited West Point, they could grant amnesty for cadets that had punishment tours. It was a get out of jail free card and applied to most cadets with area tours. This happened every few years.

Some offenses were considered more severe and included both demerits and mandatory punishment tours. Intentionally missing a class could be 30 demerits and 20 area tours on the first offense. A second offense could be 60 demerits and forty area tours. Getting caught with alcohol was major and could result in 80 hours on the area. That would require at least 16 weeks to walk off.

There was an alternative punishment to Walking the Area, serving a room tour. This sentence required cadets to stay confined in their room for two hours instead of one hour on the area. This was used for cadets recovering from injuries, an in-season athlete, or a cadet in deep academic trouble. During a room tour, a cadet must sit at their desk and work on academics.

Any cadet that was serving punishment tours was said to be "slugged." During the punishment period, cadets could not have any other privileges. A cadet that accumulated over 100 hours of punishment tours was considered a "Century Man." A "Double Century Man" served over 200 hours. That implies the cadet lost over one year of any privileges.

I believe most cadets served area tours at some point during their four years at West Point. I was one of the lucky few that never served one. I came close a few times but was able to dodge a few disciplinary bullets.

Area Birds walking off punishment tours, 1979

A new list of demerits and punishment tours was posted each week on the company bulletin board. This list was called the *Slug Sheet*, and it was visible for all cadets. The list was meant to provide full disclosure, cause embarrassment, and serve as a deterrent to others. It often had the opposite effect. Reading the Company G2 Slug Sheet often served as a means of entertainment for Plebes. We loved reading about evil upperclassman who were now slugged. To our great amusement, the most egregious conduct offenses were publicly announced to the entire Corps of Cadets during dinner in the mess hall. All 4,000 cadets would learn of a specific cadet's misconduct and the swift and firm punishment that ensued. A major offense, such as "conduct unbecoming of a human being," often lead to spontaneous loud cheers and instant fame for the young offender. The poor guy's life was ruined for the next year, but everyone in the Corps now knew and loved him.

If a cadet accumulated enough demerits and punishment tours, they would be required to face a Conduct Board. The Board of Officers determined if the cadet should remain at West Point or be separated from the academy. It was a serious situation, and one's entire future was at stake. Several classmates fell victim to the conduct boards. The exploits of one former classmate, "Ranger" Bob G, were legendary.

There was a famous Regimental Tactical Officer named Colonel Moscatelli, who had a reputation for strict enforcement of cadet regulations. During one Saturday morning inspection, he entered a cadet's room with an assistant who was prepared to record any demerits. Moscatelli inspected the cadet's clothing to ensure it was properly folded and marked with the owner's name, as required by USCC regulations. To his surprise, he found a pair of non-regulation underwear in the cadet's dresser. The skivvies had a big Burger King hamburger printed on the front and boldly displayed a "Home of the Whopper" logo above it. The room went silent. Without missing a beat, Moscatelli turned to the assistant and announced the charge, "Conceit and attempt to deceive. Ten demerits." Colonel Moscatelli had a sense of humor after all. The cadet was probably thankful that he did not face honor charges. Later, some cadets demonstrated their own sense of humor by relocating Colonel Moscatelli's Triumph convertible from Central Area to the entrance of Thayer Hall, blocking the doors to a major academic building.

* * *

Life as a cadet was demanding, especially during Plebe year. But attending the academy was also an honor and a privilege. Every cadet had a full four-year scholarship, including room and board. After the U.S. Government had collected taxes and fees for uniforms and books, the discretionary pay for a Plebe was $50 per month.

After a foreign dignitary had toured the U.S. Military Academy, he remarked that West Point was the last remnant of ancient Sparta in the western world. I thought his comment was spot on. Several foreign leaders sent their children to the academy to prepare them for future leadership positions in their countries.

CHAPTER 17

ARMY FOOTBALL

Army Football

Army has been deservedly proud of its football tradition, which has produced three national championship teams and three Heisman Trophy winners over the course of its history. Given the high academic standards and small student body, it has recently been difficult for all service academies to field a nationally-ranked team.

During our senior year, the team captain was an offensive lineman, Rick Waddell. He was later a Rhodes Scholar at Oxford University and earned a Ph.D. from Columbia University. You won't find football players with academic qualifications like that at most Division I schools. Rick later deployed to Iraq and Afghanistan eight times during his career and has held numerous command assignments. He is now a two-star general and was named deputy national security advisor.

Our football team played a broad range of opponents, including a few top national teams like Stanford, Notre Dame, Pittsburgh, Baylor and Penn State. In these games, our offensive and defensive lines were typically outweighed by 50 pounds per man. If we kept the score close against a major team, we considered it a moral victory. During our sophomore year, a Plebe named Gerald Walker scored the winning touchdown against nationally-ranked Stanford on a 71-yard run. The 17-13 win was a great day for Army football and all of the Class of 1983. Those Plebes were allowed to take big bites of food in the mess hall for the next 24 hours. They were even permitted to eat the dessert.

Another big game was against Pittsburgh, who was ranked #2 in the nation. The Panthers wanted to run up the score on Army to take over the top ranking. Pittsburgh had gone 11-1 for three consecutive years. Army lost by more than 40 points that day, but our team intercepted the Pittsburgh quarterback six times; three times by our classmate Dale Love alone. In fact,

Army defensive backs were among Pittsburgh's best receivers that game. The Pittsburgh quarterback? Dan Marino, who later played for the Miami Dolphins and is in the NFL Hall of Fame. And Torin Bussey, a fellow G2 Gator, provided another Army highlight when he blocked an extra point.

When Baylor came to West Point, they brought their college mascot, The Baylor Bear. And it was real, the carnivore kind. The mascot in Company I-4 was a cadet in a polar bear costume. Yes, it happened. The I-4 Polar Bear made a bad decision and went over to tease the real bear. After the I-4 mascot almost had his face ripped off, he retreated back to the safety of the cadet seating area.

Another tradition at football games was lifting the opposing team's cheerleaders over our heads and passing them up the stands. Once at the top, cadets would throw the cheerleader down several rows at a time. Cadets preferred to pass up the lady cheerleaders. If we had a male cheerleader, his ride was a bit wilder.

Pass him up

The night before a home football game, West Point loosened up the rules for cadets to get the excitement pumping for the football game. "Joe College Night" was held in the mess hall. All cadets could wear a civilian shirt at dinner. The intent was to improve morale and support the Army football team. Even Plebes were permitted to wear a civilian shirt and allowed to eat extra chow. The most spirited Plebes demonstrated their "Go Army" spirit by standing on their chair and drinking an entire bottle of A-1 sauce or ketchup. Their choice. The tradition was called "validating the A-1 sauce." I saw one motivated beanhead drink a bottle of each. That dude did not look so good when he was done.

Motivated Plebes could also volunteer to take a "silver bullet." This involved a jar of Jiffy peanut butter and a big serving spoon. A baseball sized (minimum) lump of peanut butter was dug out of the jar and then inserted into the young soldier's mouth. It could take the trooper 20-30 minutes to consume the whole thing. Smooth peanut butter went down easier than the chunky stuff.

G-2 Gator Plebes validating a bottle of A-1 Sauce and Ketchup

Fidel Castro takes a hostage at Central Guard Room, Snoopy is powerless to help

Later that evening, a spontaneous cadet rally would occur. Cadets would drop their textbooks and run outside in outrageous and sometimes bizarre costumes. Togas were common; they only required a bed sheet. I once put on an old Fidel Castro mask, grabbed a cigar and borrowed an Army uniform from my classmate, Rawlin Castro (no relation to Fidel). Geared up, armed with my ceremonial bayonet, I decided to infiltrate "Central Guard Room" and take hostages. My mission was successful, and I made an announcement over the public-address system that "Fidel Castro is now in control of the academy. You capitalists will pay!" Snoopy attempted a counterattack during the standoff, but he was powerless to stop Fidel. We took a picture to document the breaking news story, and then I sped out of the building before some steroid laden MP shot me. Unfortunately, the media did not notice the international incident nor did top officials in government and the Department of Defense. I realized that when the next morning President Reagan had not declared war on Cuba.

Please Pass the... Potatoes

The following vignette was relayed to me by two Army football players while I was a cadet. We were drinking beer at Eisenhower Hall at the time the story was told, so I believe there is a factual basis for the account. No one lies while drinking beer. Quite the opposite, beer often liberates a story that would otherwise be suppressed.

Lt. General Willard Scott, a big supporter of Army football, became the new Superintendent, "Supe," of the Military Academy in 1981. Each week, he invited several football players to his house for dinner. The invitation was rotated to different players each week. One week he hosted the offensive backfield, and another week he invited the defensive line, etc. The intent was to build morale and team spirit.

Being invited to dinner with the Superintendent and his wife was a rare occurrence. As a Lieutenant General, Willard Scott was nine levels of rank above a senior cadet. The Supe and his wife served wine at these dinners—wine consumption was authorized—a rare opportunity for cadets. The meal was served, and there were generous portions, of food and drink, on the table. Serving dishes were passed among all the guests, and soon plates and glasses emptied—and refilled. More than once.

The cadets were feeling relaxed, and some let down their social guard. "Please pass the meat... sir, please pass the corn... send the gravy down here when you get a chance." Everything was relatively tame until one of the football players dropped a bomb. "Pass the f***ing potatoes." The table went dead quiet. The potatoes were sitting next to Mrs. Willard, and the cadet immediately realized he made a gross error in judgment. After several seconds of awkward silence, Lt. General Scott turned to his spouse and said,

"You heard him, honey, pass the f***ing potatoes." The bond between the Amy football team and the new Superintendent was truly—and well—sealed. Go Army!

Army—Navy Game

The big football game every year was Army-Navy: The United States Military Academy versus the United States Naval Academy. The game was usually played in Philadelphia, in the bitter cold.

As a Plebe, the Army-Navy game was my first time away from West Point in five months. It felt strange walking around Philadelphia in uniform. I could look around and walk in a relaxed manner—not having to square the corners. Re-entering the civilian world felt eerie; the environment was foreign. There were guys with long hair and earrings. They did not walk with a sense of purpose. Yet I still felt compelled to call everyone "Sir."

The week that that led up to the Army-Navy game was an ideal time for Plebes to pull pranks on upperclassmen. One of the more popular ones was pulled in several companies, including A2 and G2. It started by turning off the circuit breakers in Central Barracks late at night. Next, the Plebes quietly snuck into the Firstie rooms, turned on their stereos and cranked the volume knob up. On the way out the door, they flipped the light switches on. Of course, nothing happened while the circuit breakers were off. To further aggravate the upperclassmen, the A2 Plebes also took the shoes from the Firsties' and Cows' rooms and lined them up in a military formation in Central Area. The beanheads then went back to bed. At about 3:00 AM, the circuit breaker was thrown, and the power snapped back on. All the lights immediately came on, stereos blasted loud music, and upperclassmen leaped out of their beds. The Firsties immediately knew the Plebes were collectively guilty, and retaliatory hazing followed shortly after that. It was a glorious evening.

Then there were the pranks that these two service academies played on each other. West Point cadets managed to steal the Navy mascot, a goat, three of the four years we were there. We considered putting goat soup on the menu in the Cadet Mess Hall. However, the smelly, flea bitten, demonic animal was eventually returned to Annapolis unharmed. Navy had a tougher time trying to kidnap the Army mascot, a mule. That's a much more powerful and noble animal, and significantly harder to hijack. The bottom line, stealing mascots requires mostly land combat skills: ground reconnaissance, terrain navigation, deception, stealth. Army had a distinct advantage in those types of operations.

As the Army-Navy game drew near, the Commandant of Cadets, General Bard—the Comm—who was in charge of all discipline at West Point, sought to "bring spirit back to the Corps." Cadets wanted to honor the Comm's intent. To demonstrate that the warrior spirit was alive and well at West Point, all 4,000 cadets started the largest food fight in the history of North America. As soon as the USMA pep band began to play Army fight songs in the Cadet Mess Hall, the dining facility became a high intensity, asymmetrical, combat zone. Platters of food were airborne, pizza slices thrown like boomerangs, and cakes were randomly launched while pitchers of water and juice rained down on the masses. The culminating event was when Plebes picked up a ten-man table and carried it through the mess hall with a Firstie, sitting in a chair on top, yelling "Stroke, Stroke, Stroke." like it was a Roman troop ship preparing for an attack. The Firstie wore a steel ice bucket on this head to serve as his centurion's helmet. It was an awesome scene. The collateral damage was widespread and indiscriminate. Scores of waiters ran for cover. The fight ended when the food supply was exhausted; we simply ran out of ammo. The battlefield was littered with muck and goo. Surprisingly, casualties were light. General Bard must have been incredibly proud of the warrior spirit we exhibited that evening (but thankfully, this was before anyone had video cameras). The mess hall staff had to work extended hours to clean up the massive debris. Perhaps, we should have left a tip for the waiters that night.

Each year, the nationally-televised Army-Navy game kicked off in early December. Upperclassmen had the option to travel to Philadelphia the evening before, but most cadets rode to the Army-Navy game on a chartered bus and had a few free hours after the game. It was just enough time for the newly liberated cadets to tie one on before having to return. Several were carried horizontally through the streets of Philadelphia and loaded on the bus back to West Point. Some of the more inebriated and boisterous Plebes were slugged—awarded punishment tours—upon their return. A story was told that in the late 1960s, a Plebe staggered on the bus and stuck his head out the window to get sick. Well, Colonel Alexander Haig, the 3rd Regimental Commander, was standing there and got spew-slimed. Haig later became a four-star general, the Supreme Allied Commander of Europe, White House

Chief of Staff and the Secretary of State. As a result of the incident, the intoxicated Plebe became an instant "double Century Man."

If the kickoff time was at 1:00 PM, West Point wanted their cadets assembled in formation outside the stadium, the day of the game, at about 8:00 AM. Once accountability was taken, cadets stood in the cold for the next few hours until they could march on the field at about 11:00 AM. Windy, freezing weather was typical, and standing in it for hours before kickoff sapped the energy out of everyone.

The service academies exchanged a few cadets/midshipmen each year. Before the opening kickoff of the Army-Navy game, these cadets would meet at midfield and be repatriated to their own academy to cheer during the game. This ceremony was called a prisoner swap. The Exchange Cadet Program only selected the best scholars for the semester-long experience. For a West Point cadet, getting to serve a semester at the U.S. Naval Academy, the U.S. Air Force Academy, or the U.S. Coast Guard Academy was a get out of jail free card. The discipline and regulations at the sister academies were significantly less rigid. Navy midshipman and Air Force and Coast Guard cadets attending West Point on the exchange program received a culture shock.

My parents and several friends came to my first game, which was played, that year, at JFK Stadium. At one point, Navy was winning 21-0. Despite the freezing temperatures, Army ripped off their overcoats and uniform tops in the 4th quarter and displayed their 12th Man t-shirts while the pep band played the William Tell Overture. Cadets were throwing anything they could get their hands on hats, coats, popcorn and other cadets. Four thousand cadets were screaming, "The 12th man is here! The 12th man is here!" You would have thought Army was crushing Navy.

By deep in the 4th quarter, my parents asked if I could leave the game early and come home to see all our friends and relatives and celebrate my father's birthday. I only had one night off in the past five months, and this was it. I was fairly sure that leaving early was a major regulation violation, but no one specifically warned us. I waited until Navy scored its final touchdown, and I sprinted out of the stadium with my parents. It felt like a jailbreak as we jumped in their car and sped off ahead of the traffic jam that followed the conclusion of the game. I laid low in the car for the first ten minutes, and then I sat up. In our haste to leave, my dad left a pewter West

Point mug I gave him as a birthday gift at the game. He felt terrible, and so did I, but the feeling soon wore off as I was approaching my home.

We pulled into the driveway and stopped. I got out of the car in my uniform. As I walked in the door, a flood of memories came over me. I saw my dog, Queenie, outstretched my arms and called her name. She was thoroughly confused. My voice was familiar, but she did not recognize me. My long hair and blue jeans were gone; I was wearing a long gray overcoat. I took off my hat and fell to my knees. Queenie was spazzing out. She wasn't certain if I was her old friend or a new threat. After a few seconds, she was jumping all over me with excitement. She was man's best friend.

At home with family after Army-Navy

Cadet Rocky Kachejian

Everyone at home wanted to try on my cadet uniform. First, it was dad, then my brother, Kevin. My best friend Mike Willover suited up and bayoneted me with a WWII rifle. Life doesn't get much better than that moment.

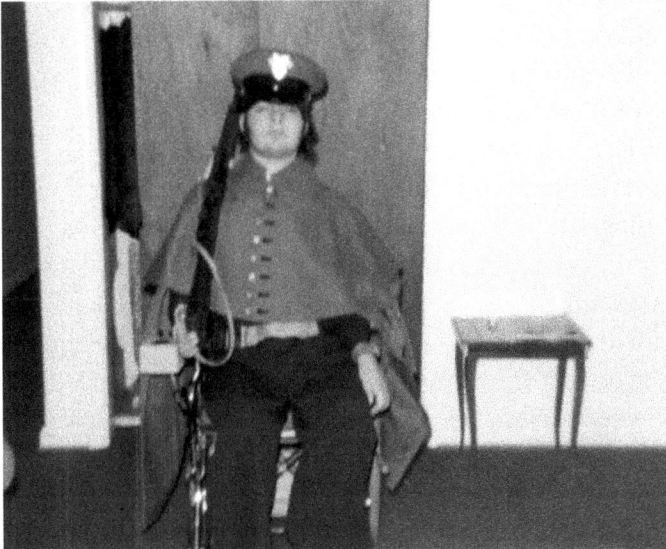

Cadet Kevin Kachejian—wheelchair sentry

Mike Willover sticks it to me

The night passed quickly, and after lunch the next day, my father made the 320-mile round-trip drive to get me back to West Point before the 8:00 PM curfew. It was a brief but welcome taste of freedom. My first real break as a Plebe would occur three weeks later at Christmas. My class would return to West Point in early January and face final exams. About 10% of our class would fall victim to the Dean that first semester; a typical academic attrition rate for freshman classes.

I experienced three more Army-Navy games as a cadet. There was an old proverb at West Point that foretold the future, "Lose four and go to war." Any class that lost four consecutive football games to Navy would be facing a war shortly after graduation. I don't know if there was any truth to the legend, but we did not want to test it. Going into our senior year, our class had lost three consecutive games to Navy, all by wide margins. December of 1981 was our last chance to beat the Squids. The game was played at Veterans Stadium in Philly and was a defensive battle the entire game. The Army punter, Joe Sartiano, had an incredible day. He set an NCAA record, averaging over 57.6 yards on five punts. Each team managed to kick a field goal. The game ended with the final score Army 3, Navy 3. Army won.

Despite the Army victory, our class went to war the year following our graduation. It was the big one: WW Grenada. In October 1983, the United States invaded Grenada as part of Operation Urgent Fury. Rangers, Special Forces, the 82nd Airborne Division and the Marine Corps rescued U.S. medical students on the island and sent the Cubans, East Germans and Russians packing. A number of our classmates were directly involved in the invasion.

CHAPTER 18
LEGENDS, AIRBORNE HAMSTERS & DISTINGUISHED VISITORS

USMA Stories / Legends

Soon after I arrived at the academy, I began to hear stories of legendary cadets from years past. I didn't know if these stories were true, but they sounded amazing to a paperboy from Pennsylvania. There was no internet or Google available at the time to validate if the accounts were true or just urban legends. But if the stories weren't true, they ought to be. Once a cadet borrowed a Russian tank that was used for training and drove it onto the main post. He intended to drive it into the mess hall and reportedly damaged the granite stairs in front of Washington Hall. A story like that should have made the national news. He must have been angry at the academy or perhaps at the mess hall staff. Another story that circulated concerned a Plebe with the last name "Mister." He officially became "New Cadet Mister," or was also called "Mister Mister," sharing the name with a rock and roll band of the day. Furthermore, when an upperclassman did not know the last name of a Plebe, they often would simply bark, "Mister, halt!" That command was uttered dozens of times each day by scores of Firsties. And there was normally a crowd of Plebes in the area; most would start scurrying for cover. Poor Mister Mister had no idea if "Mister, halt!" was referring to another nearby Plebe or was specifically ordering him to stop. I bet he had a long summer at Beast Barracks. I later conducted a little research and found evidence of a "New Cadet Mistler" who entered with the class of 1965, but he did not graduate.

In the late 1960s, the Secretary of the Army declined an opportunity for the Army football team to be considered for the Sugar Bowl. In his judgment, playing in college football bowl games was inconsistent with the mission of the military academy. West Point was intended to produce combat leaders. When the Corps of Cadets learned about the decision, cadets protested by removing all the sugar bowls from the mess hall.

152

Airborne Hamsters

One of my favorite West Point legends involved airborne hamsters. Summer training for rising juniors often included attending the Army's Airborne School at Fort Benning, Georgia, where cadets received paratrooper training. Cadets who came back to the academy in the Fall with new airborne wings pinned on their chest were proud of their achievement.

During the academic year, all cadets were required to take extensive leadership classes. Some of these involved experiments with hamsters in the Behavior Sciences Laboratory. Well, the new cadet paratroopers decided to borrow a couple of hamsters from the lab and conduct advanced airborne testing. Rigged with small harnesses and parachutes, the rodents leaped from the 6th floor of Washington Hall. Unfortunately, there was a design flaw in the system; the parachutes did not fully deploy, and the little fellas died on the concrete drop zone about 50 feet below. They were buried on the Plain, the USMA parade field, in a candlelight ceremony with full military honors.

Back to the drawing board, the cadets of Company H3 redesigned the parachute and tested it more thoroughly with a dummy payload. They went back to the lab and acquired a couple of new hamster volunteers. During the next parachute drop, the little guys wriggled out of their harnesses—mission failure again. The casualties were piling up— the lab's hamsters could not reproduce fast enough to replace the fallen troopers. After further improvements to the parachute and harness system, the next set of hamsters successfully parachuted onto the concrete apron in front of Washington Hall. Morale and confidence improved for both the cadets and hamster population. Hamster parachute drops became regular events at the daily lunch formation. Hundreds of cadets would assemble in company formation, get accountability of their personnel, and witness airborne hamsters drop from the top of the barracks. Of course, all of this violated some USCC regulations and would have sparked vigorous PETA protests if the animal rights group had been active at the time. So, the daily parachute drop was done quickly, and everybody kept quiet. At this point, the hamsters were highly trained and enjoyed the daily jumps; a textbook case of operant conditioning. America had a new secret weapon.

Now, keeping pets in a cadet room was also against regulations. The hamsters were hidden while the cadets were at class. At lunch, they were rigged up with a parachute, the cadets opened the windows, and readied for the drop. Understand that drop means the process of freefall and chute opening—it does not mean the cadets threw the hamsters out the window—the hamsters were trained to run off the window ledge. It was a well-executed process. Unfortunately, the cadets were running late to class one day and left the window open. The hamsters got loose in the room and—being well-trained troopers—ran for the window. Hamsters are cute, but they aren't that smart. Tragically, they made their final jump without parachutes. That brought an abrupt end to America's secret airborne hamster brigade. For years, the Company H3 mascot was the hamster, a symbolic gesture intended to honor these brave rodent commandos. After the last of the hamster's "Greatest Generation" was buried on the Plain, the Company mascot was changed to the Hurricanes.

Soviet General

The Cadet Mess Hall was a popular place for VIPs to dine with the entire Corps of Cadets. The "Poop Deck" was an elevated dining room in the center of the granite building used for distinguished guests. It towered about 20 feet above the six wings where 4000 cadets sat for meals three times each day. This was the iconic location where General MacArthur made his farewell address to the Corps of Cadets. During one lunch meal, the adjutant announced that we had a special visitor dining with the Corps. Everyone went quiet with anticipation, eagerly waiting to learn the identity of our guest. The announcer stated that our guest was a Soviet General. I can't recall his name, but the entire Corps began to grumble and scowl that our arch enemies were now our guests. The announcer paused for the Corps to quiet down. When the noise subsided, he noted that the Soviet General had recently defected to the United States. The mess hall exploded with cheers. Another victory for democracy and the West.

Princess of Thailand

Another distinguished visitor was the Princess of Thailand. Cadets and former paperboys were scurrying around trying to get a good look at a royal princess. The visit included a meal in the Cadet Mess. She came into the gymnasium and briefly watched a few of us playing racquetball. Man, I was giving it 150%, hoping she might ask for my phone number. No such luck. She was soon whisked out of the gym by her officer escorts.

My classmate, Mike Canavan, got to meet the princess up close and personal. He literally ran her over when he was running back from class for the lunch formation. He had his hat tilted into the cold winter wind to keep it from blowing away. As Mike was cutting across the mess hall steps, he accidentally leveled the princess. Several colonels picked her up, and Mike began apologizing profusely. The officers told Mike that she was the Princess of Siam. Mike returned to his room and asked Scott Williams where Siam was. Scott replied, "Thailand, you meat head and you sure leveled that lady!"

I guess she forgave the incident. Before she left the academy, in a tradition afforded to visiting heads of state, she granted a pardon to all cadets. All punishment tours were forgiven.

General Omar Bradley

General of the Army Omar Bradley was the last living five-star general from WWII. Bradley commanded all U.S. ground forces in the war against Germany. He had 1.3 million men under his command, including General Patton. He was a member of the West Point Class of 1915, which produced 59 generals, including President Dwight Eisenhower.

General Bradley visited West Point on several occasions while I attended. He would often want to meet with one of our fellow G2 Gators, Robert Bruce Abrams. "Abe" was the son of a legendary tank commander in WWII. His father, General Creighton Abrams, served under both General Patton and Bradley and later became the Chief of Staff of the U.S. Army. In WWII, then Lieutenant Colonel Creighton Abrams spearheaded the Allied break-out from Normandy across France and later relieved the 101st Airborne at Bastogne during the Battle of the Bulge. The Army's main battle tank, the M1 Abrams, bears the family name out of respect for his historic service. Cadet Abrams had several older brothers who also served the Army with distinction, but he was humble and rarely spoke of his family's heritage. Abe was at West Point to earn his way through the same ranks. He took no special privilege.

When General Bradley died in April of 1981, he was granted a State Funeral. The funeral honors for the President of the United States, the Vice President and a five-star general were similar in many ways. A small contingent of USMA cadets was on call to be in a State Funeral. It was a temporary unit referred to as a provisional company. Abe and I were among the cadets assigned to the company, and he served as the First Sergeant due to a lack of Firsties. Abe had every reason to be in the detail. I barely made it. There was a minimum height requirement for members of a State Funeral. I was stretching every vertebra in my neck to make the cut. I was the shortest male permitted to march.

We traveled to Washington, D.C. USMA cadets were the lead contingent in the order of precedence for parades. This was no different. We were the first military unit following the military band. The funeral route started in the U.S. Capitol and marched to Arlington Cemetery. There was a threat of rain, so cadets were directed to wear their gray raincoats. As soon as the funeral procession started, the sun came out and bore down. We sweated heavily under the rubber raincoats, but it was an honor to be part of the funeral for such a great American.

General Omar Bradley at West Point and funeral detail (photo Wikipedia)

Olympic Torch

The United States hosted the Winter Olympics at Lake Placid New York in February 1980. On its way there, the Olympic torch made a stop at West Point. It was mounted on the Poop Deck for the entire Corps to enjoy as we ate lunch with the team escorting it to the Winter Games. Several weeks later, the U.S. Olympic Ice Hockey team, composed mostly of college players, beat the Soviet Union, for the chance to play Finland for the gold medal. It was one of the most powerful moments in sports history. Every cadet had permission to watch the game, and we went bonkers after the 4-3 victory. The U.S. went on to defeat Finland and win the gold medal.

CHAPTER 19
HOSTAGES, QUINCY & MSG ROY BENAVIDEZ

U.S. Hostages from Iran

In 1979, 52 Americans were taken hostage and held in Iran for 444 days. The hostage crisis consumed the attention of our nation and led to the election of Ronald Reagan to succeed Jimmy Carter as President of the United States.

The New York Times

REAGAN TAKES OATH AS 40TH PRESIDENT; PROMISES AN 'ERA OF NATIONAL RENEWAL'

MINUTES LATER, 52 U.S. HOSTAGES IN IRAN FLY TO FREEDOM AFTER 444-DAY ORDEAL

The American public and press followed the unfolding drama every day. The lowest point happened during a failed rescue attempt where eight American patriots died. The U.S. hostages were eventually released the day Ronald Reagan was inaugurated. The New York Times headline the following morning summarized the situation well.

G2 Gators welcome home hostages.

After stopping in Germany for medical evaluation, the hostages returned to the United States. Their aircraft landed at Stewart Air Force Base on 25 January 1981. From there, the 52 newly freed Americans were bussed a few miles to West Point to be reunited with their families for a few days. The entire route from Stewart AFB to West Point was lined with yellow ribbons and American flags. One of our fellow G2 Gators, Mike Bruhn, escorted the hostages during this powerfully emotional ride. Mike was a rock-solid guy and told us how the experience shook him and every other soul on the trip.

I was initially selected to be on that escort detail but regrettably did not make the final list. Instead, I raced about a mile from our barracks to the Hotel Thayer, where the hostages would be arriving. When the buses pulled up, there was not a dry eye for miles.

Several helicopter news crews were flying overhead, but West Point offered a sanctuary from the press for a few days. It was an incredibly proud day to be an American. Our fellow citizens had endured barbaric acts, including mock executions. But now they were safely home, and our great national humiliation was finally over. During the next few days, our guests ate with the Corps in the mess hall, and the cadet glee club sang "America" to an emotionally moved audience. It was an inspiring and unforgettable moment in our nation's history. When the hostages finally left West Point, the entire Corps of Cadets formed a cordon and saluted the departing buses. Every cadet could see the faces of the hostages one final time. Ironically, I would meet one of those former hostages again at the National Defense University (NDU) twenty years later. Paul Needham was serving on the NDU faculty when I was a student at the Industrial College of the Armed Forces (ICAF). Neither of us will ever forget this collective experience.

Quincy Mass trip

In the spring of my Plebe year, G2 scored quite well during parades, and the Gators won the drill streamer for best performance among the 36 cadet companies. The drill streamer was a decorative ribbon that was attached to our company guidon or flag.

The following September, the city of Quincy, Massachusetts requested the U.S. Military Academy join their bicentennial parade. That invitation was accepted, and Company G2 was assigned the mission. Quincy is known as the City of Presidents as it was the birthplace of former Presidents John Adams and John Quincy Adams. The town was also the birthplace of other famous Americans such as John Hancock.

It was a rare weekend off post for our company, and we would sleep overnight in a hotel. Kyle MacGibbon and I took full advantage of the freedom and stayed out all night and walked to Boston to find some fun and adventure. We did not have enough money to get into any real trouble. At about 3:00 AM, Mac and I started the walk back to our hotel. We arrived at the front door just as our Tactical Officer, Major Larry Cousins, was stepping outside in his uniform. We confessed that we had not been to sleep yet. He told us we had only a few minutes to change for the parade and pack our gear. At this point, we were exhausted but had to soldier on.

We quickly cleaned up, shaved and met our colleagues as they were boarding the bus. We had no sleep or breakfast, but that night of liberty was worth it. Our company marched in the parade through that historic city, and the citizens and the weather were great. After the parade, all cadets were transported to the historic home of President John Adams and met with his descendants. Mac and I finally got some sleep on the long bus ride back to West Point.

MSG Roy Benavidez

Master Sergeant (MSG) Roy Benavidez visited West Point after being awarded the Congressional Medal of Honor in a ceremony hosted by President Ronald Reagan on February 24, 1981. When the president presented Benavidez the award, he reportedly commented to the press: "If the story of his heroism were a movie script, you would not believe it."

MSG Benavidez joined us for a meal in the Cadet Mess. He was introduced, and his Medal of Honor citation was read to the entire Corps of Cadets from the Poop Deck. He had performed a series of incredible acts of valor that left 4,000 cadets in tears and speechless. Google the Benavidez MOH citation now and read it for yourself.

The short story is that he was assigned to the 5th Special Forces Group in Vietnam. When a 12-man Special Forces Reconnaissance Team was heavily engaged by an enemy battalion (typically 250-500 soldiers), every American was either killed or wounded. MSG Benavidez had volunteered to board the returning helicopters to extract the trapped patrol. He was armed only with a knife and a medical kit. The ensuing account, validated by an eyewitness, described how he exposed himself to withering enemy fire and saved the lives of at least eight men. He suffered 37 separate bullet, bayonet, and shrapnel wounds during the six-hour engagement and was thought to be dead by his comrades and an examining doctor. As he was being placed in a body bag, he spat in the face of the doctor, to alert him he was still clinging to life. In addition to the Medal of Honor, MSG Benavidez's awards included five Purple Hearts.

MSG Benavidez attended a number of functions at West Point including a Sprint football game (a version of the game, at the time, using players with a maximum weight of 158 lbs). Two of my fellow Gators, Bob Scurlock, and Rich York, played on the team. MSG Benavidez came in the locker room and gave an inspirational speech to our team. I was able to meet him during the game, but as an awestruck cadet, I had little to say to a man that exemplified military courage and selfless service.

CHAPTER 20
BAD BOYS, DUMPSTER FIRE & MILK ARTILLERY

Dumpster Fire

There was a fire in the huge dumpster next to Tony's in Central Area before the Army-Navy game in 1980. Tony's, the only pizza place open at West Point, was in the basement of an old barracks building, and cadets could get a calzone or pizza there up until about 10:00 PM.

The fire department arrived and put out the blaze. However, they did not properly investigate the cause. Any cursory arson inspection would have revealed fireworks that failed to launch properly. The failure to identify the cause of the fire provided much relief for Company C2's infamous John "Nac" Naccarelli. Although he is no longer subject to USCC regulations decades after graduation, Nac is still not admitting guilt. He did, however, suffer several sleepless nights after the incident.

John was one of the luckiest men at West Point. He had a lot of fun at the academy, yet he was rarely caught in the act. This included a stunt where he helped to chase a skunk into the barracks elevator. Imagine the surprise of the Regimental Tactical Officer when he stepped in to get a ride. John had the potential to become the academy's first Millennium Man (1000 hours of punishment tours), yet he never broke into the ranks of a Century Man. He had a unique gift for escaping and evading authorities.

Incoming

Cadets were innovative. Despite the Spartan-like environment of West Point, they always strove to develop new ways to relieve the stress and have fun. John Naccarelli had a front row seat to one brilliant stunt.

West Point had a campus of tall, granite barracks buildings that made it feel like a medieval city. Central Barracks was a six-story high major structure that served as a home for 2nd Regiment. On the north side of the building was the Central Area where cadets walked their punishment tours for several hours on the weekends. On the south side of Central Barracks were another barracks that housed 1st Regiment. Nac and I lived in Central Barracks and could overlook dozens of cadets walking off their punishment. Nac was in C2 on the first floor. I was in G2 on the sixth floor.

One weekend, cadets in 1st Regiment set up a powerful slingshot in their rooms. Fabricated using highly elastic rubber surgical tubing, which they tied off to their window frame, they could pull the slingshot back the length of their room. Their munition of choice was an 8-ounce milk carton that they placed in its pouch. When the slingshot was released, the milk carton would rifle out of the window and fly several hundred yards, exploding on impact and spewing white liquid shrapnel. It was an impressive indirect fire weapon system, and the non-lethal ammo supply was readily available. The milk cartons were served daily in the Cadet Mess, and those unused would otherwise be disposed of.

1st Regiment began to target the cadets walking across Central Area as they exited the mess hall after dinner. Their milk cartons were launched from their rooms, over Central Barracks, and landed in Central Area. To improve their accuracy, 1st Regiment had forward observers in Central Barracks calling in the fire as cadets moved across Central Area. It was a brilliant application of the summer field artillery training and novel utilization of improvised artillery rounds.

Airborne Stereo

Graduation week is a time of celebration for senior cadets who are about to get their diplomas. Four years of highly challenging work was finally to be rewarded.

Mike Mizusawa, Class of 1980, was a few days from his graduation. He roomed with Rich Repetto next door to me, and things over there were usually quiet. But one evening, Scott Stangle, a football player (Class of 1981), suddenly burst into Mike and Rich's room. Stangle started wrestling with Repetto and Mizusawa to celebrate the pending graduation. We—in my room—heard the furniture being knocked around the room. It sounded like a professional wrestling match, and that Stangle had the upper hand. We went to see what was going on just in time for the climactic point when Scott turned to Mike and exclaimed, "Mizu, I can't believe you're

163

graduating! Let's celebrate!" Stangle then ripped Mike's stereo off his dresser, walked over to the window, and tossed it out. The room went dead silent as gravity took control of the situation. Three seconds and six floors later, we heard it impact on the asphalt, a muffled crash and crunch sound.

We all looked at each other and couldn't believe what we had just witnessed. There was only one logical thing to do, close the window and run like hell. We needed to get away from the scene before some Nazi storm trooper ran up the stairs and tried to ruin the graduation celebration. It felt like a Class One slug was coming, and nobody wanted to be on the receiving end of that. Fortunately, the flying stereo was not witnessed by any officers, and it sat in a splintered pile all night. The following morning, I left the barracks and turned the corner. Lying in front of me was its metal carcass with parts strewn all around. Standing over it was an Army major looking down at the wreckage and glancing upwards to mentally calculate which window the stereo came from. I saluted and bolted out of the area. I am sure Stangle was relieved that Mizusawa had not inscribed his name on the stereo—this was a situation where claiming ownership would not be wise. As for me, as the great Sergeant Schultz from *Hogan's Heroes* always said, "I see nothing! I know nothing!"

Dental Casualty

During my Plebe year, the military dentists decided to extract my wisdom teeth. I made an appointment during lunch. I was authorized to miss the noon accountability formation and the lunch meal to attend the appointment. I arrived at the dental clinic on time, as directed. The dentist injected anesthesia in my mouth. It was the first time I had my mouth numbed at a dental office. Then the dentist really went to work. He jacked open my mouth and pulled out some pliers, a chisel, and a hammer. The next thirty minutes were like a scene from a comedy horror show. The dentist wore glasses with Coke bottle lenses. I could see the entire dental procedure in the reflection of his glasses. He cut the gums and started using the chisel to hammer on the tooth. Then he pried it upwards. It felt like he banged on the tooth for ten minutes, and my head rocked back with each blow. I probably suffered a series of concussions. After the first tooth had popped, he began his assault on the second one. My jaw took another beating. Finally, the two teeth were removed, and the dentist jammed a wad of cotton in my mouth. I asked to keep the teeth—recall my tendency to collect things—and surprisingly, they gave them to me in a jar, along with some flesh still attached. At this point, I had only ten minutes to get to my next academic class. So, I sped out of the office climbed the six floors in Central Barracks to get my books and headed to class. I arrived just before I was recorded as late. I wasn't sure if having my teeth hammered out at lunch was a valid excuse for being tardy. This was West Point, after all, the un-college. I sat down and was thankful we did not have a pop quiz. However, the Professor did ask me to answer one of his questions. After I had gurgled a mixture of saliva and blood for him, he realized I was a dental casualty and gave me a pass on any further questions.

Medical Casualty

At this time in our history, Army medicine was scary. Knee surgery on one cadet went very wrong. When the cadet awoke, he was quite upset. The doctor HAD operated on the wrong knee, but he had no recourse. Cadets were considered government property and had few rights. He needed to heal, rehab and then get the other knee operated on. When the cadet went in for his second surgery, he used a big marker and wrote "This One!" on the bad knee and drew an arrow. The Army doctor was offended and wanted the cadet punished for disrespect. Today, writing on the knee requiring surgery is considered a best practice. In another incident—another knee surgery—one of my classmates was the victim. At his request, I won't mention his name. However, the medical team decided to film the operation. What the doctor did not expect was that the high intensity lights used for filming would actually burn the tissue inside the cadet's knee. The filming caused significant damage and put his military career at risk. Years later, I remembered these horror stories. After I came back from the war in Iraq in 2004, I needed five knee surgeries. I could have used the military or VA health care system, but I opted to use my own private insurance and paid thousands of dollars out of pocket for copays and deductibles. But they did operate on the correct knee.

Three-Day Weekend

During President's Day weekend our senior year, we had three consecutive days off. Cadets asked each other where they wanted to go. Many lived too far away to get home. Rich Wassmuth and some other cadets decided to throw a dart at a map of the United States. Wherever the dart landed, they would visit. Well, the dart landed in some small town in Colorado. Rich and his buddies had three days to get from West Point, New York to Colorado and back. It was a 3,600-mile round-trip.

So Wassmuth and company ripped across the United States trying to get to their objective. A few hundred miles short of the town, they were pulled over by the police for doing about forty miles per hour over the speed limit. Wassmuth was worried the cops would soon find his boot knife, and things would get much worse for him. But Rich explained who they were, that they had a rare three-day pass, and were trying to get to Colorado. The cop became sympathetic, made them all knock out 50 pushups and then let them go. Rich continued on to his objective and made it back to the academy. The only permanent casualty was some road kill. Although he has a good story from the trip, I bet Rich no longer picks his travel destinations using darts.

Haunted Gym

Cadet Margaret Williams (now Margaret Williams Burcham) was playing racquetball with her roommate Roberta Baynes (now Roberta Baynes Chrissy) inside the colossal Arvin Gym at West Point one evening. Suddenly, the lights were shut off, and the gymnasium was locked up while they were still inside. They had clearly lost track of time. The bugler began playing TAPS, and the two cadets faced being reported as missing from their barracks during bed check. Demerits and punishment tours would soon follow. For Margaret, this seemed like a potential career ending event.

Dark, quiet and musty, the Arvin Gym had been constructed in the early 1900s and had few windows to provide outside illumination from the moon or stars, not to mention letting any fresh air in. To make the situation more anxious, the academy pumped dust into the gymnasium each day to make sure cadets were even more deprived of sufficient oxygen during their physical training.

To Margaret and Roberta, the dark building was haunted. The ghosts of a thousand Old Grads patrolled the halls and scared the living crap out of them both. They desperately tried to feel their way down the concrete hallways and stairwells and find an exit out of that medieval dungeon. Moving through it was slow going and dangerous work, like clearing an underground bunker in Baghdad. Who knew what tripwires and booby traps had been emplaced by the ghosts of the Long Gray Line after the lights were shut off.

Somehow, they both managed to escape and survive the harrowing ordeal. When they snuck back to their barracks, no one knew they had been missing. That was a bit disappointing, as no search party would have come looking for them. The guard was probably asleep on duty. Cadets Margaret Williams and Roberta Baynes eventually graduated from West Point without an AWOL conviction.

CHAPTER 21
BOB HOPE, REAGAN, TOWER, AND DOZIER, ROCK STARS & IKE HALL

Bob Hope Show

Bob Hope hosted an All-Star Comedy Birthday Party at West Point in late May 1981, just before graduation week. We were all glad to see such an iconic figure who had entertained troops since WWII. The show was televised from Michie Stadium.

The 78-year-old still had it. The show started with "A-Man" (a caped superhero that wore an "A" for Army) rappelling from a helicopter onto the stage. After landing, A-Man unmasked and revealed his true identity, Bob Hope. It was a fun start to a show that included Brooke Shields, Marie Osmond, Sugar Ray Leonard, Glen Campbell, George C. Scott (who starred in the movie *Patton*), Mickey Rooney, and actor Robert Urich.

During the show, Bob joked about being a special guest in the Hotel Thayer, the only hotel on the West Point grounds. Hotel Thayer is a historic building with a reputation for quaint but often tiny rooms. Bob noted he was staying in the Presidential Suite at the Thayer. However, he was "not sure what president they were so pissed off at."

I was given front row seats for the special event, and I screwed up. I did not realize the tickets were special seats, and I gave them to several of the G2 Yearlings and Plebes. They thought I was incredibly generous. This donation left me sitting about forty rows behind the underclassmen. Ironically, the Vice President of the United States, George H. W. Bush, was also in attendance and was seated nearby, next to my roommate, Rich Wassmuth. Rich attended with his sister and calmly introduced his sister to the VP as they sat down.

The show had a series of skits, and one of them involved a comedy boxing match between Sugar Ray Leonard and Bob Hope. At the end of the match, dance music kicked in, and Brooke Shields entered the boxing ring to dance, but her partner was late arriving on the scene. That's when our classmate, Pete Keller, immediately climbed on stage and started dancing with Brooke. It was a gutsy and completely unscripted move, and Pete became an instant hero.

President Reagan

About a week later, the Class of 1981 graduated in that same stadium. President Ronald Reagan was the graduation speaker and security was tight. Reagan had been shot by John Hinckley only a few weeks earlier in Washington, D.C. Reagan's appearance reassured our nation he was well on the road to recovery. This was the first time I was able to see an American president in the flesh. Reagan gave a strong speech, and no indication he had been recently wounded.

SEN Tower and Brigadier General (BG) Dozier

May 26, 1982, was the scheduled graduation date for my class. We all waited with anticipation to learn who our speaker would be. The duty often rotated among the service academies between the president, the vice president, and some other senior government official.

We were informed that Senator John Tower, the Chairman of the Senate Committee on Armed Services, would be our commencement speaker. He was a WWII veteran and still serving as a Master Chief Petty Officer in the Navy Reserve. The prior evening, we had a special guest speaker at our graduation banquet. Brigadier General James Dozier had been kidnapped by the Red Brigades terrorist group in Italy the prior December. This Marxist-Leninist group posed a real threat to Italy's domestic stability. They had kidnapped and murdered several Italian officials and politicians, including their former Prime Minister, Aldo Moro. After forty-two days of captivity, BG Dozier was successfully rescued by the Italian Special Police in the largest manhunt in their nation's history. His conduct during the ordeal was both disciplined and courageous. As cadets, we followed the kidnapping and rescue of this senior alumnus each day, so the selection of BG Dozier as the keynote speaker was both timely and absorbing.

169

Special Lecturers

We periodically had distinguished lecturers visit the academy. These thought leaders covered an incredibly diverse range of topics. Two that I recall were Dr. Carl Sagan and tennis legend Arthur Ashe. Sagan was a globally recognized expert in astronomy, the Search for Extraterrestrial Intelligence (SETI), and other natural sciences. He designed the plaque on the Pioneer spacecraft and the Golden Record on the Voyager. Ashe was the first African-American to win the men's singles at Wimbledon and the U.S. Open, and the first black American to be ranked No. 1 in the world. He courageously battled discrimination in the 60s and 70s.

During another visit, Ralph Nader, an environmental lawyer, and consumer advocate, spoke to the Corps. He asked if it would be possible to get some West Point cadets as summer interns. The cadets began to laugh. We were not a civilian institution where students had time off in the summers. Our summers were highly structured and filled with military training. The probability that USMA would release a cadet to support a summer internship instead of military training was incredibly remote. The odds were about the same as finding extraterrestrial life on the sun. Nader, however, was not accustomed to life at USMA and sincerely wondered why we were all laughing.

Rock Stars and Fine Arts

As a youth, I never had the money to attend any form of professional entertainment. I did win two tickets to a Philadelphia Phillies baseball game, and once I went to a college football game with my father to see the University of Delaware Blue Hens. Outside of these, my exposure to big-time professional entertainment was confined to watching TV and listening to the AM radio in my room.

That changed radically once I arrived at West Point. I was amazed to learn that major recording artists played in the 4,400 seat Eisenhower Hall ("Ike Hall") auditorium. Cadets could buy a season ticket, which was deducted from our monthly salary. During my Plebe year, I was able to see live performances of REO Speedwagon, Southside Johnny and the Asbury Jukes, The Captain and Tennille, and Harry Chapin. During my Yearling year,

I saw Elton John, Peter Frampton, The Beach Boys, Chicago, and The Doobie Brothers. The fun continued my Cow year as Kansas, The Spinners, James Taylor, Anne Murray, George Carlin, and Atlanta Rhythm Section played at Ike Hall. My Firstie year concluded with performances by the J. Geils Band, Marshall Tucker Band, The Pretenders, Gordon Lightfoot, Gary U.S. Bonds, Clarence Clemons, and the Cincinnati Pops Orchestra. Also, the Cadet Fine Arts Forum brought further entertainment to the academy, including The Sound of Music, Steve Allen, Maynard Ferguson, Marcel Marceau, and Bill Cosby. All of this exposure to culture enriched my life well beyond what I thought was possible when I was a paperboy.

Ike Hall

Ike Hall was also an important social center where cadets could meet their friends and families, see a show, or attend a dance. We had the option of wearing a USMA issued blazer uniform to make the atmosphere feel less regimented. Cadets over the age of 18 were also permitted to purchase beer for consumption on the premises on Saturday evenings. It was watered down beer (3.2% alcohol), but it was very popular. I met many new classmates and friends while conducting beer drinking operations at Ike Hall.

Chapter 22
Rocket Science & Branch Selection

Rocket Science

The academic curriculum at West Point was difficult, and every cadet was required to take certain core science and math courses. Sometime during the second year, we needed to declare an area of academic concentration. At that point, the engineers separated from the rest of the pack, which focused their studies on management, languages, social sciences, history or some other discipline. I was a relatively good math student, and I decided to concentrate my studies in aerospace engineering.

Perhaps my childhood fascination with the U.S. space program influenced my selection. I always recalled the Apollo lunar missions and the day I watched the Apollo 11 lunar landing. As cadets, we watched the first space shuttle launch on live TV from our classroom.

The fundamental reason for my selection was simply illogical; I thought being an aerospace engineer sounded cool. With that title, I might seem smarter than I actually was. I knew that wouldn't make me a chick magnet. However, I did believe an aerospace education could help me when I applied for the Army's flight school, and that was the ticket—chicks liked aviators.

I took a series of thermodynamics, physics, mechanical and structural engineering classes. It included the theory of vibration and experimental stress analysis. I learned about the Bernoulli equation and why heavier than air machines can stay aloft and maneuver in the atmosphere. Some of the aerospace labs included actual flight testing, where we would instrument a T-41 aircraft and take it through a series of maneuvers to collect data. We needed to determine if actual aircraft performance was similar to the theoretical performance predicted in the lab. We took off from Stewart Air Force Base and conducted several "touch and go" landings in Danbury, Connecticut. It was a cool class led by Major Kip Nygren.

172

Weeks later, our class took a trip to Bethpage, New York on Long Island. We were scheduled to tour a production plant where the Navy manufactured its F-14 fighter jets. We flew down in Army Huey helicopters with an Air Force aviator sitting in the co-pilot seat. As we crossed Long Island Sound, the Air Force officer asked to take control of the stick from the Army pilot. One second later, the helicopter plunged from 800 feet. For a brief moment, I thought we were going to splash, and our bodies become food for the local crabs. Fortunately, the Army pilot grabbed the controls back and recovered the bird. I am not sure if the Air Force officer had any qualifications to fly a rotary wing aircraft. But I was sure I was going to tackle the guy if he tried to touch the controls again.

We landed at the Northrop Grumman plant in Bethpage and began our factory tour. As the tour wrapped up, we were brought into a room with a couple of F-14 Tomcats undergoing flight testing. I noticed one aircraft had five fishing trawlers painted on its side. In WWII, U.S. pilots painted a Japanese Zero silhouette on their aircraft for every enemy fighter they shot down. The time came for questions, so I asked, "Why are there fishing boats painted on the aircraft?" The answer was quite satisfying.

"The Soviets keep electronic surveillance ships off the coast of the United States to spy on our flight testing. Those ships are often disguised as fishing trawlers. Since we—the U.S.—could not stop the spying which occurred in international waters, the F-14 pilots wanted to give the Soviets a good look at the new U.S. fighters. They occasionally dropped down on the deck and blasted over the spy ship on full afterburner. If Soviet spies were blown overboard by the ear-shattering concussion, the U.S. pilot was entitled to paint a fishing trawler on the side of his aircraft."

That explanation was the highlight of the trip. I almost thought, Go Navy! Almost.

Branch Selection

In our senior year, cadets could choose what branch they would serve in as an Army officer. The choices were: infantry, armor (tanks), aviation, engineers, field artillery, intelligence, military police and several other branches.

There were limited slots for each branch. Infantry and engineers were often the most popular branches, so the selection order was based on a merit list mainly determined by a cadet's grade point average (GPA). Better students could pick first. They usually chose a more prestigious branch and were assigned to Hawaii. The students with the lowest GPA usually had no choices left and were assigned to the Air Defense Artillery in Nome, Alaska.

I intended to apply for flight school, but after an eye exam, I was told I had an optical defect known as astigmatism. My eyes were not perfect. I was an aerospace engineer but was not allowed to apply to become an aviator. Instead, the Army probably offered the aviation slot to a history major. Go figure. It worked out later because I had a chance to go into the Engineers and then to Ranger School. If I had to choose between being an aviator and being a Ranger, I got the better deal. Apologies to all my aviator friends.

CHAPTER 23
WOMEN AT WEST POINT, FOREIGN AFFAIRS & FALLEN FRIENDS

Women at West Point

During the fall of 1978, West Point agreed to support the filming of a TV movie entitled, *Women at West Point*. The story was about the first women to enter the U.S. Military Academy. The introduction of women to the military academies was controversial and led to much speculation about how they—and the institution—would (could) face resultant problems. Andrew Stevens was the leading cadet actor, and actress Linda Purl played the new female cadet.

Linda Purl was single and beautiful and became an instant cadet magnet. Cadets would continually report on her location as she moved about the academy. If she were reported to be in the gym, cadets would run over to play some racquetball. If she was in Central Area, heads stuck out of countless windows to get a look. While working at West Point, she probably received several marriage proposals.

During the filming of some R-Day scenes, New Cadets wore the highly stylish in-processing uniform consisting of gym shorts, a white t-shirt, and black dress shoes with black knee-high socks. R-Day always happened on a hot day in July, but the filming of this scene occurred on a sub-freezing day in November. Andrew Stevens and the cadet actors shot the scene and did their best to appear hot and sweaty for the cameras. The nervous looking New Cadets in that scene were actually shivering from the cold air. Whenever the director yelled, "Cut!" we would run off the set and put on our winter coats.

I was filmed in several outdoor and indoor scenes. One scene was of several Plebes running down a staircase at the position of attention and squaring each corner. That scene survived the final editing, but when I saw the film, the cameraman had only zoomed in on the shoes of the Plebes as they squared each corner. My shoes were in that scene! I could tell by the way

I polished them. It was my first opportunity for global fame and fortune. I should have held out for a piece of the back-end movie royalties. At that point, sure that the camera loved me, I decided to sit back and wait for an offer from Hollywood. It has been 35 years since I was discovered, but I am certain that offer is finally being prepared.

Foreign Affairs

All cadets took mandatory foreign language training. Mine was Spanish. I was offered an opportunity to travel to several South American nations during my third summer. However, I declined and planned to spend my limited leave time with my family and friends in Pennsylvania. I wish I could have done both, as it was a rare chance to see and learn about different cultures on a continent all but unknown to me.

West Point hosted international cadets from several South American countries for a few weeks as part of the Foreign Academy Exchange Program (FAEP). Our classmate, Walt Tollefson, was the Cadet in Charge (CIC) of supervising the foreign cadets and had recently returned from the Ecuadorian Military Academy.

Walt and Jerry Nowotny took the FAEP cadets to see the movie *The Final Countdown* in downtown New York City. Well, that was the plan. Instead, a few of the Argentinean cadets' broke ranks and headed to a house of ill-repute. There, the Argentinean cadets fell in love with their new girlfriends. When they refused to leave, the cadets were roughed up and ejected by the bouncers.

Walt reported the details; there was no way to cover up the international incident. Government funds, intended for wholesome entertainment, were used inappropriately by the FAEP cadets though up until the point where the bouncers slammed them, they probably thought it was money was well-spent.

Since Walt and Jerry were supposed to be "supervising" the foreign guests, they got fried on the bus ride back to West Point. Walt has fond memories of standing in front of his legendary Regimental Tactical Officer, Lt. Colonel Moscatelli, trying to explain how the incident unfolded:

"Tollefson, what were you thinking?"

Walt resorted to the reliable Plebe-like answer, "No excuse sir."

The situation was made more uncomfortable because Walt was the Sunday School Teacher for Lt. Colonel Moscatelli's daughter. Walt did not escape the disciplinary hammer, and Area time followed.

Fallen Friends

During our senior year, we had three classmates tragically killed in car accidents. Our memories of the academy include these fallen friends.

I met Ronald Robinson at Ike Hall the night he died. His car overturned at West Point, on the mountain behind Michie Stadium. It was a freak low-speed accident, he was traveling less than twenty-five mph. Badly hurt, he crawled several hundred feet, but no one found him until the next morning. Cadets Mike Charbonneau and Richard "Brent" Washburn were killed on Christmas break in 1981 when they fell asleep while driving in Texas. Mike was a particularly good friend. I spent one spring break with him in Florida with his aunt. His uncle was involved in the NASA astronaut program. These three cadets were all good men with bright futures and had their lives cut short. I still recall the sound of the lone bugler playing taps to the Corps of Cadets on the parade field in the pitch darkness during the evening memorial ceremony. We moved on with heavy hearts.

CHAPTER 24
MYRTLE BEACH, KNOX & BUCKNER

Myrtle Beach

We had a few weeks of summer vacation after our Plebe year so Bob Scurlock and I, along with my hometown friend Mike Willover, decided to head to Myrtle Beach, South Carolina for one of them. Willie and I left Pennsylvania and spent the night in Charlotte at the Scurlock home where we picked up Bob and his brother, Dave.

Bob warned us that Dave, a body builder, was a bit wild and crazy. And Dave did not disappoint us. We arrived at the beach the next day and found a cheap motel with a swimming pool. After paying the room rent, we had a $120 budget between the four of us for food and beer. Bob suggested we go to the nearby Air Force Base to buy our supplies at the lowest prices. Good call. We came back with $106 in beer and booze and $14 worth of snacks. We had clearly set our nutritional priorities. Bob and I jammed a year's worth of fun and decompression into seven days. When it ended, we returned to the academy for our summer training.

The Best Summer of our Life

Summer training that year involved an intense training program at Camp Buckner, New York and Fort Knox, Kentucky. The training was billed as "the best summer of your life." It was officially called Cadet Field Training (CFT).

We were assigned to new companies and platoons for the summer training. I was in Sixth Company and met new classmates like Rocky Gay, Paul Mooradian, Bill Mayville, Rick Stevens, Chip Armstrong, Don Reich, Tom Lynch, and Peter Mansoor. The training was exciting and varied. We climbed and rappelled from cliffs, fired machine guns, tanks, artillery, mortars and Light Anti-Tank Weapons (LAWs), tossed hand grenades, patrolled in the mountains and entered the gas chamber with protective masks.

Fort Knox

Our entire class flew in C-130 cargo aircraft to Fort Knox, Kentucky. Most Americans recognize Fort Knox as the location of the United States Bullion Depository that secures most of the gold owned by the U.S. Government. At the time, it was also the home of the U.S. Army Armor School where troops learned to operate and fire tanks and other armored vehicles.

After arrival, I had an afternoon free and headed to the nearby Patton Museum. They had General George Patton's staff car and his pearl-handled pistols on display.

During that week, we moved into some old WWII barracks and trained on M-60 main battle tanks, M-113 armored personnel carriers, 155mm self-propelled artillery, Dragon and TOW anti-tank guided missiles, the Vulcan Air Defense System, RedEye and Stinger anti-aircraft missiles, and .50 caliber machine guns. The Vulcan was especially fun. Its rotating barrels fired 3,000 rounds per minute in short bursts. When used to support ground troops, it was an excellent street sweeper.

Part of the air defense training was firing small arms at an unmanned aircraft. The instructors warned us it was tough to hit the small aerial target and doubted our ability to shoot it down. A couple dozen cadets put up a large volume of fire with their M-16 rifles as the small drone cruised by, and we hit the bird which immediately dropped to the ground. Upon recovery of the drone, we found a bullet had hit the engine. Every cadet claimed it was their round that hit the aircraft, and to this day, I refuse to withdraw my claim.

Camp Buckner

The Stinging Ambush

On one patrol, our squad was attacked with machine gun fire. We all dove for cover, and I landed behind a log and began to return fire with my M-16 rifle. The action was loud and confusing. I felt stinging on my face and neck. After about ten seconds, I realized that I dove into a wasp nest. Wasps were now inside my helmet. A surreal flashback to that Little All-American Football game with the bees in my helmet came to me as I tried to return fire with my right hand while beating off wasps with my left.

Someone popped CS gas on us. CS was a riot control agent, like tear gas, that was used to simulate a poisonous gas. It made your eyes lock up and caused violent coughing and mucus to blast out of your nose. We had a few seconds to don our gas masks to survive the simulated chemical attack. At this point, the wasps were really pissed off and tearing at my face. If I put on my mask, I would likely trap wasps inside it.

Small arms fire and artillery simulators exploded all around, and I made a command decision that was counterintuitive. I jumped up from my prone position and ran into the center of the gas cloud without donning my mask. I continued firing with my right hand and beating wasps with my left. To the enemy, I had to have looked like a crazy man, hitting himself in the head while attacking their position through a poison gas cloud. *This nut has no regard for his personal safety. He's on a suicide charge and probably doped up.*

My only intent was to use the riot gas to force the wasps to retreat. After a few seconds, the planned worked. The wasps took off. The gunfire and explosions stopped. All combatants ran hundreds of meters away to avoid the gas cloud that was now my refuge. But I was hacking up both lungs and my face—leaking a quart of mucous from my nose—was a wreck from dozens of self-inflicted slaps and wasp stings. Decades later, this incident makes a great story, but I don't want to go through that misery again.

Recondo & Survival Meal

Recondo was the final training event of the summer at Camp Buckner. It consisted of some challenging events with land navigation, patrolling, obstacle courses, and a Slide for Life over Popolopen Lake. The culminating event was a punishing Enduro Run performed while loaded with equipment that featured a tough uphill finish. Historically, only about 25% of cadets completed all requirements and earned the coveted Recondo patch authorized for wear on the field uniform. I was one of the lucky ones.

On one patrol, we learned how to prepare a survival meal using government issued live chickens and rabbits. We learned how to kill and eat them with limited tools. In some tactical situations, behind enemy lines, starting a fire was not possible without being detected. We killed the animals with our hands and ate some organs raw or created a cold stew with the flesh and some other vegetables. If we did not have a knife, we were trained to kill the chickens by pulling their heads off. It was a quick death, but the birds would flap around headless for another minute. Some instructors taught us how to bite the chicken's neck to facilitate yanking the head off.

The survival meal was required training, everyone had to participate. As soldiers, we might need to kill our enemy. If we couldn't kill an animal in a peacetime survival training exercise, were we really warriors—could or would we kill our enemy when we had to?

This was a new—unpleasant—experience for many of us, but we carried out our duties. Several cadets were selected or "volunteered by their peers" to demonstrate the different killing techniques. One female cadet, however, was humiliated by the experience and went to the New York Times with her cadet boyfriend to report the story. The two resigned from the academy. The newspaper article painted the survival training as harassment of female cadets who were still being integrated into the academy. Hundreds of angry cadets and faculty were left with no choice but to remain silent and take the unfair criticism. It was Fake News!

Camp Illumination

Camp Illumination was a formal dance and social, held along the banks of Popolopen Lake, that concluded our summer training. Hundreds of friends and family members came to visit their cadets and celebrate the conclusion of the summer. Several of my high school friends from Pennsylvania made the trek: Mike Willover, Julie McNamara, and Debbie Potthoff. Being with them always lifted my spirit, and I looked forward all summer to seeing them.

The experience at Camp Buckner and Fort Knox included the thrill of firing fantastic weapons (tanks, machine guns, artillery, rockets, mortars), throwing hand grenades, climbing and repelling from cliffs, surviving gas attacks, and eating raw chickens. We had all this fun while we were getting fed and paid! So, here's a big "Thank You" to Uncle Sam and the American taxpayers who funded "the best summer of my life."

CHAPTER 25
CADET TROOP LEADER TRAINING (CTLT) & AIRBORNE

The Black Lions

During the third summer at West Point, cadets had an opportunity to train with regular Army units. The program was called Cadet Troop Leader Training (CTLT). I was assigned, for six weeks, to train with the 249th Engineer Battalion, known as "The Black Lions," in Karlsruhe, Germany. My job was to be a "3rd Lieutenant;" an intern to an active duty commissioned Lieutenant.

I left for Germany after a brief vacation in Pennsylvania. The Army asked me where I wanted to depart from either Philadelphia or McGuire Air Force Base. I selected Philadelphia since it was a few minutes closer to my home. That was a big mistake, and I learned much about military air transportation during the journey. I assumed the flight from Philadelphia was direct to Germany. That would have been too simple. Instead, the airplane left Philadelphia for Charleston AFB in South Carolina. I knew that was the wrong direction. After sitting in Charleston for several more hours, I boarded another aircraft that flew me to... wait for it... McGuire Air Force Base near Philadelphia.

At that point, I realized I had just wasted about eight hours of my life. Fortunately, I did not pay for this ride. Unfortunately, I was required to travel in service uniform, which was like wearing an insulated strait jacket. I sweltered in the summer heat. At McGuire AFB, we took on new passengers. I had a pounding headache and was not ecstatic to sit next to the loudest screaming infant in North America for the overnight trip to Germany.

The only bright spot of the flight was the beautiful view overflying the southern tip of Greenland. After a sleepless night, we landed at a Royal Air Force Base near Mildenhall, England. The aircraft refueled, and we headed to Germany. I finally landed in Frankfurt in a stinking uniform and with a full days' beard.

An escort for the 249th Engineer Battalion was supposed to meet me at the terminal in Frankfurt. I had no idea who my escort was, and I had never been in a foreign country before. I found my duffle bag and hung around for an hour as most of the passengers moved on, and I continued to wait for my escort.

After ninety minutes, a First Lieutenant Beasely, who had been standing there for a while, finally asked me who I was. I told him I was Cadet Kerry Kachejian looking for my Army escort. His eyes widened and seemed surprised. He looked down at his clipboard and then up at my name tag. "I was told you were a female cadet."

I assured 1st Lieut. Beasely I was 100% male and was who he had been sent to escort. I was a bit offended by the Army's gender mix up but relieved I would not be spending the night at the Frankfurt Airport. A few hours later, I reported to the battalion headquarters late, looking a bit rough from significant jet lag.

The 249th Engineer Battalion was a "Combat Heavy" unit equipped with bulldozers, backhoes, cranes, dump trucks and other engineering equipment. With the Reagan presidency, there was a renewed investment in the military. Our battalion was building new facilities to preposition war materiel in Europe.

I was sent to Monchengladbach, near the Dutch border, with 1st Lieut. Joe Muscarrella's platoon, to construct special storage buildings called "stress tension structures." We stayed on a nearby British military base and met the UK Major in command. During lunch, for some reason, he told us his career had been stalled because he shot someone. It sounded like an accident, but we did not inquire further.

Toga!

A couple of weeks later, we returned to Karlsruhe. Joe Muscarella, Al Estes, and Jeff Bemis threw an excellent Toga Party at the bachelor officer's quarters. A dozen German friends showed up. I met some classmates also on six weeks of CTLT: Tom Wuchte, Tom LeBlanc, and Lonnie Carroll. We all liked to work and play hard and often met at the Officer's Club in the evenings. Life was good. Germany was becoming a fun place.

Rugby Match

1st Lieut. Pete Rowan, another platoon leader in our company, asked me if I played rugby. Pete was a West Point grad and had established a local rugby team. The team was invited to play a demonstration game against a British team at a sports festival in Wurzburg that weekend. Pete was short on players. I told him I had played football and lacrosse; any contact sport was fine with me. We had another platoon leader on the team named Jim Lamon. He was about six feet four inches and weighed two hundred fifty pounds. In college, Jim had played football at Alabama. He was our secret weapon. Roll Tide.

On the ride to Wurzburg, Pete tried to explain the rugby rules to me. I picked up some of them but figured it would be on-the-job training. We arrived at the festival and found hundreds of Germans watching multiple sports.

We started the exhibition game in a driving rain. It would be a muddy game, and I had no cleats, only cheap cadet tennis shoes.

We figured the Brits were experienced rugby players, so we just wanted to keep the game close. Pete knew how to play and had the ball skills and tactics. Jim Lamon was a one-man offensive line and crushed lesser mortals under him while he ran. I was still unsure of the gameplay, so I just played American football, with high-speed blocking and tackling.

We jumped out to an early lead and did not stop. I scored a few touchdowns, or whatever you call them in rugby, but Pete was irritated at me. I always ran for the corner of the end zone, which was fine in American football but not in rugby. I learned that Pete had to kick extra points from the location where we crossed the goal line, so he had some difficult oblique kicks. In the end, it did not matter. We won something like 52-17. Several guys on the British team were injured and went to the hospital. They must have been run over by our secret weapon, the Alabama rhinoceros. We were a bit amazed that we had played so well. Muddy, tired and soaking wet, we hung around the festival for several hours and toasted our German hosts.

Troop Troubles

I learned a lot about enlisted troops while I was on CTLT. The biggest lesson was that they can get into trouble. I walked into the platoon leader's office on

Monday morning, and Pete and Jim were sitting there laughing while reading some document. It was a U.S. Military Police (MP) report of an incident that had been translated from a German police report. They asked me if I had heard what happened to one of their troops, PFC Boyer (name changed to spare the soldier embarrassment).

On Saturday night, PFC Boyer was looking for some action in downtown Karlsruhe. All five feet three inches, one hundred forty pounds of PFC Boyer went to the Cheri Lounge and picked up a local girl. He wound up in a bedroom and soon discovered his date was not a girl. The scene got ugly. Alerted to the incident, the German police found Boyer in his skivvies, wearing a gold chain around his neck, running away from his transvestite "girlfriend" who was chasing him with a knife. The Polizei arrested both of them, filled out a report, and turned Boyer over to the MPs. The suspect "girlfriend" was a German male, about six feet two (without wearing heels) and two hundred ten pounds. Apparently, Boyer liked his women big. Pete and Jim tried to compose themselves so they could go out to the morning formation to get accountability of all the troops. We were all sympathetic to PFC Boyer, who was now quietly standing with the rest of his squad.

A few weeks later, the MPs forwarded another interesting report to our unit. A noncommissioned officer (NCO) had "borrowed" a military supply truck and entered it into a cross-country road rally. The vehicle was called a "deuce and a half" because it had 2.5 tons of load capacity. The only reason the NCO was caught misusing the U.S. Government vehicle was that he had been awarded a prize for his 7th place finish, and he had been showing off the trophy.

When my six weeks of CTLT in Germany ended, I was scheduled to return to the United States and attend the Army's Airborne School at Fort Benning. This three-week course was held in the baking, blistering August sun in Georgia. I knew I would soon be sweating out all of the German beer I had sampled during my CTLT experience. But when it was all over, I hoped to be able to join the ranks of thousands of other American paratroopers who had served since WWII.

Airborne School

After the flight from Germany, I rode a hot bus on the final leg of the trip to Fort Benning. On arrival, I met some of the other cadets. and we immediately went to the barber to get "high and tight" haircuts before reporting for duty. You did not want to stand out—and get extra attention—from the Airborne Instructors (AIs). So, we shaved our heads like every other soldier and had our boots professionally polished every night.

Several G2 Gators were also at Airborne School with me. Rich Wassmuth and John Madrid had arrived a day earlier, got their heads shaved, and then headed out to the Officer's Club pool that afternoon. At the time, sunscreen was either not invented or an unnecessary expense that came out of a cadet's personal beer fund. Their bald heads were torched in the burning Georgia sun. The next morning, Rich and John got their airborne helmets issued (it was a steel pot). The instructors always made sure student helmets were tightly secured on their heads just in case they landed on it. Every time Rich and John took their helmets off, part of their scalp came with it. That first week was brutal for them. Eventually, John's hair grew back, but I can't say the same for Rich.

Robert Bruce "Abe" Abrams was another G2 Gator in that Airborne course. He had spent the first six weeks of that summer serving in the cadre of the first Beast Barracks detail. He was intensively indoctrinating the new Plebes at West Point, while I was exploring Germany on CTLT. I got the better deal on that one.

At Benning, we lived in WWII-era training barracks. This was the Old Army. These noisy open-bay barracks had metal bunk beds, sweat-soaked mattresses and were like living in an oven. Daytime temperatures were well over 90 degrees F with high humidity. Night time temperatures cooled off into the 80s. There was no air conditioning. If you were lucky, you found a bunk located near a free-standing fan.

Noncommissioned officers ran the airborne training, and they also ruled the barracks. Each Airborne instructor wore a black hat and t-shirt. They were all physically fit, motivated and ready to rip into new Airborne students.

The first morning of training started with a large military formation. Our leaders introduced themselves and laid out the rules. It was evident this course was going to be three weeks of hazing sprinkled with some parachute training. At this point, an Airborne Master Sergeant (MSG) took charge of the formation. He wanted to shock us and succeeded.

"I shot twenty-two G** D*** gooks in Vietnam!" he screamed, and everyone was dead silent. It was the first time I heard such an explicitly racist comment from a military leader. My first thought was that this guy was at the My Lai massacre. His message was clear, don't mess with me! We all steered clear of him for the rest of the course.

Ground Week

The first week of Airborne School was called Ground Week. New students were whipped into physical shape with plenty of running, pushups, and calisthenics. Students were regularly dropped for pushups for any small infraction; unauthorized sweating, for example.

Much of the first week of training was designed to wash out the physically weak and unmotivated students. Airborne students were not allowed to carry canteens. We were dying of thirst while roasting in the summer Georgia sun. We had a five-minute break every few hours and had to drink water from big Lister bags hanging near the 34-foot training towers. Dehydration and heat casualties were constant threats. The most senior soldier in our class was an Army captain who had been selected as the class leader. He shocked us by quitting the course after a few days. The instructors informed us at morning formation that our leader wasn't up to the task. Although he complained of "back problems" the cadre clearly felt he just washed out. The next senior officer was appointed as the class leader.

We learned how to load into an aircraft and used the Swing Landing Trainer to practice hundreds of parachute landings. We called some of the training "suspended agony," as we hung for hours in a harness while enduring a never-ending wedgie; our shorts ended up going above and beyond their call of duty… I mean way up.

We learned how to perform a proper parachute landing fall (PLF) by distributing the impact over our entire body, reducing the chance of breaking an ankle or leg. In a round T-10 military parachute, we expected to hit the ground at 22 feet per second. When loaded with 80 pounds of military gear and blowing laterally across a jump zone due to high winds, paratroopers could get severely injured while hitting the ground. PLFs taught us how to collapse on impact in a smooth sequence from feet to knees to seat and then rolling. The goal of the repetitive PLF training was to make proper landing technique an instinctive reaction.

Tower Week

The second week, we learned more technical skills. There were several 34-foot towers on the training site. The top of the tower was built to look like the inside of a military cargo aircraft. Students wore parachute harnesses and practiced moving toward the open aircraft door and jumping out. They would fall about 15 feet before the risers on their harness would fully extend and snap tight. Then, they slid diagonally down a cable about 100 meters long. At the end of the cable, each student hit the ground and executed a good PLF.

The 34-foot tower was a good simulator for jumping out of an aircraft, experiencing the shock of the parachute opening, and practicing PLFs. The key to safety was to make sure both risers on your harness were connected to the cable BEFORE you jumped. If a soldier wasn't attached, they'd fall 34 feet straight to the ground. This has been known to cause serious injury and should be avoided.

Since dozens of paratroopers jump from an aircraft in a few seconds, being properly rigged is an important safety issue. One of my classmates was in the tower and had not been properly rigged. As he approached the door, he yelled at the instructor, "I'M NOT HOOKED UP! I'M NOT HOOKED UP!" The NCO thought the cadet was just panicked and shoved him out the door. Fortunately, one of his two risers had snared the cable and saved him. He slid to an awkward PLF dangling from a single

250-foot Tower at Ft Benning

riser. The instructor immediately realized his error and moderated his tone.

Toward the end of the week, we moved on to a 250-foot-high tower for training. With a full parachute and harness on, we were lifted by a pulley to the top of the tower. Once elevated, the cable was released, and we fell. The parachute would quickly catch air, and we would steer the chute away from the steel tower. A few seconds later, we would hit the ground and execute a good PLF. During the drop, we needed to be careful not to collide with the

188

tower, as our chutes could collapse, resulting in a potentially deadly freefall to the ground. Every student practiced three to five jumps from the big tower.

Jump Week

The final week, we would board C-130, C-123 or C-141 aircraft and make a minimum of five parachute jumps to earn our coveted airborne wings.

The night before our first jump, our class was assembled in the stands, and the instructors discussed safety hazards that could impact our jumps. What we learned was eye-opening.

The first hazards are inside the aircraft. There are typically 80-100 paratroopers packed into a noisy and smelly aircraft. After takeoff, most of the communications are conducted by hand signals and loud voice commands. When the aircraft door opens, the deafening noise from the engine and wind fills the fuselage. Every paratrooper has a main parachute attached to their back and a spare (reserve) strapped to their belly. We were instructed to always keep our hand on our reserve chute, but to be careful not to accidentally pull it open. If a soldier popped the reserve inside the aircraft, the chute could get sucked out the door, and the paratrooper attached to it will immediately accelerate to about 120 mph and smash into the frame of the door while exiting the aircraft. That can be fatal and bloody. The bottom line, don't mess around with your reserve parachute inside the airplane! If your buddy accidentally popped it open, other troopers should jump on it before it was sucked out the door.

Some paratroopers will get motion sick, particularly during low-level flights and turbulent conditions. For any paratroopers or parachutists reading this: If you need to vomit, spare your buddies. Please pull the collar of your fatigue uniform forward and throw up inside it. All your hot stomach contents will soak into your shirt. It just feels like more sweat, except it stinks more and has bigger chunks. Another technique is to take off your helmet and vomit in it. This actually happened to the jumper next to me. Unfortunately, he still had to put his helmet on a few minutes later to make his jump. There was a stinking mess running down his face and neck. He was a classmate, so as long as he buys me a beer at our reunions, I will not reveal his name. That's a big hint, Tom.

The next hazards were different parachute malfunctions. As we sat in the stands, the instructors directed our attention to the nearby 250-foot tower. They hoisted a 200-pound dummy to the top of the tower and began to demonstrate a series of parachute problems.

The first was a partial malfunction, called a "Mae West." This occurs when a suspension line in the parachute lies over the main canopy, effectively dividing the chute. A Mae West parachute has the appearance of a brassiere, and the paratrooper under it will fall significantly faster. If the guy survives, he will certainly be seriously injured.

Next, they demonstrated a total malfunction called a "cigarette roll." This happens when the parachute is wrapped in its suspension lines and looks like a hand-rolled cigarette while streaking toward the ground. Although we were a few hundred meters away from the tower, we felt the ground shake when the 200-pound dummy plowed into the earth. The students got quiet.

Now our first jump from an aircraft was scheduled as a simple daylight, mass tactical jump from an altitude of 1200 feet. This was often referred to as a "Hollywood jump." It looked good for the cameras but was not faithful to any sort of jump that would happen in combat conditions. As we gained experience, we learned that jumps got more complex and hazardous. The instructors illustrated the differences. For example, a real combat jump would be at 800 feet, not 1200 feet. Remember, enemy forces would be shooting at the airplane and the descending paratroopers. High jumps are often more dangerous than low jumps. The longer you're in the air, the more you can be shot at. The only problem jumping at 800 feet is that there is very little time to open a reserve parachute if the main chute fails. In fact, when Army Rangers assaulted the Cuban defenders on the island of Grenada (in 1983), they jumped at only 500 feet. The Rangers did not pack reserve parachutes as they could not be opened in time. Instead, the assault force packed extra ammunition. There was another reported complication on this combat jump. One of the Rangers remained attached to the aircraft after he jumped. This situation is called a "hung jumper." He dangled behind the aircraft while enemy forces shot at him. The Jump Master could not pull him back into the aircraft and couldn't cut him loose because he didn't have a reserve chute. The aircraft returned to a friendly airbase where they put "super suds" on the runway. As the plane touched down, they cut the hung jumper loose, and the soldier slid on the runway hundreds of meters. He survived the ordeal.

Other airborne hazards are caused when scores of paratroopers are all descending in the same airspace. Some troops fall faster than others and may actually land on another soldier's deployed chute. If this happens, you must run off the parachute and continue your descent. If you fail to run off the other chute quickly, your own chute will collapse. At that point, you may still be hundreds of feet above the ground. When a parachute passes under another, it will "steal air" from the upper parachute causing the upper chute to fall faster than the lower one, and it will leapfrog past the bottom chute. The last chute that leaps will hit the ground hard.

Military equipment makes combat jumps challenging. A combat jump means that soldiers are carrying machine guns, rifles, rockets, grenades, explosives, food, water, medical supplies, radios, batteries, and clothing. A 180-pound paratrooper may have 120 pounds of equipment strapped to him. Under that kind of load, it's a great relief to finally jump out of the aircraft. Military Police may drop with an attack dog strapped to them. If the dog gets excited, by the gunfire and explosions during a jump, the canine may throw its muzzle off and go after the nearest thing, not in anger but fear and reflex. The MP may get his own face chewed off during descent.

More hazards face paratroopers when they are landing. Landing in a lake or river with over 100 pounds of equipment and a parachute strapped to you is a sure way to drown. If they are over water, paratroopers may unbuckle their harness during the last 20 feet so they can freefall the last few feet and swim away from the chute to avoid getting tangled in suspension lines. Unfortunately, lakes look flat and black at night and so do parking lots. Rivers look level, with bends and turns, and so do roads. It is also tough to judge your height from the ground in the dark, even when staring at the horizon. A paratrooper, believing he is a few feet above a lake, could instead jump out of his harness at 50 or 100 feet and pancake into a parking lot. Power lines are a common hazard. While I was at Ranger School, we heard about a student who hit a power line while parachuting. He lost his leg. The guy was a standout athlete and a contender for the U.S. Olympic wrestling team.

The Airborne instructors told us what to do if a jumper landed in the forest at night. It was often too dark to tell how high you were when snagged in the trees. The best technique to estimate your height was to remove your helmet, hold it out in front of you, and release it. Count the number of seconds it takes for the helmet to hit the ground. Gravity has a fall rate of 32 feet per second squared. We can estimate our height based on the drop time. If the jumper was 30 feet or so from the ground, they may be OK to climb down in the dark. The best way to do it was to pull the reserve parachute and let it fall about 20 feet below. The paratrooper can then climb down the outside of the reserve parachute to get onto the ground.

One infamous jumper found himself hanging by his parachute in a tree at night. Remembering his training, he removed his helmet, held it out and released it. He counted, "A thousand one, a thousand two, a thousand three, a thousand four." There was no noise. This was clear evidence he was entirely too high to attempt to climb down in the dark. He decided to wait until the sun rose so he could assess the situation more clearly. The trooper fell asleep in his harness. Hours later a search party found him and woke him up. His feet were dangling a foot off the ground. He had dropped his helmet in the bush in front of him, and it sat there all night.

One final hazard that the instructors covered was high winds. There were real safety issues when jumping in winds gusting above 20 mph. Troops could get blown horizontally across the drop zone and dragged over rocks, brush, and trees. There were actual cases where paratroopers were killed when they smashed into military vehicles in the drop zone. There are other conditions that make military combat jumps complicated and dangerous. Most drops occur at night, preferably with little moonlight. The airplanes are not lit. The drop zones are not lit. Once hundreds of troops are scattered on the ground, they need to find each other and not accidentally shoot at each other. Once the instructors finished telling us about all the hazards, we could face conducting a military parachute jump, we were free for the rest of the evening. I went to the mess hall with some friends and ate dinner. On the walk back to the barracks, we learned that one of the airborne students was convinced he was going to die during his first jump the following morning. The guy was giving away everything he owned to his friends including his car, stereo, and cassette tapes. We thought it was a humorous overreaction. However, I was tempted to stop by and see if he had anything left for me. The guy was probably pretty embarrassed the next day when he survived the jump.

Rookie Jumper

The day of our first jump arrived. We arrived at Lawson Army Airfield early, but the C-130 cargo aircraft had mechanical problems which caused a delay. We sat on the baking hot airfield for 4-5 hours. The repairs were finally completed, and we strapped on our equipment and boarded the aircraft. The smell of JP8 fuel was awful; we couldn't wait to get out of this aircraft. There would be no hesitation to jump from this flying death trap. We checked and double checked our equipment. The bird took off in the hot Georgia sun. The aircraft doors were opened, and a strong draft came through the aircraft. The engine noise was deafening. The exit doors were located behind the engines for a good reason - paratroopers do not want to jump into the massive propellers.

Parachute jump from C-141 aircraft

After climbing to 1200 feet, the Jump Master began to give a series of commands; all paratroopers loudly repeated them. The first was a warning,

"Six Minutes!" Soon after came, "Inboard personnel, stand up!" Then, "Outboard personnel, Stand up!" All jumpers were now wide-eyed and standing. Further commands were issued. "Hook up!" directed us to connect our static line to the anchor cable running along the inside of the fuselage, which would automatically extract the parachute as we fell. "Check equipment!" directed each soldier to inspect their own parachute harness and connections, as well as the rig of the soldier in front of them. Once the inspection was complete, the jumpers shuffle stepped toward the exit door. The next command was "Stand in the door!" This directed the first jumper to put their toes on the threshold and prepare to leave the aircraft. All other jumpers followed closely behind. I was the third man in the line.

It's a cliché, but there is something inherently wrong with jumping out of a perfectly good airplane. But I was going to do it anyway, as I watched the two small lights next to the door. The red light meant STOP, do not jump. The aircraft was not over the drop zone. The green light meant GO - we were over the drop zone, and it was time to take a walk on the wild side. There was no yellow light in airborne operations; it was STOP or GO.

As I approached the aircraft exit, the soldier in front of me froze in the door. This was bad. We had only a few seconds to get scores of jumpers out of the bird, or we would be widely scattered and land miles from our planned drop zone. The Jump Master supervising the operation wasted no time. He grabbed the metal anchor cable with both hands. He then performed a powerful pull-up and dropped kicked the frozen trooper in the ass, launching him into the atmosphere. The rookie jumper left the aircraft head over heels. After watching that, I knew I did not need any assistance. I stepped out, into the breeze, and counted to four as a 120 MPH wind blew through my uniform. It was an exhilarating feeling. I felt the parachute shock when it opened, and I looked up to check my canopy. It was oscillating open and closed, but it soon stabilized.

The world was now incredibly quiet. The aircraft was gone. I looked down to spot the colored smoke on the drop zone to see which way the winds were blowing. I rode that silk for a few dozen seconds as I approached the earth then pulled on my risers to turn into the wind. I hit the ground and executed a decent PLF. I rolled over and detached one of my risers so any gusts wouldn't drag me across the drop zone. I stood up in the waist high grass, elated that I had just completed my first jump. I looked up and saw dozens of other paratroopers still descending. As a one-jump veteran, I was now confidently shouting encouragement to all those rookies that had not yet reached terra firma.

I gathered up my parachute and ran, an "airborne shuffle," back to the collection point about half a mile away. One jump down, four more to go. I met my classmates in the mess hall that night for dinner. We were all beaming and telling stories.

We had no fatalities, but several students suffered injuries during jump week. I watched one soldier land and do a leg split, breaking both his legs. Most of us completed the five required jumps from both C-130 (propeller) and C-141 (jet) aircraft. At the conclusion of the course, I was among dozens of colleagues who proudly earned airborne wings and a course diploma.

I have many fond memories of my experience at Airborne School. However, tragedy struck two years later. As I mentioned earlier, my former Beast Barracks friend, Barry Dominick, died while training at Airborne School. He had a heart condition that the Army felt was not significant. Ironically, Barry had already completed the much more challenging and hazardous Ranger Course with this condition. The loss of this close colleague and friend still saddens me. Miss you, Barry.

Decades later, some my classmates would rise in the airborne ranks and serve the nation with distinction. Colonel Billy Mayville would lead the 173rd Airborne Brigade on a nighttime combat parachute assault into northern Iraq. Major General John "Mick" Nicholson would command the famous 82nd Airborne Division, leading rapid deployment missions around the world. Decades earlier, Mick had his first taste of combat in Grenada as a young lieutenant with the 82nd.

I had an opportunity to return to Airborne School in July of 2015. I watched a few hundred new paratroopers make their final jump at Fryar Drop Zone.

After one of the young "Five Jump Commandos" landed, he shuffled past me and said, "Hey, you ought to try this someday."

I replied, "Welcome to the club, son. I made my first parachute jumps here 35 years ago."

Welcome to the Fryar Drop Zone

CHAPTER 26
EXCHANGE CADETS, SPRING BREAK, BACK TO BEAST & GRADUATION

Exchange Cadets

During the fall semester of our junior year, we had several exchange cadets join West Point. Two were assigned to our company. Thad Sliwinski from the U.S. Coast Guard Academy in New London, Connecticut was my roommate. He fit in quickly, and we enjoyed his stories about the USCG Academy.

For a few weeks, we were joined by Damien Hess, an exchange cadet from Australia. He fit into the American culture well and had an awesome accent. Damien liked to tell people shocking stories to see how they reacted. He told one story—several of us knew was a total fabrication—about dropping napalm bombs on kangaroos and watching the flaming animals hop around. Some of the animal lovers in the room were left speechless. I immediately put Australia on my bucket list. It would be another thirty years before I was able to travel there and see at least part of it. For the record, I love kangaroos. Medium rare.

Spring Break

During spring break in March 1981, Mike Charbonneau, Greg Gerovac and I decided to drive to Florida. It was my first trip to the sunshine state. We drove in an old car that Greg had purchased for one dollar. The clunker made it to South Carolina where a mechanical problem with a wheel that, nearly caught fire, delayed us for four hours. Fortunately, we found a mechanic that would work on Sunday and paid him seventy bucks to get it fixed. Our beer money was severely depleted by the unplanned expense, but we were back on our way.

We arrived near Patrick Air Force Base and stayed at a house owned by Mike's aunt. At one point, her husband had been in the astronaut program.

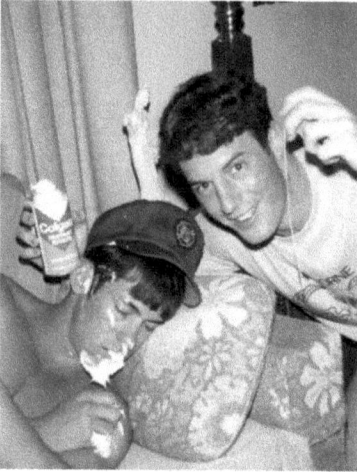

She was a kind hostess and put up with our horsing around, constant noise and practical jokes. For example, when Mike fell asleep on the sofa, I loaded his hand with shaving cream and dangled a string on his face. He started scratching his face and smeared himself with shaving cream. Greg and I were in tears laughing. When Mike finally woke up, he was a good sport about it.

Meanwhile, Greg found a wicker laundry hamper with a dog's head for the lid. Drinking a beer, he stuck it over his head and started dancing. My sides hurt from laughing at this ridiculous sight. It was one of those moments where you just had to be there to fully appreciate. This was what young men did when they tried to have some fun but had no money.

On our first full day in Florida, we laid out on the beach for hours without suntan lotion. My skin was fried, and I had the cold shakes all night. However, we were able to watch an unmanned rocket launch from nearby Cape Canaveral.

Later that week, we toured the Kennedy Space Center. I was able to see an Apollo Saturn V rocket for the first time. We also saw the solid rocket boosters and the fuel tank for the space shuttle Challenger, standing upright on a launch pad. Less than a month later, its sister shuttle, Columbia, made its first flight. I watched the launch on TV, with great anticipation, from my aerospace engineering class when we returned to the academy.

Horsing around with Mike and Greg

The following day was my 21st birthday. By coincidence, Greg, Mike and I went to The Magic Kingdom at Disney World. The one-day entrance ticket price at the time was $11.50 - two weeks of pay for a paperboy. It was expensive but worth it. We stayed all day through the closing parade and fireworks.

Spring break passed quickly, and it seemed we had just got there and then had to pack the car and start the long drive back to West Point. It was a fantastic trip for me, and the experience with Mike and Greg made me long to see and do more. I wanted to explore as much of the world as possible.

Tragically, my friend Mike Charbonneau never graduated from West Point. He was killed in a car accident during Christmas break our senior year along with another classmate, Brent Washburn. Our class was deeply saddened by the loss of these brothers.

Back to Beast

During my last summer at West Point, I served in the cadre that ran Beast Barracks to train the incoming freshmen. As a platoon leader, I was responsible for about forty Plebes. I roomed with the platoon sergeant, cadet Mike Minear. We were now the Firsties that New Cadets feared. Our platoon was informally known as "Kachejian's Legions." Our platoon was several thousand troops short of being a full-strength legion, but our Plebes had a lot of attitude.

Graduation

After four tough years, it was time for our class to graduate and join the Army officer ranks. Our class was reminded that the journey had just begun.

Dad, mom, and Kevin visited for several days during graduation week in late May. For my parents to take several days off of work and make the trip was a major financial commitment. I deeply appreciated all their sacrifice and support to get me to that moment. In gratitude, I presented my parents the USMA saber I had carried in my graduation parade. There were two inscriptions, one on the saber, and one on the case which mounted it:

To Mother and Father. With all my love, Kerry, Class of '82
To Mom and Dad. Thanks for making this day possible. Love, Kerry

My dad had long suspected I would give him a saber as a graduation gift, but he never mentioned a word. When I presented it, he and I broke into tears. Feeling the pride my parents had that day was one of the most memorable moments in my life.

Presenting my parents a saber after the Graduation Parade

Departing Hudson High

Located on the Hudson River, we sometimes referred to the academy as "Hudson High School." We had some humorous and satirical expressions about cadet life and feeling trapped at West Point: "West Point, fifty thousand people trying to get in. Four thousand trying to get out." And "The most beautiful sight in the world is West Point—in your rear-view mirror," were just a couple of them. Cadets also had some internal jokes about their alma mater: Q: What do Orange County California, Orange County Florida and Orange County New York have in common? A: California has Disney Land. Florida has Disney World. New York has West Point.

From the moment we set foot in the institution, we poked fun at it and could not wait to graduate. But truly, once inside and part of West Point, cadets, developed a different view of their daily life and leaving it came with mixed emotions. I felt the elation of accomplishment and excitement of going on to serve our nation around the world. And there was the regret I would leave many of my academy classmates behind and might not see them again.

As graduation day approached, I realized how much had changed for the kid who once zoomed around West Chester diligently working his paper route. Since graduation, the sense of loyalty to the academy and to my classmates, that shared this common experience, has continued to grow throughout the years. I look forward to seeing old friends at reunions and special events.

* * *

The academy hosts nearly three million visitors each year. A trip to West Point should be on every American's bucket list. The institution is rich with history and heritage. It is a National Historic Landmark. Graduates have made a profound impact on our nation since President Thomas Jefferson supported its founding in 1802. I was honored just to join the ranks of thousands of others that preceded me.

The scenery is stunning. West Point has been cited as the most beautiful campus in America; its dramatic granite buildings, the cadet chapel, museum, the historic cemetery, and dozens of monuments and cannons. The campus is surrounded by the spectacular Hudson River Valley with its imposing mountains. During the autumn, the leaves add brilliant colors, especially when a full-dress parade and a home football game make the atmosphere exceptionally appealing.

The four years I spent at West Point was a turbulent time in our nation's history. While the Iranian Hostage Crisis dominated the news, there were revolutionary labor strikes in communist Poland that rocked Soviet-dominated Eastern Europe, John Lennon was murdered in nearby New York City, and there were assassination attempts that wounded Ronald Reagan and Pope Paul II. In the same period, our nation launched the first space shuttle and beat the Soviet Union in ice hockey at the Lake Placid Olympic Games.

More Class '82 Stories

As many of the military officers in my class approached retirement, we shared scores of cadet stories via email — recollections of the humorous, surreal and fantastic events that occurred that made daily cadet life more bearable. A word of caution: retirement has been described as a state where people have increasingly vivid memories of events that never occurred. I wanted to capture some of these events while I was still in the lucid period of my life.

Many thanks to Joe Hajost, Jeff Irwin, Ben Bergfelt, John Proulx, and a dozen other classmates for sharing their memories:

- Being late to class was a reportable offense drawing immediate demerits. Intentionally missing a single class was serious misconduct, resulting in area tours. When the academy was hit with three feet of snow, cadets were granted an extra five minutes to get to class. The Commandant made it clear - there was no excuse to be late.
- Some of our Plebe classmates were required to wear black armbands when Keith Moon of The Who died in September of 1978.
- When fifteen spirited cadets tore up the Officer in Charge's (OC) room as a prank, only Bob Neilson got caught. He was the sacrificial lamb. Bob, thanks for taking one for the team!
- One stunt involved Company F1 Plebes who "called minutes" several hours early at 2:00 AM, waking up the entire company and yelling out they had only "five minutes to be in breakfast formation." Upper-class cadets, believing it was 6:00 AM, were scrambling to get on their uniforms, shave, and sprint outside for the mandatory formation and roll call. You may need to be a cadet to enjoy this story, but believe me, this was a hilarious stunt that confused and disoriented everyone in the company. I am laughing to tears just writing about it.
- We watched the world's biggest opossum waddling across Central Area after midnight one night. The animal was actually a three-foot-long rat fleeing the Cadet Mess Hall as workers replaced the stoves in the basement. The mess hall chow kept the rodents well-fed, and so they grew into Jurassic beasts.
- While attending an assembly where the Commandant was going to address the Corps of Cadets, the announcer started the introduction with,

"Ladies and gentleman..." and then paused for just a second. Someone in the back yelled, "The Rolling Stones!" It was perfectly timed, and cadets all burst out laughing. Ironically—and perhaps best for all concerned, especially the shouter—nobody entered the auditorium. The Commandant was late and arrived later.

- During finals of our Plebe year, we wondered what all the colored bits of plastic were scattered on the Area. We later learned it was debris from Firsties, who had thrown their 4-function calculators out the windows after completing their last final exam.

- In one company, Plebes were required to go trick-or-treating during Halloween. One room of Yearlings had wired their doorknob to the transformer of their desk light and put water on the floor. The naïve Plebes were shocked when caught in an ambush.

- Cadets would post a "Dear John" letter from their girlfriend on the company bulletin board for others to review, mock, and make grammatical corrections. One college girl sent her cadet photos of herself being affectionate with her new boyfriend. The cadet re-mailed the pictures to the girl's mother.

- When Ladycliff College, the all-girl school adjacent to the West Point, permanently closed in 1979, cadets went into mourning. The number of dance partners at cadet socials in Cullum Hall and Ike Hall diminished significantly. Several rumors were started, speculating how the former Ladycliff facility would be used. There were two leading suggestions. First, the old Ladycliff campus might be converted into a mental institution. However, there was a political issue; a New York State law prevented having two mental institutions next to each other. The other main rumor reputed that Ladycliff would be converted to a stewardess training academy for Eastern Airlines. The CEO of Eastern at the time was a USMA grad and former astronaut Frank Borman. We all had hopes that Borman would step up and help out his alma mater.

- A leading sports magazine rated West Point intramural lacrosse as the roughest, most dangerous intramural sports program in the country. The report was based on some factors including injuries and fatalities. The bottom line: we threw twenty-two gladiators on a lacrosse field and taught them how to beat each other with sticks. The amateur players had few ball skills, but they could wield a lacrosse stick like a shillelagh. I had several six-foot-long wooden defense sticks broken over my body. Any such experience was considered a badge of honor.

- The one civilian food establishment near the cadet barracks was "Tony's." Their calzones and pizzas were cadet favorites. We made plenty of late night runs to Tony's. Grab it and go, whatever was already made, and figure out what you bought later. The academy awarded the follow-on contract to another small business, and the quality and portion sizes declined dramatically. This was the only commercial food provider we could access, and the cadets felt ripped off by the new monopoly. To make a point, cadets left a calzone on the Superintendent's front porch, along with a note reporting extreme dissatisfaction about the poor quality. The administration acknowledged receiving the calzone.

- We marched in so many parades, cadets decided to start praying to Odin, the legendary Norse God, who we thought, could change the weather, and bring a major thunderstorm. In the thirty minutes before each parade, cadets would open their windows and call "Oooooo-din! Ooooo-din!" out the window to invoke a storm that would cancel the parade. A cancellation would give cadets an extra hour to nap or work on homework. Perversely, on one occasion the parade went on despite a threatening storm. When we marched out on the parade field, the skies darkened and a torrential storm hit. Winds blew full-dress hats off, and every civilian in the stands ran for cover. The cadets continued with the ceremony, in their soaked wool dress uniforms. It took a few days to dry uniforms that reeked of sweat and mud. Since my days as a cadet, I have learned that Thor, not Odin, is the Norse storm deity. Perhaps that is why Odin rarely answered our prayers.

SECTION 5
ARMY

CHAPTER 27
ENGINEER OFFICER BASIC COURSE
& SOMALI CAMEL

Somali Camel

After graduation from West Point, I attended a four-month-long course at Fort Belvoir, Virginia to learn how to be an Army Engineer, the Engineer Officer Basic Course (EOBC). We were trained on tactical engineering skills, such as building bridges, roads, and airfields, emplacing and removing minefields, and using explosives to destroy similar things. We also trained on common soldier skills such as marksmanship, physical fitness, and land navigation.

To strengthen military relationships, the U.S. Government invited officers from foreign nations to train with their American counterparts. Consequently, we had six allied officers, two each from Sudan, Zimbabwe and Somalia, in our EOBC course. English was not their native language, so learning about U.S. military equipment, operations and tactics was often difficult. For newly commissioned American second lieutenants, the course was interesting, and we had time to mentor some of the foreign officers.

1st Lieut. Abdullah Mohammed Shire was one of the Somali officers in our class. He told us about how his country had been allied with the Soviet Union for a few years, but then the Somalis rebelled, and a gun battle ensued. Abdullah was shot several times by his former Soviet instructors. He showed me some nice scars on his torso and legs. That story earned him considerable respect among the American officers.

Abdullah asked me for some help with bridge design, and I agreed. He was not familiar with the U.S. "float bridging" equipment. His English-speaking skills were basic but much better than my Somali speaking skills. I reviewed some typical problems with Abdullah. For example, if U.S. military forces came to an 80-meter wide river where the existing bridge was destroyed, and we needed to get 60-ton tanks across, our task was to design a floating bridge to get it done. A problem like this on an exam might only allow a student twenty minutes to solve. During field training exercises, we would only have a few hours to actually build the bridge and get the first tanks across the river. The design and build had to be done quickly, as enemy aircraft and tanks would be attacking the bridge while we were building it.

After a few hours of help, Abdullah was much better prepared for the test, and once the exam was over, he thanked me for the tutoring. Then he surprised me with a gift, a camel. Abdullah explained that he was a wealthy man in Somalia and owned 400 camels.

Owning a camel in Somalia was the equivalent of owning a car in the United States. The only caveat was that my camel was still in Somalia. If I made the trip to Mogadishu, he'd let me have the beast. I wanted to give Abdullah an Army mule in return, but I didn't actually own one. I thanked him for the camel, but I never made it to Somalia to claim my little part of his fortune.

American Slang

Tim Hopper and Max Huey were excellent engineer officers, and they were also outrageously funny. No field exercise was complete without them lifting the morale of their friends. What happened in EOBC stayed in EOBC. Except for the following story:

Our Somali colleague, Abdullah, sought help from other EOBC classmates. Tim Hopper graciously offered to help him learn the American version of English, particularly slang. Few Americans spoke the Queen's English that Abdullah had been taught.

This was 1982, before personal computers and word processing were widely used and before the internet. So, Tim manually compiled a dictionary of American slang. For completeness, the guide included every locker room swear word in the American subculture. Abdullah dutifully studied Tim's unofficial dictionary.

He was appreciative of Tim's efforts and genuinely wanted to improve his social skills. Unfortunately, 1st Lieut. Shire did not fully understand when and where it was socially appropriate to use the slang. I remember attending our formal dinner at the end of EOBC where Abdullah was introduced to an American colonel. Abdullah's enthusiastic greeting started with, "How's it going M#$%&@ F@*%&$!?" A bunch of American lieutenants quickly bolted out of the receiving line so they would not be asked about Abdullah's newly acquired vocabulary.

Now You Owe Me

We had a great group in the EOBC class, and some had also been classmates from West Point. I enjoyed the special times we had during the course, both on duty and off. So, I wanted to give my fellow Engineer officers a "shout out" in this book. In return, I expect every one of them to buy me a beer at our next reunion:

Charlie Baldwin, Monica Balkus, Rene Belanger, Steve Bigari, Brett Boerema, Joe Bonometti, Jim Boyle, Steve Buc, Greg Burgamy, Chuck Chase, Brett Comolli, Paul Cunningham, Tim Devens, Mike Deitz, Mark Easton, Duane Gapinski, Debbie Gillette, Bill Goetz, Bill Graves, Kevin Griffith, Dave Hanauer, Jim Heavner, Mark Hoffman, Tim Hopper, Max Huey, Ken Kennedy, Kevin Keough, Rich Kubu, Knute Leidal, Mike Mazzuki, Everett McDaniel, Bob Metz, Mike Minear, Bob Moore, Bill Murphy, Scott Pasolli, Bill Patterson, Rich Plasket, Mike Proulx, John Pulliam, Randy Richardson, Rob Rockwood, Bill Rogers, Gene Rohrer, Mike Rossi, Chris Schopfer, Skip Setliff, Mike Slavin, John Snyder, Rick Stevens, John Taylor, Pete Taylor, Tim Torchia, Martin Von Tersch, Joey Warwick, Bill Waugh, Ron Welch, Frank Weston, Dave Williams, Margaret (Williams) Burcham, Mike Wilmer, Tey Wiseman and Dan Worth. Other EOBC classes included more engineer colleagues: Randy Fofi, Ed Cardon, Tim Gallagher, Steve Hill, Bob Carlson and John Naccarelli. There's a lot of free beers coming my way.

CHAPTER 28
RANGER SCHOOL

Ranger Preparation

During EOBC, new lieutenants could apply for the U.S. Army Ranger School. There were 126 U.S. and foreign officers in the EOBC class. Approximately 115 of the officers were American males, and all were permitted to apply for the course. Seventy-five of the EOBC students started the selection process, which included two months of additional physical fitness training called "Ranger PT." The odds of getting one of the five Ranger slots allotted for my EOBC class were not good.

The competition was stiff. It required an officer to complete EOBC with a perfect academic record on over 40 exams and to achieve a maximum score of 300 points on the Army Physical Fitness Test (APFT). There were many other assessments of each officer's tactical and technical skills including land navigation and weapons training. We also had to complete a twelve-mile road march in boots with a loaded rucksack, weapons, and water, in three hours.

Serious Ranger candidates resisted the temptation of going to the pubs in Old Town Alexandria and Georgetown at night. Much of my free time was spent studying for exams or practicing the APFT each day. However, we reserved our weekends so we could still have a social life.

The physical conditioning and self-discipline paid off. Knute Leidal, Everett McDaniel, Rich Kubu, Tim Hopper and a former paperboy from Pennsylvania were selected to attend Ranger Class 3-83. Now the hard work was about to begin.

Vietnam Veterans Memorial

Our Ranger class started six weeks after EOBC graduation. From mid-October until late November 1982, the five Ranger candidates needed to find a "snowbird" job in the Army, while awaiting our next assignment. Fortunately, we found one. Knute, Rich and I volunteered to serve as DOD Project Officers for the National Salute to Vietnam Veterans. On November 13 of that year, our nation planned a special day for Vietnam veterans in Washington, D.C. It kicked off with a parade and included a flyby of military jets and helicopters. That afternoon, the Vietnam Veterans Memorial was officially dedicated on the National Mall. Our job was to coordinate the participation of 900 Vietnam Vets expected from the State of Virginia.

The National Salute was long overdue. Vietnam veterans had been ridiculed and abused for their service, and this ceremony was the beginning of the healing process. On the day of the dedication, we wore our Class A uniform and attended the ceremony. The parade started with General Westmoreland in front. Former Pittsburgh Steeler Rocky Bleir, who had lost part of his foot while serving in Vietnam, followed in a jeep. That special day went smoothly. The Thanksgiving holiday was approaching the following week, so I took leave to see my family in Pennsylvania before flying to Fort Benning to begin Ranger School. I picked up a couple of extra pounds eating turkey. I knew I would be losing it very quickly once I started training.

Enroute to Fort Benning

On the flight from Washington National Airport to Benning, the young lady in the seat next to me began to panic. She was convinced the aircraft was going to crash. Ten months earlier, Air Florida Flight 90 had crashed while taking off from National Airport, hitting the 14th Street Bridge. I reassured her that we were fine and used some of my aerospace engineering training to explain all the aircraft noises and vibrations; they were normal and expected. She was able to contain her fear but needed occasional reassurance. I wanted to tell her I was also a paratrooper, and if we needed to jump, I would take her with me. Better judgment told me to not make this offer. The aircraft eventually landed, and as promised, we both survived the flight.

When I finally arrived at Fort Benning, I met Rich Kubu and Knute Leidal. A couple of dozen other West Point classmates also came from other Army branches including infantry, armor, and field artillery. It was a brief but welcome reunion. We would all be on this journey together. The first order of business was to shave our heads. We would not be meeting any new girlfriends here; no need for stylish haircuts. We needed to blend in and not attract unwanted attention from Ranger Instructors (RIs).

2LTs David Anstay, Knute Leidal, Rich Kubu arrive at Ranger School

The Training

Ranger training has three distinct phases: Fort Benning "Darby" Phase, Mountain Phase, and Florida Phase. Each is a grueling three weeks in simulated combat conditions. Every activity was designed to create physical and mental stress. Living outdoors in the freezing cold. Sleep deprivation. Lack of food. Physical exhaustion. The cumulative effect was almost unbearable, and there was no safe haven—no respite. Typical weight loss was 20-30lbs from fit young men who started the course with little body fat. It was highly competitive just getting into Ranger School, and incredibly difficult to complete. About one-third of each Ranger School class was recycled if they failed a critical task in one of the phases. They would need to repeat the entire three-week stage with the next class. Consequently, each class added and dropped students as they moved from phase to phase. Attrition was almost 50%. But for those able to succeed, they were authorized to wear the highly-respected Ranger tab for the remainder of their career. I had heard it was a good idea to keep a small diary of activities during Ranger School. I am very glad I did. Over the years, reading it has been a source of inspiration when I thought life was tough. And it helped to refresh my memory of some of the stories that follow.

Fort Benning Phase

Ranger School kicked off with a harsh physical assessment that lasted several days. This included a Ranger Physical Fitness Test (pushups, sit-ups, chin-ups and 5-mile run) where the standards of performance were high. Students must strive to achieve a maximum score. Conserving energy by completing only the minimum passing scores was viewed as a lack of commitment and motivation. We underwent a Combat Water Survival Assessment (CWSA). This included the "Log Walk Rope Drop," an obstacle that required a Ranger candidate to climb a 35-foot tower, then walk 70 feet across a narrow log (climbing three steps in the center), and conduct a commando crawl along a rope suspended over the water. It concluded with the 35-foot drop into Victory Pond and swim to shore. I thought I had broken my hands when I hit the water with my arms extended out. Everyone made it through, but we had some injuries and one case of hypothermia from the 55-degree water.

Ranger Nate Curley conducts Commando Crawl
on the Log Walk Rope Drop obstacle

The next obstacle was the "Slide for Life," and always a thrill. We climbed a 75-foot tower and slid 150 meters down a cable over Victory Pond. Before hitting the water, we released the handle bar and splashed down at nearly 50 mph.

The Land Navigation test was conducted during day and night. We had to find several small markers in the woods using a map, a compass and terrain association skills. This was before we had GPS. We counted each step to estimate the distance we traveled between each waypoint. For example, if I took 71 steps, I figured I had moved 100 meters. The course is timed and spread over 10 kilometers. We used every natural and man-made feature to our advantage, including road intersections, streams, and prominent terrain. It was a foot race to locate enough of the small markers and return to the finish point within the allotted time. Completing the course one second late resulted in failure.

Patrolling

After the physical assessment period was over, much of the training covered the fundamentals of patrolling and small unit tactics. Initial patrols were led by Ranger Instructors (RIs) that demonstrated what "right" looked like. Patrols then become student led and were graded as a GO or NO GO. To pass, students need to receive a GO on at least 50% of their patrols. Some patrols included airborne insertions where we would parachute into the area of operations.

There are three types of combat patrols: raids, ambushes, and reconnaissance (recon). The raid involved friendly troops moving to an enemy location (missile site, command post, bunker, etc.) with the purpose of killing, capturing and destroying enemy personnel and equipment. The ambush involved friendly troops waiting for enemy forces (troop convoy, etc.) to move into a kill zone with the purpose of destroying enemy personnel and equipment. The recon patrol involves friendly troops moving to an enemy location or area (airfield, missile site, road network) to collect and report intelligence about enemy activities. Each patrol had to be carefully planned and executed. Speed, stealth, and security must be properly used, or the mission may fail.

Band of Brothers

We started the course with 177 Ranger candidates; that number fell off rapidly at first. We found a lot of old friends and quickly made new ones and became close brothers in our shared struggle to push through the course each day.

The oldest guy in the class was a Special Forces Captain named Ernie Davis, a Green Beret seeking his Ranger qualification. Bo Dyess and Steve Salazar reported in with me. Thirty years later, they became Army generals. Rich York was a G2 Gator and former roommate from the academy. Lewis "Skip" Setliff was another classmate and fellow engineer; years later we served together during combat operations in Iraq. There were dozens of other guys I should mention, including: Frank Asencio, Chuck Chase, Mark Easton, Scott Fedorchak, Craig Fox, Steve Gerras, Kevin Hackney, Scott Hampton, Mike Jasenak, Tom Juric, John Keely, Craig Langhauser, John McElree, Bob Nakamoto, Casey Neff, Mike Rossi, John Piatak, Chris Schopfner, Benny Schrivner, Manny Silva and John Zemet. I would buy these guys a beer anywhere. Of course, I would expect them to stick around and pay for the second round.

We had one Allied officer assigned to our Ranger class, 1st Lieut. Jasuant Singh, a Sikh warrior. He was the only guy in the course not required to get a haircut or shave. Since Sikhs are prohibited from drinking intoxicants, I would skip the beer and buy this guy a cup of tea.

I briefly saw two more G2 Gators, who arrived for Ranger Class 5-83: Bob "Bosco" Scurlock and Robert Bruce "Abe" Abrams. Abe was the Company Commander, and Bob was the Executive Officer. Two decades later, both would lead thousands of troops in combat in Iraq and Afghanistan. Gene Skinner and John Garrison were also in that class. John later became the president and CEO of Bell Helicopter.

We had a few dozen other classmates coming through other Ranger classes, including Kenny Dahl, John "Mick" Nicholson and Rob Baker. All three became Army generals with extensive service in Iraq/Afghanistan. Mick would go on to command the 82nd Airborne Division and lead all forces in Afghanistan. A few classmates went through Ranger School in the summer of 1980 when we were USMA cadets. They included two fellow lacrosse players, Sammy Johnson and Phil Connolly; an E2 Dog, Alex Gorsky, would later become the CEO of Johnson and Johnson; and two more Gators, Kevin Merrigan and Rod "Junior" Mateo, who had arrived at USMA with his tab.

Ranger Diary (Benning)

Below are some extracts from my Ranger diary during the Fort Benning Phase. The daily log provides some feel for the day-to-day activities and challenges we faced. I redacted some names to protect identities:

- 29 Nov—Head shaved clean! Reported with 177. Swim test fails 3 today. No real hard asses yet—all admin. 10 pushups. Tomorrow PT test at 0300. 1 hour 45 minutes sleep.
- 2 Dec—Ranger Committee (Morgan) busted into barracks at 0230 and made us do fatigue drills in our underwear on the gravel road. 40 minutes of hell. Practiced patrolling the rest of the day. 450 pushups. 4 hours of sleep! 150 Rangers left.
- 3 Dec—2 hours hand-to-hand combat. 8 hours patrolling. 2 hours survival training. So damn tired. 149 are left. Need more sleep. 425 pushups. Had 4.5 hours sleep last night.
- 4 Dec—3.5 mile run so damn fast—lost 1/3 of Rangers in it. Down to 148. Land Nav Course for 7 hours. Worm pit again tomorrow. 1.5 hours sleep.
- 6 Dec—Hand-to-hand combat at 0230. Only 150 pushups today. Medical and demolition classes. Packing for Darby tonight. 3 hours sleep last night. Rich Kubu →injured his knee. 1 hour sleep. 350 pushups.
- 9 Dec—Airborne insertion into Ledo DZ from 1250 feet. Jumping from a chopper is great. Patrolled 17 hours. No sleep. No food today. I was Patrol Leader to recon an enemy missile site. Ungraded exercise but I did a reasonable job. 100 pushups.
- 10 Dec—"Darby Queen" obstacle course. 28 obstacles / confidence challenges up to 50 feet high. 138 assigned to company. 175 pushups.
- 12 Dec—Jump canceled. Right now, I am on the perimeter of an ORP. We are raiding an enemy camp shortly. I had breakfast 14 hours ago and won't eat again for another 6 or so. It is so cold. I'm shivering intensely. I want to fire my weapon on automatic, so it will heat up. I only expect an hour of sleep tonight. Left the swamp (ORP) at 1830—only 20 degrees F.

Did not get a wink of sleep tonight. 3 men medically evacuated for frostbite. My C-rations were frozen too.

- 14 Dec—We were trucked out to the front lines. Hit by artillery as soon as we crossed into enemy territory. Reconned a missile site and bunker. I was appointed Assistant Patrol Leader (14-man patrol) at about 1430. Old Patrol Leader Majer (E-3) replaced by M—- (E-3). I was still APL. He got us lost on the patrol and started using roads! He failed the patrol. It is so cold. Hands and feet are numb, and skin is torn up from the bushes at night. 3.5 hours sleep.

- 15 Dec—Wake up at 0400 (Slept in). 2nd squad joined up in a link up operation of 28 men. After 16 hours of APL, they appoint me Patrol Leader. Recon a new patrol base 300m away and move out. Set up LP/OPs with commo, R&S teams, emplace M-60s and squad positions, alert plan, evacuation plan, and alternate patrol base within 1 hour. Also, must do sector sketches with fields of fire and a fire support plan. Then I must do field planning for a new ORP for the raid on the missile site. I passed the patrol! Only 37% passed. Relieved at 1330 by Murphy and patrol was a success. Ambushed a troop convoy at 0200 and returned to front lines at 0530. I lost the TA-1 phone on return. I caught hell, and they sent the entire patrol back out in the woods. A truck drove by and threw it out. Another patrol found it and saved my sweet ass. No sleep. No breakfast.

- 17 Dec—5-mile run. Had 135 people left before the run. Nine people fall out including Al W—- and my Ranger buddy Ken R—- (SP-4). R—- dropped back one step to let the old cadence caller into formation. The RIs pulled him for falling out. Down to 126. Next was the Comprehensive test of all skills (maps, OPORDS, coordinating, signals, codes, etc.) Four failed including Don R—- the 1st SGT. He was such a <u>stud</u>. You could see his eyes as he packed his gear. Damn! Finally, the retest for Land Nav took 7 more. Down to 119 at the end of 3 weeks. This includes recycles from earlier classes. 100 pushups.

Other notes from my Ranger journal include:
- It poured freezing rain, and they would not allow us to put on rain gear because it "shines." Streams of water going down my back. Vines snag you everywhere.

- You carry a 70-lb. rucksack, wet uniform BDUs, M-60 machine gun w ammo (30 lb.), radio PRC-77 w batteries (20 lb.), or any other gear (telephones, mines, LAWS, etc.). Every damn vine has thorns too! My hands are shredded. 35 cuts on my right hand alone. They have been numb, swollen and infected for 1 week now. Feet are shot too. No skin and all blisters.

Droning

"Droning" is a term used to describe a Ranger student so exhausted they would fall asleep while standing on their feet. Droning was also accompanied by confusion and hallucinations. I fell asleep on my feet numerous times while patrolling at night. We typically moved through the dark woods in a single line called a "Ranger File." The patrol would periodically stop for a quick map check at 2 or 3 AM. That's when we usually fell asleep, while stopped and standing upright. I'd wake up a minute later and forget my dream. I would then struggle to see if the guy five feet in front of me was still there or if he had moved out of sight. It was very hard to see someone only a few feet away in the woods on a cloudy night, particularly when you are exhausted.

I fell asleep three times one night standing in the same spot. The Ranger behind me was concerned

Notes taken by author during a Ranger class when severely sleep deprived

about my lack of motion. He hit me with the butt of his rifle and said, "Hey, you're droning! Did our patrol move out?" That was an instant shot of adrenaline. If the front of the patrol was gone, then my droning caused the break in contact. If the RIs found out, I would get severely disciplined, and

217

the rest of my squad would be found collectively guilty. I shook my head and strained to see if there was still a Ranger in front of me. There appeared to be a short, stocky guy two steps ahead. Over my shoulder, I told the Ranger behind me, "No worries. The patrol hasn't moved." I turned back to the Ranger in front of me and asked him why the map check was taking so long. He didn't answer, so I accused him of droning. I thought he mumbled something in reply, but that's when I fell back asleep, still on my feet.

Two minutes later, I was hit with another rifle butt in my back. "Hey, Ranger! You're droning!" I snapped awake, looked up and was glad I still saw the stocky man in front of me. The best defense was a good offense, so I took a step forward and accused the Ranger of droning. The guy stayed still and didn't say a word. I lifted my M-16 rifle and drove the butt of it into his back. "Wake up dude!"

That's when I realized there was no Ranger in front of me. I had been talking to a small tree for the past few minutes. The front of the patrol left at least five minutes earlier.

"Oh S***! We broke contact. Follow me!"

I started running in the pitch-black woods in the general direction I thought the patrol had gone. Half a dozen Rangers were running behind me with machine guns and radios, swearing they were going to kill me. We tripped over logs and rocks and pushed through thorny vines that sliced us up. We made as much noise as a herd of elephants, desperately trying to catch up to the rest of the patrol before the RIs figured out we were missing. After sprinting blind for several minutes, I ran into the back of our patrol. Halleluiah! I was breathing hard, but the panicked run warmed me up in the 20-degree weather. The rest of the patrol came crashing in over the next minute. Fortunately, our Patrol Leader did not change the original azimuth, and the RIs did not catch us. We had a near death experience and averted disaster. A minute after we rejoined the patrol, the RIs demanded a head count, and all the Rangers were present.

We walked, sleep-deprived—it's like being in a drunken stupor—at night along the top of cliffs up to 60 feet high without regard for our safety. The RIs called the cliffs "erosion ditches." The cliff to our right was hard to see, but it was a bit darker than the ground to our left. We just trusted that the guy in front of us was walking on firm ground.

Ranger Majer was carrying the M-60 machine gun and was two men behind me on one dark night patrol. I heard someone warn him, "Watch the cliff!" It came too late. Woosh! Majer left claw marks all the way down an erosion ditch 18-feet deep. The M-60 landed on his face, and he had to be evacuated for a few dozen stitches. He rejoined our patrol a day later. The hospital had given Majer a shower and cleaned him up. Maybe a hot shower was worth getting smashed in the face with an M-60. But we could smell him—the sweetness of the soap—from 20 meters. That meant the enemy could smell us too.

Cheap Cigars

We had a solid week of hand-to-hand combat training in the "Pit," a large area filled with wood mulch. All 150+ Rangers would usually start the training at about 2:30 AM. The freezing rains and cold temperatures in December often turned the pit into a pile of ice encrusted wood chunks. When we threw another Ranger to the ground, the frozen mulch did little to absorb the impact. It was almost as bad as training on a concrete slab.

In the pit, we learned how to beat and kill other human beings using different throws, choke holds, punches, and gouges. It was like participating in a professional wrestling match, but what we were doing was not theatrical and decidedly not entertaining.

We had an unusually aggressive RI named Sergeant First Class Swackhammer. He loved screaming at Ranger students and often threatened to inflict severe physical pain. Swackhammer was the primary instructor in the hand-to-hand combat pit. We heard a rumor that he had been recently transferred to a regular (non-Ranger) military unit. Within days of arriving, he threw an uncooperative soldier through a wall. Swackhammer was immediately transferred back to the Ranger Training Brigade where his bone crushing skills could be better utilized.

Having Swackhammer screaming at us at 2:30 AM every morning, while he directed us to beat the crap out of each other, was one of my fondest memories at Ranger School. If he did not think you were fighting hard enough or were pulling punches, he'd make the entire class do fatigue drills. Swackhammer's favorite scream was, "I'm going to smoke you, Ranger! I'm going to smoke you like a cheap cigar!"

One morning, we had a rare two-minute break during hand-to-hand combat training to get a sip of water. That's when our classmate, John Keely, passed the word: the next time Swackhammer started screaming, Keely told us he would break ranks, run up, get in his face, and scream back, "Smoke Me! Smoke Me!" We thought Keely was nuts. What he was proposing to do would be insanely funny, but it was a suicide mission. Perhaps John just wanted to crash and burn out of Ranger School that day. Then Keely requested something from us in return. When he screamed "Smoke Me! Smoke Me!" to Swackhammer, Keely wanted the other 150 Rangers to drop their pants and yell, "Smoke This! Smoke This!"

Well, the break ended a minute later. Swackhammer took charge and immediately started making life more miserable for us. Not long after, the whole sequence played out.

Swackhammer: "I'm gonna smoke you, Ranger! I'm going to smoke you like a cheap cigar!"

Keely: "Smoke Me! Smoke Me!"

150 Rangers: "Smoke This! Smoke This!"

Swackhammer won. He smoked us for the next hour. We were dying of exhaustion, but we were all dying together. And Keely became a Ranger legend.

Chow Hall and a REMF

When we were in garrison—in camp and not out in the field—we could eat an occasional meal in a small mess hall. Even this was a haze. We only had two minutes to eat. Some other soldier was ordered to stand next to our table and continuously scream in our faces during those two gluttonous minutes. "Get the hell out of my mess hall, Ranger!" We were only provided one utensil for eating, a large serving spoon. Chewing food was a luxury, so we usually sought to eat mashed potatoes or something that already looked partially digested. We were swallowing fists full of food and had no regard for social etiquette. After two minutes of gorging, we were kicked out of the mess hall and had to run back to our barracks. Some guys puked out their meal during the run.

Once, as I left the mess hall, I was disgusted to hear a female enlisted soldier complaining that she had "to eat C-rations again!" ("C-Rats" were canned meat, veggies, and crackers. The quality was similar to dog food.) She was an admin or supply clerk that issued equipment to students. She was a REMF (Rear Echelon M—F—) and had no idea what sacrifice and hardship was. Any one of the hungry Rangers at the camp would have been elated to have a C-Ration. Food was the most valuable currency in Ranger School.

Another time, after returning from an extended patrol, our squad had a brief opportunity to shower outdoors in freezing water. A dozen of us were completely naked and exposed to the cold, windy weather. We could be observed by anyone nearby. That same female supply clerk was intentionally sitting in a nearby jeep playing "Peeping Tom." And laughing at us. This time, I was angry about her disrespect, and I wanted to drag her REMF ass out on the next combat patrol or have her face Swackhammer in the hand-to-hand combat pit at 2:30 AM. He would smoke her. She wouldn't last five minutes in any stage of Ranger School.

8-hour break

After each 3-week phase of Ranger School, students had an eight-hour break. We could shower, wash our uniforms, pay bills, sleep or eat. By the time we were released from our military duties, the break was as little as five hours. Almost every Ranger student piled into a car and headed to an all-you-can-eat restaurant. Our stomachs had shrunken, but we shoveled in as much food as we could. We could not bring food back to the camp, or we risked expulsion from the course.

* * *

Every day of the Ranger School felt like a week. But at the end of every phase, I would feel like I earned two of the letters in the word RANGER. After I had passed the Benning Phase, I had secured the R and A. I had two more phases to complete and pick up the remaining four letters.

CHAPTER 29
RANGER SCHOOL - MOUNTAIN PHASE

Christmas Break

Going through Ranger School at any time of year was tough, but the winter was particularly challenging. Winter Rangers often used white thread to sew their Ranger tab on their uniform to emphasize the point. However, there was one distinct advantage to being a Winter Ranger. Our class spanned the Christmas season, and the school shut down for a couple of weeks. Class 3-83 had a holiday break between the Fort Benning and the Mountain Phase, and I was very grateful.

Casey Neff was driving 950 miles up to New York, and offered to give me a ride to Delaware, within 20 miles of my home in West Chester, Pennsylvania. Casey had an older model Porsche, and we quickly packed it and left Fort Benning. The night before the break, the RIs screwed with us and made us clean the barracks for five hours, so we had one hour of sleep. The long ride was a bit risky, but we would be Ranger buddies during this movement. Neither of us could fall asleep.

We bought a ton of junk food. I consumed a large pizza, several bags of chips and two pounds of peanut M&Ms. I washed it down with a couple of two-liter bottles of soda. At that point, my stomach became a battlefield; chemical warfare was raging in my gut. I needed to make an immediate pit stop, or things were going to turn biological. That's when we got caught in rush hour traffic outside Washington D.C. As we crawled along in traffic, I was about to explode.

I told Casey I had to bail out of the car and would be back shortly. So, I jumped out of his Porsche on I-95 and ran across several lanes of traffic for the woods. Mission accomplished, a few minutes later, I came running out of the woods onto the interstate highway and sprinted to catch up to the Porsche. Traffic inched forward as I ran to the car and pulled open the door. A cop, in a nearby lane, alarmed by my behavior jumped out of his squad car. He must have I thought I was a skinhead carjacker. I saw him, his hand on

222

his pistol as he yelled at me, "What are you doing?" My reply was simple, "I had to go! I had to go!" I jumped in the passenger seat and buckled up. The cop stood there trying to figure what just happened. I was glad he didn't shoot me, I had another big bag of peanut M&Ms to eat.

Hours later, Casey dropped me and my duffle bag at a strip mall near Wilmington, Delaware at midnight on a cold, windy evening. Wearing only a light jacket, I shivered as I found a pay phone and made a collect call to my dad. My father had planned to pick me up but yielded to my brother-in-law, Peter Curley, who insisted he could get me. Dad called Peter to let him know where to get me. Peter answered the phone, acknowledged the mission and then promptly fell back asleep.

I stood outside a deserted strip mall waiting for another two hours and then decided I would just walk the last 20 miles to get home; just another night mission from Ranger School. Then I thought Peter might arrive after I left the area and that would make matters worse. I called my dad collect again. Dad correctly assumed Peter fell asleep and went ballistic. An hour later my father picked me up, and we finally arrived home at 5:00 AM. I was very glad to be there and have some heat, food, and sleep. Peter was in the dog house with my parents for the next week. There's some sideways irony to this. As I mentioned in another chapter his son Nate, decades later, also became an Army Ranger.

Mountain Phase

Ranger School started back up the first week of January. Our class was now entering the Mountain Phase in Dahlonega, Georgia. I remember one of the RIs standing in front of our formation and preparing us for what was to come.

"If you thought it was cold last phase, you got plenty more coming! You're in the Mountain Phase now, Rangers. It is not just cold—It's F****** COLD!" His words turned out to be prophetic.

The Mountain Phase added rugged terrain and extreme cold to the sleep deprivation and hunger. It would be physically and emotionally taxing. We would climb cliffs, repel, cross freezing rivers, and patrol under harsh conditions.

Just before reporting back to the Mountain Phase, some us went to "Ranger Joe's," an equipment store where we could buy last-minute supplies.

We were looking for 'snivel gear,' any clothing or device to keep us warm and stop us from sniveling. We hated people that sniveled.

It was an open secret that some Rangers wore pantyhose under their uniforms to keep the wet cloth off their skin. I had some of that, just in case, but the latest technology for extreme cold was special long underwear that was webbed like a basketball net. When you were soaking wet, it kept the cold uniform a few millimeters off your skin, creating an insulating air pocket that helped to delay hypothermia. Unfortunately, Ranger Joe's was out of stock. I rarely asked for help from my parents, but I immediately sent my mother a brief but direct letter:

> *Mom,*
> *If I do not get webbed underwear immediately, I will die.*
> *Sincerely,*
> *Kerry*

I included a drawing of what it looked like. She immediately found a pair and rush shipped it to me. The package arrived just before we went on a patrol. It was a huge morale lifting experience.

Patrols

I would dream of a big bag of peanut M&Ms on the top of every mountain we were climbing. If I could just get to the top, my prize would be waiting for me. We did anything we could to keep morale up while patrolling. We would rib each other and use self-deprecating humor. We acted like there was no other place we'd rather be. What made the experience more tolerable was that everyone else was enduring the same hunger, pain, cold and lack of sleep. There was no rank, no special privilege or safe haven.

We had Rangers who earned the names like, "Stump" and "Horse-face." We all agreed that every Ranger had a right to be ugly, but old Horse-face abused the privilege. Everett McDaniel became a rock star and was dubbed the "Solar-Powered Ranger." During daylight, he was unstoppable. He powered his squad through many patrols and obstacles. But when the sun went down, Everett's energy level faded. His squad had to tie a cord around him to pull him along. They needed him alive in the morning to drive the next daylight shift.

Frank Asencio became an inspirational figure. His father had been the U.S. Ambassador to Columbia when we were cadets and among a dozen diplomats taken hostage by the M-19 guerrilla group in 1980. Frank joined our Ranger class after recycling in the Mountain Phase. He had a great attitude and was a welcome addition to our team. We were determined to do our best when Frank was the Patrol Leader, but we immediately let him down. An ambush we set up went poorly. The temperature was near zero, and we were all shivering and sniveling. When the enemy convoy came down the road, most of us had fallen asleep, and no one fired a shot. The RIs went ballistic. When the next convoy rolled through our kill zone, the demo blew late, the M-60 machine guns jammed, and everyone ran out of ammo at the same time. There was a big lull in fire while we tried to reload our weapons with frostbitten hands. Then we swept across the objective to take prisoners and destroy enemy equipment and ended up detonating explosive charges under a truck that was not supposed to be damaged. The RIs were furiously pissed and blew a gasket. Frank was off to a bad start on his mountain patrols, and it was entirely our fault. Characteristic of Frank, he just shook it off. But we didn't let him down again, and Frank finished the course strong. He was the guy rallying us when we were stumbling.

One pitch dark night, I thought I lost my eye while patrolling. A sharp tree branch jammed in it, and the stick snapped. I dropped to my knees, in excruciating pain, holding my face trying to feel the eye socket and assess the damage. While I was on my knees, the Patrol Leader walked by and saw what he thought was a Ranger kneeling and taking a break in the darkness. He proceeded to kick me in the gut and punch me in the back of the head. I wanted to pull out my bayonet and gut the ass, but I couldn't see crap. If I had been shamming, I would have deserved the beating. Seeing that I was injured and not screwing off, the RI came over and inspected my eye. We got under a poncho and turned on a flashlight to keep the enemy from seeing us. My eye was raked, but fortunately, not punctured or popped out of the socket. I patrolled the rest of the evening with one eye closed and kept pouring water on it to reduce the burning sting.

Mount Yonah

We moved on to Mount Yonah to begin upper mountain training, climbing the cliffs and rappelling. We started with a 120-foot free climb up the face of the cliff. The climb was made all the more difficult because the rocks were freezing cold, and my hands, with their numerous cuts, were numb. But like all the other Rangers, we sucked it up and worked our way up the cliff.

At the top, Scott Hampton and I prepared for a buddy rappel. When we started, Scott was simulating a wounded soldier. I had to strap him on my back and get down the cliff with him. Ice coated everything, and the footing was tricky. I backed up to the face of the cliff and checked to make sure there was a belay man at the bottom that could brake—slow—us if we fell. With a 200-pound Ranger on my back, I could barely reach the rope with my brake (right) hand. It wasn't looking good. I was top heavy and about to back my way down off an ice cliff. I stepped backward off the edge and tried to get in a good L-seat position. Well, my feet did not hold on the ice, and I immediately dumped upside down. My feet were pointed at the top of the cliff. My head was toward the ground. Scott, still strapped to my back, was also upside down and had no ability to control his destiny.

Fortunately, the belay man, 120 feet below us, was pulling our rope taught, preventing us from plunging onto the rocks at the base of the cliff. I wasn't exactly sure how to recover from this vulnerable position and was concerned I might somehow wriggle out of my Swiss seat which would likely be fatal for both Scott and me. That's when Scott spoke up. "Kachejian, if you get me out of this alive, I'll buy you a beer." That did the trick. I accepted his offer, and we managed to inch our way down the cliff while upside down.

Once we got to the bottom, I had to climb the cliff with Scott again. This time at the top, it was my turn to be the wounded soldier. I strapped onto Scott's back, and we replayed the same scene. Scott dumped upside down on the icy cliff while I dangled from his back. I was ready. Experience had taught me how to handle this delicate and dangerous situation. I told Scott, "Hampton if you get me out of this alive, I'll buy you a beer." We made our way to the bottom and lived to talk about it. However, decades later, I am still waiting to collect that beer and so is Scott.

We then made a 220-foot buddy climb and some Australian rappels, where we ran face first down the cliff. I enjoyed repelling a lot more than climbing, as gravity was your friend, and going up was a lot more work. On one rappel, I lost my grip on the rope and fell the last five feet. I was wearing a rucksack with 70 pounds of equipment and landed hard on my butt. The shock stabbed through my spine, and I could not feel my legs for several seconds. My first thought was that I had suffered a back injury, and my mother now had a second paralyzed son. After a few minutes, the feeling came back, and I was able to stand. But my rear end hurt for weeks. I was glad an RI did not see the incident. There was no way I was going to be medically evacuated and possibly not get to return to the course.

Later during the training, a severe ice storm came in and hit us on Mount Yonah. One of the RIs was injured in a fall on a rock shelf, and we were directed to immediately get off the cliff tops. The freezing weather that followed would have made our scheduled evening sleeping on the mountain top awful, possibly deadly.

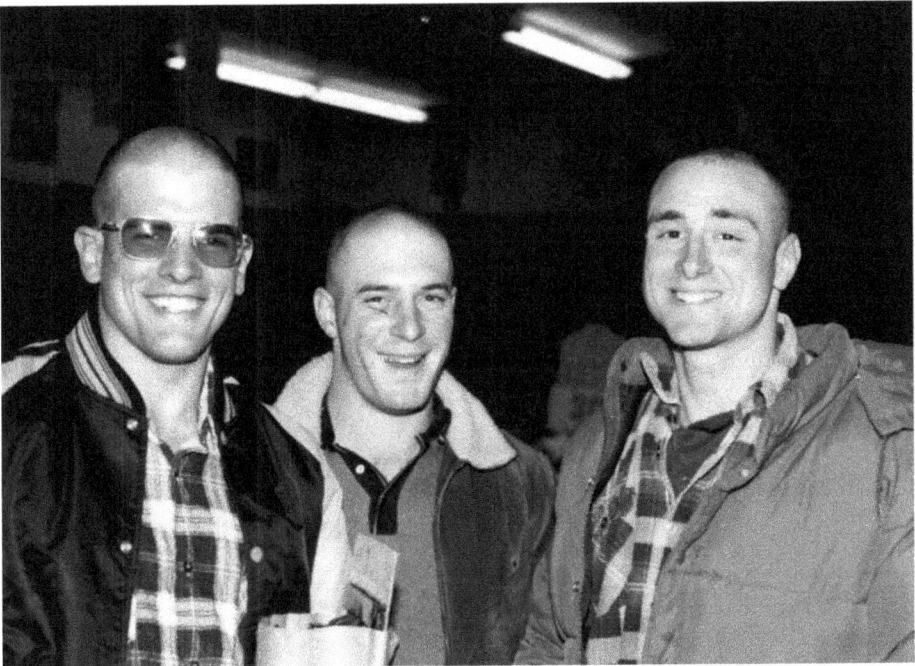

Frank Asencio, Kerry and CJ Eccher during a break after the Mountain Phase

Excerpts from my Ranger Diary (Mountain Phase):

- 09 Jan—12 mile road march with 50 lb pack. Feet are beat. 3 hours of patrolling tactics followed by 2 mile squad run up and down a mountain. 30 pushups. 5 hours sleep.
- 12 Jan—Wake up 0130 for announcement of new Patrol Leader, APL and I am RTO. H—- is PL. He failed the planning phase. We humped 5000m through the mountains, up 2000 feet. We were dying. It snowed all

morning with the temperature around 25 degrees F without the wind chill factor. About zero degrees F with it. Contouring mountains claimed a lot of feet. Reconned an ambush site on TVD Road (Tennessee Valley Divide Road). Humped to patrol base by 2200 on a mountain slope. I stayed up all night to call in situation reports hourly on the radio. Temperature dropped to minus 28 degrees F. Two people had frostbite and are gone. Down to 122 (116 from Darby 112 from original class). 40 minutes sleep. RIs let us wear extra clothes and start a fire. The Colonel ordered it since his job was on the line over the cold weather injuries in his unit. Some people lost fingers and toes.

- 13 Jan—RIs change at 0700. I am now APL. Move to new patrol base and conduct PB activities and field planning. I felt I did well, but the PL (T—-) screwed up the patrol order. I got a "GO" and a compliment from the RI. He said the only reason the PL passed was because his APL covered for him. Humped 5000m just outside friendly lines on a mountain top. Passive patrol base—yeah! 4 hours sleep. Temperature in patrol base was zero with wind chill factor.

- 15 Jan—Mountaineering today. Knot tying, 2-man bridges, rappelling. Made my first Australian rappel. Face first running down the cliff. Quite a few guys crashed and burned. 6 hours sleep. 135 pushups.

- 16 Jan—HUMP DAY. HALF WAY THROUGH! Rappelling off the 60 ft cliff, buddy repels, belaying, etc. Good training but the cliffs were extremely icy. A lot of people fell, but the belay man caught them. I carried Scott Hampton down on my back (simulated wounded man). We crashed and burned on the ice cliffs. The rope was frozen. 3 hours sleep. 60 pushups.

- 17 Jan—Last day of lower mountaineering. Two failed belay test. 15 failed the knot test. I got 75% (9 of 12). 8 of 12 was passing. I was pretty worried. About 8 failed rappels including our APL (P—-). We practiced falling off the 30 ft ramp for our free climb at Mt Yonah. Also covered suspension traverse and vertical pulley system to climb a 25 ft cliff. This was followed by walking a 3-rope bridge without safety lines 35 ft above the rapids (100 feet long). 2.5 hours sleep. 75 pushups. Chopper ride over all LZs for patrols.

- 18 Jan—Wake up 0130 for 36 hour patrol. Knute Leidal is PL, and Frank Asencio is APL. Temperature is 3 degrees F, and the patrol order is given outside. I am the new PL for the movement. We are air mobile and dropped off on Tildon Field. Hump up 3154 feet to Wilcott Mt. We recon a road with enemy movement. Passed the patrol and am now 3-0. The best record in the company (from an RI). Temperature dropped to +5 degree F with wind chill factor about -12 degrees F. Presnell, our APL, got frostbite on his toe and dropped from the course. 40 minutes sleep.

- 19 Jan—Move out of patrol base and do another road recon. RI makes us stop and start a fire. His hands are frostbitten. He made us feel them, and they were rock hard. Picked up a chopper at PZ (Pick Up Zone). One of the UH-1s lost an emergency door on the flight back. 5.5 hours sleep.

- 20 Jan—First day on Mt Yonah for upper mountaineering. The last 1/3 of the mountain is bare faced cliffs. I made two 120 ft free climbs, and you could see everything for miles. We did Australian rappels down. Then I made a 220 ft buddy climb with another Ranger. He was more nervous than me, and I was worried about doing it with him. He almost pulled me off the cliff while belaying me. We started about 150 ft up the cliff so any fall would have been close to 400 ft. I Australian rappelled down (there was ice on top). This severe snow storm hit us, and one RI fell down a rock shelf and screwed up his ankle. They made retrievable rappel lanes and rescued everyone off in 45 minutes. It was very cold, and they canceled all other climbs. We left Yonah a day early, and we missed the overhang rappel and the 250 ft night rappel. It was definitely frostbite weather, and we got about 3 inches of snow. Everyone was soaked. 5.5 hours sleep. Thank God we did not sleep on Yonah in our tents as planned.

- 21 Jan —2 rope bridge, vertical hauling line, etc. 5 day patrol starts tomorrow, and it's freezing rain for the next two days followed by a blizzard on Sunday or Monday. The word is out that if the Colonel has one more frostbite case, then he lost his job. If we stay out in it for 5 days, I know someone will die. It is so cold, wet and miserable. We get 4 meals in 5 days. 4 hours sleep.

- 22 Jan—Wake up 0200. Write OPORD for 0900. 25 degrees F. Leidal PL. Humped 6 kilometers over mountains. I was tactical squad leader. Tortorella and Washechek hurt knees. (twisted and strained ligaments). Hit objective at 2400 (3 hours late). Moved on 4 K to patrol base. No sleep.

- 23 Jan—Link up with 1 and 2 Squads at 0700 for a platoon mission. Hump to ambush Soviet Garrison. 6 clicks on map = 12 clicks on ground. Ambush went well. I was made PL after raid and had to take platoon back to Patrol Base 1800 m at night and initiate Patrol Base activities. It was difficult setting up the PB when everyone wants to bag at 0230. Passed the patrol. I am now 4-0, which only one other person has a record that good. 40 minutes sleep. Warm night 34 degrees F.
- 24 Jan—New PL (Langhauser) takes us to new PB. Mission is to raid enemy camp. We humped across many ridge lines. It seemed like forever. I carried M-60 machine gun the last 3000m (map distance) through woods to new patrol base on mountain top. 3200 ft up and windy. Temperature around 14 degrees F. 45 minutes sleep.
- 25 Jan—Wake up and hump 5 kilometers to another ORP (Objective Rally Point) on a mountain top. Tortorella rejoins our patrol from medics. His leg is still twisted, and he is in intense pain but guts it out. I'm in charge of the support section (4 M-60s), and we rip up the camp and vehicles while the assault team rolls across. 4 dead and 3 POWs. Pack it up and hump to new PB outside Camp Merrill. 1 hour 10 min sleep. 15 degrees F.
- 27 Jan—0230 wake and move back to Benning. Pack for Florida. Get 5.5 hour break to do laundry, shopping, ½ lb of M&Ms, all-you-can-eat restaurant. 3.5 hours sleep.

Chapter 30
Ranger School - Florida & WW Grenada

Florida Phase

The final phase of Ranger School was in Florida. My initial thoughts of Florida were pleasant: palm trees, warm sunshine, white sandy beaches, cold beer, and bikinis.

Unfortunately, that is not where Rangers train in Florida. Think of dark, dank swamps, waist-deep muck, wet weather, insects, alligators, snakes, and having to eat animals you caught or captured and killed yourself.

The Florida Phase taught Ranger students how to operate and survive in a jungle warfare environment. The patrols covered longer distances, and the phase culminated with a twelve-day patrol.

It started with a wake up at 2:30 AM. Soon we were fully combat loaded and airborne in a C-130 aircraft. The plane tossed around, and the guy next to me had motion sickness. He repeatedly filled his helmet, spewing up his guts. It was a sight and smell you never forget. Six minutes before the jump, the Jump Master canceled the drop due to high winds. But just as I made a mental note not to sit next to that airsick guy again, the Jump Master changed his decision.

We flew over the drop zone at 1000 feet, and I was the eighth Ranger out the door. My parachute fell more quickly than the others ahead of me, and I was the first man on the ground. The drop zone was moist and sandy; my feet penetrated about 8 inches into the soft soil. I was now in—no pun intended, well maybe—enemy territory, Florida. We spent the next couple of days training on the skills needed to survive in the jungle.

River Crossings

Rivers run through jungle areas, and we trained on how to cross them tactically. The single rope bridge required one Ranger to swim across a river and tie a rope off to a tree or anchor point on each side. Once the rope was taut, each Ranger would tie a Swiss seat harness, snap link themselves and their equipment on the rope bridge and pull themselves across. Each Ranger's head would stay above water, but everything else, including weapons, radios, and equipment, were immersed in the cold water. We used large waterproof bags to seal our uniforms and gear, hoping they would not completely soak.

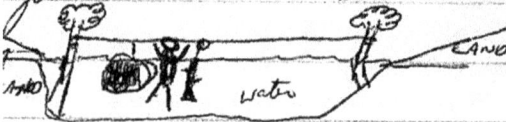

③③

patrol until lunch, carried the M-60. Classes in the afternoon. 6 hrs sleep.

30 January 1983 Wake up 0330. RB-15 assault boat drills. Conduct capsize drills in the Gulf of Mexico at 0800 (58°F water temperature). We threw both tactical officers in (SFC SCHRIVER + CPT AUGUSTINE) and then buried them in the sand. Conducted two crossings of the Yellow River using single rope bridge. Everyone got soaked in the 53°F water. About a 105' wide crossing. Fireguard tonight. 4½ hours sleep. Smoke

Single Rope bridge diagram from Ranger Diary 30 Jan 1983

The first Ranger had to strip off his gear and uniform, then swim in his underwear while carrying the rope. Once across the Yellow River, he tied the rope to a tree and returned to get his gear and weapon. We crossed quickly, as the water temperature was only 53 degrees.

Now that the RIs had taught us how to make the single rope bridge, it was time for the Ranger students to demonstrate it. The RIs asked for a volunteer to jump in the river, set up the bridge and swim back. John Piatak immediately stepped forward. John had a negative spot report on his record and thought volunteering would earn him a positive report to offset it. The RI liked John's initiative and told him to take his gear behind the formation and prepare for the swim.

The RI had his back to the river, and we faced him, while John was stripping off his equipment and uniform. The RI kept talking to us, directing our attention toward the river. After a couple of minutes, the RI was ready for the demonstration and directed Piatak to run to the front of the formation and prepare to enter the river. Piatak immediately came streaking out of the jungle, buck-ass naked, yelling "RANGER! RANGER!"

Seeing his pasty-white butt accelerating for the cold river was incredibly hilarious. We were all in tears laughing at his unexpected sight. [Side note: it was a common practice for many Rangers to not wear underwear because it would cause crotch rot.]

Piatak jumped into the icy waters, made it across, and secured the rope on the far shore. The sight of him swimming with his ass gleaming and barely above the water gave a whole new meaning to the word moonshine. He swam back and emerged from the river, naked, shivering and remarkably untouched by the alligators and leeches known to infest Florida's waterways and swamps. They must have fled in fear as Piatak's blinding albino flesh crashed into the river and tore through the water. For taking the initiative that day, John earned a positive spot report from the RI and a footnote in the Ranger Hall of Fame.

Miserable Night

On a later mission, our patrol approached another river we needed to cross. The air temperature was bitter cold, 22 degrees, and it was very windy. The wind chill temperature was reported as minus 17 degrees F during a safety call over our tactical radio. The water temperature was 45 degrees.

Excerpt from Ranger Diary

No one wanted to go in the water, but if we wanted to be Rangers, we had to earn it. We proceeded to cross the river using a single rope bridge. The water was paralyzing. As we emerged from the river, there was a safety call on the radio directing us to stop the training because it was life-threatening: "Do not conduct river crossing operations." It was too late, though. I believe the safety call was intentionally delayed a couple of minutes to make us go in the water and get the full Ranger experience.

Once the life-threatening call was acknowledged, the RI gave us one hour to "sleep" or change clothes. We had only slept an hour total in the previous two nights. We had to have some rest, so about a dozen soaking wet Rangers got in a pile and hugged each other like newlyweds in the freezing cold. There were no 'queer' jokes. We all wanted to be on the bottom of the man pile. Anyone lying on top of the pile was welcome to urinate on the frozen guys beneath him. It was a few seconds of shared warmth between brothers.

After about 45 minutes of precious sleep, the Ranger Instructor started kicking the pile to wake us up. Our wet uniforms were now frozen together. We had to pull each other apart. It was the most miserable night I had in Ranger School, but it makes a great story now. Years later, my friend, Major General Bo Dyess, vividly recalled the same night and told me it was the coldest he had ever been in his life.

Boat Movements

Rangers also moved through enemy territory via rivers and other bodies of water in inflatable rubber boats, officially known as RB-15 assault boats. In Florida, other creatures shared the water with us. We knew there were 12-foot gators in the area, and one named 'Big John' was kept as a mascot at the local Ranger camp.

During one boat movement, there was a safety-related radio call, "There's a 16-footer in the water." Although our minds were mush from the cold, lack of sleep, and hunger, we all sat up higher believing a 16-foot alligator was stalking our rubber boat. Every paddle became a defensive weapon. We knew that alligator had to be the world's largest and needed to eat hundreds of pounds of meat—maybe a couple of Rangers-in-training were on the menu. In hindsight, the RIs likely exaggerated the size to induce more psychological stress and have some fun.

On another night boat patrol, we attempted to move stealthily down a swampy river during freezing rain. However, several air compartments in the rubber boat had gone flat, and it immediately filled with water. I sat in the rear of the boat, for what seemed like hours, in waist-deep frigid water.

My feet were so numb I thought I had lost them. I literally prayed to God to get me out of the water or to just take my life. My body could no longer shiver, and I was ready to die.

Fortunately, the conditions were deemed life-threatening. The RIs stopped the patrol and directed us to paddle ashore then cut brush and tall grass to build a fire in the middle of the swamp. Frozen to the bone, with no chow and no sleep, I was grateful when that night ended.

Jungle Chapel

One early morning, our patrol ambushed an enemy convoy. We seized some live chickens and rabbits from the trucks and stuffed them into our ammo cans so we could eat them later. Then we moved about ten kilometers away from the carnage so nearby enemy forces would not find us and retaliate.

When we arrived in a more secure area of the jungle, we took a break and were offered a twenty-minute chapel service. Our patrol sat in a clay pit as the Chaplain introduced himself and led a prayer for us. A dozen bleary-eyed Rangers fought to stay awake. Then he dropped a bomb. The Chaplin was scheduled to attend Ranger Class 7-83. He was in a future class. Everyone sat up. I had confusing images in my head of a Chaplin throwing hand grenades and bayoneting communists. I guess he would become one of God's warriors. But collectively, we thought to have a Chaplain with a Ranger tab was an awesome decision by the Army. We wished him well. I don't know how the guy did, but with a little faith, he could endure the rigors.

Survival Meal

Later that day, we opened the ammo cans with the chickens and rabbits. The animals looked scrawny and quite shell-shocked, but the worst was yet to come. Our patrol boiled a pot of water and tossed in some potatoes, rice, and vegetables. We were in a relatively secure area, so we started a small fire and looked forward to the meal.

It was my job to kill the chickens. I hypnotized two of them briefly, stepped on their heads and pulled on their legs as if doing a dead lift. Both heads popped off immediately. Now with a flapping headless chicken in each hand, I wanted to help improve the team's morale, so I ran around the campfire holding the flapping chickens upwards seeing if I could take off like Superman. Unfortunately, the chickens could not generate enough lift to get me airborne, but my Ranger buddies enjoyed the spectacle. After a couple of minutes, the chickens stopped flapping, and we carved them up and tossed them in the pot. The rabbits met a quick and honorable end with a karate chop to the back of the head. I tried to save the fur to use later as insulation for the cold, wet nights still to come.

The survival meal was great, but it was our only one for the day. There was not enough food for the patrol. I was hoping we could get our hands on a goat, a small pig or perhaps a stray cat. Anything that moved was a potential food source.

Raining Chow

Another patrol began with a parachute jump. I failed to secure my gear well, and my rucksack opened as I was exiting the C-130 aircraft. By the time my parachute fully opened, my winter gloves and four of my meals (MREs) fell out and were plunging toward the ground. Hungry Rangers, already down on the drop zone, scrambled to catch these meals falling from the sky, obviously gifts from Heaven. I was desperately tracking where my chow hit the ground and who got it. One of the RIs recovered my gloves for me, but I was still short some food. That wasn't good; every calorie was worth fighting for.

Santa Rosa Island Assault

On the last day of the 12-day patrol, we conducted our final mission; an assault on Santa Rosa Island. Our target was a 'Soviet missile base.'

We approached the island in RB-15 assault boats. We came ashore and reconned the site. There were vehicles, missiles, and dummy personnel moving about the target site. Our patrol was large, about 30-40 men.

We set up sixteen Claymore mines and eight M60 machine guns. Each Claymore fired hundreds of metal fragments in a 60-degree arc, creating a casualty radius of 50-100 meters. I crawled forward and emplaced a Claymore mine to my front and pointed it toward the enemy sentries. I ran the detonation wire back about ten meters and laid in a prone position with a single sandbag in front of my head. I had 4 inches of cover, not enough to protect me from the backblast of the powerful landmine, but it was all I had. I carefully wriggled my body another inch or two into the sandy soil thinking, "Get low Ranger, the earth is your friend."

The attack commenced. Every weapon system was live: bullets, explosives, mines. The only things not live were the Rangers; everyone was half dead from utter exhaustion. We were completely spent. During the assault, I saw that a teammate had fallen asleep while firing his machine gun; a deadly dangerous thing to observe.

The attack was initiated with our most casualty causing weapons: the claymores. Sixteen simultaneous explosions, immediately to our front, ripped apart the sentries and the missile site. It was too tempting not to watch, so I peeked out from behind the single sandbag that protected my body. Thousands of ball bearings from the landmines violently shredded the people, equipment, and nearby trees.

Our M-60s opened up after the last Claymore exploded, and thousands of bullets tore into anything still vertical. Once the machine guns ceased fire, our assault team swept across the objective to kill, capture and destroy remaining enemy personnel and equipment. Within minutes, the objective was secure, and the world was now safe for democracy. God Bless America.

During this final patrol, we had spent eleven cold nights in the Florida swamps. I now understood what homeless people in Philadelphia must endure every winter. Over that time, we had a total of 14 hours of sleep, an average of one hour and sixteen minutes each day. The cumulative effect of the cold, sleep deprivation, hunger and injuries took their toll on our class.

Graduation

Finally, Ranger training was complete. It took a few days for us to clean up, move back to Fort Benning, and turn in equipment. We were fed two Super Suppers, one in Florida and one at Benning. These were big meals, and we shoveled the chow in. They allowed us to regain some strength.

As our graduation ceremony neared, I was informed I was a candidate for Honor Graduate. I knew we had some good men in our class that had performed with distinction. I was honored to be considered, but I knew I had faded while in Florida. My classmate, Craig Fox, was selected as one of four Honor Graduates. I had been on an extensive patrol with Craig when he had given a remarkable operations order; outdoors in the freezing cold, late at night after days with little or no sleep, he showed no sign of mental or physical fatigue. His leadership abilities were in a different class. He earned the award and my profound respect. But the class had only one Distinguished Honor Graduate – Steve Salazar. Steve was a classmate and future Brigadier General. He received the William O. Darby Award for best tactical and leadership performance during the course. During his last mission, Steve served as the patrol leader for 24 grueling hours, enduring far beyond the normal 4-10-hour shift assigned to most others. It was the final evidence the Ranger Department needed to select him as a cut above the rest.

About eighty of the original 177 men we had started with in November graduated with our class that February. We also picked up about a dozen more Rangers that recycled from previous classes. We had our Ranger tabs pinned on at a simple ceremony on at Fort Benning's Todd Field. The official photo of Ranger Class 3-83 is an enduring reminder of this great test of our minds and bodies.

Ranger Class 3-83

After graduating, I began to heal and get my strength back. My fingers were shredded and infected from dozens of cuts. I would not regain most of the feeling in my fingertips for six months. Fortunately, I could still hold a beer mug while my hands recovered. I flew to Ft. Lauderdale for spring break two weeks later with my friend Mike Willover and moved to Germany in mid-March. I conducted beer drinking operations in both locations. I also used my temporary duty paycheck, earned at Ranger School, to buy a timeshare condo while in Ft. Lauderdale. So ironically, I got a beachfront condo out of my Ranger experience.

Excerpts from my Ranger Diary (Florida Phase):

- 28 Jan—0230 wake up and pack ruck and duffle bag. Jump Master briefing, etc. and take off in C-130 from Lawson Army Airfield. 45-minute flight via Alabama to Eglin AFB. We are fully combat loaded. Jxxx got sick continuously. Six minutes before jump they scrub it but change their mind before we land. Eighth one out the door at 1000 ft. Low jump and fell quickly (First one on the ground). Sandy DZ and penetrated about 8 inches deep. Now in Florida. 2 hours sleep.

- 30 Jan—Wake up 0330. RB-15 assault boat drills in the Gulf of Mexico at 0800 (58 degree water temperature). We threw both tactical officers in (SFC Schriver and Captain Augustine) and then buried them in the sand. Conducted two crossings of the Yellow River using a single rope bridge. Everyone got soaked in the 53 degree water. About a 105 ft wide crossing. Fire Guard tonight. Snake and reptile class. Lots of snakes.

- 1 Feb—Pouring rain all day and lightning. Wind gusts to 60 mph. Ambush during cadre led patrol. Survival, Evasion, Resistance and Escape classes. Slaughter a chicken, rabbit, and goat. 101st Abn chicken head. Slit the goat's throat—lots of blood. Pack for 12-day patrol.3.5 hours.

- 2 Feb—12-day patrol begins. Fox was the PL. Air Mobile insertion is canceled. Winds are too high for choppers (25 mph+) so no food from student pilots. Great OPORD by Fox. Ambush goes well. Humped 15 kilometers. One hour sleep. Very cold nights 22 degrees F.

- 3 Feb—Day 2 of 12 day. I was now platoon leader to plan and conduct the foot movement (1100 m), boat movement (5000m), foot movement (2000m). Did fairly well but I think I failed due to a break in security. Damn! I sent out an R&S team to kill some aggressors on our perimeter. Our team was caught in a hasty ambush. One hour 15 minutes sleep. Mission fragged to boat movement and raid. (droning).

- 4 Feb—Team Leader. Received major plus spot report, so I am all even now. 8000m boat movement ends in disaster as freezing rain, and leaky boats fill them up. My feet were so numbed thought I lost them. Built a fire in the swamps. No chow, no sleep, so cold.

- 5 Feb—Made PLT SGT for actions on the objective. Humped 25 kilometers today. Finally got new water. Lived off 1 gallon for last 5 days. 5100 meters back to patrol base. But D—- fell asleep (RTO), and we left him about 400m behind. This break in contact probably cost me the patrol. 1 hour 15 min sleep.

- 6 Feb—Crossed a neck deep creek (water temp 45 degrees F) at night. One hour sleep. Woke up with frozen feet and clothes.

- 7 Feb—Early morning ambush on convoy. I'm right flank security. Move to clay pits for 20 minutes of chapel. Chaplin is going to be in 7-83 (Ranger Class). Move on for survival meal. Our squad had 4 rabbits and 3 chickens. Hypnotized chickens first to make tender meat. Good meal— boiled with onions, potatoes, lettuce, cabbage, rice, and celery. Not enough for squad, though. Only meal for the day. Move back to garrison to clean up and shower. I feel so clean! My hands and feet are all cut up and infected. Skin is split open at joints on fingers exposing raw flesh. They do not function well as you can tell by my handwriting. 5 hours sleep.

- 8 Feb—0330 wake up and move out for new mission. Hump 22 kilometers. Practice live-fire. Long night moves are brutal. No sleep.

- 9 Feb—Day eight of 12-day patrol. Air Mobile extraction canceled. Moved on foot. Crossed "Turkey Gobbler" Creek. Ambush. One hour sleep.

- 10 Feb—Day 9 of patrol. I am squad leader. Hit by artillery in Patrol Base in morning. 3 casualties. 1 sucking chest wound, 1 blown off leg, 1 shoulder wound. Carry them 500m and call in MEDEVAC choppers. Blocking position that night goes well. Return to FFU (Friendly Forward Unit) for airborne mission next day. 3.5 hours sleep.

- 11 Feb—Jump in (Mass Tactical Combat Equipment) from C-130. Assembly area takes too long. Move 8000m to ambush and 5000 more to Patrol Base. No sleep.

- 12 Feb—Mission is fragged to an ambush. We do too many ambushes -not enough raids. Kept moving through East Bay Swamp (2400m). Then access East Bay River at night and continue another 1000m through swamp. This is where 2 men froze to death in 1977. Cold son of a bitch too. Go 1500m more to patrol base. Mud up to waist in swamp. No fire in PB. No sleep. Prepare for "Santa Rosa Island" attack.

- 13 Feb—DAY 12! Road march and pick up RB15s for boat assault across Gulf of Mexico to Santa Rosa Island. Really dragging. Drive on. Hit the beach on another ambush. Back to boats and withdrawal. Trucked to live-fire site. Moving targets and live ammo. One guy fell asleep 5 times. Very hazardous. Trucked back and clean up. Training is done!
- 17 Feb—1100 hrs. Silver Wings HALO jump in. (High Altitude, Low Opening) and we get our TABS on Todd Field. At last an AIRBORNE RANGER!

(39)

10 Feb   Day #9 of patrol. I am
squad leader. Hit by artillery in
patrol Base in morning. 3 casualties
1 sucking chest wound, 1 blown off leg,
1 shoulder wound. Carry them 500 m
and call in MEDDEVAC Choppers.
Blocking position that night goes well.

ENEMY WITHDRAWAL → 2ND PLT AMBUSH   RETURN TO FFU

3RD PLT BLOCKS RETREATING ENEMY — ROAD — (FRIENDLY FORWARD UNIT)

FOR AIRBORNE MISSION NEXT DAY. $3\frac{1}{2}$ HRS
Sleep.

11 FEB   Jump in (MASS TACTICAL COMBAT
EQUIPMENT) FROM C-130. Assembly Area takes
too long. Move 8000 m to Ambush + 5000 more
to Patrol Base. No sleep

From Ranger School Diary—Florida

[Side note: Twenty-eight years later, my nephew, Nathaniel Curley, went through Ranger School after he graduated from West Point and completed a combat tour in Iraq with the 82nd Airborne Division. I was flying back from a business trip in Australia, and I did not make it to his Ranger ceremony in March 2011. I regret I could not get there in time to pin his tab on. Fortunately, I was able to watch him perform during the Army's 'Best Ranger' competition in April of 2012 and for his Special Forces graduation in November of 2013. Nate now has four tabs: Airborne, Ranger, Sapper and Special Forces. Every one of them must be earned, and they mean something. Only a handful of Americans have all four of these remarkable tactical qualifications.]

World War Grenada

Eight months later, in October 1983, many of the Rangers I had trained with were involved in Operation Urgent Fury. President Reagan authorized the U.S. invasion of Grenada to rescue U.S. medical students and to spank the new communist government that had seized power.

I was stationed in Germany and had no direct role in the operation. However, Grenada was the first major use of U.S. military forces since Vietnam, and only a few weeks after a Hezbollah car bomber destroyed the U.S. Marine barracks at the Beirut Airport. The successful combat action helped to restore the credibility of our military forces. Rangers, other Special Operations Forces, 82nd Airborne Division troopers, and Marines conducted the assault. They were later able to brag about fighting in "the BIG ONE," also satirically referred to as "WW Grenada."

CHAPTER 31
DEFENDING GERMANY

From 1983-1986, I was a Platoon Leader with the 237th Engineer Battalion based in Heilbronn, Germany. As a new lieutenant, I led a 40-man platoon tasked with defending a small sector of the inter-German boundary.

During the Cold War period, Germany was a divided nation. West Germany was on the side of freedom and backed by the United States. East Germany, the Deutsche Demokratische Republik (DDR), was on the side of communism and the Soviet Union.

Combat Engineering in the Cold War

Our nation was prepared, so I thought, for World War III and to fight against the spread of communism. The Army's mission, as part of the North Atlantic Treaty Organization (NATO), was to defend Western Europe from a Soviet-led invasion by the Warsaw Pact. Deploying rapidly from the 237th Engineer Battalion Headquarters at Wharton Barracks, my platoon's mission was to slow down the invading forces (in their tanks and armored vehicles) by emplacing minefields, blowing up bridges, cratering roads, turning towns to rubble and creating other obstacles. If we could slow the enemy and bottle them up into small pockets called 'kill zones,' the good guys from the U.S. Army and Air Force would then be able to destroy them with our tanks, artillery, attack helicopters, and aircraft. This was how we would protect democracy and capitalism in Western Europe. Before my deployment to Germany, as I've told in earlier stories, I was trained at Fort Belvoir, Virginia as a Combat Engineer (often referred to by their specialty code, 12B).

BRIDGEX Goose

Within days of arriving in Germany, I was sent on an annual military exercise called BRIDGEX. As Combat Engineers, one of our wartime missions was building or repairing bridges so our tanks and vehicles could move on the attack. Our mission also included blowing up bridges, to prevent the enemy from using them to attack us. BRIDGEX tested our unit's capabilities.

The outdoor exercise began in March of 1983, on an inlet of the Rhine River near Speyer, Germany. We had classic German weather for that time of year, cold and rainy. There was also plenty of mud. Living outside in the cold, wet rain for a few weeks tends to sap the morale of soldiers. Each of us was usually provided with a semi-hot meal to eat and would sometimes receive a letter from home, but there was not much to look forward to. Despite the cold and wet isolation from the outside world, we knew that this training was necessary and that we were volunteers.

Building an M4T6 Bridge across a dry gap

About a week into the exercise, a hot lunch was delivered to the Float Bridge site on the river bank. Everyone had been looking forward to the meal—you don't realize how much you take hot food for granted until you go without it for a while—and our work immediately stopped. We were all muddy, wet and cold to the bone. As the meal was served, one of the sergeants broke out a loaf of bread and put some peanut butter on it. It smelled great, and he looked perfectly content to enjoy this small pleasure as he sat along the river's edge.

That's when a bold goose, probably from a nearby nest, walked up to the NCO and demanded a piece of the action. All eyes were now on the sergeant and the goose to see what would happen next. The NCO took out a piece of bread and tossed it to the goose. The bird snatched it and quickly scarfed it down. The NCO took another bite of his food. The goose came in closer. The soldier offered another piece of bread, and this time, the goose took it directly from his hand. They were quickly becoming buddies. This was followed by a third piece of bread. The goose was thoroughly enjoying the free meal.

But that's when the sergeant turned the tables on Big Bird. He pulled out the next piece of bread, flashed it to the goose, and then opened a bottle of Texas hot sauce. After soaking the bread in the jalapeño juice, he offered it to the trusting goose. The bird confidently waddled up and snatched the oozing bread from the NCO's hand and woofed it down. The reaction was immediate and very human-like. The goose's eyes popped open to the size of marbles. Now at the mercy of the fiery Texas Pete, the goose flung its beak wide open and let out a panicked scream. Immediately turning and sprinting for the water, the goose thrashed its wings violently and stuck its head under the surface in an attempt to consume the entire contents of the Rhine River.

By this point, those of us watching the show were rolling in tears as this goose tried to shake off the fire that burned within. I can't recall laughing so hard in my entire life and am glad I wasn't drinking milk at the time. This incredibly funny sight paid for at the expense of an overly bold goose, was exactly what we needed to brighten our cold, dreary day and lift the morale of our troops.

But it didn't end there. After spending several minutes in the water trying to recover, the goose waddled back on shore and approached the NCO again. We couldn't believe an animal could be so stupid. The sergeant shook the bottle of hot sauce and soaked another piece of bread. Yes, the bird took the bait and replayed the theatrical scene all over again. Luckily for the goose, the lunch break was soon over, or else it probably would have returned for a third round. My gut hurt for several days due to laughing so hard. This incident was the highlight of the multi-week exercise. Whenever someone mentioned Speyer to me in the following years, I immediately thought of the battle of brains between the NCO and goose.

For those readers who are members of PETA, let it be confirmed I was just a witness to these events. The goose lived. Additionally, justice was served as the goose was able to exact some measure of revenge by crapping all over our project site.

Grafenwoehr, Germany

Shortly after my arrival in Germany, I was deployed for four months to the major Army training area in Europe, located at Grafenwoehr. My unit, the 237th Engineer Battalion, was part of the larger 18th Engineer Task Force involved in a major construction project, called the 'Range 42 Upgrade.' Our mission was to upgrade the 3.7-kilometer training range so the new U.S. Bradley Fighting vehicles could train effectively against simulated Soviet forces.

During the project, our unit installed 42 enemy vehicle silhouettes and 132 enemy soldier silhouettes, targets for the new Bradley vehicles while they were on the attack. The computerized enemy targets would move on tracks as they were fired on by American gun crews who needed to 'qualify' on their new Bradley's. We also built the other infrastructure and facilities for the new range: roads, five troop barracks, a dining facility, and 19 kilometers of underground cable - all high-speed technology for 1983.

The project had special meaning to me. A few years earlier, I had been on the military funeral detail for Omar Bradley, the last 5-star general from World War II. The new U.S. vehicle was named after General Bradley.

The range had been actively used for tank and artillery gunnery since the 1870s by the Prussians, the Germans, the Russians, the Brits, the French, the Americans, Canadians, and probably other military forces. Consequently, there was unexploded ordinance (UXO) all over the place, including tank rounds, artillery, mortars, and anti-tank rockets. In many ways, it was like working in a massive minefield.

Combat Engineers spent weeks clearing these potentially lethal devices across the entire range area before the real construction began. The initial clearing operations successfully removed or destroyed 80-90% of the unexploded ordnance our troops could find on the surface. They could not, however, find what was buried beneath. Our construction crews found plenty more after they began digging.

Most of the UXO was inert, not designed to explode. However, among the thousands of rounds we uncovered, hundreds were live and potentially unstable. Early in the project, one of our vehicles ran over an old artillery shell which detonated. The driver survived, but the vehicle was badly damaged.

Remains of an armored vehicle used for target practice

Tragically, we had a young sergeant killed when his front-end bucket loader overturned. Driving too fast and not strapped in, he was thrown out of the 12-ton construction vehicle. Unfortunately, the 'roll cage,' designed to protect the driver inside, crushed his head when the equipment turned over. I arrived at the site, a gruesome scene, a few minutes after the accident. The loss was particularly tragic as the soldier's wife, and child were moving from the U.S. that week to join him in Germany.

By October, we had successfully completed the project and returned to Wharton Barracks in Heilbronn. There, I finally got to live in the apartment I had been renting since March. For our extensive efforts, everyone in the battalion received a medal, a certificate of appreciation, or a kick in the ass. One of the best rewards after returning home from Grafenwoehr was pizza. We learned there was an actual Pizza Hut only two hours away in Frankfurt.

Some of us had not eaten American pizza for two years, so we piled into a car and made a four-hour round-trip to satisfy the urgent desire.

Pay Day

At the end of the month, we had to pay the troops. This was before the direct deposit of electronic checks, and the Army paid its soldiers with a check or in cash. It was the soldier's choice. Consequently, I was often given the additional duty as "Pay Officer," officially called a "Class A Agent."

On payday, I carried up to $100,000 in cash–both U.S. and German currency–drawn from the local military finance office. I had an armed guard (with an M16 rifle), and I carried a .45 caliber pistol. Soldiers lined up to visit me in an office. It was an interesting day. Soldiers I had not seen all month miraculously showed up and presented their paycheck to me. I would pay them

Time to Pay the troops

in U.S. dollars, German marks, or a combination of both. That meant I had to convert U.S. currency, and the exchange rate varied daily. What a pain in the butt. If I was any amount of money short, I was accountable for the difference. To reduce errors, Pay Officers counted the currency twice and then made the soldier also count it. As soon as the troops got their check, they had the rest of the day off for 'Payday Activities.' They would have a few hours to pay their rent, utility bills, car loans, as well as buy groceries. After a few days, some them were out of money after investing their monthly earnings at the local bar or buying some companionship at the local "50-Mark Park."

Explosives Training

Combat Engineers like to build things. But it's far more fun to blow stuff up. And the Army paid us to do it. What an awesome job for a former paperboy. Once again, I'd like to thank the American taxpayers for funding all my explosives training and three-year tour in Europe. Trust me, it was money well-spent.

I was initially trained on landmines and demolitions at the Engineer Officer Basic Course at Fort Belvoir, Virginia. Safety was always emphasized during the instruction. Nobody wanted to make a mistake and be the poster child for the Army safety program or possibly win the next "Darwin Award." [Google that one. Okay, okay... to not sidetrack you with that, I'll give you this. The award's tagline and motto is: "In Search of Smart."]

There was, however, a greater purpose for all the explosives training. The U.S. Army was preparing for World War III in Europe. If 'the balloon goes up' (this phrase you should Google), thousands of Soviet and Warsaw Pact tanks and vehicles could pour into Western Europe. We (the U.S. and our Allies) needed to slow them down by creating impediments like blowing up bridges, cratering roads or blocking them with downed trees. We would also place minefields around these obstacles to prevent the commie bastards from simply driving around (bypassing) them.

If the combat engineers could slow down and jam up the invading communist forces, our attack helicopters, tanks, and artillery could counterattack and finish them off. That was the tactical war plan. My platoon was one of the pawns in this much-anticipated chess match. We hoped it would never come to pass.

We learned how to handle plastic explosives and to calculate how much charge we needed to blow up a bridge, knock down trees, or crater roads. We learned where to place the charges and whether they needed to be tamped (covered or buried) or elevated to maximize their effect.

But if the Combat Engineer wasn't sure of his calculations, he risked not placing enough explosives on the target, which would render them less effective or possibly ineffective. The solution—as taught us—was to round up the quantity. We called that equation "P for Plenty." If you calculated that five pounds of composition C-4 explosive was enough to cut through a steel bridge girder, and wanted to be sure it was destroyed, then round it up to 6-8 lbs. There's a caveat, though. Sometimes the 'P for Plenty' rule did get soldiers in trouble.

Once we had mastered the basics, we got more sophisticated. We practiced how to set up a series of explosive charges on a ring main, a big loop made of detonating cord (aka "det cord"). Det chord came in a big roll, resembling a plastic clothesline, only stiffer. Once ignited, ring main would burn in both directions to ensure that all the charges would explode, even if the loop were cut by enemy fire or artillery.

Det cord burns extremely fast, at approximately 20,000 feet per second. That's about four miles per second. Don't blink. In fact, it appears to explode rather than burn. The burn is incredibly fast to make sure all the charges on the ring main blow up at or near the same time. If you wrapped enough det chord around a tree and set it off, the tree could be cut in half. Important safety tip #1: don't use det chord as shoe laces or to tie up enemy prisoners... unless you don't like your feet or the prisoner.

We would usually dual prime each circuit. That means we used two different ways to set off the explosion. We liked to use both an electric and a non-electric (burning fuse) blasting cap. The electric cap was initiated with a small handheld blasting machine. Important safety tip #2: Don't let another soldier play with the initiating device while you are setting up the explosives, or he may blow up all your soldiers. That type of accident happens more often than we'd like.

Now if everything was set up correctly, we could connect a dozen or more explosive charges to the ring main. The C-4 explosive we used was very stable stuff, and it could take some abuse. You could burn it, and it would not explode. You could throw it against a wall, and it would not explode. A blasting cap is needed to create both the simultaneous heat and shock required to detonate the plastic explosives. This was important because we carried C-4 in our backpacks and would also parachute with it. Nobody wanted our paratroopers exploding when they hit the ground. But, if C-4 was subjected to intense heat and shock at the same time... BOOM! Important safety tip #3: Don't burn C-4 as a fuel and use it to warm your military rations. And don't stomp out the burning C-4 after the meal is cooked. You will blow off your foot and maybe a lot more. Short guys, closer to the ground, are in particular jeopardy.

In addition to C-4, there were several other kinds of explosives, including Semtex (from Czechoslovakia) or commercial dynamite. If we didn't have any of the good stuff, we learned how to make Improvised Explosive Devices (IEDs) like those that, twenty years later, became widely used against the U.S. in the Iraq and Afghanistan wars. Ironically SUV was attacked with an IED in Iraq, but fortunately, this paperboy had nine lives and lived to talk about it.

Okay, now back to the story.

No matter how carefully you prepare all the demo charges and set up the ring main, things don't always go well. If an explosive charge did not detonate when it was supposed to, we would wait a few more minutes. It could be a slow-burning fuse. If the wait got to be more than 20 minutes or so, some (un)lucky guy from the demo team—usually the one who set up the charges—had to go back to the area and determine why the explosion did not occur. You don't want to be this guy. But if you are that guy, take the blasting machine with you, so some other soldier doesn't push the plunger again while you are troubleshooting ring main (see safety tip #2 above).

During one exercise at Fort AP Hill, Virginia, we set up 200 pounds of road cratering charges and dual primed the circuit. We measured off a five-minute fuse, lit that puppy and quickly walked about 500 meters to get out of the danger zone, where flying debris could not injure us.

Just as we got to our safe spot and prepared to observe the explosion, two *superior* officers decided to visit the range and inspect the demo training. So 'Major Einstein' and 'Captain America' came rolling up in a jeep, looking for a dozen lieutenants that were now hunkered down 500 meters away waiting for the blast. They unwittingly stopped their jeep about 10 meters from the buried explosive charges. The fuse continued to burn. The two officers did not see the ring main lying in the tall grass. We yelled to (at) them to clear the area, but they couldn't hear us from that distance, particularly with their engine running. When Einstein could not find us, he got back in the jeep and sped off. We let out a big sigh of relief as they cleared the area about one minute before the explosion.

But the show wasn't over. Seconds later, we heard helicopters approaching. Then, four Bell UH-1 Iroquois (aka Hueys), flying a trail formation (in a line) at treetop level, came directly over the demo site. Really. You can't make this crap up. There were only about 20 seconds left on the burning fuse, give or take 15. I was convinced we were going to kill at least one aircrew. My career was going to end before I got to see my tour in Germany. A few seconds after the last bird passed over the charges, they detonated, launching rocks and debris a few hundred feet in the air. The explosion created a small mushroom cloud. A few seconds earlier, and we would have knocked those guys out of the sky. The pilots must not have read their map, where it clearly marked the location as an impact area—one to avoid.

* * *

We used explosives, demolitions, and land mines to prevent the enemy from capturing important objectives. However, some really big jobs needed special-purpose explosives. On a scale far above conventional explosives, a few 12Bs also were trained on the employment of atomic demolitions (ADMs). ADMs were small 'backpack' nuclear weapons used to quickly blow up a major airfield, autobahn crossing or seaport to keep it from being captured. As you can imagine, there were very sensitive issues concerning the use of these weapons. Our soldiers had to be carefully screened for personal reliability. A 2nd Lieutenant with a backpack nuclear weapon gets instant respect, outranking any four-star general. That lieutenant was potentially the world's most dangerous suicide bomber.

During one ADM training mission in Germany, we flew to our target area in a Black Hawk helicopter and set up the weapon, an inert replica. Once we set the timer, we jumped back into the chopper and sped off. After passing a few nearby hills, we dropped the aircraft to the ground, jumped out and quickly disconnected all the helicopter electronics to protect them from being fried by the weapon's electromagnetic pulse (EMP). We immediately crawled into a sewer to await the imminent nuclear explosion. When the pilot asked what he should do to get ready for the (simulated) blast, I told him, "Take your helmet off," I gestured for him to do that, to pretend it was the real deal. "Put your head between your knees." Okay, done. "And kiss your ass goodbye."

Surviving an actual ADM mission was possible, but far from certain. A nuclear detonation had multiple characteristics, including a massive blast, searing heat, shockwave, nuclear radiation, and EMP. Fun stuff. Good luck getting through that day, Ranger. And if you screwed up... it wasn't just drop and give me 50... the penalty could be not just your own life but those of a lot of other people, including civilians in the area. Fortunately, the United States never had to use this weapon, and these battlefield nukes have since been removed from our nuclear arsenal.

During my final ADM exercise, I was in a remote location with limited communications. Once I had returned from the mission, I was told that my father had died. It was like an ADM had gone off; I was numb at first and then felt the pain. Let me back up and tell you the rest of this story: I spoke to my mother before the exercise, and she told me father was very ill and unlikely to survive the next few days. I told my company commander, thinking he would offer to get some other lieutenant to lead the exercise. That thought did not even cross his mind, so I just drove on with the mission. Maybe he had no other ADM qualified officers, or maybe he was just an insensitive ass. Then, perhaps proving the latter, when my father died, my CO withheld the news until I returned from the field the next day. That really soured my thinking about staying in the Army.

Hohenfels

At the demo range near Hohenfels, I was no longer being trained. I was leading the training for our troops.

Demo training

Hohenfels was the site of a legendary incident where a variation of the 'P for Plenty' rule got some soldiers in trouble. It almost necessitated creating a new rule, 'T for Too Much' as a common-sense check.

The troops were training on steel-cutting charges with their unit. Part of a steel 'I-beam' was rigged with charges and detonated. If it were done correctly, the steel would be cut in two. Now steel can fly hundreds of meters during an explosion. To prevent injuries, the I-beam and explosives were placed in a special bunker to contain the shrapnel.

The lieutenant in charge wanted to get rid of all the remaining explosives. It was near the end of the training day and turning in unused explosives and ammunition meant his platoon would be working for several more hours. The standard practice was to blow up everything you were issued that day and shoot up all the ammo. There would be nothing left to turn back in. The lieutenant put all his remaining explosives, over 150 pounds, inside the steel-cutting bunker which was only certified to withstand about 10 lbs. He threw in road cratering charges, shaped charges, blocks of C-4 plastic explosive and several rolls of detonation cord. He primed the fuse and backed his unit away from the bunker. The massive blast shattered the bunker and threw metal and rocks all over the training area. The seismic wave shook the nearby housing areas. Within minutes of the unauthorized detonation, the lieutenant, his battalion and the entire chain of command were thrown off the Hohenfels training area. There certainly were further punitive consequences.

Our unit, the 7th Engineer Brigade had a new deputy commander who liked to hold all soldiers financially accountable, for any damage they negligently caused. That included vehicle accidents on icy roads (if you weren't using chains), a fire that burned down the field kitchen (if you failed to clean the grease traps), missing equipment, etc. That's fair, but the command emphasis on docking pay made many soldiers want to avoid any risks.

In a supreme irony, one day the deputy commander visited the demo range. My platoon had set up explosives and moved to a bunker to observe the detonation. We were well within the casualty radius of the blast but protected inside the bunker. The deputy brigade commander parked his military vehicle (CUCV) next to the bunker and moved inside, with us, to safely watch the explosion. His choice of parking spot was unwise. A big rock from the blast hit his vehicle's roof and caused extensive damage. We all knew it was a foreseeable accident—none of us would have parked there—for which our soldiers would have been held financially liable. But no one wanted to ask if the deputy commander was going to pay for this damage to his vehicle. It seemed like a double standard.

ENTEC

Military training in Germany was always interesting. One of my favorite events was the Euro-NATO Engineer Training Course (ENTEC), where we trained with Combat Engineers from Germany, France, the United Kingdom, and Belgium, among other nations.

During this two-week course, we studied each other's equipment and capabilities, learned how to jointly prepare target folders, and emplace demolition charges secured in special bunkers near the border.

The best part of ENTEC was its location, Munich, the undisputed beer capital of the world. When the training day was over, many of the ENTEC students headed for the pubs. And so, it was in this way that beer, always the foundation of diplomacy, became the single most important component for forming collegial relationships with our NATO allies.

It was a tough job—protecting democracy and capitalism in Western Europe—but someone had to do it. If we were all going to die in World War III, we wanted to make sure we enjoyed these pre-war years.

The Border

We did not routinely work on West German-East German border, so I took my platoon there to see what conditions were like at the "Iron Curtain" where communism faced off against the free countries of Europe. The communists were serious about keeping their citizens captive behind it. They had built a formidable obstacle and guard system, to prevent those in East Germany from escaping to the West.

Only a few East German citizens, such as farmers, were permitted to live within five kilometers of the border. Nearby trees were cut down to allow the communist guards—in their towers placed every few hundred meters—to see and shoot anyone sneaking toward the border. Dogs would patrol in some areas, along where two fences had been built about 50 meters apart to slow escapees so they could be trapped and shot. Inside these fences were land mines.

The vertical obstacle closest to the border was 12 feet high and had razor sharp edges to cut the hands of anyone attempting to climb it. Along the top of the fence were a series of "self-shooting mines" that fired a shotgun-like blast along the fence line to kill anyone who had gotten that far. Not many East Germans were successful getting across this barrier to freedom.

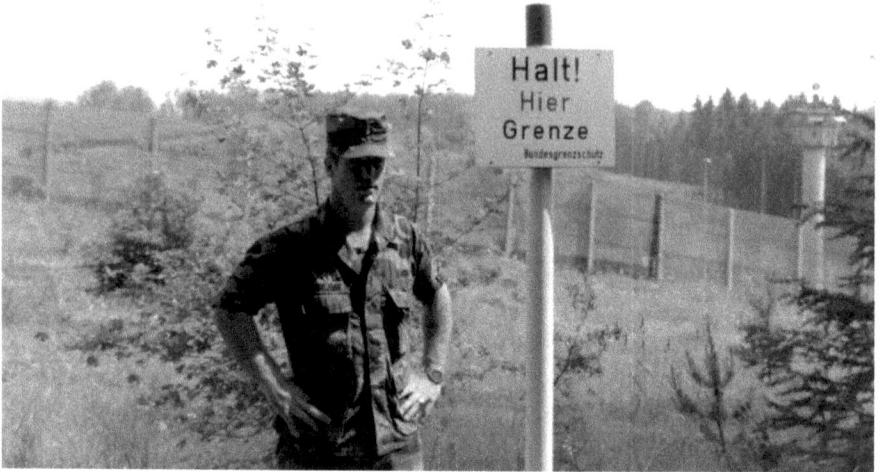

Patrolling on the East German Border

Obstacle system outlined at East German Border

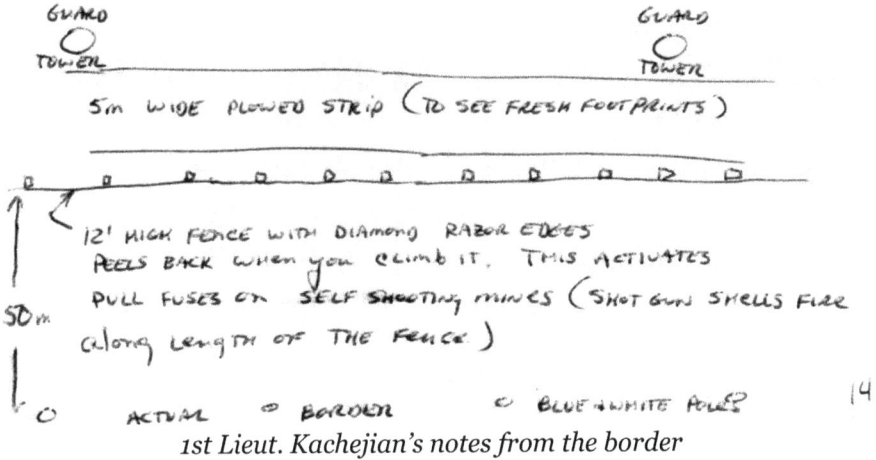

1st Lieut. Kachejian's notes from the border

East German guard outside the minefield

East German Patrol passes by

Highway 19 passed through this area, one of the few legal crossing points connecting East and West Germany. This was the site of many escape attempts by desperate East Germans. Occasionally, they were permitted by their government to travel briefly to the West for a family funeral or some other important event. Once in the West, many would not return. The communist government would often punish the relatives of these defectors by throwing them in jail or stripping them of their careers.

To catch potential escapees, a fake West German checkpoint had been constructed inside East Germany. East German citizens, with official permission to travel to the West for a few days, would depart an official East German checkpoint on their side of the border.

The travelers would be sternly reminded that they would be soon entering West Germany and must return in a few days. The next checkpoint they approached flew a West German flag and had guards in West German uniforms. Unfamiliar with the border and believing they were finally in a free country; some East Germans would declare themselves political refugees to the guards—who were not West German—and ask to defect. The travelers were immediately arrested and sent to jail. Viewers on the Western side of the border could see the false flag and guards but were powerless to stop the deception.

Fake West German Border Checkpoint inside Communist East Germany
(Highway 19)

Screwing with the Commies

One of my friends, Pete DeMarco, was on the border while conducting summer training as a West Point cadet. He noticed the East German guards intensely staring at him across the border. Every time Pete exposed his left shoulder to the communist guard tower, the East German soldiers would glare through their binoculars, try to take photos, and start looking through a reference book. They would shake their heads, pick up a field phone and evidently were calling higher authority at their headquarters.

Pete quickly realized they were looking at the strange shoulder patch sewn on his left shoulder. Each U.S. Army unit has a unique patch to signify what division or brigade a soldier is assigned to. The East Germans studied all the American patches and, consequently, could report which U.S. Army units were patrolling the border. The First Infantry Division had a big red '1' on their patch. The 101st Airborne Division had an eagle's head with the word Airborne embroidered above it. Since Pete was a cadet, he wore a shoulder patch with a Spartan helmet unique to West Point. Since cadets don't usually patrol the border, the East German guards were baffled by the new 'Special Unit.'

Pete decided to start screwing with them. After he had finished his patrol that day, he headed to the Post Exchange, a military store like a K-Mart or Wal-Mart, where soldiers and their families can shop. Pete found some sew-on Disney patches intended for children's clothing. He cut off his West Point patch, and with a quick few stitches sewed on Daffy Duck.

The next morning, back at the border, as Pete approached the communist guard tower, he shielded his left shoulder, trying not to overtly reveal the patch. Occasionally, he would make an abrupt movement, ensuring that the guards got a brief glimpse of it. The binoculars came out, and cameras started clicking as East German guards frantically flipped through their field manual trying to determine which U.S. Army Division had a duck on its shoulder patch. The East Germans picked up the field phone and called their local headquarters to report a new special U.S. Army unit was patrolling the border. Perhaps the duck signified an amphibious unit. That morning behind the East German line, intel on the 'Duck Brigade' was priority number one. No doubt communist patrols were strengthened along the inter-German border.

On another day, Pete showed up wearing a Goofy shoulder patch. The East Germans were ready. They assigned more guards and more cameras on this sector for the border. Something suspicious was going on with the Americans. Pete gave the commie bastards a couple of quick glimpses of this strange dog patch. Heavy work with binoculars, cameras, field manuals and telephone calls soon followed. Perhaps Pete belonged to a special canine assault unit of the U.S. Army. Would they use German Shepherds or American-bred Pit Bulls?

Later, Pete had an opportunity to patrol the border between Germany and communist Czechoslovakia, which was not as heavily defended. Every few meters, a small stump marked the actual border, and Russian soldiers would patrol on the Czech side of the stumps. Rarely did the patrols see each other, but the border stumps encouraged the free market system to flourish. Whenever Americans patrolled, they would leave a few goodies, such as Playboy magazines, on the stumps. The implied message: "Yes, the chicks in the West are gorgeous. You should defect and meet some." A few hours later, a Russian patrol would pick up the Playboy and leave behind a Soviet Army belt buckle, prized by the U.S. military as a souvenir of their time protecting Western Europe. This low-level trading helped keep the peace and made the day interesting.

Eventually, Pete ran out of Disney patches and Playboy magazines, and his brief summer training in Germany concluded. He headed home to

West Point and shared his epic stories of military deception with many of his friends.

During my tour in Europe, we always tried to acquire pieces of uniforms and equipment used by the communists—like the aforementioned Soviet Army belt buckle. Some items were rather difficult to obtain, but they made great collectibles. I was able to get some buttons from an East German soldier. While he was a bit drunk and distracted, a German friend of mine named Udo cut them off his uniform.

Hollow Force

Our military is a national insurance policy, and its primary purpose is to deter war. If it needs to fight, it must do so as quickly and inexpensively as it can (measured in lives and treasury).

That sounds good, but one of the glaringly obvious problems I found after I was commissioned in 1982 was that the U.S. military was a hollow force. Our military had been cut so deeply after Vietnam that it could not defend the nation properly.

I arrived in Germany in 1983 in the early stages of that recovery, but the scars of neglect were still visible—and felt. For years, the Army could not afford to buy new equipment. My platoon's wartime mission was to emplace minefields and blow up bridges to slow down the advance of thousands of Soviet tanks and armored vehicles attempting to penetrate Western Europe. I was responsible for five military vehicles and 40 men. However, our vehicles averaged about 30 years old and constantly broke down. We often joked that they were older than our troops. Due to past budget cuts, none of my five vehicles worked, and there was little money for repair parts. If war broke out, my platoon had no means to travel the 150 miles to the border to defend our sector of Germany. The Soviets would capture key bridges, airfields, and major cities, which would result in dramatically increased casualties among our fighting forces.

I left Germany wiser about how things really were and with the hope that our nation's leaders would also see these readiness issues and correct them. Fortunately, President Reagan when he was elected made a decision to re-invest in the military. It slowly began to recover from years of neglect.

CHAPTER 32
PATROLLING, P2 & WALDHEIDE

The Patrol

Twice a year, John Guidotti, Erik Fleischner and I would volunteer to take some young soldiers on a three-day tactical exercise to teach leadership skills. It was part of their training and development to become new Noncommissioned Officers (NCOs). John, Erik and I were all recent graduates of the Army Ranger course and considered subject matter experts in small unit military tactics. We had outstanding support from Staff Sergeants Michael Akins and Michael Cabrera.

The exercise included a 24-hour patrol through the German woods. We started in the afternoon. Moving stealthily through the forest, we needed to get to the top of a cliff before nightfall. At that point, we would teach the soldiers how to rappel down the cliffs. Along the way, we would 'pop smoke' to simulate a chemical attack, be attacked by sniper fire, set up an ambush on an enemy patrol and conduct a raid on an enemy-held position. The next day, our patrol would return to the barracks and review how we did.

Not all of these training exercises went according to the plan. Germany was a crowded country, and we often operated near civilian areas. Several times we startled locals with our simulated combat operations. And that leads me to sidetrack a bit here, to give you a sense of how tense things were at times.

Pershing Missile Base

Our training was complicated because our patrol area ran near the highly secure Waldheide site, where the United States had just deployed Pershing 2 (P2) nuclear missiles. Authorized by President Reagan, these missiles pointed at the Soviet Union and were intended to counter the threat of Soviet SS-20 nuclear missiles targeting Western Europe.

Anti-nuclear protesters—rumored to be supported by the Soviet Union, often camped outside the Waldheide site. Through heightened political tension, they attempted to force the withdrawal of P2s from Europe. We wanted to avoid contact with these protest groups during our training. Tragically, a P2 missile (one without a nuclear warhead) had exploded at this base, killing three soldiers and causing a major international incident. It was rumored a nearby protester equipped with a sniper rifle, from a tree outside the perimeter of the site, had fired at the missile and set off the solid rocket propellant. I was in the medical clinic at Wharton Barracks on January 11, 1985, when they brought in the charred remains of one of the soldiers.

Immediately after the incident, our engineer battalion was tasked with installing vertical camouflage nets around the missile site. The nets formed a visual screen blocking reporters and demonstrators from easily seeing inside the site. Captain Chris Young had his troops working for many weeks, in the bitter cold, to complete that urgent project. There were no more major incidents, but the Cold War was still in full swing.

Now, back to the patrol.

Things You Find in the Woods

After we snuck our 23-man patrol across a German road, we stopped about 50 meters inside the woods. I fired off some blank rounds from my M16 rifle and announced that our patrol leader had just been KIA'd (Killed In Action). It was another soldier's turn to be graded on how well they led their men. I assigned a new soldier to take charge as the patrol leader, telling him to continue the mission in five minutes.

As soon as I finished talking, SSG Akins grabbed me by the arm, and said: "Sir, we have a problem."

I looked at him. "What's up sergeant?"

Still holding my arm, he turned me and pointed. The sun was setting; the German forest was getting dark. At first, I didn't notice what he meant for me to see. I glanced at him, and he stabbed his finger toward a tree not far from us. Then I saw it. "'Houston, we have a problem,'" was my first thought as I focused on the object.

"I think that's a dead guy," said Akins. "Hanging from that tree."

The body was tied to a limb. This was not a part of the training activities planned for this patrol. My mind raced to grasp what my eyes were seeing. Something about the scene seemed off. The victim had a rope around their neck, and they were sitting on the ground. The rope was taut, tied to a branch only five feet off the ground. Somehow this person had hung themselves by simply tying the rope and then sitting down. The line—not long enough to let their weight entirely rest on the ground—had stretched their neck up and back, as if they looked at the sky, choking them until they had asphyxiated. How could anyone have that amount of self-discipline? The instinctual will to live would cause almost anyone to stand up. The sergeant and I moved closer to inspect it. I shook my head as I looked down at the corpse. Definitely, no CPR was required.

Badly decomposed, the body's neck had stretched, distended to about 15 inches long. The ears were like cauliflower, and gray flesh had sloughed off the face and scalp like a large glob of wax melted on the side of a candle. The torso had shrunk inside its clothes and had evidently been exposed to weather for some time. Maybe it's a prank, I hoped. Perhaps a rotted pig, dressed in clothing, made to look like a human suicide. I had a couple of my soldiers illuminate the body with their flashlights to help me inspect the carcass. Then I saw the ulna and radius bones exposed on one arm. No, it was human. And I was quite certain the victim was a German. The guy had brought a coat hanger with him to the woods and hung his jacket on another tree branch before he died. Germans were tidy like that.

What a strange—and sad—way to die. And it was only 100 meters from the fence line of the Waldheide P2 missile site. Could this be a protester? Why would they kill themselves so deep in the woods? Surely, if this were a protester, it would have served their cause to have done it near the main gate of the missile base. Somewhere that would guarantee local news coverage. The main entrance was a much more plausible location for suicide.

That's when my Ranger training kicked in. Maybe the body was booby-trapped, an attempt to create a bigger story by killing some first responders. I quickly checked the area for trip wires but found none. My suspicions took another direction. Was this a murder set up to look like a suicide? Were we now disturbing the evidence at a crime scene? Oh crap, I had just fired off blank rounds, and my ammo casings were lying somewhere nearby in the woods.

After assessing the situation for two or three minutes, we decided to alert the authorities. We made a radio call to our military team near the cliff site, which had a medic on hand. I also decided to step out of the woods and flag down a German vehicle to ask the driver to report the situation to local authorities.

Unfortunately, our radio call to the team at the cliff site was misinterpreted. They thought a U.S. soldier had been killed. One of the team members, dressed in camouflage and carrying a rifle, ran to the Waldheide fence line screaming to get some help. The guards at the nuclear missile site were confused and thought it might be a terrorist attack. Fortunately, they did not shoot the messenger.

Meanwhile, there I stood, heavily camouflaged, in the road trying to wave down a German car in the darkness. I broke out a flashlight to help me signal. When a car with two young German women pulled over, I used my best broken German to explain that our patrol had found a dead civilian in the woods. "Please notify the police and have them send an ambulance." Surprisingly, they understood my message, but I had doubts it would be passed on soon enough to matter. Being a multi-tasking bachelor, for a fleeting moment, I thought about getting their phone numbers, but it wasn't quite the appropriate time.

Staying on the dark road, I flagged down the next vehicle, a taxi. He stopped, and I repeated the story. This guy had a dispatch radio in his vehicle, and this time, I was confident the message would get through to the local authorities.

I then went back into the woods to check on the patrol. The young soldiers were now clustered in a small group waiting for further instructions. They looked up at me.

"We're taking a tactical pause in the exercise until authorities arrive," I told them.

One of the troopers looked over at the body then at me. "Sir, who do you think the dead guy is?"

"We aren't sure yet," I caught the eye of one of the sergeants then looked back at the young man who had asked the question. "He could be a soldier that got separated from us during our last patrol." That was a false rumor we joked about later back at the barracks. But I knew it would discourage the troops from wandering off for the rest of the night.

A few minutes later, in the distance, I heard the distinct sound of a German krankenwagen (ambulance) approaching. Herman the German was on the way, and it was time for me to get back on the side of the road and flag them down. The siren sound got closer and closer. Then I saw the lights come over the crest of a hill and the vehicle screeched to a stop. The two-man ambulance crew jumped out and started to run toward me. I held both hands up and yelled, "Langsum, Langsum." You're not saving anyone today buddy. I led the two men into the woods and showed them the body. The nearby troops moved away. I explained to the ambulance crew, "We found the body just a short while ago. When you search the area, you're going to find M16 ammunition shell casings from our patrol." I was not sure if they even paid any attention to what I had just told them. They were both on their knees studying the body.

One medic turned to the other and said, "Drei monate" (three months). The other medic replied, "Nein, sechs" (No, six).

I gave the medics my contact info and told the troops to ruck up, as we were behind schedule and needed to move out. When we returned to the barracks area the next morning, I had to go to the local military police station and give a statement. The only word back I heard was that the victim was a German who had attempted suicide before and had been missing several months.

Attacking the Cliff Site

On another patrol, we moved toward the top of local cliffs to raid an enemy position holding the terrain. Our young troops attacked the site using grenade and mortar simulators along with machine gun fire to rip apart the enemy stronghold. All of these explosions are thunderous, but they typically do not create shrapnel or inflict injury. Unfortunately, some Germans were having a cookout in the woods at the bottom of the cliff site and had no idea what was about to happen. They had inadvertently joined our training. When the explosions started, the picnickers panicked and ran for their cars. They sped off leaving their food behind for 23 hungry troops. Yum. We didn't touch the chow, but it sure was tempting.

Later that evening, a German man, walking his dog on a leash, unknowingly approached our perimeter. Our soldiers had set up a tripwire on the trail that triggered a land mine (simulator) and an illumination flare. In combat conditions, the real thing would kill any approaching enemy and allow our troops to see any others nearby. The civilian and dog were quickly at the wire, and we had no way to warn him. Boom! Whoosh! The surprised and stunned German took off running with his dog. The guy probably crapped himself. Our troops knew this man was not their intended target and held their machine gun fire. At least we knew our tripwire worked well.

Rappelling site

Once the cliff site was captured, John Guidotti set up the rope lines, and we taught our soldiers how to rappel off a 70-foot cliff. For most troops, it was their first experience, and they were a bit nervous. John and I demonstrated how it was done, emphasizing the safety precautions. Then we inspected each soldier's Swiss seat (rig) and snapped them into the rappelling line.

It was nearing dark, and for safety reasons, we wanted to complete the rappels with some daylight left. Most of the troops went over the cliff edge with a little encouragement and bounded their way down to the base, but some men needed a bit more prodding. One soldier simply could not step off the cliff. He was extremely nervous and spent several minutes backing up to the edge, only to change his mind. The entire patrol waited on him. He was scared and embarrassed, but I needed to get him moving.

"If you want to pass this leadership course, you need to get the hell off my cliff!" I pulled out a 12-inch Bowie knife that I used as a motivational tool. I wanted to impress on him that if he did not get off the cliff, I might cut the rope. He could rappel, or he could fall, the choice was his. "Now move out soldier."

He took me seriously, and immediately stepped off the edge and clumsily slid down the rope. His teammates cheered him to the bottom. He had saved face but didn't volunteer to do it again. I knew he was relieved and proud he had passed the test. No one ever asked me if I was really going to cut his rope, so I left them thinking I was dead serious. After all, that's how the Ranger instructors had taught me a few years earlier in the mountains of northern Georgia.

On another patrol, we were accompanied by a reporter, SP4 Craig Beason, from the brigade newspaper. This paper published stories each month, and the 237th Engineer Battalion's Basic NCO Leadership Course was the feature story. Luckily for Beason, we had more drama at the cliff site again. This time, one of our soldiers failed to tuck in his uniform, and his camouflage blouse got jammed in the D-ring of his harness. Hanging ten feet from the top of the cliff, he could not descend any further. SP4 Richard Ziehr, an experienced mountaineer, ran an emergency line down the cliff alongside the original one. Ziehr then climbed down and tried to cut the soldier's uniform free to unjam the harness, a fruitless effort. After a while, the soldier complained that his legs were numb from blood circulation being cut off.

After a few minutes of discussing options, we decided to pull him back up the cliff. This approach had risks, as the soldier could break free and fall during the attempt. There weren't any better ideas. Two of the troops started to pull the soldier back up. Unfortunately, it was an overhanging cliff, and the soldier was scraping his face and body during the hoist. Tied into a rope at the top, I got down on my belly, leaned over the edge and grabbed the guy under his armpits. He struggled to hold the line as I desperately tried to do an arm curl with this 200-pound soldier and pull him up the last three feet.

Now we had *two* guys in a bad position. I was worried that both of us would dump out of our Swiss seats and smash on the rocks. Hey, at least the brigade reporter would get exclusive photos of our deaths. At that moment, SSG Akins jumped into action. He crawled my back, grabbed my Swiss seat with his left hand, and reached over the cliff with his right. His effort made all the difference, as the combined pulling by the troops on the rope, Akins, and myself propelled the soldier over the top of the cliff. We dragged him away from the edge and had the medics check him for injuries. Meanwhile, I tried to appear cool and calm about the whole thing, but that situation was more excitement than I was looking for.

Here's a toast to SSG Akins and the rest of the BNCOC cadre that made the story published in the brigade newspaper end well. I still owe those guys a nice German beer. Each of them is welcome to collect on that debt at any time.

Lonely Soldier

Later that evening, the patrol conducted a reconnaissance mission. At about 3:00 AM, I led three soldiers toward an "enemy-held" building in the woods. I dropped two troops off near a road intersection and told them to observe and report any enemy activity on the roads. They kept our only radio.

I took the remaining soldier deeper into the forest to a position where he could watch the small building at the site of the pending U.S. raid. This soldier was to observe and gather information such as, how many enemy soldiers were in the area, what kinds of weapons and vehicles they had, and what their intent was or seemed. I made sure he was in the proper location, and before I left him, I added to my instructions.

"Don't make any noise or move from his position. I'm returning to the patrol to lead them up for the attack." When he realized, I was leaving him he got nervous and appeared concerned about being left alone. I knew he was a city kid, and it seemed he was afraid of the dark forest.

I reassured him. "I'll be back in 60 minutes. Don't be detected. Don't move. Observe and report when I return. Here's some extra ammo but use it only if your position is compromised."

I quickly left the surveillance position and headed back for the rest of the patrol which laid in wait about two kilometers away. As an instructor, I needed to be in several locations at the same time, so I took a privilege and ran part of the route along the paved roads. I linked up with the main patrol and updated them on the two surveillance teams. I pulled out a map and gave them the route to move on. "Move with stealth. Be in position for the raid no later than 5:00 AM."

I turned around and headed back to the surveillance teams, leaving the forest and running on the road again to cut down the travel time. Back in the woods, I linked up with the two-man team surveying the road. Everything looked good. The troops were confident and learning a lot from this exercise.

I felt good. The patrol was going to be a success. Just one more thing to do. I moved toward the lone troop who was watching the target site.

As I approached within 200 meters of him, I could hear an animal thrashing in the woods. I thought it could be wild boar, and that an encounter could get exciting. I had a grenade simulator and a Bowie knife for protection. That was good enough to handle the situation. I crept closer to the last soldier and could now hear more clearly. There was no boar. It was this guy, who was panicked and thrashing around. I heard him weakly call out, "Is anybody out there? Help me!"

I was angry. In real combat, this guy would have compromised the entire mission. As the noise continued, I wanted to rip him apart. Once I was within 50 meters, I could literally hear the guy breathing, heavily. Then he pulled the ultimate Hollywood stunt and fired his M16 in the air so someone could find him. It would either be the enemy or one highly ticked off instructor, and I was now within hand grenade range. I closed within 2 meters, and he had no idea I was right friggin behind him. He let out another cry for help. I got right up in his ear and whispered, "Soldier, what the $&@!

are you doing?" The guy was startled and spazzed like a squirrel hit by a truck, flopping on a hot highway. I chewed into him for a minute in a firm tactical voice. He had blown the mission. I told him, "When you have an M16 and an attitude, you are the biggest predator in the forest. There is nothing to fear. Other animals fear you. You are at the top of the food chain. Act like it. I was gone for only forty minutes. Trust your leaders." Enough said.

I did not tell his fellow soldiers about what he had done, the story stayed between the two of us. I am sure the incident was deeply engrained in his mind for the rest of his career. Hopefully, that experience made him a better soldier and leader. It was much better, I thought, that his breakdown happened during a peacetime exercise than a wartime mission. We can survive an exercise.

CHAPTER 33
BERLIN—THE DIVIDED CITY

East Berlin

While stationed in Germany, I made two trips to Berlin. That city, at the end of World War II, had been divided between the Allied forces and the Soviets and became the face of the Cold War. Its stark contrast was an international symbol of where freedom faced off against communism. West Berlin, an enclave located 110 miles inside East Germany, was the free part of the city. Each time I traveled to it, I would cross into communist-controlled East Berlin, the capital of East Germany.

On my first visit, I was with First Lieutenant (1LT) Lonnie Long and 1LT Chris Fortner. Since I was only a 2nd LT and therefore outranked, I was *persuaded* to drive my car. I had a black and gold, souped up, Mercury Capri with a glass T-Roof. It looked a lot better than it ran.

Speed is what you need on the German autobahn, but my car could not make 90 mph even if it were dropped out of an airplane. However, that Capri had the world's first onboard vehicle navigation system. It was a prototype, not based on GPS since such a satellite system did not yet exist. My Capri shook badly at autobahn speeds and would throw parts off, but that was a significant benefit. If I ever got lost, I could follow these parts back home like a breadcrumb trail, kind of a PGS (Parts on Ground System) navigation system.

My first trip to Berlin was during Labor Day weekend in 1983. The Soviet Union had just shot down Korean Airline flight 007 on September 1st, which had drifted over Soviet airspace, killing 269 innocent people in that attack, including a U.S. Congressman. The world was outraged. The Soviets at first denied the incident, then claimed the plane was on a spy mission and hid evidence (it was not released until eight years later, after the dissolution of the Soviet Union). The breaking news and public relations battle were global.

At the border, we were briefed by the American authorities at the Helmstedt post (Check Point Alpha) on the procedures for crossing into East Germany. We left West Germany and approached the first checkpoint inside East Germany. I pulled up in my car with the glass roof removed. The Soviet guards stared curiously at the vehicle. There must not have been many T-top sports cars running around in the communist world. I got out of the car and approached the Soviet guard. We exchanged salutes and greetings. I immediately noticed he had rough hands and stubs for fingernails, the kid had been living a hard life.

Helmstedt Border Crossing looking into communist East Germany

I then proceeded to the guard house to check in, where I was required to slide my military ID card under a narrow slit in a darkened window. I could not see who was on the other side, but I could hear a photocopier working. Stuck in an austerely furnished waiting room until I was cleared to travel, I sat down on a wooden chair and noticed several communist newspapers on the table. One was Pravda, a major propaganda magazine from the Soviet Union. On the cover was a cartoon of Ronald Reagan portrayed as a fanged devil. He was riding on top of a Pershing 2 nuclear missile, and he had cruise missiles for arms. I laughed. I had a copy of the American *Stars and Stripes* newspaper in my car. On its cover was the headline, 'Soviets shoot down Korean airliner, Kill 269.' I wanted to take the Pravda magazine with me and leave behind the Stars and Stripes but was being watched and still had 110 miles of East Germany to cross. I could not make the swap undetected, and

274

when caught, would likely be charged with some crime like spreading the truth. Now, I look back on that moment as a missed opportunity to stick it to the Soviets. After waiting about 30 minutes, we were given permission to proceed. We jumped back in the car and headed for Berlin. We had a precisely defined route which we were permitted to use; take a wrong exit and we could be detained for espionage. We were forbidden to take pictures, and the commies also monitored our departure and arrival times to see if we were speeding during the trip. Ironically, any speeding fines incurred during the journey were to be paid off with Western currency as it was more valuable to the communists than East German currency. Along the way, we saw people driving their little Trabants. These vehicles were cheaply made in East Germany, but outrageously expensive for locals to own. The Trabant was only rated at about 18 horsepower, and many East Germans admired our Western cars—even my hot-looking, though relatively underpowered, Capri—as we drove across their country.

Capri vs. Trabant

A few hours later, we arrived at Check Point Bravo, the last Soviet Checkpoint in East Germany. Once we had passed that checkpoint, we finally entered West Berlin and freedom.

Looking back into East Germany from Check Point Bravo

At the Reichstag

We spent the entire first day touring West Berlin. A dramatic contrast to its eastern half, this was a fun city with lots of nightlife. We went into one of the largest department stores in the world, Kaufhaus des Westens (Kadewe). It had dozens of restaurants that served exotic meals and meats including lion, bear and other animals I thought were endangered.

Other West Berlin sites included the Reichstag (Parliament), the 1936 Olympic Stadium (where American Jesse Owens won four gold medals in front of Hitler) and Charlottenburg Palace.

At lunchtime, we sat down at an outdoor café. I ordered a wheat beer (Weisse bier), and the waitress asked if I wanted a Berliner Wheat beer. I said "Yes," thinking it would be from a local brewery. I soon learned that a Berliner Weisse was flavored with raspberry fruit syrup. The drink was so thick it was delivered to my table with a straw. That was one of only two beers in my entire life that I honestly could not finish.

We then went up to the famous Berlin Wall, built by the communists to fence in East Berlin and keep its citizens from escaping. At all hours of the day and night, East German guards were in their towers on the wall, much like at a federal prison. Little patrolling was done by them because even the guards would try to escape. They were ordered to shoot anything that stepped into the crossing area.

Hundreds of East Berliners were killed or imprisoned attempting to escape to the West. White crosses (crucifixes) were placed on the western side of the wall to remember the fallen.

Dennis Faker and Kerry

Site where nine East Germans were killed attempting to escape

We were able to walk up to the wall on the West Berlin side, which was decorated with humorous or often crude graffiti. Some scribbles were in German, some in English. I remember one that read, "Last Coca-Cola for 5,000 miles." I took a piece of concrete out of that evil wall; it felt like an appropriate act that both supported the reunification of Germany and undermined the brutal communist system.

We worked our way around several sections of the wall and spent about an hour at Brandenburg Gate, the site where Presidents Kennedy and Reagan made famous speeches decades apart. From there we could overlook the East German obstacle system that included two walls and a 'no man's land' between them that had anti-vehicle barriers and guard towers. We were also able to see the bunker area where Adolph Hitler had committed suicide.

The next day, we decided to drive into East Berlin. U.S. soldiers were allowed to enter this sector of the city as a result of the post-WWII Status of Forces Agreement. We were required to wear our "Class A" uniform (military coat and tie) when inside East Berlin, so that we could be clearly identified as American soldiers, but we were directed not to wear name badges to prevent communists from knowing our specific identity.

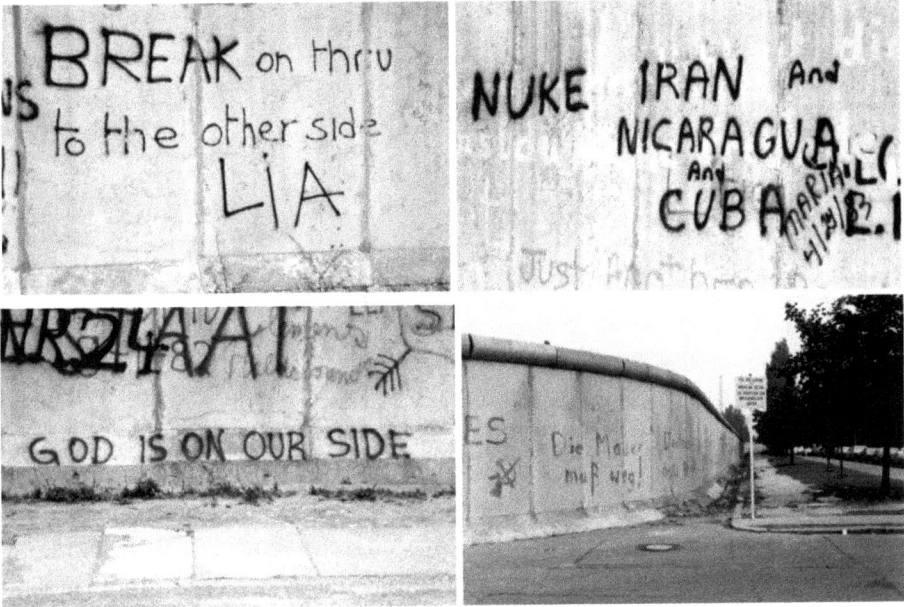

Graffiti on the Berlin Wall

Before leaving, we exchanged money at a rate of 10 East German marks for 1 West German mark. Outside East Germany, its currency had little value. Inside, the East Germans demanded a one-for-one exchange rate to collect highly prized Western money. Soldiers, however, as we had done, picked up their East German marks at a much cheaper rate in the West. We felt no obligation to subsidize their empire of evil.

East German Marks

We jumped in the Capri and headed for the infamous "Check Point Charlie," the legal road crossing from East to West. Many famous escape attempts happened at this checkpoint, some successful, some ending in

279

tragedy. We were now driving through one of the most visible—and visceral—symbols of the Cold War.

Check Point Charlie (Post Cards)

Once inside East Berlin, we rolled through the communist capital encountering a lot less traffic, as few citizens could afford cars. The architecture near the main government buildings was nicely modern. Then, we toured the older parts of the city and were surprised to find that many old buildings still had bullet holes and scars left over from World War II bombings.

TV Tower and Pope's Revenge

At Alexanderplatz, the social center of the city, we saw the tall TV tower which, near the top, had a restaurant in a glass sphere. A West German tour guide told us how it was built. The Pope had donated money to East Germany to rebuild a major church in East Berlin. However, the godless commies used the cash to build this enormous TV tower. Obviously, this was a major insult to the Pope. After the tower's construction, the large glass and metal sphere at the top were visible for many miles. Ironically, when the sun's rays hit its glass panels, the reflected light created the shape of a massive, elevated, white cross. This reflection was dubbed "The Pope's Revenge."

We ate lunch in a restaurant at the base of the tower. As we sat down, dozens of East Germans stared at us, trying to get a good look at the Westerners and to judge our lifestyle and wealth by studying our clothing, our watches and how much shopping we did. It was illegal for them to talk to us, which could lead to suspicion of disloyalty, collaboration or even espionage. If we walked near them, they changed their path or looked away to avoid eye contact.

At the restaurant, I ordered a wurst, some bread, and a cola. The total bill was the equivalent of 15 cents in Western currency. The wurst could have been better, and the drink was just brown water. It did not taste even remotely like a Western cola, but this was all a part of the communist experience. As we sat there, well-aware we were under constant surveillance, I decided to break the suspense. Grabbing a small candle stick on the table, I held it up to my mouth like a microphone and started saying, "Testing: one, two. Testing, testing." My friends began to laugh, and so did some of the East Germans seated nearby. Humor is universal.

East German Guards at Tomb of the Unknown Soldier

Soviet Guards change at War Memorial

A year later, I returned to Berlin. This time, we flew into West Berlin and then took a tour bus to East Berlin. After we had passed through Check

Point Charlie, a female East German Army Major demanded everyone get off the bus for identity checks. She was angry and scowled at everyone, declaring that only U.S. military personnel could stay on the bus. Inside the bus, with an even nastier look at us, she confirmed that only U.S. soldiers remained on board. At that moment, I actually felt sympathy for any man who married her.

After the tourists had piled back in, the bus was required to go to a particular shop that had a sign outside marked, "Nur für Reisegast," which meant 'Only for Travel Guests.' The intent of this establishment—its sole purpose—was to get Western tourists to spend their Western currency in the state-sponsored store. Since the bus did not stop anywhere in East Berlin to exchange money, no one could legally have East German marks. American soldiers, however, did have East German marks. Having found some souvenirs to purchase, I headed up to the check-out counter to pay. The young girl working the register told me I owed thirty marks. When I handed her thirty East marks, she was shocked and demanded West marks. I immediately asked, "DDR geld is niche gut in DDR?" (Translation: East German money is not good in East Germany?) Even though I had caught her off-guard and embarrassed her, I paid her in West marks so that the situation did not escalate.

CHAPTER 34
SKI TRIPS

Learning to Ski

I learned to ski as a cadet at West Point. Since I didn't have money to pay for individual lessons, I took a free Physical Fitness class on skiing. I came out of the class as a basic skier with limited control, no style, and absolutely no brakes. Technically, I was no more than a moving hazard on the slopes. After practicing on the bunny slope for about half an hour, I decided it was time to move up the mountain.

On my first run, I hit an Army captain. I really cleaned his clock, and mine too, and then just laid there in the snow. I didn't know how to stand back up on the steep slope, so he showed me how to get my legs under me. The guy was really nice, told me "no worries" and to keep at it.

Thankful that I was not going to face a military courts martial for assaulting an officer, I got back on the lift and headed for the top of the slope. And then, of course, the inevitable happened. I was gunning it like a one-man avalanche when I nailed an Army major. That collision wasn't quite as intense as the last, but we both ate a lot of snow. He was another good guy, telling me everything was okay and gave me a few skiing tips.

I made my way down the mountain, hopped on the ski lift and headed back up. Determined to strike yet another superior officer without consequence, I started looking around for my next victim, ideally, an Army colonel since I didn't want to jump the chain of command and nail a general. Fortunately for colonels, most of them are too old to ski, and I did not get one that day. To warn others that I was dangerously approaching them like an errant golf ball, I would occasionally yell "Fore!" when I got within ten yards of them. I didn't want to hurt anyone and needed to limit my liability if I had another collision.

My final run of the day was nearly a success. I made it all the way to the bottom without falling, but my braking system failed. Unable to come to a stop, I zipped out of the snow area and onto a gravel parking lot. Although

I did crash, I considered the run complete once I had gotten past the lift. Thankfully I was using rental equipment. I got my money's worth out of those poor skis.

Skiing in Italy

The next time I attempted to ski was while I was stationed in Germany for three years. Many of the officers in my battalion would take a week off each year and ski in Italy, Austria or France. These were considered team-building events.

My first trip, in January 1984, was to the Dolomites in northern Italy. Ron Claeys, Billy Fortner and I traveled from Germany through Austria and the Brenner Pass. After a long ride, we arrived in Pozza DiFassa, Italy.

I decided not to take any formal ski lessons. My friends were all eager to hit the slopes, and I didn't want to slow them down. My plan was to follow them down the mountain and learn from observation, trying to mirror their movements and mimic how they handled themselves on the slope. Lieutenant Mike Anthony was a good skier and set the pace for our group.

Thankfully, I had played a lot of sports in high school and at the academy, most of which I was more talented at than skiing. Football, lacrosse, and wrestling all required good balance. I also was built like a professional midget wrestler and had a low center of gravity. Since I was low to the ground, there'd be less wind resistance.

I got to the top of the slopes and set up in a wide stance, like a linebacker lining up on a football field. There was no one around to hear me, so I coached myself. "OK Kachejian, lean forward, lead with your head, and don't stop until you hit something." Perhaps not the best coaching advice, but practical with odds in my favor that I could get that done.

During my first run, I cut off my battalion commander, Lt. Colonel Bruce Malson. I had finally found the colonel I was aiming for a few years earlier on the ski slope at West Point. It was a high-speed strafing run and near miss, and I made no effort to stop. He was angry and yelled, "Hey, who is that guy?" Fortunately, he couldn't recognize me, but my unstylish, ugly clothes marked me as an American, and probably one of his troops. We are both retired from the Army now, so here's a decades-long overdue apology to my former battalion commander: "Sorry Sir."

The prevailing language in this part of Italy was German. As I made my first few runs down the slopes, some skiers were yelling "Langsam! Langsam!" I wasn't sure what that meant, but I knew it wasn't good. Later that night, my roommate, Lonnie Long told me it meant: "Slow down." If they had spoken to me in English, I could have done something about it. At least they did not realize I was an American. My reckless skiing could have seriously damaged the relationship between the United States and its NATO allies.

Sella Ronda

When we arrived in Italy, each member of our group bought the Dolomiti SuperSkiPass, which allowed us to ski throughout the entire region. We had fun the first two days, but on day three the excitement really picked up when our group decided to tackle the Sella Ronda.

Sella Rhonda is an incredible ski route that loops around the massive Sella mountain range. An entire circuit covered about 38 kilometers of lifts and downhill skiing and traversed four mountain passes, four valleys, and three Italian provinces. We were advised to start early morning to finish before it got too late. It sounded like a good challenge for a bunch of lieutenants who had spent much of the previous night celebrating at a promotion party hosted by new 1st Lieutenant's Max Hughey and myself.

We started the route at about 9:00 AM. It was a beautiful day, and we were surrounded by rocky peaks. At the top of several, we stopped at ski lodges for shots of grappa, a local alcohol that both served as a painkiller and provided liquid courage to go down the next run. We skied as fast and hard as we could and wound up back at our start point at about 2:00 PM. Our legs were tired, but we were very proud we had conquered the Sella Ronda.

Unfortunately, that's when we made a gross error in judgment. Ron Claeys said, "Let's do it again!" My brain was saying, "Are you nuts? Isn't once enough?" However, I found myself joining the rest of my friends by responding, "Yeah, let's go!" Nobody wanted to go for this ride, but no one had the guts to bail out.

We headed back up the slopes. It was still beautiful, but now the wind was picking up, and the temperature dropping. But the grappa was still being served, so we pressed on. A few hours into the trip, the sun started to get low. We were about half way around the second circuit when the lifts abruptly closed. Stuck between mountain passes, we were probably 15 kilometers short of our final destination. You don't want to be in those mountains at nightfall, so we started cross-country skiing in our downhill skis. Now, no one was having fun. It took us four or five more hours get back to our hotel. By then, it was completely dark, and we were all exhausted. Nobody muttered a word about trying to go for a third lap. We went to our rooms and collapsed.

The next morning, my legs felt like burning rubber, and I could barely walk. Our group did not reconvene until late in the morning, and we had no desire to go skiing that day. In the afternoon, we toured several Italian towns and then sat in a hot tub. It was a great trip, and the highlight was lap one of the Sella Ronda. Lap two, however, was undoubtedly the worst part.

Fasching with St Nick

Before driving to Italy, Lonnie told me it was the time of year when the Europeans celebrated a holiday called "Fasching" or "Carnival." It is the rough equivalent to Marti Gras.

Many Germans, Austrians, and Italians would wear festive clothes and celebrate the season. Being a bachelor with limited German language skills, I decided to pack a costume for the ski slopes in hopes of having fun and meeting some new friends. The costume had to be cheap, as I needed to conserve my limited funds for more important staples like beer and wine. Fortunately, my mother had given me a Santa suit previously used by my father. So, I dressed up as Santa and headed to the slopes with the rest of my friends.

St Nicholas in Bad Gastein, Austria

287

The costume was an immediate hit. Skiers stopped to greet me everywhere. I was asked to pose for some photos with families. Germans, Austrians, Italians, and Spaniards... they all wanted in on the action. I can still hear their voices. "Nicholas! Nicholas! Un momento, fotographía!"

What a power trip. This suit made me an instant rock star and a chick magnet. It was going to be a good day. I realized, however, that Santa still needed to be a gentleman, as dozens of children were now trying to get my attention.

I got off the lift at the top of the mountain and looked down the slope. After straightening my beard and red hat, I started my descent. I wasn't wearing goggles during that run, and with the stinging cold and wind, my eyes began to form tears.

Unfortunately, I only knew one way to ski, fast and hard. But this time I needed to exert some control—there were civilians all around, and I didn't want any collateral damage.

I zipped past some ski schools, each with an adult ski instructor leading a dozen or so little kids who trailed behind them in a single file. The instructor glided down the mountain and showed the little ones the mechanics of skiing. The kids watched their leader's every move and imitated his or her style. They demonstrated great discipline and quickly learned the higher-level skills of skiing.

But there was a disturbance in the Force that day. No one knew Santa Claus was in town and ripping down the slopes. When I zoomed past each ski class, the cries became louder, "Nicholas! Nicholas!" I gave them a gentle wave of acknowledgment and a big "Ho, Ho Ho!"

As you might expect, the kids lost focus on their instructors—I distracted them. The instructors let me know they were not happy with me, verbally.

I tried to speed off, but I was skiing half-blind, with my eyes full of tears and beard all over my face. Struggling to see which direction to ski toward, I hadn't gotten far when the kids broke ranks to chase old St. Nick. I was probably breaking a dozen laws and had no candy to give these kids once they cornered me. I had to hold it together, or those angry instructors would catch me and impale me with their ski poles while a hundred kids picked my pockets like vultures.

Gravity pulled me down the slope. Picking up speed, I was completely snow-blind as I careened out of control. And then, the inevitable happened as I entered the friggin moguls. Somehow, in my escape attempt, I had gotten to that part of the downhill. I hit the first of them, crossed my ski tips while moving at autobahn speed and exploded. My poles flew off to the side in one direction, my skis in another and my body... well, it stuck to the plan and followed gravity.

I plummeted head first, on my back, down the ski slope hitting mogul after mogul. I grabbed very little air as I slammed over each one. If someone had caught the catastrophe on tape, it would have belonged on the 'Agony of Defeat' video from ABC Wide World of Sports.

After pounding downhill at least 200 meters, I finally came to a complete stop. My Santa suit was full of snow that jammed down my neck, stuffed into my pants, filled my ears, and stung my eyes.

While lying on my back and taking an inventory of all my body parts, I thought I had broken my nose and hoped that nothing major was permanently damaged. I looked up at the clear, blue Italian sky expecting my view to soon be blocked by a ski instructor standing over me like a victorious gladiator preparing to give me the final sword thrust to my chest. "It's been a good life," I thought, "I might as well have a good death. Let's get it over with."

But I was spared. Dozens of little kids had seen Saint Nicholas explode on the ski slopes and raced to my rescue. They picked up my skis and my poles, brushed me off and helped me up. Not one of them said a word about my beard now being on my head backward, as these kids were expecting something big in their stocking next year. I started taking toy requests while thinking, "I hope your parents deliver."

The ski instructors then quickly restored discipline, collected their classes and sped away from Santa Claus. After I had composed myself, I slithered back down the slopes and headed for a little café in search of a shot of grappa. I'd had enough skiing for that day.

Skiing in Austria

Officer Ski Week in February 1985 was in Bad Gastein, Austria. It was another week of well-spent youthful overindulgence. Two of my friends from Pennsylvania joined me: Mark Potthoff and Mike Willover. This was their first trip to Europe, so we made use of every minute.

Mike Willover — "Look, Mom, No Skis!"

We skied hard during the day and found fun places to hang out at night. Trying to repeat my previous success in Italy, I brought a European-style St. Nicholas suit with me and wore it one day. The Austrians were less enthusiastic, and clearly, Italy was a friendlier place for St Nick.

The first day, instead of renting equipment, I bought skis, boots, and poles. I really liked this sport and thought I should have my own equipment. I could also save money by not renting equipment. I got a great deal on some white skis. They had a catchy name, "Blizzard Wizard." What a mistake that was. Whenever they came off, it was extremely hard to find the white skis in the white snow. No wonder they were on sale.

We had several new lieutenants in our battalion that year, including John Guidotti, Erik Fleishner, Ted Jennings, John Shuman and Eric Wolf. Guidotti, who had both speed and style, was a ski animal from Vermont. He and I had some intense drag races on the slopes. I coined a new phrase to describe this style: "Ski Ballistic." Go fast, go straight, don't stop until you hit something or disintegrate.

One afternoon, there was no one else on a broad downhill slope, and we were going at it. I had the lead for a few moments, but Guidotti had a lower coefficient of drag and started to pass me. We were both laughing hysterically. I caught the tip of one of my skis a few moments later, wiped out and exploded again. My equipment flew in all directions, and I must have bounced down that slope for 20-30 seconds before I came to a stop. It was an awesome ride, but it took the better part of an hour to find my white Blizzard Wizard skis.

On another day, several of us left the marked trails and went through some soft powder. "Rocket Ron" Claeys found a snow drift up the side of a small barn and used it as a jump ramp, providing an impressive aerial display. We cut across a farmer's field in some deep powder, and I let Ron take the lead. If there was barbed wire fence under that snow, I wanted Ron to hit it first. He would be launched out of his boots—something I had already experienced—and I intended avoiding a repeat. Besides the possible bodily injury and certain wounded pride, I would have never found my white skis in that powder.

Return to Italy

In February of 1986, our battalion headed back to Italy. This was my final chance to ski in Europe before the Army shipped me back to the United States. It was another week-long team-building event, but this time, St. Nick did not join us. We spent one day in Cortina, the site of the 1956 Winter Olympics, and hit the slopes and shopped for trinkets in nearby Italian villages. We discovered some fine Italian white wine for 78 cents a bottle. The price was excellent, but the ensuing hangover was not. Buyer beware!

CHAPTER 35
A TREK THROUGH HISTORY

In June of 1983, the 237th Engineer Battalion began a four-day Officer Professional Development (OPD) trip through France and Germany, retracing the battles and routes our unit had experienced during World War II.

Our job was to follow the historical trail and understand the military decisions made during these epic battles, and of course, we could also enjoy the journey—an excellent deal. The trip was considered an official training event and approved by Lt. Colonel James Campbell, our Battalion Commander. In fact, Lt. Colonel Campbell gets great credit for many of the innovative training ideas that our battalion used to build teamwork while preparing for war. We started with dining at the Heilbronn Officer's Club the evening before we departed. A formal dinner, the officers wore their Dress Blue uniform, performed some ceremonial duties, made a few toasts (to the president, to the ladies, to the bartender, etc.), ate some good chow and made highly forgettable speeches.

The group included Lt. Colonel Jim Campbell and his wife Emily, my boss Captain Al Wheatley, our Company XO, 1st Lieut. Ricky Stennet, Captain Bob Basinger, Captain Charlie Waters, 1st Lieut. Chris Bowling, Major Moon, Major Coffee, and about ten other lieutenants. Spouses were permitted to join us on the trip. The one officer that spent weeks planning the entire event, Captain Chris Young, was rewarded for his efforts by being ordered to stay behind in Heilbronn with his spouse to lead our battalion in case a war with the Soviet Union broke out.

The next morning, at 5:00 AM, the officers, and their wives jumped on a German tour bus to begin our journey. From the battalion HQ in Heilbronn, Germany we traveled to the D-Day beaches, where the 237th Engineer Battalion came ashore on June 6th, 1944. In the late morning, we stopped in Reims. It was my first experience in France. There was a statue of Joan of Arc in the square and a massive Cathedral similar to Notre Dame in Paris. We stopped at a local restaurant, but I didn't know what to order.

French toast and French fries weren't on the menu. So, I ordered pastries and beer. The locals immediately suspected I was either American or German. But a notable distinction clearly made me a ringer for an American; I could not dress in matching clothes.

Gold Beach

When we arrived in Normandy, our first stop was a very scenic view of Gold Beach. The British forces had assaulted this area on D-Day. Their primary objective was to establish a beachhead near Arromanches so the Allies could later deploy an artificial floating Mulberry harbor. The Allies needed this man-made port to rapidly move supplies ashore. Wreckage from the landing, as well as German military equipment, was still visible forty years later.

Omaha Beach

Our next stop was Omaha Beach, where the American 29th and 1st Infantry Divisions came ashore. The German defenses in this sector had superior observation and fields of fire. They could easily track and target the landing force, and the first wave of Americans suffered horrible losses. It was a slow and costly assault, and the men of our battalion fought and bled on these sands to help make it ultimately successful. We made a solemn stop at the American military cemetery where Chaplain Stagner of the 237th Engineer Battalion led a memorial service.

Map of Landing Beaches and German view of the Omaha

Pointe du Hoc

The highlight of the Normandy tour was Pointe du Hoc, considered critical terrain during the D-Day invasion. The Germans had 155mm artillery positioned on the top of these coastal cliffs that posed a significant threat to the U.S. landing zones on Omaha and Utah Beaches. It gave the Germans a great tactical advantage. Although heavily bombed by Allied aircraft and ships, the German artillery position was not destroyed. The mission to seize Pointe du Hoc was assigned to two hundred and twenty-five men from the 2nd Ranger Battalion.

On the morning of June 6th, 1944, the Rangers climbed 100 feet with grappling hooks and rope ladders, fighting their way up the cliff as German soldiers directed fire and dropped hand grenades from the top. Many of the ropes the Rangers used to climb the cliffs were cut by the defending Germans, and many soldiers fell to their death. It was a brutal assault. American casualties were about sixty percent, but they secured the cliffs and destroyed the German defenders as well as their artillery. Decades later, this epic battle was depicted in the opening scene of the movie *Saving Private Ryan*.

Several of the officers in our battalion were Ranger-qualified and were in awe of what our forefathers had achieved that day. We walked on hallowed ground. The site is preserved as a Ranger Memorial and covers over 30 acres. The following year, President Reagan made a D-Day speech in that very same spot.

This place also carried another significance, one of a personal nature. A West Point classmate's father had climbed Pointe du Hoc with the Rangers on D-Day. I had a chance to meet his father when visiting their family home a few years earlier. He was among the wounded on D-Day. For the rest of his life, he was very humble about his service. He has since passed away. His son asked me to keep his actions anonymous, as his father never wanted public recognition. Humility runs in their family.

We had some free time to explore the area atop the cliffs. Fortunately, the signs telling tourists not to enter the battle-damaged bunkers were written in French, and being ignorant Americans, we had an excuse to go straight inside.

Chris Bowling emerged a few minutes later with a link of Russian machine gun ammunition. We immediately huddled around the ammo belt and concluded that the German defenders had used weapons and ammo captured from the Russian front to defend their famous "Atlantic Wall."

Ricky Stennett inspecting a German bunker at Pointe du Hoc

Greg Schwalb inspecting a German Bunker

Utah Beach

Our battalion's primary landing zone on D-Day was Utah Beach. As engineers, their mission had been to clear (blow up, remove) German obstacles that kept the Americans pinned down on the beach. The longer you were stuck there, the greater likelihood you would die from the murderous hail of gunfire and mortars coming in from above the beach.

In this coastal area, the Germans had constructed a concrete wall along the shore designed to slow American troops and prevent their tanks from moving forward. It was the engineer soldiers from our battalion who, armed with Bangalore torpedoes and other explosives, blew a hole in that wall as well as the surrounding barbed wire obstacles.

As a result, American forces poured through the gap and continued the attack inland. This D-Day scene was immortalized in the film *The Longest Day*.

Billy Fortner and Chris Bowling exploring Pointe du Hoc history

Anti-Tank wall breached by the 237th Engineers on D-Day

After inspecting that historic wall, our tour group moved inland a few hundred meters. There remained the famous red-roofed house on the beach that was present during the invasion. This home served as a useful landmark for American troops trying to establish where they were on the beachhead. It had certainly been heavily damaged by the fighting. But there it was. It was unbelievable that this house still existed 40 years later (at that time).

Red Roof Inn—Utah Beach

As we explored the area beyond the beach, we found more signs warning visitors that the area was a WWII German minefield. Again, these

297

signs were primarily in French, and most of the lieutenants I hung out with could only speak English, Canadian, Australian and Pig Latin.

Being young, unmarried and not quite fully mature has its advantages. It was a liberating feeling, not worrying about the consequences of our actions. Given we were engineer soldiers and had the proper training required to emplace and clear minefields, this was an awesome opportunity to test our technical and tactical skills. We marched right out into a WWII minefield looking for some action. No worries, we covered our ears with our hands to protect from a potential hearing loss just in case we struck an old German mine.

Clearing a WWII minefield: Bowling, Kachejian, Fortner, Medina

St. Mere Eglise

The final stop in the Normandy area was the village of St. Mere Eglise. On D-Day, in the early hours of the morning, American paratroopers landed directly in the village. In one famous incident, the chute of an unfortunate soldier, John Steele, snagged on the spire of the local church. He hung there for hours, unable to free himself while the battle raged on around him. Although John feigned death for several hours, the Germans eventually captured him. He later escaped when his unit captured the village. The story of John Steele is yet another D-Day scene in *The Longest Day*.

Paris

There were several sites on which our WWII battalion conducted military operations while moving across France. On the way, back from Normandy we briefly stopped at a few of these locations. The big prize left was Paris, as our group had a chance to tour the French capital. We hit all the popular spots, thoroughly enjoying ourselves.

While in Paris, I stopped at an outdoor café with four buddies. We weren't sure what to order, so we chose beer. Yes, we drank beer in France, the wine capital of the world. We must have offended the locals because when the check came, we were shocked to discover that each beer had cost the equivalent of $7.00 U.S. This was back in 1983, and a beer should have cost a buck or two. One thing was certain, we needed to stop dressing like the ugly Americans we were.

Later, we walked toward L'Arc de Triomphe and decided to give it a closer look. As we approached the monument, I noticed the street around it was an incredibly wide traffic circle. I could not find any crosswalks. There were at least six lanes of traffic to cross to get to the monument, and French cars were flying around the circle with reckless abandon. "Yikes Batman," I thought to myself, "I have to cross this thing twice!" I timed the traffic as best I could, but I got trapped in the road like in the video game *Frogger*. I felt like a squirrel trying to cross an interstate highway during rush hour. I made it across by the skin of my teeth. I looked up, wiped the sweat from my brow, and saw my buddies arriving from a different direction. They weren't sweaty and jacked up from having dodged fast-moving Citroens and Peugeots.

"We found a tunnel." They gestured behind them.

Then I saw the sign for it, which was, of course, written in French. "Thanks, guys," I remarked, "I'm following you back across."

In the late afternoon, it poured rain, and we stopped to take cover in another café. Seated outside, just under an awning, we wondered what we could do next. We had a full day and night left in Paris and did not want to waste any opportunity for fun and adventure.

A taxi pulled up to the curb near our table. That's when a (my) lightbulb went on: we were going to race taxis in Paris! I left my colleagues at the table and jumped in the cab. I told the French driver in a mix of English and German that I wanted him to race around the block as fast as he could and get back to our table. The driver gave me a strange look, clearly not understanding my intent. I told him again, this time louder and drew circles in the air with my finger. "Go around the block. Snell!" He got it this time and sped off.

There was plenty of traffic, so getting a good lap time was going to take both skill and luck. We pulled back up to the table in about seventy seconds, by our unofficial clock. I paid the driver some Francs and told him to wait for the next rider. I waved over one of my buddies who took his lap and had a respectable time. We did a few more laps, and then the rain stopped. With this improvement in the weather, the novelty of taxi racing soon wore off. And so, we headed to Moulin Rouge in search of French ladies who liked to meet American men with more money than common sense.

CHAPTER 36
EUROPE TRAVEL

I lived in West Germany for three years, and I had ample opportunity to see much of Europe. When traveling on the German autobahn or the Italian autostrade, speed limits were often determined by personal comfort so you could get to most destinations quickly. The only place I did not like to drive was in the United Kingdom. The Brits drove on the left side of the road and navigating through a crowded roundabout was intimidating for Americans.

In addition to its great cities, Germany offered numerous first-rate attractions that were clean and easily accessible. The castles and palaces were incredible, and the beer was even better. The downside was that the summers were too short, it rained too much, gas was expensive, and stores were rarely open on Sundays. None of this detracted from the fact that Germany's central location in Europe meant I could easily travel with friends to many other countries on the weekends. We could be in as in as many as five countries in one day, as they are roughly of similar size to our states in America.

Thank You Taxpayers

Our men and women in uniform earn their paychecks, which are generously funded by American taxpayers. As an added benefit, military personnel can visit many interesting and exotic parts of the world. I certainly would have never traveled to dozens of countries had I kept my job as a paperboy in West Chester. It was a blessing to have experienced so many countries, some of which no longer exist. So here is a big "thank you" to the American taxpayers who funded my European tour.

Luxembourg

Luxembourg is a small, landlocked country about the size of Rhode Island, pinched between France, Belgium, and Germany. You could drive through it in an hour or less.

In WWII, the Battle of the Bulge was fought there and in nearby Belgium. We stopped at a U.S. military cemetery in the countryside. General George S. Patton is buried there, along with his troops, in a military formation of perfect columns and rows. Patton's grave is in front of the formation, where he would have been as the Commander. The American white grave markers were a stark contrast to the dark tombstones at the nearby cemetery for German soldiers. That cemetery was not as well-traveled.

WWII Memorial sites: U.S. and German cemeteries

Ironically, some of the land in Luxembourg had been reserved as a graveyard to bury the thousands of American dead anticipated if NATO had to fight the Warsaw Pact in World War III. Thankfully, we did not need to use it.

Salzburg

Salzburg, the Austrian city home to the Von Trappe family and the movie *The Sound of Music*, was among my favorites. Walking through it was like stepping back in time several hundred years. I felt my stress level fall as I walked through this remarkable city. Everyday scenes included horse-drawn carriages in the streets, big chess games played in the town square, as well as pleasant little cafes and shops. The great composer, Mozart, was born in Salzburg.

When my mother and brother traveled to Europe after my father had died, I made sure they visited this historic city. I recall pushing my brother's wheelchair up the steep gravel slopes of Hohensalzburg, the main fortress overlooking the city. It was one of the best physical workouts I had ever had. I was pouring sweat, and a couple of local Austrians joined in to help. We finally made it to the top and were served a great lunch while enjoying a fantastic view.

Now as bachelors, most of us—my fellow soldiers—had no clue about how to dress fashionably. I was perhaps the most clueless of the group and a complete fashion disaster. I grew up in a frugal house and kept every scrap of clothing for years. Nothing was thrown out. I owned a lot of tacky, torn t-shirts and athletic shorts. Little of the clothing I owned matched. The Europeans could easily pick an American out of a crowd. Me most of all.

Can you find the American fashion disaster in this photo?

Munich

Munich is one of the great cities in Germany, and I frequently traveled there with friends. Although it was about 200 miles from my apartment in Bad Wimpfen, I moved at autobahn speed. If traffic was light, the trip to Munich could take only two hours. Once we arrived, we would explore the city's great mix of the old and the new.

I usually traveled with Lonnie Long, "Rocket Ron" Claeys, Tom Reed, Tom Schmutz, Erik Fleishner, John Shuman or one of several other bachelor lieutenants. The married guys, like Dan Cummings, Todd Skoog, and Ted Jennings did not join us, as they were usually more responsible, had newborn infants, or just could not get a kitchen pass on short notice. Tom Reed was an unusually useful tour guide on these trips. He was rumored to be a half-Cajun and half-hound dog. That unusual genetic combination gave Tom a rare navigational gift; he could find a dive bar in a Mormon cemetery.

Tom introduced us to his favorite Munich hangout, Schwabinger 7, where the lights were dim, the beer was cheap and the bartenders, Eddie and Hans, ruled. Many years later, an unexploded 500-pound bomb from World War II was found under Schwabinger 7 and had to be detonated in place, damaging many local homes. I regret this tragic end to a great chapter in my early adult social development.

We often hit some of the famous pubs and biergartens in the city. Several times we started at the 'House of 1001 Beers.' Our group of six would each order a beer and share it, like wine tasting only with some German brau. After we had polished off biers #1-6, we ordered a second round, biers #7-12. We occasionally hung out for a third round, climbing the bier list to #18. At that point, we moved on to other pubs or fests near the university. On the next trip to Munich, we had usually forgotten what bier number we had stopped at on the previous visit. We would start all over with bier #1. After three years of living in Germany, I never got to try biers beyond #19. Our mission to conquer the House of 1001 Beers was never completed. Perhaps I'll get another trip to Munich and have another crack at sampling the remaining beers.

There was always something interesting and fun to do. Munich, a city rich in history and culture, had impressive architecture, and I saw much of it: Nymphenburg Palace, Deutsches Museum (similar to the Smithsonian

Institute), Marienplatz, Rathaus, BMW building and the Hofbräuhaus. Munich was a must-see city, and I often took friends and family to visit.

Helen and Kevin Kachejian exploring Munich

The Germans, however, are a bit quirky by American moral standards. This was evident when we took a tour through Munich's renowned 'Englisher Garten,' a public park along the Isar River. While the park was a pleasant place to visit, we weren't prepared for a shocker when the sun came out, and the temperature warmed up. Within minutes we walked along a path crowded with dozens of naked people. This immediately gave rise to several concerns. First, what do you say to a naked person? How do you get away from a naked man without looking too obvious? Are these people expecting us to get naked too? Sorry, that's not part of my job description. That was way more than we bargained for on a walk through the park. We later checked into it and learned that up to 50,000 nudists use the park on a beautiful summer day. I should have opened a kiosk and sold suntan lotion. Apparently, the German nudist movement 'FKK' (Free Body Culture) was fairly popular throughout the country.

Each year Germany holds Oktoberfest in Munich. However, if you arrive in October, you will miss the event, as it is usually held in September. Ironically, Stuttgart hosts the lesser-known Bad Constadt Fest at the same time. The dueling festivals allow Germany's international travelers to enjoy the local culture and are a great place to practice your German language skills.

If you are ever hungry at a German festival, a useful phrase might be, "Halb Hanchen mit pommes und ein litre bier, bitte" (roasted chicken half, fries, and a liter beer, please).

Munich hosted the Summer Olympic Games in 1972, and they were the first ones I can recall watching on television. The Germans preserved the Olympic Park where so much history was made. During these games, American swimmer Mark Spitz won seven gold medals and set seven world records. Soviet gymnast, Olga Korbut, dazzled spectators and showed the world that humans did live behind the Iron Curtain. The U.S. Men's basketball team lost the gold medal in the final to the Soviet Union after the U.S. had initially won it, but referee's reset the game clock. Runner Dave Wottle won gold in the 800-meter run, coming back from last place. As a young wrestler, I watched in awe how Dan Gable shut out every opponent on his march to gold. And then there was Frank Shorter, who won the marathon for the United States, despite the presence of a

1972 Olympic Village –
Kerry K and Lonnie Long

hoax runner, who had entered the stadium ahead of him. I was incredibly impressed by the Olympic athletes in the 1972 games, and now I stood where those giants had captivated the world.

Great tragedy, however, befell the 1972 Olympic Games when Palestinian Liberation Organization (PLO) terrorists from the 'Black

306

September Group' attacked the dorms where the Israeli athletes lived. Two athletes were killed in the initial assault, and nine other athletes and coaches were taken hostage. Hours later, the horrifying standoff tragically ended at a German military airport. The nine Israeli hostages, a West German police officer and five of the eight terrorists, were killed. The "Munich Massacre" was an appalling day in world history, and the Olympic Games were temporarily stopped. It was my first real exposure to manifest evil in the modern world.

Dachau

Just outside of Munich lies the town of Dachau, a notorious concentration camp in World War II and part of a dark chapter in German history. It was a grim and sad reminder of the potential for evil in Man. I visited Dachau four times, often with guests who came to see me in Germany.

Dachau Memorial—Author with Mark Potthoff and Mike Willover

The wrought iron sign on the camp gate included the phrase "Arbeit Macht Frei" (Work makes one free). This sign gave false hope to thousands of internees that would be murdered within its fences. It was always sobering to see the barracks, execution ranges, gas chambers and ovens used in Hitler's "Final Solution." A lesser-known fact is that the Holocaust was the second great genocide of the 20th century. The first took place during World War One, claiming the lives of approximately 1.5 million Armenians, including my relatives. The world's failure to respond to the Ottoman Empire's methodical slaughter of the Armenians gave Hitler confidence that the Nazi's could exterminate their adversaries without fear of global retribution. A week before the invasion of Poland, he delivered a speech that included, "Who, after all, speaks today of the annihilation of the Armenians?" Many years later, I saw this quote inscribed on a wall at the U.S. Holocaust Museum in Washington, D.C. During my three-year tour in Germany, I also visited the Flossenberg concentration camp near the Czech border. It was a smaller scale operation, but nonetheless one of many camps built to bring about the Final Solution.

Heidelberg, Germany

Heidelberg was another vibrant German city less than an hour north from my apartment in Bad Wimpfen. Its local university attracted a lot of young Germans and offered plenty of things for tourists to do and see. I never turned down an opportunity to visit scenic and festive Heidelberg. The major landmark is the historic castle (Schloss). Many old European structures are often called castles, but most are really palaces and better suited for luxurious living rather than siege warfare.

The castle in Heidelberg, however, is the real deal. A tough-looking, battle-tested fortress built for defensive warfare; Heidelberg Castle sits on a hill more than 250 feet above the city. No frou-frou architecture, it's a manly structure that dominates the city and river beneath it. It is the ultimate man-cave.

Burning of the Castle - Heidelberg

Over the years, the castle suffered significant damage during battles. The most severe incident occurred when lightning struck the gunpowder stored inside the walls. Part of the castle was blown off during the massive explosion, and the structure was further damaged by the resulting fire. The "Burning of the Castle" is an annual event each summer that uses lights and fireworks to recreate the castle's rich history. Put this exhibition on your bucket list.

Vienna, Austria

I traveled with Army friends, Mike Anthony and Greg Schwalb, to Vienna, Austria for a long weekend in October 1983. Vienna, Prague, and Budapest (the capitals of Austria, Czechoslovakia, and Hungary) were often referred to as sister cities. They shared a lot of similar culture and architecture. But two of them, Prague and Budapest, were behind the communist Iron Curtain.

Only Vienna was considered "free." We took a sightseeing tour that included Schönbrunn Palace (where President Kennedy and Khrushchev met on June 3, 1961), Belvedere Palace, as well as the Parliament, Rathaus, and Burgtheater.

Although Austria was officially a neutral country, it was still impacted by World War II and the U.S.-Soviet Cold War that followed. The Soviets liberated Vienna from the Nazis in the final month of WWII. Before returning control of Austria back to the Allies, they built a large war memorial to commemorate the 17,000 Red Army troops killed during the battle for Vienna. The transfer agreement required the Austrians to grudgingly keep the memorial in the capital. After the Soviets left, the Austrians built a major fountain in front of the Soviet monument. When turned on, the fountain shoots water several dozen feet in the air and effectively masks the memorial from view. A perfect "engineering" and architectural solution.

Soviet War Memorial

Amsterdam

Lonnie Long and I traveled to Amsterdam during Thanksgiving weekend in 1983. We had high expectations for a great weekend. However, it turned into the worst trip I have ever taken.

We had driven about six hours from Bad Wimpfen, Germany to learn the traffic in the city was horrid. We spent another three hours trying to find a parking spot. The lack of parking was compounded by a month-long garbage strike by local unions. Rotting trash was piled up on the sidewalks, in the streets, and in parking lots.

Lonnie Long in Amsterdam

Lonnie and I finally found a parking space and began an hour-long search, on foot, for a hotel. Finding one with a room available—we could afford—was easier said than done. But we eventually did and checked in. After being assigned a room on the fourth floor, we learned the hotel did not have elevators. We hauled our bags up an unusually steep and curved stairwell that was only wide enough for one person. We made another run back to the car to get the rest of our gear. As we came downstairs, we caught the two male receptionists kissing behind the check-in counter. Okay, we were probably staying at a gay hotel, at least for one night.

Back at the car, which was several blocks away, everything looked normal. We were legally parked and no signs indicated otherwise. We brought the rest of our bags back to the hotel and climbed to our room. Both of us were sweating from the ten-plus hour trip and hustling several city blocks back and forth and up and down steep stairs. We wanted to go out and enjoy the Amsterdam nightlife but needed to clean up. Lonnie asked, "Where's the shower?" We looked around to discover there wasn't an in-suite bathroom. I went down the hall and found a community bathroom and shower. Great. So, I stood guard outside the bathroom while Lonnie showered. When he was done, he stood guard for me. We were ready to get the hell out of that hotel.

We went out on the town and ate some dinner, then found a lively pub and met some people. At the bar, a tall girl approached me and started talking. Something was strange—maybe it was her Adam's apple—and I began to suspect "she" was a he. Lonnie and I ducked out of that pub and looked for a place that had biologically honest women. Around midnight, Lonnie and I got back to our hotel room, locked the door and crashed.

The next morning, we agreed to check out of the hotel and try to find another one. We paid the bill in cash (we did not have credit cards then) and hauled our bags back to the car, only to find the parking space but not our car. It was gone. No fricking kidding, the car was missing. We could not speak a word of Dutch but tried to ask locals what happened to our car. Holy smokes. Stuck in Amsterdam, our bags on the sidewalk around us, with no idea what had happened to our car. After about 15 minutes, we realized there were no other cars on the side of the street where we had parked. Perhaps it was towed away. We walked across the street and saw traffic signs in Dutch. We suspected they said something about parking in the evenings was permitted, but not during morning rush hour. There were no signs on the side of the road where we parked, so we felt like we had been sucker punched.

After running down a local policeman who spoke English, he suggested we go to an impound lot about a mile away. So, we dragged our bags through the city, breaking into another good sweat. We found the impound lot and spent 30 minutes looking for someone who could help us. Finally, we did, and sure enough, my car had been towed. We had to pay about 150 Dutch guilders to get it out of impound. Lonnie and I scrapped together the cash. I was ready to go back to Germany, but we talked about it and figured the next 24 hours would be better.

Driving back through Amsterdam we looked for another parking space, found a parking lot and pulled in. An old drunk walked up to our car and appeared to want some money. I didn't know if he was the attendant or just offering to protect my car for a fee. I gave him a few guilders, and we went to find a new hotel. Our cash was now low due to the towing fee, so we went cheap. We found a Youth Hostel on a back street. We checked in, paid for the night, and then went inside to see what the rooms looked like. Shocked to find it just a big room filled with several bunk beds and smelly men lying on them, it reminded me of the concentration camp at Dachau. No fears. Lonnie and I were Army Rangers and had seen much worse. We left our bags in the car so that they wouldn't be pilfered in the Youth Hostel.

Day two was now half over, and it was finally time to actually tour Amsterdam. We walked the streets and saw some of the famous canals. It was cold and misty, and the city's scenery and smells were dominated by the trash strike which was visible everywhere. The highlight of the day was touring Anne Frank's House. Frank was the young Jewish girl who wrote a diary while in hiding from Nazis during WWII, a sad story that most American school children are required to read. She was eventually betrayed, deported, and ultimately died in the Bergen-Belsen concentration camp. We later visited the house and museum of Dutch painter Rembrandt, a less sobering moment.

We drifted across the city and could not find much more to do. Approached several times by residents who wanted to sell drugs to us, I ignored the first two or three offers. But my patience wore out. I was irritated that these people thought I looked like a druggie. The next guy that came up asked, "Coke? Hash?" I screamed at the top of my lungs, "NO. I DON'T WANT ANY %$#@ DRUGS!!" The little twerp scattered back into an opium den. Lonnie politely suggested I take a more tactful approach in declining any offers. When other scumbags continued to ask me if I wanted any drugs, I emphatically answered, "No, but I do need peanut butter! Do you have peanut butter?" This answer would confuse the idiots or make them think I was mentally unstable.

After eating dinner, we went to find some nightlife. We hung out until about 1:00 AM, and then made the long walk back to the Youth Hostel. When we arrived, we found the door locked and heard that the management did so at 11:00 PM. Bummer. The bright side of being shut out was that we would not get head lice from one of those bunks bed. And so, we executed plan B: sleep in the car. At about 2:30 AM, Lonnie and I arrived at the car. I tried to open the driver side door, but there was a big hole in the lock. Some dirtball had tried to break into my car by jamming a screwdriver in both locks. They did not succeed in breaking in, but now I could not open either door. Fortunately, the hatchback lock was undamaged. We crawled into the car from the rear, and Lonnie and I slept until 6:30 AM.

On awakening, we both agreed we'd had enough. There was nothing left for us to see and began our drive back to Germany. As we left Holland, we were stopped by the German border police. Germany was a more conservative country. They saw a couple of American soldiers in civilian clothes and figured we might be smuggling drugs into their country. My car was pulled into an inspection pit, and the border agents started to pull off the wheels. We had nothing to fear, but this was yet another delay and inconvenience caused by the Amsterdam visit. We had been there only about ten minutes when a beat-up old van pulled up to the border with a couple of guys who looked like Cheech and Chong. The German border agents started salivating and pulled the minivan into the secondary inspection point. They then realized Lonnie and I were just regular tourists and let us go. As we pulled out of the checkpoint, I could see the Germans getting out power tools and putting on rubber gloves. We both laughed about how we had blown our Thanksgiving break and swore we would never return to Amsterdam. Since that visit, I've spoken to some friends who said they had a great experience in the Dutch capital. Over thirty years have passed so I might give it another shot. I think it is safe to say, however, that it's not on my bucket list.

Arnhem, Netherlands

On the way home from Amsterdam, we had an opportunity to visit a famous WWII battlefield at Arnhem, Netherlands. The Allies had attempted to seize strategic bridges in German-occupied Netherlands during *Operation Market Garden*, a U.S. and British military operation that did not go well. Capturing the final bridge was the objective of British paratroopers performing a high-risk mission deep in enemy territory. The lightly-armed soldiers surprised the Germans but ultimately were unable to hold out against German reinforcements with tanks. Much of the British force was killed or captured. The epic battle was eventually dramatized in the movie, "A Bridge Too Far."

Copenhagen

During Labor Day in 1984, I took a four-day weekend trip to Copenhagen. A tour bus ride through a sleepless night was the cheapest and easiest way to get there from my apartment near Heilbronn, Germany.

Arriving in the Danish capital early, my hotel room was not ready, so I set out to see some of the city. Some of the interesting sites, included Amalienborg Palace, Christianborg Palace, Marble Church, Houses of

Parliament, the Stock Exchange, Tivoli Amusement Park, the Royal Theater, and the Little Mermaid statue.

The Little Mermaid was perched on a rock at the edge of the harbor. Based on the fairy tale by Danish author Hans Christian Andersen, the small and unimposing statue is a Copenhagen icon and has been a major tourist attraction since 1913. In recent years, vandals have targeted her, and occasionally, some drunken sailor would sneak up in the dark and saw off her head. I am certain the sight of a decapitated mermaid probably terrorized all the little kids who came to visit. Fortunately, she had her head on her shoulders during my visit. And in true European fashion, she was nude.

The city tour ended in the early afternoon, and the bus dropped me off in the main square. I wanted to check into my hotel and take a nap but sleeping that early would mess up my body clock for the rest of the trip. So, I went over to a nearby pub to get more flavor—the liquid kind—of what Copenhagen was like.

I went inside and must have stood out as a typical American tourist: mismatched clothes, a camera dangling around my neck, and a city map hanging out of my back pocket. There was a Brit at the bar, who had clearly been there for a while enjoying his stay. I grabbed an open stool and looked over at the beer taps, debating on my choices.

As I took a seat, the Brit leaned over and gave me some words of advice. "Don't drink the Elephant Beer." I paused for a moment and gave him a puzzled look. He repeated, "Trust me. Don't drink the Elephant Beer!"

I had never heard of Elephant Beer but hoped it did not actually originate from an elephant. Maybe it was just a bad brew with a catchy name, like Billy Beer or some other cheap American brand. But he had me hooked. It was the perfect sales line for someone selling Elephant Beer.

This was clearly a challenge to my manhood, but a 25-year-old Airborne Ranger is not about to publicly relinquish his "man card" in a foreign pub. I had to know and turned to the bartender and immediately ordered an Elephant Beer. The bartender filled a glass, and I sat there and enjoyed it. I followed it with a second.

At this point the Brit staggered off his stool, mumbling as he went out the door, "Don't drink the Elephant Beer."

He was clearly a half-wit. The beer was excellent. I was feeling fine. Score: American 2, Elephant Beer 2, nitwit Brit 0.

My hotel was only a five-minute walk from the pub. The customer traffic had picked up, and maybe some interesting ladies would come in, so I hung out for another hour. I had no fear of the elephant. I took on an entire stampede of them, a glass at a time.

Then it finally hit me. Feeling no pain, I had reached my culminating point. And I was out of cash, no U.S. dollars or Danish crowns. If I drank any more, I would probably begin to grow beer muscles. I decided to walk back to my hotel and recover from the long bus ride and the fine Copenhagen beer. I paid the tab and left a customary American tip, which was not something the Europeans typically did.

As I left, a couple of guys walked into the pub. I stopped and told them, "Don't drink the Elephant Beer! Don't do it." I felt like it was my obligation to continue this interesting social experiment. They looked at me without saying anything then walked straight up to the bar and placed their order, Elephant Beer. I thought the brewer, Carlsberg, had a great marketing approach. Challenge a customer's manhood. Declare that Elephant Beer a forbidden fruit, and the sinners will fight for it. I was probably one of the dozens, if not hundreds, of tourists snagged in this verbal-chain-letter scheme. It was an early form of viral marketing, long before the development of the Internet or Twitter.

Sweden

The next day was Sunday. Things were slow in Copenhagen, so I decided to take a one-hour boat ride to Malmo, Sweden. I had never been to Sweden, the mysterious land of beautiful blondes (something I hoped was true having seen pictures). I needed to see it for myself as I may not have the opportunity again. I jumped on the boat and started the journey.

The trip crossed a narrow channel—it couldn't have been more than ten miles wide—in the Baltic Sea. This channel was a maritime choke point where Soviet submarines tried to sneak in and out of their Navy base in the Baltic Sea. I had read accounts where Scandinavian fishermen occasionally caught a Soviet sub in their fishing nets, resulting in some of the boats being dragged under the water. Other times, the sub surfaced, and Soviet sailors would climb out and cut the fishing nets and then escape back to the depths. I kept an eye out for subs during the ride but had no luck.

I wanted to check Sweden off my bucket list, so I documented my visit. Upon arrival, I immediately got my passport stamped and bought a postcard and stamps and scribbled, "Having a blast in Sweden" and addressed the card to my family in Pennsylvania. Ten minutes had elapsed, it was now time to look around and find where the Swedish blast was to back up my words. I only had about two hours until the return boat trip to Copenhagen.

It was Sunday, so most of the stores were closed. Initially disappointed, then I found an ice cream stand open for business. I walked up and, sure enough, a beautiful blonde Swedish girl stood behind the counter. She spoke perfect English. It was too early to propose to marry her, so I ordered some ice cream first. I already loved this country and was ready to defect. Reluctantly I left her, ice cream in hand, to see as much as I could in the limited time I had.

There was a lieutenant in my battalion named Todd Skoog, who was of Swedish descent. I thought he might have some family nearby, so I looked for a phone book. Maybe some of Todd's relatives could show me the town. Then I realized that the surname Skoog in Sweden was probably like Smith in England. There would be six pages of Skoogs in the Malmo phone book. I decided to explore Malmo on my own. I bounced around the city on foot for the next hour and a half, then headed back to the dock to catch the boat to Copenhagen. The ice cream stand was now closed, my future fiancé gone. I felt sad that I had to ship out before I could order another cup of ice cream and get engaged. Sometimes, life can be cruel.

Neuschwanstein Castle

In the late 1800s, the German state of Bavaria had a crazy king named Ludwig, who spent most of the royal treasury building three huge castles: Neuschwanstein, Linderhof, and Herrenchiemsee. They were all impressive, but his erratic behavior and excessive spending caused significant distress in the Kingdom. In 1886, a day after being officially declared insane, Ludwig died under suspicious conditions.

Neuschwanstein is perhaps the most famous and is rumored to be the inspiration for the Disney castle. I visited it at least five times and never tired of its striking architecture and dramatic scenery. There is a pedestrian bridge nearby that provides great photo opportunities. Visible from Neuschwanstein is Hohenschwangau Castle, built by King Ludwig's father, where Ludwig spent much of his time.

Linderhof & Herrenchiemsee

The other two palaces, Linderhof & Herrenchiemsee, included architecture and features inspired by the Palace of Versailles in France. Linderhof was the smallest of the three palaces and featured a Hall of Mirrors, a Moroccan Tea Room and an indoor Venus Grotto where the nutty king would row his swanboat while illuminated by changing colored lights. It also had impressive gardens for those who appreciate landscaping.

Whereas Linderhof was inspired by Versailles, Herrenchiemsee was intended to be a faithful replica of the Louis XIV's palace. Construction ceased after King Ludwig's death and shortly afterward, the unfinished palace was opened to the public. It is still an impressive royal residence, located on an island in Bavaria's largest lake, Chiemsee. Ferry boats are the only way to get to and from the palace. I was able to tour Herrenchiemsee one weekend after running a half marathon race at Chiemsee.

Bad Wimpfen

For a time, I lived in Bad Wimpfen, Germany located on the Neckar River. It was a picturesque old walled city with a fascinating history, including settlement by both the Celts and the Romans. The Blue Tower, which dominated the skyline, was fun to climb and provided a commanding view of the Neckar River valley. Bad Wimpfen made me feel like I lived in a storybook.

On Saturday mornings, I would walk through the stone streets, among the well-preserved historic buildings and shop in the outdoor market. Occasionally, I would run into an American tour group and welcome them to my new hometown. I rented an apartment with several other lieutenants, and my roommates rotated as we were all serving on three-year tours at staggered times. They included Lonnie Long, Chris Bowling, John Moeller, and Ron Claeys. We all worked late and often saw each other only on the weekends. The Schimmel family were our landlords. The parents, Fritz and Klara, had three grown children: Artur, Carmen, and Ingrid. They learned about my family in the United States from my stories and informally adopted me. I spent many memorable birthdays and Christmas holidays with the Schimmel family. Carmen Schimmel had a child a few years after I left and named him Kevin, after my paralyzed brother. When my brother died, he left some of his estate to Kevin Schimmel.

Burg Guttenberg, Berg Hornberg

A few miles north of Bad Wimpfen, also on the Neckar River, were two more medieval castles: Burg Guttenberg and Burg Hornberg, which were favorite places to take visiting family and friends. Guttenberg Castle is over 500 years old and is more than just a ruin, as it includes a museum, a restaurant and offers another great view of the valley. The castle's massive stone walls have been well-preserved and are used for flying demonstrations by birds of prey: eagles, falcons, and vultures.

Hornberg Castle is located on a steep hill above the village of Neckarzimmern. The castle was once in possession of Götz von Berlichingen in the 1500s. On a later trip, my wife and I ate dinner in the castle with the Schimmel family who pointed out that a suit of armor, worn by Götz von Berlichingen, was on display in the restaurant. The Germans then told us the rest of the story. At one point, the castle was under siege, and a messenger from the opposing king carried an ultimatum to surrender. Undaunted by the threats of his enemy, Götz von Berlichingen delivered his famous reply to the opposing king: "Sie können mich am arsch lecken." That loosely translates to tell your king, "He can kiss my ass." It was the first known use of this well-known phrase, uttered by a bold German nobleman exercising his first amendment rights.

The Castle Ball

Each year Army Engineers hold "The Castle Ball" to celebrate their profession and to build personal relationships. A castle is a symbol of the type of fortresses built by military engineers through the centuries. The Castle Ball is simultaneously held in many locations around the world. Officers and NCOs wear their formal Dress Blue uniform. While I was stationed in Germany, the 7th Engineer Brigade Castle Ball was held at the historic Ludwigsburg Palace near Stuttgart. Most of these formal balls were a bit stuffy for young bachelor officers. Senior officers would bring their spouses and catch up with long-time colleagues. The bachelors always wanted to get rowdy but felt as if the eyes of seniors were on them—and they were—to keep them in check. Most of the bachelors intended to stay at the Ball only as long as socially required and planned to peel off and find more fun elsewhere.

But that year, things were different. Jaws dropped when they announced contestants of the Miss America Pageant planned to attend this Castle Ball, and the ladies needed escorts. There were probably 15 bachelor officers in the battalion and only two or three beauty contestants. The big question was who would be selected as the lucky escort officers.

The competition started as a classic power play. The captains immediately pulled rank on the lieutenants, it—rank—had its privileges. The captains it was decided, led by the devious and cunning Tony Roucco, would represent the battalion for the escort mission. Captains were naturally more seasoned, more mature, and the ideal choice. The bachelor lieutenants fired back, "We're younger, fitter and have outgoing personalities. The ladies will have more fun with a dashing lieutenant!" We noted that the captains who weren't married yet–probably for good reasons–had been passed over in the Darwinian natural selection process for mates. Lieutenants were clearly a more suitable choice for this critical international, diplomatic mission. To our dismay, the captains won the day. Although we were the ideal candidates for the job, they had the upper hand in the game of politics. They had rigged the selection by telling their friends in Battalion Operations to assign them to the escort duty. It wasn't fair to the lieutenants, but we simply rolled over to appease the senior officers. Ever-hopeful for another shot at escort duty, we consoled each other with the fact that lieutenants eventually become captains.

Czechoslovakia

During Thanksgiving of 1985, I traveled to Czechoslovakia, another communist country in the Warsaw Pact, and toured Prague and Karlsbad. Accompanied by another lieutenant in our battalion, Dennis Faker, we both wanted to see how the communist society lived, some of the historical sites, and shop for prized Czech crystal.

The Czechs were known to hate the Soviets and had an affinity for the West, but their government was politically tied to the USSR. The people of Prague had revolted in 1968 against Soviet oppression to little avail; their hopes were quickly crushed by Soviet tanks. After this uprising, however, it became apparent if war were to break out in Europe between the nations of the Warsaw Pact and NATO, the Soviets could not rely on the Czech military to fight willingly for the communist cause.

The Czechs had an underground economy that prized Western goods. These items, however, could only be purchased with Western money, such as U.S. dollars or West German marks. As in East Germany, communist money could be legally exchanged at a controlled (artificial) rate only at stores run by the State. The average Czech citizen would eagerly pay ten times more for a U.S. dollar because the communist Czech crowns (their currency) had little real value. It was a game, and the doctrine of capitalism played out behind the scenes.

On this trip, we traveled in civilian clothes and crossed the Czech border on a tour bus. I immediately noticed security was less strict compared to that of East Germany, a satellite nation the Soviets had a much firmer hold on. As we rode through the countryside, I saw multiple military installations, convoys, and overhead a MiG fighter jet practicing bombing runs. We weren't allowed to take pictures of Warsaw Pact military forces, having been forewarned by threats of detention for spying. We didn't want to spend time in the gulag, so we took pictures of lots of other things. Despite our best efforts to avoid taking pictures of anything that could get us hauled off to prison, there were so many military personnel around it was hard to avoid them.

Interesting Clouds, partially obscured by MiG Fighter jet

There was an unusual cloud drifting in the sky that day, and I aimed my camera at it. Just as I snapped the picture, a pesky MiG fighter jet flew into the lens' field of view. Rude. I attempted to take two or three other cloud pictures, only to watch the MiG fly back into the shot and ruin the photo. As an engineer, I had studied road construction. While taking a picture of a Czech road, a military convoy drove into the scene. Another photo ruined. Film and film development weren't cheap, and I was frustrated, knowing that I needed to make every shot count.

Czech road, partially obscured by Military Truck

It snowed when we arrived in the nation's capital, Prague. We toured many of the attractions it had to offer: Charles Bridge, Jewish Cemetery, and the Astronomical Clock to name a few. We later visited the nearby Karlstein Castle. Fortunately, there weren't as many military planes and vehicles in the city to mess up my photos. At this point, we had seen enough cultural sites, and it was time to check out the shops.

Dennis and I flagged a taxi that took us across Prague to a store that sold crystal. The driver told us his fare. I did not have any Czech crowns, handed him a $20 bill and asked for change in Czech crowns. The driver was thrilled. He gave me the unofficial exchange rate, ten times higher than the official rate. Using this rate, I calculated the cost of the taxi ride to be 17 cents. I was happy with this transaction.

Dennis Faker and Kerry in Snowy Prague

The experience taught us how to exchange money in a communist country, buy something cheap, and pay for it with big U.S. bill. Also, make sure to ask for your change in crowns (or the local currency). Pretend you are an ignorant American and walk off with wads of commie paper. Changing money on the street with a random shopkeeper was relatively safe, but I was suspicious of the dozens of people who walked up to us on the street and asked to exchange money.

Dennis and I knew this could be a set up by the police to trap Westerners into an illegal exchange of currency. If we agreed and demanded an unofficial rate, we might have been arrested.

The strangest of these encounters was when an old lady knocked on my hotel room door at 11:00 PM. I opened the door, and she asked me to "change money." She was probably a poor pensioner, but I could not take the risk. It might have been a trap. My suspicions were further reinforced by another American who informed Dennis and I that he had found a surveillance bug hidden in a radio in his room.

Back to the crystal shopping.

Dennis had it all figured out. I watched how he gamed the communist system. First, he bought a big suitcase for about $3, then went to the crystal store and bought about 50-60 items, many were wine and water glasses, part of a matching set. He paid for it all with cheap crowns.

Back at the hotel, Dennis packed the suitcase with the crystal but did not put his name on the bag. He then put the suitcase in the baggage compartment under the tour bus as we boarded to leave the country. At the border crossing, the guards only checked a couple of bags for items that needed to be taxed. Any Czech crystal leaving the country—exported—had a large tax levied on it. If Dennis's bag were one of the ones inspected, it would have no identity on it, and he would not claim it. The bag and the investment would be lost, but he would not be at risk of being questioned by communist authorities.

Dennis was true to his last name, 'Faker.' He beat the odds and returned to Germany with a lot of highly-valued crystal acquired for less than $70.

We felt good that we stuck it to the commies. We had no obligation to subsidize their military. Instead, we felt as if we had undermined the evil empire. Regrettably, this clandestine operation was not recognized by the U.S. government, but I assured Dennis that he deserved a medal. The citation could read: "For conducting covert operations while surrounded in a hostile communist environment, Lieutenant Dennis Faker single-handedly weakened the economy of the Czech puppet government and contributed to the economic collapse of the Warsaw Pact and Soviet Empire. His fearless actions reflect great credit upon himself, the United States Army and the United States of America." Well done, lieutenant!

As we departed Czechoslovakia, we made a final stop in the city of Karlsbad. I walked into a small chocolate shop to get some last-minute souvenirs—not just chocolate, mind you. As I turned into the aisle, I looked up and saw Rich Hook, a West Point classmate, staring me in the face. We were both surprised as we had last seen each other about two years earlier and over 4,000 miles away. The chance encounter was a bit eerie. It's a small world after all.

CHAPTER 37
REFORGER, MANEUVER DAMAGE, ROCKET RON

REFORGER (REturn of FORces to GERmany) was an annual exercise conducted, during the Cold War, by NATO (the last was held in 1993). It was a major test to determine how quickly the United States could send more Army troops and equipment from the United States to Germany in case WWIII broke out. REFORGER deployed up to 100,000 troops from the United States. Although this may seem like an impressive number, it is only a fraction of the manpower that would be deployed in a third world war.

In January 1985, I was an evaluator for a National Guard battalion (about 700 soldiers) that had flown across the Atlantic for the exercise. I was a coach and mentor tasked with evaluating a company of about 130 soldiers. Once the unit landed, the battalion needed to quickly get all its troops and equipment from the airport and into the woods to conceal itself from a Soviet attack.

I met the company commander, an Army National Guard captain after his unit arrived. Wherever the captain went, I tagged along. It was a long and tiring trip from the United States, but there was much work to do. The company headed to their field site, located near a small German town. When we arrived, a bitter snowstorm was hitting the area.

The commander directed the mess tent be set up and to get the coffee brewing. This order was good for moral, but a tactical error. The priority of work in wartime is always security first. Establish a perimeter and develop a defensive plan; put out concertina (razor sharp wire), set up a gate for vehicles to enter and put guards out to monitor and secure the perimeter. Security is always the number one task, not creature comforts like food and coffee. I spoke to the company commander about the issue and acknowledged the unit was tired and hungry, but told him, "Our first objective is secure our position and keep them alive." The captain outranked me, but I wore a Ranger tab, and he could not argue with my tactical position. The teaching point was made, and we continued the exercise.

While the unit set up their perimeter, I noticed an older German lady watching all the activity. She was old enough to remember WWII, and her facial expressions spoke volumes. All the noise and traffic from the Army vehicles, generators and soldiers would disturb their little town for the next week. I wanted to have a good relationship with the local residents and walked over and greeted her, "Gruss Gott." A big smile spread on her face, and she spoke to me in German. She seemed happy to see American soldiers but was curious as to what we were doing. I explained it was an exercise and that we would be there for a few days. She was shocked when she learned we were going to sleep outside in the snow.

"It is so bitter cold, please... you and your soldiers can stay at my house and be warm." She waved her hand at a house not too far from our site.

I was touched. "Thank you for your generous offer, but we have tents, and we're," I gestured around at all the men busy with their work, "trained for these conditions."

She nodded. "But perhaps you," she pointed a finger at my rank, "can come to dinner."

"Thank you but I can't. I have to set an example for the other soldiers and can't accept special privileges."

She nodded, "Still, I will bring you something" and headed toward her house. Shortly she came back with a cup of hot tea, which I accepted, and we talked for another twenty minutes. It was a nice conversation that built some good will with her and the other locals. Throughout our friendly talk, I felt the presence of our troops had brought back memories of her youth in WWII. She seemed thankful the United States Army was there, deterring another war from happening. It felt reassuring to know we were appreciated, but we would need to respond by being good neighbors during the training exercise.

The next evening, I rode in the back seat of an Army Jeep with the captain and his driver in the front. The jeep, a small but rugged vehicle, was officially called the M151A2. Built to take a beating, it was slow to accelerate and had few comforts. During wartime and military exercises, we could not use headlights for fear that the enemy might detect us. Instead, we drove on the back roads and on trails using 'black out drive,' very small low-powered lights on the front of the vehicle. The driver could see perhaps only 20 feet in front, but it helped us navigate at night. However, other vehicles would not be able to see us, which, unfortunately, resulted in collisions. Any collision between a 60-ton tank and an Army Jeep had a disastrous outcome. Off-road, blackout drive also made it very hard for drivers to see soldiers sleeping in the woods. Each year, Army vehicles ran over a few dozen soldiers, whose crushed bodies were often not found until after sunrise. The tanks, weighing sixty tons, and armored personnel carriers (APCs) were the worst. The drivers can't see much, and they don't feel the crunch of a body. We were always careful in selecting our sleeping spots, no one wanted a multi-ton wake-up call… or worse, having it listed as a cause of death.

As we drove the jeep in darkness on a German road, we strained to see the left turn, on a small trail, that led through the forest and back to our bivouac site. I was quite good at terrain navigation and told the driver to slow down, we were approaching the turn. He didn't and missed it, blowing past the turn by about 100 meters. Quickly putting the jeep in reverse, he started to back up on the road. Alarm bells immediately went off in my head. Jeeps did not have back up lights! If a local Herman the German was flying up behind us in their car on this road, he would not see us until it was too late. I turned my head around, and sure enough, headlights were closing on our position. We needed to get off the road, or the German car was going to plow into us at full speed. The only steel between my body and the oncoming car was a full 5-gallon gas can that would probably ignite and explode, right on my back. Our driver ignored my urgent warnings to pull off the road, and he kept backing up. The German headlights raced over a rise in the road. A violent impact was imminent. I thought my life was going to end and that I had seen my last beer festival.

CRASH!!!

Well, Praise the Lord for MILSPEC equipment. That jeep and that gas can were evidently designed to withstand a nuclear explosion. The front end of the German car was crushed, and we were driven forward by the impact. But the gas can and jeep frame were barely scratched. I couldn't believe it. There was another Octoberfest in my future.

Maneuver Damage

REFORGER was sometimes held in January, the cold season, as was the case in 1985. That meant the German soil was frozen and would not tear up under the weight of hundreds of American tanks. Major exercises always caused some 'maneuver damage' where farmer's crops were crushed, forests and streets were damaged, and fuel would be accidentally spilled requiring an immediate environmental cleanup. All this damage to German property needed to be paid for, so the Army did its best to minimize it.

If an Army exercise killed a German farmer's chicken, the farmer would be reimbursed for not only for the value of the chicken but also the eggs it would have produced.

In one case, an Army soldier drove an M60 tank over a historic stone bridge. The centuries-old bridge was designed to carry ox carts and maybe light vehicles. The tank caused severe damage, reportedly well over a million dollars in repair cost.

One of our battalion's well-regarded soldiers, Staff Sergeant (SSG) Michael Akins, told me about his vehicle accident during a previous tour in Germany. He had been driving his M-113 tracked Armored Personnel Carrier (APC) on an icy German road. Now, the M-113 carries a squad of infantry soldiers, weighs about 13 tons and can travel at over 40 mph. Once it starts moving, it has some irreversible momentum.

Akins was doing fine on the frozen road until he encountered an unusually steep downhill slope, immediately followed by a sharp right turn. He tried to stop the APC, but gravity and momentum were stronger than the negligible traction on the slippery surface. His APC left the road and plowed through a farmer's barn. He blasted a massive hole in the side of the barn, ran over a cow, flattened some chickens, and continued through the other wall of the barn. His armored vehicle finally came to rest in the nearby field.

Akins called his military unit on the radio and reported the maneuver damage. The German police (Polezi) were alerted and raced to the scene. Meanwhile, the cow though terribly injured was still alive and screaming. It's distressing to hear an animal suffer, but SSG Akins did not have any live ammo and was also not authorized to shoot the cow. Akins knew he was probably going to be charged with driving at excessive speeds on an icy road and might be facing other disciplinary action. As valued as he was viewed in the company, his stock price was declining by the minute. Just then, a small miracle happened. The Polezi racing to the scene came over the same icy hill. Their vehicle lost control and crashed through the same barn and put the cow out of its misery. Fortunately, the German police officers were not hurt. Even better, the Polezi could not charge SSG Akins with negligent driving, or they would also need to charge themselves. Akins was off the hook for the damage. The farmer got reimbursed for a new barn, some new animals and had tenderized beef steaks as a bonus. The Polezi got a new squad car.

Rocket Ron

During my last year in Germany, my roommate was Ron Claeys, and he was a bit of a daredevil. He had bought a superbike, a motorcycle capable of extremely fast speeds. I wasn't a big motorcycle fan—or of stunts on two-wheeled vehicles, as my brother had broken his neck as a young boy on a bicycle and was a quadriplegic for the remainder of his life. And I knew it didn't matter who was at fault in a motorcycle accident. The loser was always the unprotected rider.

But Ron was close to immortal, and he did not share my aversion or opinion. He was confident in his ability and managed the risk by buying "a good helmet and good leathers." He zipped around southern Germany and earned the nickname "Rocket Ron."

One Saturday morning, I was at the apartment when Ron came out of his bedroom wearing his leathers and carrying his helmet. He announced, "See you later, Kerry. I'm going to Nuremberg." I told him to have fun.

About 30 minutes later, the phone rang in our apartment. We rarely received an incoming phone call, so I picked it up thinking it was a wrong number.

"Hello." I could only hear someone gasping heavily. My first thought was that it was an obscene caller. But then I heard my name during the panting.

"Kerry? Kerry? I'm OK. I'm OK." It was Ron. "I wrecked my bike."

He settled down and asked if I could borrow another friend's pickup truck to come get him and help recover his bike.

I got to the scene about an hour later. The German Polezi were already there and had issued Ron a ticket for excessive speed on the off ramp. Given the favorable exchange rate, the ticket was only about $20. I asked Ron what had happened.

"I was flying down Autobahn 6 and looked up and saw this castle I've always wanted to visit." He shook his head then continued. "I made a snap decision to take the exit for the castle. Too late... and too fast." I was standing at the exit he had tried to take. It was a 270-degree spiral off ramp. "I was at 225 kph (140 mph) and braked hard." He rubbed his chin. "I got the bike speed down to 160 kph (100 mph) as I entered the curve but couldn't hold it. I shot off the ramp partway into the turn."

It was my turn to shake my head. Ron had been incredibly lucky. He had gone off the ramp into dozens of small trees rather than into an unforgiving metal guardrail. Sliding in bike first, he had managed to shear off six trees which had absorbed the energy of the impact. Amazingly, he survived mostly intact with only a sprained thumb. His motorcycle, however, was KIA. The superbike suffered significant damage and had come apart, its pieces were strewn across the area. I am sure Ron considered it a character-building experience. Years later, he got his law degree and became a prosecuting attorney in Colorado. I have often wondered what vehicle he drives to work nowadays.

CHAPTER 38

PORSCHE - THE MOBILE MONEY PIT

One of my roommates in Germany, Lonnie Long, had bought an old Porsche 924. He shared the driving with me during some long trips on the autobahn but did not want me to exceed 160 kph (100 mph) when I was behind the wheel. But as soon as Lonnie dozed off, I pegged that baby. I was one with the engine, the flow of machine and highway, but I watched for signs of him waking and would then back off. He never caught on, and it was his fault for trusting me. That little taste of high-speed made me think about getting my own German sports car.

Another friend of mine, 1st Lieut. Bill Hargraves, also worked at Wharton Barracks in Heilbronn, Germany. Bill and I were former roommates at West Point, where we both played lacrosse. One day, Bill came rolling through our battalion headquarters area in a red Porsche 928S, an impressive eight-cylinder grand touring, luxury, sports car. It looked hot, and I immediately needed one. I asked Bill the details. He gave me the inside story, and I went straight to the same dealership in Zuffenhausen, just north of Stuttgart.

Financially, the time was right for me to act. I was single and had no debt. U.S. soldiers did not need to pay the German sales tax on cars. The exchange rate of the U.S. dollar against the German Mark was at a favorable rate of 3.4 to 1. Servicemen in Europe paid low U.S. prices for gasoline (we did not need to pay the stiff tax on fuel).

My exotic car strategy was to buy a used Porsche 928, test it out on the autobahn, and then ship it back to the USA. When I finally got back to the States, I could cruise the streets in my new chick magnet. Maybe I could even go back to my old neighborhood one day and deliver newspapers in it. The possibilities were endless.

I arrived at the dealership and looked at several 928s on the lot. I settled on an affordable one, five years old and relatively low mileage. I drove it for a few months in Germany to have some fun and see what it could do - up to 260 kph (160mph) on some stretches of the autobahn. I never completely pegged it but was very close. I backed down when I realized that a tire blowout, at that speed, would leave parts of me and the car scattered across southern Germany, Austria and perhaps northern Italy.

Near the end of my three-year Germany tour, I prepared the Porsche for shipment back to the United States. Now this car had been built to European specs and was considered a 'gray market' car. I had to complete a safety conversion to comply with U.S. Department of Transportation standards. That meant installing an upgraded rear bumper, steel bars in the doors to protect from a side impact, and an anti-spill valve on the gas tank to prevent fuel from leaking during a rollover. Additionally, the autobahn tail light was not a U.S. standard, so it needed to be disconnected. The U.S. import policy allowed for a one-time EPA waiver on emissions. That meant this car did not need a fuel conversion and could run on leaded or unleaded gas. I signed a contract with a car conversion company that also included shipping back to the USA.

Everything seemed to have gone well with the conversion and shipping until I picked up the car in the United States. The hood was dented, and the exterior of the car was scratched and scuffed. This was pure negligence. Inside, I discovered the Blaupunkt radio had been stolen. It was probably taken by a German, as there was no other damage to the interior. A German thief would use precision tools and do a professional job. I almost expected a "Danke Schoen" note on the dashboard or in the cavity where my radio used to be. I was thankful an American hadn't stolen the radio. They probably would have used a crowbar to rip apart the dashboard.

Now I had to file a damage and loss claim with my insurance company. Everyone knows what a hassle that can be. USAA wanted proof there was a radio in the car before it was shipped. My word was not sufficient. I was a bit offended by their claims rep and felt my integrity was being challenged. Fortunately, I had taken pictures of the car interior and exterior, in Germany, before shipment. The policy eventually covered the radio replacement and hood repainting.

A few months later, the repaired hood had already faded and looked awful, the result of a bad paint job. I decided to repaint the entire car at my expense. This was the beginning of a new chapter with this Porsche which quickly became a money pit.

Before I repainted the car, there were a series of mechanical problems. First, the coolant hose broke on the way to my uncle's funeral. Edward

Kachejian, aka Uncle Eddie, was the last of six siblings on my father's side. I was now stranded on the shoulder of a highway in Virginia and thought I was going to miss his services later that day in Pennsylvania. Fortunately, a local pastor stopped to help me. We patched the hose since I had no time to go to the dealer and get the special 928 coolant hose. The temporary repair worked, and I made to Uncle Eddie's funeral in time to mourn with the family and console my Aunt Helen.

Upon my return to Virginia, the coolant hose broke again and the car overheated. I was towed to the local dealer in Alexandria. During the ride, the tow truck operator repeatedly insisted I use a particular customer service rep at the Porsche dealership. I thanked him for his advice, but it smelled like a he was getting referral kickbacks for each customer he corralled.

I entered the dealership looking confused, possibly because I was. One of the customer service representatives yelled, "Here, I'll help you!" I walked over and saw his nametag, something like "Ed Malek." This was not the name of the guy the tow truck operator insisted I use, but I was now committed. I felt ambushed. This facility was feeling like hostile territory, and my radar lit up.

The tow truck driver came into the dealership a minute later and saw that his buddy, the service advisor, was not getting my business. He gave me a hostile glare. I shrugged and turned back to the man behind the service counter.

Ed had half a dozen certificates on the wall behind him; each cited he was "Porsche Certified." He took my information and booked the repair. I waited a few hours for it to be done. They replaced the bad hose, handed me a bill for about $500 and told me the car was also due for a service. I scheduled the service with them and planned to return the following week. I drove out of the dealership and headed home. When I was five miles from the dealership, red warning lights came on the dashboard, and the engine began smoking. I immediately pulled over and popped the hood. The new hose they had just installed did not have a clamp on it. It had simply blown off, and radiator fluid drenched the engine compartment. I was pissed off. This was pure negligence. How could a Porsche Certified maintenance team miss something that simple?

This was 1986, and nobody had cellular phones, so I walked a few blocks to the nearest pay phone and called the dealership. I demanded they immediately send a tow truck to get my car. I wanted it repaired, and the engine steam cleaned. An hour later, I was back in the service area with Ed. Two hours from then I was back on the road, and most of the day had been wasted. I now had doubts that being a Porsche owner was worth the aggravation.

I returned to the dealership a week later and dropped off the vehicle for its scheduled service. Returning a day later, I was handed a bill for about $2200. I was shocked. In 1986, that was a month of base pay for an Army captain and almost six years of pay at my paperboy job. They handed me a detailed invoice five or six pages long. I wanted to talk to the mechanic and review the bill. The mechanic came out and told me my car had needed a lot of work and claimed he had saved me hundreds of dollars. I didn't feel that grateful. I suspected I was being ripped off.

I inspected the invoice and was shocked at the prices. Parts cost about five times more than an American car. The air filter was $75. I had shipped a brand new one with me as a spare from Germany, where it cost me about $25. Each of the nine distributor wires cost about $40, but they must have been excellent quality as they were cited as 'gold tipped.' Then I saw a charge for two new distributor caps. I thought that was strange. I approached Ed who was standing in front of his wall of "Porsche Certified" qualifications.

"Why was I charged for two distributor caps?" I asked.

He replied, "Your car needs two."

I had never heard of a car with two distributors and was puzzled. My automotive engineering course in college had never covered a two-distributor engine, and it was something new to me.

"Ed, I believe you, but I want you to show me where those two distributors are in the engine." He didn't move from behind the counter. "Come on, show me," I insisted.

We went out to the parking lot and popped the hood of my car. We both looked around. I found the one distributor, but he could not find the other one. Now I was feeling somewhat redeemed, but also more suspicious of every charge though I couldn't prove anything further. Ed reduced the bill by the price of the second distributor. As I drove away from the dealership, I thought, "What have I done to deserve this?"

A few weeks later I went back to the dealership to buy some accessories. As I walked in, I overheard two customer service reps openly arguing about stealing each other's business. The fight for my business seemed to be their next battlefield. What a toxic work environment! Where was the leadership in this place? Before leaving, I approached a lady employee near the front office to ask some questions about my car, I didn't trust those guys in the back to give me honest answers. Where could I get a good paint job? What could I do to reduce the maintenance costs?

"Germans run their cars hard," she commented.

I knew that was true, having seen it for myself.

She continued, "But they don't maintain them."

I knew that to be false. I had witnessed exactly the opposite.

"I think the best thing for you to do is trade yours in and buy a new Porsche." She studied me for a moment. "I can help you pick a good one," she swept her arm around the showroom floor.

I thanked her for her advice and politely left. No way, José, I thought, *that* is not going to happen for a *long* time. I was done with Porsche dealerships.

A few weeks later, I got serious about having the car repainted. Since it was running better, I wanted the car to look good. I went to the Porsche recommended paint expert who specialized in high-end vehicles. He quoted me $4500 for a paint job. BOHICA! Over two months of pay?

My verbal reaction was unfiltered, unmuted and included some profane literary gems that surprised even me. The price was 3 to 4 times more than other paint shops charged. I pointed that out and got a highly defensive response about how they disassemble every part and use the best paint in the world ($125/quart). But I needed a best-value paint job, not the most expensive paint job. I moved on.

But wait, there's more! The saga continued when the Porsche failed an inspection for the exhaust system. It was going to cost me about $3500 for a new tailpipe and muffler. That was not in my budget. I found another manufacturer that made a compatible exhaust for about $900 and paid an Army buddy to install it one weekend for about $250 in labor. The car's new exhaust sounded different, but that was okay. It passed inspection, but I was still hemorrhaging cash.

My car was parked in an open lot near my apartment, and I thought it smart to install an anti-theft alarm. That cost about $500, but it worked well. Too much so. A neighborhood cat occasionally jumped on the hood at night and triggered the alarm. I decided it was more important to keep my neighbors happy and shut the alarm off.

I still had to get the car painted but wanted a quality paint job at an affordable price. Unsure where to go, I poked around at a few different places. One day I drove past a paint shop that had a Porsche 911 parked outside. It had a high-gloss black paint finish that looked spectacular. Ironically, it was a MAACO paint shop that had a reputation for low-budget work. I stopped in the shop and talked to the manager. He confirmed the 911 paint job was his work. It sold me. If he could do the same with my car, he had the deal. We signed a contract for about $1200.

Before MAACO began the work, I briefed his team on unique issues with the car. "We're changing the color from the factory Forest Green to Black. Do not forget to pop up the recessed headlights before you paint. The back of the headlights need to match the car. The headlights can only be popped up with the ignition on. The car has a 5-speed racing gearbox, 1st gear is located where you would normally find reverse on most other cars." They nodded their understanding and my parting words to the manager were, "Please call me if you have *any* questions."

I dropped the car off on a Monday and was told it would be ready on Wednesday. On Thursday, I called to ask if the car was done. The paint shop said they needed more time. Maybe it'll be ready early next week, I reassured myself.

The next week came around, and the car was still not painted. When I called MAACO, I asked what the delay was. Then came the confession. There had been an accident with the car. A painter had been seriously injured, and the car severely damaged. The incident happened the prior week, and they had been stalling for time to repair the vehicle before I learned of it.

I immediately drove to the MAACO to see the car. Upon arrival, I met with the manager. English was not his native language, so we kept the discussion slow and simple. The events leading to the mishap with my Porsche apparently happened very quickly. It all started when the painter pulled the car into the paint bay. He was about to spray the vehicle when he realized the headlights were not popped up. He opened the door, reached in, and turned the knob to pop the lights. They did not rise. Then the painter inserted the key in the ignition while standing outside the car with the door open. He did not realize the vehicle was in reverse gear. When he turned the ignition switch, the powerful engine started, and the car immediately drove backward. The painter had been knocked down by the open door, and the front end of the Porsche had run over his chest. The car continued backing out of the paint shop until the open door had caught the wall and was snapped off when it hit the exit. The car stopped a few moments later.

The painter was rushed to the hospital. He was in bad shape but survived because he was a very fit kick-boxer. He would need several weeks to fully recover. We were all relieved about his prognosis.

I asked why the shop had delayed contacting me. The manager fessed up. He had intended to fix the car and not inform me about the incident, but they could not get the repairs done quickly. Porsche doors were reportedly made with an aircraft metal alloy that was expensive, and the special-order door required a trained mechanic to mount it.

The manager pleaded with me to allow him to make the repair and pay for my rental car. I was not confident they knew how to fix a Porsche. The manager assured me his team could do it. He did not want it reported to his insurance company and would pay for everything out of pocket. I felt torn, sympathetic for the manager but also concerned the repair would be made improperly. But I caved in and gave him the option to fix it. I later regretted this decision. Fortunately, I had taken pictures of the damage.

The MAACO manager started researching Porsche parts. He told me the door shell was about $7000. The electronics in the door were also pricey. He kept shopping for cheaper parts, and weeks stretched into two months. I went to the shop to see what progress had been made and was shocked to see my car still sat in a paint bay, its door still missing, completely uncovered the entire time. Paint dust had covered the inside of the vehicle. The thick coating of industrial dust was embedded in the seats, the dash, and in every other place imaginable. My car had been neglected, and no special precautions had been taken to keep the vehicle from further damage, some of which had already occurred. I took more pictures.

I voiced my concern to the manager, who agreed to sign a statement as to what, specifically, he was going to do to complete the repair to my satisfaction. This repair had gone on long enough. The next a week, I got a call that the new door was on, and the car was being painted. I stopped by to see the final paint job. The paint job was awful. There were half a dozen areas where the paint had been applied too thick, and then was baked on while running down the side. These were major flaws in the finish. I took pictures. The manager acknowledged the workmanship was poor and agreed to repaint it.

The next week, the manager called and said the car had been repainted. I visited the shop to find it was a flat black, a dull finish when it was supposed to be a high-gloss. The manager said he would give me a discount for the paint job. I told him it was not the paint job we agreed to, and I was not going to take the car. He promised to check into it. Later that day, the manager called and told me his paint team did not bake the paint after it was applied, which resulted in the dull finish. He offered to repaint it a 3rd time. At this point, I completely regretted my decision to buy this car. It was not worth the time or effort I had invested in it.

I took the gloves off. I wrote a detailed letter to their corporate headquarters and sent them photos. A few days later, I received a call from a MAACO executive who offered to fly down to meet me at the shop. I was surprised how young the executive was, but I was glad he was personally involved. I showed him a few dozen photos and recounted the situation which was now well into its 3rd month.

The third paint job was not perfect, but it was good enough. The door was re-hung, but it did not always close cleanly. Sometimes it needed a hip check to latch properly. I took the car and spent a week cleaning out the remaining paint dust.

Admittedly, the car now looked fairly good. I was finally able to cruise through Old Town Alexandria with some measure of confidence about its appearance. Girls would turn their heads and no doubt, one of them would remark, "Look at that guy - he has more money than common sense!" Yep. She got that right.

Given the aggravation I had with the Porsche, I decided to only drive it on the weekends. I bought a little Subaru for $1200 and drove it to work on weekdays. I kept the car for about two more years, and by then, I was married and needed a different vehicle—a truck—to move furniture to our new home. It is now 25 years later, and I'm still happy I sold that money-sucking nuisance. But I must admit that it felt cool being in the driver's seat of a Porsche. However, the pleasure was not worth the pain.

SECTION 6
CAREER

CHAPTER 39
ARMY ENGINEER SCHOOL
& CAREER TRANSITION

I returned to the United States in 1986 from my tour of duty in West Germany. My mother hosted a family reunion, and it was so good to see all my relatives converge on our small house in West Chester. My father and many of his siblings and cousins had passed away while I was overseas. Dad, George, Florence, Adrina, and John had all died in 1984. My father's youngest brother, Eddie passed soon after I returned. But the next generation of Armenians and Irish in our family stepped up their game at the reunion.

Army Engineer School

My next assignment was at Fort Belvoir to take the Engineer Officer Advanced Course (EOAC), where I found plenty of time to stay physically fit. I was in the best shape of my life, and I could smoke the Army Physical Fitness Test (APFT). Now that I am 30 years and 8,000 bagels past my prime, and I would struggle to simply pass this test. My mind still wants to believe I am that once invincible youth, but the law of gravity is always telling me otherwise. Each morning I rise early, stumble into the bathroom, and wonder who in the hell that guy is in my mirror.

After I had completed EOAC, I was assigned as an instructor and taught military Engineer officers how to design and build roads and airfields in a combat zone. If a war broke out, and the main airports in the combat zone were destroyed, our soldiers needed to know how to rapidly design and construct a new airstrip so cargo aircraft could take off and land. I was now considered an Army expert in soils engineering, flexible pavements, asphalt, concrete, and the California Bearing Ratio. Ugh! This was not sexy stuff, but it was my new mission.

One day, an Air Force Air Combat Controller came into my office carrying a cone penetrometer, a device that measures soil strength. He stated that a C-130 cargo aircraft was stuck in the Bolivian jungle, and he needed our help figuring out what happened. The aircraft had been supporting a counter-drug raid and had landed on a crude airfield. As the aircraft was preparing to take off, it had to turn around at the end of the airstrip. The outside landing gear broke through the thin hard layer of soil and sank. The wing of the C-130 then hit the ground and cracked.

When news of the damaged aircraft was reported, many senior officials got involved. The immediate problem was getting the aircraft and people out of the jungle. The Air Combat Controller visited us to try and make sure the incident would not occur again. He explained what had happened. Before the raid, a special operations team had crawled out on the airstrip at night to measure the soil strength using the cone penetrometer. The team did not want to be detected and carefully, quietly, drove the penetrating rod into the ground and measured the resistance. Unfortunately, they only measured down to 12-18 inches and not to the depth required. The top layer soil was strong enough to support the C-130. However, the soft soil layer below was not. Consequently, the landing gear broke through the top layer crust while turning around. There was no real mystery as to why the accident happened, but it was an expensive lesson to learn. It was proof that even boring studies of soils engineering can make the difference between success and failure in a military operation.

During this period, I studied for hundreds of hours to prepare for the Professional Engineering (PE) examination. The Army fully supported my preparation as having a PE license was an excellent qualification. Although I studied aerospace structures in college, the Army needed me as a civil engineer, so I took the civil engineering exam. I was told the historical pass rate on the eight-hour exam was about 30% and that applicants can take the exam up to three times. I bombed the first time, getting a score of 49%. I doubled down on my studies and passed the second exam with an 81%.

I was quite relieved but unsure what the Army wanted me to do with this new qualification. Later in my career, the PE certification came into play when I was assigned to the Headquarters of the U.S. Army Corps of Engineers and supported numerous natural disasters and military contingencies. In 2004, the Army assigned me to be the Operations Officer for the reconstruction of Iraq. That required rebuilding oil fields, electrical power plants and distribution lines, hospitals, border forts, bridges and other infrastructure. It was high adventure trying to perform this mission in a combat zone. Scores of our government and industry teammates were killed by insurgents and terrorists during these operations. I wrote my first book, *SUVs SUCK in Combat*, several years after I returned. I wanted to capture the hard lessons learned during the war, so they are not repeated.

I worked with some outstanding colleagues at the Engineer School. Bob Carlson and John Naccarelli were academy classmates, and we enjoyed the nightlife in Washington D.C. and Old Town Alexandria. Garrett Moore was a no-nonsense Marine engineer assigned to our branch. John Rivenburgh was our boss and was a smart and seasoned officer. Ed Boyajian and I were both of Armenian descent and could each speak about 20-30 words in Armenian. We'd walk around the office and speak random Armenian words and point to things and to other soldiers. We pretended to have a conversation, and no one else in the office could understand us. They all wanted to know what we were saying. If you translated the 'discussion' into English, it would typically be something like this:

Kerry (in Armenian): "One, two, three, four, five."
Ed (seeming to agree in Armenian): "How are you today?"
Kerry (nodding approval): "Pizza, chin," followed by a hearty laugh.
Ed: "Five, one, three, two."

That "conversation" would be followed by back slaps or high fives. The ~~suckers~~ soldiers and civilians in the office never caught on to us.

While assigned at Fort Belvoir, I was able to take a couple of memorable business trips. The first was a tour of the Gettysburg Battlefield and was particularly interesting as we first flew over the historic battlefield in Huey helicopters. I had studied Gettysburg in the classroom but spending time on the terrain made the experience incredibly meaningful. This battle was the turning point of the American Civil War, and every one of the 46,000 casualties was an American. The number killed in three days at Gettysburg exceeded all deaths during ten years of war in Iraq and Afghanistan.

I took another trip to Vicksburg to attend a two-week Pavement Design Course. The best part was the excursion to New Orleans during the weekend. It was my first time visiting the French Quarter. We stopped in Pat O'Brien's for their famous "Hurricane" drink. It was sweet-tasting, and I was thirsty. I needed to re-hydrate after a day of walking around the city and consumed six of those concoctions thinking they were a just a refreshing fruit drink. Within 30 minutes, my brain whirling, I felt like I was in a Category 5 storm. The next day, Sunday was a day of rest, and my best friend was a bottle of aspirin.

Transitioning from the Military (1988)

Fort Belvoir was a good place to transition from the military back to civil life. At this point, I had served ten years; four years as a cadet and six years on active duty. I was now engaged and had set a wedding date. My future spouse, Alice Bush, wanted me to settle into a corporate job. Fortunately, my Army assignment was near Washington D.C., which made the transition from the military to the civilian sector relatively easy. The economy was recovering under President Reagan, and good jobs were available for junior military officers.

A corporate recruiting firm contacted me and scheduled interviews with about a dozen companies. One of them, Phillip Morris, paid well, but my father had been a career smoker and died of cancer, so I declined to follow up with them. The handful I did follow up with included Booz Allen Hamilton (consulting), Michelin (manufacturing), Air Products and Chemicals (sales), GE Aerospace (defense), and Honeywell (industrial services). It was a good mix of different industry sectors. After a few trips to South Carolina, New Jersey, and Atlanta, the decision came down to GE Aerospace or Honeywell.

My best friend, Mike Willover, was working for Honeywell at the time. That made the company attractive from the start. Recently engaged to Alice, Honeywell agreed to fly us both to Atlanta. The company offered us our choice of twenty locations in the southeastern USA. They treated us very well, and I was grateful for their hospitality.

I recall my interviews at GE Aerospace with Mike Collins and Earl Turner. The job required a security clearance and involved a rotating shift. They were seeking employees that could perform in a team environment. They could not tell me any further details, so the specific duties were a mystery. Earl was a seasoned manager. During my interview, he asked one of the best questions I have ever heard, and I still use it decades later when I interview prospective employees. Earl simply asked, "How do you get ahead in an organization?" I paused and replied with a list of desirable behaviors: "Work hard, don't watch the clock, be punctual, keep your technical skills current, be professional in your appearance and conduct...." Earl listened politely and then replied, "I think you get ahead in an organization by helping other people." BINGO. Earl nailed it. That was the right answer.

At that point, I knew the culture at GE Aerospace would be a good fit for me, and they were my choice. The position with them would allow me to serve my country in the defense industry, something I felt comfortable with. We could also stay in Northern Virginia, where Alice could live near her parents. I would only be three hours from my family in Pennsylvania. Staying in the Washington D.C. area also allowed me to continue my military career in the Army Reserve. Alice and I would stay rooted in the national capital region for most our careers.

Jiffy Sniff

While I was busy interviewing with several companies, I also considered starting my own business. I had what I thought was a killer idea, certain to be successful if I could get it going.

Our country was in the midst of a "war on drugs." U.S. law had a zero-tolerance policy, and any assets associated with a drug crime could be seized by the government. Private owners of boats, planes, cars or houses, could have their property taken if drugs were found in them. The problem was many innocent owners were at risk if a guest at their home or on their boat carried drugs with them. Law abiding citizens were concerned that they would become unsuspecting aiders and abettors.

My idea was to provide a business service to inspect homes, boats, and cars before or after an event to certify that the owners were acting responsibly. I would use retired military working dogs and trained handlers who were deputized by local law enforcement. We would inspect a boat before and after a party and certify the boat was drug-free. We would verify a car being purchased was also clean. Customers only needed to contact one of our local offices located near boat docks, car dealerships, or other key locations. Parents could subscribe to our service if they wanted to know if their teenage children were hiding drugs in the house. Real estate agents could reassure potential buyers their houses were 'clean.' Responsible citizens who used our service would have legal protection from property seizures. Any drugs found by our inspections would be turned over the police with immunity. I contacted some colleagues to identify where I could get access to retired military/police working dogs and trained handlers. I even came up with a catchy name for our new service, "Jiffy Sniff." We could get the job done quickly and professionally. Just call 1-800 JIF-SNIF.

However, Jiffy Sniff—I think to some people's relief—never came to pass.

Get-Rich-Quick

I did have one other get-rich-quick idea at that time. I recalled that someone had made a ton of money selling "Pet Rocks" in the mid-1970s. Collecting those rocks became a fad for a few months. They were a perfect pet that did not require walking, feeding, cleaning or vet bills. The rock came with an instruction manual and a carrying case.

My idea was to sell "Pet Water." You could buy your pet in different colors, and it was highly trainable. For example, you could teach it to roll, splash or wave. I had no idea how to take this product to the market, so that particular business plan just dried up.

GE Aerospace 1988-1990

I started my new job at GE Aerospace, and it involved a 24-hour operational environment and a rotating shift. Week one was a typical day job from 7:00 AM to 3:00 PM. Week two was a swing shift from 3:00 PM to 11:00 PM. Week three was a seven-day night shift that started with two 12-hour evenings on the weekend.

At the same time, I transferred into the Army Reserve and began performing weekend duty. Ironically, Bob Carlson and I served in the same unit and were both assigned to operations. On one noteworthy Sunday, we attended a military dinner wearing our formal Dress Blue uniform. When the event was over, I left for my night shift job at GE Aerospace. Bob pulled out the Reserve unit about a minute later in his RX-7. About 200 meters into the trip, Bob smashed into two whitetail deer. Both of the deer were badly injured. Bob contacted the local military police to report the incident. The MP that arrived was willing to shoot the deer to put them out of their misery. But the MP could not lawfully discharge his firearm without permission from his superiors. The MP made several radio calls to no avail. The deer were in really bad shape, and Bob "the humanitarian" found a screwdriver in his car and was considering killing the deer with it. That would have made a mess of his full-dress uniform. Fortunately, a hunter soon pulled up in his pickup truck, and he had a more suitable knife to finish the deer. He gladly took the remains with him. After it was over, Bob was standing next to his wrecked car in his full-dress uniform near a pool of blood, holding a screwdriver, trying to figure out what just happened. I was on the way to my night job and completely unaware of the situation. (It was before cell phones were widely available.)

This period of my life was very busy with trying to do everything and get it all out of the way. For example, I finished a 12-hour Friday night shift at GE, immediately changed into a military uniform on Saturday morning and worked a 10-hour shift in the Army Reserve. After finishing Reserve Duty, I changed and pulled another 12-hour shift that Saturday night. After work on Sunday morning, I shaved quickly, threw my uniform on and went back on military duty. Fortunately, my reserve duty was at Fort Belvoir, near my home, so travel time was minimal. Sunday night began the more manageable eight-hour shift. But by the time the weekend night shift ended, I was a certified, card-carrying zombie.

During the weeks, I was on a GE day shift I also attended the U.S. Army's Command and General Staff Officer's Course in the evenings. Simultaneously, I started working on a Master's Degree in Systems Engineering at Virginia Tech.

The 24-hour, non-stop, sleep-deprived schedule was like Ranger School, except I was warm and well-fed. Alice and I rarely saw each other for two years as she worked a day job with GE Capital and made an extended commute to Columbia, Maryland. I would come home at weird hours and often startle Alice, who thankfully did not have a concealed carry permit. To further pile on the schedule, she and I also served as Youth Group Leaders at Immanuel-Church-on-the Hill in Alexandria, on the grounds of the Virginia Theological Seminary. The Youth Group service provided good insight about how hard it would be to become a parent. Alice and Reverend Robert Trache, discussing the demands of my work and adding to my education, would often ask me what kind of race I was running. But I was sprinting... not running. My plan was to get everything done in life up front so I could coast for the next 30 years. I was paying it forward. It took five years to complete the master's degree. I finished it shortly after the birth of our first child, Kent.

The extra money I earned working shift work was nice, but I had no time to spend it. Fortunately, I bought a lot of GE stock as part of my retirement plan. The company's share prices appreciated 4000% during the twenty-year reign of CEO "Neutron Jack" Welch. I enjoyed part of that ride.

The work we performed at GE Aerospace was classified. We could not tell others where our jobs were located and certainly, could not discuss what we did. Security was serious and strict. Gate Guards were armed. Employees were specially selected because they were considered reliable, trustworthy and stable. However, I wanted to bring some humor to the night shift. On Christmas Eve 1988, I wore a Santa Clause suit to work that evening. The desk guards asked St. Nick for his photo ID badge. Prepared, I handed the guard my credentials with the previously placed sticker of Santa's face over my own in the photo ID. The guard cracked a smile and said, "Sorry Santa," as he peeled the Santa face off. "Please take the mask off." Not even old St. Nick could bluff his way into this facility. I told the guard, "You're gonna get coal in your stocking." It didn't faze him, so I followed up with, "Santa is treated better in Philadelphia." Not a blink from him as he handed me back my ID. My parting shot was, "I should have come down the chimney."

After two years of shift work, I knew I needed to change my lifestyle. I could not sleep well during daylight hours, and my body never adapted to the constantly rotating schedule. I was burned out from the rotating shift work and other demands. Thankfully, Bob Carlson introduced me to my next employer, System Planning Corporation. Shortly after I left GE Aerospace, the company was bought by Martin Marietta, and a few years later, it merged with Lockheed.

CHAPTER 40
SYSTEM PLANNING CORPORATION: SASS/ARL 1990 -1995

System Planning Corporation (SPC) needed a person with Army experience to work on two counter-narcotics programs that supported U.S. Southern Command (SOUTHCOM), the military organization responsible for operations in Central and South America. The programs were managed at Vint Hill Farms Station, Virginia, an old Signals Intelligence (SIGINT) post located about 40 miles west of Washington D.C.

My new boss was Dr. Alton Wallace, who had a Ph.D. in Mathematics and was a smart guy with a huge heart. Always considerate of others, he fostered a collegial environment. As a young man, Al Wallace was an Army Engineer who built roads and cleared minefields in Vietnam. Occasionally, Al would offer a war story and use it as a teaching point for his corporate troops. His Vint Hill team included Jeff Harris, Derek Baker, Gerald "Jerry" Bate, Bob Elwell and some other dedicated colleagues.

The customer at Vint Hill was The Program Executive Office for Intelligence and Electronic Warfare (PEO IEW), where Lt. Colonel Nelson Johnson was rapidly developing new capabilities to detect drug smugglers coming from South and Central America. He liked to work hard and to play hard and was later promoted and selected to serve as the Program Manager for Night Vision, with a charter to develop advanced sensors, scopes, and googles that allow the military to see at night. Johnson was succeeded by another great American, Lt. Colonel Stan Niemiec, an Army aviator empowered with rapid acquisition authority.

The new job provided an exciting opportunity to apply both my technical background and tactical skills. I was part of a small team of contractors supporting them with the program management, technical assistance, and testing.

The first counter-narcotics program was called Airborne Reconnaissance Low (ARL).

Airborne Reconnaissance Low (ARL)

This program converted a commercial DeHavilland Dash-7 aircraft into a flying intelligence machine. It was outfitted with a day/night video camera (EO/IR), and it later added a moving target indicator (MTI) radar and a signals collection capability.

Airborne Reconnaissance Low

The ARL system was designed to cross-cue one sensor to another. One sensor would detect something suspicious, and then tip off another that would track and identify it. Ideally, the SIGINT system would hear the bad guys talking on the radio and locate them. Next, the radar would track them as they were moving in a boat, a pickup truck or a pack mule. Finally, the day/night video camera would zoom in to confirm who they were and what they were doing. In the early 1990s, this surveillance mission was performed in a manned aircraft. Today, it's often carried out by an unmanned aerial vehicle (UAV), now commonly called a drone. We experimented with drones during this period: the CL-227 Sentinel "Flying Peanut" launched and recovered from the deck of a ship, the CM-44 "optionally piloted vehicle," and an unmanned airship dubbed the SASS-Lite.

Small Aerostat Surveillance System (SASS)

SASS – Carlson Tide

The other counter-narcotics program in development at Vint Hill was the Small Aerostat Surveillance System (SASS). The Army leased three large ships, each about 300 feet long, named the Jan Tide, Dickerson Tide, and the Carlson Tide. Westinghouse outfitted the ships with sensors, communications and a large tethered aerostat that flew at an altitude of 2500 feet. Tether Command (TCOM) was the subcontractor that provided the 32-meter (101 feet) long aerostat. The aerostat hoisted a modified F-16 fighter radar above the ocean that would detect aircraft, boats, and vehicles along the shore.

There were some known smuggling routes and gaps in land-based radar coverage, and the SASS would be moved to these spots to strengthen the defenses. Since a SASS boat could move freely about the Caribbean, the smugglers would need to constantly guess where it was to avoid detection.

System Testing

Our team was responsible for designing and conducting the tests on each new system to make sure it worked properly before it was handed over to U.S. military personnel supporting SOUTHCOM missions. Much of our testing of ARL and SASS sensors occurred at Fort A.P. Hill, Virginia, Elizabeth City, North Carolina, Lakehurst, New Jersey, as well as Key West and Pensacola, Florida. These tests were coordinated with the Army's Communications and Electronics Command (CECOM) and the Night Vision Lab at Fort Belvoir, Virginia.

Mr. Charles Crook, the U.S. government lead for sensor testing, had a good sense of humor and loved anything related to the state of Alabama. He had a small collection of special flying machines and sensors that our team would test and evaluate. Working with Charles was like shopping at Toys R Us; he always had some new gizmo for experimentation.

To support all the ARL and SASS tests, Jerry Bate rapidly designed and built two unique vehicles that served as a command center. The first vehicle, the Remote Receive Station (RRS), was constructed in a large recreational vehicle and appeared similar to the Urban Assault Vehicle from the movie 'Stripes.' The first fifteen feet of the vehicle interior seemed to be a cozy motorhome. However, the last twenty feet was an impressive collection of high-speed electronics that included a telescoping mast with a day/night video camera, an auto-tracking dish antenna that received full motion surveillance video from aircraft, and a full suite of radios, including HF, VHF, UHF, cellular and satellite communications. This was state of the art stuff in 1991. The second vehicle, the Ground Exploitation Station (GES), was similar to the RRS, but it was integrated into a camouflaged military shelter carried on the back of a truck. The GES had few creature comforts but featured a multi-sensor workstation, designed by our teammate, Bob Elwell.

ARL Testing

Occasionally, we used a Black Hawk helicopter to flight test a new airborne radar. One of the tests was conducted at the Naval Air Station in Lakehurst, the site of the Hindenburg airship disaster. On May 6, 1937, the great German airship caught fire in front of live news crews, and thirty-six people perished. Those old airships used flammable hydrogen gas. The newer SASS aerostats used a safer helium gas.

When we needed to conduct an airborne test of new cameras, radars, special sensors or antennas, Major Mike Farmer would show up with a D-18 twin-engine Beechcraft test aircraft he called "Blue-2." Mike was an Army test pilot and a great guy with a *can-do* attitude. He would do anything to support the mission. I flew missions with him in the Caribbean, at AP Hill and a very memorable one in California in May 1991. It was my first trip to California, and I was excited to see the west coast. We had a lot of testing to do on this trip and had to work extended days. After the test preparation was complete, Jerry Bate and I were able to take Sunday off and see the sights in San Francisco and the surrounding area. We had a chance to visit Alcatraz Island, the Bay Bridge, Sausalito, and took a drive on Lombard Street, the Crookedest Street in the World. It was a fun city surrounded by impressive terrain.

The testing began early on Monday morning. As the Test Director, I was responsible for the success or failure of the effort. Our mission was to collect data on the performance of a new conformal antenna that could receive high frequency (HF) radio signals and identify which direction it was coming from. The antenna was mounted on the skin of the Blue-2 aircraft. Our team set up an HF radio transmitter on the ground, and we would try to locate the transmitter at various ranges while flying over the California desert and later while flying over the Pacific Ocean. I had been warned that flying over the desert in a small aircraft could get rough when the temperatures spiked around mid-day. I told Mike we needed to be wheels up from San Jose Jetport at 6:00 AM to get an early start. That meant a 3:00 AM wake-up to have the aircraft ready for the test. I arrived at the Jetport commuter terminal and expected to find some place to eat a quick breakfast. I was surprised there was nothing open. The only food available was from vending machines. I bought two 6-packs of Oreo cookies and two Diet Cokes in the terminal. I was running late, so I wolfed down the dozen Oreos and two sodas for breakfast. That was a big mistake.

Minutes later, Mike was rolling Blue-2 down the runway. I was in the back of the aircraft with an engineer responsible for collecting the HF radio signal data. We both studied the little computer screen as Blue-2 flew over the mountains and headed for the first test mission over the California desert. We began to fly oval racetrack patterns at altitudes as low as 2500 feet.

Things were fine for a few minutes, but as the sun rose over the desert, the thermal updrafts began buffeting our aircraft. The test engineer and I were in the tail of the plane, focused on the computer screen, and could not see the horizon. The smell of fuel and oil permeated the cabin, and it seemed to grow stronger as the plane was tossed about. I quickly realized my Oreo breakfast was going to make a round-trip. I grabbed an in-flight sickness bag and—yes—I literally lost my cookies. Thankful we had two bags, I filled them both. The poor engineer had to sit there like a professional, breathing that foul smell, as he continued collecting data for several hours. At mid-day, running out of fuel, we headed back over the mountains and landed in San Jose. I was very happy to finally be back on terra firma.

The test plan called for a second signal collection flight over the desert that afternoon. So, a couple of hours later, Mike Farmer was rolling old Blue-2 back down the runway. Having learned a lesson, I skipped lunch, so I had nothing left in my stomach. It was still an uncomfortable flight, but we completed a few dozen 40-mile oval racetracks at various altitudes.

When we finally finished our desert collection runs, Mike turned Blue-2 westward toward San Jose. As we approached the mountains, I could see and smell smoke coming into the cabin. I said nothing for a minute, but it thickened. I looked down and saw nothing but crags below; there was no place nearby for an emergency landing. I got on the aircraft intercom system and told Mike about the smoke. He paused for a second, stayed calm, and theorized that some of the oil on the cabin heater was cooking off, causing the smoke. The engines were not showing any signs of a fire. In the back of the aircraft, we covered our faces with our shirts to filter out the smoke so we could breathe. I hoped Mike's theory was right and looked, through the small window, to find someplace in the mountains below for an emergency landing. After about ten more minutes, San Jose appeared on the horizon, and not long after that, I was relieved again to touch down on planet Earth. The day's testing was over. Tomorrow's would be over the water and had to be a better day.

The following morning, Mike piloted Blue-2 on another data collection mission over the Pacific. We started the test at twenty miles offshore and worked our way out to a range of eighty miles, conducting flat turns at different distances and altitudes to characterize the accuracy of the antenna. Flat turns meant the aircraft flew in circles without banking. The intent was to keep the antenna, on the belly of the aircraft, level relative to the ground. Our circles were big, about five miles in radius. When were about sixty miles offshore, we completed a flat turn at 5500 feet and asked permission from the FAA air traffic controller to climb to 7500 feet to conduct a similar turn. We had just received approval, about to start to change our altitude, when suddenly, a Navy P-3 Orion aircraft climbed right in front of Mike's windshield. We were so close to the big four-engine propeller aircraft that I could clearly see the face of the other pilot. Facing an imminent mid-air collision, Mike let out a loud "WHOA!" and immediately banked Blue-2 hard to the right, narrowly missing a disaster. Seconds later, the P-3 was out of sight, and Mike and I were trying to figure out what had just happened.

Mike called the FAA on the radio and reported the near collision. The air traffic controller immediately admitted he had made an error putting both aircraft in the same airspace and gave us his identification number. I was just glad that Mike's quick reaction saved us. Tragically, Mike was killed the following year in another test flight over Georgia. While flying a C-23 Sherpa, conducting stall maneuvers with a simulated sensor payload, the airplane became inverted and caught in a slow, flat spin. Mike and two other men could not get out of the aircraft, and all three were killed on impact. Mike had been scheduled to retire from the military less than a week later, and this flight was his last one in uniform. I was deeply shocked and saddened when my colleague, Jeff Harris, broke the news. Mike was a great soldier, pilot, husband, and friend. After the accident, Lt. Colonel Stan Niemiec put three pairs of Army jump boots in a memorial display in the ARL Program Office to remember our fallen friends. It was a dignified and respectful tribute.

TAClink

Although I was working in industry, I was trained by the Army in tactical operations and continued to serve in the Army Reserve.

As I worked on the ARL system, I realized that its full potential could not be achieved unless troops on the ground could benefit from the same video being viewed on the aircraft. I intuitively knew that giving a tactical team a live aerial view of everything around them significantly improved their situational awareness, physical safety and their potential for mission success. The aerial video served as a 'guardian angel' enabling troops to see where they were, where the enemy was and to adjust their plans to maintain the tactical advantage.

I wanted to develop a portable capability to deliver live ARL video to troops on the ground. Though I was motivated to build the new system, I did not have the technical know-how to make it happen. Fortunately, one of my SPC colleagues, Jerry Bate, was a legendary engineer who shared this same goal. Jerry was a HAM radio enthusiast, and largely self-trained in radio frequency "RF" propagation. I honestly believe he could see radio waves transmit through the atmosphere, although they were invisible to all other mortals.

I once saw Jerry make a bet that he could transmit his voice over a VHF handheld radio signal from Key Largo, Florida to a team located near an aerostat anchored at Cudjoe Key, a distance of almost eighty miles. A military intelligence officer flat out refused to believe it was possible for a low-powered handheld radio to transmit a signal that far. Jerry's credibility had been challenged, and the heated debate was witnessed by several of us.

Jerry set up a test the following day and took his doubters to school. What Jerry knew was that an above ground electrical powerline ran the length of the Florida Keys. Jerry set up the radios on both ends of the test, so they were near this power line. Jerry believed that the weak radio transmission would couple to the power line as a "hitchhiker" signal and ride its way through the Keys. It worked. Jerry was able to talk to the other person 80 miles away. After that demonstration, anything Jerry said related to communications was taken as a fact.

On another occasion, the prime contractor was having problems transmitting signals up and down the aerostat's tether. The company proposed to study, not solve, the problem for $750,000. The customer was irritated and asked Jerry to look into it. Within one day, he had improvised a solution that bypassed the tether with a wireless transmission system. He installed the work-around solution on the SASS boat inside of a week and for less than $12,000. To protect the electronic components and antenna from corrosive salt water, Jerry glued an upside-down mop bucket to the deck of the ship. The improvised "radome" cost the U.S. Government about two dollars.

After I had spoken to Jerry about my vision to transmit live video from an aircraft to troops on the ground, he began to work on a solution. Having already integrated video receivers into the GES and the RRS vehicles, he had a head start. Now, we had to make it smaller, lighter weight, battery operated and easy to use by a small team. Jerry worked during nights and weekends, and he emerged a few weeks later with a prototype product we coined "TAClink," short for Tactical Link. We tried to trademark the name, but the corporate lawyers said it was not possible.

Jerry taught me much of what I know about radio signals, including meteor burst communications. I further benefited by working with Jerry as I took a digital and analog communications course in the evenings at part of my master's degree at Virginia Tech. When it came time to present my final project for the systems engineering degree, I used our TAClink development project as the case study.

Mike, Marge, and Frank

About this time, I met Mike Hollingsworth, an incredibly smart, innovative and helpful entrepreneur who owned a small business that serviced the video and surveillance market for the FBI, DEA, and other law enforcement customers. I soon learned that Mike was half-Armenian, and we Armenians are a rare breed that sticks together. Mike is also part Native American and affiliated with the Leech Lake Band of the Minnesota Chippewa Tribe.

Mike started his career carrying a tool bag and often traveled to install and maintain radars and communications on specialized Navy ships. Based on his exceptional technical skills, he built a successful business, and his reputation for integrity and candor were widely respected throughout the community.

About this time, I also met Mike's mother, Marguarite, a full-blooded Armenian and a really sharp-witted lady. I don't know what "Marge" eats, but I need to get some of that stuff too. Marge deserves great credit for raising such a fine son.

Mike reviewed our TAClink design and immediately offered some ideas that helped us to address the space, weight and power issues we were trying to overcome. We selected video transmitter and receiver modules used in air-to-ground missiles, as they were rugged and compact. Every time we had a technical challenge, Mike offered potential solutions.

I soon had the honor to meet Mike's business partner, Frank Nulton, a retired U.S. Navy Lieutenant Commander and aviator, who I learned had an incredible reputation in the military. Frank was the personal pilot for General Douglas MacArthur during the post-WWII occupation of Japan. He later commanded a naval aviation unit during the Vietnam War and was the commanding officer for the future Senator John McCain.

Decades earlier, while Frank Nulton was at Alameda Naval Air Station, a maintenance chief asked him to take a new SNJ Navy prop trainer on a test flight. Frank agreed, and he immediately jumps into the cockpit and takes off. It smells and rides nice. He goes into a simulated dogfight with another pilot, and the loser buys the drinks. Frank pulled some Gs, runs into some clouds and goes inverted with the canopy open, ready to pounce on the other aircraft. Then there was total silence. His airplane was gone, and Frank was free falling back to earth. He comes out of the cloud and pulls his parachute. The other airplane circles around him and radios in the incident. The pilot-less aircraft splashed into the ocean about eight miles off Alameda. Frank lands, pops smoke and a rescue helicopter eventually picks him up. He tells the helo crew to drop him at the aircraft maintenance shop at Alameda. Upon arrival, he finds the chief and asks, "Tell me Chief, do you happen to have one spare ejection seat retainer pin?" The supervisor found the pin and immediately realized his team had failed to properly bolt the pilot's seat into the aircraft, resulting in Frank being unceremoniously thrown from the cockpit. That was a costly mistake.

Over the years, I met several of Mike's other colleagues that served the nation in the military, law enforcement, and industry. It was clear Mike hung out with a great group of patriots. One was John Conrad, a member of the Army Special Forces, twice wounded in Vietnam. He has a few dozen amazing stories that he needs to write down if the government will permit him!

Mike and Marge were genuinely kind and thoughtful. Marge enjoyed making jewelry by hand that she shared with my wife and daughters. For Kent's fourth birthday, Mike bought him a remotely controlled toy truck. Mike and I assembled it and installed the batteries. However, we could not get it to work. After ten minutes struggling with it, I jokingly asked Mike, "You bought my son a broken toy?" It was a classic case of "No good deed goes unpunished." A few minutes later, Mike presented the toy to Kent believing my son would be disappointed that the truck was just a dead toy. To our surprise, Kent excitedly grabbed the truck and turned it upside down. He flipped a well concealed "On/Off" switch on the belly. The lights immediately came on, and Kent drove the monster truck across the room with the remote control. Mike and I stood there in stunned silence. How could this four-year-old boy have outwitted two guys that had years of science and technology experience? Clearly, neither of us would be successful contestants on the TV show, *Are You Smarter than a 5th Grader?*

TAClink II and III

About this time, Steve Griggs joined the SPC team. He was a Ranger-qualified West Point graduate and had a strong technical background. Steve redesigned the original TAClink system using the new missile parts. We called the improved version TAClink II. The system fit in a small metal tool box and could be carried in a rucksack. The new receiver design was more rugged, easily carried, and operators could quickly use it to view and record video. Steve and I worked together on the design of the TAClink transmitters, which could be readily installed into a helicopter or fixed wing aircraft. We also developed a wearable receiver we called TAClink III. The wearable model was highlighted on a TV show about advanced technology in the hands of law enforcement. There was no official military requirement for TAClink systems.

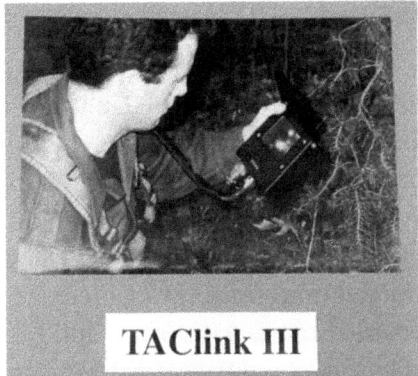

TAClink II Receiver and TAClink III Wearable Receiver

We initially designed and built TAClink II systems largely on our own time. We were a couple of entrepreneurs that had our own little Skunk Works project. Steve and I knew if we built it, the customers would come to us. Our company liked what we were doing, and funded product components, marketing literature and allowed us to make a product video on TAClink. I only had a $15,000 budget for the film, so I wrote the script in my spare time. We shot and edited it during a weekend, and the final video came out remarkably well. I kept Major Mike Farmer's memory alive by including his voice; our friend was still with us on the program.

TAClink Testing

The ARL aircraft was used in an exercise with the 18th Airborne Corps and Army Special Forces. It had an infrared video camera that could zoom in on activities on the ground. The aircraft tracked a Special Forces (SF) team as they inserted on the enemy drop zone at night. The SF team thought they were undetected. After landing in the darkness, one of the troopers, believing he was unobserved, decided to relief himself on the drop zone. ARL beamed live infrared video of the event into the 18th Airborne Corps command post, entertaining the battle captains and staff controlling the exercise. At the conclusion of the training, the SF team reported they had inserted undetected. To their surprise, the operations team then replayed the unedited infrared video of the SF insertion and commented, "That's BS, we had your ass!"

TAClink in Haiti

During the invasion of Haiti, ARL was able to broadcast live video of the Marine Corps amphibious landing to troops on the ground and to the command ship fifty miles offshore. As a result, the JTF Commander of the invasion force dubbed ARL and TAClink "the CNN of the Battlefield." Our company CEO, Dr. Ron Easley, later received a very kind letter of appreciation from Lt. Colonel Stan Niemiec for the support our team provided to the ARL office and for the development of TAClink, which made a significant contribution to military forces.

Advanced Concepts

Not only was TAClink adopted as a part of the ARL program, but the system was also used with many other aircraft. Apache attack helicopters and AC-130 Spectre gunships were able to broadcast full motion gunsight video to troops on the ground. This allowed ground forces that were in "danger close" range to see exactly where the aircraft was targeting. TAClink was also used at the Dismounted Battle Lab in Fort Benning, Georgia. When they put the transmitter in the AC-130 Spectre gunship, they coined the system "Spectre Vision." Later, TAClink was also invited to an Advanced Concept Technology Demonstration (ACTD) called the "Rapid Force Projection Initiative" (RFPI) where it flew missions inside the Apache attack helicopter.

The National Guard and Border Patrol

The fun did not stop there. The National Guard had a fleet of OH-58D observation helicopters with a mission to support domestic counter-drug operations. These aircraft were part of the Reconnaissance and Interdiction (RAID) program. These same helicopters had a secondary mission for emergency response to natural disasters so the live video could be used to help assess the damage and rescue those stranded by a hurricane, flood or earthquake.

During this period, I met an amazing guy named Bob McVey. Bob was a retired Special Forces officer; a helicopter pilot who had served two tours in Vietnam. After he retired from the military, Bob founded and managed a company that helped us market TAClink. He coordinated our support for National Guard RAID missions and to operate with U.S. Border Patrol helicopters detecting drug smugglers near El Paso. As a former Green Beret, Bob commanded instant respect, but he was also remarkably kind, caring and helpful. He was not only a business colleague; he became a personal friend.

Bob took a personal interest in my family and their well-being and shared many stories with me. He once traveled to Korea with the Adjutant General of the State of Missouri, a Major General that Bob nicknamed CINCMO (Commander-in-Chief, Missouri). While in Korea, Bob ordered two leather jackets. He told the Korean tailors to embroider the word "CINCMO" on the one jacket for his colleague. And he carefully told the tailor to "put nothing on the second jacket," as Bob wanted it for himself. When he picked up the two jackets the following day, he laughed hysterically when his had the word "Nothing" perfectly inscribed across the chest. Classic Bob McVey, he was not angry, accepted the mistake, paid for the service, and took the jacket with him. So, the two walked around Seoul, Korea proudly wearing their *CINCMO* and *Nothing* leather jackets wherever they went.

I worked with Bob for several years and was deeply saddened when he suddenly passed away. He is now buried in Arlington Cemetery among thousands of other brothers who served our nation with distinction.

Bob McVey - a great American

After making the TAClink infomercial, Bob introduced me to Captain Jeff Henderson, a Georgia National Guard helicopter pilot. I learned that Jeff had recently competed in the 1994 World Helicopter Championships in Moscow and reportedly came in second place. That earned him the respect of his peers as a highly skilled pilot. Jeff was using TAClink in his helicopter during a drug raid in Lenox, Georgia. He called this mission "The Great Lenox Bust." The police had conducted a nighttime drug raid on a building. As a few dozen bad guys scrambled from the building, and Jeff tracked them on his infrared camera. He reported where they were hiding, and agents successfully pursued them. A few dozen vehicles and weapons were seized in the raid. Jeff later invited me to Echols County, Georgia to patrol with some local police.

Shortly after I arrived, it became apparent this was a dangerous area, because the police officer I was patrolling with handed me a loaded pistol "for self-defense." I was wearing a Ranger patrol cap, and I think he wanted me to be his back up shooter.

Visions of Hollywood

After working together for a few months, Jeff told me he had a problem and needed my help. Jeff's high school friend was the actor, Robert Patrick, who was famous for his role as the T-1000 liquid metal villain in the blockbuster film *Terminator 2: Judgment Day.* Robert was planning to produce a Hollywood movie and asked Jeff to help write the script. The film would be called *Unlimited Resources,* and the story would be about a police force with access to every possible crime fighting technology. He approached Jeff based on his experience flying ducted-fan helicopters and using TAClink. It seemed like a good fit. However, Jeff wanted more help developing exciting technical ideas while Robert was working on getting funding for the movie. Jeff knew I was supporting advanced technologies at the Defense Advanced Research Projects Agency (DARPA) and had some ideas that could contribute to the story. Armed with a six-pack of beer and a long weekend, Jeff and I worked together to outline a convincing script that included unmanned aircraft, robotic ground vehicles, future combat systems, nanotechnology, flat panel displays, non-lethal weapons, covert tracking devices and advanced surveillance sensors.

These were cutting-edge technologies in the early 1990s. I mapped out how the future police could use these new capabilities to fight bad guys. A few weeks passed, and I asked Jeff for an update on the project. We had hoped to meet Robert in Orlando to move this exciting project forward, but Jeff told me the funding had not come through for Robert. Once again, my dreams of Hollywood fame, this time as a screenwriter, collapsed. I would need to keep working at my day job.

SASS Testing

Anytime we conducted testing related to the SASS boats, we had to travel to some hardship location such as Key West or Pensacola. These tests normally involved working with a team of colleagues, including Jeff Harris, Jerry Bate and Derek Baker. We worked extended hours, but it was good duty.

The Test Director role was initially filled by Jeff Harris, who was a veteran of the program. Later, Derek and I also led tests, depending on the scope and timing of the event. The Test Director had significant power and oversight responsibilities.

We had our own Army, Navy, and Air Force that served as test targets and simulated bad guys. Our radars, cameras and intercept systems tried to find and track test targets at various ranges and altitudes. The ground targets would include pack mules and small groups of men walking. The sea targets were often provided by the U.S. Coast Guard Auxiliary. These included Boston Whalers, Zodiac boats, and Cayugas, a small riverine boat used in Central America. The Civil Air Patrol provided a single engine Cessna to act as a smuggler's aircraft. Mike Farmer also joined in with Blue-2 to serve as a test target or to hunt the bad guys operating on land or sea.

Jerry Bate was the wizard, the man behind the curtain who kept everyone communicating. When he was not available, we used a new technology called, "Cell Phones," to communicate between the widely-dispersed test targets. Cell phone service was outrageously expensive at the time, and our team racked up a $10,000-dollar bill for just one night of testing while using only two phones.

GPS was also a relatively new and expensive technology. I bought a new GPS receiver for use in our testing. It was the size of a large brick and had only a single channel to receive satellite data. It cost $8,000 and was slow, requiring at least two minutes to get its first location reading after it was turned on. The receiver gave us a numerical reading of latitude and longitude, but it had no map display. We had to plot the coordinate on a paper map to see where we were.

One of my first uses of the GPS receiver involved a U.S. mail run to a covert nudist colony. It happened on Santa Rosa Island, at the western tip of Eglin Air Force Base in the Florida panhandle. It was a relatively desolate and quiet spot. I was alone on the island as the sun rose. I was surprised to discover Florida panther tracks on the nearby sand dunes. I carried a big stick as I walked around, so I did not look like panther food.

About 150 meters from the surf and hidden behind a sand dune, I operated the communications suite inside the Ground Exploitation Station (GES) as part of a SASS acceptance test. The SASS boat was about twenty miles offshore, staying in a fixed position for the duration of the radar test. Several members of our team were onboard and had no means to communicate with their loved ones at home. Getting U.S. mail once a week, routed to me through the government program office, was a big morale booster. That duffle bag of letters needed to be delivered to crew on the boat, but I had no means to get the mail out to sea. One of the soldiers assigned the SASS program, SFC Boone, volunteered to pilot a small motorized rubber boat (RB-15) to shore to pick up the bag. Boone was Special Forces qualified and had a reputation for getting things done. We spoke via radio and agreed he would get the mail at about noon on the following day. Boone needed me to give him a good grid coordinate so we could meet on the beach. I committed to send him one later that day.

An hour later, I walked out of the GES, across the dunes, and toward the ocean to get a good GPS location for the mail pickup. What I saw surprised me. About fifty people, buck-ass naked, were sunbathing on the beach. I was confused. This was Federal property and part of a U.S. military reservation. I soon learned that the nudists started the day sunbathing at nearby Navarro Beach. When the local police came to arrest them, they scampered across the boundary of Eglin Air Force Base, where the local police had no jurisdiction. The Eglin MPs would be called, and they would respond a few hours later and chase the nudists back to Navarro Beach. It was a cat and mouse game.

The nudists wondered who I was. But since I was not in uniform and did not appear as a threat, they carried on. Some of them were grossly out of shape and had no right to be naked. I seemed disinterested, and they ignored me as I quietly used the GPS receiver to record the location of the nude beach. After a few minutes, I walked back toward the dunes where the GES was parked. I made a radio call to SFC Boone and gave him the location for the mail pickup.

The next day, SFC Boone piloted the small boat over the horizon to the agreed location. He got out of the boat in the waist-deep water and pulled the boat ashore. After getting on dry ground, Boone looked up and saw a few dozen naked people all around him. The confused look on his face was priceless. I ran over the dune toward him, laughing, with the mail bag over my shoulder. "Surprise! Hope you enjoy the view. Life is much better here on the beach. Here's your mail." Boone broke out laughing, then wasted no time, jumped back in the rubber boat and motored back to the SASS boat.

Aerostats vs. Airplanes

The SASS program had to continually justify its existence. Why should the government use aerostats rather than airplanes to conduct surveillance missions? As an airborne platform, aerostats provide many advantages over conventional planes. Aerostats have no airborne crews, so they are safer to operate. They can stay aloft for weeks at a time, only needing to be reeled in to add helium every few weeks. Aircraft must repeatedly land and refuel, causing gaps in surveillance coverage or a need for multiple aircraft and crews to keep continuous eyes on an area.

Aircraft had some advantages as they can move faster to a location that needs to be surveilled. The airplane proponents noted that an aerostat that was anchored to land or on a slow-moving ship (SASS) was less responsive. The drug smugglers could quickly relocate and avoid the aerostat's radar coverage. However, the SASS boat could move a few hundred miles each day to keep the smugglers guessing. Constantly changing the SASS location was something of a shell game to those trying to sneak contraband into the United States. Smuggling routes needed to be regularly changed to avoid detection. Also, SASS allowed our government to plug gaps in any existing coverage when a land-based radar was down for maintenance. The biggest advantage of aerostats at that time was cost. An hour of flight time for an aerostat was far cheaper than an aircraft. The United States could get the same surveillance coverage for less money.

Pilots did not (probably still don't) like large aerostats for safety reasons, as the tether that holds them to the ship or ground is a flight hazard. The airspace near a land-based aerostat is often treated as a no-fly zone. The SASS aerostats were moving hazards to flight. I recall a Navy pilot screaming on the radio when he flew out of a cloud to discover he was on a collision course with a big gas bag with a cable under it.

Aerostats Gone Wild

Ironically, bad weather was a problem for both aerostats and aircraft. One of the Army's early SASS aerostats was land-tethered in South Korea, presumably keeping an eye on events in North Korea. High winds in the area caused the tether to break. The free flying aerostat, and its sensitive radar, then reportedly sailed into North Korea. I don't think the U.S. government every got it back, as the North Koreans considered it a gift.

Our operations in the Gulf of Mexico and Caribbean meant the SASS boats were constantly on alert for thunderstorms and hurricanes. If bad weather was approaching, we would quickly lower the aerostat back onto the ship and secure it for the storm. Sometimes the squall came up too fast and simply outran us. In February 1992, two aerostats and their multimillion-dollar payloads were lost in storms at sea. The loss of both aerostats, in such a short time, raised a question about the fundamental performance of these systems. Consequently, our team assembled an independent panel to conduct the world's first aerostat failure review board. The leading authority on the panel was Dr. John Attinello, a highly-respected aerospace expert, who had designed the wing flap used on modern aircraft. The board recommended several aerostat design changes to improve the performance in high winds.

Fortunately, severe weather was also a problem for the drug smugglers. Their aircraft and boats took a pounding during storms, and they suffered losses that were rarely reported. However, the smugglers accepted these risks as they were paid much better than we were.

UFO Sightings

While SASS was testing and operating in the Gulf of Mexico, there was a spike in UFO sightings. Local news media picked up on the reporting. At least one book was published on UFO sightings in the Gulf and mentioned Lt. Colonel Nelson Johnson. Since aerostats made no sound and their military intelligence mission made them a bit mysterious, we were quite sure much of the UFO chatter was about SASS. The aerostat had lights on it at night to avoid collisions with military and civilian pilots. To keep things lively, we should have issued some Roswell-type alien masks to the SASS crew to further fuel the UFO speculation and hype.

SASS vs. the Honduran Military

On one mission, a SASS ship was approached by a Honduran military gunboat. The armed Hondurans had no idea what it was and approached the strange ship with weapons drawn and intent to board it. There was a standoff for several hours while messages were sent through official channels and made their way to the U.S. Embassy. The Honduran gunboat got the word that the SASS ship was friendly. However, the conversation soon changed. There were several Honduran paratroopers on the gunboat, and they asked if they could practice parachute jumps from the aerostat. This request was a bit crazy, as they would likely land in the ocean and potentially drown in their parachutes. The request was respectfully denied to avoid an international incident—and a lot of paperwork. But in hindsight, if the SASS crew had permitted the jumps, we could have issued the Hondurans some UFO alien masks and taken pictures. We could have slipped the photos to the press. The news headline would read, "Alien Paratroopers Descend from Spacecraft and Seize U.S. ship." We could have had some fun with that one. But then again— it would have attracted too much unwanted attention to the program—it's probably best we didn't.

SASS & SBA Merger

SASS was an Army program. Congress directed that SASS be merged with the U.S. Coast Guard's Sea-Based Aerostat (SBA) program. Both programs had a similar counter-drug mission. SASS had three ships, and the SBA program had five. The new combined program was called the Ocean Based Aerostats (OBA). The SBA contractor was General Electric, and our team conducted extensive side-by-side testing in April and May of 1992 to assess the two different configurations to see which program had the better performance. Derek Baker led the test. We evaluated each subsystem, including the aerostat, the radars, the communications suite, data processing, and system availability.

Moving On

After completing this extensive SASS-SBA testing, SPC asked me to change my duties. Lisa Willey had joined the Vint Hill team to continue the mission support. I was moving to lead the corporate team supporting the Defense Advanced Research Programs Agency (DARPA). I was a mission-focused guy and did so with great reluctance. I found the experience supporting the ARL and SASS programs absorbing and professionally rewarding and was unsure how DARPA would compare. I was a team player, though, and agreed to the new position.

Letter of Appreciation

In late 1995, I left SPC for a new job at Raytheon E-Systems, and Jerry Bate soon followed. In February 1996, the CEO of SPC, Dr. Ron Easley, received a very kind letter of appreciation from Lt. Colonel Stan Niemiec. The letter cited six years of exemplary performance by the small team that supported his Program Management Office. Although we were supporting contractors, hired to advise and assist the government, we always felt like a part of the official government SASS and ARL team. We were honored to be recognized.

As for the TAClink product line we developed, SPC eventually sold it to another small business. We knew digital video technology was maturing, and TAClink's analog video would eventually be surpassed. But Jerry Bate, Steve Griggs and I have fond memories of the entrepreneurial environment that gave it birth and the many missions it served for our nation.

After serving about ten more years with Jerry at Raytheon, he retired to his farm in Pennsylvania and had more time for his inventions and HAM radio passion. He passed away a few years later. I will always remember Jerry Bate for his patience in helping me understand the basic principles of radio communications, his friendship, and for serving his nation's military from industry.

1990 Testing a Cellular Repeater in Elizabeth City, North Carolina

CHAPTER 41
DARPA

My new assignment was to lead a team supporting the Electronic Systems Technology Office (ESTO) at the Defense Advanced Research Projects Agency (DARPA). Don Wickstrand, a retired naval officer, was my new boss. Our Vice President in the Center for Battlefield Technologies was Don Shaw, a retired Army colonel. Both Dons were professionals, friendly and provided a very supportive environment. I felt I was off to a good start.

I quickly studied up on DARPA. It was the Department of Defense's high-risk, high-payoff technology organization and employed some of America's smartest people. It had been involved in some exciting technical breakthroughs. The agency had funded ARPANET, the earliest version of the Internet and also helped develop the Global Positioning System (GPS), stealth technology, unmanned aerial systems (drones), and served as America's first space agency. The DARPA headquarters was located only a few blocks from my SPC office in Arlington, Virginia.

DARPA had about one hundred entrepreneurs, called Program Managers (PM), with a lean organizational staff. This allowed new technical ideas to be quickly reviewed by a PM and rapidly receive funding. Many interesting technical ideas were pinging around the halls, and PMs were often unaware of the work ongoing in other offices. Soon after I arrived, I heard an interesting description of the organization, "DARPA has 100 entrepreneurs, connected by a common travel agent." Well said.

I was the new Program Manager of the Advanced Technology Team. Our task was to provide direct technical and program management support to ESTO whose mission was to develop a broad range of technologies, including interface systems; sensors, actuators, and displays; signal processing; and packaging and interconnect systems. Although I had a decent technical background, I was now being asked to support a bunch of customers with PhDs. When I initially read the technology programs that ESTO was pursuing, it gave me pause. The list sounded like it was the MIT version of Ranger School:

- Microelectromechanical Systems (MEMS)
- Microwave and Millimeter Wave Integrated Circuits (MIMIC)
- Application Specific Electronic Modules (ASEM)
- Low Power Electronics (LPE)
- Tactical Information Assistants (TIAs)
- Wireless, Adaptive Mobile Information Systems (WAMIS)
- Rapid Prototyping of Application Specific Signal Processors (RASSP)
- Microwave and Front-End Technology (MAFET)
- High-Density Microwave Packaging (HDMP)
- Head Mounted Displays (HMD)
- High-Definition Systems (HDS)

My job was to support the ESTO Director, Dr. Lance Glasser. Our team also helped several other Program Managers, including Dr. Ken Gabriel, Eliot Cohen, Ellison (Dick) Urban, Nick Naclerio, and Dr. Jim Murphy. Henry Girolamo was a DARPA Agent that helped to accelerate the technology development. This talented team worked on advanced microelectronics that would transform the global market in the 1990s. It turned into a great partnership. The DARPA Program Managers understood advanced technology, and I recognized its military applications. I often served as ESTO's subject matter expert, determining if their new technologies had military relevance and identified strategies to transition them to the Department of Defense. Our company had some talented employees working at DARPA in three major offices. Ann Stone joined us soon after I arrived, and provided exceptional administrative support to Lance Glasser, and most importantly, she kept me out of trouble. We also had a few husband and wife teams, including Chris and Susan Miles, and Stephen and Kathleen Griggs.

Fort Hood –DARPA Testbed

I often flew to Fort Hood, Texas to bring new DARPA toys to military intelligence officers in the 2nd Armored Division. Lt. Colonel Maxie McFarland was a dynamic and enthusiastic guy that loved any advanced concept or capability he could get his hands on. Whether it was flat panel displays, TAClink or a number of other futuristic tactical gizmos, Maxie was all in. He invited me to his command post during a field training exercise at

2:00 AM so I could see how the Intel and Ops came together at the peak of the war game; a culminating event of "high adventure." Maxie later introduced me to Major Gus Green and his eventual replacement, Lt. Colonel Barbara Fast.

Meanwhile, Dick Urban asked me to come up with some ideas for his new Tactical Information Assistants program. He wanted to know how we could embed new technologies into military equipment to produce an immediate and compelling benefit for warfighters. This was 1994, and years before smartphones were commercially available. However, I could foresee many separate devices merging into a single handheld device.

After visiting some smart guys at Fort Belvoir that worked for the Program Manager for Night Vision, I believed the MELIOS Laser Rangefinder was a good candidate for a DARPA technology insertion. What I wanted to do was to make the job of a U.S. Army scout or forward observer much easier. Scouts had to locate enemy targets (vehicles or soldiers) a few kilometers away, by scanning through a laser rangefinder, and then manually plotting the estimated position on a paper map. This took time and potentially introduced location errors of hundreds of meters. The scout would follow up with a radio call to verbally describe the target and its location. If the target were moving, it would make efforts to hit it with artillery almost impossible.

Our idea was to take a standard MELIOS Laser Rangefinder and augment it with an embedded processor, micro-high-definition display, GPS chip, digital camera, tactical map software and a secure communications link. The enhanced MELIOS would allow a scout to detect an enemy target, push a button to immediately get a precise location, snap an image of the target, and rapidly fill out a digital situation report (Size, Activity, Location, Unit, Time, and Equipment). The operator could then digitally transmit—burst— the report and a photo within a few seconds of the detection.

I ran the idea past Maxie McFarland and the Commander of the 2nd Armored Division, and I received two big thumbs up. I flew back to DARPA and presented the idea to Dick Urban and Ken Gabriel and got a couple of big smiles.

Shortly after that, a Business Development Manager at Motorola, Mr. Dave Carroll, visited my office. I mentioned how excited DARPA and Maxie were about the enhanced MELIOS concept. Dave apparently took the idea to his engineering team and came back to DARPA with a plan for how to rapidly build a prototype system, they named TAMER.

DARPA jumped on it and wanted quick action from Motorola. I was the honest broker, flying out to Scottsdale every few months to check on progress. The project attracted the attention of the DARPA front office. During testimony to Senate Armed Services Committee later that year, the Director used the enhanced MELIOS (TAMER) as an example of what DARPA was doing for the warfighter.

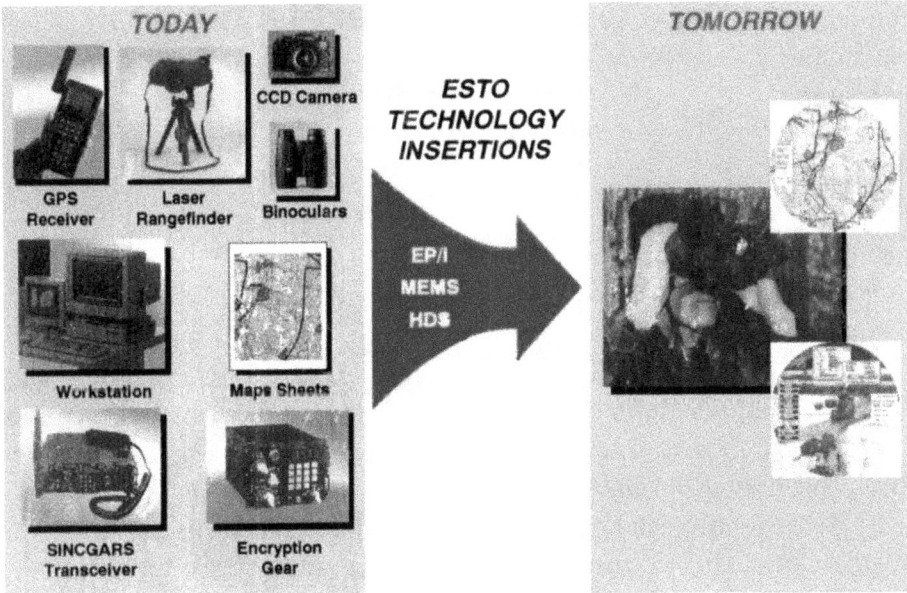

The Enhanced MELIOS Concept

Part of my job was to connect DARPA technologists directly with their warfighting customers. This was important to build professional relationships, to share a mutual understanding of capabilities, and to strengthen collaboration on new technologies. Working through Maxie, the Commander of the 2nd Armored Division sent a formal invitation to Lance Glasser and Dick Urban to visit Fort Hood and meet with the command group and other senior staff officers. Maxie arranged an executive tour of the Division Command Post. This was followed by some field time, where Lance and Dick were able to drive in an M-1 Abrams main battle tank and a Bradley Fighting Vehicle. It was here, at the tactical edge of the battlefield, that

DARPA's electronics technologies needed to make an impact. The trip was quite successful and provided a renewed sense of purpose for the ESTO team.

I ran into Maxie McFarland in 2011 at a trade show and learned he had retired from the Army. He was a senior executive working at the United States Army Training and Doctrine Command (TRADOC). That job was a good fit for him. He paid me an exceptionally kind compliment, "You were ahead of your time." That comment, coming from Maxie, was incredibly meaningful. Frankly, so was he. Maxie made my job supporting DARPA easy and exciting. He deserved much of the credit for helping us develop advanced technologies for our troops. Sadly, Maxie passed away a year later. He was a great soldier and a patriot, and I hope others will get to know him through this account.

MEMS

Working with Dr. Kaigham "Ken" Gabriel was another bright spot in my career. We shared a common Armenian heritage. His family had relocated to Baghdad, Iraq to escape the genocide of the Armenians early in the 20th century and later moved to America. Ironically, almost twenty years after I met Ken, I would be deployed to Baghdad during the war and learned more about the local Armenians. They were a minority Christian population trying to live peacefully while an insurgency raged on the Iraqi streets.

Ken's family celebrated Christmas on January 6th, the traditional Armenian date. He told me this had significant advantages; toy prices were deeply discounted, and the shopping in the stores was light.

Ken was leading the microelectromechanical systems (MEMS) program at DARPA, and one of his first actions was to send me to a training course to help me understand the technology. That course helped me get up to speed.

MEMS were microscopic systems packaged on a computer chip, such as accelerometers, chemical sensors, radio frequency filters, and medical devices. They enabled everyday objects to be smaller, lighter weight, lower power and become much smarter and useful. The breakthroughs in the technology were exciting and offered great promise, as they could be embedded in hundreds of devices, including helicopter rotor blades, truck tires, automotive airbags, as well as inside the human body.

One of my more interesting tasks was helping Ken with a major DOD study to identify the military applications for MEMS. Ken's revolutionary program rapidly gained attention, and he was asked to brief Secretary of Defense William Perry at the Pentagon. Years later, Ken served another tour at DARPA, as the Deputy Director.

Special Operations Command (SOCOM)

During this period, there were several opportunities to work with U.S. Special Operations Forces (SOF). SOF included Special Forces (Green Berets), Rangers, SEALS, Special Boat Units, Air Combat Controllers, and some elite counterterrorism units including Delta Force. It was a natural alignment: SOCOM was at the forefront of developing American military tactics, while DARPA was on the cutting-edge of advanced technology.

[Decades ago, there used to be a humorous description of U.S. Special Forces that was used on t-shirts and posters. It painted a rosy picture of SOF, until the final line: "U.S. Special Forces travel all over the world, to strange lands; they meet exotic people, and then they kill them."]

While on a military flight to Fort Bragg, Lance Glasser and several other DARPA executives were briefed by a senior SOCOM commander. When the briefing was over, the commander stated, "We'll see you on the ground," at which time the crew opened the aircraft doors, and the SOCOM team immediately parachuted from the plane. The DARPA guys were quite shocked by the abrupt exit and realized they were not on a routine business trip. When the airplane landed, the Special Ops team met the DARPA execs on the airfield and led them to special training facilities that featured live ammunition and hostage rescue training scenarios. Life doesn't get much better than that.

Later, Ken had a chance to brief some SOCOM operators on his MEMS program. After his talk, there were a few moments of silence. One of the operators stood and respectfully told Ken that he apparently knew a lot about his technology, "but I don't understand why it's important to our military unit."

At that point, I had an opportunity to help translate the technical benefits into operational benefits for SOF which these operators could fully appreciate. I asked the special operator, "What do you do at SOCOM?"

"I operate special mission aircraft."

"Do you have accelerometers and gyroscopes on the aircraft?" He nodded, so I continued, "How big are they... what do they weigh?"

"There's six of them of different weights and sizes."

I told him, "What if they could be manufactured on a computer chip with minimal size, weight and power consumption?"

The light bulb went on for the Special Ops guy. "I could fly 30 minutes longer and carry more troops or payload; it'd be a real operational benefit."

"Accelerometers are just one type of MEMS device," I told him. "Undoubtedly, many other aviation subsystems could also be improved." The energy level in the room spiked.

On another trip, Dick Urban arranged meetings with U.S. Special Forces at Fort Campbell, Kentucky. There we worked with Operational Detachment (ODA) 596 that experimented with new equipment before deploying it to the Middle East. We learned about their current tactics and procedures and later conducted training on some surveillance missions and set up an ambush.

On a DARPA trip to San Diego in 1998, we observed training for the Navy SEALs, formally referred to as the Basic Underwater Demolition/SEAL (BUDS) school. I enjoyed comparing their training to what I experienced at the Army's Ranger School. We arrived at a pool where the SEAL trainees were conducting drown proofing. Their hands and feet were tied together, and they had to survive in a deep pool of water for an extended period of time. I was not a great swimmer, particularly while carrying a hundred pounds of gear. Trying to stay afloat was just too much work, so my preferred technique for crossing a river was to simply sink to the bottom and walk across.

Our next stop was at the waterfront where we met a Special Boat Unit and boarded the Mark V, a high-speed vessel that delivered SEALs to their mission area. The Mark V can transport a 16-man SEAL platoon 500 miles and achieve speeds of over 65 knots.

In rough seas, that is a back-jarring experience. We strapped into the boat and went off on a wild ride. It was like riding a motorcycle on the autobahn full of potholes. We were told the Mark V could also stop within one boat length and conduct a U-turn in two boat lengths, AT FULL SPEED. I didn't believe this claim when I got on the boat. Holy smokes, I do now.

When we returned to the Naval Special Warfare facility, we received a briefing from a Navy SEAL named William McRaven. He gave us an overview on the command and discussed current and future SEAL technology. All of the DARPA visitors also received a copy of a book authored by him on Special Ops Case Studies. Many of us asked him to sign it. Thirteen years later, ADM McRaven organized and oversaw the Special Ops raid, code-named Operation Neptune Spear (a reference to the trident in the SEAL insignia), that killed Osama bin Laden. Since then I have been tearing apart my house to find that darn book, he signed in 1998.

We finished off the day by going to a rowdy pub called Dick's Last Resort. The place was reportedly a SEAL hangout, and the place was a fitting stop to finish our trip. The servers were intentionally rude, obnoxious and constantly insulted customers. I decided to launch an aerial counterattack—they'd never expect that from an Army Ranger. The dining area was full of picnic tables, and helium balloons were tied to each table. I tied a paper cup, full of beer, to a few helium balloons and then poked a small hole in the bottom, so it leaked. I released the balloons, and the beer cup climbed above the tables. Then the ceiling fans pushed the balloons around the barroom while beer dripped indiscriminately across the staff and customers. As the balloon bomber lost beer, it climbed higher and moved faster. Other tables retaliated by making their own balloon bombers, and it soon rained beer throughout the restaurant. We laughed until our guts hurt.

Unmanned Ground Vehicles

In 1993, DARPA had an Unmanned Ground Vehicle (UGV) program led by Lt. Colonel Erik Metalla. He was developing autonomous navigation technologies for robotic vehicles. Lt. Colonel Metalla saw a demonstration of our TAClink video system, recognized it could be used with robotic vehicles and invited me to his DARPA UGV Conference in Keystone, Colorado.

I was glad to attend, and many of the conference attendees enjoyed the local skiing during non-working hours. Unfortunately, I was within two months of completing my master's degree in Systems Engineering, and I needed to dedicate every free hour toward preparing my final course work. I did not get a chance to enjoy the ski slopes or any of the nightlife. Someday, I would like to get back to Keystone and see what I missed. I'll put it on my bucket list.

Years later, I met Lt. Colonel John Blitch who led the DARPA Tactical Mobile Robots (TMR) program. He was a rare breed: a Ph.D., a West Point graduate, and also Special Operations qualified. He was working with industry to develop small, backpack-sized robots. iRobot was one of the contractors that developed a family of "PackBot" military robots. A decade later, these were widely used in Iraq and Afghanistan to detect and clear IEDs and roadside bombs. While I was at Raytheon, we developed a tactical glove that could communicate with the robot by providing hand gestures. These tactical hand signals were similar to those used by soldiers when they need to remain silent and undetected. The PackBot could recognize and respond to commands such as turn right, left, speed up, stop and others.

Lt. Colonel Blitch also worked on advancing a new category of robots called "throwbots." These small robots could be literally thrown into a window, a room or a hallway and surveil the area for enemy personnel, equipment, and activity. The machines were also intended for urban search and rescue.

Space

Ironically, my former company commander from Germany, Al Wheatley, also worked at DARPA. He was now an Army major and directly involved in the Advanced Space Technology Program (ASTP). This program had some projects intended to reduce the cost of space launch vehicles, the Pegasus and Taurus rockets among them, along with the development of micro-satellites. I believe Al was re-using nuclear missiles, no longer required for the Cold War, as potential launch vehicles to put satellites in orbit. The effort sounded fascinating as it resonated with my aerospace engineering training. Unfortunately, Al finished his DARPA tour as I was just arriving, so our overlap was short.

Advanced Battlefield Medicine

Our SPC team supported two doctors on the DARPA staff that worked on advanced medical technologies. One of the programs involved using telemedicine for faster battlefield care.

To highlight its benefits, DARPA was planning to demonstrate telerobotic surgery at a major conference in 1994. A surgeon would operate on a patient remotely—theoretically as far as thousands of miles away—using a robotic arm and a satellite link while monitoring the progress on a display.

This advanced technology allowed future soldiers to be operated on sooner and closer to the battlefield, potentially saving more lives. We focused on providing life-saving treatment during the "golden hour," the first hour after a traumatic injury.

The day of the conference, the DARPA PM gave us an urgent task to bring "two buckets of fresh pig guts" to the conference. The surgery would be performed on the pig innards, rather than a real human volunteer. The task to acquire the raw pig guts was assigned to our colleague, Joe Gill. Joe was a former member of "The Old Guard," the military unit that guarded the Tomb of the Unknown Soldier and the White House. Joe had a can-do attitude, and the mission always came first. So, he contacted a local butcher shop and explained the urgent need. When Joe arrived at the butcher shop, a man walked out from the back room holding two small squealing pigs. He asked Joe if the pigs were okay. Joe nodded, and the guy threw the pigs in some kind of hot pressure washer that immediately killed the little guys and sanitized them. Within minutes, the man handed Joe two buckets of pig guts, on ice, and Joe raced back to the conference to deliver the goods. Mission complete.

Dr. Satava was one of the DARPA PMs that had developed the Personnel Status Monitor (PSM) for use by soldiers. PSM was a wrist-worn device that remotely monitored a soldier's vital signs (including pulse, blood pressure, respiration, and O2 level) to determine if he was wounded, in shock, dehydrated, or had some other life-threatening condition. Using the PSM, local medics would quickly locate and diagnose soldiers in distress, leading to higher survival rates. Twenty years later, the Fitbit became a commercial product that was remarkably similar to the vision of the DARPA PSM program.

CPR

One morning, I left Lance Glasser's office at DARPA and walked down a long hallway. About thirty meters away, I could see Dr. Satava conducting what I figured was CPR training on a dummy. As I came closer, I thought it odd that the training was in the hallway and not in a separate room. Within seconds, my understanding of the situation radically changed. He was attempting to resuscitate a young woman, an administrative assistant, who had collapsed. Dr. Satava was trying to keep her alive.

I dropped my briefcase and immediately asked if he needed help. He said yes, so I took off my suit jacket and began to provide artificial respiration and chest compressions. I had been trained in life-saving in the military, but this was the first time I was directly involved in a real-world situation.

While waiting for the ambulance, we tried to talk to her, but she was unresponsive. I spoke to other co-workers and learned the young woman's name and that she had a small child. Her boyfriend was in the Navy and might be deployed. I asked the others in the office if they knew if she was pregnant. No one was certain. I feared someone might say "yes," and then we would need to try to save the child.

We kept performing CPR for 10-15 minutes until the paramedics arrived. The rescue team injected a large needle in her chest. Nothing happened. They asked Dr. Satava if he wanted to declare her deceased at the scene. He preferred she was transported to the hospital and have the attending physician in the Emergency Room make the call. The woman was taken in an ambulance.

I stayed at the scene for a few minutes contemplating what had just happened. We had failed to revive the young lady, and her family would get some terrible news. Deep in thought, I snapped out of it when a member of the DARPA security staff, trying to be professional and respectful, asked me if any unsecured classified documents were lying about. I looked around and saw nothing significant. I headed back to my office and let Don Wickstrand and Don Shaw know what happened. I could not focus on my work and went home early that day. The lesson learned was clear. We never know when life will end. Every day we have is a gift.

Mac Attack

Mercer "Mac" Dorsey, a retired Army colonel and an incredible man, worked with us at SPC. He had served in the Special Forces in Vietnam and later as the Assistant Commandant of the JFK Warfare School at Fort Bragg, North Carolina. He would occasionally tell us stories of his adventures. Some of the training he conducted as a young Green Beret involved snatching high-value targets (bad guys) or swimming past German guards to emplace demolition charges on a key dam. He also shared some combat stories from Vietnam.

After he left SPC, Mac took a job as the chief of security for the United Nations in Bosnia. We told him to stay safe; war was for young men, not retired colonels. Six weeks later, I saw an article in the local newspaper about a man, from the area, who had been wounded in Bosnia. It was Mac. He had been in a Russian Antonov aircraft when it was hit, as it took off, by Serbian anti-aircraft fire. The round came through the bottom of the plane and tore into Mac's leg, and he bled profusely. The Russian aircrew did not have a first aid kit; they had sold it and probably used the money to buy vodka. The flight immediately diverted to Split, Croatia where Mac was evacuated to Germany and finally to Walter Reed Medical Center. Throughout the ordeal, Mac needed over 80 units of blood to stay alive. He caught a horrible infection and spent almost an entire year recovering at Walter Reed.

Secretary of State Baker

SPC had a reputation as a fun place to work, and the company was often involved in big events. For example, after the Cold War ended, SPC sponsored the SS-20 Soviet missile exhibit at the Smithsonian National Air and Space Museum.

In 1993, SPC held its annual holiday party at the Willard Hotel. It was a first-class event at one of Washington's finest hotels.

While walking about the Willard, I unexpectedly ran into Mr. James Baker, the former Secretary of State during Operation Desert Storm, under President Bush (41). He had also served some presidents as the White House Chief of Staff and Secretary of the Treasury. It was not long after the Gulf War ended, and although I was in civilian clothes, Secretary Baker recognized me as a member of the military based on my haircut and bearing. He stopped me in the hallway and thanked me for my service. He was an incredibly kind and respectful man. He did not even ask if I deployed to Desert Storm. I had not, and I did not feel that I deserved the gratitude. I was just a former paperboy, and he was one of the truly great Americans of that period. But I will never forget how gracious and impressive he was.

CHAPTER 42
RAYTHEON / E-SYSTEMS 1995-2001

My former colleague at SPC, Jeff Harris, joined a company called E-Systems and then disappeared. After a few months, he called me and asked if I was interested in also joining E-Systems. I told him things were going well, I liked my work at DARPA and thanked him for thinking of me. Jeff was persistent, and he visited me three or four times after regular business hours. Every time he stopped by, I was the only one still at work. My extended work days were often twelve hours long, and I added a forty-five-minute commute to either side.

It was 1995, and our young son, Kent, spent much of his first year in the hospital in intensive care. I started wondering why I was turning the lights on at work each day and turning them back off in the evenings. Perhaps there was a rewarding position somewhere with some better work-life balance.

Jeff finally convinced me to come to E-Systems for an interview. The interview process went remarkably well. I was offered three positions to choose from. The new job came with a 35% pay raise, a pension, and an annual bonus. That was very attractive, and after weeks of deliberation, I gave SPC notice that, regrettably, I was resigning. I offered SPC six weeks of notice so I could transition my duties to another employee. I was surprised that several senior corporate leaders personally met with me and counter-offered to try to retain me.

The DARPA contract was considered strategic, and I was playing an important role on it. It was awkward. I had given my word to E-Systems that I was joining, and then SPC significantly upped their counter-offer if I would stay.

It was my first real lesson on salary negotiations. You get what you negotiate. In a matter of days, my market value was much higher, yet I was essentially the same former paperboy. But I knew I could not accept the SPC counter-offer. I had given my word to E-Systems and needed to honor it. The new job and better pay were reward enough. I had accepted a position in the Reconnaissance Systems organization of E-Systems working for a bright guy named Mark Neuhausen. Recon Systems supported major Air Force programs related to the ground stations for the U-2 high-altitude aircraft and the Global Hawk Unmanned Aerial Vehicle. The U-2 was a legendary spy plane from the Cold War, and the Global Hawk was an unmanned aircraft the size of a Boeing 707. The new job sounded pretty cool.

Ron and Linda Easley at SPC held a farewell event and thanked me for my service. I returned their thanks for allowing me to work on such interesting programs and felt like I was leaving my family behind. They wanted to give me a gift and asked me what I would like. I did not need anything and did not want a lot of attention drawn to my departure. However, I told them I had a paralyzed brother and caretaker mother, who had never seen Orlando and all the theme parks. So SPC gave me a very meaningful gift; three airline tickets to Orlando. It was another classy move from a highly-respected company.

A few weeks before starting my new job, Jeff told me that E-Systems was being acquired by Raytheon. Big changes would be coming. I wasn't sure what this meant for me, but Jeff said not to worry.

I arrived at E-Systems in early September 1995. I could immediately sense there was some panic in the building. The Raytheon acquisition was playing out, and a major reorganization had been announced. That meant personnel layoffs to create a more efficient organization. Two of the three senior leaders that had offered me my new position were now gone. The building was eerily quiet. People had scattered, probably hiding under their desks as if there were a gunman in the hallways. Who was the next casualty? As the new recruit, and perhaps an easy target, I naively bopped down the hall, playing the extrovert, trying to meet new friends. People avoided eye contact and moved away quickly as if I had leprosy or Ebola. Perhaps seeing a new guy walking around meant someone else would be getting the ax.

After two weeks, the re-org ceased and the dark period ended. There were new signs of life in the hallways. Unshaven managers and engineers peeked out of their offices. By now they were pretty hungry, and they worked their way to the cafeteria like zombies headed to a food festival. I went to the cafeteria to meet some of the survivors.

I started to learn about the company's technical capabilities and its core competencies. E-Systems was excellent at building remotely controlled systems, processing and disseminating large streams of information, and building Signals Intelligence (SIGINT) systems. The truth was, there was little I could do to help the company's existing programs. These were mature programs with seasoned staff.

What I focused on was using my DARPA and tactical reconnaissance experience to propose new ideas and develop new programs. Mark Neuhausen gave me a broad charter to do whatever I saw fit. His guidance was to add value; that was a perfect job for me.

I met with a senior engineer named Matt Harding, a nice guy. But I think I offended him by one of my early comments, "SIGINT is tactically irrelevant."

He became defensive. "Our SIGINT sensors are world class." As he continued to explain, I quickly realized that Matt's view of a tactical tip was alerting a fighter aircraft in the area of operations.

"That's great for aircraft operations, but what about tactical ground support? As an Army Ranger that needs to operate in enemy territory, I never once got a tip from a SIGINT sensor." That got his attention, and I continued, "Ground warfighters are blind in the radio frequency (RF) spectrum. Soldiers can see enemy targets in daylight with their eyes, and at night with night-vision goggles and infrared sensors. They can hear threat noises with their ears and smell battlefield odors. But our troops are completely blind in the RF spectrum. They have no capability to know if enemy tactical radio communications are nearby. Soldiers need to know, within five seconds, the location of an enemy radio that turned on near their position. That would immediately alert them their mission might be compromised, and their small unit in imminent danger. An enemy radio transmission may be reporting their location and requesting enemy artillery to hit them unexpectedly." I paused a moment. "I want this future capability to be owned, operated and carried by soldiers, and it should work against Low Probability of Intercept (LPI) signals that are hard to find. The system needs to show the location of friendly forces and where the enemy radios are. It would serve as a guardian angel and give our troops a competitive edge on the battlefield."

Matt had listened intently. "The current technology to do that is big, bulky, heavy, expensive and requires a lot of power. It can't be used by tactical ground warfighters."

That immediately made me think of DARPA. I wanted to reduce the size, weight, and power consumption of current systems by at least 10 times, so it could be battery operated and carried by a warfighter. It had to detect tactically relevant LPI communications used by enemy forces. We did not want the system to require a new or unique antenna. It needed to use the same single whip antenna the troops already carried. All of these technical challenges, addressed at one time, made this project a DARPA-hard problem.

I started with a vehicle-mounted concept, where tanks and Humvees could find the direction of enemy signals while our vehicles were continuously moving on the battlefield. I initially called the idea "Tank-mounted DF."

I wrote a concept paper to DARPA about it that sparked some initial interest and worked with a team of smart guys to refine the idea. Bill Reinard, Doug Vujcic, Chip Edwards and others helped us brainstorm. The team concluded that a "time-difference of arrival" solution approach was needed to reduce the size of the antenna needed. The technology also required revolutionary breakthroughs with advanced packaging, low power electronics, and signal processing algorithms. Several engineers thought the idea was too high-risk and probably impossible, so I did not want them on the solution team. DARPA's mission was to prove the impossible was possible. This effort was not for the faint hearted.

Since the proposed system detected an enemy radio, alerted local friendly warfighters, and cued them to the enemy location, I re-named the system "Combat-Cueing" or "Combat-Q" for short. DARPA funded it, and our team was off and running. The goal was to develop small brick-sized modules that could be installed anywhere: in a tank, Humvee, robotic vehicle, helicopter, drone, on a tower or carried in a soldier's rucksack. These modules would discover and communicate with each other and then share information and alerts about nearby enemy radios.

Our team shifted to a "time-difference of arrival" technical approach that used a single whip antenna. After brainstorming for several weeks, the team developed an innovative, break-through technical approach that reduced the amount of data that needed to be shared between different modules by 1000x. This was a huge advance. The Combat-Q development took a couple of years, and our team used many pioneering approaches to overcome daunting technical obstacles. At the conclusion of the program, we conducted successful field testing at Fort AP Hill, Virginia.

Meanwhile, I briefed the emerging capability to the Dismounted Warfighting Battle Lab at Fort Benning, Georgia. The Lieutenant Colonel I met with immediately recognized the tactical value of the system in urban areas and called it "RF Patrolling." There was a lot of momentum building.

Combat-Q's technical advances made during the program were used for several follow-on communications programs for DARPA and other customers. These included RF MEMS, PCMCIA-Embedded National Tactical Receiver (PENTR), UltraComm, the Airborne Comms Node (ACN), WolfPack, and Future Combat Systems (FCS). Along the way, we built a small "Skunk Works" for advanced communications and intelligence technologies.

Walt Havenstein

About this time, Walt Havenstein became the new general manager for our Strategic Systems Division (formerly Melpar) in Falls Church, Virginia. He was the new sheriff, at the top of the food chain.

Walt was a Naval Academy graduate still serving as a colonel in the Marine Corps Reserves. As the Chief of Staff of the Fourth Marine Division, he flew each month, at his own expense, to his unit in New Orleans to perform military duty. His corporate duties at Raytheon E-Systems and in the military were both very time-consuming. He was a patriotic American, serving the nation virtually for free. In fact, he had a negative annual income from the Marine Corps Reserves once he paid his own travel costs (airfare, hotel, and rental car) to report each month for the weekend of duty. Having senior positions in both industry and the military was an incredibly heavy load for Walt to carry, particularly when there was no financial benefit from his military service. It was an indisputable hallmark of patriotism and professionalism.

Walt and I had a spirited rivalry going on related to the Army-Navy game. As a graduate of West Point, I had a solemn duty to mess with all Naval Academy grads during the months leading up to the annual classic, known as "America's Game." The chatter would increase as the game approached each December. During that period, I developed a three-phased operational plan to increase the corporate energy level.

Phase I involved conducting psychological operations to mess with Walt's mind and get under his skin. I started by posting the scores of the last five Army-Navy games at key locations around the building: in every stairwell, along the main hallways and most importantly in the company cafeteria near the ice cream machine. Army had won all five of these close games. The total margin of victory for all five was only 10 points, but I enjoyed the rare prolonged Army winning streak and rubbing some salt in the wounds of the Navy alumni. The sign read:

Go Army! Beat Navy! Again!

1992	Army	25–24	Veterans Stadium	Philadelphia, PA
1993	Army	16–14	Giants Stadium	East Rutherford, NJ
1994	Army	22–20	Veterans Stadium	Philadelphia, PA
1995	Army	14–13	Veterans Stadium	Philadelphia, PA
1996	Army	28–24	Veterans Stadium	Philadelphia, PA

I now had Walt's attention and followed up with Phase II of my plan, a direct assault on him during a leadership staff meeting. While his team was seated in the main conference room, I drove a small robotically controlled model tank through the entrance door, with a black and gold "Go Army, Beat Navy" sign on it. The war machine, with its realistic engine noises, grinding and squeaking of gears, entered several feet into the room, stopped, and rotated its main gun toward the leadership team. BOOM! A simulated tank round was fired into the Navy sympathizers. I followed up by sweeping the staff with the co-axial machine gun, to make certain there would be no survivors. The tank turned and hastily departed the room with another sign on its rear bumper presenting the last five game scores. I quickly picked up the tank, tucked it under my arm and scurried back to my office to work on my alibi. I was thinking, OK, Havenstein, "How are you going to top that?"

The retaliation did not take long. Walt warned me he had something planned for the Army fans. His family had painted a large "Go Navy, Beat Army!" sign using a cloth sheet. It was proudly displayed a few days later in the main foyer of the Falls Church building.

Coincidentally, I had a similar idea, but it was less artistic. A week earlier, I took my design to a sign company, and they made a 4x8 foot black and gold banner. It read, "Go Army, Sink Navy!" and had a graphic of a Navy ship, the USS Squid, sinking below the waves. I drove the sign to work, strapped to the roof of my car, at about 4:30 AM the next morning and entered the building. The security guard wanted to know who I was and what was I doing. I told him it was a secret mission, and he needed to act like Sergeant Schultz on *Hogan's Heroes*. "I see nothing! I see nothing!" I made my way to the balcony and hung the new banner near Walt's sign. Then I zipped off to my office to develop another alibi.

I wasn't present when Walt saw the new sign, but I heard rumors he was getting irritated at my persistence. I was poking the bear in the eye. The owner of the building, Mr. Al Forte, came into the foyer the following day and seemed a bit disturbed by all the spirit signs and juvenile antics. I told him it was an Army-Navy rivalry thing and reassured him it would end the second week of December. I asked him what side he was rooting for; he needed to declare.

"I like Air Force," he said.

I gave Mr. Forte a look of disapproval. "Air Force never has won, and never will win an Army-Navy game. Ever."

I should explain something here. Any discussion about the Army-Navy football rivalry often upsets graduates and fans of the U.S. Air Force Academy. They probably felt left out, overlooked, or their team was marginalized by the Army-Navy hype. Not wanting to be ignored, my Air Force colleagues would often butt into an Army-Navy discussion. Typically, they would interject with some disruptive comment such as, "Well, Air Force beat Navy this year" or "Air Force is going to a bowl game."

Phase III of the plan involved a covert attack behind enemy lines, deep into hostile territory. Yes, it's what Rangers do. It was time to infiltrate Walt Havenstein's executive office suite and let him know there was no safe haven for Navy fans. So early one morning (Army early—not Navy early), I placed some "Beat Navy" bumper stickers in prominent locations about the office and left one staring him in the face above his doorway. His mouse pad needed an upgrade, so I swapped it out for a much better "Go Army" model. I wanted to install a new Army screen saver on his computer, but the rascal was using a password.

I went into his private conference room where he had his corporate strategy neatly written all about on white boards. Knowing I was pushing the limits, I hesitated. If I erased or altered anything in this room, I was messing with our future business. Stock prices might plunge. And there might be an Army casualty the following day. I was a bit bold but not that stupid. This room was out of bounds. I was pushing my luck and decided to exfiltrate. Time was running out, people would be showing up for work soon, so I headed back to my office to develop another alibi.

The big game finally came in 1997, and it wasn't pretty. Navy spanked Army 39 to 7 in East Rutherford, New Jersey. All good things must come to an end. Clearly, Navy must have played the game sober. Having been soundly defeated, I needed to act quickly to limit the potential damage to my reputation. I came into work early the following Monday and took down my big sign. Sergeant Shultz was still on duty, and he still saw nothing. I needed to quickly sanitize the rest of the building to eliminate any evidence of my existence. During that week, I avoided taking the main hallway past Walt's office, knowing I'd be walking into an ambush. Despite the significant ribbing I had delivered in the prior months, I kept my job. Walt only stuck me once with a verbal bayonet, "How about that Navy victory!" and then returned to being a gentleman.

Inter-service rivalries occasionally popped up during meetings. I had to brief Walt on a technical innovation that Jerry Bate and I had developed - a new handheld receiver that could be used to tune into battlefield video. I had an opportunity to demonstrate it to Walt, so he was made aware of the project. I recall the presentation vividly:

Kachejian: "Sir, this is Tactical Video Link, also called TVL. It allows ground warfighters to see live battlefield video. It is designed to be extremely simple to use. The operator turns it on using this switch, and then tunes to different channels, just like a television."

Havenstein: "We don't build radios here at Falls Church. That's done by another division."

Kachejian: "Yes. This is only a video receiver. It is an experimental capability that the advanced technology group has prototyped." That was a quick-thinking BS answer, receivers are half of a radio. I did not give Walt a chance to push back and kept driving on with the demo. "I am turning on TVL now. As you can see, I am tuned to Channel 1 which displays overhead video from a Predator unmanned aerial vehicle. I flip the dial to Channel 2, and I am looking at gunsight video from an Apache attack helicopter. I change to Channel 3, and I am watching video from a ground robot. Now Channel 4 is reserved for the Marines—it's the Cartoon Channel."

Havenstein promptly replied: "And Channel 5 is for you, The History Channel."

Kachejian: "Yes, Sir! We can do that."

Awesome. My project was approved. We could continue with the TVL development.

Walt, his wife Judy and their family moved to New Hampshire to for an executive position at BAE, and the Army-Navy rivalry in Falls Church fell off. He later rose to become the CEO at BAE Systems Inc. and at SAIC. After his corporate retirement, he ran for governor of New Hampshire.

Business Development

During this time, I worked with a great team of professionals that were responsible for developing advanced systems and new business for the company. Many of these colleagues were military veterans: Roger Bache, Bob Guerra, Pete Johnson and Greg Bartholomew were among them. They made coming to work a pleasure. One weekend, we had a chance to escape and do something even more enjoyable, fishing. We had great success catching striped bass at Solomans Island.

Striped bass fishing with Roger, Pete, and Greg

CHAPTER 43
THE INDUSTRIAL COLLEGE
OF THE ARMED FORCES

Application

In 2000, my boss, Bob Guerra, asked me what training courses I wanted to take to continue my professional development. He mentioned a few, such as attending a seminar at Harvard or enrolling in a short course at the Defense Acquisition University. I told Bob I wasn't sure and needed a week to think about it.

After talking to a few colleagues and friends, I decided to attend the Industrial College of the Armed Forces (ICAF) at the National Defense University. My father-in-law, James Bush, had been an ICAF graduate thirty years earlier. ICAF was a one-year executive leadership course sponsored by the Chairman of the Joint Chiefs of Staff. Considered a national war college, its curriculum was focused on the strategic acquisition and logistics that enabled our country to have the right equipment needed to win wars. All ICAF graduates earned a master's degree.

Active duty military officers (Army, Navy, Air Force, Marines) comprised the majority of students carefully chosen to attend ICAF. Other federal government leaders were selected from the Departments of State, Justice, Homeland Security or the Intelligence Community. Also attending were two dozen International Fellows, foreign military officers from allied nations. Only a handful of ICAF candidates were selected from industry. I was asking for one of these rare industry slots.

I met with Bob the following week and told him I wanted to attend ICAF. It was an expensive request, and I told Bob he had screwed up by giving me a choice. Bob was a former Marine, and an awesome guy. To my great relief, he was immediately supportive. We elevated the request to our VP, Dr. Hank Orejuela, a retired Navy captain. Hank did not flinch and quickly agreed. With both Bob and Hank's support, I was nominated as Raytheon's corporate candidate to attend the ICAF class the following year.

There was rigor in the ICAF application and selection process, but in this case, it seemed too easy. This was an incredible gift to me. I was going to serve with 300 senior U.S. and international government leaders for a year, receive my full salary, travel to far off places and earn a fully-funded master's degree. The paperboy was embarking on a new adventure.

Having Bob and Hank's support was huge. My attendance at ICAF meant their team would be short-handed for an entire year. Perhaps they just wanted to get rid of me, but it was an expensive way to do it. And after I completed the course, it was likely I would be assigned elsewhere in the company. It was not in their personal interest to endorse me to attend ICAF, but good leaders support their employees and make tough calls. So, I am forever indebted to these two men for giving me this extraordinary opportunity.

Arrival

Although ICAF had a significant number of military officers, the culture was designed to foster long-term relationships across U.S. agencies and international governments that would benefit our nation. To this end, all students, including military officers, wore civilian business attire. There was no rank, and all students were on a first name basis to break down formal barriers and promote teamwork. This policy reminded me of Army Ranger School, where every soldier, officer and enlisted, stripped off their rank and rotated leadership assignments.

I reported to ICAF in August of 2001. Upon arrival, I learned I was the only U.S. Industry student for the Class of 2002. Europe sent one other, Julian Bott from EADS. I proceeded to the administrative office and informed them that though I was attending from Industry, I also served in the Army Reserve. That allowed me to also get military credit for war college attendance. Being an ICAF graduate would help to advance both my civilian and military careers. I was killing two birds with one stone. My apologies to any animal rights activists.

ICAF was organized into two semesters with 20 groups called "Seminars," each with 15 students. As the only student from U.S. Industry, I brought a different perspective that was highly valued. Before my arrival, I was told there was some serious debate among the faculty as to which seminar the Industry student should be assigned. It seemed like a lot of fuss over a former paperboy.

My overall goal that year was to understand the strategic environment facing our nation and to network with new colleagues. I was pleasantly surprised to learn that many of my fellow government students were networking just as hard with me.

First Semester

The first semester, I was assigned to Seminar 9 and met my new teammates. From the Air Force were John "JJ" Torres, Marcus Caudill, Doug Cooke, and Dominique Myers. Navy shipmates included Scott Spencer, Gary Haben, and Sande Layton. My Army teammates were Paul Hilton, Neal Patterson, Dan Sheahan, and Lynne Caroe. Steve Williams was our sole representative from the State Department. We also had two international students, Colonel Ron Howard from the Canadian Forces, and Colonel Te-Chin Liu of the Taiwanese Army.

The curriculum required a lot of reading and many papers to be written throughout the year. Since several of the papers were on topics related to industry, I was often approached by fellow classmates to review and comment on their individual papers. I was flattered to be asked and happy to help my new friends, but it often meant I had significantly less time to write my own paper. But I knew it was part of my duties as the "industry guy," and I was able to balance the workload. Ironically, even at ICAF, the government relied on contractors to get their mission done. ;-) wink wink.

The first semester was packed with interesting courses, taught by a highly qualified staff. Historical Studies in Grand Strategy (Colonel John Charvat); Strategic Leadership: Leading and Managing Change (Dr. John Bokel); Military Strategy and Warfare (Colonel Terry Kerrigan); Political Science (Phillip Gary); Regional Security Studies: China (Captain Jeanne Vargo and Colonel Mike Falvey); and Economics of National Security Strategy (Dr. Nicole Crain). I also took two electives: National Security in the Information Age (Dr. Dan Kuehl) and Space and National Security (Stephen Randolph). My faculty advisor throughout the year was Dr. Alan Whittaker, an expert on national security issues and an advisor to the National Security Council. Another notable member of the faculty was Paul Needham, one of the former 52 American hostages held by terrorists in Iran for 444 days, enduring torture and mock executions. He was among the hostages my fellow cadets escorted to West Point after they were released from captivity the day Ronald Reagan was inaugurated.

9/11/2001

However, this particular year at ICAF was far from normal. Our nation was attacked on September 11, 2001. We witnessed the attack live. The Pentagon was hit by hijacked American Airlines Flight 77 within direct sight of our seminar room. Many ICAF students lost friends and colleagues who were on duty and killed at the Pentagon. Four of my fellow Raytheon employees were passengers on the doomed aircraft. Several ICAF students were medical doctors, and they immediately ran several miles to the Pentagon to render assistance.

It was a shocking day that awoke our nation. The ICAF curriculum and our global security perspective were permanently changed. One of our colleagues suggested that we all write down our personal accounts of this tragic day, so our memories were not lost. It was a smart idea. My account is presented at the end of this chapter.

ICAF vs. NWC

There was a friendly rivalry between the National War College (NWC) and ICAF. Both colleges were part of the National Defense University at Fort McNair. NWC was focused on preparing future military and civilian leaders for high-level policy, command, and staff responsibilities. ICAF focused on preparing selected military and civilians for strategic leadership in developing our national security strategy and managing resources in its execution. NWC felt their program was more elite, as their graduates commanded military forces in war. ICAF graduates provided the technology, equipment, and logistics needed to win the war.

After serving a career in the government, many ICAF and NWC graduates retired and moved on to a second career in industry. At this point, ICAF grads had a competitive advantage. They were generally more marketable, as they had industry-related experience and social networks.

This observation led to an interesting sound bite that could be heard in the NDU hallways, "Eventually, every NWC graduate works for an ICAF graduate."

Team-building Events and Travel

In addition to the academic program, ICAF offered several team-building events including exercises, intramural sports, field trips and class socials. When a major speaker came to NDU, both the ICAF and NWC students assembled in Baruch Auditorium to share the experience.

On September 17th, less than one week after the 9/11 attack, our class visited the U.S. Capitol Building. It was a somber day. The Capitol had been targeted during the assault, but that aircraft had been deliberately crashed in Pennsylvania, short of its target. The passengers fought back and saved our nation from a major blow to this site—and icon—of our government. That day we stopped at some locations, including the House Ethics Committee and the nearby U.S. Supreme Court. As we walked about outside the Capitol, I kept looking up for another inbound aircraft, but the skies were eerily empty. All air traffic overhead had been halted. We were now at war.

Seminar 9 Visits the House Ethics Committee

Seminar 9 at the U.S. Capital

A few days later, our class traveled to Gettysburg Battlefield in Pennsylvania. On July 1-3, 1863, this epic battle, during the Civil War, forever changed the course of our nation. We walked the terrain and re-traced, day by day, the battle. It culminated when Pickett's Charge failed to break the Union lines. Thousands of Union and Confederate casualties littered the battlefield for weeks. Tragically, they were all Americans.

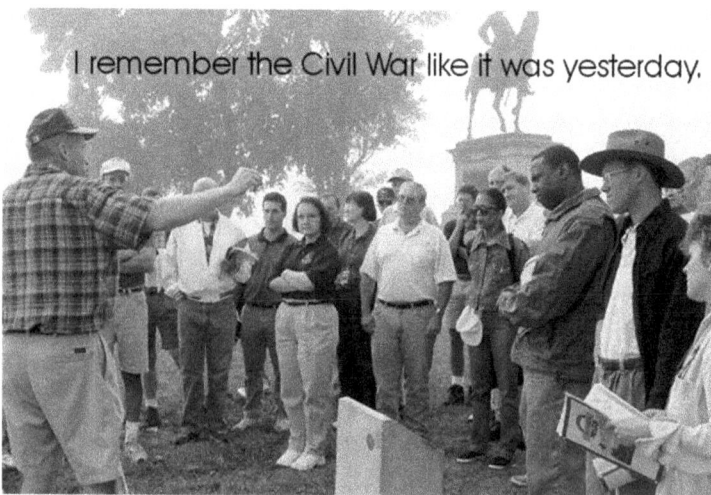

Terry Kerrigan provides a battlefield overview

394

Fall semester also involved participation in several intramural sports. There was something for everyone: softball, soccer, bowling, tennis, volleyball, etc. The culminating game for each sport was the big rivalry match between the National War College and ICAF.

Seminars 9 and 19 formed a softball team. I was a player-coach along with Air Force pilot JJ Torres. We were all mentally 20-years-old but playing with 40-50-year-old bodies. We played hard and pulled a lot of muscles. I fell back in on my old Little League position as a shortstop. Colonel Te-Chin Liu was our Taiwanese star outfielder, and Cliff Tompkins could hammer the ball like a cannon.

Meanwhile, intramural soccer was the sport where many of our international officers excelled. ICAF players from Europe, Latin America, and the Middle East joined in the action. It was a physical game. Paul Hilton suffered a significant head wound, but the old infantry colonel wiped up the blood, slapped on a bandage, and went back into the action.

A few weeks after the 9/11 attacks, the Commandant of the U.S. Coast Guard, Admiral James Loy, came to Fort McNair to present a major lecture on maritime security to almost 500 students. During the talk, I had a spirited exchange with our VIP guest. I introduced myself as a Raytheon employee, and said he could, "Expect Great Things!" It was the Raytheon corporate tagline at the time. Admiral Loy seized on my introductory comment and quickly fired back, "I'm not going to just expect great things, I am going to *demand* great things."

The packed lecture hall broke into hearty laughter. I replied, "Okay Sir, here comes your first great thing, from industry at no charge." I then suggested an idea to help improve cooperation between government and industry. It involved a voluntary approach where shippers could pre-register their cargo and shipping information to identify and mitigate potential security risks. In return for giving the U.S. government more insight on their proprietary supply chain, companies would receive expedited screening of their goods (less than 24 hours). Those shippers that did not join the program would be considered higher risk and their cargo could face increased inspections, resulting in higher costs and port delays of a week or more. Those companies joining the program would have a competitive advantage for delivering goods.

Admiral Loy enthusiastically supported the idea and said he would take it back with him for action that day. The exchange ended on a very positive note.

Immediately after the lecture, Vice Admiral Gaffney, the NDU President, invited me to his office for a private discussion. I was surprised by the sudden invitation. He made me feel welcome and said that my contributions as an industry fellow at the University were valued. When the meeting ended, he gave me the NDU President "Commander's Coin," something that is reserved for special occasions. He followed up by calling a senior executive at Raytheon to let them know what had happened. I was taken aback. I really had not done much to deserve this attention. Two years after his NDU lecture, Admiral Loy was selected as the nation's second Secretary of the Department of Homeland Security (DHS) following Governor Tom Ridge. The government had chosen well.

The voluntary supply chain security idea was soon adopted and became the basis for a successful program called the Customs Trade Partnership Against Terrorism (C-TPAT). I know many others in our government greatly contributed toward the launch of this new program. C-TPAT now accounts for over half the value of all merchandise imported into the United States.

In November, Colonel Ron Howard invited our Seminar to lunch at the Canadian Embassy. We toured the Embassy and learned a bit more about our northern neighbors. We capped it off with a great meal and enjoyed a fantastic view of the U.S. Capitol from their rooftop terrace.

ICAF had an excellent fitness center. Many of us would travel into Fort McNair early to get ahead of the abusive D.C. rush hour traffic and work out. My battle buddy was my friend Tim Gallagher. Press Marshall, Tim and I were West Point classmates and fellow Army Engineers. Tim kept me motivated and on track with my fitness goals. I know I would have slacked off

Conducting beer drinking operations with Tim Gallagher

without him. We both got into good physical shape. We even found time to grab a beer after school while we planned how America should strike the Al-Qaeda terrorists that had just attacked our nation. Our planning got better with each successive beer. I was advocating the use of flame throwing robotic vehicles to attack those hiding in the caves of Afghanistan. I wanted to cook the bastards.

Seminar 9 Christmas Party 8 Dec 2001

Second Semester

In mid-January 2002, students were assigned to their new Seminars. I was now in Seminar 1 which focused on Advanced Manufacturing. With the semester's focus on U.S. industry (including its overseas operations) and its relationship to our national security, the curriculum expanded and included domestic and international travel. The courses included: Acquisition (Jeanne Vargo); Economics of National Resource Allocation Strategy (Marc Wahl); Industry Study - Advanced Manufacturing (Vargo, Mike Falvey, and Terry Kerrigan); Information Strategies for Strategic Leaders (Dr. John Bokel);

Strategic Logistics (Dr. Fae Davis); and Strategic Mobilization (Dr. Alan Gropman).

I also took two electives at the Information Resources Management College (IRMC) on relevant topics: Information Age Policy Issues (Dan Kuehl); and Information Operations in Military Strategy (Lt. Colonel Michael McNamara).

My new teammates came from different government organizations and disciplines. From the Air Force were Doug Cooke (acquisition), Pete Micale (intercontinental ballistic missiles), Gary Plumb (F-22 flight testing), and Cliff Tompkins (test and evaluation). My Navy shipmates included Bill Carrico (F-18 fighters), Andy Li (advanced technology), Kelly McDowell (nuclear submarines), and David Meyr (strike operations). New Army teammates were Jim Heverin (artillery), Rob Cook (finance), and "Neal" Patterson (contracts). Joel "Coach" Kane (helicopters and V-22 tilt-rotor aircraft) was our feisty Marine. Ben Duffy (diplomacy) hailed from the State Department. We had two senior international students, Brigadier General Obaid Al Ketbi from the UAE Air Force (logistics and procurement), and Brigadier General Ali Azaizeh of the Jordanian Army (artillery).

We started with a professional development trip to the Norfolk area, a region full of vital military installations. It was a cold and rainy weekend when we toured the Newport News shipbuilding yard and saw the construction of a new nuclear submarine and an aircraft carrier, the USS Ronald Reagan. I did not realize how complex aircraft carriers were. There were more than 900 miles of cables running through them.

We followed up with a visit to the Navy SEAL training facility at Little Creek, a tour of the USS George Washington aircraft carrier at Norfolk Naval Base, and a stop at a U.S. Coast Guard installation for an inspection of a cutter and buoy tender. We wrapped up the trip with an overview of aircraft maintenance at the Naval Air Station (NAS) at Oceana, the new home to the F/A-18 Hornet fighter. On the return trip to Washington, D.C., we made a final stop at an Army cargo handling facility at Fort Eustis. That was a lot of interesting stuff to digest during a long weekend.

In February, our Seminar took a day-trip to the National Institute of Standards and Technology (NIST), a federal agency that partners with industry to develop and apply technology, measurements, and standards. We toured the Manufacturing Engineering Lab and received briefings and demonstrations related to precision manufacturing and measurement equipment. One of the more impressive presentations was on Intelligent Robotic Control of unmanned military vehicles. I had worked on some related technologies a few years earlier at DARPA.

That same month, our first overseas trip was to Panama. We boarded a new C-40 aircraft at Andrews Air Force Base and flew direct. The trip was focused on global shipping through the strategic Panama Canal and its famous Miraflores Locks. Major security issues about international shipping arose after the 9/11 attacks, and much of the world's trade flowed through the canal. How could our government really know what potential threats were inside the thousands of ships and millions of shipping containers transported around the world each year? A nuclear weapon or a dirty bomb could be in one of the containers shipped to the United States. Furthermore, an attack on the Panama Canal that damaged the locks or sunk a ship in the channel could severely damage the global economy.

We made another key visit to the Manzanillo International Terminal (MIT) near Colon where we were able to observe how shipping containers were handled. The big question was, "How could our nation improve security by inspecting every container, without slowing the speed of commerce?" The stop at MIT helped us all better understand the security threats discussed earlier that year in the lecture by the USCG Commandant, Admiral Loy.

We also made eco-friendly stops at the Smithsonian Tropical Research Institute where they studied marine animals (whales and rays) and the rain forest in El Valle. Our group finished off the day in Panama City by having dinner at Jimmy Parrillada's Restaurante. I pounded a few brew dogs with an old Air Force friend, Rick Ingalsbe, and a new friend, Boyd Robinson from the Australian Navy.

The following morning, we spent our last two hours relaxing on Santa Clara beach, before catching the flight back to D.C. with a refueling stop in Puerto Rico. One thing was clear, although few government employees became wealthy from their careers, they sure knew how to enjoy life through official travel.

In mid-March, our Seminar went through Pennsylvania and Delaware to visit manufacturing plants and to better understand their capabilities. We began with a stop at General Dynamics Ordnance and Tactical Systems, an ammunition manufacturing facility supplying our military. We moved on to York, Pennsylvania to tour the Harley-Davidson motorcycle manufacturing plant, which was making the sleek new V-Rod model. There, we bet that Terry

Kerrigan and Gary Plumb were going to whip out their credit cards and drive one of those chrome ponies off into the sunset.

The next morning, we visited the Boeing plant near Philadelphia. This facility upgraded helicopters for our military. Ironically, my aunt, Helen Kachejian, was an employee there, and I got to see her for the first time in over a decade. It was a brief but heartfelt reunion. Her husband, my Uncle Eddie, had passed away sixteen years earlier. Before I left, I looked the Boeing managers in the eye and sternly told them to make sure they were "taking good care of my Aunt Helen." I was wearing a business suit, and they thought I was some big shot government executive on a VIP tour of their plant. They had no idea I was just another government contractor and a former paperboy. I chuckled as I walked out of the plant.

The afternoon stop was at the Saturn Auto Assembly plant in Wilmington, Delaware. We were able to see and understand some of the best practices used in the U.S. auto industry. They were exceptional hosts, and very open about the domestic and international challenges their industry faced. After the meeting ended, we climbed back on the tour bus and returned to Fort McNair.

Easter came at the end of March, and the ICAF Commandant, Major General Harold Mashburn, and his wife, Susan, invited students and their families to an Easter Egg Hunt at Fort McNair. Alice and I thought it was a great idea. We loaded up a few dozen plastic eggs with toys, candy, and coins, belted our kids in their seats, and headed off for Washington, D.C. After we arrived, Alice and I met a dozen other families with children. Kent, Kara, Katie had a great time searching for their eggs. The Mashburn's were genuinely kind and generous. They had prepared some elaborately decorated eggs to share with all the children. I had never seen eggs this large and ornate. They looked like they were from Tiffany's.

In April, our Seminar embarked on another domestic trip to several companies in North Carolina including Thompkins Associates (supply chain), Flextronics (electronics), Caterpillar (construction), Siemens (power distribution) and GE Aircraft Engines. Being a professional trip, we all wore business suits. However, when we reached Caterpillar, a big part of the learning experience was hands-on. We were encouraged to jump into some construction equipment and began operating it in their "big dig" playground. We took off our neckties and went at it like kids in a candy store, trying out backhoes, graders, bulldozers, and other fun toys. No licensing required. Our

Marine colleague, Coach Kane, was having a great time ripping up planet Earth.

Seminar trip to Caterpillar

Coach Kane tearing up planet Earth with a backhoe

Inspecting a turbine at GE Aircraft Engines

We wrapped up our domestic travel by flying from North Carolina to Albuquerque, New Mexico for a tour of Sandia National Labs. The night we arrived, we decided to eat at a restaurant at the top of a local mountain. Visitors had to ride a tram to the peak, which provided a great view of the area. So, our group drove to the tram only to discover it was not in service. We needed an alternative place to eat, and it was getting late. There were few restaurants open. I recalled passing a casino a few miles back, and it likely had a decent restaurant. My teammates agreed, so we proceeded back down the slope to the casino, where we parked our cars. As we walked toward the entrance, I realized that General Obaid (United Arab Emirates) and General Ali (Jordan) might feel uncomfortable going into a casino. I asked them if our choice of restaurants was acceptable, and they agreed. We were all hungry.

As we stepped into the casino, the lights and sounds of slot machines dominated the foyer. We all paused for a minute to look across the gaming hall. I asked Obaid and Ali if they knew how the slot machines worked. They seemed a bit curious, so I said, "Watch this" and confidently strode up to the first machine. I pulled a quarter out of my pocket, stuck it in the machine and pulled the lever. Seconds later the bell was ringing loudly, and the strobe light was flashing. Dozens of quarters paid out in the metal pan. "Ching, Ching, Ching, Ching ...."

I was as surprised as anybody but tried to calmly act like it was just another day in the casino. As I stuffed my pockets with pounds of quarters, Kelly McDowell and Doug Cooke theorized that "The industry guy must have rigged the slot machine." I did not push my luck with a second pull on the slot handle. I had already won a year of paperboy pay with my first quarter. So, my pockets bulging, we waded through the gaming room, found the restaurant and ordered big steaks to cap off the night. I was tempted to pay my bill with quarters.

The next day, we toured Sandia National Labs and met a lot of smart people. Unfortunately, with the previous late night and time zone change, we were a bit low on energy. But Sandia Labs had some incredible technology, and that's why we often heard news reports that the Chinese and Russians continually tried to hack into their computer systems.

My nephew, Peter Curley, was a cadet in the West Point Civil Prep Program at the New Mexico Military Institute, about 200 miles away in Roswell. He rode a bus several hours that day to visit us in Albuquerque. When our seminar went to dinner that evening, I introduced Peter to the group. Although Pete was 25 years younger and seven levels lower in rank, he was immediately accepted as another colleague at the table.

China

The best part of our second semester was the two weeks of international travel. Each ICAF seminar needed to understand how other nations operated their industries. For the Advanced Manufacturing seminar, our travel destinations included the People's Republic of China, South Korea, and Japan.

It was an international custom to give a small gift of appreciation after each business meeting. We planned a few dozen business meetings during our overseas trip, so we needed a large number of small gifts. Our seminar surveyed the ICAF gift store and decided we would purchase sixty ICAF monogrammed pocket knives. The souvenir knives were gifts from Americans but ironically were made in China. The knives were of good quality, small and easy to carry in our checked baggage. However, one of our classmates had a major brain cramp and took all of them on the airplane. He sent his carry-on bags straight through the metal detector. Amazingly, the TSA did not find the sixty knives, but they did seize two suspicious bottles of water.

After we arrived in Shanghai, China, we checked into the Ritz-Carlton Hotel and went to a local restaurant. We were in an exciting new country and had a day to recover from the jet lag. We wasted no time and went out shopping. I could not read or write any Chinese, so I just followed the pack. We found ourselves in a crowded outdoor market. Everything was on sale. Mont Blanc pens sold for $1. DVDs were $1. Lots of things for... $1. Scores of Western brands were being pirated and sold.

We few Americans stood out in the crowd and were magnets to local merchants. There were about 17 million people in Shanghai, and at any moment, I felt like 15 million of them were following me, trying to sell me a Ro-Rex watch for $5. We were surrounded but fought our way out of the open market to a series of local shops. I found a store that sold neckties for about a dollar each. I bought thirty of the neckties and took them all home to see which five my wife liked that I could keep. The remaining ties were donated to AMVETS.

The following day, we awoke and had breakfast in the hotel. We saw several clean-cut All-American looking guys eating chow at a nearby table. They were eyeballing our group and asked us who we were. We confessed we were visiting from the National Defense University, and it was our first trip to China. We started sniffing back at them. "Who are you with?"

Surprisingly, they immediately told us they were with the U.S. Secret Service. It was clearly a poorly kept secret. I asked them if they were the advance party for an official visit, and they replied they were with a protection detail. They would not say who they were protecting, but it was a short list of candidates. Then came the invitation. We should meet the Secret Service detail in the hotel lobby, near the elevators at 4:00 PM that day. "Don't be late." We had a full day already planned, but we now had another surprise coming.

We left breakfast and headed to the U.S. Consulate office for an official meeting. While there, we discussed some policy and trade issues related to intellectual property (IP) rights.

China had passed several IP laws, but they were not well enforced. Pirated DVDs could no longer be manufactured on Chinese soil. The fake DVDs were now being produced on ships twelve miles offshore and then brought back into port in the evenings. Somehow, that—to the Chinese—represented progress for protecting American intellectual property.

As we left the Consulate, one of the staff members told us where the best place was to buy good quality pirated DVDs. We were all proud that our government was fiercely protecting U.S. business interests in China.

Meeting at the U.S. Consulate

We jumped back into our motor coach and departed the Consulate grounds. As we left the compound, we got a close look at the Chinese guards on duty outside the gates.

The truth was, these guards were not actually protecting the Americans. They were actually keeping Chinese citizens from defecting.

The guards sneered at us as our bus departed the Consulate. Their behavior reminded me of the communist East German and Soviet guards I faced during the Cold War in Europe. One of the guards stood on a podium directly in front of the Great Seal of the United States to mask the eagle from being seen by the public. However, they could not conceal the U.S. flag proudly flying over the Consulate wall.

As we drove off, I looked back at the Consulate. I noticed that all the Chinese guards were wearing pants that were too long. They clearly needed to find a good South Korean tailor to hem them up.

Communist Chinese guards at the U.S. Consulate

Our next destination was at the Jade Buddha Temple, a local cultural site. We piled out of the bus near the temple and decided we were hungry and wanted to eat some lunch before starting the temple tour. Someone suggested we go to a local "tofu" restaurant, which did not sound very appetizing to the rest of the group. I recall one of the responses, "Tofu? Really? I'm not going to eat that crap!" After a few minutes of debate, many of us agreed we would try tofu for the first time. We entered the restaurant with a lot of caution and a bit of curiosity. We ordered a variety of tofu foods to get a good sampling. When it was served, we were all amazed. The fake meat and fish not only had a realistic look, texture, smell, and feel, but it also tasted great—like real meat.

After lunch, we waddled a few blocks back to tour the Jade Buddha Temple. It was my first exposure to Buddhism. There were dozens of giant Buddha statues in the temple area, some guarded the temple entrance. Each had a different facial expression showing a particular emotion. Some were happy, sleepy, grumpy, or angry. No disrespect, but these statues reminded me of *Snow White and the Seven Dwarfs*. However, I am not sure Walt Disney was inspired by Buddhism while making the popular film.

Happy and Grumpy Buddhas

Sleepy

We found the tour interesting. I was surprised the temple was so well maintained and had not been destroyed by the communist government, which believed the State was supreme to any religion. Most communist governments professed atheism and saw organized religion as threats to their power. But these communists were also capitalists, so they probably considered the temple a revenue-generating tourist business.

Our tour wrapped up, and we headed back to the Ritz-Carlton, following the instructions from the Secret Service to be in the lobby near the elevator at 4:00 PM. Most of us had arrived early and waited for something to happen. Some people in business suits came through the glass doors and entered the lobby. Among them were former President George Bush (41) and former First Lady, Barbara. They stopped for a moment to greet a mother and child that happened to be in the lobby. President Bush and Barbara were then whisked into an elevator by both U.S. and Chinese bodyguards and suddenly vanished.

The place got quiet. Was that it? We wondered if the event was over but stayed in the lobby a few more minutes. A couple of our ICAF colleagues still hadn't shown up. Then our clean-cut American breakfast friends arrived and told us to get into the elevator—no waiting for stragglers. We rode the elevator to the penthouse suite and walked into a foyer. President Bush was talking to six off-duty Marine guards, likely assigned to duty with the U.S. Embassy. After a couple of minutes, President Bush approached our group and chatted with us. It felt like we were talking to our grandfather.

President Bush was very gracious and kind. He was incredibly humble for all of his lifetime achievements. He was awarded the Distinguished Flying Cross as a World War II naval aviator. A graduate of Yale University, he became president of a petroleum company, was elected to the House of Representatives, served as ambassador to both the United Nations and to China. He served as Director of the CIA, became the U.S. Vice President during President Reagan's two terms, and was later elected President of the United States during the collapse of communism in Eastern Europe, the invasion of Panama, and Operation Desert Storm which liberated Kuwait. His was a remarkable life. Few Americans in our history have had such a distinguished career. However, I learned that he had never served as a paperboy. I had that going for me.

Being a Navy pilot, the president wanted to know who in our group was in the Navy, and who was a pilot. Bill Carrico, David Meyr, Gary Plumb,

Cliff Tompkins, Andy Li and Coach Kane all had something to say. The air and sea stories started to flow. The group talked for a few minutes about aircraft carriers, F-18 and F-22 fighters, Marine helicopters, and deployments in ships. I stood by quietly, listened and waited, while the Army was ignored in all the stories. Then I had a chance to edge into the discussion and change the topic. "Sir, I just want to remind you that Army beat Navy 26-17 in the last football game. We Army guys should get a chance to tell some stories too." That line got a good laugh. My strategy worked, and I was able to talk to President Bush for a few precious minutes.

Our group spent about twenty minutes with President Bush. He was very generous with his time and allowed us to take some photos to remember the encounter. When the visit was over, we were escorted back down the elevator and thanked the Secret Service agents that arranged the meeting. It was an unforgettable day and the highlight of the entire trip. It was a bit ironic that we had to travel to a foreign country to meet a U.S. President. Unfortunately, our two ICAF colleagues that arrived a few minutes late missed an elevator ride to remember.

Seminar 1 meets President George Bush in Shanghai

We had some other official meetings while in Shanghai. Many were with large U.S. companies with international business operations. During these discussions, we learned about how business was conducted in China

409

and within the Shanghai Free Trade Zone. Among our visits were Honeywell and an Intel facility where the U.S., Chinese, and Intel flags flew over the factory.

I had participated in a Regional Study on China during my first semester at ICAF. Much of what I learned in that class helped me to better understand the political and economic issues of this mysterious land. These classroom discussions were now played out during this trip. The senior leaders in China are members of the Communist Party. However, they have completely embraced capitalism as a means of making economic progress. Their primary goal is to retain personal power and privilege. China's political leadership thinks and acts strategically. They are calculating and cunning. After seeing the 9/11 attack on the United States, the Chinese Premier's first reaction reportedly was not shock or remorse. It was, "How can we benefit from this?"

But the greatest threat to their leadership is not an external threat (the United States) but an internal revolution. Consequently, the party leadership is constantly on guard for internal threats and actively working to suppress them. High unemployment, poverty, independence movements (Tibet, Taiwan), selected organized religions (Falun Gong, Muslims, Christians), and freedom seeking Chinese citizens (remembering the Tiananmen Square Massacre) are among the perceived threats to the Communist Party's grip on power. To counter the popular appeal of these internal threats, the communist government must regularly demonstrate how the Chinese people are making progress under the regime. The political message is, "The Government is restoring China as a world power."

Examples of progress the Chinese government points to include: joining the World Trade Organization (WTO) in 2001; launching their first manned space flight in 2003; hosting the 2008 Summer Olympic Games; and the military's rapid development of aircraft carriers and stealth fighters. Still to come are the 2022 Winter Olympics and announced plans for a manned space station and missions to the moon and Mars.

I saw evidence of the rapid economic progress in the scores of modern skyscrapers all over Shanghai, each with impressive architectural features. They represented billions of Yuan (China's currency) invested in new structures. And many construction cranes were scattered about the city, clearly indicating the continuing building boom. I was curious about who was actually paying for all this work, and who was going to occupy these new skyscrapers. Was this building boom really a bubble that would eventually burst?

To maintain domestic stability and demonstrate economic progress, China needs to create 20-30 million new jobs each year to keep their citizens employed. The Chinese government has done this by industrial espionage, stealing U.S. intellectual property (new ideas and product designs) and helping their own factories win in the global marketplace. In essence, China has stolen millions of manufacturing jobs from the United States which has damaged our economy.

There is also a significant migration problem within China. The country's population has been described as 5% living in the first-world and 15% living in the second-world, while 80% of the citizens were living in third-world conditions. Most of China's poor live in the rural farming areas. When they learn of good paying jobs in the cities, they attempt to move to cities to improve their family's lifestyle. However, the Communist Party strictly controls this migration, so the most prosperous cities are not overrun with the homeless and indigent populace. At one point, Shanghai had a population of 17 million people of which three million arrived via illegal migration from rural areas.

On the last night of our China trip, our seminar wanted to experience something cultural, so we attended a professional acrobat show. I had low expectations when I arrived, but when dozens of gymnasts took the stage, I found the performance quite impressive. These acrobats performed amazing feats of strength, balance, flexibility, and agility. Some of them appeared to defy gravity and bend themselves in ways anatomically impossible, particularly for a paperboy. The show was a great way to conclude our very rewarding visit to this exotic country.

South Korea

Upon landing at Incheon Airport, one of our seminar colleagues failed to clear Korean Customs. The inspectors found a sword in his checked baggage that he had bought in China. It was a gift for his son, but he was not allowed to bring it into the country. To resolve the matter, he had to immediately ship the sword from the airport to the United States. This caused an hour delay in our schedule and our team held a mock trial and sentenced our classmate to buy us all a round of drinks as compensation for the inconvenience. He never paid up.

While we waited for the sword to be shipped, another classmate was stopped by inspectors because he was wearing five Ro-Rex watches. He explained, "They're all gifts." The Korean officials were not sympathetic. But once he presented a military ID card, the Customs officer let him pass through. It appeared U.S. government officials were given special privileges. Any other offender would have received the rubber glove treatment.

We checked into the Seoul Grand Hyatt and looked around for any Secret Service agents hanging out at the hotel bar. We did not find any and set off on our first visit, a tour of the Hyundai Asan plant. We followed that up with a visit to Samsung, where we visited their corporate campus and were briefed on their product manufacturing process. We removed our shoes before entering the facility, so we did not bring contaminants or electrostatic charges into the electronics manufacturing area.

Andy Li and Bill Carrico at DMZ shrine

The most interesting visit we made was along the Demilitarized Zone (DMZ) separating North and South Korea. We drove along the DMZ highway that hugged the Han River. There were miles of razor wire and scores of border forts defending South Korea from a potential ground attack by North

412

Korea. Many of the local fields were flooded and used by farmers as rice paddies, which in wartime would help to bog down any invading tanks.

During the border visit, we toured the DMZ Plaza and a shrine to the Korean War. However, one of the most historic attractions was Freedom Bridge. Symbolically important, it was the site where 12,773 captives returned home during the first prisoner of war exchange after the Korean War armistice.

Kerry at Freedom Bridge

There was a nearby railroad bridge connecting North and South Korea used to promote economic development between the two countries. While we were there, a train rolled across the border from a manufacturing area in North Korea. During a surprise attack, the train could be packed with invading North Korea troops. The South Koreans were prepared and fortified the train station on their side of the border and patrolled it with armed guards.

Freedom Bridge (timber) and Railroad Bridge across river toward North Korea

At another site, we toured a border overlook near Imjingak where an abandoned, bullet-riddled train has been rusting, since the war, in the DMZ between North and South Korea. It's an eerie reminder of that devastating war fought from 1950-1953.

We spent several days in Korea and had some time to shop. I needed a new suit and wanted to get it made while staying in Seoul. Several of my colleagues had previously been stationed in Korea, and they took me shopping in an area called Itaewon. There were dozens of tailor shops there, and each had a large picture of the Chief of Staff of the Army, in his full military uniform, prominently displayed. Each store implied that they personally tailored his uniform. It was highly unlikely that the most senior Army Four-star general owned several dozen uniforms, each made by a different Korean tailor.

We picked a decent looking shop, went inside and met the owner. I told him I needed to have three "CEO" suits made. He immediately broke out his tape measure and showed me a few different fabrics. I wished my wife was with me at that moment because I could have really screwed this up. Fortunately, the tailor steered me to some good choices. I had intentionally packed an old suit on this trip with the intent of ditching it and having a new one made. The plan worked out well, and I was also measured for several custom-made shirts. My new clothes were later shipped back to the United States.

Japan

Our final stop on the international trip was to Japan. We landed in Nagoya, southwest of Tokyo. The country was densely populated; packed with people. Our first order of business was to find a good Japanese restaurant. We were in luck. There were hundreds of them all over the city. Imagine that.

The next morning, we made a visit to the nearby Toyota manufacturing plant. The company featured its new hybrid vehicle technology. That afternoon we visited the Denso plant, where they made automotive parts.

The following day, we made a stop at Yamazaki Mazak, where we learned about machines and "the machines that made the machines." It sounded like a bad Hollywood sequel to The Terminator. Amazingly, Mazak only needed one guy on the manufacturing floor to maintain all the machines.

At every stop we made in Japan, Korea, and China, we were treated with great respect. Our hosts were all kind and gracious. We felt our visit also contributed to international diplomacy. But there was one glitch in Nagoya. We went out for a tofu lunch, and the food looked good, but unlike in China, it tasted awful. I am not sure what kind of cardboard they made it from. It was so bad that even us Army guys could not eat it. The Chinese tofu was so much better. We re-named the place the "Terrible Tofu Restaurant." Maybe the Japanese were trying to get us to leave their country early or were retaliating against us for dropping a couple of nukes on them at the end of World War II. Whatever it was, something atomic was now raging in our stomachs.

We wrapped up the Nagoya trip with a stop at Sony and then jumped on a bullet-train that took us past Mount Fuji to Tokyo. We sliced through the Japanese countryside between 150-200 mph. We checked into the New Sanno Hotel in Tokyo and went to dinner at its steakhouse. The food was awesome, and we enjoyed some spirits. Our chef disappeared for a few minutes, so I jumped behind the grill, picked up a steak knife and spatula and started taking orders; entertaining the troops in my seminar.

When the real samurai chef came back, he was armed with a set of razor sharp Ginsu knives. I immediately bowed and let him relieve me of my new duties. I did not want to be on the menu. My career working as a Japanese samurai chef was very short but memorable.

My new job at the New Sanno Restaurant

Our Tokyo itinerary also included visiting a Toshiba facility and a stop at Mitsubishi Heavy Industries. During our visit, we were curious as to how Japanese industry prevented their intellectual property from being stolen by China. The story we heard in response was illustrative of the philosophy "if you can't beat them, join them." There was a prominent case where Japanese motorcycles were illegally copied by nineteen different factories in China. The Japanese company owning the design bought two motorcycles from each of the illegal manufacturers and determined which Chinese factory made the best quality copies. The Japanese then licensed the best two factories to manufacture their motorcycle in China and then told the Chinese government that there were seventeen illegal plants stealing business from the two authorized ones. The Chinese government then cracked down.

On our big night out in Tokyo, I went down into the subway system that was famous for packing thousands of people onto the rush hour trains. I was also a bit curious to see the subway as it was the site of a major poison gas attack in March 1995. Sarin nerve agent was released in several locations by a domestic terrorist group, killing twelve people and injuring dozens more.

The Tokyo stop was brief, but we could get a real sense of the Japanese lifestyle and culture. The country was clean, and the food—other than at the Terrible Tofu Restaurant—and service were excellent. On our last evening, we had another meal at the New Sanno where we linked up with another ICAF seminar that was traveling through Southeast Asia along with our

416

Commandant, Major General Harold Mashburn. The following day, somewhat reluctantly, we began our return trip to the USA.

Memorial Day 2002

The weekend following our return from Asia was Memorial Day. Alice and I took the kids to see her father, "Pop Pop," who had died a few months earlier, shortly after the 9/11 attack. I was glad he had been able to meet his grandchildren before he died.

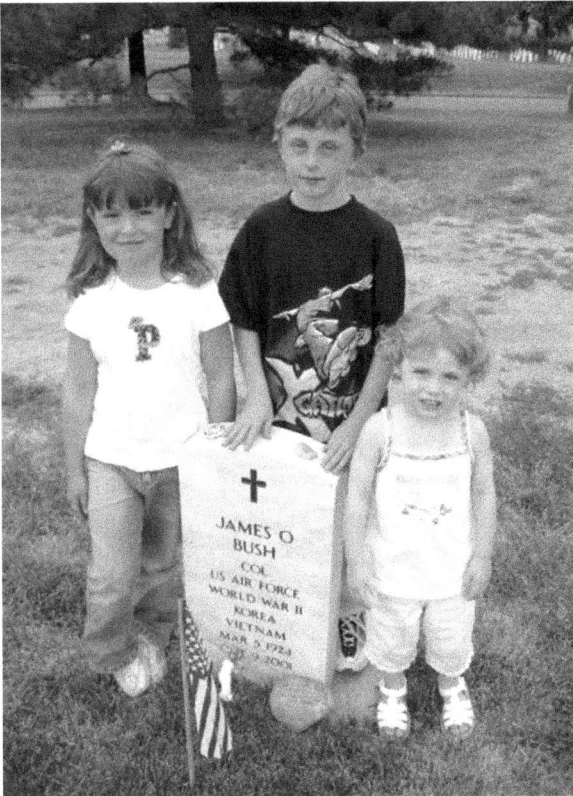

Kara, Kent, and Katie visit Pop Pop

Ironically, I had just returned from Japan, the country Jim Bush had flown over on the first B-29 mission as a young man during World War II. Colonel James Bush was now buried in Arlington Cemetery within view of the

Air Force Memorial and the Pentagon, where he had served much of his career.

Distinguished Lecturers

Most of the discussions at ICAF were in a "not for attribution environment." Consequently, we were able to get frank perspectives from many leaders in government, industry, and academia.

As the academic year drew to a close, I was asked to introduce the President and CEO of Lockheed Martin, Dr. Vance Coffman, during a major ICAF class lecture. His company had an impressive list of accomplishments, including the Hubble Space Telescope and the new Joint Strike Fighter. I took a few liberties as I read his biography to hundreds of students and concluded his introduction with great theatrical emphasis much like Vince McMahon did during a professional wrestling match:

> "In this corner... standing six feet three inches... weighing 225 pounds of taaaa-wisted steel and sex appeal... from a small town in Iowa... please give a warm, ICAF welcome to the Paaaa-resident and C-E-O of Lock-heeeeeed Martin, Dr. Vance Coffman!"

The intro worked great. Pandemonium broke loose in Baruch Auditorium. Hundreds of government officials leaped to their feet and cheered and screamed for this giant of industry now climbing into the ring to wrestle with them. The noise persisted for about a full minute. Dr. Coffman was now a certified ICAF "Rock Star" and owned the audience.

As he approached the podium, he privately told me, "I have never had an introduction that good."

"Too easy, Sir. We industry guys need to stick together." I resisted the temptation to hand him my resume.

When I turned the microphone over to Dr. Coffman, he asked me to hold his corporate Blackberry phone during his 45-minute lecture. I remarked "Yes Sir! Thank you! As one of your top competitors, I'll be downloading all your contacts while you're speaking!" We both laughed, and I headed off to my seat. I had one more duty to perform at the conclusion of the lecture, presenting Dr. Coffman with an ICAF coin. I took a few more social liberties with the microphone: "Sir! On behalf of the Commandant of the Industrial College of the Armed Forces, Major General Harold Mashburn... he's that clean-cut All-American looking guy over there in the first row, wearing the spotless uniform. I want to present you with this ICAF coin to thank you for accepting our invitation to speak today... And I also want you to have one of these priceless Raytheon coins. You should keep it on your desk to remind you of your fiercest competitor."

Late in the academic year, the Secretary of Defense, Donald Rumsfeld, presented a major lecture at the National Defense University. Afterward, he took questions from the audience. I had my hand raised as he panned toward the section where I was seated. We made eye contact. I stood up to begin my question, but a moment later, an allied officer from South America stood up in front of me and took the microphone. My opportunity to speak to the SECDEF in person had just been hijacked. I chuckled, yielded to my colleague, and sat down. I had a great question prepared about how unmanned systems would transform warfare. Instead, the SECDEF was asked a question about the "armor threat in South America." Like most Americans, Rumsfeld was unaware of any potential South American invasion plans involving tanks and armored vehicles. It was a baffling question, and the SECDEF handled it with great respect, but I knew he would not seek any further questions originating from our section of the audience.

As ICAF graduation approached, I began to reflect on the year. Undertaking a strategic curriculum, engaging with senior government and industry leaders and traveling to see and experience so many places made ICAF an incredibly rich experience.

Graduation

The day before graduation, Alice and I hosted a potluck lunch at our house for my ICAF friends. My nephews, Pete and Nate Curley, manned the grill while my classmates all gathered one last time before graduating and spreading our wings. I was honored that everyone made it, including my new international friends General Obaid Al Ketbi and General Ali Azaizeh.

The following day, we assembled at Fort McNair and listened to our graduation speakers, Dr. Condoleezza Rice, the U.S. National Security Advisor, and General Richard Myers, the Chairman of the Joint Chiefs of Staff. It was a beautiful day and great way to wrap up the year. After the ceremony, many of us lingered to take photos with family and friends.

Final ICAF gathering at the Kachejian ranch

My first-semester colleague, Colonel Te-Chin Lieu, of the Taiwan Army, approached me and introduced me to his family as "his American brother." I was incredibly surprised by his kind comments. Te-Chin told me that his ICAF experience allowed him to earn his master's degree, something he highly prized and that could not be easily achieved in the Taiwanese Army. He had placed a high value on the help I had given him while we were writing several papers. It had been my pleasure to help, and I had learned much from him. Taking an executive level course in a different country, in a different language and using a different alphabet, was tremendously difficult. I was impressed he could keep up with the coursework.

Before we departed, Te-Chin gave me a small gift of gratitude and said, "I hope you can come to Taiwan someday and speak at our War College."

"It would be my honor, my friend," I told him.

Major General Te-Chin Liu later served as Superintendent of Taiwan's Military Academy.

After graduation

After graduation, I returned to Raytheon and was invited to have lunch with the Chairman and CEO, Dan Burnham. We had a great conversation. I gave him an overview of the course and how our company could benefit from the investment. Although ICAF was designed to be a one-year curriculum, I jokingly offered to come back for a sophomore year.

Attending ICAF was a game changer for my industry career. I was offered a two-level promotion at Raytheon and joined the new corporate Homeland Security team. My new boss would be Ed Woollen, a Corporate Vice President and a member of the Raytheon Board of Directors.

In June of 2003, my ICAF classmate, Commander Kelly McDowell invited me to his assumption of command ceremony for the USS Louisiana, a strategic ballistic missile submarine, in Kings Bay, Georgia. The vessel was huge, and Kelly had the tremendous responsibility for it, the crew and its arsenal of nuclear missiles. I was honored to attend and spend time with his family and his lovely wife, Naida. Kelly arranged a tour of the Louisiana for a few of his special guests, and I was grateful to be included.

These missile boats are often called boomers; a huge communist-killing strategic weapon. The sub even had torpedoes to defend itself. We could not bring cameras on board, but I still have vivid memories of the tour. Every square inch of space on the ship was used. Sleeping areas were very tight. Some sailors slept between the missile silos. Submarine crews work in shifts for several months while underwater. They had no external sense of day or night, except through a periscope. There were no windows or screened doors. Everyone on board trusted their lives to American technology, exceptional training, and seasoned leaders.

The hallways were narrow, and there were plenty of trip hazards. There was a spiral stairwell on the ship. At the bottom of it, someone installed an exercise bike in a small open area. One of the guests asked what the machine was. I told them it was an auxiliary power generator should the nuclear reactor quit.

We visited the missile room and were briefed on the two-man rule to initiate a launch. The room had a lot of buttons with colored lights. I realized that World War III might be started from that very room. When the sub surfaced, a few weeks following a nuclear missile attack, the crew might be among the world's few survivors.

While at the pier, I had an opportunity to observe the security practices used for ports. I learned how subs and other ships were protected from surface and underwater threats while they were in the harbor. These insights helped me make informed security decisions the following year when I was serving in combat operations along the Tigris River in Baghdad.

In 2006, I met another classmate, Brigadier General Ali Azaizeth, at the Special Operations Exposition (SOFEX) in Amman, Jordan. I had spent much of 2004 serving in Iraq, and Ali and I had much to discuss about the ongoing war and its impact in his country. I was also able to see King Abdullah II and meet his brother Prince Feisal as they moved about the exhibit areas. Since then, my friend has been promoted to Major General and served as the Director of Royal Artillery in the Jordanian Armed Forces.

In 2007, I met with Major General Obaid Al Ketbi and Brigadier General Nasser Al-Ali at the International Defense Exhibition (IDEX) in Abu Dhabi. Obaid was now the Director of Logistics for the UAE Armed Forces. His responsibilities were vast, and he led the entire IDEX operation.

Since graduating, I have been invited to return to ICAF as a guest lecturer on several occasions. My military experiences with reconstruction in both Iraq and Afghanistan from 2004-2007 were topics of keen interest to the new ICAF classes. The first book I authored, *SUVs SUCK in Combat*, illustrated many of the severe challenges the United States faced rebuilding these countries during raging insurgencies.

About ten years after I graduated, the Industrial College of the Armed Forces was re-named The Eisenhower School. There was a lot of grumbling by alumni and significant internal resistance to the name change. ICAF was the branded name of this respected national institution. Despite the name change, the mission and curriculum remain mostly intact and evolve with America's national security needs. I hope it all works out.

* * *

As I noted earlier in this chapter, the following are my personal recollections as a witness to the terrorist attack on the United States.

Personal account of the attack on the United States 9/11/2001
By Kerry Kachejian, Raytheon. Industry Fellow at the Industrial College of the Armed Forces.

Seminar 9 was on the fourth floor of Eisenhower Hall at Ft. McNair in Washington, D.C. Our seminar room overlooked the Potomac River and the Pentagon.

On September 11, 2001, Seminar 9 was preparing to conduct a Military Strategy class involving a Civil War Cabinet exercise. The weather was nice. The atmosphere of the seminar was festive.

At approximately 9:30 AM, Colonel John Charvat came into our classroom and interrupted our preparations. He did not say much but turned on the large screen projection TV. We were puzzled at what he was doing until we saw the live news footage of the first World Trade Tower burning. Thick black smoke. An intense fire. It reminded me of the movie "Towering Inferno."

At first, we weren't certain it was real. But the commentary told us it was. How could an aircraft accident like this happen? It was broad daylight.

A few minutes later, when the second airliner hit the other tower, I knew it was clearly no coincidence. This was a directed attack. A huge fireball burst from the second building upon impact. We were shocked. This can't be happening to our country. The TV kept replaying the scene of the impact.

I immediately started estimating casualties to get a sense the scope of the disaster. There was probably a 25,000-person capacity per tower. Tower 1 was probably ½ full (12,500) at the time of impact. The impact occurred ¾ the way up. All those above the impact in Tower 1 would likely not escape (3,000) the fire and smoke. Tower 2 was probably only 25% full as it was likely being evacuated during the first fire (6,000). It was hit about 1/3 from the top. Possibly 2,000 casualties in Tower 2. My total initial estimate was 5,000 dead or dying.

Sometime later the second tower collapsed. It pancaked down, floor by floor. There was now no hope. Anyone inside or near the tower was now dead. The civil engineer inside me instantly knew the steel had yielded from the heat. The steel columns were designed to carry the loads from above, not the individual floors. Each floor failed as it was overloaded. The lower impact of the second aircraft into Tower 2 meant that more weight from above was being supported by the weakened steel.

The pancake collapse was tragic, but it was much better than the tower toppling over and taking out several city blocks. I knew there was a good chance the first tower would also fail. I was hoping that the higher impact would limit the collapse to only the top floors. Shortly later, we saw it totally collapse as well.

I realized that this was a brilliant use of our own assets and technologies to attack us. The only investment was the cost of some airline tickets. Cunning and devious. Not cowardly. These terrorists were willing to die. Someone in the room or on the TV said that the Pentagon was hit. We lifted the shades and saw the smoke out our window across the Potomac.

View of the Pentagon attack from our ICAF window on 9/11

I was furious. Our people were cooked and crushed.

The adrenaline was flowing. There were TV reports of another airliner in the air. We were not sure how many there may be. I started to determine what the other targets likely were. Primaries: The White House, Congress, monuments... Where was NDU on the target list? Possibly an alternate. NWC looks a bit like the U.S. Capital from the air. Are we an alternate target? Unlikely but possible. Colonel Terry Kerrigan also thought it was unlikely.

I wondered what was the extent / scope of the entire attack? What about suicide boats loaded with explosives taking out the bridges over the Potomac? What if the attack was combined with a Bio or chemical agent? Was there a dirty nuke? If the bridges went, and the city was contaminated, I was considering using the boats in the marina outside ICAF for my exit strategy.

The city had no air defenses. I hoped someone would pass out small arms to the NDU students so we could attempt to defend the capital from a Potomac River approach. Soon thereafter, there was a boom, and I looked out the window and saw an F-16 flying over the city. It was a welcome site. However, I could not tell if it had any weapons. If not, it could only stop another airliner by crashing into it.

I called my wife, Alice. Her father attended meetings several times a week at the Pentagon. It took several hours to account for his whereabouts. He was not in the Pentagon that day and was safe.

There was a TV report that a fourth aircraft crashed in a remote section of Pennsylvania. I turned to Terry Kerrigan and told him there were probably some heroes on that flight that attempted to resist the hijackers. He agreed. The voice data recorders would tell us more.

We received a report of a truck bomb detonating at the State Department. Steve Williams quietly slumped in his chair. He had many colleagues at State. We all felt sympathetic for Steve's situation. Later, we discovered that the reported bombing was inaccurate. State survived.

Many of us stayed glued to the TV. Watched the events unfold. At 1500, Tim Gallagher and I drove out of D.C. on I-395 past the still burning Pentagon. We wondered how many of our friends were killed or injured. We stopped off for a beer to clear our heads and recount what just happened. We speculated about other potential attacks on our infrastructure. This enemy was willing to die to kill as many Americans as possible. There was only one thing this country could do. We needed to identify who was responsible for slaughtering our people and kill that entire organization. As President Bush later said, you are either with us, or you are with the terrorists.

The next day I discovered that four of my colleagues from Raytheon were on hijacked flights out of Boston and Dulles.

It was ironic, but our class was scheduled to visit the Capitol about a week later to meet with Congressmen and have our ICAF class photo taken in front of the Capitol. The visit was much more meaningful due to the recent attack.

A few weeks later, an anthrax attack occurred through the D.C. postal system. There was much speculation about the source and the scope of the attack. Our auditorium (Baruch) was quickly modified to serve as an alternate location for the Congress if the capital required evacuation.

This concludes my account of the 9-11 attack, and I am sticking to it. The following is an email that I sent the following day as we were trying to get an accounting of our West Point classmates following the attack.

-----Original Message-----
From: "Kerry Kachejian"
To: usma1982@xxxx
Cc: "Tim & Linda Gallagher"
Sent: Wednesday, September 12, 2001 11:48 PM
Subject: Re: usma1982: Status of Classmates

Tim Gallagher, Press Marshall and I are at ICAF (NDU). Tim and I watched the Pentagon events live from our seminar rooms at Ft. McNair. We had a line of sight to the Pentagon.

It was good to see the first F-16 over the city. We also owe some passengers in the fourth airliner our deepest gratitude. They likely prevented another successful attack on the capital. The cockpit recorders will tell us more.

Thanks for reporting the status of all 82er's.

- Kerry Kachejian

CHAPTER 44

RAYTHEON / HOMELAND SECURITY—
STANDING UP THE TEAM

After I had joined the corporate Homeland Security team in September 2002, things started to happen quickly. I was initially hired by Hugo Poza, but my new boss would be Ed Woollen, a Corporate Vice President and a member of the Raytheon Board of Directors. Ed was bristling with ideas and energy. He saw opportunities where others only saw barriers. Ed was a Vietnam veteran with some exciting stories and a compassionate leader that made our work fun.

My initial area of focus was on Information Analysis, how we could find a specific needle in a pile of needles. The enemy was hiding in plain sight. We needed better ways to identify who they were, where they were, and what their intentions were.

This was a huge and ambitious task in the aftermath of the 9/11 attacks that involved using both human and open source intelligence. It required screening travel and financial records, lawfully intercepting communications, collecting biometrics and accessing a dozen other information sources that had to be shared between national and local agencies in real-time.

The path ahead for how the government and industry would be able—and capable—to do this was unclear. It was hard to get traction in this area for several reasons. Federal laws and policies allowing information to be shared between agencies had not been approved. That process involved reshuffling the deck on who had specific authorities and funding. There was political infighting on the roles and missions of the dozens of agencies involved. The new Department of Homeland Security (DHS), led by Governor Tom Ridge, was in its infancy. It lacked the staff and facilities needed to be fully capable. DHS was attempting to merge twenty-two separate agencies, with different missions, cultures, personnel systems, and acquisition systems, into a single seamless organization.

There were few new addressable business opportunities for industry. Time was of the essence, so the government modified existing contracts to quickly acquire new services and capabilities. This gave a significant advantage to incumbent contractors that could staff quickly and demonstrate agility. Raytheon had much to offer, but the company had little existing work with the twenty-two agencies being integrated. We were an outsider to the new DHS. Fortunately, we could leverage our significant presence in the FBI and DoD.

One of my new colleagues was Vice Admiral Tim Josiah, who had recently retired as the Chief of Staff of the U.S. Coast Guard. He brought exceptional relationships with government executives and a deep understanding of maritime security operations. His USCG connection was highly relevant, as the Coast Guard became a major law enforcement organization within the new Department of Homeland Security. His insight allowed us to understand the big issues that were facing the government, who the key decision makers were, and what actions industry could take to help our nation.

Charlie Blaich had also joined the original Raytheon corporate team. He was a retired Battalion Fire Chief from New York City and a retired colonel in the USMC Reserve. Before 9/11, he was the Deputy Chief of Department, Commander of 15th Division in Brooklyn. It was a one-star billet. Charlie was recovering from neurosurgery on his back the day of the 9/11 attacks, but he left his home on Staten Island and took the ferry to the scene of the collapsed World Trade Center towers.

After arrival, Charlie assumed command of one of the four sectors he and the other Deputy Chiefs had established. The scene was pure chaos, but one of the first orders of business was to turn off gas lines that ran into the area. Shortly after the second tower collapsed, there was a famous photo taken of Charlie. He was standing on the rubble—among the pulverized remains of almost 3,000 people, reading a blueprint, trying to determine what part of the building was beneath him. Charlie soon realized that he had been given the building plans for the 97th floor, which no longer existed.

The next week, Charlie reported to Fire Department HQ in Brooklyn to get a Medical Officer to declare him fit for duty, which was a bit ironic considering he was still recovering from surgery. At that point, told "Because you're a Marine," he was assigned as the Logistics Chief for the WTC Incident Command Post. He stayed in that position for five months.

Charlie's new role on the Raytheon Homeland Security team was to lead our products and services in the Emergency Response market. As a retired military officer, he offered many words of encouragement during my deployment to Iraq in 2004.

Charlie Blaich at WTC (white shirt in lower right)

The original Raytheon Homeland Security team grew over the next few years. New corporate leaders hired other distinguished experts to address our evolving national security strategy and the markets they created. The expanded team included experts like: Kevin Stevens, the retired Deputy Chief of the U.S. Border Patrol; Curt Powell, who had survived the 1983 Hezbollah bombing of the Marine Barracks in Lebanon and later stood up the first Transportation Security Agency (TSA) Operations Center; Frank Larkin, the former CTO of the U.S. Secret Service; Dan Snow, a distinguished U.S. Secret Service Agent; Adam Isles, the former Chief of Staff for DHS; Patrick Burns, a former White House and DHS expert on critical infrastructure protection; and Darryle Conway, a Homeland Security (HLS) industry expert. Karen Steinfeld was an exceptionally bright and energetic solution architect that helped our team identify and develop new capabilities. She knew where most of Raytheon's corporate capabilities were centered within our six divisions and 72,000 employees. She had an infectious can-do attitude and was a catalyst who helped us transform an operational concept into a practical solution and business opportunity.

Working on the corporate Homeland Security team at Raytheon was a professionally rewarding experience. It allowed me to operate at the strategic and international level of the defense and aerospace industry and was an excellent assignment following my ICAF experience.

Homeland Security was not unique to the United States. Our friends and allies around the world faced similar security concerns, and our Raytheon team was prepared to help. As part of my corporate duties, I traveled throughout the United States and to several countries, including Canada, UK, UAE, Jordan, Kuwait, Israel, and Australia, where I met some fascinating and talented people. However, my efforts on the corporate Homeland Security team were interrupted because I still served in the Army Reserve. I was recalled to active duty twice during the next six years to support U.S. military operations in Iraq, Afghanistan and the Middle East.

Ambassador Bremer

Our new corporate Homeland Security team frequently held exploratory discussions with other companies to see if there were business opportunities of mutual interest. During a morning staff meeting in October 2002, Ed Woollen announced that he had invited a "heavy hitter" from the counterterrorism world to a meeting at our Reston office. Later that week, we met with Ambassador Paul "Jerry" Bremer, the Chairman and CEO of Marsh Crisis Consulting, a risk management company.

Bremer was the former Ambassador to the Netherlands and an ambassador-at-large for counterterrorism. During the meeting, we discussed some of our open source intelligence capabilities and cyber-tools that could be used to combat terrorism. It was an engaging session that successfully identified some potential business leads.

What was more interesting was what ensued during the following year. The war in Iraq broke out in March. Lieutenant General Jay Garner (retired) became the Director of the Office for Reconstruction and Humanitarian Assistance (ORHA) for Iraq following the U.S. invasion. Garner was later succeeded by Ambassador Bremer, who was appointed as the head of the new Coalition Provisional Authority (CPA), headquartered in Baghdad.

Upon his return to the United States, Garner became a consultant to Raytheon. I greatly valued the time our team spent in strategy meetings getting his perspective on how the war was unfolding. I listened intently to everything he said and used the information to help develop sound technical ideas we could offer to our military forces.

Coincidentally, Hugo Poza, the VP of Raytheon Homeland Security, was asked by the Bush administration if he was interested in being a candidate for an executive position in the CPA, as a deputy to Ambassador Bremer. Ironically, in early 2004, I was recalled to active duty and deployed to Iraq to serve as the operations officer for the Gulf Region Division (GRD), a military unit created to rebuild that nation in the middle of the raging insurgency. Ambassador Bremer and his staff occupied the Republican Palace in Baghdad, while my unit was headquartered nearby in the Iraqi White House. As the head of the CPA, Ambassador Bremer was at the top of the food chain for the entire country. The first time I saw him Iraq was in the Republican Palace during Easter service. We were both 6,000 miles away from our last meeting in Reston, and our new missions were now strategic and daunting, with daily life or death consequences. We stood near each other during the Easter service, but I did not reintroduce myself. I felt it was an inappropriate setting. We both had things we needed to pray for, and Bremer's duties were enormous. He had the weight of the world on his shoulders. And that morning I was particularly sullen, as our GRD team was grieving the loss of one of its finest security men, Johannes "Fish" Visagie, who had died of wounds suffered a week earlier in Fallujah.

431

Tom O'Connell and Robotic Bobcats

Tom O'Connell was a senior manager at Raytheon focused on new intelligence and information systems. As a former Army Intelligence officer with service in the Joint Special Operations Command, Tom was deeply respected by his peers.

Over several years, Tom and I held engaging discussions on emerging DARPA programs, including Combat-Cueing, Tactical Video Link, and the UltraComm radio. Tom liked to explore the advantages that these new capabilities could bring to the U.S. military. He was an out-of-the-box thinker with excellent connections inside of DoD. When I started working on the Corporate HLS team, Tom approached me about his idea to robotize the Bobcat family of construction equipment for use in Homeland Defense missions. Given that some missions were extremely hazardous, Tom wanted to make the Bobcats remotely controlled, to move the equipment operator out of harm's way. One dangerous mission was the removal of unexploded bombs. Another was to bury all the contaminated waste after the detonation of a dirty (radioactive) bomb.

Tom approached Bobcat executives about the concept, and they expressed significant interest. Tom asked me to travel with him to their headquarters in Gwinner, North Dakota. I liked the idea and quickly agreed.

Our flight landed in Fargo on a freezing day in December of 2002. We picked up a rental car and began the long drive to Gwinner. Along the way, Tom asked me if I had ever seen a herd of Buffalo. I had not, so he pulled off the road next to the entrance of a large Buffalo ranch. We got out of the car and walked toward the main gate. Tom pointed out a herd of a few hundred Buffalo on a nearby hill. The Buffalo saw us standing at the gate and began to approach us with some urgency. Apparently, they thought we were there to feed them. Every Buffalo tried to be at the front of the pack to get the first crack at some fresh chow, so they picked up the pace and trotted. With every second, the massive beasts closed the distance. They looked hungry and determined. If we hung out at the gate much longer, the stampeding herd would be on top of us, and we had no food to make them happy. We both decided to avoid the confrontation and live to fight another day. So, we jumped back in our rental car, buffaloed the buffalos, and sped off to the factory

Tom and I spent the rest of the day inspecting the Bobcats and their electronic control interfaces. We had some fun driving them around in the parking lot, testing out their ease of use and agility. It didn't last long, as the outside air temperature was about nine degrees Fahrenheit, and I only brought a lightweight jacket and had no gloves. Having gone through Army Ranger School in the winter, I thought the bitter North Dakota cold would not be a problem. That was a bad assumption. Though I smiled on the outside, I sniveled inside.

A few weeks later, our Raytheon engineers were modifying the Bobcats for robotic operations. Unknown to me at the time, Tom was interviewing with Secretary of Defense Rumsfeld for a job as the Assistant Secretary of Defense for Special Operations and Low-Intensity Conflict (ASD SO/LIC). Tom briefed Rumsfeld on the robotic Bobcat project, who commented, "that's great thinking." SECDEF noted that he wanted to drive one. Soon after, Tom was selected for the job and served in that position for almost four years, until April of 2007. When Tom left Raytheon, I felt I had lost a good battle buddy, but his selection as the ASD SO/LIC was a big win for our nation.

Kuwaiti MOI—Colonel Yousif Al-Mudahaka

In February of 2003, our HLS team hosted a delegation from the Kuwaiti Ministry of Interior (MOI) in the United States. The purpose of the trip was to show the Kuwaitis some of the best commercial surveillance technologies that could be used in their national Emergency Operations Center to detect threats inside their country and along their borders. Colonel Yousif Al-Mudahaka, the senior MOI official, and his team arrived at National Airport and spent a week with us.

The visit started in Arlington, Virginia with demonstrations of 3-D modeling technologies for cities. We followed up with a 911 Call Center visit near Atlanta and a tour of the Los Angeles Sheriff's Department. The final stop was in Las Vegas, which used state of the art technologies for facility access controls and surveillance technologies based on biometrics (the identification of people using facial recognition and fingerprints).

For this project, we partnered with a Kuwaiti firm, Gulf Technology Electronics and Systems Company (GIT), led by billionaire Fouad Alghanim. Privately, we learned that Mr. Alghanim was highly respected in Kuwait for his actions resisting the Iraqi invasion in 1990. We did not get the specific details but knew he had fortitude. Ed Woollen, Charlie Blaich and I had dinner with Mr. Alghanim and his project lead, Mr. Steve Mathews, a few weeks earlier to discuss the business aspects of the overall project. We spent several hours at dinner, building a relationship and establishing personal trust. To facilitate travel during the Kuwaiti visit, Mr. Alghanim allowed our team to use his Gulfstream jet to stay one step ahead of the visiting delegation.

Steve and I worked out the details regarding which company would cover what expenses. I had to spend a few weeks with our corporate legal/ethics team well in advance to make sure anything we paid for was in compliance with U.S. laws. Legal and ethics issues were always a high priority for Raytheon, and handled, or better said... mishandled, they could stop any business deal. In some cases, the compliance requirements were so onerous the lawyers involved were referred to as the business prevention team. Any gift, meal or any trinket (coffee mug) worth more than $5 had to be pre-approved. Fortunately, everything we planned to do was pre-approved so we could move forward smoothly. It was fortunate my company was not paying for any hotel rooms. Steve was quite surprised when he got the Four Seasons hotel bill in Las Vegas. There were a lot of "incidental room charges" incurred by some of the guests.

Before leaving the Las Vegas area, I stopped at nearby Lake Powell and the Hoover Dam with another corporate colleague, Taz Hofmann. Hoover Dam was massive, and there was a new highway bridge under construction that would allow future traffic to bypass the narrow road running across the top of the dam. The new bridge was another impressive civil engineering project. Both the dam and the bridge were part of the U.S. transportation infrastructure that would need to be protected from a terrorist attack.

In April, our corporate team traveled to Kuwait for ten days to follow up with the MOI. We met with Colonel Yousif every day. Our team worked extended hours to develop a better understanding of the customer's requirements and operational environment. As our host, Colonel Yousif asked me several times if I had visited the "Old Market" in Kuwait City. Each time, I reassured him I would do so before I left the country. At one point, I worked about forty hours straight putting together a proposal. I finally went to bed for a short nap. When I awoke, I saw Colonel Yousif and told him I would be heading back to the United States later that evening. He asked me again about the Old Market, and I promised him I would go that afternoon. He gave me his MOI business card. One side of it had his contact information in English, and on the other side, it was in Arabic. I thanked him and put it in my pocket. Off I went.

I had no idea where the Old Market was, so I jumped into a taxi and directed the driver, who spoke no English, to take me to the Old Market. We had trouble communicating, but he got the idea I wanted to go shopping. The taxi dropped me off in front of a very modern shopping mall along the Arabian Gulf. I walked around the mall for a few minutes and saw nothing that looked like an Old Market. I saw a large metal pier near the mall, and I immediately recognized it as the structure that an Iraqi Silkworm anti-ship missile hit during the Gulf War a few years earlier. The Iraqi missile thought the metal pier was a large ship and attacked it. It was an interesting sight, but I was concerned I was running out of time for my primary mission.

I went back to the front of the shopping mall to find another taxi to take me to the Old Market. I tried to flag down a few, but they just sped past me. I did not see any taxi stands nearby. Still tired from the lack of sleep, I saw a Kuwaiti police officer and thought he probably reported to the MOI. He looked serious and was wearing a pistol at his waist. I walked up to him and asked for help. I handed the Officer Colonel Yousif's business card and explained, "My friend, Colonel Yousif, wanted me to visit the Old Market. I can't find it. Can you help me?"

The police officer appeared a bit puzzled at first, but then he flipped the business card over and read Colonel Yousif's name in Arabic. He immediately snapped to attention and became quite animated. He told me he would immediately help. The officer put his right hand on his pistol and stepped out into the busy street. He pointed sternly with his left hand at a taxi that was approaching at high speed. The taxi locked his brakes and stopped just in front of him. The Kuwaiti cop directed the cabbie to roll down his window. I could see through the windshield that the cabbie's eyes were getting big. He wasn't sure what he had done wrong. The officer leaned down to the window and began to bark out stern instructions in Arabic. The cabbie was shaking and nodded affirmatively at the orders. The cop stepped back on the sidewalk, opened the rear door to the taxi and politely invited me to sit inside. I thanked him, gesturing with my right hand on my heart, and said, "Colonel Yousif will be grateful that you helped me." I slid into the taxi and put on my seat belt. The officer closed the door, and the cabbie took off. It was clear that Colonel Yousif's business card was respected; it was a powerful weapon, and my get out of jail free card for any travels in Kuwait.

While riding in the cab, I thanked the driver for helping me. His English was broken, and he was still quite nervous. I assumed he was a foreign guest worker, and any slight infraction or misconduct would mean the loss of his job and expulsion from the country. I tried to reassure him I appreciated his assistance and his job was not threatened. We finally arrived at the Old Market, and I asked the cabbie how much the fare was. He insisted there was no charge. I countered and told him I would pay. I tried to hand him some Kuwaiti dinar, but he refused to accept it. I dropped the money in the front passenger seat and thanked him again. I wished him well and went into the market.

I had less than an hour to shop and bought some gold charms for my children, Kent, Kara, and Katie. I raced back to my hotel and headed off to the airport. I asked my colleagues to let Colonel Yousif know I had made it to the Old Market and to express my thanks. I made sure I took his business card with me as I departed the country.

Iraq War Planning

In the weeks between the Kuwaiti visit to the United States and our corporate team's trip to visit the MOI in Kuwait City, I conducted my annual military training for the Army Reserves. It was March 2003, and the United States was planning the invasion of Iraq. My two weeks of duty was in Wiesbaden, Germany with the European District of the Army Corps of Engineers. The U.S military wanted to launch the attack from Kuwait in the south and from Turkey in the north. While on duty, our Engineer team was determining how to support the invasion from Europe and Turkey. It would be difficult to move American tanks and military equipment through the mountainous terrain in Turkey. Part of our job was to determine how to do it using the existing Turkish roads and railway. While I was in Germany working on war plans, the Turkish Parliament voted to not allow the United States to use their territory to launch the invasion. This meant that none of our war planning efforts would be utilized.

The invasion began on March 19th, the last day of my annual Army Reserve training and my 43rd birthday. Little did I know that in the coming months, I would be recalled to active duty and serve in Baghdad at the height of a raging insurgency.

Athens Olympics

During this period, our Raytheon team was continuously engaged with our allies and partner countries. We developed and proposed solutions for several markets, including border security, port security, critical infrastructure protection, immigration control and identity management, as well as emergency preparedness and response.

Our company bid on the 2004 Olympic Games in Athens, and we were initially informed, via a phone call, that we had won the prime contract. However, the Greek Government suddenly changed course and decided to reopen the bidding. Rumors were that the Prime Minister of Germany called the Prime Minister of Greece and threatened to close a Siemens factory in Athens if their company was not part of the winning team. Facing the layoff of thousands of Greek workers, the bidding was re-opened. Siemens (a German company) was on the competing team and had partnered with SAIC (a $15B U.S. defense company). It appeared the Germans did some political arm twisting on the Greeks. The contract was awarded to SAIC, who was the prime with Siemens as the major subcontractor.

This decision to reopen the bidding set off alarm bells on our corporate team. There was already insufficient time to make the required security preparations for the Olympics. This added delay in getting started made the project schedule extremely critical. There was no more time to compress out of the schedule. We knew the winning contractor would be blamed for not getting all the work done, no matter if it was an impossible timeline. Furthermore, every reasonable cost reduction had already been squeezed out of the bid. More cuts meant a suboptimal security system would be deployed. The unfolding situation reminded me of the old saying, "If you want it bad, you'll get it bad."

There was a lot of emotion with winning this prestigious contract. The prime contractor would get global recognition for their security qualifications. But our team was not going to agree to a price and a timeline that could not be met and risk a contract failure that would tarnish our corporate reputation. We submitted our final proposal, and shortly after that, were told SAIC won, and that we lost. However, it was the best loss our

437

company ever had. SAIC fought a ten-year legal battle with the Greek Government, resulting in getting paid for only a fraction for their work on the contract.

Fortunately, there were no terrorist attacks during the Summer Games. The following year, I was able to watch some of it on a satellite feed while I served in Baghdad.

CHAPTER 45
THE TOUGH ROAD TO BAGHDAD

The fall of 2003 began the toughest year of my life. I documented many of the events in my first book, *SUVs SUCK in Combat: The Rebuilding of Iraq During a Raging Insurgency*. I summarize them in this chapter to capture the flavor of what happened. It was a difficult period, both physically and emotionally.

It started with Hurricane Isabel hitting the North Carolina coast. The storm damaged our newly acquired beach home, and it would be months before it was again habitable. But we were spared. Hundreds of other homeowners lost everything.

In the following weeks, my mother's health began deteriorating rapidly. Helen Kachejian was the sole caregiver for my paralyzed brother, Kevin, for thirty years and in doing so had neglected her own health. She finally went to the doctor and discovered she had stage four lung cancer, emphysema, and a mass in her heart. I stayed in West Chester for a few weeks helping my sister, Gina, take care of Kevin and while watching my mother's health decline. She passed away before Thanksgiving.

At my mother's funeral, I approached Gina and told her I had some bad news. Now, she was thinking that my house had been hit by a hurricane, our mother had just died, and we both now had to provide full-time care for our quadriplegic brother. What could be that bad? I told her I was expecting orders to deploy to Iraq.

For the next month, I drove back and forth from Virginia to Pennsylvania, sometimes round-trip overnight, to help my sister with the estate and to care for my brother. I was running out of time before my deployment, and we needed a better solution before I disappeared. Gina was a single parent. Her husband had died a few years earlier, and she was self-employed. Caring for Kevin continuously meant she would be virtually unemployed. And I felt I was placing the entire responsibility of Kevin's care on her by going to Iraq.

I broke the news about my pending deployment to Alice over the Thanksgiving holiday. She took it hard. Her family had their own health issues. Alice's mother, Elizabeth "Betty" Bush, was seventy-nine and had emphysema and osteoporosis. She was on oxygen 24/7. She lived alone in her Virginia home after her husband, Jim, died two years earlier. Alice was trying to care for her mother's medical needs while I attended to my family in Pennsylvania. I felt guilty that I would be flying off to Iraq and abandoning my post as a father and husband.

On top of this, I was responsible for a military team in the Contingency Response Unit (CRU) that would be soon going into combat to engage in a special mission to rebuild Iraq. My teammates all knew our lives were going to change radically and the timing couldn't be worse for me personally. The order was given. It was time to salute and execute.

We began to train hard for our imminent mission, acquiring the right equipment, studying the terrain, firing our weapons, conducting drills and sharpening our technical and tactical skills. I was shocked to learn we had no ammunition for rifle training, so we bought our own.

The stress meter with our families was pegged. It could get lonely on both sides of the ocean during a deployment, and we wanted our wives and children to get acquainted so they could support each other while we were gone. Then we began to update our wills, powers of attorney and life insurance policies. Then each of us had "the talk" with our wives: "If I am killed, captured or missing, this is what I need you to do...."

Lt. General Flowers, the Commander of the U.S. Army Corps of Engineers had a farewell ceremony for us in his Command Conference room in Washington, D.C. Then we flew to Fort Bliss, Texas for our final training which included a completely inadequate two-hour PowerPoint briefing on Improvised Explosive Devices (IEDs). We'd have to learn about IEDs the hard way when we got to Iraq.

We completed the Ft. Bliss training and four members of our team from the Contingency Response Unit (CRU) were on the next flight to Iraq: Captain Charlie Driscoll, Lt. Colonel Hal Creel, Major Chris Kolditz and Lt. Colonel George Clarke. Major Bob Cabell and I would follow in the coming weeks. The Advanced Party, Lt. Colonel Whit Sculley, and MSG Tom Jankiewicz had already deployed weeks earlier. We were getting early reports back about daily IED and rocket attacks. It sounded like we were all in for fireworks once we arrived.

As the deployment date approached, my brother's health took a turn for the worse. He was hospitalized, and his condition continued to degrade. He was moved to the intensive care ward. As my team flew on to Iraq, the Army agreed to delay my flight date as Kevin was gravely ill and on a respirator. His survival was uncertain. I returned to the east coast until Kevin's life or death struggle played out. I was embarrassed that I was not flying with my fellow soldiers, but my CRU teammates all understood.

I spent a few more precious days with Alice, my children, Gina and Kevin. I continued shuttling from Virginia to Pennsylvania. Every time I drove back home, I wondered what else could befall us. Then Aunt Barbara, Uncle Haig's wife, died. After driving back to Virginia from the funeral, I finally received some good news from Gina. Kevin had come off his respirator. He had come back from the brink of death several times over the last three years. It appeared he was going to cheat death again. It was a sign that I could finally go to Iraq.

The next day, March 15, was departure day. I played basketball with Kent, Kara, and Katie. We took a walk. Katie rode along in her Barbie Jeep. Then we went to Dulles airport for a long farewell at the gate. It was a tough scene that every departing serviceman has played out. It was very hard to say goodbye. Alice was steady with the kids, but I knew she felt the burden of what lay ahead for her. The aircraft doors opened; a big lump grew in my throat as I walked away from my family to a long, lonely flight to Iraq.

After stops in Frankfurt, Germany, and Cairo, Egypt, I wound up in a large tent in the Kuwaiti desert. My final travel leg to Baghdad was in a C-130 aircraft. It was baking hot inside the plane. We were packed in like sardines. The woman in the jump seat across from me took her body armor off and struggled to stuff it under her seat. There simply wasn't enough room. I offered to stuff it under my seat. She thanked me. I said, "No... thank you. That body armor will protect my ass when someone starts shooting through the bottom of the plane." The look on her face was priceless.

We took off. While in flight, the C-130 made several evasive maneuvers and fired flares to distract potential heat seeking missiles during the hour-long flight. During the final minutes, we made a steep dive on the approach to the Baghdad airport. We landed, and I offloaded my gear. A few hours later, I was at the headquarters of the Gulf Region Division on the Tigris River in Baghdad. The building was the home of the last monarch in Iraq,

King Faisal II, and a former residence of Saddam Hussein. It would be where I lived and worked during my tour of duty.

I was now involved in an unbelievable mission, to rebuild Iraq while the U.S. military was fighting a raging insurgency. The soldiers and civilians of the Gulf Region Division (GRD) began the largest, most dangerous and most complex reconstruction project ever undertaken by our nation. Our mission included thousands of projects that were spread throughout a hostile country, including schools, hospitals, police stations, border forts, barracks, oil production, electrical power and water treatment plants. To "Git-R done," our team faced daily car bombs, snipers, rocket attacks, improvised explosive devices (IEDs) and kidnappings as we worked throughout a chaotic war zone. The mission was so important its progress had to be reported daily to the SECDEF and often the President.

GRD was a new military unit that did not exist prior to the war. It was hastily created, staffed, equipped, and then rushed into combat. We went to war with what we had and what we could quickly acquire. Over 90% of the Division staff were civilians, all volunteers, that served as construction managers, engineers, contracting officials, quality assurance representatives, and translators. They were difficult to recruit because the work was hazardous and high-risk, but they were critical to our mission. Most of the GRD team met for the first time in combat. I was the Operations Officer for the Division. I led a military cadre largely responsible for keeping the GRD civilians safe.

There was no spare Army equipment for GRD. Since we were largely a civilian organization, many of our people were not trained or authorized to operate military vehicles, radios and to carry weapons. Everything had to be quickly outsourced, including the security contractor teams that protected our project sites and transported reconstruction civilians on the battlefield. For transportation throughout Iraq, GRD leased 200 SUVs, only twelve of which were manufactured with armor protection. The rest were simply standard commercial vehicles, with no actual protection. We moved around Iraq at high speeds, often approaching 100 mph, to avoid IEDs, dodge drive-by shootings or to outrun enemy ambushes. Driving each day on "the most dangerous highway in the world" was like living in a Mad Max movie. There were hundreds of attacks on our unit that killed scores of people involved in our reconstruction operations. Most of the casualties were contractors who took risks every day while operating in a complex and deadly environment.

I recounted the details of this strategic mission in my first book. It is a personal account of an important historical and political episode in our nation's history, based on the events but also filtered through my eyes and experience. I wanted to tell the rest of a story that was largely ignored by the mainstream media as "not newsworthy" or reduced to mere sound bites. The book also was intended to make certain our country does not forget—or repeat—what we learned during this seemingly impossible period. And I wanted to remember my friends and colleagues and to honor those that had fallen. **The lives of those who served with me during the early days of Iraqi reconstruction are forever changed**.

A few of the everyday harrowing stories:

- On my first day in Baghdad, while in a meeting in Saddam Hussein's former palace, a 1000-lb truck bomb detonated, leveling the nearby hotel Mt. Lebanon Hotel, killing 27 people. The blast wave threw us all to the ground. It was the first of nearly 150 car bomb blasts I personally experienced during my tour.
- Our team set up a local chop shop to rapidly add after-market armor, bullet-proof glass, and run-flat tires to our SUVs to better protect our personnel riding in convoys. We also removed the tailgates, and put a tail gunner, armed with a Russian machine gun, in the back of the vehicle to engage enemy BMWs that would attack us from the rear at speeds up to 120 mph.
- One of our security teams was ambushed in Fallujah and then ran out of ammo—a firefight in which a colleague was killed. The quick reaction force sent to rescue the beleaguered team encountered another overwhelming ambush.
- We witnessed a parade of Congressional Delegations on "fact-finding" tours that diverted precious resources and attention from the war effort.
- After insurgents had blown up an oil pipeline, we sent a security team to inspect the damage. They became lost and then "accidentally" rescued an American hostage.
- Our unit initially lived and worked in the Iraqi White House, but we were later evicted by the Prime Minister.

- After publicly announcing the successful opening of a new school for Iraqi girls, terrorists came in and murdered all teachers in front of their students.
- We created thousands of construction jobs to employ local Iraqi men that keep them from becoming part of the recruiting pool for insurgents.
- One of our SUVs accidentally plunged into the Tigris River with two civilians inside. The vehicle was wrapped in concertina wire and rolled upside down as it submerged in the Tigris River. We attempted to rescue one of our interpreters trapped in the wreck, but we failed.

There are scores of other amazing stories that I brought back from Iraq. Many shocking. Some hilarious. All true. And I have hundreds of photos to back them up. They are now documented in *SUVs SUCK in Combat*, and the book details how this former paperboy spent his summer vacation in 2004.

Assassin's Gate Bombing

CHAPTER 46
HOMELAND DEFENSE 2005-2006

Transition to Peace

In late October of 2004, I came off active duty. The following day, I went straight back to work at Raytheon. I needed more time to decompress from the stress of protracted combat operations, but felt I had been gone from my civilian job too long. I had to get back to a normal routine.

But it was a new and changed normal. Being exposed to hundreds of enemy rockets, scores of car bombs, IEDs, sniper fire, drive-by shootings, kidnappings and beheadings in Iraq made my perspective on life in the United States quite different. Our work on the Homeland Security team, providing solutions to detect, protect, and respond to threats, now had much more meaning.

One question that I never had to worry about while in Iraq was, what am I going to do when I return to the United States? Fortunately, I worked for a great company that took care of any Reservist that had been deployed in Iraq and Afghanistan. My office and my position in Rosslyn were still waiting for me thanks to my boss, Ed Woollen. I was very glad to be home, and the company's support, while I was deployed, helped me stay focused on our military mission.

To show my appreciation to our corporate leadership for their support, I presented American flags to Ed, Hugo Poza and our CEO Bill Swanson. These were special flags, flown in the face of the enemy in Baghdad, often following an attack.

Kuwait Border Guard

Soon after returning, Ed asked me to organize a team to help the Kuwaiti government. Their Ministry of Interior had become very concerned about their border security following a recent car bombing. Our team was stretched thin, simultaneously working on solutions for three other major customers. Demand for our services was exceeding our capacity and our solution architects, the engineers that helped to develop our technical approach, were fully committed to other projects.

During a two-month period, I was assigned four different lead engineers, each one required a week to "spin up" on the project requirements. The lead engineers on this project worked for Raytheon Systems Limited in the United Kingdom, so our team was also battling time zone changes during the planning phase.

When our initial design was ready, I flew to the UK and met the program team. Our work included analyzing the potential threats to the Kuwaiti border and developing a plan to cover it with sensors, including radars and cameras. Our solution approach traded off the sensor performance (ability to detect a person or vehicle at different distances) and the total system cost to determine the optimum design.

The team flew on to Kuwait, where we met another border security colleague, John Baggott, a retired Army colonel who had spent several months surveying borders in the Middle East. His experience and insights were welcome.

Our team spent a full day with senior Kuwaiti MOI officials, going over the details of the proposed plan. They were impressed with our terrain graphics which made a large, complicated design much easier to understand.

At this point, the work of the corporate team was complete, so we handed leadership of the project to the Raytheon UK team and moved on to the next big project.

Major General Larry Arnold

We had several consultants that supported our team. One of them was Larry Arnold, a retired Air Force Major General. He was the former Commander of 1st Air Force, the military unit that controlled the U.S. airspace on September 11, 2001. I was fascinated to hear his personal account of what happened that day. In the chaos of that day, there was considerable uncertainty about other potential hijacked planes. However, two F-16 fighters were ordered to intercept the terrorist attack on Washington D.C. There was no time to arm these jets, so their plan was to ram the hijacked aircraft. It didn't come to that, as the passengers on board Flight 93 fought back against the hijackers and crashed the plane.

Secretary Norm Mineta

My father-in-law, Jim Bush, often mentioned his work with Congressman Norm Mineta. They were close colleagues, and Jim considered Norm, a true friend. Both served on the House Intel Community, while Jim was an SES staffer.

In October of 2005, I met Norm Mineta, then Secretary of Transportation, at an Asian-American awards dinner. I introduced myself as Jim Bush's son-in-law, hoping he would remember their work together. Secretary Mineta lit up and immediately treated me like family. Then he recounted the same story that Jim Bush had told me years before.

With Secretary Mineta

Jim had completed a major intelligence project, and it was particularly well received. Norm was quite pleased and showed his gratitude by spontaneously kissing Jim on the top of his bald head, in front of some senior colleagues. The kiss caused an uproar of laughter throughout the room. Secretary Mineta then asked about Alice and our family and gave me his business card. He was a natural leader, with a warm and endearing personality. Honored to meet the man, I now understood why Jim Bush thought so highly of him.

Border Security Workshop

There were many stakeholders in border security and few of them shared information well. A Raytheon colleague, Ray Wheeler, proposed a workshop in El Paso, Texas in February of 2006, on "Border Security Information Sharing and Intelligence." Our company partnered with the New Mexico State University and the University of Texas-El Paso which agreed to host the event and invited some Federal, State, and local agencies. The goal was to enable government, academia, and industry to improve our collective understanding of border security issues and develop better professional networks. Industry could not help solve problems if they weren't understood. The workshop was an unqualified success. Both Brigadier General Jose Riojas, the Commander of Joint Task Force (JTF)-North, and Mr. James Mavromatis, Director of the El Paso Integration Center (EPIC) were keynote speakers. The event brought dozens of executives together to share ideas on how to better secure the border. Tunnels were identified as one of the most pressing problems, and Raytheon had several technical approaches to detect them.

Honorable Paul McHale

My position evolved over time, and in 2006, I became the Director for Homeland Defense, Combating Terrorism, and Intelligence Program Support. I frequently attended industry association events that invited senior government officials. At one power breakfast, I was seated at a table with eight attendees including a vice president from Lockheed Martin and the Assistant Secretary of Defense (ASD) for Homeland Defense, Paul McHale. The Assistant Secretary was also a Marine Corps Reserve colonel with a pending deployment to Afghanistan that October.

During the breakfast, McHale seemed a bit reserved. He probably had a lot on his mind. I was trying to break the silence and engage in some light conversation during the meal. When the coffee and tea were served, I reached for the sweetener. There were white sugar packets and three colors of artificial sweeteners: pink, blue and yellow. I grabbed a blue packet, tore it open and poured it into my cup. Without looking up, I jokingly commented that I figured out the difference between the three different colored sweeteners. "The blue ones were for the boys; the pink ones were for the girls, and the yellow ones were for those that weren't certain." As I chuckled at my joke, I looked up to see McHale pouring a yellow packet in his coffee. He was not amused. My first inclination was to smear a competitor and invoke plausible deniability by introducing myself as an employee of Northrop Grumman. But my nametag proudly had Raytheon printed on it in large font. That hastily conceived deception plan was dead on arrival. Having my foot now solidly lodged in my mouth, I had to quickly extract it and go into damage control mode. I immediately shifted the discussion to McHale's Marine Corps service and pending deployment. It was an uphill fight to save face and redeem my good standing, but I did make some progress. When the breakfast concluded, I quietly slithered out of the dining area. The real lesson here was for my corporate leadership at Raytheon. They should have never sent a former paperboy like me to this important customer event. You reap what you sow.

Jordan Special Ops Exhibition

In March of 2006, I attended the Special Operations Exposition (SOFEX) in Amman, Jordan. While in the country, I planned to meet with my ICAF classmate and friend, Brigadier General Ali Azaizeh. I sent my travel dates to Ali's staff via our Jordanian country manager. I was informed that Ali and I could meet on the last day of the conference.

Curt Powell, a retired Marine, and I arrived a few days early to coordinate with our in-country business team and ensure our exhibits were set up. Security was a major concern leading up to the conference. My usual strategy was to stay in non-American hotels while traveling in the Middle East because they were less likely terrorist targets. Three American-brand hotels in Amman had been bombed only a few months before the conference. Al-Qaeda in Iraq claimed responsibility for the attacks which killed sixty people.

The Grand Hyatt, where the conference was being held, and the Radisson SAS, where Curt and I stayed, were two of the hotels that were bombed. At the Radisson, the suicide bomber detonated near a wedding party while they were celebrating in the Philadelphia room. The repairs in the hotel lobby were still ongoing. The good news for us was that hotels previously bombed usually had better security afterward. The Radisson now had a security guard and a metal detector in the lobby to screen their patrons. Terrorists prefer to hit new targets with poor security.

Although there was a war raging in neighboring Iraq, Amman was peaceful and felt safe. We had some spare time, so Curt and I toured the capital city. It had an impressive history, and the Jordanian government had preserved the archeology. We briefly visited nearby Mount Nebo, where the Prophet Moses climbed to overlook "the Promised Land" before he died. We still had a few hours to explore so we made a dash to the Dead Sea, the lowest point on Earth. While zipping through the desert countryside, I saw a couple of Bedouins riding camels. As we streaked by, I asked Curt if he had ever ridden a camel and if he wanted to. We stomped the brakes hard and backed up on the highway. We got out of the car and began to negotiate a camel ride. We did not speak Arabic, and they did not speak English, so we used the international language, U.S. dollars. They wanted a lot. I knew the prevailing wage and countered with less. For ten bucks, Curt and I jumped on the camels and started our ride in the Jordanian desert. The first few minutes were a blast. But then, an army of fleas covered my body, and the stench of the camel was overpowering. We dismounted the animals, thanked the Bedouins for their kindness, and got back into our clean, air-conditioned rental car. Unfortunately, we had picked up some pesky little hitchhikers.

Jordanian Camel Jockeys—Kerry & Curt

The rest of the ride to the Dead Seas was miserable. I still had sand fleas biting my skin and my clothing now reeked. When we arrived at the Dead Sea, I wanted to go in for a swim, but I had no shorts. I took off my shirt and just walked in. There were sharp rocks on the bottom that cut my feet. The dense salt in the water stung the cuts, but fortunately, the salt also killed the remaining blood-sucking fleas still on my body. Curt and I floated in the Dead Sea for about twenty minutes until we were bored and then headed back toward Amman. On the way, we stopped at a gift shop near the site of Christ's baptism in the Jordan River. I bought a silver cross for my sister Gina and some Holy Water bottled from the baptism site.

Once back in Amman, the conference kicked off, and we worked extended days in continuous meetings and exhibits. Many senior leaders and officials attended, and I was able to see King Abdullah II and his son several times and met his brother, Prince Feisal, as they moved about the exhibit areas. We watched a gutsy demonstration by Jordanian Special Forces as they rappelled from helicopters and conducted a hostage rescue on a moving bus.

Finally, I was able to meet with my friend, Brigadier General Ali Azaizeh, now the senior Artillery Commander in the country. Ali and I discussed what had changed in the three years since we were at ICAF. He lived in Irbid, and two of his children were in medical school. He had much to discuss about the ongoing war in Iraq, and its impact in his country. I told him I had spent much of the previous year serving in Iraq.

With General Ali Azaizeh in Amman

451

I was surprised by Ali when he wanted to take me on a tour of his country and specifically to the historic city of Petra. Unfortunately, it was my last day in Jordan, and I was unable to see the country with him and felt awful as I declined his invitation. Somehow the dates of my visit were miscommunicated, or he thought I could extend my trip. Regardless, I hoped to get back to Jordan one day and complete the tour with General Azaizeh.

Israeli Security Practices

In April of 2006, Raytheon was invited by the Israeli Ministry of Defense (MOD) to meet with their defense contractors and to observe their government's best practices for border and airport security as well as emergency preparedness and response. Curt Powell, Tom Bonsaint and I were among the Raytheon representatives that attended.

Israel had learned security practices the hard way, having suffered from many terror attacks that were mainly perpetrated by infiltrators from the West Bank and Gaza Strip. We toured a recently constructed "Anti-Terror Fence" that ran along their border. It was credited with dramatically decreasing the number of infiltrations. Ironically, it reminded me of the fence the East Germans built when I patrolled there during the Cold War.

We also toured an Israeli Defense Force (IDF) battalion command center that monitored the security and responded to any threats. Later, we visited a Land Port of Entry (LPOE) where Palestinian pedestrians could legally cross into Israel each day to go to work. The LPOE automatically screened thousands of workers for weapons and explosives, and it was designed to minimize the damage caused by a suicide bomber, including handling poison gas. In the following days, we received an overview of the security procedures at Ben Gurion Airport and their First Responder capabilities, should an attack or disaster happen.

The official tour included patrolling with IDF soldiers in Palestine. At the border, our team was provided an armed security escort. The area was quiet, and there were no indications of an imminent threat. We stopped on a high bluff in the West Bank and looked across the entire width of Israel to the Mediterranean Sea. At its narrowest point, the country is only nine miles wide, giving us an excellent perspective on why the nation is so vulnerable.

Border Inspection with IDF in West Bank

While in Israel, I also participated in two separate tours of Jerusalem: one commercial and the other led by the Israeli government. Jerusalem has three major religions, all on top of each other in a few square blocks of land: Christianity, Judaism, and Islam. The tours were highly informative from multiple perspectives: religious, political and security.

The city is divided into four uneven quarters: Christian, Jewish, Muslim, and Armenian. The naming convention is a bit deceiving because the Armenians are a nationality that adopted Christianity before the Romans. While in the Armenian sector, I bought a gold cross for my sister Gina.

The Wailing Wall is the last visible remnant of the Temple of David. Muslims later built the Dome of the Rock mosque on top of the original Jewish temple. Around the corner from it is where Christ was crucified, buried and rose again. Any Christians that have not visited Jerusalem need to get off the sofa and experience it. A tour puts much of their faith in perspective. I was able to visit many important sites, including:

- Mount of Olives
- Golden Gate
- The Last Supper

- The Church and Garden of Gethsemane - where Jesus Christ was arrested.
- Via Dolorosa - the route on which Jesus carried his cross, from the Judgment Hall to Cavalry Hill, where he was crucified.
- The Church of the Holy Sepulchre Cavalry—the site where Christ was crucified. Inside this church is the stone on which Christ's body was anointed with oils and the tomb in which his body was placed.

A final note on the visit: I found the Mediterranean coastline near Tel Aviv beautiful, and enjoyed a long walk to the Ancient Port of Jaffa. When the trip ended, I departed for the United States, and Curt took a short flight to Beirut International Airport in Lebanon to look at airport security issues. Curt had not been there since 1983 when he was a young Marine in the barracks that were blown up by an Islamic Jihad truck bomb.

Active Denial System

Raytheon had many innovative people and technologies that could be used to support Homeland Security missions. Engineers in our Missile Systems division had developed a millimeter wave, non-lethal, directed energy weapon called the "Active Denial System" (ADS).

The system was designed for area denial, crowd control, and perimeter security. When the focused beam of energy illuminated a person, their skin felt like it was on fire. The nerve endings exposed to the beam were tricked into sending signals to the brain that the skin was burning. This was a temporary effect without any permanent cell damage. But ADS did alter the immediate behavior of aggressive people, making them comply with orders or flee the scene.

ADS gave law enforcement and military security personnel an option between shouting at dangerous suspects and shooting them with lead bullets. As with other non-lethal weapons, ADS was designed to save lives and deter crime. There was a truck mounted version of ADS and a smaller handheld version, called Silent Guardian.

One of our teammates, Frank Larkin, the former Chief Technology Officer (CTO) for the Secret Service, helped develop ADS interest within the Department of Justice (DOJ) and other agencies. He set up a major demonstration where volunteers could stand in the beam and feel the effect. I wanted to understand ADS's capabilities, so I also volunteered as a target. The beam warmed quickly and felt like I was getting too close to a hot grill. At some point, you must move your hand to a cooler spot. Frank later returned to government service and worked in the Joint IED Defeat Office (JIEDDO). In 2015, Frank was sworn in as the Sergeant at Arms of the U.S. Senate.

Army Reserve Duty

Meanwhile, I continued my duties in the Army Reserves. In 2005, Colonel Walt Chahanovich asked me to serve as the Deputy Commander for the Contingency Response Unit (CRU). Our unit not only supported operations in Iraq and Afghanistan but also responded to Hurricane Katrina which ravaged the Gulf Coast. As the new deputy, I needed to understand how our teams supported their global missions. I was familiar with our work in the Middle East involving the U.S. Central Command but needed to become familiar with the other regions, including the European Command, Pacific Command, and the Northern Command.

I took brief trips to these regions, which were much safer and more pleasurable than combat tours the Middle East. In Germany, I reviewed our operations with Major Jeff Kwiecinski. While there, I briefly stopped in Bad Wimpfen, my former home during the Cold War. Our CRU support in the Pacific was headquartered in Hawaii. Lt. Colonel Mark Canale gave me an overview of our operations and led colonel Chahanovich and me on a World War II professional development tour of Pearl Harbor and Hickam Airfield. My stop in Alaska was in support of a Northern Command Homeland Defense Exercise. The military exercise took a short break during the weekend, so I met with my friend, Colonel Tim Gallagher, who was the USACE District Commander for Alaska.

It was my first trip to Alaska, and Tim took me on a quick tour of the Kenai Peninsula, Seward harbor, the Iditarod Trail, the incredible blue ice at the Exit Glacier Trailhead, and finally, we stopped at the Russian River for some salmon fishing. Upon arrival, I walked out into a river packed with salmon and caught one by hand. After a few seconds, I threw the fish a few yards upstream, thinking it helped the exhausted fish with his journey. Other nearby salmon immediately attacked him as if he was cutting in line and violating some social order. To avoid the fight, the salmon turned and sprinted to the back of the line. It was weird behavior, and I will undoubtedly need more trips to Alaska to conduct important salmon research. Perhaps I can get funded by a government grant. There were some brown bears in the area, and occasionally, they would steal salmon from the fishermen. Tim was carrying a bear repellant spray with him and did not seem too concerned about being attacked by a 1200-pound carnivore. Personally, I would have felt more comfortable with a shotgun. I let Tim walk in front of me with his Walmart bear spray. Later, Tim and I joined Linda and his family for an exceptional grilled salmon dinner and toured the new home they were building that overlooked Anchorage. On the way back to the military exercise, I saw another unusual sight in his neighborhood, a huge bull moose dancing over a lawn sprinkler, getting an underbody wash. Only in Alaska.

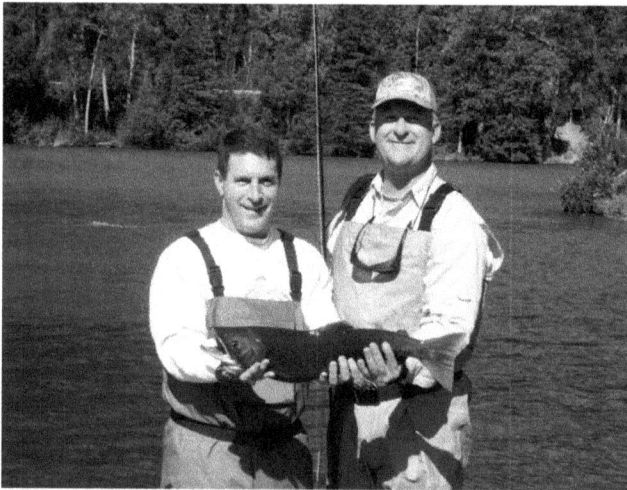

With Tim Gallagher on the Russian River

Promotion to Colonel

The following June, I was promoted to colonel. I don't know what the Army was thinking at the time, but I was a happy dude. We held the ceremony at USACE Headquarters in Washington, D.C. with my family and teammates. Colonel Bob Korpanthy led the ceremony. Alice, Kent, Kara, and Katie helped to pin on my new rank. My sister, Gina, traveled from Pennsylvania. And the Army's newest Second Lieutenant was there also, my nephew, Peter Curley, who had just graduated from West Point the previous week and was headed to Fort Sill, Oklahoma. Four of my Raytheon Homeland Security colleagues also joined us: VADM Tim Josiah, USCG (ret), Curt Powell, Courtney Banks and Darryle Conway. Darryle's grandfather, Private Frank Bart, was awarded the Congressional Medal of Honor (MOH) during WWI in France. Darryle informed me that PVT Bart lied about his age when he joined the Army, so he may also be America's youngest MOH recipient.

In the Army Reserve, once you are promoted, you need to find a new military position to keep working at your new rank. Fortunately, a colonel slot opened in Winchester, Virginia so I could continue to serve as the Military Chief of the Emergency Operations Center. That meant I had another chance to work with great Americans like Scott Lowdermilk and Tom Jankiewicz.

In August, the CRU had a Change of Command. Colonel Walt Chahanovich was departing, and my new boss would be Colonel Bob Korpanthy. Lt. General Carl Strock, the Commander of the Army Corps of Engineers, was the senior official presiding. As a farewell gift, I gave Walt a flag flown over the GRD HQ in Baghdad. When General Strock saw the flag, he approvingly blurted out, "Nice!" That was a three-star general unintentionally telling me he'd like to have one too. Unfortunately, I did not have a spare one to give to him.

Other Travels

Working on the corporate team at Raytheon meant significant business travel. Fortunately, some of the destinations were quite interesting and exotic, particularly for a former paperboy. One of the places I visited, for a Homeland Defense Symposium, was the Broadmoor Hotel and Resort in Colorado Springs. While in the area, I donned my uniform and made an official visit to US Northern Command (NORTHCOM) where my classmate, Colonel Tom Muir, gave me an exceptional operations briefing in the command center. NORTHCOM was responsible for defending the United States against all global threats. Tom introduced me to the NORTHCOM Deputy Commander, Lieutenant General Joseph Inge. While standing on the operations floor, I could see how our nation integrated an amazing array of intelligence, defense and law enforcement capabilities and information. I wanted to have Tom's job, but he was clearly the best man for the mission.

Months later, our Raytheon team hosted a widely-attended gathering at the John F. Kennedy Presidential Library and Museum in Boston. Hundreds of industry and government executives attended. Toward the end of the year, we held an Executive Off-site at the Wye River Conference Center. This was the site of the Middle East Peace Talks where an agreement between Israeli Prime Minister Benjamin Netanyahu and Palestinian Chairman Yasser Arafat was negotiated.

MOAA Award

Soon after taking command of the CRU, Colonel Bob Korpanty nominated me for a National Leadership Excellence Award from the Military Officers Association of America (MOAA). I was honored that he considered my service worthy of nomination. After a few months, I received letters from both Lt. General Jack Stultz, the Commander of the U.S. Army Reserve Command, and from Major General George Read, the Commander of the U.S. Army Reserve Readiness Command, congratulating me for being selected.

In December of 2006, I flew to Atlanta to receive the award from MOAA President, VADM Norb Ryan Jr, USN (ret). I had my three minutes of fame and was profoundly grateful. But as with every award, my family, friends, and colleagues helped me along the way. It was not my award. It was ours.

CHAPTER 47
DUAL CAREERS IN TRANSITION

The year 2007 felt like a major roller coaster ride. My industry duties required significant international and domestic travel. However, I was abruptly recalled to active duty and stepped out of my Raytheon career a third time to serve. My military duties included travel to several Middle East countries from Egypt to war-torn Afghanistan.

During that year, I made important career choices that shaped the future for my family. And after much encouragement from others, I began to draft my first book, *SUVs SUCK in Combat | The Rebuilding of Iraq During a Raging Insurgency*. When the year ended, I was back at my industry desk at Raytheon.

Force Protection

Protecting our nation against terrorist threats was part of the charter of the Homeland Security team. In early March, I was invited to speak at a three-day brainstorming event on "force protection" at the Raytheon Missile Systems facility in Tucson, Arizona. I had some relevant experience to offer from my combat tour in Iraq. I prepared my ideas about new innovations that our company could develop which leveraged the use of advanced technology with new tactics. Upon arrival in Tucson, I met another invited speaker, Mike Thornton, a Navy SEAL who was awarded the Medal of Honor in Vietnam. He had some amazing stories to share which motivated the technical team.

"You have to Write a Book!"

Later that month, Peter Probst, a distinguished terrorism consultant, asked me to co-chair a panel at a major American Society of Industrial Security (ASIS) conference. The other chair was Dr. Anne Speckhard an Associate Professor of Psychiatry at Georgetown University Medical School. The panel focused on the "Psychology of Terrorism." The conference was to be held at the Ritz-Carlton Hotel in Pentagon City and coincided with my 47th birthday.

I had previously told Peter about some of my experiences during the insurgency in Iraq. He thought I could use them to complement the research that Anne had done on terrorism psychology and resilience. At first, I was reluctant to accept the offer. I was not a trained psychologist. Peter insisted and introduced me to Anne. After a brief discussion with her, I agreed to speak.

The panel session worked out great. Anne covered her research on terrorism. I focused on describing my experiences in a terrorist-filled environment, and how it affected the mental state and the behavior of our civilians and workers. My presentation was filled with actual stories of car bombs, kidnappings, intimidation, insider threats, and drive-by shootings, including ones of personal loss. The audience was captivated. Immediately following the presentation, Peter and Anne told me that I "had to write a book." They were insistent, and again, I was reluctant. Writing a book was a massive project. It was far easier to talk about—tell my stories—than to write them down.

After another week of encouragement from Peter and Anne, I agreed to write the book with the intent to dedicate it to my brother, Kevin. He had been a quadriplegic for over thirty years. I knew he would be my motivation to finish the book. I also wanted to recognize other family, friends, classmates, and teammates, some of whom died in our combat operations. It took three years to draft and publish the nonfiction account of Iraq reconstruction activities. My marketing philosophy was that I had a story to tell, not to sell. I have since given away hundreds of copies of the book to those I served with because it was their story too.

Career Changes

In early April 2007, Bernie Elero asked me to join the Intelligence and Information Systems (IIS) business unit of Raytheon, where he was the Vice President of Business Development and Strategy. Soon after, I was appointed the director focused on the IIS Homeland Security (HLS) business. My new mission was to drive strategic growth, and I would rotate off the corporate team. IIS had a lot of talented people and impressive technologies, so I was excited about this new opportunity.

During this same period, I was also on Army Reserve duty with the Army Corps of Engineers (USACE) at the Transatlantic Programs Center (TAC) in Winchester, Virginia. My military supervisor was the Commander, Colonel Robert Suthard. The unit's mission was to provide military engineering, construction, and related services in the Middle East and Africa, including the ongoing wars in Iraq and Afghanistan. During the peak of the war, TAC contracted or executed up to$5 billion worth of projects each year throughout the region.

Colonel Suthard asked me to come back on active duty to serve as the Deputy Commander and to help stand up a new USACE Division. The current Deputy Commander, Lt. Colonel Jim Langan, was retiring that month. Colonel Suthard was retiring that summer. There was a pending leadership gap at TAC, and I was being asked to fill the gap until the new active duty officers arrived. I recognized the Army could simply order me to duty, and I would have no choice. Out of respect, Colonel Suthard and I privately discussed the conditions and timing of the recall order. He knew I held a significant position in industry and had already stepped out of my company twice. I appreciated his consideration.

Letting off the Gas—Industry

I now faced a huge career dilemma. Going back on active duty would be the death of my civilian career. The company had recently announced my new leadership position. Furthermore, I had been privately pulled aside and told that the IIS Leadership Team had just concluded an executive off-site meeting to discuss leadership succession. During that closed session, they had identified me as the top high potential candidate within the business unit. I was surprised and flattered. However, if I stepped out of my company a third time in six years to serve my country, it would raise substantial doubts I would be available to assume senior leadership duties. Another military tour meant my corporate career would likely not advance to the next level.

It had been a great ride for many years. Until that point, I kept both of my feet on the gas pedal and balanced two simultaneous careers for nearly two decades. But I had reached a culminating point where I could no longer do that. I did not like having reached this crossroad, but I accepted it. Our nation was at war, and it needed to call on their reserve soldiers. Duty called, and I needed to salute and execute. My career at Raytheon would reach its plateau.

Ironically, a few months earlier, I had another career dilemma. I was approached by an executive recruiter about leading a new division within a $2B technology company. I agreed to an interview, and it went exceedingly well. I fully disclosed my association with the Army Reserve. After many rounds of discussion, I was privately told I would need to quit the Army Reserve so I would not be at risk of a recall. The company could not have a senior executive that might "suddenly disappear." I declined to stop serving, and that meant I was eliminated from consideration from the new corporate position. I stayed at Raytheon.

Now I dealt with virtually the same situation: advance my corporate career or stay in the Army.

Letting off the Gas—Military

There is a big race in the military to climb the ranks. The most successful officers make it to General Officer. Probably less than one percent of all officers get there.

While being a general is prestigious, it is also an all-consuming leadership position. A typical Army Reserve general works a full-time civilian career, and also performs military duty many evenings each week and three weekends each month. It is a life with little personal down time, and the Reserves did not provide their soldiers with holidays, vacations or leave. In fact, many Reservists use vacation time from their civilian job to meet their military duty commitments.

One of the essential steps to reach the rank of general is to command a unit while a colonel. I was privately asked to submit a package to compete for a colonel-level command. The top job at the Contingency Response Unit (CRU) was opening, and I knew that unit extremely well. I would be very competitive for the position.

I paused and reflected on where I was in life, and where I wanted to be. I realized I could not do everything and needed to make a choice and hope it worked out for the best. I had missed enough family events. I endured four knee surgeries after coming out of Iraq. I was only getting three or four hours of sleep at night and did not have the stamina of ten years earlier. I considered the fact that my father and all of his siblings had died before the age of fifty-

462

five. Longevity was not guaranteed. I had served honorably for many years and never imagined that a paperboy would make it to the rank of colonel, see and do all that I had done in life. Considering all this, I declined to apply for a command. Barring a miracle, I was purposefully eliminating myself from the competition for promotion to General Officer ranks. I could still serve another five years and quietly retire. During that time, I would have a few more nights and weekends to enjoy my family and focus on being a father and a husband. And I would write a book. My new goal was to finish my Army career strong and become a published author so I could leave behind some good stories for my family and friends.

My new career target was to retire from the military in 2012 after thirty years of service. And coincidentally, that year I would also be eligible for an early retirement from Raytheon. At that point, I would transition to one career. I would be done burning the candle at both ends, and I would start working on my bucket list.

Active Duty Tour at TAC

In April of 2007, I reported for active duty in Winchester, Virginia. My primary mission was to design a new organization, which would later be called the Transatlantic Division (TAD). That new division's mission was to align all military construction in the Middle East and North Africa. My efforts focused on a bottom-up design, working with all the units and offices in Winchester (TAC), Iraq, Afghanistan, Egypt, UAE, Qatar, Kuwait, and Jordan, that would be absorbed in TAD. My colleague, Colonel John Plumley, led the top-down design. He was the Chief of Plans for HQ USACE in Washington, D.C. Together, we could develop a solid plan for the organizational structure, including military and civilian staff, policies, and the roles and missions.

My second mission was to serve as the Deputy Commander, backfilling Lt. Colonel Jim Langan. While I was just leaving my industry job to serve in the military, Jim was now leaving the military and transitioning to a career in industry. Jim was a smart guy with a Ph.D. I had first served with him in Iraq in 2004. Fortunately, I had a few days to work alongside him and understand his duties. I asked Jim where he was hoping to work in industry, thinking I might recognize the company. Jim noted that he had a couple of offers, but the one he liked best was a company called UTD. Surprised, I paused and then asked him if it was a small business in Springfield, Virginia, and he confirmed that was the one. I started to laugh. I explained that Raytheon had recently bought UTD, and I had been on the team that helped to buy it. I knew a lot about the company, its technology, and its leadership. UTD was a first-rate organization with an excellent professional reputation. The conversation was beyond ironic, it was unbelievable. Jim had a pending job offer from the same company that I had just left!

My third mission at TAC was to lead the conversion of the workforce to a new pay system called the National Security Personnel System (NSPS). This new system replaced the existing government promotion system that featured predictable government-wide annual raises. Pay raises under the NSPS system were merit-based, a pay for performance approach. Employees needed to have annual goals and measure their performance against them. The NSPS system was similar to what industry used. Everyone would not get the same pay raise. The pending conversion caused a lot of anxiety in the civilian ranks. This job was made much easier because I worked alongside some very talented and experienced leaders, including Pam Kelly-Farley and Paul Rosensteel in the Resource Management Directorate.

In industry, my staff consisted of a single administrative assistant that I shared with three other business leaders. As the Deputy at TAC, I led a large primary staff of over a dozen functional area leaders. These included Engineering and Construction leaders, Roger Thomas and Roger Vogler, who designed, managed and delivered projects throughout the Middle East. The Plans and Operations Directorate, led by Scott Lowdermilk and Tom Jankiewicz, who were responsible for the military aspects of the mission. They oversaw an Emergency Operations Center and a USACE Deployment Center that trained and equipped civilians for deployment to Iraq and Afghanistan. We also had staff leaders for Information Management, Logistics, Security and Law Enforcement, Resource Management, Business Management, Legal Counsel, Public Affairs, Civilian Personnel Advisory Center, Equal Employment Office, Internal Review, Safety/Occupational Health, and Contracting. It was a talented and experienced team that quickly helped me to understand their responsibilities, and most importantly, they kept me out of trouble.

There were a lot of leadership changes during the summer. Colonel Ron Light was the incoming commander, scheduled to replace Colonel Bob Suthard. However, Colonel Light would be delayed by about two months so

Colonel Larry Sansone would be the interim commander. And Larry had to step out for a period, so I took the command. It seemed like a game of musical chairs, and when the music stopped, Ron Light was finally in charge of the center. During the summer, I also handed off some duties to the newly arriving Deputy Commander, Lt. Colonel Don Johantges.

25th USMA Reunion

In early June, I had an opportunity to join my classmates at West Point for our 25th reunion. I always enjoyed seeing hundreds of old friends and catching up on where their journey had taken them. Our class had a big loss that year. In January, Colonel Brian Allgood and several other soldiers were killed when their helicopter was shot down in Iraq. His wife, Jane, was also a classmate. Brian was serving as the senior surgeon for our forces in Iraq. At the reunion, I was able to visit my nephew, Nate Curley, who had just completed his junior year at West Point and would graduate the following year. He was making the most of the experience and enjoying the fierce Sandhurst competition.

USMA Engineer Classmates (left to right): Ron Welch, Kerry,
John Naccarelli, and Joe Schulz

Offensive Driving Course

To prepare soldiers and civilians for deployment to Iraq and Afghanistan, TAC sponsored a five-day course on the "Dynamics of International

465

Terrorism" and "Security Driving." One of the attendees at the training was Brigadier General (BG), Jeff Dorko. He later deployed to Iraq to assume command of the Gulf Region Division (GRD) in Baghdad.

The first part was a short course focused on terrorism surveillance and counter surveillance exercises. The last two days of the course were hosted at Summit Point Raceway in West Virginia. The course taught offensive driving techniques to prepare us for deployments in a combat zone. During this phase, we conducted live-fire weapons training and drove automobiles at high speeds while dodging ambushes. We learned how to throw "Starsky and Hutch" 180-degree J-turns to escape a roadblock or a trap. We performed "pit maneuvers" to force hostile vehicles to spin out, allowing us to get away. And the best part of the training was ramming parked cars that blocked our escape path. Only in America could we have this much fun and get paid to do it. But one of the most valuable lessons learned during the training—having forgotten what happened flying in Blue-2 over the desert years before—do not consume two cheeseburgers and two Diet Cokes for lunch before doing a dozen J-turns. That nine-dollar meal made a round-trip.

We had plenty of other entertainment. We shot at unarmored cars to understand how the engine block could help protect us from enemy fire and learned that car doors provided very little ballistic protection. During an ambush exercise, our vehicle was shot up, so we cross loaded the wounded into another vehicle. We now had nine armed men in one vehicle trying to return fire, administer first aid and drive like a bat out of hell to get out of the enemy's kill zone. I wished I had this training before my first trip to Iraq.

Middle East Trip

In October of 2007, I headed back to the Middle East to meet with the organizations that would become part of the new Transatlantic Division (TAD). It was a "Back to Iraq" trip, but also included stops in Qatar, UAE, Afghanistan, Kuwait, Egypt, and the Africa Command Headquarters in Germany. I wanted to get a "boots on the ground" perspectives of how TAD should be organized, staffed and equipped. I traveled with Lt. Colonel Don Johantges, who had been recently assigned to TAC as the new Deputy Commander.

We landed in Kabul, Afghanistan on October 6, 2007, the sixth anniversary of the U.S. invasion that overthrew the Taliban. We arrived on a commercial flight and wore civilian clothing to maintain a low profile. A security team was supposed to meet us at the airport with our body armor, helmets, and weapons and then escort us to the Afghan Engineer District (AED) compound in downtown Kabul. The security team was not there, and I felt uneasy. Suddenly, dozens of armed Afghani police/military swept through the airport terminal. We determined that some Afghani VIP was coming through the airport, probably President Hamid Karzai. When our security team finally arrived in two SUVs, about an hour late, they explained the delay. The Taliban marked the 6th anniversary of the U.S. invasion by exploding a car bomb on the main road between the U.S. Embassy and the Kabul Airport. One soldier had been killed just before we landed. Don and I put on our body armor and headed to AED headquarters to meet with the Commander, Colonel Miroslav Kurka.

Kurka provided us with a good feel of the country, and how Afghanistan compared and contrasted with Iraq. We toured several project sites for the Afghan National Army and conducted a road trip to Gardez, near the border with Pakistan. It was located near the end of the world. The terrain was rugged and barren. There was a local saying, "Where the road ends, the Taliban begins." And this was clearly Taliban country. Our convoy attracted a lot of hard and angry stares. One of the project sites near Gardez was an Afghan National Army Brigade Headquarters. We met the local Afghan Colonel and used a translator to have a frank discussion about his needs. The project site included a barracks, a dining facility, a wastewater treatment system, and a fuel storage area. The Afghan Colonel wanted us to modify the new prison under construction. He wanted to have a large room with a high ceiling and a sloped floor with drains. He was a bit ambiguous about the purpose for the modified room, but we believe it was intended for indoor executions by firing squad.

A few days later, I returned to the Gulf Region Division (GRD) in Iraq, three years after I left it. I immediately recognized what had changed. The surge in Iraq had made considerable progress with security in Baghdad. During our three-day stay, I only heard one bombing, one local rocket attack, and one small arms fire incident. It was strangely quiet. GRD was much better staffed, and the security teams had significantly better equipment and vehicles. Intelligence and operations were better integrated, providing improved awareness and security for reconstruction convoys. I did have an eerie qualm as we passed under the bridge where the vehicle I was in, on my last trip, had been hit by an IED. This time, we rode through without incident.

The GRD senior staff provided Don and me with a detailed update on their operations, intelligence, logistics, security and program management. I met briefly with the new GRD Commander, BG Dorko, who I had recently trained with during the Dynamics of International Terrorism and Security Driving course. A few weeks after we left Iraq, BG Dorko was severely wounded by an IED while riding in an SUV. He appeared to have been specifically targeted by an insider. At the time, he was the only General Officer to be wounded in Iraq. During the visit, we conducted an updated tour of Saddam's bunker located under the rubble of Believer's Palace. After three years, the air in the massive bunker was now utterly vile, the walls covered in black mold and putrid water had filled many of the areas. But the overall situation in Iraq was positive. GRD was starting to plan how to wrap up its mission over the next few years. The bottom line was the "Surge" was working. But tragically, all those gains were later lost when the United States rapidly and completely withdrew from Iraq, against the recommendation of our military leadership. Much American blood, sweat, and money were wasted as the Iranians, and ISIS filled the power vacuum.

TAD Stand Up

A month before the Middle East trip (29 Aug 2007), Colonel John Plumley had briefed the Chief of Engineers, Lt. General Robert Van Antwerp, on the proposed plan for the new Transatlantic Division. The Chief agreed, and it went to the Department of the Army for final approval. The proposed change in "force structure" required more approvals from senior stakeholders, but the Army finally agreed. Two years later, on 29 Sep 2009, Brigadier General Ken Cox became the first TAD commander in a ceremony held at the historic courthouse in Winchester, Virginia. A few years later, my long-time friend and classmate, Bob Carlson, took command.

Mission Complete

With my three primary missions at TAC now completed, I came off active duty that December and returned to Raytheon.

CHAPTER 48
FINISHING STRONG

During the next few years, I was determined to complete both careers at Raytheon and in the Army. However, I did not want to glide in for a soft landing. I wanted to finish strong. So, from 2008-2012, I dug into new projects, explored new places, assumed new responsibilities, built more relationships and along the way, enjoyed the ride.

U.S. Border Security

Now that I was back at Raytheon, I could return my attention to advancing Homeland Security (HLS) solutions related to intelligence and information systems. Fortunately, our corporate HLS team now included Kevin Stevens, the former Deputy Chief of the U.S. Border Patrol. Kevin had a wealth of knowledge about border security issues which he openly shared with his new colleagues. With his knowledge, we could better understand the threats to our borders and develop better solutions.

Southern Border

Through Kevin's introductions, I had opportunities to meet senior Border Patrol leadership officials, including Chief David Aguilar and Chief Mike Fisher. Our team's initial focus was improving security at the U.S. southern border. We conducted several visits to understand the current techniques and technologies in use.

Our engineers had developed special sensors and software to detect, recognize and track potential border threats at longer ranges. I will not divulge the specific technologies and approaches. It was cool stuff. Trust me. Some of those sensors sniffed for threats hidden inside vehicles at land border crossings. Other technologies were used to detect tunnels dug under the border. Other techniques were used to conduct surveillance on long stretches of border that were not protected by fences or agents. But new threats continually emerged. For example, smugglers began to use swarms of ultralight aircraft to simultaneously penetrate the border in different locations. This approach dispersed and outran pursuing Border Patrol units.

The smugglers ran an extensive and profitable business and had plenty of money for innovation—they quickly adapted new smuggling methods. Contrast that with the U.S. government's slow and bureaucratic process to acquire and deploy potential solutions. Consequently, the threat always had the tactical initiative, so we focused on developing intelligence approaches to help anticipate their next move. If the Government could only get out of its own way, our border security could be more effective.

Our company became a sponsor of the Border Patrol Foundation, a non-profit organization that helped the families of fallen agents. These professionals served as the last line of defense for our nation's borders. I was proud that Raytheon recognized their service and their families and looked forward to the annual dinner.

Northern Border 2009-10

While much attention was being paid to the security of the U.S. southern border, our nation's northern border also had daunting security challenges. While the U.S. and Canada were friendly neighbors, each country had concerns about the threats that crossed our shared border.

In February of 2009, I had lunch in Washington D.C. with Paul Girard, the Deputy Minister of Public Security for Quebec, to discuss issues facing security for the U.S. northern border (from his perspective, the Canadian southern border).

We had a polite but frank discussion on transnational issues such as the migration of thousands of North Africans to France, and their easy travel access to Quebec. Once in Canada, they could cross into the United States, sometimes over the frozen Detroit River in the winter. I learned much from our extended discussion, realizing that our concerns were two-sided: while the U.S. was most concerned with terrorist threats, Canada had economic risks due to illegal smuggling.

Mr. Girard then changed the topic. "Do you speak French?"

"Not very much," I apologized, wondering why he asked.

"What do you think is the best way to learn the French language?"

470

Still unsure where this was going, I told him, "Probably, cultural immersion. Practical—and daily— use has to be the fastest way to learn any new language."

He nodded, "But there is an even better way to learn French." Now he was smiling. "You must get a French girlfriend."

We both laughed at the innovative approach. [Note to Alice: I did not test this theory!]

In August of 2009, our team made an interesting trip to get a first-hand look at the security issues. We spent the entire visit with the Royal Canadian Mounted Police (RCMP). Curt Powell set up the visit, and we were also accompanied by Chris Peterson, a Navy Reserve intelligence officer, who had significant experience in open source intelligence.

Upon arrival, we immediately met with Mike McDonell, the RCMP Assistant Commissioner of Ontario province, for a briefing at the RCMP facility in Cornwall. The Canadian government was concerned about drugs and cigarettes being smuggled into their country from the United States and had identified several smuggling organizations and their techniques.

Much of the activity occurred near the St. Regis Mohawk Reservation, also known as the Akwesasne Indian Reservation. The territory of this nation spans the international border and is in both the United States and Canada. This geopolitical reality facilitated smuggling, as residents could move freely within the reservation and across the border.

The St. Lawrence Seaway crossed through the reservation and demarked the international boundary. Consequently, some smugglers used fast boats and WaveRunners to race across the river and around islands to get their load to the other side. Many of these runs were at night with no lights, which occasionally resulted in a violent and fatal collision with large ships moving down the river.

We saw graphic images of the results of these accidents washed up on the nearby shore. The smarter runners used night-vision goggles and maintained radio communications with local spotters to avoid physical contact with the U.S. Border Patrol, the U.S. Coast Guard, the RCMP, and merchant ships.

We spent several hours patrolling in RCMP coastal boats throughout the area and observed smuggling routes on both the water and the adjacent shoreline. There was a significant amount of activity reported, and we could readily see the positive economic impact it had. There were new upscale homes built—presumably with the proceeds from profitable smuggling—next to old shacks. The RCMP officers told us they were occasionally shot at by angry residents who did not appreciate local law enforcement activities. Many of these shots originated from the U.S. side of the border.

We patrolled westward until we reached a massive hydroelectric dam that spanned across the border. We could go no further, so we turned back and took a course around the southern side of Cornwall Island.

Patrolling with RCMP

With dusk approaching, we concluded the patrol and went out to a local restaurant that overlooked the river. We were all casually dressed and began to relax as we ordered a round of appetizers and beers. We quickly realized we were sitting at a table next to several spotters, supporting the smugglers, that were enjoying a meal and calling in situation updates to their runner. The spotters constantly watched the river and seemed pleased to report there were no law enforcement officials in the area. They had no idea that some of the law enforcement officials they could not see were actually sitting at the table behind them, observing their activities. I will say no more about what happened next, other than it was an excellent way to wrap up a very insightful trip.

During our visit, we were pleased to learn that there was a lot of cooperation between the U.S. Customs and Border Protection, the U.S. Coast Guard and the Canadian RCMP along this section of the border. They frequently held joint exercises to make sure their communications, safety procedures and tactics were well honed.

A week later, Chris Peterson worked his magic and used his Open Source Intelligence tools and tradecraft to identify the infrastructure, finances, and personnel associated with potential smuggling operations. We shared the results of our work with both the U.S. Border Patrol and the RCMP. No charge. We were grateful for the opportunity to see the border first-hand and wanted to help the authorities with their critical mission.

In April of 2010, I met with Rowdy Adams of the U.S. Border Patrol. He was the Division Chief of Northern and Coastal Operations. Our team had been studying the tough problems associated with surveilling the long northern border. Much of the western region had thick forests that covered the terrain, and the Border Patrol could not see what was going on beneath the forest canopy. It was too vast to patrol on foot, and aircraft pilots could not see through the thick trees. The Great Lakes posed another daunting challenge. It was difficult tracking all the boats on the Great Lakes. How could the Border Patrol sort out which boats had originated in Canada and later pulled up to a pier in the United States without declaring they had entered? It was a huge weak spot and law enforcement risk.

Fortunately, our team had studied these two major problems, and I briefed Chief Adams on some innovative ways to solve them. I will not disclose the technical approaches, but our team was confident these offered operational breakthroughs. But as in all government agencies, implementing new solutions costs money. Obtaining the necessary budget and getting the approval would take years. Once again, it was clear that solutions for border security were delayed and diminished by both a large bureaucracy and outdated policy. Technology was ten years ahead of both U.S. policy and its painfully slow acquisition system.

Homeland Defense

My corporate duties also included pursuing business opportunities related to Homeland Defense (HLD), the Defense Department's contribution to Homeland Security. Many of the HLD opportunities that Raytheon could address involved identifying, tracking and if necessary, shooting down threat aircraft over our national airspace.

While the U.S. military was historically intended to fight wars on foreign soil, after 9/11, the U.S. Northern Command, NORAD, and the National Guard all assumed broader roles in protecting U.S. territory. Even NATO played a military role in defending the airspace of the United States.

During this period, Improvised Explosive Devices (IEDs) were a huge threat to our troops in Iraq and Afghanistan. They also posed a global menace to airlines, trains and other critical infrastructure (electrical power transmission, dams, nuclear plants, communications, etc.). Given my first-hand experience in Iraq, I was appointed to the Raytheon IED Task Force that worked on solutions to detect and defeat improvised explosive devices and the networks behind them. This included using intelligence and biometrics to identify the financiers, bomb makers and those that transported them.

Lightning Strikes

In December 2009, I became the Chief of Staff of the 78th Training Division at Fort Dix, New Jersey. To save money, the Army, Navy, and Air Force merged their separate installations into a single one and re-named it Joint Base McGuire/Dix/ Lake Hurst (MDL). My former Army Reserve boss from the Contingency Response Unit, Walt Chahanovich, was now a Brigadier General and the 78th Division Commanding General.

I soon learned that the 78th Division's history included distinguished service in both world wars. The Division's nickname is "Lightning Strikes." Its 20,000 soldiers fought in three major campaigns during World War I and suffered 7,144 casualties: 1,169 killed and 5,975 wounded. In World War II, the 78th fought in Belgium, France, and Germany in the push to Berlin. It was engaged on the Siegfried Line, the Roer and Rhine rivers, the Cologne plain, the Ludendorff Bridge at Remagen, and the Ruhr pocket. The soldiers of the Lightning Division were awarded numerous honors, including One Medal of Honor, Nine Distinguished Services Crosses; 599 Silver Stars; 3,909 Bronze Stars and 5,454 Purple Hearts. The Division had 1,368 Officers and Enlisted men killed.

Brigadier General Chahanovich and his team were now part of this impressive lineage. Our Division staff was honored to meet one of the distinguished members of the WWII Division, Lt. General Frank Camm, a young Engineer officer in the 78th when the Division fought its way through Europe. He was awarded three Bronze Stars and later in his career, served in wars in Korea and Vietnam. After retirement, he became the Deputy Director of the Central Intelligence Agency for Collection. In 2005, he received the Distinguished Graduate Award from West Point. We were deeply saddened when Lt. General Camm passed away a year after we met him.

Being the Chief of Staff of an Army Division was a demanding job. It was especially difficult for me because I also worked 60 hours each week at my full-time industry job. My military duties oversaw senior staff officers responsible for Human Resources, Intelligence, Operations, Training, Planning, Logistics, and Communications. Simultaneously, the Army Reserve was undergoing a major reorganization, changing our Division's mission, our staffing levels and having us now report under the 84th Training Command. On top of this, our unit had to physically relocate its headquarters from Edison, New Jersey to Fort Dix. The combined impact of all this change was a very busy and stressful operational environment. Fortunately, the 78th Division had a good team that pressed hard and got it all done.

Many active duty military units often viewed the Reserves as soldiers that were less trained and less committed. We were considered the Junior Varsity team. I know this because I was on active duty for many years. And during it—the first tour—I had no idea how much the Army Reserve worked, nor how much they sacrificed from their civilian careers and their families. While most Army Reservists worked one weekend each month, key leaders needed to invest much more time and effort. For example, I led conference calls with senior staff several nights each week. Each month I made a 450-mile round-trip drive to Fort Dix for mandatory Battle Assemblies. Additionally, we traveled on 3-4-day weekends to perform duty at other military locations. During any month, I felt lucky to have a single weekend off. And like many colleagues, I took personal vacation from my civilian job to work these extended hours. Reservists also paid for their own travel expenses (hotels, mileage, tolls) when they worked at their home station. I was surprised to learn that some of our Division officers flew to Fort Dix each month, at their own expense, from Kansas, Indiana, and Massachusetts. Those guys were either extreme patriots or just plain nuts. Regardless, it was clear they were committed to serving our country.

The 78th Division's primary mission was to train Army Reserve units for their pending deployments to Iraq and Afghanistan. We led two premier military training events at Fort McCoy, Wisconsin during the months of July and August. The Warrior Exercise (WAREX) and Combat Support Training Exercise (CSTX) involved about 8,000 soldiers from dozens of military units. Training all these Reservists in our back yard at Fort Dix would have been infinitely easier, but the training areas at Dix were dedicated to preparing active duty forces for their combat rotations. Our Army Reserve division could not touch the local training facilities, so we had to plan and conduct our exercises about 1000 miles from where we worked. That made coordination much more challenging and expensive.

My job was made easier because our staff was dedicated to getting it right. Many of us had combat experience, and we wanted the troops to get the best preparation possible. Let me salute a few of them. Major Jeff "Duke" Dukavas was a squared away officer who supported the Commanding General and kept me out of trouble. Colonel Alan Neidermeyer was the operations officer (G3). It was a huge job, and I don't think he ever slept. When not in uniform, Al worked at the Department of Homeland Security. Colonel Joe Lampert led our Human Resources (G1) staff, and he kept the medical readiness levels high. Joe had an infectiously good attitude, even though he commuted each month from Indianapolis. Colonel Bruce Martin led our logistics effort (G4). If Bruce told me everything was under control, I could sleep well at night. And when I needed more adult supervision, I would dial up my counterpart at the 84th Training Command in Fort Knox, Colonel John Cardwell. John always had a level head and sound advice.

To prepare for CSTX and WAREX, we wanted to understand the latest training and facilities being used at the National Training Center (NTC) at Fort Irwin. Fortunately, the Commander was Brigadier General "Abe" Abrams, a long-time friend and classmate from West Point. So, in February of 2010, we traveled to Fort Irwin, met with Abe and were able to see the best practices used by our nation. It was impressive to see the full-scale Iraqi villages and very realistic training taking place there. From our observation point above the village, we saw U.S. military units entering the village, and insurgent actors firing at them with small arms fire and rocket-propelled grenades. NTC set the standard on which all other training should be based.

The following months were packed with training conferences, rehearsals and extensive coordination and planning sessions. Summer eventually came, and the two major training exercises were successfully conducted at Ft. McCoy. About a dozen VIPs came to observe the training, including Major General Jeff Tally, the Commander of the 84th Training Command. Tally had commanded the 926th Engineer Brigade in Baghdad, held a Ph.D., and was the President and CEO of Environmental Technology Solutions (ETS Partners). I also knew him from our civilian careers, where we had crossed paths. His combined military, industry and academic qualifications were quite unique, and two years later, he pinned on a third star and served as both the Chief of Army Reserve and the Commanding General, United States Army Reserve Command. That new job put him at the top of the food chain.

78th Division Headquarters Staff at Ft McCoy

Pete and Nate Curley Deploy

For much of 2009 and 2010, my two nephews Peter and Nate Curley were deployed in Iraq. I tried to get a military assignment that would take me back to Iraq, even for a short period so I could share the experience with them. However, there were few positions open for old colonels like me that required a lot of care and feeding. But there were plenty of combat jobs for the younger soldiers. I did not have the honor of serving with them in theater.

Peter was an artillery captain and supported a Provincial Reconstruction Team from Forward Operating Base (FOB) Warhorse. He had a few close calls. In one case, several Iraqis, who worked in his office, attempted to kidnap him. If he had been snatched, Peter would have probably wound up on a terrorist video being beaten or even beheaded. Fortunately, Peter had a pistol that day, and he knew how to use it. He turned the tables on his would-be captors and held them at gunpoint until other soldiers arrived.

Nate was a Combat Engineer and a First Lieutenant assigned to the 82nd Airborne Division in Ramadi. He had already been through the rigorous Sapper course. During his deployment, he led scores of missions clearing roadside bombs from convoy routes, and he also trained Iraqi troops.

Both Peter and Nate were in harm's way every day while deployed. Our family was very relieved when they both returned home safely in the summer of 2010.

Publishing

Around that time, while waiting for a flight at National Airport, Curt Powell introduced me to one of his business associates, Rich Irwin. Rich had served a career in the government, working for the CIA and later the Department of Homeland Security (DHS). He was now in industry, working for an Alaska Native company called Alutiiq. Over his career, Rich had been to many interesting places and remained well-connected with government leaders.

During the next month, I had a few follow-up business meetings with Rich. I soon learned that Fort Irwin in California was named after one of his relatives, Major General George Irwin, Commander of the 57th Field Artillery Brigade during WWI. Rich had a gift for telling stories of his adventures, complete with facts, dates, and anecdotal information.

Several weeks later, I received a surprising email, inviting me to a book signing. Rich Irwin was publishing a book about his life in the CIA and at DHS. I immediately called to congratulate him and ask him how he had found a publisher. I told Rich I had also written a book about my military experience in Iraq, but I did not know how to get it published. Rich said he could save me two years of effort, and he put me in touch with Dennis Lowery, president of Adducent, Inc. (a publisher) and his colleague, Jim Zumwalt. I reached out to them, and their immediate support was fantastic. I owe a big thanks to Rich for making this valuable introduction.

The title of Rich's book was *KH601*, which was his badge number at the CIA. His draft manuscript required two years to get approved by both the CIA and DHS. The former DHS Secretary and Governor of Pennsylvania, Tom Ridge agreed to attend Rich's book signing. Rich introduced Governor Ridge to me at the event. I was honored to meet him and commented about how he had used to work for me. Ridge hesitated and had a puzzled look on his face. I followed up, "Yes, sir. I voted for you when you ran for Governor of Pennsylvania. That means you were working for me and all the other citizens of our state."

GEOINT in New Orleans

In mid-2010, I took the lead for the development of Raytheon's geospatial-intelligence business. I teamed up with Kevin Brown, a very bright and respected senior engineer and program manager. Kevin taught me much about the customers and the companies that served this market.

The biggest customer was the National Geospatial-Intelligence Agency (NGA), but many other members of the intelligence community and the military were involved in geospatial information. I was put in charge of identifying key exhibits and marketing messages for a large symposium on geospatial-intelligence called GEOINT. After surveying the capabilities from six divisions within Raytheon, Kevin and I selected the top eight exhibits for the show. We coordinated closely with our Marketing Communications team to make certain all the details were worked out. The conference was held in New Orleans, Louisiana in November.

Once we arrived in the Big Easy, I was told that GEOINT TV would film at our booth the following day. I was the corporate spokesperson selected to walk the TV crew through each exhibit. It was to be a glitzy, fast-paced, four-minute infomercial, and I had to write a script and memorize it overnight. That meant I could not go to the French Quarter that evening with all the other conference attendees. I would need to stay sober and break out the 3x5 cards and write down my talking points. I started with the overall theme for our company, "Actionable Intelligence to the Edge." Then I recruited my secret weapon, my friend and colleague, Doug Guthrie. Doug was the master of sound bites and fed me some great one-liners. I stayed up late that evening refining the talking points and rehearsing the entire script.

The next morning, I went to the conference a few hours before the show started and rehearsed my lines as I walked around the empty booth. I had slept very little and needed to get some caffeine in me to get the cobwebs out of my head. Doug came early, gave me a few more pointers and reassured me all would turn out well. Before long, the GEOINT TV crew arrived, led by a stunning lady named Diane. I was about to melt in my shoes when I turned and looked at Doug, who gave me a big smile and the thumbs up sign. That's when all the rehearsals paid off. Diane and I walked around the eight exhibits, and I confidently knew what to say. It was over in about twenty minutes, and the film crew moved on. I gave Doug a high five.

When the infomercial tour was aired later that day, it looked great. My colleagues and corporate leaders seemed quite pleased. Once again, I hoped Hollywood would discover me, but so far, the call has yet to come.

While the symposium was the premier intelligence event of the year, and all the agency rock stars attended, the real fun happened in the evenings after the work was done. New Orleans wanted to show us the best their city offered.

One of the evening social events, sponsored by Lockheed Martin, was at the Super Dome. Hundreds of GEOINT attendees were invited to run into the stadium and onto the field like NFL football players. Fireworks went off, bands played, and professional cheerleaders screamed for us.

We immediately got into it. The legendary Archie Manning was at the stadium signing autographs. Many of us participated in an adult version of punt, pass, and kick, where we were able to return punts, throw passes, and kick field goals, all while drinking beer! It does not get any better than that. I felt like a kid again, catching touchdown passes and spiking the ball in the end zone... of THE SUPER DOME! We received points for each event and were eligible to win great prizes like iPads. I was crushing it, well on my way to NFL fame and fortune—when I lined up for the mandatory 20-yard field goal. They teed up the ball. I stepped up and kicked that pigskin with everything I had.

I completely toe mashed it. It flew low and wide right like an opossum hit by a tractor trailer. That was it. In an instant, my dreams of a professional football career went up in smoke, and I would never qualify for one of those prized iPads. I sunk my head in disbelief, and slithered off the field, not making eye contact with anyone. I reached the sideline and looked up. There was a bar there for all the losers, so I bellied up and got a big draft beer to relieve my injured pride. It helped.

GEOINT in San Antonio

In 2011, GEOINT was hosted in San Antonio, Texas. That's another great town. Kevin and I identified the corporate exhibits again. This time, I was better prepared for Diane and GEOINT TV crew. In the evening, our Raytheon team, led by Jane Chappell, recognized more than twenty-five military families by sponsoring an appreciation dinner for wounded warriors. These soldiers were receiving treatment at nearby Brooke Army Medical Center, while they lived at the Operation Homefront Village. Our team proudly served a Texas-style barbecue meal and held craft events for the children. Spending time with these wounded veterans was a worthy cause.

Down Under

In April of 2011, I traveled to Melbourne, Australia for the Avalon Air Show. It was my first time "Down Under," and it would be a quick visit. Avalon was a 40-minute bus ride from our hotel. Our company had a large pavilion at the show and significant business interests in Australia and the broader Southeast Asia market. My duties were focused on developing geospatial-intelligence business. Each day, thousands of visitors were entertained by the flight demonstrations and gravity defying stunts. On display were the world's most advanced aircraft: The F-18 Super Hornet, F-35 Lightning (Joint Strike Fighter), new stealth F-22 Raptor, B-1 bomber, Global Hawk Unmanned Aerial Vehicle, and C-5 Galaxy. Also, on display was the seemingly eternal C-130 Hercules transport, the type of aircraft I first parachuted out of thirty years earlier at Airborne School. Some of the aircraft had tight security restrictions. However, I was permitted to climb into the cockpit of a C-5 and play with the controls. There was always a friendly rivalry between the Army and the Air Force, but I refrained from leaving a big wad of bubble gum on the seat.

The city of Melbourne was clean, safe and quiet. I could walk around the city alone. Everyone spoke English. No one was panhandling. It was much like an American city, only better. One evening, I was invited to a social function at the Melbourne Cricket Ground, a beautiful stadium in the middle of the city. I spoke with some Aussies and learned some of the rules of Cricket. The game started to make sense, but within a few days, I had already forgotten what I learned.

I had barely recovered from the 12-hour jet lag from flying to Australia when it was time for me to return to the United States. The airshow ended, and I raced back to the airport. There was an important family event happening that I did not want to miss. My nephew, Nate Curley, was graduating from Ranger School at Fort Benning, Georgia. Unfortunately, the long flight and 12-hour time zone change crushed my hope of making it. I felt awful that I let him down.

Best Ranger

At this point, my military career was winding down while Nate's career was just taking off. I was still smarting from missing his Ranger School graduation, but Gina, Peter and I were able to be there when he competed in the annual Best Ranger competition the following year. He was already an Airborne, Ranger, Sapper and was on his way to getting his Special Forces qualification. Very few soldiers ever achieve that level of tactical expertise. I would now be able to enjoy his stories.

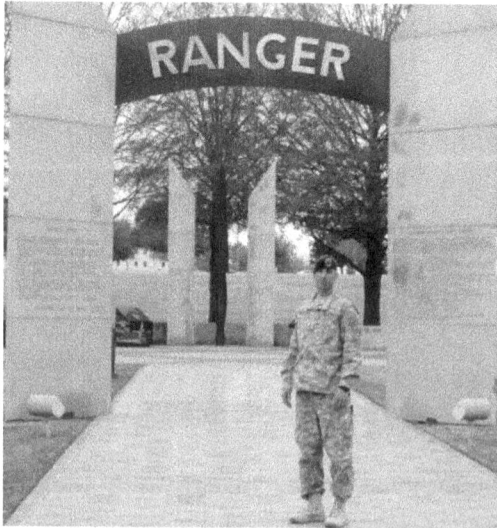

1st Lieut. Nate Curley after Ranger School Graduation

Earthquake

August 23, 2011, was a typical hot summer day in Virginia when I visited some business associates at OG Systems in Chantilly. I had just arrived at the reception area and was signing in at the front desk as a large screen high-definition TV on the wall broadcasted the latest global news. The breaking news story described how NATO aircraft were making bombing runs on Muammar Gaddafi's compound in Tripoli, while Libyan rebels assaulted it. Video of large explosions filled the television screen. I moved closer to the big screen to get a good look at the action. Another explosion occurred, and suddenly, the floor beneath me heaved upwards, and the lobby I was standing in shook with great force. I was thinking "Man, that is one heck of a television!" The video, audio, and seismic effects felt like I was at the scene of the bombings.

But the seismic wave that ran through the building was too big and too real for a wall-mounted television. It turned out to be an incredibly rare earthquake that hit the Washington, D.C. area during the Gaddafi news report. A magnitude of 5.8, the earthquake was a big one for the east coast of the U.S.

The building I was in withstood the shock wave without damage. However, my sister, Gina, 150 miles away in Pennsylvania, felt the same tremor. Knowing the epicenter was about fifty miles from our home, Gina sent us an urgent note to make sure my family was safe and not injured. That led to a humorous exchange.

```
From: Gina Curley
To: Kerry Kachejian, Alice Kachejian, Kara Kachejian
Date: 08/23/2011 02:15 PM
Subject: R U OK?????

Tried to get thru to all of you via
phones....... I am worried! I felt it all the
way up here!!!!!!! Try to contact me to let me
know you are safe, PLZ!!! THX

==============================
```

From: Kerry Kachejian
To: Gina Curley
Date: Tuesday, August 23, 2011, 2:45 PM
Cc: Alice Kachejian, Kara Kachejian
Subject: Re: R U OK?????

My car plunged off the bridge, and I am at the bottom of the Potomac River. Running low on oxygen and beer. Please send more beer.

Just kidding of course. I have plenty of beer.

Farewell Discovery

The best day I had at Raytheon in 2012 was on April 17th. On that day, the Space Shuttle Discovery was flown to Dulles airport on the back of a Boeing 747 jet, its final flight before being retired to the Smithsonian Museum. Before landing, it made a spectacular flyover of the National Mall in Washington, D.C., then turned toward Dulles. Our office building was directly under the shuttle's flight path, and it made several low-level passes. We watched the end of an era, with both great pride and sadness.

Farewell Army

By 2011, I had been working two simultaneous careers for over 20 years. I needed an end game. My strategy was to finish both careers strong and transition to a more balanced lifestyle. I still intended to work, but I sought something different and less demanding. I needed to catch up on an enormous sleep deficit and work on my bucket list. The magic year for me to make this shift was 2012. During that year, I hit a mandatory retirement date from my military service. Old colonels are put out to pasture after thirty years. In mid-2011, I changed military positions from Chief of Staff of the 78th Training Division and began my final assignment as the Deputy Commander (Forward) of the Transatlantic Division in tranquil Winchester, Virginia.

I retired in June of 2012 in a formal ceremony led by Major General Michael Eyre. I was honored that so many friends and colleagues from the military and Raytheon could celebrate with us.

Former high school troublemaker Mike Willover with Kerry

In October, our West Point class gathered for its 30th reunion. Only a few dozen classmates were still in uniform, and most now wore General Officer stars. Many had moved on to new careers in industry or government. It was unbelievable to see where life's journey had led them. And we did not forget the fallen. We held a very emotional memorial service for 27 classmates who had died since our cadet days. We concluded by singing the alma mater. The final verse really hit hard:

And when our work is done,
Our course in Earth is run,
May it be said, "Well done;"
Be thou at peace."
E'er may that line of gray,
Increase from day to day,
Live, serve and die we pray,
West Point, for thee.

And 2012 was also the year I would qualify for an early retirement from Raytheon. In early August, I made a quiet exit after 17 years. It was a great ride with an internationally respected company. I stayed there so long

485

because they had such interesting programs and many good people, like Lynn Dugle, Mike Capps, and Scott Oakes, that made me feel valued. Although I had resisted several opportunities to leave over the years, it was now time to try something new.

CHAPTER 49
BOLD SOLUTIONS, PUBLIC SPEAKING, SSIC, HARRIS & 1 WTC

Transition

In the months preceding my departure from Raytheon, I had discussed potential employment with two different companies. The first was a global aerospace firm that sought to fill a Director–level position. The executive recruiter, conducting the search, screened over seventy candidates. After three months of interviews, I was informed I had been the final one selected, and the position was virtually assured. It was just a matter of negotiating the compensation and duties. My confidence about a pending offer was further increased because I knew some of the principles who all previously worked at Raytheon E-Systems.

The second company of interest was privately held and focused on advanced analytics. The company helped customers detect fraud and cyber threats while protecting critical networks and improving the financial bottom line. I had been negotiating this position with the Senior Vice President of Corporate Development for six months. My final interview with the CEO was reassuring. Quite confident I was going to have a choice of two executive positions to choose from, I felt self-assured as I left Raytheon. I thanked all my former colleagues for the honor to work with them over the past seventeen years. During the following month, I planned to finalize the negotiation with both prospective companies and select the new position best for my future. In the meantime, I intended to work on my bucket list throughout the month of August. That list started with a bucket of chicken followed by a bucket of popcorn, a bucket of shrimp, a bucket of ice cream, a bucket of golf balls, and I would cap it off with a bucket of beer.

All my careful planning was abruptly disrupted when the U.S. government decided to implement "budget sequestration" as a means to reduce federal deficit spending. Hard caps were placed on public spending, and across-the-board budget cuts would be automatically imposed. Sequestration was immediately harmful to every agency and program involved in the process.

Dark clouds gathered over the defense industry as any hope of starting new programs or opportunities were crushed, and the existing programs that formed the industry's business base were expected to be slashed.

One of the immediate reactions to the looming budget sequestration was a broad hiring freeze in both government and industry. The aerospace giant preparing my offer held a senior level off-site strategy meeting over that first weekend after the sequestration announcement to discuss the budget situation. They decided it was the wrong time to make a new executive hire. I learned of their decision when the recruiter called me in a panic the following day, at the very moment I was signing out of Raytheon. The executive recruiter lost his placement fee, and I lost my new job after months of intense discussions. I felt completely abandoned, like a soldier that had parachuted out of an airplane into enemy territory without a radio, ammunition or even food. I was shocked and angry. I had demonstrated my complete commitment to this new company, and in return, they crapped all over me.

Later, I learned that the aerospace executives, I previously knew, had bailed out of their corporate positions with golden parachutes. While I streaked past them in a flaming parachute. This experience shattered my trust in recruiters and large corporations. But at the end of the day, I learned a huge lesson: always get the offer in writing. Meanwhile, my second job opportunity, with the advanced analytics company, was still in play. I was provided a draft of the compensation plan at the end of August. Things still seemed optimistic for a few weeks, but then that situation also went south. The company decided to focus on near-term sales with existing clients rather than the longer term development of new customers. The new position I sought was not needed, and within a few weeks, the SVP who was negotiating with me hastily left the company. With the unexpected loss of both major job opportunities, I was now the Lone Ranger. I needed to chart a new course.

Bold Solutions

In September 2012, I added one more item to my bucket list, run my own company. Through the years, I had been fairly good at identifying and winning new programs. I had maintained excellent contacts in both industry and government. Along the way, many companies had asked me to join their team.

I thought it would be interesting and fun to work for several different companies at the same time. So, I started Bold Solutions, a consulting company that provided business development and strategy services to clients in the Defense, Intelligence, and Homeland Security markets.

While setting up the new company, I learned quite a bit about being a small business owner. It was like being a paperboy all over again. I now had total profit or loss responsibility. I also directly controlled the strategy and business climate. I was an Army of One, and the best boss I had ever worked for. I had great human resources policies, flexible work hours, and a relaxed dress code. I just needed to land a few clients so I could pay myself.

It took a while to get traction, but over the next few months, I picked up seven clients. Each compensation agreement was different. And the client businesses were very diverse and included geospatial-intelligence services, command, and control software, military construction, high-performance ammunition, unmanned surface vessels (USVs), and Russian rail transportation.

The continued budget sequestration in the federal government put great stress on my new clients. Resources were lean. Some paid by the hour or on a monthly retainer. Others sought contingency contracts, where I would only be paid if the year-long business venture was successful. Some clients that had lean start-up companies offered me an equity position as part of the compensation.

With each new client, I was able to learn about their business processes, executive leadership, corporate culture, investment plans and their strategy to position for break-out growth in their respective market. Some asked me to work for them full-time. It was simply too soon. I wasn't ready to give up my new company quite yet, but it was nice to have options.

Expert Witness

One day, I received an unusual email from the United Kingdom. I was asked to provide consulting services, but this situation was most unusual. The U.K. attorneys wanted to interview me about a combat incident that occurred in Iraq. I cannot disclose the specific details, but a U.K. security contractor was injured during an attack on a convoy. A lawsuit ensued, and the attorneys wanted my perspective. My former role, as the GRD Operations Officer and as the author of the book *SUVs SUCK in Combat* (SSIC), made my opinion a significant contribution to this case.

I was willing to help, but two important questions came to my mind. First, how much does an expert witness charge in a case like this? Second, if I had to fly to the U.K. to testify in one of their courtrooms, could I wear a white wig while I was on the witness stand? That experience would definitely make it on my bucket list. I was too embarrassed to ask either self-serving question, so I let the elephant sit in the room.

The attorneys asked me to prepare a detailed witness statement in advance of the trial. The statement expressed my personal views on the sufficiency of the armor protection afforded to the plaintiff. A few months later, I was informed that both parties settled out of court. I believe my statement proved to be an important piece of evidence. I was glad it all worked out for both sides involved, but I felt left out with no compensation, no flight to the U.K. and no photo wearing the white wig.

Publishing & Public Speaking

In early 2011, I was surprised to learn that *SUVs SUCK in Combat*, was selected for the Literacy Hero Award. Apparently, my elementary school principal and his wife, Dave and LaRue Morgan, submitted the nomination, and it was chosen as the winner of the Uniformed Service Category. In early April, I attended the awards breakfast at Longwood Gardens in Pennsylvania, still wondering what happened. I was even more surprised when the award was presented by Tracy Carter of Lockheed Martin. Her company was an event sponsor and a respected competitor in the defense and aerospace market in which I worked. The award was accompanied by several certificates including ones from the Pennsylvania Senate and House of Representatives.

That year was particularly fun. I spoke on about a dozen radio shows, and media events including WKRC, KSSK, KZIM, KGAB, Point of View, and You Served Radio. In September, I spoke at a Leadership event at Gillette Stadium, home of the New England Patriots, in Foxborough, Massachusetts.

In January 2012, I received my first invitation to speak at the National Defense University. It felt like a homecoming, as I recalled my time as a student there a decade earlier.

In March, I was contacted by Rob Bluey at the Heritage Foundation. They were working on a project highlighting the risk of a dramatic decline in military readiness due to pending budget cuts. Even though our nation was coming out of two wars, the world was still a dangerous place. Our country cut too deeply coming out of Vietnam and after the Cold War. We now faced a repeat of the same mistake. The story of the Gulf Region Division (GRD), a unit that was hastily created, staffed and equipped for its mission to rebuild Iraq during an insurgency, was a good illustration of the lack of readiness. Since I was the former Operations Officer of GRD and had recently written on the topic, I was asked to help. After checking with my military chain of command and my civilian employer, I agreed. Rob and Brian Slattery came to our home and filmed a short documentary entitled, "America at Risk: Real Stories from the Front Lines."

Rob's team did a first-rate job on editing and producing the piece. A few weeks later, I was invited to speak at a Bloggers Briefing at the Heritage building on Capitol Hill. When I arrived, I met Senator Tom Coburn, the author of *The Debt Bomb*, who was the other speaker at the event. There were about forty attendees on-site, and the event streamed live to other viewers.

The Heritage Foundation reached out again later that year asking if I could travel to New York City to speak at the National Security Roundtable. The event was canceled due to Hurricane Sandy hitting the city the same weekend. That storm ravaged the city, and I was glad the speaking event was rescheduled for the following spring.

I continued to receive interesting opportunities to speak both publicly and privately on topics related to the war on terrorism, defense spending and readiness, contractors on the battlefield, and the recent wars in the Middle East. I did not seek these roles, but I almost always accepted. I never requested any compensation, although my transportation or lodging expenses for a long trip might be covered.

Over a two-year period, I spoke at the National Defense University four times. Each time, I enjoyed the opportunity to spend a day at beautiful Fort McNair on the Potomac River and tell war stories to an audience of bright emerging leaders in national security.

After the Heritage Foundation had made their initial "America at Risk" video, they invited me to several more events in Washington, D.C. and New York City. I gained great respect for the Foundation. They had very talented, mature and patriotic experts, serving their country as conservative thought leaders. I was honored to work with James Jay Carafano and Dr. Steven Bucci, who are among the organization's most talented staff. After supporting several Heritage events, the Huffington Post Live also asked me to participate in a few broadcasts. I knew they had a reputation for being politically liberal, but I was glad they were reaching out. The first discussion was focused on military and national security budget cuts. I felt the Huffington Post was trying to play catch up on the same topic. The interview went remarkably well. The hostess was polite and respectful, and she seemed to want to learn more about the issues.

The second broadcast, a few months later, was completely embarrassing. The topic dealt with a political battle between the Army and Congress on upgrading the Abrams battle tank. The topic was in the news and worthy of a good discussion. The production crew needed someone to provide a rational, balanced point of view, so I agreed to be on the panel. However, I quickly discovered that the host was completely uninformed and irrational. He wasn't even an American citizen. This was not his debate, and he had no skin in the game. He was the first Australian I ever met that was a real irritant. In fact, he was a certified, card-carrying gas bag. The host made repeated ludicrous arguments about tank technology and our production capabilities that were grossly unfounded and dangerous. It was clear the Aussie and the panelists had never operated or fired a tank, and they could not distinguish an Abrams tank from self-propelled tracked artillery. The unprofessionalism of that broadcast epitomized why the Huffington Post lacks credibility.

Heritage and Freedom Tower

In early May of 2013, The Heritage Foundation asked me to participate in a panel on Military Readiness to be broadcast on C-SPAN. Dr. Steven Bucci led the group that included two other members, Mr. Baker Spring and Mr. Richard Dunn. Each of us had strong views about the risk of the United States having a Hollow Force (a military that looks good on paper but can't adequately defend the country), especially since we were coming out of long wars in Iraq and Afghanistan. Ten years of war had caused major wear and tear on equipment, and a series of defense cuts were creating a great risk to America's military capability. The panel went exceptionally well, and our message was also delivered during follow-up interviews.

The following week, we were invited to discuss Military Readiness at the National Security Roundtable (NSR) held at Harmonie Club in New York City. The original trip had been planned the previous October but canceled due to Hurricane Sandy. Steve Bucci and I made the train trip to the Big Apple where we joined the other panelist, Lt. General (ret) David Deptula, the former Air Force Deputy Chief of Staff for Intelligence, Surveillance & Reconnaissance. Ronni Shalit, the NSR President, kindly made all the arrangements.

Before traveling to New York City, I contacted two of my former Army buddies, Colonels (retired) Mike Donovan and Steve Hill. Both colleagues were former senior leaders in the Army Corps of Engineers and were now executives at Louis Berger Group, Inc. and responsible for the most significant construction project in our nation. They both served as consulting program managers for One World Trade Center (1WTC), also called Freedom Tower.

This project and its completion were an iconic symbol that both America and New York City were back after the destruction of the original World Trade Center complex during the 9/11 attacks. Mike and Steve had previously invited me to tour the new tower, which had been under construction for several years. We agreed to meet early on May 10, 2013, the morning following the NSR panel discussion.

When I arrived at Mike's office on Broadway that morning, we exchanged greetings. He immediately told me this was a "big day." In fact, it was historic. The ironworkers were installing the final piece of the spire that capped the building at 1776 feet. Mike told me Matt Lauer, the host of the Today Show, was doing a live TV broadcast at the top of the building.

The tower was still an active construction site, so Mike gave me a hard hat and asked his colleague, Alicia Roberts, to take me to the top. Minutes later, we were making a beeline for the tower, passing security checkpoints and trekking through the mud.

Alicia led me through the building, where hundreds of workers were making progress on the complex structure. We rode two elevators to the 104th floor at the base of the spire. Several helicopters were orbiting the building with TV news crews. The scene reminded me of the day in 1981 when the American hostages came home from Iran and stayed with us at West Point. Every American wanted to see the action on live TV. We moved to the 103rd floor where there was more space to walk around. The views were incredible. There were no exterior walls, just massive steel beams, a few safety ropes and sheets of clear plastic. If someone fell off the building from this height, they would probably die of old age before they hit the ground.

This floor would later become the observation deck. Alicia handed me a black marker, and I was able to write a special message that would be permanently encased at the top of the tower. I picked a steel column that faced north, up the Hudson River toward West Point. The message read:

> *10 May 2013. The final spire is now in place. To my children and wife: Kent, Kara, Katie, Alice Kachejian. I hope for a safer world. —Dad*

Throughout the tour, Alicia told me interesting facts about the new building. I recall the evacuation stairwell was built in the center of the structure with concrete walls three feet thick. Any occupant on any floor could simply move into the center stairwell for protection should there be any threat to the building. And the firefighters had their own dedicated stairway so they would not be impeded by thousands of occupants coming down the stairs during a building evacuation.

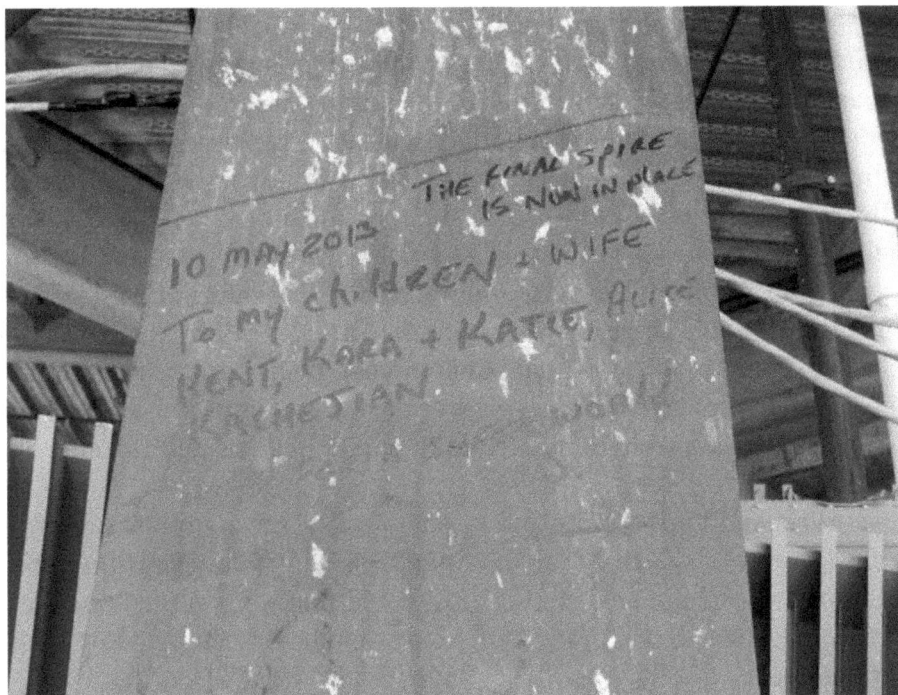

Message at the top of Freedom Tower

Freedom Tower—Final Steel placed at the top—1776 feet

On the elevator ride down, I met Mike O'Reilly. He was the lead ironworker on the project that day and had set the final piece of the spire in place an hour earlier. Mike was one of a handful of men that connected the tower's steel skeleton as it was built floor by floor. He mentioned how long he had been working on the project, and he was glad the major steel work was finally complete. I shook Mike's hand and thanked him for what he had done to help our nation heal. "Millions of Americans will be able to see your work from miles away, for the next one hundred years," I told him and asked to get his picture so I could show it to my children. I later learned that Mike's father was a connector on 7 World Trade Center when he had an accident that left him paralyzed from the waist down. After the terrorist attacks on the original WTC, Mike decided to become a connector and help rebuild the site. That took guts.

Alicia and I left the site and headed back to the management office a few blocks away. I was able to thank Mike Donovan and Steve Hill again for hosting me on such an amazing day. If I could have only picked one day in my life to tour One World Trade Center, it would have been that day. What a gift it was.

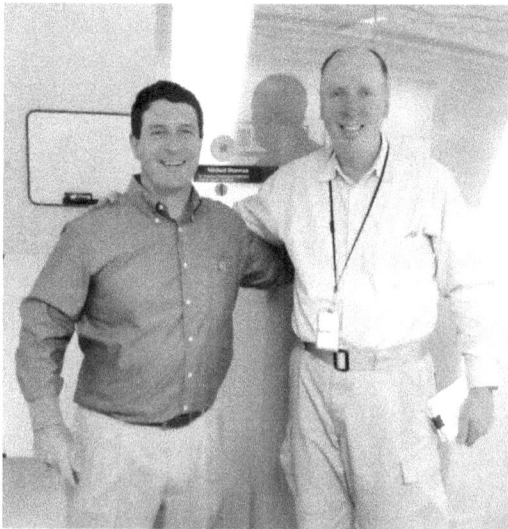

Kerry with Mike Donovan

I headed off to Penn Station to catch the train back to Washington D.C. I reflected on how great this brief trip to New York City had been. And suddenly, it got even better. As I was standing in the train station, I met

Cardinal Timothy Dolan, who had been appointed the Archbishop of New York by Pope Benedict XVI. He was a man who loved both God and beer.

In December 2015, I was on another business trip to New York City with some colleagues from Harris Corporation: Amy Miller Feehery and John Weaver. While there, we were able to meet with Mike Donovan and his new colleague Jeff Ryscavage. We were joined by my friend and former NYC Deputy Fire Chief, Charlie Blaich. Jeff gave us a tour of the now completed One WTC building and a preview of the major transportation hub, called the Oculus, that was nearing completion. The magnificent structure will be an architectural icon of NYC for many decades to come.

Inside the Oculus (left to right): AM Feehery, Charlie Blaich, Kerry, John Weaver

Record-breaking Territory

In March of 2015. I woke up and celebrated my 55th birthday. None of my father's siblings lived past 54. My brother died at 43. I started to pinch myself to verify I really was still alive. That caused me to ponder why I had I lived so long. Perhaps I was adopted.

SECTION 7
FAMILY & FRIENDS

CHAPTER 50
KERRY & ALICE

Santa Claus is Coming to Town

In October of 1986, I was stationed at Fort Belvoir, Virginia and spent many weekends in Georgetown with my roommate, Mike Willover, and several other friends. There was fun and safety in numbers.

We decided to attend the Halloween festivities that year and selected our costumes. Mike and his future wife, Lisa Kirk, made a convincing ZZ Top duo. Chad Harrison was a Cone Head, famous on Saturday Night Live. Donny Bellenthin was a cigar-chomping Rambo. Charlie Restivo was dressed as a bumble bee. He had large antennas on his head and strapped a toilet plunger to his ass that served as his stinger. I needed a costume that would be an instant chick magnet, so I dressed like Santa Claus. With the suit came great power, I could quickly find out who were the good girls and the bad girls. I loaded my sack with candy bars to give out to all the girls, the good and the bad.

Preparing for Halloween in Georgetown

499

We packed into a single car and joined the traffic jam entering Washington D.C. After parking near the Potomac River, we headed a few blocks up the hill to the main drag in Georgetown, M Street. The streets were open only to pedestrians, and large crowds of party-goers walked by in costumes. The energy in the city was picking up, and police were patrolling on horseback.

As soon as I stepped out onto M Street, I knew my strategy was going to work. I was the only Santa Claus in town. Everybody wanted to say hello to old St. Nick. Life was good... for a few moments.

Suddenly, I was approached by three cave women. They were among the very bad girls. They started screaming and hitting Santa Claus with their plastic baseball bats, trying to take my sack of candy. I warned them, "You're getting coal in your stockings!" That comment really pissed them off. I absorbed their blows with my left arm and fought to hold on to my sack of candy with the right. I figured this theatrical scene would end soon, but those cruel women kept pounding away on me. Down on one knee, taking a beating, the welts from the plastic baseball bats were starting to sting. A large crowd formed around the beat down hero of the Christmas Holiday Season. But nobody helped old St. Nick. A cop on a horse was nearby... laughing at me. There were no elves to protect me with their professional midget wrestling moves. Where was ZZ Top, the Bumble Bee, Rambo and Cone Head when you need them? Finally, some dude in a Superman suit jumped out of the crowd and started to beat back the cave women. He made quick work of them and even found my hat, dusted it off, and gave it back to me. I took note. Superman was definitely getting a big stocking this year.

At this point, ZZ Top and the Cone Head showed up and hustled me off the street for my own protection. They led me a block away into an alley to a sports bar called Champions. I definitely needed a beer. Inside, it was noisy and crowded. Within a few moments, girls started seeking Santa, and my luck had begun to turn. I gave out a bunch of candy bars and was pulled onto the dance floor. ZZ Top and the Cone Head had some good dance moves. I was doing a spastic dance called the Santa Shake. But good old Charlie was a very aggressive Bumble Bee. He got out on the dance floor and whipped his toilet plunger stinger at a crowd of girls. It was hilarious to watch him back into the girls and drive them over toward the rest of his friends. Charlie may have over done it, but to my benefit. The girls left the dance floor and sought refuge with Santa. One of them, Margy Jahn, complained about the obnoxious bumble bee. I expressed sympathy, threw Charlie under the bus, and did not mention that I knew him.

I was now standing next to a pretty girl named Alice, and I asked her, "Would you like some candy?" She replied, "My mom taught me to never accept candy from a stranger." It was a good answer as I realized I was out of candy bars anyway, so I bought her a drink. We went back out on the dance floor for a few more songs, then took a break. I was now cooking inside the Santa suit—all that ho ho'ing is hot work. I told Alice I was going to disappear for a minute but would be right back and went upstairs to the men's room. I took off the Santa suit and packed it inside my red sack. Under the Santa suit, I wore blue jeans, a red "Airborne" t-shirt, and black paratrooper boots. I went back downstairs feeling much cooler. The bar was still noisy and packed, and it took a few minutes to find Alice. I picked up the conversation again. She seemed a little distracted. I did not realize it, but she had no idea I was her Santa. She thought I was some different guy. After a few minutes, she looked down and saw my black paratrooper boots, and blurted out, "You're Santa Claus!" I smiled and told her, "See, I came back as promised."

We chatted for a few more minutes. She noticed my t-shirt and my class ring, and stated, "You went to West Point." Now I was thoroughly impressed. I had not said a word, but she had figured it out. I had found a beautiful girl who was also smart. But she gave me fair notice, "If you're staying in the military, you'd better find another girl."

I didn't listen to her warning and took her out on a date the following night. And we have been together ever since.

Vicksburg

When I met Alice, I was still on active duty in the Army stationed at Fort Belvoir, teaching civil engineering. In December of 1986, I went on two weeks of travel to attend a training course on Pavement Design and Construction held by the Army Corps of Engineers in Vicksburg, Mississippi. While there, I toured the historic Vicksburg Battlefield. History is always so much more real when you walk the ground. Vicksburg is a great southern town that has kept much of its history and charm. And if residents needed to add some spice to their life, New Orleans was only a four-hour drive to the south.

Long distance phone calls were expensive at the time, so I always felt the need to communicate quickly. I normally had five minutes to talk to family and friends every week, so I prepared a list of things to say before I placed the call. Trained to be honest and forthright, I occasionally blurted out comments before I considered their impact. I called Alice from Vicksburg one night to tell her about the trip. After a few minutes, our time was almost up, and I unexpectedly announced, "I love you." There was a pause as we realized what I had said (I think we both were floored). What I had said was out there, alone in that silent moment. But Alice did not leave me hanging in suspense for long. She replied, "I love you, too!" That was an awesome phone call.

Several of my new-found friends at the training course decided to head to New Orleans over the weekend and invited me to join them. It was my first time in the French Quarter. On a relatively warm and sunny day, we walked around the city for a few miles. After stopping at a few piano bars, we went to Pat O'Brien's, a famous tourist pub. Somebody suggested I try their famous drink called a Hurricane. I was thirsty and rapidly poured down four of them.

That's when the Hurricane started to come ashore. The weather forecast in my head changed quickly. The drinks were sweet, and I wasn't smart enough to stop. Taunting the storm, I drank two more. Six Hurricanes delivered the full fury of a Category Five storm, and our night on the town had just started. I am glad my friends took care of me, and from that point on, I only remember the horrible taxi ride back to the hotel. I did not get out of bed until the following afternoon. FEMA could have declared my body a federal disaster area, and I spent the second week of the engineering course recovering from the Hurricane.

Studying for PE

In the early spring of 1987, Alice and I were anxious to get outside, enjoy the weather, and meet our friends. However, much of my free time was consumed studying for the Professional Engineer exam (PE). While lawyers needed to take a Bar exam, engineers were certified by passing the PE exam. In college, I studied aerospace, but I was now preparing for a civil engineering exam, a very different technical discipline. The PE exam was eight hours long and included eight design problems. About 30% of the people taking the PE exam pass it. I spent hundreds of hours in the evenings and on the weekends working on sample problems and organizing my notes. I was trying to pay forward to have more opportunity later in my career. But that left little time for enjoying the spring weather with Alice.

Engagement

As previously mentioned, I occasionally blurted things out. One weekend in May 1987, while I was in the den studying for the PE exam, Alice came in looking for someone to talk to. I was buried in books and a bit distracted.

Among all the engineering textbooks, she spied a thick shopping catalog. Alice knew that I never shopped and had no interest in catalogs either. She asked me why the catalog was on my desk. I was trained to be honest and forthright and blurted out, "I was looking for an engagement ring."

Alice gave me a surprised look, and she replied with great enthusiasm, "We're getting married?" She paused for a second, and the question turned to a statement, "We're getting married!"

Holy smokes. I was still mentally hung on answering her question. And technically, I had not asked her yet, but she had apparently already accepted. I went from boyfriend to fiancé in a few seconds. Feeling like I had been lured into a friendly fire ambush, I thought, "What the hell just happened?"

I hate catalogs. This was not the way I envisioned proposing. I had never been very good at being romantic but sitting at my desk with an engineering textbook set a new record low. The moment was completely unplanned and unimaginative, but the rocket motor was now ignited at full throttle. Within minutes, Alice started calling relatives, friends, co-workers, and the pizza delivery guy. I wasn't sure what to do next, so I put my tail between my legs and played dumb. Alice wanted to see the rings in the catalog. Of course, none of them was the right one. She suggested we spend the next few weeks visiting local jewelry stores. To avoid another screw-up, I immediately agreed. I didn't trust my own judgment, so why should Alice. Soon enough, we started making the jewelry store circuit. I learned about the six Cs: color, cut, clarity, carat weight, cost, and credit. That's when we met our new family jewelers, John and Jenny Caro, who had just launched their careers, and they helped us find the right ring.

I knew at some point Alice would come to the stark realization she would be changing her last name from Bush to Kachejian. She would have to learn how to spell it first. It had taken me a few years to get it right. But I didn't want to bring up the subject just yet. There were plenty of other things to keep her distracted.

During the rest of that year, we started to learn about each other's friends and families. We skied on Camelback Mountain with Margy and Rick Jahn and hit the air show at Andrews AFB with my Army buddies. Then we packed our bags for a trip to Cancun, Mexico. It had the bluest water I had ever seen. Alice started hanging out with my family more. We traveled to Pennsylvania to attend Kevin's graduation from Villanova Law School and later for his celebration when he was admitted to the Pennsylvania Bar, an incredible achievement for a quadriplegic.

Alice's father, Jim Bush, was able to get us two tickets for a VIP tour of the White House. Jim had worked on Capitol Hill for a few years, and still had connections with Representative Andy Ireland. It was an exciting visit. Ronald Reagan was president, and we were able to briefly see his daughter, Maureen.

Alice and I joined Immanuel Church-on-the-Hill in Alexandria, Virginia. It was adjacent to the beautiful Virginia Theological Seminary. It was a historical church attended by Francis Scott Key, the writer of our national anthem, the Star-Spangled Banner. We began our pre-marital counseling with Reverend Bob Trache. We also volunteered to lead the Youth Group at the church. Our mission was to teach the children a variety of lessons. Ironically, Alice and I learned much more about being responsible for children. It was not easy.

In early spring of 1988, our wedding date was near. I purposefully steered clear of the wedding planning, having heard it could be hazardous for men to get involved. Instead, I planned to resign my active duty military commission and was busy with job interviews. A few weeks out from the wedding, Alice was the honored guest at a bachelorette party with her best friends. And of course, I had my own night on the town with the men. We both survived and looked forward to our big day.

The Wedding

The weather forecast for April 16, 1988, called for cold and windy conditions with a dusting of snow. The weatherman called it perfectly. It was crisp and windy when we arrived at our church.

We had a military wedding, and it was the last formal ceremony I was involved in while still on active duty. The military groomsmen wore their dress uniforms and saved a ton of money by not renting tuxedos. My brother, Kevin, was the Best Man. Sherry Feltman (Davis) was the Matron of Honor. Mike Willover and three Army buddies were Groomsmen: Ed Boyajian, Bob Carlson, John Naccarelli. Bridesmaids were Stacey Baker, Margy Jahn, Erica Jenkins and Debby Wolf. Gina was a Reader, and her daughter Rebecca was the Flower Girl while her son, Peter, was the Ring Bearer. Lisa Kirk was our Soloist. After the wedding, we left the church in an "Arched Sabers" ceremony. Ed, John, and Bob also served as saber bearers and were joined by other officers: John Rivenburgh, John Shuman, James Moore, Charlie Restivo, Ted Devens, and Michael Horkey.

Arched Saber Ceremony

Our reception followed at the Fort McNair Officer's Club, a beautiful building along the waterfront in Washington, D.C. Fort McNair is the home of the National Defense University and the historical location where several of the conspirators of the Lincoln assassination were hung. Yes, our wedding reception was not the first group to hang out there.

We had about 200 guests and a live band that rocked the O'Club. Man, we could party, and all wound up doing the famous dying cockroach dance on the floor while the band cranked out *Shout* by Otis Day and Knights.

Alice and her family did a great job planning the entire night. And the best news was that Jim and Betty Bush paid for the open bar.

The next day, there was a rumor that one of our guests had driven their car into the Potomac River after the reception. We never got confirmation that it actually happened or who did it. Alice and I replayed the wedding video trying to figure out which guest it might have been. It's still a mystery.

After the wedding, Alice and I slipped off on our honeymoon to the Caribbean. We flew to San Juan and hit several islands. The islands were great. On the way home, we stayed a few extra nights in San Juan. That was a mistake. The police standing in the downtown tourist area near our hotel were armed with assault rifles, which made us a little nervous. Dogs were crapping all over the nearby beach. Our "luxury" hotel room came with giant insects and had a six-foot crack in the wall. The San Juan city tour we took included a two-hour stop at a library. WTF? Finally, the minivan we toured in broke down in the middle of the highway during a torrential rainstorm. The van had no air conditioning, and we steamed inside for several hours. When we asked for a refund, we were refused. As a result of that trip, I took Puerto Rico off my bucket list and put it on a different one that begins with "S."

DINKs

Life was good, and we were DINKs, double income, with no kids. Alice and I had a lot of time to travel and socialize. We went boating with the Boyajian's and the Feltman's. Later, we visited Margy and Rick Jahn in New Jersey and toured the World Trade Center. We went to the top observation deck. It was a spectacular view, and I never imagined it would be lost in a terrorist attack thirteen years later that would send our nation, and a former paperboy, into a Middle East war.

At first, Alice and I lived in a lovely condo in Alexandria called Montebello. It was comfortable and had lots of amenities. About a year later, we sold the condo and bought a new home. It was exciting seeing it as it was built. After we moved in, we had several empty rooms, so we needed to buy some furniture. There was no way I could haul furniture in my German sports car. I was now a married man, and I no longer needed the old Porsche 928 "chick magnet". I sold it and bought a used Nissan SEV-6 pickup truck. I could now haul furniture and have a different kind of manly experience. It took some time to get used to the higher center of gravity, and I soon learned that pickup trucks don't take corners like Porsches. I almost rolled the truck a few times. The guy who bought the Porsche was the President of the American Ferret Association, and he "wanted to drive his ferret in the Porsche to conventions." Then he put handicapped license plates on a high-performance Porsche. Really. You can't make this stuff up. But he paid with cash, and I used it to pay off the pickup truck and build a nice sports bar in my new basement.

Missing Stuff

Life was going well, but I started to notice some of my stuff was missing. The manly possessions I brought to the new house were being replaced with ~~fru fru crap~~ things that Alice liked. Almost everything I owned looked like junk to my new bride. I tried to explain how my stuff had good memories associated with it. That did not work, and she started secretly throwing out my childhood and bachelor memorabilia. If Alice was smiling when I came home from work, I knew something else was gone. The list kept growing:

- My green polyester bell-bottom leisure suite with platform shoes. An outfit from the John Travolta era and a style I was sure would eventually come back. I went off on travel, and whoosh, it disappeared while I was gone.
- My comfortable old t-shirts. There were fifteen years of memories in that collection. I needed those shirts for my workouts, yard work, and painting. Some had holes in them, but each hole had a story associated with it. All that history got pitched in the trash.

- My fifty wine tasting glasses from dozens of festivals in Germany. Each one had the name of a German village on it. Throwing those memories out was almost a criminal act.
- My sebaceous cyst. It had been cut off my forehead by a surgeon and floated in a small medical jar that I stored in my desk. That tissue sample contained my DNA. Guys can't give birth, but that little fellow came out of my body. I felt like Alice was throwing part of me away.
- All my baby teeth. I saved them for decades in a small box and kept them in my nightstand. The tooth fairy let me keep them and still left me some money. And I also had two big wisdom teeth in the box. They are now rotting in some landfill.
- My beer can collection. I had been to many of the world's pubs. This collection had historical value.
- My college textbooks. They made me feel educated.

Things Alice did not throw out:
- My medieval weapons collection. I had a battle ax, crossbow, sword, mace, and some other goodies. Alice wanted them gone, but I think she was afraid to touch them. They were too spooky.
- My dad's combat boots. Tossing them out would be grounds for divorce.
- Lladros and Hummels from Europe. I think Alice wanted to sell these porcelain figurines for cash.
- My Grandfather clock from the Black Forest. Surprisingly, Alice and her mother liked it. However, the cuckoo clock I bought at the same factory got punted.

We started to meet our new neighbors. Living next door were Lou and Louise, who were from Louisiana and had a dog named Louie. Living on the other side were Marty and Jane Horowitz. He worked for the U.S. Secret Service, and I'll share more with you shortly about our friendship with him and Jane. Across the street was a neighbor named Dave. He worked for the Navy, liked to fix cars, and brewed his own beer. I became one of his taste testers.

On our first wedding anniversary, Alice and I pulled our wedding cake out of the freezer. Her mother had wrapped the top tier of the cake in multiple layers of plastic and aluminum foil. We thought it would taste awful. To our surprise, it was fantastically preserved. It smelled and tasted just like the day of the wedding.

Willover Wedding

In June, Mike & Lisa (Kirk) Willover had their wedding in Minneapolis. Man, we rocked the Metrodome Hilton Hotel. Mike's college buddies were there in force. My apologies—long overdue—to the clean-up crew at the hotel. It won't happen again. I promise. I served as the Best Man, and somebody made a mistake and handed me a microphone at the reception. I gave a congratulatory pep talk to Mike and Lisa which ended predicting they would have a station wagon full of freckle-faced kids. Leah Nicole and Lauren Elise were born a few years later.

With Mike "Waldo" Waldron, Mike Willover, Stu Harrison, Ray Pidge

Cancun with Sandy and Dave

When Mike and Lisa snuck off on their honeymoon, Alice and I took off to Cancun where we met Sandy and Dave Bost. We went to a Polynesian dance show, and I got dragged up on staged, dressed in a grass skirt and was forced to perform unnatural dance steps in front of hundreds of guests. Fortunately, I was presented a bottle of tequila as compensation for my public humiliation. Amazingly, I was allowed to keep my Top-Secret security clearance after I returned to the United States. The following year, Dave and Sandy went with us on a two-week trip to Europe. In later years, we shared some other vacations with them to Florida, Jamaica, and their home at Lake Arrowhead, Georgia.

Anything for a free bottle of tequila

Victory Parade

On July 4, 1991, the Desert Storm Victory Parade was held in Washington, D.C. All the U.S. military vehicles and equipment drove down the George Washington Parkway, while fighter jets and bombers flew overhead. I was in the Army Reserve, but our military unit had not deployed. Bob Carlson and Charlie Restivo served in the same unit and were at the parade as well. We were spectators that day, just like we were during that war. While we were proud that our military teammates crushed the Iraqi Army, we felt like we had sat on the bench during the Super Bowl. We watched the war live on TV each night, drank cold beer and cheered on our brothers in arms. The parade was a proper welcome home and conclusion to the war. It was a great day to be an American.

Desert Storm Victory Parade in Washington, D.C.

New England

In October 1991, Alice and I took a ten-day trip through New England. We set low expectations and far exceeded them. The fall colors were still in view and beautiful. Our first stop was at West Point, where we stayed at a charming European Inn, LeChambord, with Blake and Mary Peck. Blake was also a USMA graduate, as well as Mary's father, Jim Bambery. Rick and Margy (Bambery) Jahn joined us for the football game against the Citadel. I needed to attend a social event with my classmates, but I screwed up and did not pack a suit. Rick Jahn loaned me his suit, and I still owe him for that one.

Next, we visited the Boyajian's in the Boston area and toured historic Concord and Lexington. We moved on to spend time in the White Mountains, Franconia Notch, Jackson, New Hampshire, the Mount Washington Resort and St. Johnsbury, Vermont. Each stop was at a bed and breakfast. We saw the Bush estate in Kennebunkport, Maine which was severely damaged a few weeks later in a Nor'easter. Ironically, we could not order lobster at our dinner in Maine as there was a festival the week before and all the lobsters were exhausted. The fisherman could not harvest anymore until the species recovered. We left Maine via peaceful Perkin's Cove in Ogunquit and stopped at Newport Beach, Rhode Island. We toured The Breaker's, a famous Newport mansion, and saw a beautiful yacht, reported to be that of Alan Greenspan, the Chairman of the Federal Reserve. On the way back to Virginia, we made a final stop at Mystic Seaport in Connecticut.

Marty and Jane

For several years, we lived next door to a nice couple I mentioned previously, Marty and Jane Horowitz. Marty often traveled to many countries with the U.S. Secret Service (USSS). When we got together on weekends, he and I shared a beer and stories about different places and situations we had been in. Marty had been to some exotic places working on technical security issues ahead of presidential visits. His team also supported former presidents and their families.

One story spoke volumes about the character and kindness of President George Bush (41) and his wife, Barbara. I feel compelled to share it. However, if Marty was not allowed to tell me this personal story from his Secret Service days, then I categorically deny he was the source.

Marty was setting up the command post and finishing his shift at the Bush family's Houston residence shortly after they left office. The president was in his den, grumbling about some kind of technical issue and asked for some help. Marty entered the room and offered to assist. President Bush was having trouble operating the remote control for his television. Marty quickly assessed the situation, programmed the remote control, and gave the president a quick lesson on how to use it. There was only one more thing President Bush needed technical support for. He handed Marty his corkscrew and asked him to open a bottle of wine. Mission complete. President Bush could now relax. He thanked Marty, and they both went about their business.

Some time later, Marty realized his rental car was blocking Dorothy's car, the daughter of the President. Marty walked outside to move the vehicle. The sun was getting low; dusk had settled. While walking across the grass, Marty dropped his car keys. He stopped and looked down, and all around but could not see them. Marty went to his knees and began to feel around in the tall grass.

Meanwhile, Dorothy and her mother, Barbara Bush, were on the steps saying their goodbyes to each other, when they both saw Marty. A moment later, Marty heard the First Lady asking him what he was doing. Marty looked up, and with some embarrassment, explained that he had dropped his car keys and could not find them. Barbara Bush giggled and advised her daughter to go and "help that nice boy find his car keys." Marty tried to decline the offer, but Barbara was determined to do the right thing. Dorothy joined Marty in the search through the grass, and both patted around on the ground while Barbara watched.

At this point, Marty felt quite awkward, wished he had a flashlight, and did not want his supervisor to know what was going on. And it could get worse, the president might come outside and join the search. Mrs. Bush and Dorothy were both chatting—as they searched—and asked Marty about his family. Marty was trying to be polite and maintain eye contact while desperately feeling about for the elusive keys. After an extensive search, Marty put his hands on the keys but waited a few moments until the ladies stopped talking, before announcing the find.

Both Bush's were genuinely thankful to know the keys were now secure and proud they had played a significant role in the recovery operation. Marty was thoroughly relieved the embarrassing incident was over, and that he had salvaged his professional reputation among his Secret Service colleagues. But most instructive was the reaction of the Bush family. They treated everyone on their team with kindness and respect. There was a great affection for this First Family within the White House. It was something probably sorely missed after the Bush's left office.

To our surprise, Marty extended an invitation to visit the White House for a Christmas party in December 1991. Alice and I immediately accepted and were very grateful for the opportunity. We had previously been on special White House tours arranged through Alice's father, but this Black-Tie

Christmas event was definitely more exclusive. It was the Christmas season, and Alice and I had been invited to four parties that day. We made a brief appearance at the other three before our visit to the White House. We had no time to change clothes for each party, so we dressed in our formal wear and made the circuit.

When we arrived at the White House, it was a magical experience. There were about a hundred guests, mostly family and friends of the USSS and White House staff. The decorations and food were fabulous. We were able to walk around The People's House freely, sit on the antique furnishings and enjoy appetizers and drinks. We were very cautious to respect everything we touched, but I was a bit surprised that some of the guests smoked cigars and cigarettes inside the historic building.

This was one of several White House Christmas parties held that month, and President Bush (41) did not personally attend. However, it was a highly memorable occasion for a former paperboy and his young bride.

Alice and Kerry at the White House

Marty and Jane at the White House

Naked Brit

The following morning, Alice and I left on vacation for the Sandals resort in Negril, Jamaica. Upon arrival, we learned that this resort was right next door to the infamous Hedonism, a resort that had a reputation for being clothing optional, and it was appropriately named. While on the beach, I took a quick sailing lesson on a small Sunfish. I took the boat out to sea about 100 meters and immediately came back to shore. Too easy. I was now a qualified sailor.

I strolled up to Alice with high confidence and told her I wanted to take her out for a sail. She was an All-American swimmer in college. I was an Army Ranger, but I swam like a rock. She jumped in the little Sunfish, and I sailed it out like an ace. Then I forgot everything I had learned and could not turn the sailboat around. I struggled to turn the uncooperative beast back toward the shore. I tried to move the sail by hand, pushing it against the breeze. As I released it to grab the rudder, the sail swung back and forcefully smacked me in the head. I resorted to swearing and threating the Sunfish, but the boat continued to ignore my orders as we drifted out to sea. After fifteen frustrating minutes, I jumped in the Caribbean and decided to get behind the sailboat and kick board it back to the shore, about 500 meters away. I made little progress. A windsurfer was nearby and noticed we were struggling.

Standing on his board, holding his sail, he glided up to Alice and me with great skill and ease. Alice was in the boat. I was still in the water. This man had a British accent and politely asked if we needed help. It was a nice offer, but he was clearly staying at Hedonism resort. The dude was completely buck-ass naked standing in front of Alice. I needed the help, but there was something blatantly wrong about having a naked man offer to help my wife. I would rather drown.

"No thank you" was our reply. He realized there was some stress in the situation and repeated his offer to help us. I looked and confirmed he was still naked. "No thank you" was our reply again. I would rather drift off into shark-infested waters during a hurricane than suffer the humiliation of being towed back to the resort by a naked Brit. Then he left.

My wife and I could now peacefully drift off to South America. Fortunately, a resort worker in a powerboat came out to give us a tow about fifteen minutes later. No more sailboats for me. I'm a fossil fuel guy.

Pass That Guy

Early in our marriage, Alice and I were traveling to West Chester, Pennsylvania to visit my family. While driving north on I-95 in Delaware, I was in the center lane following a pickup truck. We were doing about 55 mph, which was the speed limit, but it was slower than most of the nearby traffic. Since we were climbing a hill and I could not see over the crest, I did not want to pass. While in the Army, I studied terrain. I realized that a cop could be sitting just over the hill in a perfect ambush position. I intended to pass after cresting the hill. However, this was not soon enough for Alice. She wanted to get to Pennsylvania and demanded I pass the pickup truck immediately. I protested, "This is a bad place to pass. It is a possible speed trap." Alice was fed up with my excuses and demanded, "Pass the guy!" Not wanting to pick a fight, I moved to the left lane, stomped on the gas, and shot past the pickup just as I crested the hill. Within seconds, the police lights and sirens came on, and Kerry was being pulled over.

While stopped on the left shoulder of I-95, the cop walked up and asked me if I knew I was doing 72 mph in a 55-mph zone. I replied, "Yes officer. I was doing exactly 72 mph. Your radar gun is perfectly calibrated.

Don't let anyone give you any crap." I looked over at Alice who was now hiding under the dash board. As the cop took my license and was writing my ticket, two teenage boys rifled past us in a VW at a high rate of speed. They were taunting the cop who had already snared me. Seconds later, the police car was accelerating past me tearing up the grass in the medial strip and then cutting back onto the highway to give chase. The cop was franticly waving his hand, directing me to follow him. He still had my driver's license, so I followed his commands. I was now chasing a cop who was doing over 100 mph chasing two teenagers that disrespected him. After several minutes, I caught up with the police car at a rest stop. He caught the two punks in the VW and was writing them up. I parked about 20 feet in front of the police car and waited for him to finish with the other car. After about ten minutes, the cop came back up to my window and apologized. He said the teenagers buzzed him at 88 mph, and he had to pursue them. The cop handed me back my driver's license and said he had already started to write the ticket, so he had to complete it. He gave me a ticket for doing 60 mph in a 55-mph zone. After I arrived in West Chester, I told my brother about the incident. Kevin was an attorney for the county and said the police officer got me involved in a high-speed chase, and I could have the ticket thrown out. I saw it differently. I was responsible for my own actions. I was guilty of doing 72 mph and only had to pay a ticket for 60 mph. And I also have a good high-speed chase story to tell.

CHAPTER 51

FAMILY STORIES

1992-93

The year 1992 opened with great news. Alice was pregnant and to top it off, I was the father! (Just teasing honey). We were going to have our first child. No one taught us how to be parents, but we had some good role models. And Alice bought all the books on what to expect. This was the year that marked the start of our family together.

Super Bowl Party

A few weeks into the new year, the Washington Redskins, and the Buffalo Bills faced off in the Super Bowl. As an amateur coin collector, I realized that the old Buffalo nickels used in the U.S. between 1913 and 1938 featured an American Indian on the face and a noble buffalo on the tail. Since Americans were passionate about their football teams, I thought I had a get-rich-quick idea that would provide a college fund for our new child. I would acquire a few thousand old buffalo nickels, gold plate them, and market them as lucky, Super Bowl coins:

> *Just $19.95 plus shipping and handling. Act now, and we will throw in a handsome display case. Quantities are limited. Don't miss this once in a lifetime opportunity.*

Of course, I only had two weeks to take the idea to market before the Super Bowl was played, so the idea was never implemented. I had the 1% inspiration and could not deliver the 99% perspiration required to be successful. My get-rich-quick idea soon died.

Instead, Alice and I held a Super Bowl party in our newly finished basement. We had a wet bar, some tiered seating, and about twenty guests at the house, mostly rooting for the Washington Redskins. The beer flowed, and the Skins had a 17-0 halftime lead. There was a lot of excitement in the room. That's when I recalled that Alice, as an employee of AT&T, had free long-distance phone calls as part of her benefits package. It was time to use it. We were going to have some fun at the expense of the suffering fans in Buffalo. I picked up the phone and dialed operator assistance in Buffalo, New York. I asked to be connected with Mr. John Smith. The friendly operator noted there were dozens of them listed, so I asked her to connect me to the first one on the list. A few seconds later, Mrs. John Smith picked up the phone. She was a very sweet lady, but I immediately started to rub some salt in the wound:

> *"Ma'am, are you watching the Super Bowl? The Redskins are killing the Bills. Aren't you embarrassed? I thought Buffalo had a professional football team. Where's your husband?"*

> *"He ran out to the store to get some more beer."*

> *"Believe me; he's going to need a lot of beer before this game is over."*

Then, I handed the phone to some other guests at the party who did some of their own teasing. Throughout the call, Mrs. John Smith remained polite, and she seemed to be enjoying all the unexpected attention. I am sure she would be a wonderful grandmother to some lucky kids.

Spuds and Gizmo

The summer of '92 was quite busy. Alice entered her third trimester of pregnancy, and we were picking out baby names. The new nursery was being painted and furnished, and everything was looking good. In June, we celebrated my mother's 60th birthday with a surprise trip to Ireland. I was gone for ten days, and our two cats, Spuds, and Gizmo kept Alice company.

Spuds and Gizmo were brothers, from the same litter. Gizmo had been born blind in one eye, which explained why he would often come home with that side of his face torn up. He could not protect himself on the blind side. We spent hundreds of dollars at the veterinarians stitching that two-dollar cat back together.

We had a neighbor who lived down the block. Everyone referred to her as "the crazy lady," and she had a wild-eyed stare. She had a garden in her back yard where she put out bird feeders at ground level. She also grew catnip in the same garden, near the bird feeder. To top this off, she put cat food in a bowl on her front porch to feed the feral cats that lived in the neighborhood. One day, she knocked on our door and complained that our one-eyed Gizmo was in her yard chasing "her birds." I walked over to her house to look at the situation. I thought, "Are you kidding me? No cat could resist coming to your house to get fresh cat food, a bird, and a buzz." The real solution was for her to stop feeding cats in her yard, to stop growing catnip, and to raise her bird feeders off the ground several feet. Her complaint about our cat was ridiculous, but I did not want to tell her she was nuts and then have her stalk us. So, I bought her a super soaker water gun. I told her to "hose down" my cat if it came onto her property. She accepted the water gun and disappeared. It was the best $15 I ever spent.

Our cats loved going outside. So, I installed a cat door in the basement. Spuds and Gizmo came and went as they pleased. They were happy cats. To demonstrate their love for me and Alice, they would bring home gifts. It would usually be a mouse that they had shredded into pieces. They ate some of it and left the guts on the stairs to share with us. On several occasions, we stepped in mouse guts in our bare feet when coming down the stairs in the morning. Our nephew, Nathaniel, visited one weekend, and we woke, abruptly, that Saturday morning with him screaming, "Uncle Kerry! Uncle Kerry! I stepped in mouse guts!!" My reply was, "Welcome to the club, Nathaniel." On another afternoon, Gizmo walked in the cat door with a live snake in its mouth while the rest of the snake's body was coiled around the cat's head. That one pegged Alice's fun meter.

While Spuds and Gizmo were coming and going through their basement door, a neighbor's cat had discovered the same entrance. It was a big bushy, wild-looking cat. I think it was possessed. It snuck into our house and ate our cat's food. Our cats were constantly hungry because this evil freeloading cat was scarfing up their chow. I would frequently come home from work and find long cat hairs all over my basement and blood stains on the carpet. One-eyed Gizmo kept getting torn up trying to defend his house. We spent hundreds of more dollars at the animal hospital treating the bite wounds, torn ears, and gashes.

I was taking a nap one afternoon on the basement sofa when I was awakened by the sound of the evil cat coming through the door. It quietly slipped past me and headed into the tool room where the food bowl was. I snuck up behind and trapped it. The Satanic beast climbed the wall and hid in joists between the basement ceiling and the floor above it. It took me three hours and two shredded arms to get the demon from our house. And if it came back, I might need to get an exorcist to drive it back into the underworld. That evil cat continued to haunt us.

Spuds usually slept in our bed. One night, at about 2:00 AM, I was sound asleep when Spuds began hissing and screaming. For a few seconds, I wasn't sure if I was really awake or having a nightmare. I knew something really bad was about to happen.

It did! The devil-cat had infiltrated our house, ate the cat food and then come upstairs and jumped into our bed. A massive cat fight immediately broke out ON MY CHEST! Razor sharp claws came out, and fur and fabric flew everywhere. Alice leaped out of bed, but I was pinned in the middle of World War III. Fortunately, the comforter saved me from being completely mauled. I turned on the lights and immediately chased the wild animal down the stairs and out of the house. My patience had run out. I had lost enough blood, sweat, sleep and money. This was war, and I looked forward to the devil-cat's return so I could get even. Fortunately, miracles do happen—and saved me from that battle. The evil cat disappeared a few weeks later. The owner actually wanted to know if it was living in our house. I should have given her a bill for two years of cat food and medical bills.

On another night, Gizmo woke me while meowing in the bedroom. He had caught a mouse and brought it into the house, but it escaped in our bedroom and was hiding behind the dresser. It was about 2:00 AM (there's something about that hour that bodes no good), and Alice was not happy that a rodent was loose in the bedroom. My new mission was to get out of bed and catch the little guy.

I devised a trap using a paper towel roll. It worked, and now I had to release the mouse outside. It was February, and there was a hard, freezing rain. I was tired and in my underwear. I decided just to open the back door, run bare-footed through the back yard, and release the mouse at the edge of a field about 30 yards away. It would be a fast dash, and no one would see me. Just do it and get back to bed. I turned off the house alarm, opened the back door and ran out on the deck and into the backyard. That's when the two 150-

watt spotlights lit up the entire area when they detected my motion. Great. The neighbors were now awake and could see a near naked wild man in his underwear running outside in the icy rain holding a mouse. I sprinted through puddles of freezing water and mud to the edge of the field and put the mouse next to some brush. I then made a ~~wet willie~~ [NOTE: Alice wanted me to strike that out, so I have] run back to the house with my wet, pasty-white skin glistening in the beams of bright spotlights. I was concerned my Secret Service neighbor, Marty Horowitz, was filming the entire incident on an infrared camera. I made it back to the house. Freezing, shaking and fully awake, I cleaned off my muddy feet, put on some dry underwear, and got back to bed. It took twenty minutes to get my core body temperature back to normal. Finally, I fell back asleep at 2:40 AM.

A few moments later, I was awakened again by the same "meow." I thought, "Could this be happening again?" Yes, it could. The fricking cat had followed me outside and recaptured the mouse. And the mouse escaped again, and it was hiding behind the same dresser. My choices were to kill the cat or catch the mouse. Alice was barking orders, so my mission was to set up the same mouse trap. This time, I put the rodent in a shoe box. I went downstairs, turned off the alarm and made another nature-boy run into the back yard. The motion sensor lights popped on and tracked me as I streaked in my skivvies across the back yard, through the subzero rain and puddles of water, down a trail and much deeper into the woods. All the while, I was swearing unspeakable things. I looked around to see if Gizmo was tailing me and then hid the mouse near some downed trees. I ran back to the house shivering, convinced that by now some neighbor had called the police about a "pervert," and I would soon be in handcuffs. I took a hot shower to clean up and fight the pending hypothermia. I locked the cat door and dove back under the covers. I was sure Marty and Jane were going to ask me about the incident the next morning, but they never said a word.

Hurricane Kent Kachejian

The big event of 1992 was the birth of our first child, Kent Charles Kachejian, in September. Unfortunately, a month before Kent's arrival, my last grandparent, Janet Kift Browne died. I had hoped to get a family photo with four generations in it, but it was not meant to be.

After thirty-six hours of labor, some of it at home, Alice had a C-section at Alexandria Hospital, and our new son arrived! At first, Kent looked a bit like a plucked chicken. But after a few minutes, he got some more color, and the nurses wrapped him in a blanket. Watching Kent's birth was an exhilarating feeling. He weighed in at seven pounds, eight and one-half ounces of twisted steel and sex appeal.

To add to the "wow factor," the doctor took the opportunity to lift Alice's skin around the incision to look at all her internal organs. I had a front row seat to see all her "innards" while the doctor inspected them. He visually confirmed that she only had one kidney. ~~The view of all her organs was clear proof that Alice was human and not a Stepford Wife.~~ [NOTE: Alice wanted me to strike that out, so I have] While lying on her back with an epidural, Alice was unaware the doctor was doing this inspection. A few days later, I told Alice what happened. I said, "Honey, you have guts. I've seen them first-hand. Don't let anyone ever tell you different."

Kent had gone into the nursery while Alice was resting. After a few hours, the nurses came into the hospital room and said Kent was having trouble breathing. He had been immediately moved to the Pediatric Intensive Care Unit (PICU). We knew he had sounded a little noisy while breathing, but this development was alarming. He spent several weeks in PICU. Alice and I had many sleepless nights praying that Kent would pull through. Gina and my mother traveled from Pennsylvania to support us. Many friends and family offered to help. We needed prayers, and they worked. Alice and I were both thrilled, though a little scared, to take him home with us.

Our first night home resulted in a trip back to the hospital emergency room. In fact, during his first year, Kent was in the hospital five or six times. A few months later, he was rushed from the doctor's office to the emergency room via ambulance due to respiratory distress. We went home from the hospital with a machine that monitored Kent while he slept. The machine let out an ear-piercing scream if he stopped breathing. The noise level approached that of a jet engine. To shut it off required us to

Uncle Kevin with Kent at his Christening

enter a code into the control panel. The machine would constantly have false alarms, particularly if a sensor fell off Kent's body or if he was pooping. We were woken several times each night and would race into his bedroom with flashlights to see if he was still breathing. Alice and I were constantly sleep-deprived, and we looked like zombies in the mornings.

In February 1993, Kent was admitted to the PICU at Fairfax Hospital with three other infants who had viral pneumonia. All four were critically ill. I would watch the vital signs of all four babies at the nurse's station. I wanted to know how Kent was doing compared to the other three. We were deeply saddened when we learned that the other three children died a few days apart.

Alice and I balanced work with hospital visits and covered different shifts to be with Kent. Alice had been recently promoted at AT&T to a Sales Manager by Jack Harvey. We were lucky she had many wonderful co-workers who offered to cover for her. We are grateful to AT&T for having excellent medical benefits that covered much of the expense.

Kent's situation became so critical one morning, the hospital staff urged Alice to call our Reverend Bob Trache, at Immanuel-Church-on-the-Hill. We did not have cell phones or pagers, and I came out of a long meeting at work to find I had twenty-seven messages on my desk phone. I finally picked up Alice's frantic messages hours after she left them. I dropped the line and raced to the hospital. I arrived as Dr. Keller performed an emergency surgery on Kent to insert a chest tube.

For several days, it was a life and death struggle. The nurses kept drawing blood from Kent to test it. Sometimes it was hourly. I was concerned that Kent could not replace his blood as fast as it was being drawn. He looked pale and anemic, and I talked to his nurse about it. She paused, and you could see the lightbulb go off in her head. I told her I had donated blood for him, and he probably needed some new blood added to his system. She listened. Thirty minutes later, she came in with some of my donated blood and infused it into Kent. His color immediately improved. What a powerful feeling to know my blood had helped my son. I could finally do something to physically help him.

Kent turned the corner and came home in March. At this point, I nicknamed our son "Hurricane Kent" because he rocked us like a Category 5 storm. He continued to have visits to the hospital, but as he grew, his respiratory problems improved. However, in August we were told he needed heart surgery. It was not a complicated surgery, but any operation on our son's heart was a big deal to us. Alice and I were able to go into the surgical prep room with Kent. When no one was looking, I pulled a Ranger tab out of my wallet that I had carried for over ten years. I put it in Kent's sock. It was my way of telling him I loved him and to hang tough. Alice and I gave him a kiss and let the nurses take him. Alice and I waited anxiously for about two hours. The surgeon came out to update us on Kent. He told me he was a former Army doctor and had found the Ranger tab in Kent's sock. He gave me back the tab, and I put it in my wallet. More importantly, he gave us back our son. When we went in to see Kent, he was standing up in the hospital crib, trying to escape. He looked great and appeared to have no idea he had just had heart surgery. Two weeks later we had about sixty people at our house for Kent's first birthday. The kid was a rock star and got all kinds of cool gifts. Fairfax Hospital loved the Kachejian family, since Alice's medical insurance had probably paid for a new wing at the facility. [Twenty years later, I pulled the Ranger tab out of my wallet again at my Army retirement ceremony. I told Kent I had carried it with me for the past thirty years, and that I had put it in his sock for his heart surgery as an infant. I wanted him to have it to remember the tough days we had together and the deep love I had for him. I also told him not to sell it on eBay.]

Mama and Papa Perez

During Kent's first year, we met Mr. and Mrs. Perez. Gladis and Agustin Perez were born and raised in Cuba. When they applied to immigrate to the United States as a young couple, Agustin was punished by the Castro regime. He had been forced to quit his professional accounting career and sent to work in the sugar cane fields for two years, far from his hometown. Their hard life together became much harder. Eventually, they were allowed to leave Cuba with only what they could carry. But they rebuilt their lives in the United States and raised two daughters, Gladys and Magalys. When Alice went back to work after maternity leave, Mr. and Mrs. Perez became Kent's surrogate grandparents. Kent knew them as "Mama" and "Papa" Perez. They took incredibly good care of Kent during his early years. Mama would hand make his food, bathe him, wash his clothes and taught him good manners and how to behave. Kent even learned Spanish. They loved him like he was their own grandchild. We were blessed to have Mama and Papa there to support us during the first few years of Kent's life. Alice always said, "God gave us a sick baby, but He also gave us Mr. and Mrs. Perez." We can never repay them for their love, kindness, and compassion. Alice, Kent and I were so proud to join Mrs. Perez at the ceremony when she became a U.S. citizen in May of 1993.

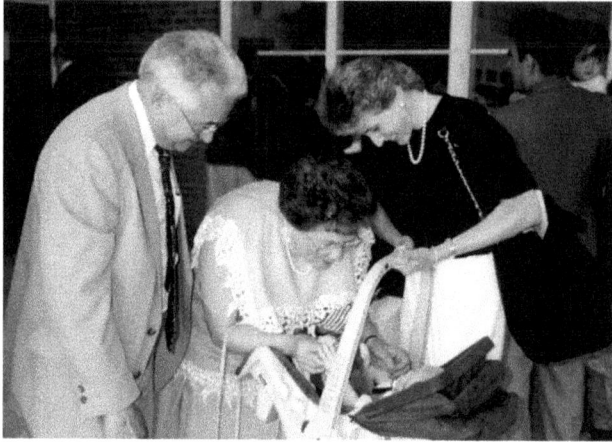

Papa and Mama Perez with Kent

Air Jamaica Mistaka

In May of 1993, Alice and I were able to get away with Sandy and Dave Bost for a week to the Ciboney Resort in Jamaica. It was a much-needed time to decompress from the stress of work and hospitals. We felt comfortable with Mama and Papa watching Kent during the week. Kent's doctors all knew the Perez's personally and were as fond of them as we were. On the trip, we enjoyed visiting Dunn's River Falls, our quiet meals, and playing a few rounds of golf. Things were perfect until the day of our departure.

The return home was full of delays, and it obliterated the stress-relief and relaxation we had gained at Ciboney. It started with the long bus ride to the airport, avoiding chickens and goats on the road. Then we dodged shady characters at the airport who wanted to sell us drugs or other contraband. When finally airborne on Air Jamaica, we hit severe storms that caused traffic problems along the east coast of the United States. With lightning crackling all around us and violent turbulence, the pilots were directed to divert and land at Cincinnati Airport in Ohio. Thankful we had finally landed somewhere; we were told we had to wait until the storms passed. There were no U.S. Customs officials at the airport to allow people off the airplane, and we sat on the taxiway for about five hours. It quickly became hot and stuffy. There was no food service, and the bathrooms were now HAZMAT zones. Lightning still struck near the grounds of the airport, and the jet could not be refueled. We had planned to pick up Kent at about 4:00 PM and were now several hours late, but we could not make a phone call to tell Mama and Papa that we were stranded. We finally received permission to take off but waited as dozens of other aircraft were ahead of us. A small cheer let out when we became airborne. Our destination was BWI Airport outside of Baltimore. About thirty minutes into the flight, the pilot announced they were having a mechanical problem and needed to divert the aircraft to Philadelphia. That announcement sounded fishy. BWI was much closer to our flight path than Philadelphia. I was confused. Why would we fly further if we had a mechanical problem? We finally landed in Philadelphia at around midnight. Once U.S. Customs Officials were called back in on duty, we were allowed to get off the plane. We collected our bags and cleared immigration and customs. Everyone on the flight raced to the pay phones to make collect calls to their families. We immediately called Mama to tell her the situation and apologized that we could not reach her sooner. She was worried about us, but Kent was fine and sleeping. Next, we raided every vending machine in the airport to get something to eat. Air Jamaica personnel told us they were ordering buses to drive us from Philadelphia to Baltimore, so we waited another hour. The bus ride took about two hours, and we were dropped at the BWI arrival terminal at about 4:00 AM. The shuttle buses to satellite parking weren't there, but after about an hour, we finally caught one and dragged our bags to the car.

Dog-tired, we got in our car and faced the two-hour ride to get home. We drove up to the parking attendant's booth to pay. The man asked us if we had flown on Air Jamaica. We told him, "Yes." He laughed and said that Air Jamaica did not have a mechanical problem. They lied to their passengers. The airline failed to pay their landing fees at BWI, and the aircraft had been refused landing rights. We were fuming mad. The attendant also noted there were two dozen travel agents on the same flight, who would be scorching Air Jamaica in their travel reviews. American Airlines would be getting their business in the future. A few days later, I wrote Air Jamaica a letter expecting an apology and some compensation. They eventually replied with a bogus excuse and took no responsibility for their part of the delay. Needless to say, Alice and I swore to never fly with them again—and we never have.

Family Gatherings

In October of 1993, four generations on Alice's side of the family got together for lunch in Hagerstown, Maryland. We took some pictures that included Pop and Lula Bush, Betty and Jim Bush, Sis, and Simon Snyder, Bobbi and Willie Yost, and Alice, me and Kent Kachejian. We were glad to get so many of the family together.

Four generations breaking bread in Hagerstown

We spent Thanksgiving in 1993 with my family in Pennsylvania. There were a lot of mouths to feed, and I wondered what food mom might prepare.

At about ten o'clock Thanksgiving morning, I thought I had heard a pig snorting outside our front door. We didn't live on a farm, so I ignored it. Then I heard the snorting again. I opened the front door and standing in front of me was a live pig. This had to be a joke played by my brother-in-law, Peter. Or was it an anonymous gift we needed to roast for the Thanksgiving meal? The animal seemed relatively tame. It took about an hour before we learned it was a pet potbellied pig that had escaped from a neighbor's house. The pig lived another day, and the Kachejian's ate turkey for dinner.

Thanksgiving 1993

In December of 1993, we celebrated Betty and Jim Bush's 50th wedding anniversary at the Fort McNair Officer's Club. It was a quiet family affair, except for Hurricane Kent, who proudly showed off his healthy lungs.

New House

In the early 1990s, the new Fairfax County Parkway was under construction in our region and, when completed, made remote areas of the county more accessible. New housing developments popped up along the new road. This mattered when I had asked Alice what she wanted to do for Mother's Day in 1993.

"I want to go look at model homes," she replied holding a copy of the New Homes Guide. She had good instincts, but I knew a car ride to the new development came with a high risk that we would be looking at getting a new home. I was reluctant to go having often moved while in the Army. The house we lived in was only a few years old, and I wasn't ready to move again.

Sure enough, we soon walked through some attractive model homes that backed up to parkland. We discussed finding the right floor plan. Alice made a smart decision to pick such a nice location in a quiet neighborhood

529

with great schools. We agreed we would stay in this new house for a long time and raise our family there. We planned to pack up our belongings and say goodbye to our Alexandria neighbors for our future move about six miles west.

The builder had some problems with site permits during the construction process, and that worked to our benefit. We wanted a large breakfast nook on the back of the house. The nook was designed to have a deck on the roof above it, and a tool room in the basement below it. Due to a pre-existing easement, the builder could not build the full-sized room. When the builder told us, the room needed to be smaller, we told them it would be acceptable only if the optional breakfast nook and deck were "no charge." The builder agreed and immediately reduced our purchase price by $25,000. Furthermore, delivery of the house was delayed several months, and during this period, home mortgage rates dropped significantly. That made the deal even better.

The builder kept making mistakes, and every time, we negotiated a solution to our benefit. Because the easement in the backyard required the house to be moved forward on the lot, we now had a smaller front yard. That was acceptable, but the house elevation was not changed. Consequently, our short driveway was very steep. When Alice's Honda Accord could not get in the garage due to the front end scraping the driveway, we told the builder we would not close on the house.

The president of the construction company got personally involved and called me. I said the problem was serious. The only way we would settle was if they jackhammered out the garage floor and driveway and lowered both by two feet. He balked and initially said they would not do it. He did agree to go to the lot and see the problem. An hour later, he called and told me he had inspected the property, and they would immediately jackhammer out the garage floor and drop it two feet. I was glad to hear this news. However, that meant our new garage required special doors two feet higher than standard. The change in the driveway and garage also required them to re-landscape the front yard, put in a retaining wall and build two sets of stairs. The total repair cost the builder significantly more time and money.

There was another serious problem with the finished basement. Before signing the contract, I had asked the sales office if I could modify its standard floor plan. They wanted to close the deal, so they eagerly agreed. Over a weekend, Alice and I redesigned the basement, moved the bathroom and wet bar, widened all doorways for storage areas, added some electrical outlets and recessed lights, and converted four hundred square feet into additional finished space.

This was a better design for us, but the change from their standard layout would cost significantly more money. I was pleased when the sales office simply agreed to my new plan and filed the drawings. Unfortunately, the construction crew never looked at the changes to the contract or the new design. They simply built the standard floor plan. After we had inspected the finished basement, we told the builder, who looked surprised, there was a serious error. They had to tear out much of the finished basement and jackhammer out part of the floor to re-run the bathroom plumbing. We had to remind them to, "install all the additional electrical outlets and recessed lights. And don't forget to widen the doors. Per the revised plan." When it was finally completed the second time, the basement looked good and added value to our home.

We moved in during a severe winter storm in January 1994. The special-order garage doors had not yet arrived. Frigid air filled the open garage, and it froze the water pipes that ran throughout the ceiling. The pipes burst, and water ran into the ceiling, causing the drywall to collapse in some areas. The repair crew immediately shut off the water supply and desperately poked holes in the garage and laundry room ceilings to allow the trapped water to drain to the floor. When Alice came home from her job to find a worker poking holes in the ceiling with a broom handle, she asked what he was doing. He replied, "Shut up lady. I am trying to save your house!" Both of our cars were parked in the garage, and water poured all over them. The water immediately froze on the cars and the floor. As water continued to fall, a thick sheet of ice formed on the cars and floor. Drywall and insulation also fell and froze on the vehicles. Icicles formed inside the garage.

The freezing temperatures persisted for several days, and we were without fresh water and access to our cars. I dug up new snow in the yard, brought it inside the house, melted it, and used it to flush toilets. Fortunately, we still had heat. We were also grateful that Mr. and Mrs. Perez offered to take care of Kent until our new home was livable. At this point, we were not happy with the builder.

Only a few days into the new home warranty, we questioned whether this house had been a terrible mistake. But to their credit, the builder began the repairs once the temperature rose above freezing.

A few years after we moved in, the builder approached us about the dead-end road adjacent to our property. Fairfax County had conducted a study and identified several hundred dead-end roads that would never be built through. The county did not want to maintain these stub roads. Any builder still under a construction bond was required to convert the street to turf and divide the new land with the adjacent property owners.

Basically, the builder told us they wanted to give us "free land." They just wanted us to sign an agreement. We balked. We liked the dead-end road. It was convenient to park a car there and offload groceries. We had already built a walkway that led from the dead-end to our new deck. Our son rode his tricycle safely in that area. If we took the deal, Kent would lose his play area. And if the builder tore it up, we would need to replace it with a separate driveway to maintain a side parking area and connect it to the existing walkway. That would cost us a lot of money. We told the builder. "Free land was not enough. We also wanted $10,000 to build the new driveway." The look on the builder's face was priceless. But he could not argue with the impact. The builder noted that our neighbor needed to get the same deal, so we had to split the free land and the money. We all agreed, and we took the new land and further improved it.

The county also benefited as they raised our property taxes and avoided the cost of maintaining a dead-end road. Everybody won on this deal, except the builder who lost another battle to Team Kachejian. Reflecting back, I believe the construction issues we faced related to our new house should be used in a case study by the Harvard Business School.

1994

Alice and I escaped all the chaos in January and took a few days off to see friends in San Francisco, visit Monterey and ski at Lake Tahoe, Nevada. We had planned to spend a few days in California, but after reaching Lake Tahoe had to abruptly fly home early. Kent was having breathing problems. All the return flights were overbooked, but we pleaded our way into some standby seats. We finally arrived at Mrs. Perez's house, picked up Kent and headed to the hospital. Fortunately, his condition was not too serious this time.

During the rest of 1994, Kent was healthy enough to travel. We made some family trips to see my side of the family in West Chester, Pennsylvania. Kent also enjoyed visiting the National Zoo. In June, we took a family vacation to Ocean City, Maryland. Kent was able to see the beach for the first time and play with his dinosaurs in the sand. In September, we spent a week with Sandy and Dave Bost who lived on Lake Arrowhead in Georgia. Kent got to play with their young daughter, Erin.

I stopped in Dallas while on a business trip in February. With my few hours of free time, I visited the Texas School Book Depository and stood at the sixth-floor window where Lee Harvey Oswald had fired the fatal shots that killed President Kennedy. I was only three years old when he was assassinated but had heard and read so much about the murder and the related conspiracy theories. Being at the scene really put the assassination in perspective. I was surprised to realize that Oswald had a relatively easy shot at a slow-moving target. I had fired enough rounds during my military training to know that this window was a good position to take the shot. I also walked to the "grassy knoll" at Dealey Plaza. I tried to envision what had happened there on November 22, 1963.

A few weeks later, I enjoyed a trip, with Alice's father, to the Smithsonian's aircraft renovation facility. Jim Bush had been a B-29 crewman during WWII, and the Enola Gay, the plane that dropped the atomic bomb on Hiroshima, was being renovated. The aircraft and its crew helped to end WWII and changed the nature of warfare forever.

1995

We had another fun year in 1995. In the spring, Alice and I boarded Norwegian Cruise lines to see a good part of the Caribbean. We stopped in San Juan, the Virgin Islands, St. Kitts, Barbados, St Lucia and St. Barts.

In the summer, our family was invited to go on vacation to Duck, North Carolina with the Peck, Bambery and Jahn families. Together, we rented a big beach house and enjoyed life in the Outer Banks. We toured the famous Corolla Light House and the monument where the Wright Brothers made their first flight.

On the way home, we stopped in Colonial Williamsburg. My Army friend, Ed Boyajian, brought his children, Mathew and Nicole, and came to visit us later that summer. We took the kids on a tour of Luray Caverns. In the early fall, Jim and Betty Bush rented a house at Cape Hatteras to get the family together. Alice's sister, Debbie Bauman, drove from South Florida with her husband, Arnie, to join us. Unfortunately, we had to leave Hatteras early, as Kent had some breathing problems.

On October 16th, Kevin came to Washington, D.C. to visit the U.S. Supreme Court with some of his law colleagues from Pennsylvania. Unfortunately, they had picked a bad day to visit. The Million Man March was in town, and the Metro system was overloaded with hundreds of thousands of visitors. It was tough getting a wheelchair onto the trains, but it eventually worked out. Kevin was able to meet some of the Supreme Court Justices and learn more about our nation's highest court.

Kevin (left front) at the Supreme Court

Kevin with Ghostbuster vehicle

A month later, while changing jobs, I had a week off, so I took Mom and Kevin to Orlando. We rented a wheelchair van to transport Kevin and had a special handicapped hotel room. Everyone we met at Disney World, Universal Studios and Sea World went out of their way to make us feel welcome.

1996

We started spending a lot of time at Chuck E. Cheese in 1996. It seemed like every child Kent's age had their birthday party there. I should have bought stock in the company. There was plenty of pizza, entertainment, and prizes for the kids, while parents could also relax and get a beer. Kent also enjoyed family outings to Burke Lake Park, where he could feed the geese and ride the train and carousel. We also rented a boat and went out fishing.

Alice and I were expecting our second child in July and wanted to see Nappa Valley and Yosemite Park in California before she was too pregnant to travel. In April, we took a romantic trip to California wine country and toured the Redwood Forest and Yosemite National Park. It was a great get away, and many thanks again to Mama and Papa Perez for again watching Kent and allowing us some cherished and needed personal time together.

The big event of the year was the birth of our first daughter, Kara Elizabeth Kachejian on July 9th. Everything was fine, but we had a big surprise in the Fairfax Hospital delivery room. The head nurse on duty was Rene Zelkin. Decades earlier, her name was Rene Wright back when she was my neighbor. We had grown up together in West Chester. As a youth, I had delivered the newspaper to her house every day. The Kachejian's and the Wright's were very close, and they had helped us in many ways after Kevin broke his neck. I even had a job working for her father, the store manager at Shop-Rite. Rene saw the name Kachejian on the list of scheduled deliveries and knew it had to be the same family. Rene scheduled

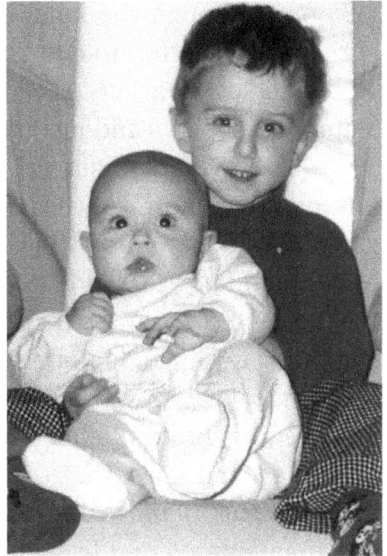

Kent shows off his new sister, Kara

the "A Team" to be on duty for the delivery of Kara. We felt relieved to have Rene supporting us that day. The delivery went well, and soon, Kent was showing off his new sister. Three years later, Rene would also help to deliver our third child, Kathryn Ann, at the same hospital. And Rene's daughter Annina would eventually play field hockey with our daughters in the same high school and travel leagues. I also learned that Rene was a highly-accomplished field hockey referee, and she was selected to referee at the 2016 Olympic Games in Rio de Janeiro, Brazil.

1997-1999

Now that we had young children, our family started taking annual vacations in the Orlando area. On our first trip, we were at the Magic Kingdom, and Kent had a Mickey Mouse balloon. He demanded that we untie it from the stroller so he could hold it in his hand. We told Kent he would lose it. He insisted—as only kids that age can—so we relented. We let Kent know, if he lost his, we would not buy another one. A minute later, when he lost his grip on the balloon, it flew away. He became hysterical and completely inconsolable. He made such a scene, Alice and I thought we'd be arrested for child abuse. Sorry, but Disney was not getting another five bucks for a rodent balloon. Although the kids enjoyed all the Orlando theme parks, we were surprised when they told us the best part of their vacation was the hotel pool. Had we known earlier, Alice and I could have saved hundreds of dollars by skipping the parks and just hanging out at the pool.

One year, we started the trip by visiting our friends, the Willover family. Mike and Lisa were hosting, and Kent chased their daughter, Leah, around the pool. I was sitting in a lounge chair reading a magazine. They were each about five years old and having a lot of fun, but I told Kent very clearly to stop running near the pool. I reminded him that he could not swim, and he was going to slip and fall in the pool. Kent stopped for a minute, but then the two started playing tag again. Sure enough, he came ripping back toward the pool and his brakes failed. He went straight into the pool, to the bottom. I looked up and knew that the next ten seconds were a teachable moment. I carefully put my magazine down and took off my watch, removed my wallet, and then jumped in. I brought Kent to the surface and sat him on the side of the pool. "Son, I told you to stop running by the pool. If an adult had not been sitting here, you would have drowned. You'd be dead right now. You need to listen to your parents. Got it?" Kent acknowledged the message, loud and clear. I then gave him a new nickname, The Anchor Man. He swam just like his dad.

Later, we rented a house at an Orlando resort with Margy and Rick Jahn. The house had a pool, so Rick and I showed all the kids how to do the "Double Dad Dive." Rick and I made up aerial maneuvers as we both leaped into the pool. Soon enough, Tori, Brianna, David, Kent and Kara created their own signature dives. Daniel couldn't walk yet, so he watched from his stroller. Alice was pregnant with Katie, who was already practicing backflips inside mom. Then we turned on the stereo and blasted some Jamaican music. We put on our favorite song, *Ragga Ragga,* and led half a dozen kids on a high-energy line dance through the house and over the furniture. It was a frenzied version of the Pied Piper. The kids thought their parents were the genuine rock stars that we always wanted to be. Amazingly, we still got our full cash deposit back when we checked out of the resort.

Breakfast with Mickey Mouse—Kara, Kent, Stacey and Cameron

Several of the Disney trips included our extended family. Alice's sister, Debbie Bauman, lived near Fort Lauderdale with her husband, Arnie. And Alice's niece, Stacy Patasnik and her children, Cameron and Kristoffer, were also South Florida residents. On one trip, the ladies reserved seats so we could attend a Character Breakfast where the children would be able to meet Mickey and Minnie Mouse. Things were going well, and the kids were having fun. Several Disney characters came to our table. Then, Alice held Kara up to meet Minnie Mouse face to face and give her a hug. Apparently, Kara was still hungry and started sucking on Minnie's nose. That's my girl! There was baby saliva dripping from Minnie's nose. After a quick wiping, it had a good spit shine, and we had a good laugh.

Road Trips

In between the annual Orlando trips, we would pack up the SUV and go exploring. The kids always loved the nearby theme parks like Kings Dominion and Busch Gardens or touring Colonial Williamsburg, Yorktown, and Jamestown. And we would visit all the relatives. Sis and Simon Snyder in Hagerstown.Willie and Bobbie Yost in Newport News. Or ride to Pennsylvania to see the Armenians: Grandma Kachejian, Kevin, Gina, Shelley, Rebecca, Peter, Nate, Haig Geovjian, John, Beth, Patty, Nancy and Audrey Klijian, and Chuck Puchakjian. There were a dozen more Armenian relatives spread throughout the country.

Armenian reunion at Patty Geovjian's wedding (Sep 1998)

538

Regardless of where we were going, when we cruised down the road, we'd be rocking out to Jimmy Buffett. The kids loved holding their hands up over their heads while making a shark fin and singing the lyrics, "You got fins to the left, fins to the right, and you're the only bait in town." After playing "Cheeseburger in Paradise, Volcano," and a few more Jimmy Buffet songs, the kids wanted to settle down and watch a movie. Of course, no two children could ever agree on the same one. To prevent a civil war from breaking out, every child in the car had to have their own portable DVD player. It was a price willingly paid to keep the peace.

Sometimes, Alice and I snuck off for a weekend to be with good friends and refresh our relationship. One of those trips was to a class reunion at West Point in October 1997. We had a great time tailgating with Blake and Mary Peck as well as Rick and Margy Jahn. They were always a fun crowd to hang out with.

USMA Tailgate with the Peck's and Jahn's

Great Exuma

Alice's parents, Jim and Betty Bush, used to plan their own get-away vacations. Back in the early 1960s, they had really enjoyed an island in the Bahamas called Great Exuma. Jim and Betty had stayed at the Hotel Peace and Plenty in George Town. They were so attracted to the island, Jim bought three undeveloped Exuma properties. They owned the land for over thirty years. Jim noted that he would probably never build on them and was willing to part with the land. I offered to fly to the island and spend a few days there to assess the real estate situation and the island's growth potential. Jim agreed. In November of 1998, I stayed in the charming Hotel Peace and Plenty and took a ferry over to the deserted beaches of Stocking Island. The water and the beaches were spectacular. During a hike, I found a lot of shells and surprisingly, the remains of a crashed airplane. I further explored the full island of Exuma and found the three family properties. While at the Hotel Peace and Plenty, I had asked about rumors that Jimmy Buffet and Prince Albert of Monaco were past Exuma visitors. The answers I received were a bit evasive as to protect the identity of their guests. The cozy bar at the Peace and Plenty held some secrets. There were some interesting development projects ongoing, so the island had potential. After the trip, Alice and I assumed ownership of the properties and have held them now for over fifteen years. The family dream to build something on Exuma has continued for over fifty years.

Kathryn Ann Kachejian

Alice and I had one more special delivery. Kathryn "Katie" Ann Kachejian was born at Fairfax Hospital in August of 1999. Once again, my childhood friend, Rene Wright Zelkin, was in the delivery room to make sure all the nurses were ready. When Katie first emerged, I knew we were in trouble. She was born holding cars keys and a credit card. Outside of that, everything went smoothly. And Katie was named after a famous relative on Alice's side of the family, the actress Katharine Houghton Hepburn. We never met the actress, but she was part of the family lineage. As Katie grew up, she developed the same fierce independent spirit that Katharine Hepburn was known for.

The Millennium / 2000—2002

As 2000 approached, there was widespread fear that many of the world's computer systems would seize up. It was known as the Y2K problem or the millennium bug. Much of the computer code in use at that time had been designed in the 1980s and 1990s, and only used a two-digit year. When the year 2000 arrived, computers would not be able to distinguish 2000 from 1900. Many financial records could be affected, but there were also widespread and unfounded fears that entire banking systems would collapse and airplanes would fall out of the sky. There was even speculation that many of the world's ATM machines would malfunction, so there was some hoarding of cash. Software programmers, who created the crisis, were now paid a lot of money in 1998 and 1999 to fix the looming problem. Many of their salaries immediately doubled. However, on 1 January 2000, the crisis passed without incident, and they all looked for new jobs.

The Kachejian clan decided to avoid all the crowds and the hysteria, so we celebrated the millennium in October, a few months early. We joined Michelle and Todd Drake as well as DeAnn and Mike Boehm for a scenic Potomac River Cruise dinner on the Odyssey. We brought some noise makers and party horns onboard. At first, the other dinner guests and the staff weren't sure what was going on with our group, but they quickly figured it out.

Our table selected a random time to start counting down the last ten seconds of 1999, and then started with the noise makers and smooching. We gave some "Happy New Year" high fives to the staff and guests. We declared the Y2K crisis as over and popped a bottle of champagne.

At the end of December of 1999, our family drove to Lake Arrowhead, Georgia and celebrated the millennium again at Sandy and Dave Bost's house. If the world's economy was going to collapse, there were plenty of fish in the lake to catch, and we had stocked up on beer. And of course, we had topped off with an impressive arsenal of fireworks.

Cub Scouts

In late January of 2000, Kent became an official member of the Tiger Den of Cub Scout Pack 435. It was time for the famous Pinewood Derby, the Cub Scouts' annual racing event. Kent and I had to make our model car from a kit that contained a block of wood, four plastic wheels, and four nails that served as metal axles. There were some length and weight restrictions on the model car, and the wheels would need to fit on a narrow race track.

Kent and I worked together on the design and whittled down the block of wood to get the basic car shape. The key to having a fast car was for it to have as little friction as possible in the axels and wheels. We sanded the nails and lubricated them with graphite. During initial test runs, our car's speed was good, but not great. There were many other experienced Cub Scout's involved in the event, and I knew they would be better at making a fast car. It was evident our car would not win the speed contest. I asked Kent if we could make a cool car rather than a fast car. He agreed.

Together, we made an awesome car. We painted it Army green and mounted a big missile on its roof. We inserted a small soldier in the back of the car, who faced the rear and had a machine gun. He was our tail gunner. We dressed it up with some stickers and went into the next Scout meeting to face our competition.

When Kent showed up at the race with his heavily weaponized car, he commanded instant respect. We lined up on the six-lane track against the other high-speed, low-drag competitors. The cars were released from the top of the steep track and accelerated down toward the finish line. We ended up dead last in our heat but turned some heads. When it came time to recognize the winners, trophies and ribbons were passed out to the fastest cars. Then Kent was called up. He won an award in an entirely new category: Most Lethal Car.

The Big 4-0 (2000)

A few months later, I was turning 40. My long-time friend, Mike Willover and I had been born only a few days apart, so we decided to go skiing in Colorado. My roommate from Germany, "Rocket Ron" Claeys, lived in Colorado and was also turning 40. I exchanged my Florida timeshare property for one in Avon, Colorado, and we hit the slopes at Copper Mountain and other resorts. It reminded us of our ski trip to Austria many years earlier.

Little League Baseball

Kent played baseball with the Central Springfield Little League (CSLL) for several years. He was our favorite player and each year picked up more skill. In 1998, he played for The Knights. In 1999 and 2000, he moved to the Aqua Sox and the Mobile Bay Bears. On both of these teams, one of Kent's teammates was Bobby Wahl, who was later drafted by the Oakland As.

In 2001, my company, Raytheon, sponsored Kent's team, the Snappers, who finished the season with a record of 17-1. The team players were young, so they used a machine to pitch the ball. He wrapped up his career with the CSLL Cubs in 2002 and the LookOuts in 2003.

The year Kent played for the Snappers I was also the teams "very unofficial" journalist and reporter. My best articles follow, and I continue to hold out hope for a Pulitzer... or maybe an ESPY (Hollywood having let me down all these years):

Raytheon Snappers Lead Central Springfield Little League

Look out Baltimore Orioles, the Raytheon Snappers are coming through. The Snappers (9-0) defeated the previously undefeated Bay Bears (8-1) in a come-from-behind thriller by a score of 14-11. This recent victory moved them into sole possession of first place among twelve teams in the Central Springfield Little League (CSLL).

The game scorekeeper, an undisclosed Raytheon employee, had a corporate auditor over his shoulder the entire game. He had this to say afterward. "The numbers add up. We won in a 'best and final' inning."

The Snappers are composed of twelve local players, ages 7-8, that play in the "A" league. When asked what was the key to the Snapper success, 2nd baseman Corey Gigliotti cited the team's star pitcher. "He's like a machine. Throws them right down the middle, a high fastball every time. We haven't walked a batter all year."

The team batting average is an incredible .690, dominating the league. One player, "Hurricane" Kent Kachejian is batting 1.000 after 25 trips to the plate. (Further investigation revealed that Kent's father is also the team statistician.) The players are a bit young to be recruited by the Major League, but the Raytheon HR department is reviewing their resumes for potential software engineers. The Snapper shortstop, Michael Nebrich, is an all-around athlete. He can hit, field, throw and program in C++. That kid is going places.

Donovan and Geoffrey Lawhorn are the team's identical twins, and they are the heart and soul of the Snapper team. Both are batting around.900 and dominate the infield. According to the coach "We can't tell which one is a better batter because our team statistician can't tell them apart."

One of the team's best power hitters is Luke "The Nuke" Bondurant. According to one of the local young ladies, Luke is "48 lbs. of twisted steel and sex appeal." Most of the other players compare him to Mark McGuire. Luke actually exceeds McGuire's batting when you compare them using a metric such as "hit distance/body mass," and he's a better value when compared using a "total bases/total salary" metric.

Kenny Lawhorn, the team manager, stated "These kids are good. Not only can they hit the ball, but they know which way to run. We don't have to point toward first base after they hit the ball and yell "That way! That way!" In a few years, some of these kids will be the emerging leaders of our defense industry."

The Snapper Star pitcher. "He's like a machine."

Raytheon Snappers Win It All!
Central Springfield Little League Champions

The Raytheon Snappers finished the regular season with an incredible 17-1 record, dominating the twelve team Central Springfield Little League (CSLL) "machine pitch" baseball league. The rival ISI Bay Bears also finished 17-1 but lost to the Snappers in a regular season showdown, giving the Snappers sole claim to the 1st place crown.

Coach Frank Gigliotti noted, "During the second half of the season, many of our unsung heroes really stepped up to the plate. Aaron Puller (a.k.a. "The Gladiator") started crushing the ball. Opposing shortstops started wearing Kevlar body armor to protect themselves from hypersonic line drives. One first baseman began to sandbag his position and would dive for cover every time someone yelled "incoming." I just have to know what Aaron's dad feeds him."

Coach Mark Nebrich noted, "The second half of the season was a lot tougher. Our opponents had improved markedly. We needed some solid play from the Snapper lineup to stay ahead. The other teams were going all out to beat the Snappers." He cited Philip Winthrop for making some clutch defensive plays during one tight game against the Lookouts, and he also had the winning hit in the final inning of the same game.

The season was disrupted by two weeks of rain that temporarily put a damper on the Snappers play. According to Adam Davis, "We couldn't practice for almost two weeks. We went into a one game slump. We lost a 17-15 nail biter to the Riverbats. Once we dried out and ate some cheese fries, we started playing a lot better."

Ian Brennan, the catcher, helped the Snappers come out of their shell when he hit a clutch double during an

18-17 squeaker over the Grizzlies. Ian drove in the tying run, and then he scored the winning run.

Raytheon Snappers — CSLL Champs

Now that the regular season is over, the Snappers are advancing to the play-off phase. The top six teams are playing in a single elimination tournament. The Snappers drew a bye in the first round. Cubby White is looking forward to the playoffs. "If we win this, my dad is going to raise my allowance by $1.00 a week. I'll be one of the best-paid second graders in CSLL." When asked what his plans were for the postseason, Cubby replied, "I'm going to Disney World."

Ruth Sherill is hoping the Snappers will wind up on the cover of Wheaties cereal. "We're really cute kids and deserve a chance. Most of us would probably eat Wheaties, but they don't taste that good, and those flakes get stuck in our braces."

2nd baseman Corey Gigliotti proposes that the team celebrate its success by making a Hollywood movie titled "Remember the Snappers."

"Hurricane," Kent Kachejian says he's going to start preparing for next season by eating cheese fries and playing Nintendo. "I need to bulk up and work on my reflexes. My rigorous diet and the Nintendo training should really pay off next year."

Kenny Lawhorn, the team manager, was particularly dedicated to the team effort. He would frequently sneak out of family reunions and birthday parties to get to the ball field on time. "Please don't tell my wife," said Kenny. "She'll kill me!"

Kenny's wife, Julie, has been a huge supporter of the team and a mother of two of the star players. "It hasn't been easy. Sometimes when Kenny sneaks out of the house to go to practice, I sneak over to Tyson's and hit the stores. Please don't tell Kenny. He'll kill me!"

The final team statistics were staggering. Five players batted over .800 for the season. Shortstop Michael Nebrich was the best slugger on the team, averaging .941 with five home runs. Mike was a golden glove defensive player. He threw many "bullets" to first baseman Luke "The Nuke" Bondurant to retire opposing batters.

Donovan "No Brakes" Lawhorn was a notorious base runner all season. He could stretch any hit into an extra base or two. "Once I start ripping around the bases, I get excited and just keep going."

Donovan's twin brother, Geoffrey, has been practicing psychological warfare on selected league officials. In a recent interview, he admitted, "Donovan and I have been switching jersey's every couple of innings to confuse the officials. I think it worked. Last week our scorekeeper was admitted to St. Elizabeth's."

The final Raytheon Snapper team batting average was 0.686, and they scored over 15 runs a game.

Summer / Fall 2000

We took a few short trips during the Summer and Fall of 2000. Mom, Kevin and I went for a weekend in Atlantic City, New Jersey and spent one day with Pete and Julie Peters, who had a house nearby. In June, Kara had her first dance recital. It was a precious moment when we gave her a bouquet of roses. With the autumn colors of October, we took the children to see the Potomac River at Great Falls. Later, Alice and I took some personal time to ride

Kara's first dance recital

bicycles in scenic Harper's Ferry, West Virginia. At the end the month, Alice arranged to have an outdoor family portrait taken at Colvin Mill Run.

We capped off November with another trip to Orlando and stopped to visit our friends, Debbie, Ryan, and Grace McDougall, in Rockledge, Florida. The kids had a great time making sandcastles at the beach, surfing and watching the small alligators in the lake. I decided to make the trip a bit more exciting by secretly putting coins in a few of the small palm trees that encircled the lake. While leading Kara and Grace on a tour around the lake, I would point to selected trees and excitedly exclaim, "That's a money tree!" The girls would run up, shake the tree and a few quarters, nickels and dimes would fall out. They were having fun making a few dollars, and I enjoyed watching their excitement.

2001

President of Armenia

In March 2001, my niece, Rebecca Curley, lived in Key West, Florida and worked at a waterfront restaurant. She urgently called her grandmother (my mother) one evening and told her that the President of Armenia, Robert Kocharyan, was at the restaurant, and she was serving his table. Rebecca could not remember any of the Armenian phrases she learned as a child. She asked how she should greet the president. My mother told her to say, "How are you?" which translated to "Inchpes ek?" Rebecca went back to the table and greeted President Kocharyan in Armenian. Surprised to learn that she was Armenian, he asked Rebecca if she wanted to join his party snorkeling off Key West the next day. The following morning, Rebecca met dockside with the president and his security detail. They went out on their day-long snorkeling trip and had a relaxing and fun day. But there was something quite humorous and unique to see on the boat. The armed Armenian Secret Service agents wore Speedos and pistols while protecting their president. I'll let you imagine that picture.

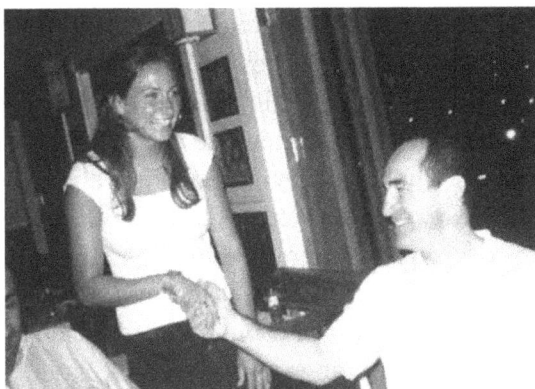

Rebecca Curley Greets President Kocharyan

More Adventures

In April, we took the three kids to the White House for another Easter Egg Roll. This time, they met the White House Mouse. In June of 2001, I traveled to the Paris Air Show with some other colleagues from Raytheon. At the end of the show, I arranged for Alice to fly in so we could spend a few days together. We had a fantastic time, enjoying the all the sites and the romance of the French capital.

In July, we packed up the Kachejian clan and drove up to Niagara Falls, Canada. We rode

by Lake Erie and Buffalo and stayed in a hotel on the Canadian side of the border, which was much more upscale. The falls were beautiful and powerful. We rode the Maid of the Mists, a boat that toured the base of the falls and offered an up-close experience. The next day, we took an excursion to nearby Toronto. On the way, we stopped at a family amusement park where we celebrated Kara's fifth birthday, and she stole the show. She hopped in one of the small race cars and ripped around the track. Passing other kids with great skill and precision, lap after lap, she handled the car like a professional. Other parents openly commented on how good she was. Alice and I were baffled at how she had become such a talented race car driver in only her kindergarten year. We knew we were going to be in trouble in another eleven years when she was able to drive a real automobile. On the way home from Canada, we drove across upstate New York to the Finger Lakes and toured Watkins Glen State Park, with its beautiful deep gorges and waterfalls.

At the end of July, we squeezed in one more family vacation to Corolla, North Carolina. We rented a big beach house with Mary & Blake Peck, Margy & Rick Jahn, and Joe & Sue Bambery. There were about twenty adults and children along for the ride. We thoroughly enjoyed our time with them. It was clear, as the children grew, our family vacations were shifting away from Orlando toward the Outer Banks of North Carolina.

The rest of 2001 was a bit of a blur. I entered ICAF in August. Kara started kindergarten in September, and a week later the 9/11 attacks occurred. Alice's father, Jim Bush, died in October, and he was buried at Arlington National Cemetery with full military honors. Before we knew it, Thanksgiving and Christmas were on top of us.

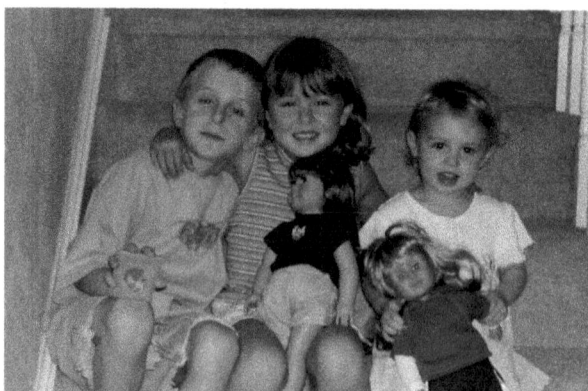

Kent, Kara, and Katie hanging out at home

First day of School

Donuts at the bus stop

Kent mans the cannon at Jamestown

2002

During the first half of 2002, I finished up my schooling at the National Defense University and graduated in mid-June with a master's degree. The next few weeks after graduation were action-packed. Kent's baseball team, the CSLL Cubs played in the league championship game. The following week, I took my Mother to Scotland for her 70th birthday, while Gina cared for Kevin - a story I shared in an earlier chapter. A few days after I returned, Peter Curley entered the West Point Class 2006. He had served a year at the New Mexico Military Institute and received his appointment a few months earlier. The entire family was proud of him.

Nate, Peter and Gina Curley at West Point

In late July, we took another family trip to the Outer Banks, but this time with the Planas family. Ramon and Suzanne have three young and gifted children, Gabriel, Maria Elena and Olivia. Another family friend, Audrey Gallagher, joined us and helped keep an eye on all the kids. She was credited with saving three-year-old Katie's life at least once in the pool. Of course, Katie found other ways to get into trouble at the beach house. She found a toilet plunger in the bathroom, picked it up—a truly toxic weapon—and walked around with it while other kids ran and hid. Suzanne was able to calmly disarm Katie using a song she spontaneously made up. The lyrics were, "Put that plunger back in the bathroom! Uh ...Uh, Uh, Uh!" which were repeated to a new dance step. You had to be there to fully appreciate the genius of her actions.

In October 2002, I was able to attend the 20th reunion of my West Point Class. It was all the more memorable, as my nephew, Peter was in his Plebe (freshman) year. That fall, Kara began her sports career with the Red Freedom soccer team. Over the next dozen years, she would be a formidable player in both lacrosse and field hockey. I also had a chance to be an escort for Kent's school trip to Jamestown and Yorktown. I probably learned as much as the kids. We took our annual trip to the Fort Lauderdale area to spend time with Alice's family during Thanksgiving. Her niece, Stacey, always prepared unbelievably good meals and was so humble about all the work she did. Since Katie had been too young to appreciate the previous Disney trips, we made a one-day run to Orlando so she could meet the Little Mermaid.

Kara and Katie meet the Little Mermaid

Kent, Kara, and Katie had entered a decade-long period filled with kid's events. I don't know how Alice managed it all while I was often on travel with my job. There were scores of medical appointments and school events. It seemed like every weekend, we had at least two or three birthday parties to attend. The week's schedule featured pre-school, soccer and baseball games, as well as dancing and guitar lessons. We had to have child car seats in both cars and extra ones ready in case we were transporting other kids. Parenthood was clearly designed for young adults. The pace was unrelenting, but there were precious moments every day.

The Jungle

During this decade, we started accumulating pets. At first, it was one cat. Then came the second cat. Throw in a parakeet, some frogs, several hamsters, an aquarium filled with goldfish, and a small bowl with a beta fish. In case that wasn't enough, we occasionally found an injured squirrel or bird. The house was a zoo. Now I know what it was like to be on Noah's Ark. And while the kids always promised they would care for each new pet; they rarely did much. Feeding, watering, cleaning cat boxes, bird cages, and aquariums, and driving to veterinarian visits, the work to keep the animals, fed, clean and healthy fell mostly on Alice. I secretly hoped the cats would eat some of the other pets, and then run away. It didn't happen. We had to wait for them to die of natural causes. (Well, Gizmo was run over by a car, but naturally, he died.) But then we quickly learned that a dead pet created an entirely new crisis. How should we break the tragic news to the kids? How long was the mourning period? What do we do with the body? And the most important question, will the kids get a replacement pet?

Dino-mania

Kent's big passion as a toddler was dinosaurs. Thomas the Train took second place. Barney was a distant third. Kent was an information sponge, absorbing every fact he could from his dozens of dinosaur books and videos. He could name many of the dinosaurs and authoritatively discuss scientific facts. His favorites were the Allosaurus, Brachiosaurus, Diplodocus, Giganotosaurus, Iguanodon, Spinosaurus, Stegosaurus, T-Rex, Triceratops, and Velociraptor.

Kent knew that the Allosaurus had three fingers, while the similar looking T-Rex only had two fingers. He was quick to point out factual errors in dinosaur books. Kent never believed Barney was a real dinosaur. In fact, Kent knew Barney would not survive ten minutes if he lived in the Jurassic period. And he had an impressive collection of dinosaur figurines. He liked taking them to the beach. His Triceratops could chase any wimpy sand crab off the beach. But his best dinosaur was a large remotely control T-Rex that Uncle Pete and Aunt Julie gave him for Christmas. That thing even scared mom and dad.

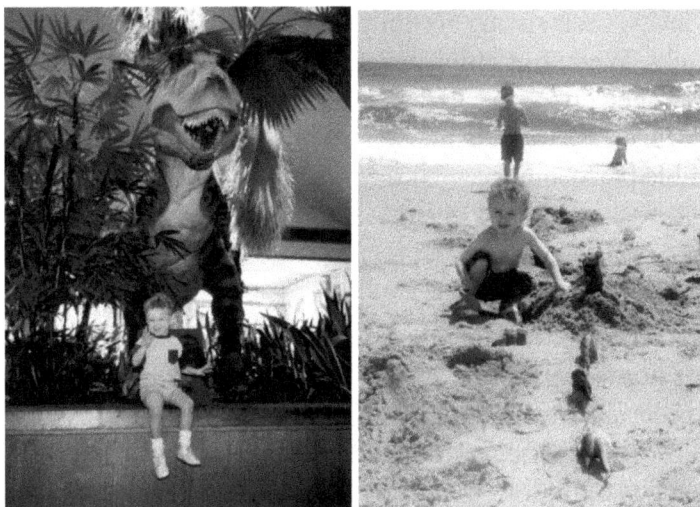

Kent with his dinosaur friends

The Money Game

I wanted to teach my kids about money and finances while they were young. When I came home from work each day, I had change in my pocket. I would hold up the coin to Kent, Kara, and Katie, when they were as young as three years old and tell them the coin had value. And that they could trade it for candy, toys or other fun things. After teaching them about pennies, nickels, dimes and quarters, I would put them to the test. I pulled out a coin, and asked, "What's this?" If they correctly identified the coin, they were allowed to keep it. If they guessed wrong, I put the coin back in my other pocket and kept it. We called this daily ritual "The Money Game." After a while, the kids had to work harder to earn their coins. I gradually asked more questions:

What's this coin? *It's a nickel.*
How much is it worth? *Five cents.*
What President is on this coin? *Jefferson!*
What building is on the back? *Monticello!*

The kids earned a few dollars each week playing The Money Game. After a while, they simply received a small allowance each week. I kept their money in "The Bank of Dad." To encourage savings, each month I would pay 10% interest on their account balance. That was an incredibly good rate. Each month I reviewed their saving accounts with them and awarded them interest or bonus bucks. When our children went to Kindergarten, their teacher gave a lesson on money and coins and Kent, Kara and Katie nailed it. They could have taught the class. The teacher was so impressed that she told Alice about their incredible performance.

Coming Home

With the arrival of Katie, Alice was handling three young children all day. When I came home from work, Alice finally got a small break. The kids came running to greet me at the door, each one competing for attention. Coming home from work and being mugged by my kids was a great feeling of unconditional love. But it was a bit unfair to Alice. She made most of the daily sacrifices raising the children, and I got much of the glory. We'd play a few games before bedtime. I would pick Kent up over my head and give him a Superman flight around the house. Kara loved her "Tinker Bell" flights up the stairs and on the balcony. Then Katie had to have her own flight. The kids kept me in good shape with these evening workouts. As I flew the kids around the house, I had a lot of power and respect. I would ask each of them a question, "Who's the greatest dad you ever had?" When they replied, "You are!" they were rewarded with an extra minute of flight time. It was pure operant conditioning.

Home Safety

As the kids grew, they got more active around the house. Alice and I tried to protect them from the typical household dangers: electrical outlets, stairs, and hot stoves. One of the biggest dangers we faced was Kent's severe allergy to peanuts. We discovered it one day accidentally. He ate a sandwich with peanut butter, and his extreme reaction was frightening, potentially life-threatening. Being an inquisitive toddler, Kent continually went to the pantry to look for candy or anything good to eat. We bought a special door knob lock and made the pantry door "childproof." That way, he could not raid the pantry, and we could monitor what he was eating. The first time Kent encountered the door lock, he was immediately frustrated. The plastic knob cover would just spin in his hand, and the door would not open. He became distressed and asked us why the special knob was put on the door. Anticipating the situation, Alice and I had already created a silly cover story. "Kent, we're getting a lot of ants in the house. They're trying to get into the pantry to eat all the food. That unique door lock keeps the ants out." Kent didn't like it, but he understood the ants were a problem. Alice and I fought back the laughter. We were glad he overlooked the fact that the ants could just walk under the door.

We had to be constantly on guard for Kent's peanut allergy in restaurants, during Halloween, and even on airline flights. On one of our early trips to Orlando, Kent was sitting in a window seat. Kent started touching the window shade and put his tray table down. He came in contact with residual peanut oil. Within minutes, his face turned red, and his eyes swelled shut. The situation worsened, and he had some respiratory distress. The flight attendant asked if the pilot needed to make an emergency landing. Someone else offered us a Benadryl pill. Within a few minutes, the symptoms subsided a bit. We did not need to make an emergency landing, but Kent's face was bloated for several days. After that incident, we packed cleaning wipes and an EpiPen in our carry-on bags. Ironically, thirty years earlier, Alice was on an airline flight with her parents. The aircraft radio was tuned to a frequency that resonated the metal wires in her new braces. Her pain was intolerable, and the stewardess ran to the cockpit and asked the pilots to change their radio frequency. The problem was immediately fixed.

Playing at Home

Before long, the kids started to play outdoors and discovered the neighborhood around them. Kara and Katie loved their new battery-powered Barbie car. Soon they were riding bicycles, and the training wheels came off.

Wearing helmets was a must. They knew their Uncle Kevin was severely injured as a young boy on his bicycle. The next phase was roller blading, and later, Kent became a talented skateboarder. He liked to ride at different skate parks in the area. Our family also had a blast playing basketball in the driveway. I lowered the rim to about seven feet and lifted each of the kids in the air so they could slam dunk the ball. Sometimes the kids wanted to hang on the rim just like the pros.

Katie and Kara in their Barbie Jeep

Breakfast Surprise (2002)

Alice and I decided to take the kids out to breakfast one Sunday morning. We arrived at a popular diner called the Magic Skillet. The waiting line was long, but the place smelled great. While we were reserving a table, young Kara wandered off. I did not want to panic but started to look around the crowded waiting area. A moment later, Kara reappeared, smiling, and holding a lollipop. I asked her where she got the candy. When she told me some man gave it to her, I was a bit alarmed. As a protective father, I told Kara to show me where the man was.

She led me around a corner and pointed to an older gentleman, dressed in a suit and tie who was seated. He was accompanied by another man in a suit and tie who was attending to him. I stayed at a distance for a moment to study them. The older man looked familiar. The younger man was talking to others and referred to "the Senator."

I immediately realized who the older man was. I took Kara by the hand and walked up to him. I introduced myself as Kara's father. "Senator Strom Thurmond, I understand that you gave my daughter a piece of candy. Kara's not usually allowed to take candy from strangers, but in this case, I'll grant a rare exception." Senator Thurmond told me Kara was a delightful young lady, and he could not resist talking to her.

We chatted for a few minutes. I thanked him for his generosity and for his service to our nation. Less than a year later, I heard the sad news that

Senator Thurmond had died at the age of 100. He had served during World War II and at the Battle of Normandy, where he landed in a glider with the 82nd Airborne Division. A decorated war veteran, he later served as a United States Senator from South Carolina for forty-eight years. I was glad Kara was able to meet him in a chance encounter.

Letters to Santa

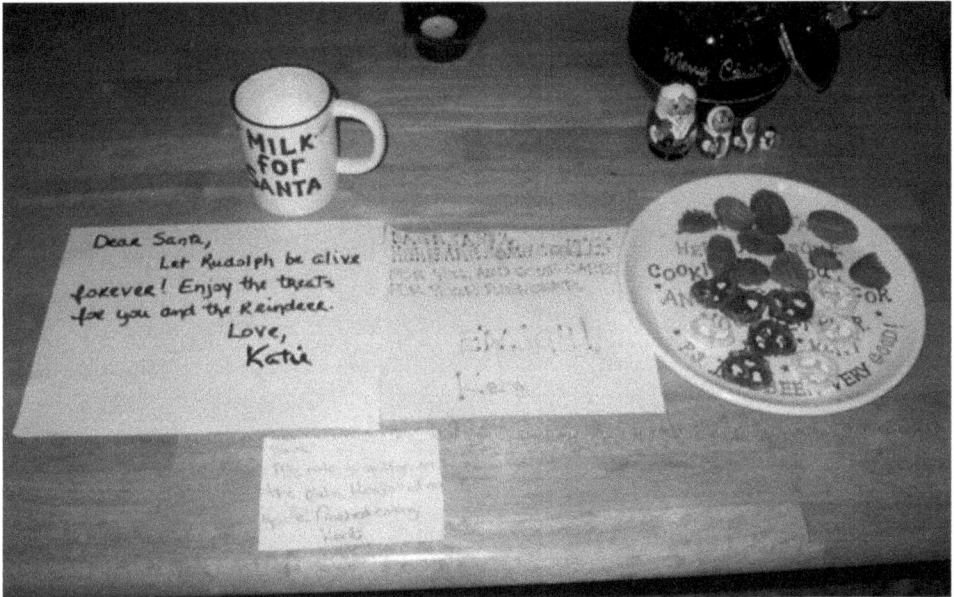

Every Christmas, the kids would write letters to Santa and leave them on the kitchen table along with some milk and cookies and a few carrots for the reindeer. Then we would read *The Night Before Christmas* as a family. We turned on the computer and would track Santa's progress on the NORAD radar as he flew across North America.

On the following pages are some of their letters.

Dear Santa,

I ♡ Christmas I wish Christmas came every day. Say Hi to the reindeer. I want to give my presents to the homeless shelter ~~but~~ but I don't want to feel like I am the only one not opening presents but my Mom and I gave some toys to a toy DRIVE!

Sincerely,

Kara E. Kachejian

P.S. I Have Been very good this year
P.P.S Get some cookies and you can have choclet chip cookies or peanut butter and choclet!
P.P.S.S. I like the peanut butter and choclet
P.P.P.SS. Write back if you have time.

♡ U SANTA ♡♡♡
♡ U SANTA ♡♡♡
♡ U SANTA ♡♡♡

Dear Santa all I want for
Christmas is. to. Some teeth
I Believe in you.

I Love Christmas.

12\24\07

Dear Santa,
Here is some ~~M~~ ~~Snacks~~ Snacks for you
and the Reindeer. I hope you enjoy
them. Thank you for visiting custom
Merry Christmas
with lots
oF
Love,

Katie Kachejian !

Thank you,
Katie!
Some bells
for you!
Love,
Santa

Ps, You Rock !

DECEMBER 24, 2002

Dear Santa,

Here are some milk and cookie's. Do not get a tummy
ache.

love,
kara Katie
and

KENT

For you
and the
Reindeer

P.S. look at note
about the Reindeer
Food

563

Vacations

We tried to pack in the vacations during the toddler years to escape the Washington, D.C. area and spend quality time together. King's Dominion was always an easy day-trip. Kara took her friend, Rachel Cotton, to the park for her seventh birthday. We had a blast riding the terrifying Scooby Doo Roller coaster.

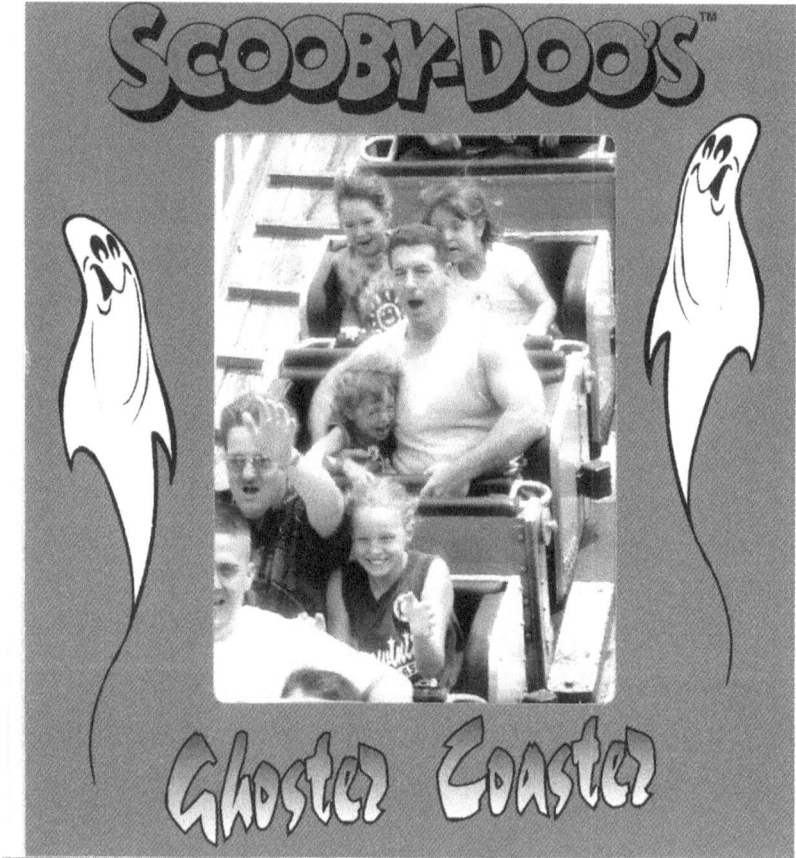

Rachel, Kara, Katie and Dad on the Scooby Doo Roller Coaster

In July 2003, we spent a week at a mountain resort at Massanutten. On the way there, we drove along scenic Skyline Drive. The resort had a lot to offer. The kids had a chance to ride horses, climb rock walls, skateboard, swim, and walk along mountain trails. At night, a bear broke into the dumpster near our house and woke up the neighbors.

The following month, Alice and I spent a romantic long weekend in Quebec. We were able to see many of the sights: Chateau Frontenac, Old Armory, local waterfalls, and Chapel of St. Anne at Beaupre, famous for many miracles that healed the sick and injured.

In October, Colonel Walt Chahanovich, the Commander of the Contingency Response Unit (CRU), led a Gettysburg Battlefield tour. All the soldiers in the unit were encouraged to bring their children. Kara and Katie met new friends, Victoria and Kelly Chahanovich and Hayden and Collier Cabell, while they toured historical sites: The Little Round Top, Devil's Den, Pickett's Charge, and the High-Water Mark.

Kara and Katie at Gettysburg

Thanksgiving and Christmas 2003

My mother passed away a few weeks before Thanksgiving in 2003. That holiday season was a sad time for the entire family. My mom was the sole caregiver for her paralyzed son, my brother, Kevin. My sister, Gina, took that on and had to shoulder an enormous responsibility to care for Kevin. At the same time, the war in Iraq had heated up. My military team was ordered to return to active duty in January 2004 for deployment to Iraq. Our mission would put us in harm's way. I would be gone most of the next year, and I wanted to get a lot of family pictures that Christmas.

Visiting Santa at Fair Oaks Mall

Family Christmas in West Chester

Christmas 2003 with Grandma Bush

2004

During much of 2004, I was deployed in Iraq and missed all the family birthdays and events. Fortunately, I made it home on Kent's birthday.

Soon after I returned, our family took a few beach vacations to make up for the lost time. I needed to decompress from the intense combat experience in Iraq. Alice and I got away to the Palladium Resort at Playa del Carmen Mexico. We also took the kids to the Outer Banks where a family of wild horses hung out at the house, eating sea oats growing in the dunes.

Later in October, we offered the use of our beach house, Watercolor, to my Iraq teammate, Charlie Driscoll, and his wife, Constance. They spent a few days at the beach with their young girls, Grace, and Claire. We were all quite shocked when Charlie died suddenly in early November. The following week, our team traveled to West Point to help bury him in the academy's historic cemetery.

We made another trip to Watercolor during New Years with another Iraq teammate, Bob Cabell, and his family. We toasted our fallen friend, who had left this world far too soon.

2005

Spring Break

During spring break, the Kachejian clan went to the Outer Banks to stay at Watercolor with the Planas family. We rode up the beach a few miles to the state border, where an iron fence separated North Carolina from Virginia. The big question we had was, "What is the purpose of the fence?" Was it to keep Virginians out of North Carolina or to keep North Carolina residents out of Virginia? Perhaps it was to keep the wild horses in North Carolina. Fortunately, the fence gate was opened after Hurricane Isabel. Local residents could drive through it to evacuate from the storm and to later re-enter to clean up from the damage.

Sitting on the NC-VA border fence

A Decade of Sports and Activities (2003-2017)

While Kent spent several years playing baseball and scouting, he also picked up a few more skills. He loved skateboarding and snowboarding. He was a bit of a daredevil, like his Uncle Kevin. Kent had some jumps that both thrilled and scared us. We were glad he wore a helmet.

Kent learned to play the acoustic guitar and started to entertain us with his songs. His favorite tune was Jack Johnson's *Banana Pancakes*. He brought his guitar on a Disney cruise ship and started playing one night on a secluded deck for his family. Within minutes, dozens of vacationers began to pack around and join in. I hoped the cruise line would make him an offer to be an entertainer. [During his high school years, Kent joined the theater and was quite an entertainer. He was recognized by the Virginia Theatre Association with an All-Star Cast Award for One-Act Plays.]

During this time, Kara and Katie had started playing soccer, swimming, gymnastics, field hockey and lacrosse. They were gifted athletes. The first time Kara and Katie entered a swim meet, they were competing with the best swimmers in the pool and often won. I think the girls got some of their mom's swimming genes. Alice was an All-American swimmer at the University of Richmond and held several school records as a sprinter. She swam several miles each day in practice.

Kara started playing soccer with the Red Freedom team. But by the time she attended West Springfield High School, Coach Brian Pulick convinced her to change sports and join the "Lady Spartans" varsity lacrosse team. There were some talented players on the team, but Kara had her share of spectacular plays. I was a bit partial to lacrosse, as I had played it in college. But those Lady Spartans had more stick skills than I ever had. Kara was 2nd team All-Conference in her junior year. As a senior, she was a team captain and Honorable Mention All-Conference. Kara also played on several club teams including Cardinal, Future Elite, and Capital.

For me, Kara's culminating lacrosse game was a tournament in Florida at the Disney ESPN Sports Resort in Orlando. The opposing team, Hagerty High School, was coached by my old high school teammate, Mike Willover. His daughter, Lauren, was also a senior and a Hagerty lacrosse standout. The game was hard-fought and became an even more intense battle in the second half. The last ten minutes were hand-to-hand combat, featuring tomahawk chops, fixed bayonets, and hand grenades. Both teams left nothing on the field. In the end, the Lady Spartans prevailed. As part of our pre-game bet, Mike had to wear a West Springfield Spartan shirt to dinner that evening at Outback Steakhouse.

Spartan fan Mike Willover (right)

During Kara's senior year, the Lady Spartans made it to the Patriot District championship game. Kara had a career high game with four goals and two assists. Her last-minute score tied the game and sent it into overtime. It was a hard-fought battle, and the Lady Spartans fell to the Woodson Cavaliers due to a failed offsides call by the referee. The game films clearly showed the game-changing mistake, but the season ended abruptly for the Spartans who felt robbed of the title.

Kara also played for the Lady Spartan varsity field hockey team. It took a while for Alice and me to understand the rules in field hockey. It seemed like Rule #1 was to blow the whistle and stop the play every ten seconds. Fortunately, Kara taught us some of the rules so we could follow the action. Kara was selected as team captain two years, and during her junior and senior years she made Honorable Mention All-Conference. The West Springfield team had a great season, reaching the final four in the region her junior year. Kara continued her field hockey career in college and played for the James Madison University (JMU) club field hockey team.

Go Kara!

Our neighbors and close friends, Dave and Charlene Salter, are a military family with children the same age as ours. Their daughter, Sydney, grew up with Kara. For many years, they both played on the same soccer, lacrosse, and field hockey teams. Dave, Charlene, Alice and I spent many games together on the sidelines and in the stands, cheering on our favorite players. We enjoyed the post-game dinners at the Austin Grill with many of the other parents and coaches. Since graduation, Kara and Sydney are both attending James Madison University where they have been accepted into the Nursing program. Dave has since retired as an Army aviator and has transitioned into the defense industry.

Katie's soccer career started when she was five years old with the Tigers (2005) and later, the Fireballs. She progressed through the years, playing on the varsity West Springfield High School team and several travel teams, including SYC Freedom and SYC Stampede. Over those years, Katie played every position: defense, midfield, forward and goalie.

Katie earned Honorable Mention All-Conference her sophomore year. A fierce competitor who often played through pain and injuries, she completely tore her PCL her junior year, but deferred surgery and continued to play in a leg brace. Katie had her knee repaired in December 2016 and was unable to play in her senior soccer season. However, she still served as a Team Manager.

Go Katie!

Katie also is a talented field hockey player. Her amazing break-away speed always generated excitement for the West Springfield team. Katie "Super Sonic" Kachejian played both midfielder and forward. As a Lady Spartan, she earned Honorable Mention All-Conference her sophomore year and 1st team All-Conference in her junior year. Katie was also a member of the highly-ranked Rampage field hockey travel team and played in several tournaments across the country. During the 2014 National Field Hockey Festival, a competition held in Palm Springs California, Katie was a 15-year old playing with the Rampage U-19 team. Their team finished the tournament undefeated. Later, they qualified for the Nationals in indoor field hockey. In her senior year, Katie was a team captain of the Spartans along with her friend Marie Laverdiere. The two were an awesome duo and helped the Spartans to be among the most feared and respected teams in the league, advancing to the Regional playoffs. Katie completed her senior year by being named to the 1st Team All-Conference and 2nd Team All-Region teams. After recovering from knee surgery, Katie played in college, making the Virginia Tech (VT) field hockey team. Their team went undefeated in 2017 and won the national championship. JMU and VT are rivals, so our family was a house divided when the two colleges faced off.

Kara and Katie have given us years of excitement playing competitive sports. We loved watching their physical and leadership skills improve each year. Go Spartans! Go Dukes! Go Hokies!

Ocean City NJ (2004-2008)

While I was deployed to Iraq in 2004, Suzanne and Ramon Planas invited Alice and the kids to Ocean City, New Jersey (OCNJ). They spent two fun-filled weeks at the family-friendly beach resort town. I always had good memories of OCNJ as I went there occasionally with friends when I was in high school.

At the end of summer vacation in 2005, I was leaving OCNJ to visit my brother Kevin for his birthday. On the way, I planned to stop at Cross Keys Airport and use a gift certificate that Gina had given me for a parachute jump. While on the Atlantic City Expressway, a few miles from the airport, my tire blew out. The lug nuts were frozen, and I could not change the

Blown tire that may have saved Kerry's life

tire. I called for a repair crew, and they needed an hour to remove the tire. That meant I missed the parachute jump I had planned for that afternoon. I continued on to Pennsylvania to see Kevin. Later, I learned that the two parachute instructors had collided during a jump at Cross Keys Airport that day, and both died. It turned out to be the best flat tire I ever had. It may have saved my life. Alice insisted that I return the unused gift certificate to Gina.

The Big Apple

A few weeks later, we took a long weekend to New York City. It was the first visit for the kids, and I had never seen many of its famous sights. The Manhattan skyline, without the twin towers, looked unfamiliar to me. We rode the train to Penn Station and then hopped in a taxi to our hotel. We packed in a lot of sightseeing during the trip. We saw Ground Zero that would eventually become the new Freedom Tower. We toured the American Museum of Natural History, the Statue of Liberty and its Museum, and Ellis Island. We split up for half a day. The girls went to tea at the American Girl Place on 5th Avenue. Kent and I went to the Brooklyn Bridge so he could skateboard at the famous Brooklyn Banks. We walked back through Rockefeller Plaza and Times Square.

When the family rejoined, we went to the top of the Empire State Building. We could feel the building swaying in the breeze. As we were taking in the panoramic view, we watched some hopeful guy drop to his knee and propose to a lady in front of us. We were embarrassed for him when she turned him down. It was the only blemish on an otherwise perfect day.

Visiting the Statue of Liberty

574

Throughout our trip to the Big Apple, we were struck by how friendly New Yorkers were. Though we had always heard they were rude and pushy, we certainly didn't experience it. Thank you, New York.

Emergency Room Visit

During the summer, Kent was at home eating an American staple, a hot dog with Mac and Cheese. The doorbell rang, and it was his neighborhood friend. Kent raced to the door and wanted to go out and play. Alice told him he could not go until he was done with his lunch. Kent swallowed the hot dog in big bites and ran out the door. For the next two days, Kent could not eat and could not hold down water. Anything he ate immediately came back up. Concerned about his dehydration, we went to the emergency room. While waiting to be seen by a doctor, Kent vomited up a big chunk of now nearly-three-day-old hot dog. The mystery was solved. Fortunately, Kent's windpipe wasn't blocked. He enjoyed eating and drinking once again.

Farewell Kevin

For all the good memories our family made in 2005, the year was marred by the death of my brother, Kevin, in late August. He had been paralyzed for 32 years and had spent the last few years of his life in and out of hospitals.

Kevin wanted to help others by donating his organs. Gina and I met with "Gift of Life" and arranged for an organ donation. We kept Kevin on life support, hoping for a miracle, while a medical review determined that his liver was the only viable organ he had to donate. A man in Ohio was identified as a recipient. The plan was for a medical team to fly in to remove his liver and immediately fly back to Ohio to perform the surgery. The team arrived. A doctor reconfirmed Kevin had no response to physiological and neurological tests. We removed Kevin from life support. It was a very hard decision to make, but Gina and I knew it was what Kevin wanted, and it was the right thing to do. Gina's two sons, Peter and Nathaniel, drove from West Point to Pennsylvania to spend some final moments with their Uncle Kevin. I held his hand and prayed. We were pouring tears. Behind us, I could hear the medical team also crying. They too were human. Kevin's heart rate declined, and after a few minutes it stopped. The doctor declared him dead and shut off the monitor. The four of us said our final goodbyes and started to leave the operating room. On the way out the door, I turned and looked at the team and said, "Make it count. Please, make it count." We left the operating room emotionally exhausted. But Kevin was a faithful Christian, and we knew he was now in a better place. We learned later that Kevin's liver was further determined not suitable for transplant. Gina and I were crushed that his final gift could not be given. We were told that even the medical team was distraught by what they found. However, Gina and I both agreed that we would be organ donors to fulfill Kevin's own wish.

Kevin's memorial service was a celebration of his life. His empty wheelchair sat next to his casket, symbolizing that he had finally left it. Many of his work colleagues, as well as high school friends and teachers, attended. Their presence reminded us of just how many lives Kevin had touched. The challenges he faced during his life inspired Kara to seek a career as a nurse.

2006

The Kachejians had another interesting year in 2006. In March, our neighbors, Tariq and Fatima Osmanzada, invited our family to visit an open house at the Mustafa Center Mosque. The mosque wanted to be more open with other citizens in the community, so many of their neighbors were invited to attend. Tariq and Fatima had escaped Afghanistan in the 1980s when the Soviet's invaded. Their children were now friends and schoolmates with our children. The Kachejian family immediately accepted the offer. I had been inside a mosque in Iraq, and I wanted Alice and the kids to have the same learning experience. Before going, I prepared everyone for what to expect, and what to wear. The Imam was very welcoming and gave us an overview of the mosque and answered many questions. The visit was an educational experience, particularly for members of the community unfamiliar with the Islamic faith.

Punta Cana

In April, Alice and I traveled to Bavaro Palace Resort in Punta Cana in the Dominican Republic. Mr. and Mrs. Perez had enjoyed their vacation there so much, Alice and I decided to see it for ourselves. At one of the comedy shows, three couples were picked out of the audience and asked to come up on stage. I tried to decline and explained in broken Spanish that I was recovering from knee surgery. That excuse did not work, and we were ushered up on the stage with the other two couples. We were made to play all kinds of silly games involving water and balloons. But we all enjoyed it. The culminating event was a push-up contest. All three men had to do pushups with their wives lying on their backs. Too easy. Pushups were my specialty, even with one leg. The other two guys could not even get off the ground. I banged out about thirty pushups with Alice on my back. We won the bottle of cheap rum and left the stage as the victors.

Later in the trip, we visited a cigar factory. The craftsman hand-rolled some cigars in front of me. He told me Dominican cigars were better than the Cuban ones. I asked why. He said Cuba had a drought and imported tobacco leaves from the Dominica Republic. Cuban cigars were being made with Dominican tobacco, though they still sold them as "Cuban." The communist Cuban government could not afford to lose sales on one of their most important cash crops. Alice and I also went to a local ranch, where were saw some of the beautiful countryside and picked fresh bananas and coconuts. All good things come to an end, so we eventually returned to the United States to reclaim our children.

More Fun

A few weeks later, I visited Scott and Carole Oakes at their cozy vacation home at nearby Lake of the Woods. I wanted to see the neighborhood that Scott and Carole had enjoyed so much. Alice and I had almost bought a house on Lake Anna five years earlier, but the 9/11 terrorist attacks caused the stock market to plunge, and we quickly withdrew our interest.

Kent and I had some of our own fun. In September, we went to Summit Point Raceway in West Virginia and watched the motorcycle races. We also celebrated Kent's birthday by inviting all his aspiring commando friends to a paintball party.

Kent (center) and his Paintball Buddies

We wrapped up the year at another great Army-Navy game celebration in a suite hosted by Mark & Carol Reynolds. Kara and Gina also joined the trip, and we met up with Cadet Nate Curley at the game.

Air Show

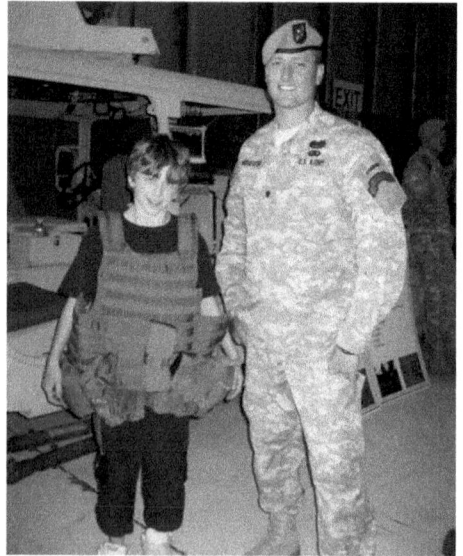

In May of 2006, I received a call from another ICAF classmate, John J. Torres. "JJ" was now an Air Force colonel and the Vice Commander of the 89th Airlift Wing at Andrews Air Force Base. That unit operates and maintains all the executive aircraft and aerial communications for the president, vice president, cabinet members, combatant commanders and other senior leaders. Earlier that year, I had seen JJ in the news escorting President Bush to Air Force One. JJ invited me to the annual air show at Andrews AFB and offered me a distinguished visitor parking pass. That was a big deal. Traffic at the show was always congested

Ranger Kent Kachejian wearing body armor

578

and getting access to a special gate, and parking lot was too good to not accept. After I had hung up the phone, I realized I should have also asked JJ for a ride on Air Force One. I took Kent and his friend for a great day at the air show. We checked out dozens of airplanes, helicopters, and armored vehicles on display. Kent's favorite part was manning the machine gun on a Humvee gunship and trying on some body armor with real Army Rangers. It was a cool father-son day, thanks to my friend JJ, (I still owe you a beer, bro. Maybe a whole six-pack).

Peter and Nathaniel Curley join the Long Gray Line

At the end of May, just when I thought the year 2006 could not get any better, my sister Gina's son, Peter Curley, was preparing to graduate from the United States Military Academy at West Point. Gina's other son, Nate, had just finished his sophomore year at the same academy. Our entire family took a road trip to New York to be there and celebrate. As I've mentioned earlier in this book, the West Point Corps of Cadets is organized into 36 companies. Ironically, Peter was assigned to the same one I had been 24 years earlier, Company G2. He also lived, as had I, on the 6th floor of the same dormitory, now called "Bradley Barracks." And as it was back in my day, cadets were not allowed to use the elevator during their four years at the academy. Peter and the rest of the senior class held their final cadet "graduation parade" in Full-Dress uniform for all the families and friends. The next day, they assembled at Michie Stadium for the graduation ceremony. At this point, our nation had been at war for over four years. President George W. Bush was personally handing diplomas to the Class of 2006, knowing most of them would be deploying to a combat zone. As Peter was called upon the stage, he boldly put his arm around the president, turned him, pointed toward the crowd, and then both waived to the area in the stands where our entire family was cheering. Someone snapped a perfect photo of the moment, which almost looks staged.

I can assure you, it happened. It was an exhilarating moment to culminate the four years of rigors at West Point. Fortunately, Peter was not shot by the Secret Service for hijacking the president, and the academy could no longer discipline him. Well done, Lieutenant Curley. Welcome to the Long Gray Line!

President Bush with Peter Curley at West Point

2007

In January 2007, 2LT Peter Curley was a fully trained Army Artillery officer, and he departed on a one-year tour in Korea. Gina, Rebecca and I said our goodbyes to him at Dulles airport. That evening, I took Katie to the VIP Dance with the Brownies.

IDEX

In February 2007, I attended the International Defense Exhibition (IDEX) in Abu Dhabi, the capital of the United Arab Emirates (UAE). It was my first trip to the UAE, and it was an impressive country. The nation carefully balanced their traditional culture with the advanced technologies and conveniences of the modern world. Everything in the country was clean, orderly and new. The tallest skyscraper in the world and many other landmark buildings were nearing completion or had been recently built in both Abu Dhabi and the nearby city of Dubai.

IDEX was a huge event that featured hundreds of exhibiting companies and tens of thousands of visitors from around the world. The president of the UAE opened the show with a ribbon cutting ceremony. The country spared no expense to make the event a first-class affair. While there, I was able to meet with two of my international classmates from ICAF, Major

General Obaid Al Ketbi of the UAE and Brigadier General Nasser Al-Ali of Qatar. General Obaid was now the Director of Logistics for the UAE Armed Forces. His day-to-day responsibilities were enormous. Furthermore, he was leading the entire IDEX operation for the UAE Armed Forces and announcing the new contract awards at an international press conference.

The Abu Dhabi trip included many memorable events and sites. Among them was a reception hosted by the U.S. Ambassador.

Armenia Trip—Back to the Future

After talking about traveling to Armenia for many years, Gina and I finally embarked on the journey in May 2007. We were joined by two other relatives, our uncle, Haig Geovjian, and our cousin, Chuck Puchakjian.

Now let's be honest, most Americans can't find Armenia on a map. They probably don't know what continent it is on and couldn't tell you the difference between an Armenian and a Romanian. So here is a hint, Armenia is in the Caucasus Mountains, where the term Caucasian derives. It is landlocked and pinched between Georgia, Azerbaijan, Iran and Turkey. Armenia's territory was historically ten times larger than it is at present and formerly included Mount Ararat, the mountain believed to be where Noah's Ark came to rest.

Haig Geovjian was the elder statesman on the family trip. Chuck Puchakjian's grandfather was a cousin of Haig's father, Parnag. Our family tree is a bit blurry back that far because many records during this period were destroyed as villages were burned and looted during the genocide. However, Chuck and Haig's family clearly have a common ancestor, at some point, several generations ago, well after Noah's Ark landed on Mount Ararat. Besides, Chuck was a retired police officer from New Jersey, and those Jersey cops never get the story wrong.

Fortunately, we cannot find any historical records that indicate our family is related to the infamous Kardashians. Our tribe of Armenians was much better behaved.

Before traveling to Armenia, we had selected an itinerary that met our interests. We wanted to see Mount Ararat, Lake Sevan, and some of the cultural heritage sites in the country. After a flight through Paris, Haig, Chuck, Gina and I finally arrived in Yerevan, the Armenian capital. After clearing immigration and customs, we met our tour guide, Marina, and our driver, Gageek. They would be our guides for the next ten days. After collecting our luggage, we went to lunch at a local restaurant. The menu was confusing, completely written in Armenian which has an entirely different alphabet. I was hungry, and a bit concerned when Marina confirmed there were no cheeseburgers on the menu. And the nearest Pizza Hut was probably 500 miles away. How could I possibly survive for the next ten days? After lunch, we began a tour of downtown Yerevan. We passed Republic Square and later the Armenian Presidential Palace. I suggested we stop there and visit President Robert Kocharyan. He needed to know I was Rebecca's uncle, the pretty girl he went snorkeling with in Key West a few years earlier. I brought some pictures of him with Rebecca to refresh his memory. Maybe the photos would give us some special privileges and top cover in case we got into trouble while in Armenia. My proposal to stop at the Presidential Palace was immediately vetoed by the rest of the group, and we moved on.

The Four Stooges at Erebouni Fortress

We spent a few hours at the Erebouni Museum and Fortress, which was founded in 782 B.C., several decades before Rome was built. From the top of this historical site, we enjoyed a scenic view of the city of Yerevan and Mount Ararat. The next stop was a very sobering visit to the Armenian Genocide Museum and Memorial. Full of documentation and artifacts from a dark period in world history, much of the evidence was recorded by prominent international observers and U.S. Ambassador Henry Morgenthau. Uncle Haig brought a few surviving old photos of our relatives from Armenia, which the historian greatly appreciated. He told us many details, including the horrible fate of the village where Uncle Haig's family had once lived.

The following day, we left Yerevan and headed to the countryside to see more cultural sites. Armenia adopted Christianity in 301, A.D., so there were many churches and monasteries throughout the country. Hundreds of other Armenian churches, now in modern day Turkey, had been destroyed by the Ottomans. One hundred years later, ISIS began butchering Christians and other religious minorities in the same region of the world. And many of these modern Christians were Armenian descendants of those driven out by the Ottomans during World War I. We visited a former pagan monument at Garni, which was a fortress and summer residence of ancient Armenian kings. It overlooked the beautiful Azat River gorge. The terrain reminded me of Switzerland. During the next few days, we visited a series of ancient monasteries. I thought they would be boring, but we found their history and architecture fascinating.

Geghard Cave Monastery

Haghartsin Monastery

Haghpat Monastery

Lunch at Lake Sevan

Along the way, we stopped at an art school in Spitak. It had been rebuilt after the city was flattened by an earthquake in 1988, a tragedy that killed over 25,000 people. Before heading back to Yerevan, we spent another day at beautiful Lake Sevan. Outside the capital, we stopped at Holy Echmiadzin Church, the original church opened in 301 AD. It is the home of "the Armenian Pope," His Holiness Karekin II, Supreme Patriarch and Catholicos of all Armenians. While we were in the courtyard, Karekin II came outside and greeted visitors. Uncle Haig worked his way through the crowd and received a personal blessing.

We traveled to Khor Virap, an impressive monastery near the border with Turkey, with Mount Ararat dramatically rising in the background. It was the historic location where King Tiridates III of Armenia imprisoned Saint Gregory the Illuminator in a pit for 14 years. Saint Gregory survived, and the pagan king later converted. As a result, in the year 301 A.D., Armenia became the first country in the world to be declared a Christian nation. Before we left Khor Virap, we released some doves as a peace gesture.

Remembering our brother Kevin at Khor Virap

We headed south toward the Azerbaijan border and stopped at the Areni Winery where we sampled some of the local wines and took a few bottles home to share with other family members. We capped off the day with a stop at the 13th-century Norovank Monastery. The terrain was spectacular, surrounded by gorges and cliffs. The church had a crazy-narrow stone staircase on the face of the building, used to enter the second floor.

Norovank Monastery and Gina Climbs the Stairway to Heaven

Norovank Monastery

At every site we visited, Uncle Haig wandered off to explore. We'd lose track of him for a few minutes, but he would later reappear. Near the end of our trip, he showed us his prized rock collection, souvenir stones from everywhere he went in Armenia. Marked by location, he brought some of the old country back to his new country.

The last day of the trip, we tried to find some old relatives using a return address written on a 40-year old letter from Haig's mother. At first, it was a bit confusing. After the Soviets had left the country, the Armenians re-named many of the streets in Yerevan. Marina was able to find an old apartment complex where our relatives had once lived. She spoke to some local residents that recalled our relatives and noted that they had resided there about ten years earlier. There were no signs of where they may have gone.

Last night in the old country

Satisfied that we had made an attempt, we headed off to the airport and back to the United States. Haig and Chuck flew to Philadelphia. Gina and I flew through an extremely turbulent storm over the Atlantic and were very grateful when we landed in Washington, D.C. We had set low expectations for the trip but far exceeded them.

Katie's Hamster

Over the years, we held several funeral services for hamsters, and I soon learned that the death of a hamster was an earth-shaking event. The situation had to be handled with great dignity and respect. "The best hamster ever" was Tigger. When Tigger died, he received full military honors. We placed him inside a comfy cardboard coffin. Katie put a personal note inside the box along with a few wild flowers. We marched outside with the little fella. Then we wrapped him in a burial cloth. Katie picked the spot in the yard where he was to be buried. I tried to find a cap gun so I could fire twenty-one rounds in the air. No luck. Instead, I saluted and whistled a solemn version of "Taps." To mark the hallowed ground, Katie found a nice smooth stone and wrote Tigger's epitaph with a sharpie.

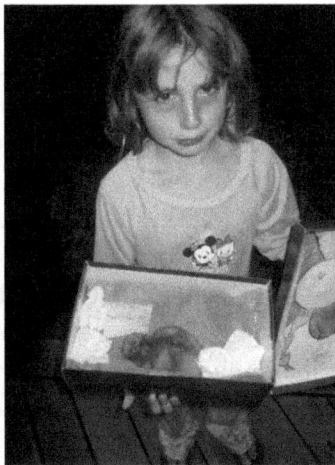

Funeral Services for Tigger, the Hamster

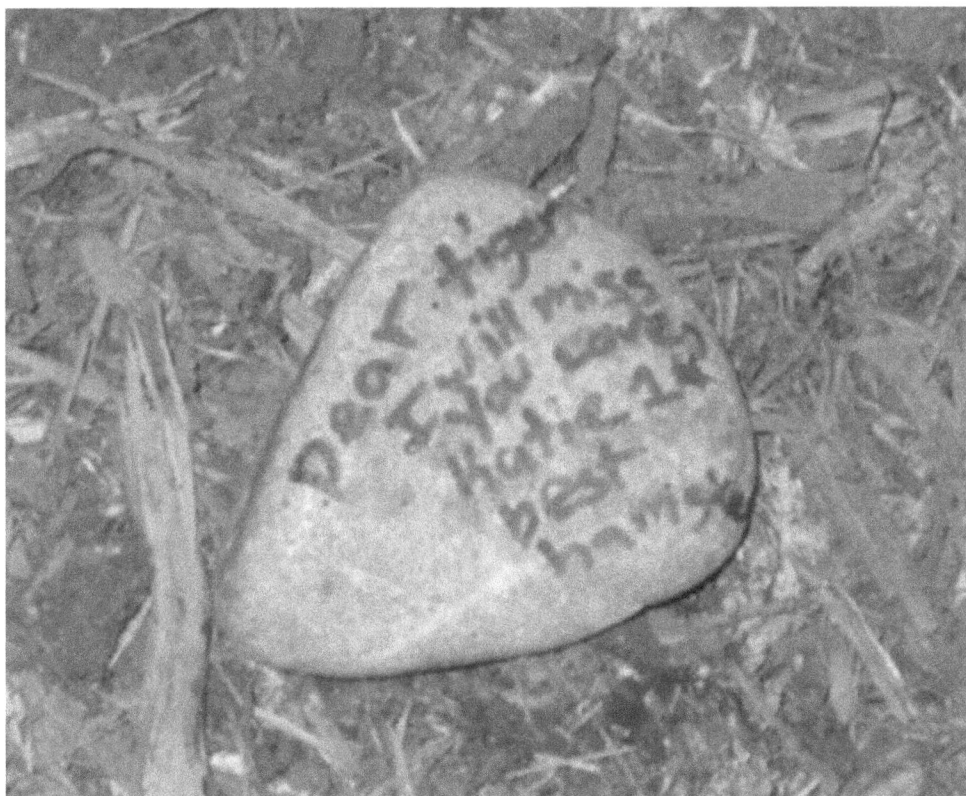

Racing at Summit Point

About six weeks after taking the "Security Driving" course with the military (offensive driving), I was invited back to Summit Point by Mark and Carol Reynolds. They were both members of a Porsche Club from Pennsylvania whose members were spending the weekend on the track. I took a quick class and then joined them riding in their Porsche 996s on the track. Both Mark and Ken Nielsen allowed me to strap into their speed machines and take a few laps in the driver's seat. The track was an American autobahn, full of curves, but we were able to get those turbocharged land rockets up to 160 mph on the straightaways. It gave me flashbacks of my tour in Germany many years earlier. They even gave me a dashboard video of our ride to document the fun. Someday, I want to go back to my old neighborhood and deliver some newspapers in one of those speed demons.

2008

Costa Rica

Our big trip that year was in March during spring break. The Kachejian's spent a week in Costa Rica and a couple of nights in the area of Tortuguero National Park, a lowland tropical rainforest. We took several boat rides to see the howler monkeys, egrets, herons, caimans, sloths and other wildlife. Later, we rode on a jungle zip line. Along the way, we enjoyed a few fruity drinks and local beers.

Costa Rica ATV Ride

Unfortunately, Kent sprained his ankle quite badly while playing basketball with some other kids at the resort. We bought him a cane in a local village, but Kent really needed a pair of crutches. We asked the resort where we could get a pair and got blank stares. They did not understand what crutches were. We then called the travel agency, and they searched for hours. They finally found a pair of used crutches about 50 miles away, through some very winding and mountainous roads. We had to pick them up the next day, during a six-hour drive to our next stop.

That stop was the Arenal volcano, and we stayed in a hotel with a great view of it. The volcano spewed ash and smoke and had a perfect cone shape. We enjoyed soaking in the hot springs, before going to dinner at a restaurant right on the slope of the volcano. Soon after we sat down for dinner, the roof of the restaurant was bombarded with rocks that tumbled down the steep slopes of the rumbling volcano. Every minute or so a large rock smashed into the metal roof, and it made a loud noise that startled the people eating dinner. It reminded me of enemy rockets that hit the roof our buildings in Baghdad. It did not seem safe, and I looked at the wait staff to see how they were reacting. Sure enough, in a few minutes, we were told that we needed to evacuate the restaurant immediately. The restaurant staff put us all in a van and drove us around to another restaurant on the other side of the volcano, which was less active. We were able to order our meals and enjoy the night views. The next morning, we went on a horseback riding tour and then explored Arenal Volcano National Park on ATVs in the afternoon. The landscape, vegetation, and rivers were incredible. We made a brief stop in La Fortuna, a picturesque town in the area. The girls wanted to buy trinkets. I looked for a sports bar. We finished up our vacation in the Manuel Antonio beach area on the Pacific Coast. On the long drive to the beach, we crossed the famous Crocodile Bridge over the River Tarcoles. We stopped on the bridge and watched about twenty crocs sunning themselves. The really fat ones laid on the water's edge right next to the bridge, eating any food or tourists that fell into the river. We arrived at the Hotel California in Manuel Antonio in the afternoon. A family of monkeys was running all over the grounds. Later, we toured the national park and saw plenty of exotic animals. It was a good place to leisurely wrap up the trip.

In the summer of 2017, Kara returned to Costa Rica to stay with a host family while studying Medical Spanish at UNIBE in San Jose. While there, she aided in the delivery of healthcare to many Costa Ricans and refugees.

Nate Graduates

Some notable military events occurred in 2008. The biggest one was my nephew, Nate Curley, graduated from West Point in late May. Many family and friends traveled to New York to celebrate the event. It was a fantastic day, culminating four years of rigorous physical and academic activity. Nate was awarded his Bachelor of Science degree in Environmental Engineering and launched his new career in the Army as a Second Lieutenant. He was commissioned in the Engineers and assigned to the 82nd Airborne Division. He deployed to Iraq where he cleared IEDs from the roads. Nate has made a career in the military and has earned numerous elite qualifications as an Airborne, Ranger, Sapper and Special Forces (Green Beret).

It is extraordinarily rare when a soldier achieves this level of tactical competence. And Nate has been very humble about his accomplishments. I regret that I missed his Ranger School graduation ceremony due to an international trip, but I was able to cheer him on when he competed in the Army's Best Ranger competition at Ft. Benning and also attended his Special Forces graduation at Ft. Bragg.

Peter, Gina, Nate and Rebecca Curley at USMA Graduation

Sadly, Alice's mother, Betty Bush, died the day before Nate's West Point graduation. Alice and Kara could not attend Nate's ceremony.

My academy class also reached a significant milestone that year. Our first classmates were promoted to General Officer rank. That included our First Captain, Mick Nicholson, who became a Brigadier General in February. There was no denying it, our class was now among the "old grads."

Farewell to Betty Bush

Alice's mother passed away in late May of 2008 after a long illness. For decades, her favorite hobby had been making teddy bears by hand. She was quite talented, and each one had a different theme. Every room in her house had a dozen or more bears perched on tables, chairs, rocking horses or shelves, smiling at you. She also collected other artist's bears from Rocking Horse Gallery in Fredericksburg, Virginia. When the owner learned that Betty made her own bears, she asked to sell them in her store. Betty called her furry creations "BB Bears." Betty was very proud that others loved her bears too. Our family and those bears sure miss Betty. She is buried at Arlington National Cemetery with her husband, Jim.

Betty Bush

Her Band of Bears

Summer of 2008

My sister, Shelley, had a big birthday in July. I won't tell you how old she was, but it was less than 51. She and I went to Atlantic City for the day to hit the casinos, the boardwalk, and some other sites. We felt like high rollers, playing on the 25 cent slot machines. We lost about twenty bucks and decided to cut our losses, so we headed over to Ripley's Believe It or Not. On the way back to Pennsylvania, we stopped in to see our cousin Pete Peters, who was a manager at West Marine. It had been about ten years since Shelley and Pete had last seen each other, and it was the best part of the entire day.

Alice also had a big birthday in August. She wanted to celebrate in style with some friends. We rented a limousine and took a party of ten to dinner at the North Mountain Vineyard and Winery in the beautiful Shenandoah Valley. We had an excellent meal on the back deck, catching up with Sherry and Dave Shultz, Tony and Glenna Hahn, Tim and Lisa Zeitler, and Mike and DeAnn Boehm. It's a shame we only celebrate birthdays once a year.

Over the past few decades, I had visited a few vineyards and taken four or five wine tasting courses. After all this training, I feel very confident that I can easily distinguish a red wine from white wine if the lights in the room are kept on.

Dinner at North Mountain

Youth Leadership Conferences

It was time for Kent to start spreading his wings and learn more about our country and how it works. In the summer of 2008, he attended the Congressional Youth Leadership Counsel in Washington, D.C. and learned about our government and its institutions. He was a bit reluctant at first, but once he was in the program, he enjoyed the curriculum, the visit to Capitol Hill, and he met many new friends. He thanked us for giving him the opportunity when we picked him up the following week.

The next summer, Kent asked to attend the Global Young Leadership Conference in China. That was a big trip, but Alice and I thought Kent would benefit immensely. He packed his bags and headed off to Shanghai, Beijing and Hong Kong. He visited many of the famous sites, including the Great Wall and the new Olympic "Bird's Nest" Stadium. During the trip, he was able to see how the communist nation had embraced capitalism. He also visited some rural villages to see the agrarian economy. Overall, Kent thoroughly enjoyed the trip. However, after he came home, Kent refused to eat meat for months. We knew he had probably seen some disturbing sights in the restaurants and markets he visited.

A few years later, Kara was invited to attend the National Youth Leadership Conference (NYLC) for Medicine and Healthcare. At the time, she did not realize the life-changing effect this program would have. During the course, she learned about the healthcare profession, while developing her leadership skills. Her conference visited some of the country's most prestigious institutions and learned from their experts. She trained on the same simulators used by surgeons to prepare for operations. In the evening, the class attended lectures from doctors and participated in leadership activities. Throughout the nine-day course, the students met some of our nation's most influential people in both medicine and healthcare. Kara realized she wanted to pursue a career in the medical field when the group visited the National Institutes of Health (NIH), where she witnessed many patients receiving tests and getting their daily treatments. It suddenly hit her that the medical field offered a career that can make a difference in the lives of others. She wants to help others recover from injuries and illnesses and provide them a more healthy and hopeful future. Kara went on to James Madison University and is currently in the Nursing program.

In the summer of her junior year (2015), Katie expressed interest in being a doctor. She also attended the National Youth Leadership Conference for Medicine and Healthcare to get a first-hand understanding of the profession. The program was similar to the one Kara attended, and it was also hosted by the University of Maryland on campus. Katie had an excellent experience, and she is pursuing a career as a veterinarian.

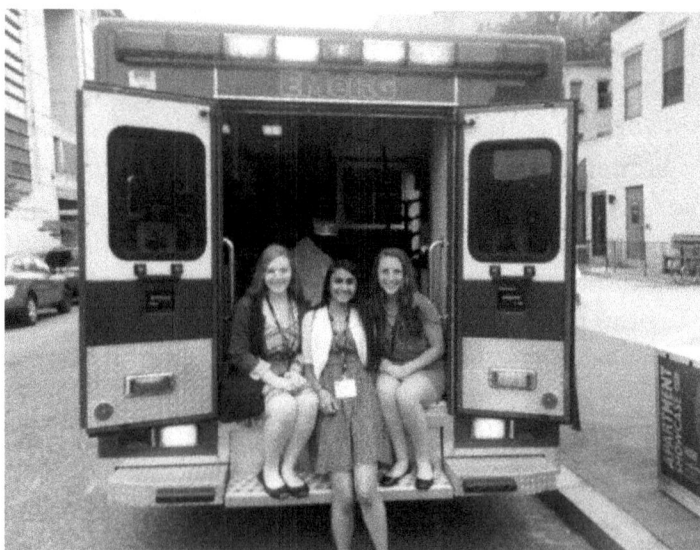

Katie (right) and friends at the NYL Medical Conference

Speaking at the Philadelphia Armenian-American Veterans Association

My Uncle Haig Geovjian was active in St. Sahag and St. Mesrob Armenian Church in Wynnewood, Pennsylvania. He was also affiliated with the Philadelphia Armenian-American Veterans Association (PAAVA). Consequently, the PAAVA President, Sandra Salverian invited me to speak at their Veterans Day event in 2008. I checked with my military chain of command and received official permission to speak in uniform. I made the trip to Philadelphia the night before and stayed with Uncle Haig. The event became a small family reunion: Haig and John Geovjian, Nancy Kliian, Gina (Kachejian) Curley and my two daughters, Kara and Katie. I was surprised that about 300 people turned out. Among them were twenty Armenian-American veterans from WWII and Korea, each being honored by PAAVA. I gave my speech and shared a few dozen interesting photos of the war in Iraq. We enjoyed an excellent lunch and were entertained by a colorful string band wearing costumes that reminded me of the Philadelphia Mummers. Those Armenians knew how to party.

Reunion with Haig, Patty & John Geovjian

Veteran's Day reunion in Philadelphia

Mount Rainier with Gina and Peter Curley

In October of 2008, I performed my annual military training at an exercise at Fort Lewis, Washington. The training was intended to prepare major units for deployment to Iraq. Coincidentally, 1st Lieut. Peter Curley was an artillery officer serving on the post. Gina flew from Pennsylvania to join us. During a day off duty, we were able to tour Seattle and hike part way up Mount Rainier.

2009

The Arts

I often wished I had some type of artistic talent. Outside of playing the air guitar or the radio, I had no real musical gifts. I did study the *Art of War* as part of the curriculum at West Point, but that is an entirely different form of art. I don't think playing poker is considered an art either. While Alice was a talented swimmer, she spent too much time in the pool to focus on any arts.

Fortunately, our kids were more gifted. Katie learned ballet, jazz, and hip-hop. She also picked up the guitar. Kara took ballet and jazz lessons, while also learning to play the piano. Kara and Katie were in several school plays in elementary and middle school and took advanced theater classes. Alice and I always enjoyed watching them perform. Kent was the most artistically talented of the three. He was spectacular in several high school plays, winning an award from the Virginia Theatre Association. His dry sense of humor and quick-witted sarcasm were always entertaining. We are especially proud of his acoustical guitar skills and his ability to sing Jack Johnson songs. It all kicked off with his first guitar recital in February 2009.

Time with Katie

Katie was at a wonderful age where she was becoming a unique person, yet she still depended on her parents. She was not embarrassed to have us around her friends. I took a day off work in April and escorted her elementary school class on a trip to Jamestown. Later that month, I had the honor of taking her to the Father-Daughter Dance sponsored by her Girl Scout Troop.

Father-Daughter dance

National Guard Conference

In June of 2009, I attended the annual National Guard Conference held in Jackson, Wyoming. The conference was an annual gathering of the Guard's military leadership from all fifty states and U.S. territories. This was an important event for businesses to attend and show their support. The Guard had two chains of command. In peacetime, each State National Guard reported to their respective Governor. Governors often called up their National Guard units to respond to State-wide emergencies, such as floods, earthquakes, and hurricanes. In times of war, National Guard units can be called into Federal service and then work for the federal government.

It was my first time in this part of the United States, and the scenery was impressive. I landed in Bozeman, Montana and picked up the perfect rental car to view it, a Mustang convertible. I put the top down and began the long drive to Jackson. This route took me through Yellowstone National Park and Grand Teton National Park. Along the way, I saw much of the natural treasures of the United States, with its spectacular scenery and wildlife. It was a great opportunity to see bald eagles patrolling the skies, buffalo and elk grazing on the grasses, the Old Faithful geyser, and several colorful hot springs. Geologically, the Yellowstone area sits atop the magma of an active volcano hidden beneath the surface. Some of the areas had an alien look and odor. As I continued south, I passed through the impressive mountains of Grand Teton, crossed the Continental Divide, and stopped at the scenic Jackson Lake Lodge. It was a place I wanted to return to someday with my family to fully enjoy its beauty. I stayed at the conference in the Jackson Hole area for several days, learning more about the Guard and its mission while building new professional relationships. In the evenings, I was able to experience some of the local culture, riding in horse-drawn wagons like the settlers did over a century earlier and being treated to Native American dances in colorful dress. It was all topped off with a round of golf. Yes, life with the National Guard was quite good.

Ron Jon Surf Camp

Also, in June, the Kachejian crew was invited to Florida by the MacDougall clan. Debbie and Alice signed the kids up for the famous Ron Jon Surf Camp. So, Ryan, Kent, Grace, and Kara spent several days in the water catching waves and improving their surfing skills. At the end of each day, the kids were worn out, making life easier for Debbie and Alice. Katie and I did not go on the surfing trip. Instead, we made a special trip to Pennsylvania to visit

Katie's Armenian relatives, including Aunts Nancy and Shelley, and cousins Faylyn, Anna and Jonie Mefford.

Partnership in West Virginia

In the summer, Kent and I took a special trip with our church to Parsons, West Virginia. Burke Community Church (BCC) has had a long partnership with First Baptist Church in Parsons, where we helped to repair homes, build wheelchair ramps, replace roofs, and work on other projects. Scores of BCC teenagers traveled to Parsons to help. Kent and I joined the construction teams, while other BCC members visited local convalescent homes. Kent's team was led by my Army buddy, Brian Soles. Justin Hansen and I led another construction team with about six hard-charging teenagers. The adults showed the kids how to safely use the tools. Everyone took pride in their work. The amazing Red Caulkin organized the trip for BCC, while Bob Aston and Richard Dick were our on-site construction experts. Kent brought along his guitar to provide some evening entertainment. It was rewarding to help so many people, and the local residents were very grateful for our efforts.

Kent on BCC Trip to West Virginia

Offensive in Pennsylvania

In October, I went to Pennsylvania for a long weekend with the BCC Men's Ministry. Many of the men in our church were current or former members of the military. Dozens of them worked at the Pentagon. They did not like to use the term "Retreat" to describe the weekend outing. It sounded like we were losing a fight. Real men don't retreat, so we called the annual event a "Men's Offensive." It was a private weekend for men to share their faith and bond. To top it off, our guest speaker was Lieutenant General (Retired) William Boykin, the former commander of the elite Delta Force counterterrorism unit. While there, I was able to get two signed copies of his book *Never Surrender* for both Kent and me.

During the weekend, several of us took the opportunity to stop by the United Flight 93 Memorial site, where the passengers and crew had fought back against the 9/11 terrorists. Their aircraft crashed in the nearby field, but their brave actions had likely saved our nation's capitol from being attacked.

The Men's Ministry has done a remarkable job inviting in highly regarded guest speakers to share their faith and experiences with us. I had a chance to meet Jim Ryun at one of the monthly breakfasts. He won the silver medal at the 1968 Summer Olympics in the 1,500-meter run and was one of the most famous track and field stars of that era. He later became a U.S. Congressman from Kansas. I was thrilled when Jim signed an old pair of my running shoes. Here's a big shout out to the scores of men of Burke Community Church who have been brother's in faith. Among them are Dave DuHadway, Curt Hammill, Bob Fimiani, Tim Lambert, Ron Hawthorne and two brothers from Egypt, Michael and Mark Ibrahim. Mark has made several mission trips to northern Iraq, the most recent was to rescue Yazidi women from enslavement by ISIS.

2010

The Big One

In the Spring of 2010, Mike Willover and I turned fifty. Alice and I flew to Orlando to celebrate with him and Lisa. While Mike and I went out golfing, Lisa and Alice set up a surprise party and packed the house with food and guests. It was a festive day. While Mike and I realized we had to grow old, we certainly did not need to grow up. We are still the teenagers we were several decades earlier.

Vacation to San Diego and LA

The following weekend was spring break. The kids wanted to see California, so we stayed in a Marriott on Coronado Island, and toured both Los Angeles and San Diego for a week. At Madame Tussaud's wax museum, Katie sat next to the model of Katharine Houghton Hepburn, the relative whom she was named after. Later, we rode an open tour bus through Beverly Hills and Rodeo Drive, strolled along the Hollywood Walk of Fame, saw the Footprints of the Stars at Grauman's Chinese Theatre, and stopped at the Kodak Theater (now Dolby Theatre), which hosts the annual Academy Awards ceremony.

Toward the end of the day, we spent some time on Malibu Beach, but we were all a bit disappointed that Barbie and Ken were not there. The next day, we went to Disneyland, where we met our friends, Steve and Kim Dameron. Their family was also visiting Southern California. The day spent with the Dameron's would kick off three years of shared spring breaks. The Kachejian clan spent another family day at Sea World with all the orcas, dolphins, rays, flamingos and turtles. We wrapped up the trip spending a day at the San Diego Zoo Wild Animal Park.

Shelley's Trip to Disney World

My sister Shelley is an Air Force veteran. Being disabled, she could not drive or travel on her own. She had always wanted to see the theme parks in Orlando.

Kent and I took Shelley on her big trip in the summer of 2010. Her nurse friend, Marcella Jenkins, traveled with us to accompany Shelley. To get around Orlando more easily, we rented a wheelchair van and reserved an ADA handicapped room at the Sheraton Vistana Villages Resort. Shelley was able to visit the Magic Kingdom, Epcot and Animal Kingdom. The only problem with the entire trip was that it was too short!

With Shelley and Marcella at Disney

Book Signing in McLean

In July of 2010, the first version of my book, *SUVs SUCK in Combat* was completed and published. We held a book signing in McLean at the home of Debbie MacDougall and Richard Levick. Their remarkable home reminded me of the Prime Minister's residence in Baghdad. Alice planned most of the event and hired a great caterer. It turned into a fun reunion with family and friends. But most importantly, many of my teammates from the Gulf Region Division (GRD) in Iraq came to celebrate with us: Alex Dornstauder (with Marion), Bob Cabell, Hal Creel, Chris Kolditz, and Scott and Michelle Lowdermilk. And riding up on their Harley-Davidson motorcycles were Jim Hampton and Ben Benner from Alabama. To top it off, the book publishers, Dennis Lowery and Jim Zumwalt, were able to join us and meet some of the soldiers they had learned so much about.

GRD Reunion

Over the next few weeks, I was involved in two less formal book signings. The first was with the Peck family. Mary and Blake Peck are former neighbors and generous friends that have become family. Blake had also graduated from West Point. In the fall, we had another signing event at the Chester County Bookstore in my hometown of West Chester, Pennsylvania. It always felt good to "go home," see many of my long-time friends and neighbors and tell them about our wartime experiences. Many thanks to Craig Surrick for helping me plan this event and extend the invitations. Over the next few years, many other new doors opened. I was invited to speak at some major conferences, media events (C-SPAN, Heritage Foundation, Huffington Post Live), radio outlets, the National Defense University and private events. I often reflected on my life and how it had changed since leaving my boyhood hometown. As a teenager, I used to deliver the local news on a bicycle. Now I was delivering it—my opinions and lessons learned on a variety of topics—in a more public forum.

2011

Bermuda Cruise

The Dameron family had planned to take a cruise to Bermuda during spring break of 2011 and asked if our family wanted to join them. Bermuda was on our bucket list, so we accepted the offer. Steve, Kim and Lauren Dameron boarded the Carnival Pride with us, and we sailed out of Baltimore. On the way out of the harbor, we saw Fort McHenry, the battle site that inspired Francis Scott Key to write the Star-Spangled Banner. We were now enroute to a beautiful island with a British heritage.

Bermuda Cruise Team

After we had docked, we began to explore Bermuda. We enjoyed great vistas from the historic gun battery at Fort Scaur. We also stopped at Summerset Bridge, famous for being the world's smallest drawbridge. We walked along the pink sands of Horseshoe Beach. A rare earthquake had hit Bermuda the day before we arrived, breaking open a huge rock outcropping on the beach. While experiencing much of Bermuda's beauty, our tour guide noted that many of the rich and famous owned homes there, including Ross Perot, Michael Bloomberg, and the Italian Prime Minister. We also enjoyed taking an "Undersea Walk" and riding on Segways through the port and shopping areas.

Katie & Kara - Undersea Walk

2011

Graduations

In June, Katie graduated from sixth grade. We had been blessed that all three of our kids spent their elementary school years at the highly-respected Hunt Valley School. The public schools in Northern Virginia had a well-deserved reputation for excellence. The "Breaking News" in 2011 was Kent's graduation from West Springfield High School. He had accepted an offer to attend Christopher Newport University (CNU) in Newport News in August. After the ceremony, Kent visited with Mama and Papa Perez so they could celebrate the moment, too.

Kent visits Mama and Papa Perez after Graduation

Our Florida relatives had flown to Virginia a few days early for Kent's graduation. We toured the Washington D.C. area with them and saw the Holocaust Museum and Arlington Cemetery with Stacey, Cameron, and Kristoffer Patasnik, as well as Mike Walker. On Sunday, Mike invited me to the U.S. Open Championship at the Congressional Country Club in Bethesda, Maryland. He had two clubhouse tickets on the 18th hole! It was the only professional golf tournament I had ever attended. It was phenomenal! During the competition, Rory McIlroy set eleven U.S. Open records, including the lowest total under par (−16) in a 72-hole competition.

Disney Cruise to the Mediterranean

Before Kent went off to college, we decided to have one more, big, family vacation: a Disney cruise through the Mediterranean Sea. We flew to

Barcelona, Spain a day early and enjoyed all the sights. The next day, we boarded the Disney Magic. [However, we made one big mistake. We used our credit card in Barcelona, and the number was immediately stolen. We did not discover the theft until the cruise was over. That's when we learned that some thief in Germany had bought first-class airline tickets to Russia and stayed in a luxury hotel. It was a hard lesson to learn. The local criminals knew which tourists were boarding the cruise ships and saw them as easy prey.]

Our first stop was supposed to be in Tunis, the capital of Tunisia, on the North African coast. However, a civil war had broken out shortly before the ship sailed, so Disney dropped the port from the itinerary. I would have paid extra to sit offshore Tunisia, so I could drink beer and watch the rocket-propelled grenades (RPGs) fly around the city. That would be high-quality entertainment.

Our cruise stopped in Valetta, Malta first, an island nation, south of Italy. Malta has a rich history due to its strategic location, and it was ruled by many different powers. Paul the Apostle was shipwrecked on Malta. We toured the island and enjoyed the beautiful scenery, fishing villages, and architecture. The Blue Grotto was our favorite spot.

Our next four stops were in Italy and started in Palermo on the island of Sicily. We then sailed on to Naples where we toured the ruins of nearby Pompeii and Mount Vesuvius. Pompeii was an ancient Roman city destroyed by the eruption of Mount Vesuvius in 79 AD. While walking around the excavated ruins, I was surprised by the size and complexity of the city. We climbed to the top of Mount Vesuvius and looked into the volcanic crater. The weather at the top was much cooler and windier. The crater was foggy at first, but the wind helped to clear the inside of the crater, providing a spectacular view.

Our next port of call was at Civitavecchia near the great city of Rome. We packed a lot of touring into this day. Our stops included St. Peter's Square, an inside tour of the Vatican, Trevi Fountain, the Coliseum, and the Roman Forum. We all left Rome feeling like we needed several more days to explore its rich history and culture, and the fine food.

The next Italian port was La Spezia, where we could choose to tour either Florence or Pisa. I had already been to Florence, so I voted to see Pisa and its famous leaning tower. It was another beautiful sunny Italian day. The next morning, we arrived in Ajaccio, Corsica, a large mountainous island that is part of France. Unfortunately, it was the only day of the cruise with rainy weather. We did not get to explore much beyond the port city. We did see the house where Napoleon was born in 1769. The rain cleared as our ship left the port.

The final port of call was Villefranche-sur-Mer on the French Riviera. Once we were ashore, we toured eastwards along the coast until we reached Monaco and Monte Carlo. It was a beautiful coastline and an exciting day. On the way back to the ship, the girls wanted to sunbathe for a few hours on the French Riviera.

Kachejian Crew on the French Riviera

Gina Curley tackles Alaska

While we were on the Disney cruise, Carol Coleman and her parents, Paul and Joanne, had invited Gina to visit Alaska. Gina and Carol were long-time neighbors and friends.

Gina spent a week exploring Alaska. They stopped in the port of Homer and visited the crew of the famous fishing vessel *Time Bandit*, from the TV show, *Deadliest Catch*. While out on a fishing trip, they spotted whales and later, flew on a seaplane to a remote area where they could see bears, caribou, and bald eagles. Gina came home utterly grateful and energized by the Alaska trip.

Carol and Gina caught in the Crab Trap

A few weeks later, Gina's son, Peter, now out of the Army, bought a house on Pensacola Beach, providing Gina with an ocean getaway on the south coast.

The Get Away

Every year or so, Alice traveled with several of her friends to Arizona or Florida for a girl's getaway, long weekend. Alice hates winters, so the break usually happened in February. Husbands were not invited, but we were expected to pick up some extra duties. That meant I had to run the household, keep the kids alive and manage all the supporting functions: school, homework, sports practices, doctors' appointments, meals, pets, and laundry. I lacked cooking skills. The kids complained when I burned the spaghetti and tried to feed them MREs. I was glad Alice was able to spend some quality time with her long-time friends, but I was always thankful when she decided to come back home!

Baptism—Take Two

I had attended Burke Community Church (BCC) for several years and finally became a member. BCC's mission is to know Christ and to make Him known. I found it a very different church. The men of BCC shared their faith openly, had high moral character, and were committed to helping each other stay on a good path. "As iron sharpens iron, so one man sharpens another," Proverbs 27:17. So the men of BCC became part of my extended family.

I knew I had been baptized as an infant because I had a nice certificate to prove it. But at the age of two, humans really don't understand their choices or the concept of free will. For many years, I had been ignorant and uncertain about my spirituality. It took years for me to reflect back on all the events in my life and how my family had persevered. I am a man of science and always sought to understand cause and effect relationships in nature. All of the wonders of the universe, all the grand laws of science, down to the authoring of the DNA code, were far beyond any possible coincidence or cosmic accident. There had to be—and is—a grand design and a Great Creator.

I did not want there to be any doubt about my faith and salvation. When I physically die, I want to be assured of eternal life. So, fifty years later, in March 2012, I decided it was time to publicly profess my faith in the Lord Jesus Christ by being baptized in front of my family and the congregation. It was so easy to do and felt so right. And now, having a relationship with God has made my life much easier to both understand and to enjoy.

Choosing whether to have faith is the most important decision every human being will make in their lifetime. Those that decide to ignore God are taking the biggest gamble they could ever make. My advice to all, don't wait until it is too late.

Eleuthera Bahamas 2012

During spring break of 2012, the Kachejians and Damerons rented a house on Eleuthera Island in the Bahamas. We all wanted to get away from the world for a week. Alice and Kim selected a house on a beautiful strip of beach that had formerly been a Club Med resort. There was plenty to entertain us. On the first day, we went on a Fishbone Boat Tour with our hosts Captain Julius and his wife Robin. We caught conch and used them in a fresh salad.

We all went snorkeling and found some massive orange starfish. Later, Cowboy Steve Dameron lept off the boat and caught a sea turtle. On land, another day, we headed north and crossed the Glass Window Bridge, a point where the island was only as wide as the road. The dark blue Atlantic Ocean was roaring on one side of the road, and the turquoise blue calm Caribbean Sea was on the other side. We continued on and took a ferry to Harbour Island where we rented golf carts to explore Dunmore Town. Golf carts are the only vehicles permitted on the island. We ate lunch, visited a haunted house and spent some time on a pink beach.

Sunset Dinner on Eleuthera

Back at the house, we took long walks on the beach. Kara and I brought our lacrosse sticks, ready to show the locals our skills. However, there was no one else on the beach. The two families had it all to ourselves! If the Jamaicans could have an Olympic Bobsled Team, then Kara and I could certainly start a Bahamian National Lacrosse Team. We traveled south, on another day, to a park called Ocean Hole. Many of the locals enjoyed this inland hole, a large lake surrounded by cliffs. The hole was connected underground to the ocean and was full of tropical fish and sea turtles. Kamikaze Steve was the first one to dive off the cliffs, and the rest of us decided to join him once we knew he had survived the jump. It's always good to have a fearless stuntman lead the way.

Best Ranger Competition

Captains: Nate Curley and Quinn McArthur

In April, Gina, Peter and I traveled to Fort Benning, Georgia to see Nate Curley compete in the "Best Ranger" competition, a grueling 60-hour event for Decathlon-caliber Soldier-Athletes. Two-man Ranger teams undergo continuous stressful physical and psychological events, and there is no sleep programmed: Extended foot marches, airborne operations, rifle, and pistol marksmanship, climbing, rappelling, first aid, grenades, demolitions, communications. The list is extensive. Only about half of the 50 teams that start are able to finish. Nate's two-man buddy team came in 17th place. I remember watching them both climb the sixty-foot rock wall like Spiderman. Following the competition, they both entered the Special Forces Qualification Course (the "Q Course") to earn their Green Berets.

Harley

In May, I received a call from Kara asking me to drive to the Fairfax Animal Shelter and see a dog. I was a bit hesitant. For some years, our house had been Noah's Ark and—with all the kids getting older—nearing what seemed the end of that, I did not want to take on a high maintenance dog. However, I agreed to see the dog and consider a new pet. I arrived at the shelter and found Alice, Kara, and Katie all playing with a good-looking caramel-colored female dog. She immediately reminded me of the two dogs I had as a boy, Scrooge and Queenie. She was a rescue animal, and Kara had already named her Harley. Harley and I got along immediately, and I did exactly what I promised myself I would not do. I agreed to adopt another animal. I could tell Harley was going to fit in well with the family. We asked the shelter worker what breed Harley was, and she stated, "a lab mix." We later gave her a DNA test and found out she was a combination of seven breeds, none of them related to a Labrador. Shockingly, Harley was half Chihuahua; hard to believe since she grew to about five times larger, at 45 pounds. So, Harley joined our family and has been a great addition. Harley loves chasing squirrels and eating cicadas. Once, while on an evening walk, she ate a toad and became quite sick. We were very concerned that she might die. Fortunately, after several days, she got rid of the deadly creature in what I called a "download of the road toad." Harley was much happier afterward and now just sniffs the neighborhood toads. She has no more desire to eat them. Harley moved to Florida with us and misses her boyfriend Bradley (Husky) and friend Shotsy (Alaskan Malamute), but she loves chasing the lizards. Yum!

Army-Navy Football in Style

I attended many of these football classics as a cadet and as a recent graduate, sitting in the freezing cold, rooting for the Army team and hoping the sun would eventually shine on our side the stadium. For five years in the mid-1990s, Alice and I hosted an Army-Navy game party at our house. Army won all five close games. We had good food, plenty of beverages and heat - all the things we were denied as cadets. Life was good. When Pete and Nate Curley were cadets, Gina and I started to go to the games again. In 2002, it was Peter's Plebe year, and we had a tailgate on another cold day. I missed attending the games in 2003 and 2004 due to the death of our Mother and the war in Iraq. Each of our children, Kent, Kara, and Katie, were able to attend one of the games.

Mark and Carol Reynolds of West Chester, Pennsylvania had hosted a suite at the annual Army-Navy football game in Philadelphia for some years, and they generously invited us to join them. There is an old adage in the

Army, "You don't have to practice being miserable." I was more than glad to accept their offer. It was indoor, heated, and stocked with all kinds of goodies. We could watch the game live in relative comfort.

Mark Reynolds with 1st Lieut. Robert Livengood,
& First Sergeant Rob Alivso

Pre-Game at Army-Navy

616

Years earlier, Mark had been an enlisted Marine, but he liked to have a few token Army guys in the crowd. He had fought his way into and through the Wharton School of Business. He and Carol have a successful business and are very patriotic. Mark supported my Army unit in Iraq and several Marine units in Afghanistan by sending hard-to-get supplies. In doing so, he built some strong relationships with tactical commanders and senior military officers.

The Army-Navy rivalry began on the bus ride to Philadelphia, fueled by fresh breakfast food and mimosas. A few dozen friends joined the annual ritual. We started telling war stories and making bold predictions about the outcome of the game. Alex and Kim Chotkowski were a Marine family and also lawyers. They knew how to fight with their hands and their words. Brian Burlingame, a former Navy Captain, was never afraid to speak his mind. We usually arrived at the suite early enough to see the march-on of the two academies.

Every year, the suite turned into a highly-spirited rivalry. Mark would invite some midshipmen and cadets to the suite to add to the flavor and let them warm up and eat. Soon after, the crazy old Army guys would challenge the Squids to a push-up contest.

Mark and Carol's other Marine guests included Jon Kenney and James Nash, who had just returned from Afghanistan. One year, we were honored to host General and Mrs. James Conway, the former USMC Commandant. On the Army side were my nephews, Peter and Nate Curley, and Cadet Jeff Nielsen with his parents, Ken and Mariana. The Curley brothers were both combat veterans from Iraq. Jeff has since graduated and has joined the Ranger ranks. We also had a distinguished Army aviator among us, Dave Salter.

In 2008, President Bush attended the game. We enjoyed watching him tee up a football and kick a field goal during the pre-game.

In 2011, President Obama attended the game which was played in Washington, D.C. Mark was resourceful and able to secure a suite at the stadium. Ironically, the suite was owned by the Embassy of the United Arab Emirates (UAE). I chuckled as I entered it. I had a friend—former colleague, Major General Obaid Al Ketbi—from the National Defense University who was a senior leader in the UAE. I sent him an email letting him know where I was and that we were enjoying the suite. I was surprised when he answered so quickly and in perfect English. General Obaid was in the UAE Air Force, so he probably was not taking sides during the game.

In 2012, Mark tried to convert me into a Navy fan. In the summer, he invited me and some his Marine friends for a day of fun and jet skiing at his house on the Chesapeake Bay. In September, he and Carol asked me to a dinner on the battleship, USS New Jersey.

In early December, Mark and I attended the Travis Manion Foundation dinner, a fundraiser for fallen warriors. While there, Mark introduced me to the USMC Commandant, General Amos. I was able to reciprocate by introducing Mark to Alex Gorsky a West Point classmate, who was the CEO of Johnson & Johnson. He was also the Vice Chairman of the Travis Manion Board of Directors. Alex told me he personally knew 1st Lieut. Travis Manion as they had both lived in Doylestown, Pennsylvania. Travis graduated from the Naval Academy and was killed while conducting

Meeting General Amos

combat operations in Anbar province, Iraq in 2007.

A few days later, we were back at the Army-Navy game. Vice President Joe Biden attended, and Assistant Secretary of the Navy Juan Garcia visited Mark and Carol's suite. After the game, Mark gave his guests a tour of his 8,000-bottle wine cellar. Mark felt so bad that Navy won another game that he broke open an old bottle of wine from the late 1800s. Despite all his valiant efforts throughout the year, Mark was unable to convert me into a Navy football fan.

The following year, Mark continued his efforts to transform me into a Marine by inviting me to the USMC Ball at the Gaylord Center outside of Washington D.C. It was a fantastic evening with a lot of celebration. Several guests had repeatedly asked me to wear my uniform. I was a recent retiree, but I was proud to do so. I was one of the few Army guys in a sea of Marines at the event.

ASN Juan Garcia, Mark, Brian Burlingame, Seamus McCaffery

A month later came Army-Navy. That year, Mark went big. He hosted two suites, one reserved for wounded warriors. During the game, we met Roger Staubach, the Navy Heisman Trophy winner and Super Bowl MVP, who was with USAA in the adjacent suite. He was rumored to be rooting for Navy. Other than that, he seemed a nice guy.

Back in Mark and Carol's suite, the noise level picked up, and we put all rank aside. Except we still called General Conway, "Sir." He and his wife seemed to be enjoying the barrage of Army and Navy jokes.

Part of the Army strategy in our suite was to divide the Marines from the Navy fans; we wanted the Marines to cheer for Army. It was planned as a three-phased psychological operation.

Cadets soften up General Conway while Burlingame surrenders

Phase One of the plan was to get the Marines drunk. Too easy. Pete and I fed them beers and asked them what they did in the Marine Corps. Then we'd start telling a bunch of war stories that were partially true. Marines were easy to read, so we knew when we had them hooked. Now it was time to get them another beer. We started to drop the names of other famous Marines that we had met, served with or read about. Sometimes it was a stretch: Al Gray, Chesty Puller, Peter Pace. The Marines listened intensely and communicated with each other by facial expressions. We got some head nods.

Phase Two began when their guard was down. We started making logical connections between the Army and the Marines.

> Army: *The Army and Marines are both ground combat forces, right?*
> Marine: *Yeah, we served alongside the Army in Iraq.*

Army: *The way I see it, the Army and Marines have a lot more in common than the Navy and Marines. I mean, do you really trust someone in the Navy with a weapon? Scary thought. Right?*

Marine: *Yeah, it gives me nightmares.*

Army: *Here, have another beer.*

Marine: *Thanks, bro.*

Army: *The Marines use a lot of Army equipment to get their job done. Abrams tanks, artillery, helicopters, rifles, radios, ammo... I mean, the Army pays to develop all that good stuff, and we let the Marines use it too. We are both land warriors fighting for team USA. The Navy doesn't spend squat to equip the Marine Corp. You guys get shorted by the Navy.*

Marine: *Yeah! The friggin' Navy treats us like dirt.*

Army: *The Navy simply signs your paychecks. In wartime, they might give Marines a slow ride to the fight. Then they quickly scoot back out to sea and leave the Marines to fight their way to the beach. Does it seem like they cut and run?'*

Marines: *Damn right!*

Army: *Your beer looks low. Let me get you another one.*

Marine: *Awesome!*

Phase Three was the final effort to win over the Marines.

Army: *So, the way I see it, the Army and Marines were really cousins, maybe brothers. The Navy was just a floating taxi and hotel. That means this game is a bit jacked up. It should not be Army vs. Navy. It should be Army and Marines vs. Navy. I mean, we are the band of brothers. The Navy hasn't done the Marine Corps any favors.*

Marine: Head nod. *Yeah, you're right. This game is jacked up!*

Now here is where Peter Curley went for the direct kill on the former USMC Commandant, General Jim Conway:

Pete: *"Sir, the Marines are just like the Army. They just need a little more training!"*

As General Conway was laughing hysterically, we handed him a "Go Army" banner, and we snapped the picture. Score: Army/Marines 1, Navy 0.

George Lindsey and USMC General James Conway says "Go Army"

So, there you have it. We revealed a deep distrust the Marines have for the Navy. Real Marines want their Army brothers to knock the snot out Navy, but they were afraid their paychecks may get docked. Our strategy worked. The Army and Marines won the third quarter of that game (7-3).

After the game, the crew all rode in an elevator to leave the stadium. Army and Navy fans packed in. Brian Burlingame, a seasoned Naval Academy grad, towered over the crowd. He spied a midshipman and asked him what field he was going to serve in after graduation (aviation, submarines, surface ships, Marine Corps, etc.). The midshipman responded with great enthusiasm, "Sir, I'm going Logistics." Brian paused for a moment and looked down at him and replied, "What's the matter? Are you broken?" When the door opened, the young middie slithered off the elevator. It was good to see that old Navy grads had high expectations for the new generation.

The ride home from the game included a discussion of why Navy football had won every game since the 9/11 attacks. The answer to Army was clear. Army football has a difficult time recruiting Blue Chip athletes during a land war. Most West Point graduates could expect to deploy to Iraq and Afghanistan soon after they graduated. Given a choice, star players will select Navy or Air Force over Army since they did not want to face a hardship tour. If they went to West Point, their slim chance of making into the NFL after a combat tour would be virtually zero.

Location plays another factor. Football recruits come to Army during a cold New York winter. It's a remote area. New York City is about fifty miles away, but recruits were told they won't have much time off and can't have a car for their first three years. So, football recruits then go to the Naval Academy in the spring and see downtown Annapolis, a beautiful, clean city with lots of bars and pretty girls.

The Navy recruiter then reminds them if they choose to join Army football, they will almost certainly be deployed to Iraq or Afghanistan after they graduate. And the statistics of the war were very telling. Nearly six times more West Pointers had been killed in Iraq and Afghanistan than Naval Academy graduates (95 vs. 16). Most of the Navy losses were Marines or SEALs, involved in land combat operations.

Breaking news! After fourteen straight Navy victories, Army football beat Navy 21-17 in December 2016. It is a clear sign that the wars in Iraq and Afghanistan are finally winding down. I went to the game with Pete Curley and his fiancé, Nicole Prochak. The only tickets we could find were on the Navy side of the field. So, we sat in hostile territory and recruited Navy fans to root for Army. Mission complete! In 2017, Army won again 14-13, and also beat Air Force, taking the Commander-in-Chief's Trophy.

Army Retirement

I retired from the Army in June 2012 after thirty years, having an exciting and rewarding career that had taken me all over the world. It was hard to hang up my uniform, but I looked forward to having only one career. We held the ceremony in Winchester, Virginia led by Major General Mike Eyre. I made one final request at the end of the ceremony, Scott Lowdermilk and I knocked out 50 pushups while in our dress uniform. Yes, the old guys still had it.

Retirement—Kachejian family photo

We had a memorable reception at our house, a reunion of family and friends. We were particularly honored that our relatives, Billy and Chrissie Martyn, whom we had not seen in years, were able to join us. And they delivered the goods, a big bottle of Dom Perignon! Alice and I have stayed in much closer contact with the Martyn's since reconnecting that day. "Live to Love, and you will Love to Live."

2013

Curacao Vacation

During spring break in 2013, we rented a house with the Dameron family on the island of Curacao, just off the coast of Venezuela. We relaxed by hanging out by the pool, visited by colorful tropical birds, and enjoyed some excellent restaurants. Kara and I took our lacrosse sticks to brush up on our skills. On most days, we went on local excursions to the Kueba di Hato caves, rode a catamaran along the coast, snorkeled over a shipwreck, and explored the backcountry using off-road ATVs. We spent some time at the beach and rode banana boats on the ocean. We spent an afternoon in Willemstad, the capital, enjoying the sights and walked across the harbor on the 550-foot Queen Emma Pontoon Bridge to explore Rif Fort village. The floating bridge swung open to allow ships to enter and exit the tropical port.

Bank of America—Near Miss

In April 2013, I connected with Emma Nelson who was casting a TV commercial for Bank of America. The company was seeking military members and their families that had family trees with a military legacy. They wanted to incorporate these stories into an advertising campaign. About twenty veteran families were being considered, and each needed to document their military heritage as far back as possible. The casting crew wanted some artifacts to use in the commercial. Only one family would be selected.

I had already developed a family tree, so I started to call our relatives to confirm their service and those of previous generations. Uncle Haig knew all the Armenian relatives. I also collected some photos and documents to validate their service. I verified our family had over twenty veterans that served during most of America's history, in the Army, Navy, Air Force and Merchant Marine. We did not have all the records, but I suspected there were more veterans from earlier generations.

Alice's side of our family was established in America much earlier, starting in 1630. When younger, she had been informed that her aunt was a Daughter of the American Revolution. In fact, Alice's ancestor, Peter Stearns served during the Revolutionary War in the Rhode Island Campaign. She had two old military artifacts from her family stored somewhere in the house, but we could not find either in our initial search. The first was a letter from a mother to her son, who was drafted during the Civil War. Enclosed with this letter was a $5 gold piece. The mother instructed her son to use the coin to help him come home after the war ended. The second item that we could not locate was a set of silver spoons that had belonged to Captain Roland Luther, West Point Class of 1836. He had initially served in the Florida Indian War and on May 8, 1846, was wounded at the Battle of Palo Alto during the

Mexican War. General Zachary Taylor was the Commander of American Forces and later became the 12th President of the United States.

Our family made it to the final round of the Bank of America selection process. I offered the casting team a few dozen artifacts from World War II, Korea, Vietnam, and Iraq, but these were not old and unique enough for the final selection. The casting team really wanted our family to produce an older and more unique artifact, the gold coin, the letter or the spoons. I tore apart our house and still could not find them. Consequently, our family did not make the final selection for the commercial.

The family that was selected was able to trace their lineage to the Battle of San Juan Hill on July 1, 1898. That was when Teddy Roosevelt led the Rough Riders to victory near Santiago, Cuba.

Two years later, I found the spoons from Captain Roland Luther, far too late to be considered for the commercial. The spoons had been wrapped in felt and sitting in a kitchen drawer, right in plain sight. They were accompanied by an old note. In 2018, I found the gold $5.00 coin, dated 1861, and a note that confirmed it was "carried by great, great grandfather Samuel Ringwalt in the Civil War."

Family note accompanying Captain Luther's spoon

On the following two pages are a summary of our family's veterans that I would like to recognize and the Bush Family Tree:

Family of Veterans

Name	Rev War	Fl Ind War	Mexico	Civil	WWI	WWII	Korea	Vietnam	Cold War	War on Terror	Notes
Peter Stearns	X										Served in the Rhode Island Campaign
Roland Luther		X									Captain, wounded, USMA 1836
Samuel Ringwalt			X								Civil War note and $5 gold coin
Aram Kachejian				X							Horse Cavalry (Armenia)
Archie Kift					X						Military Police Auxiliary (age 60)
Albert Kachejian						X					Registered, but died
John Geovjian						X					Navy PT boats
Morris Arabian						X					Army. Liberated concentration camps
Alex Kachejian						X					Navy
Paul O'Koorian						X					Navy
James Bush						X	X	X	X		Colonel, Army Air Corps, USAF, DIA, 30 yrs
Haig Geovjian							X				Army Signal Corps
Anthony Klijian									X		Army
Karabed Kachejian									X		Army, 101st Abn & Merchant Marine
George Kachejian									X		Cadet at Penna Military College
Arnie Bauman									X		USAFR
Phil Baker									X		Navy
Rochelle Kachejian									X		USAF, Reconnaissance Imagery Dev
Charlie Puchakjian									X	X	USAF Security, Aerial Refueler
Nancy Klijian									X		2LT, USAR Nurse
Kerry Kachejian									X	X	Colonel, Engineer, USMA 1982, 30 yrs
Peter Curley										X	Captain, Artillery, USMA 2006
Nathaniel Curley										X	Captain, Special Forces, USMA 2008

Family Veterans

627

James Houghton Bush
b 9-16   Hagerstown, Md

Deborah Ann Bush
b 10-25   Hagerstown, Md

James Odell Bush   m   I Elizabeth Luther Houghton
b 3-5-1924 Roanoke, Va   12-7-1943   b 2-11-1925 Akron, Ohio

II Ira Luther Houghton   m   II Alice Stearns
   b. 6-25-1895 Baltimore, Md.   9-4-1923   b. 9-7-1896 Fredericksburg, Va.

III Ira Holden Houghton   III Frank Percival Stearns
    b. 5-7-1865 m. Louise Luther Ringwalt   b. 8-3-1868 Washington, D.C.
    d. 10-7-1942 Cincinnati, Ohio   d. 6-25-1932 m. Betty Lewis
IV Charles Emory Houghton   IV Doran Harding Stearns
    b. 8-24-1827 Harvard, Mass.   b. 11-5-1841 Lincoln, Vt
    d. 1-2-1908   m. Caroline S. McMurray   d.   -1904? m. Emeline Jackson Gilham
V Steadman Houghton   V Joseph Merrill Stearns
    b. 8-28-1799 Still River, Mass (Houghton House)   b. 10-7-1815 Ripton, Vt.
    d. 5-9-1888   m. Ann Cragin   d. 11-12-1884 m. Phila Smith
VI Thomas Houghton   VI Nathaniel Wheat Stearns
    b. 1-8-1767 Still River, Mass   b. 3-22-1784 Plymouth, N.H.
    d. 5-1-1848   m. Betsey White   d. 5-5-1856 m. Levina Harding
VII Elijah Houghton   VII Peter Stearns
    b. 6-2-1739 Still River, Mass   b.   -1734 Ho. is N.H.
    d. 7-20-1819 m. Mercy Whitney   d. served 1813 m. Abadil Wheat
VIII Thomas Houghton   Revolutionary War, Rhode Is. campaign
    b.   -1696 Still River, Mass   VIII Samuel Stearns, Jr.
    d. 3-9-1764 m. Maria Moore   b. 3-7-1702 Lexington? Mass
IX James Houghton   d.   1787 m. Keziah Robbins
    b. Charleston or Woburn, Mass.   IX Samuel Stearns
    d.   -1711 m. Mary Sawyer   b. 1-11-1667-8 Lexington, Mass
X Ralph Houghton   d. 11-19-1721 m. Phoebe
    b.   -1623 Lancaster, England   X Isaac Stearns, Jr
    d. 4-15-1705 Milton, Mass   b. 1-6-1633 Watertown, Mass
    m. Jane Stowe. America between   d. 8-29-1676 m. Sarah Beers, d. of
    1635-1647. He signed Lancaster   Captain Richard Beers slain by Indians
    Covenant in 1652. Home in   (King Philips War 1675)
    Lancaster, Mass. burned by Indians 1675   XI Isaac Stearns
                                                     b. England m. Mary Barker. (Landed
                                                     d. 6-19-1671) Salem Mass 6-12-1630

MALORE LE TORT

ABSQUE LABORE NIHIL

Bush Family Tree

628

Workouts with Rick

For over a decade, Alice and her friends had fitness workouts with Rick Bucinell, an amazingly talented trainer. We were introduced to Rick through his former roommate, Joe Massimino. Every week he came to our house and led Alice, Charlene Salter, Krista Busky, Mary Elizabeth Morris, Karen Massimino and several others in an hour of challenging workouts. Rick is a man of many achievements, yet he always remained humble. As a world champion power lifter, he is built like a battleship. He competes in the International Weightlifting Federation (IWF) and has won five IWF Masters World Championships and seven National Master Championships along with forty-three U.S. and international records. Rick was recently inducted into the Strength and Power Hall of Fame in his home state of New York.

Rick Bucinell and the Girls

Emergency Room Visits

In 2014, not wanting Kent to have the lead in emergency room visits, Katie opened a soda, snapped off the metal top, and dropped it into the can. She then—not thinking about she'd just done—gulped down the soda and swallowed the top. We spent the next couple of days at the hospital getting X-rays and a bronchoscope to locate the elusive cap. The medical staff never found it, but we did help a few of the doctors pay off their mortgages that month.

2014 & 2018 / Kara Graduation

The big family event in 2014 was Kara's graduation from West Springfield High School. She attended James Madison University (JMU) in Harrisonburg, Virginia, where she played club field hockey, joined Tri Delta and entered the School of Nursing. Kara was selected for two academic nursing scholarships during her junior and senior years. In 2017, she accepted a competitive internship at Georgetown MedStar University Hospital as a summer nurse technician on a medical-surgical intermediate care unit that specialized in cardiac, vascular and hepatology patients. Kara graduated magna cum laude from JMU in 2018 and started a position in the New Graduate Nurse Residency program at MedStar Georgetown University Hospital in the Surgical ICU after passing her boards. Kara is currently a Magnet BSN, RN and has completed her nurse residency. She hopes to sit for her Critical Care Registered Nurse (CCRN) certification soon and eventually apply to CRNA school where she'll become a Doctor of Nurse Anesthesia Practice (DNAP).

2016, 2018 & 2019 / Kent Graduation

The big family event in 2016 was Kent's graduation from Christopher Newport University (CNU). As a student, he had been selected to present his academic work at the annual Paideia Conference. He was also admitted to Sigma Tau Delta, an International Collegiate Honor Society for English. While working on his undergraduate degree, Kent helped to charter the Delta Upsilon Fraternity. Kent continued his studies at CNU and received a BA in Classical Studies in 2018. He followed up by attending Maharishi University and received a MA degree in Consiousness and Human Potential in 2019. Kent continues to pursue language studies and discovered his affinity for Greek, Latin, Persian and Arabic.He is excited to see what comes next.

2017 / Katie Graduation

The big family event in 2017 was Katie's graduation from West Springfield High School. Her academic achievements were remarkable, and she was selected as an Honor Graduate. Katie accepted an offer to attend Virginia Tech in Fall of 2017, where she continues to play field hockey. The Virginia

Tech Field Hockey team won Nationals in the Fall 2017 and Spring 2018. Go Hokies!

Katie entered the Honors College and will major in animal and poultry sciences. She loves animals and plans to follow up her undergraduate studies by attending veterinarian school. She was a scholar-athlete in high school, and she intends to apply all her talent and energy to helping animals. Katie joined Zeta Tau Alpha and serves on the Philanthropy Committee. We can't wait to see what the future brings.

With Kent, Kara, and Katie entering their adult years, Alice and I are very relieved that we had three "good launches." Our children turned into remarkable young adults; despite the fact they had a paperboy for a father. I have to give most of the credit to Alice.

CHAPTER 52
FAMILY MEMORIES

WATERCOLOR

Alice and I enjoyed our family time in the Outer Banks of North Carolina so much that in August 2002 we returned. But this time, it was on a house hunting trip. Our real estate agent, Margaret Allen, was a pleasure to work with. We fell in love with a property called "Watercolor." It was in a four-wheel drive area of the beach where wild horses roamed.

We made an offer, and to our surprise, in September, Alice and I closed on our own beach house. We made one of our first trips there with our neighbors, Regina and Richard Cotton and their young children, Rachel, Ricky, and Renee.

Watercolor - The new family beach house in Corolla.

Roasting marshmallows with the Cotton clan.

Watercolor was a semi-ocean front house. There was a privately-owned lot with a sand dune in front of Watercolor. The owner of the dune was not permitted to build on the oceanfront lot, so the property actually preserved our view and protected our house. At the settlement table, I made a humorous and foretelling remark. "I am signing for this semi-ocean front property with the expectation that I will be upgraded to ocean front during the first hurricane." The comment drew a few laughs.

One year later, in September of 2003, Hurricane Isabel, the costliest, deadliest, and strongest hurricane of the season plowed into the North Carolina coast. At its peak, Isabel was a devastating Category Five storm, and the projected landfall for the eye was directly over our Watercolor. For several days, we were extremely concerned that we would lose the entire property.

To make the situation more stressful, one of my Springfield neighbors, a certified, card-carrying imbecile, who worked for the federal government, taunted me in the street about it, much like an immature fifth grader. He gleefully danced around saying, "Your house is going to be destroyed! You're going to lose everything!" He laughed in my face. I was enraged and about to completely unload on the jackass when his embarrassed wife dragged him back in the house. I was ready to go to jail to have the pleasure of disemboweling the jerk and then wrapping his intestines around his neck. It took every ounce of my being not to commit a fully justified murder that day. I know many of my fellow neighbors would have applauded his demise.

Fortunately, Hurricane Isabel weakened to a Category Two storm and drifted further south just before making landfall. The storm hit the coast with 105 mph winds and damaged or destroyed hundreds of homes. Our realtor, Margaret Allen, called us with a report of the damage the following day. Two of the homes near us were destroyed. The sand dune in front of us was flattened, but it saved our house. We had some wind damage. The storm surge had come up to the house, undermined our well and disrupted the power and phone service. There were a lot of repairs and cleaning to do, but Watercolor had survived.

Out of adversity comes opportunity. I told Margaret I wanted to make an offer on the lot in front of our home. It had no value to the current owner. But I wanted to control our own destiny. If we owned it, we would rebuild the dune. The following day, I made a very low offer for the lot, and it was accepted. Alice and I were now upgraded to oceanfront.

I saw my immature neighbor the next day and told him my property survived and was being upgraded. I got in a final shot, "But you sir, are still a complete jackass."

During the fall and winter season, we visited Watercolor and continued to clean it up. We bought a generator and spent a week inspecting and repairing the damage. Our good friend, Michelle Drake, volunteered to help with the clean-up. We worked hard every day, and then went to another house with electrical power to shower. We are grateful that Twiddy, our rental company, arranged for owners to have access to other homes.

We invited Debbie MacDougall with her children Ryan and Grace in the late fall. The Boehm family celebrated New Years with us. That winter, we collected many of the dead Christmas trees from local residents and put them in front of the house. The trees and some sand fencing collected a lot of sand from the winter storms, and by the Spring, we had rebuilt much of the protective dune.

Farewell to Watercolor

In December 2005, we made our final trip to Watercolor. It was another sad parting for the family. Our kids were more interested in other activities as they were getting older, and they enjoyed their vacations in Ocean City, New Jersey. We needed to move on. We had had three good years of memories in North Carolina, filled with family and friends. Our family was closing one chapter and opening another. The new owner wanted the beachfront experience and made a timely and rewarding offer to us.

OCEAN CITY, NEW JERSEY (OCNJ)

In 2005, our family wanted to go back to Ocean City for another summer vacation, so we rented a condo. There was plenty of fun for all. Kent took surfing lessons. The kids enjoyed Wonderland Pier, an amusement park on the boardwalk with lots of rides like bumper cars and a log flume. We rented a bicycle built for two to ride around the town. Gina and Peter came to visit. We also spent time with our friends, Mark and Carol Reynolds, who had rented a separate beach house nearby. Their son, Tyler, stayed with us for a few days in Ocean City.

Wonderland Pier in OCNJ

At this age, the kids liked it better in OCNJ than North Carolina because there were so many activities for them. We decided to look for a place to buy and searched all around the town. Ironically, Alice fell in love with the condo we were renting, so we bought it. Our new place was also near the town of Longport, where my cousin Pete and his wife Julie had a beach house.

We did not rent out our little condo in Ocean City. It was ours to use. Alice and the kids spent several summers there beginning each Memorial Day weekend. Birthdays at the beach were popular for Kent, Kara, Katie and Alice. On Kara's 10th birthday in July, the girls went on a Pirate Cruise and fired water cannons at the bad pirate attacking our ship. Kara and Katie then opened the treasure chest and split up the booty with about a dozen other kids. (It contained about a thousand cheap plastic toys made in China.) Kent liked to go surfing. Everybody enjoyed the rides and excitement on the boardwalk and the many celebrations and great meals with the extended Planas family.

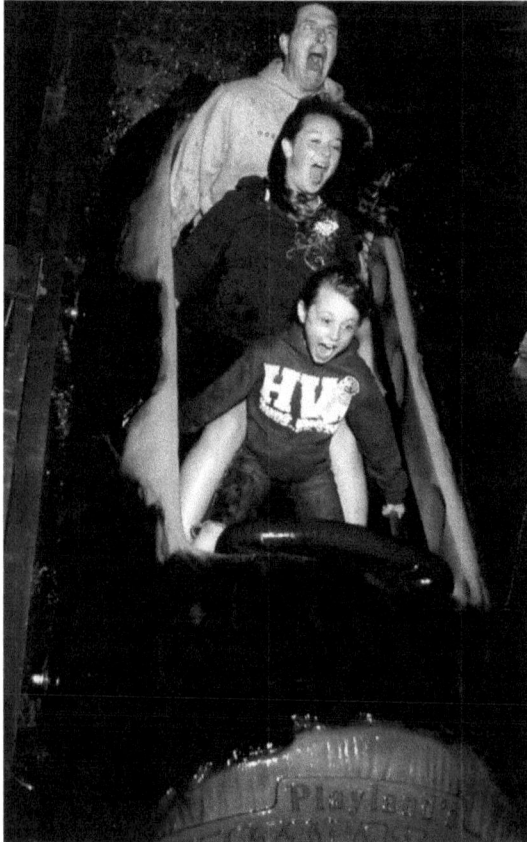

Ocean City Log Flume

We held onto the condo for several years until the kids entered high school. At that point, their schedules dictated that we stay near home for sports and other activities.

THANKSGIVING IN FLORIDA (2002-2015)

The timeshare condo in Fort Lauderdale that I bought during spring break in 1983 had turned into a good deal. Years later, I upgraded to a larger unit, and we reserved it for Thanksgiving week each year. This allowed us to make an annual trek to visit Alice's family for a big feast and some sunshine. Her sister and brother-in-law, Debbie and Arnie Bauman live in the local area along with Alice's niece, Stacey Patasnik, and her children Cameron and Kristoffer.

Sometimes we ventured to Orlando for a few days to hit the theme parks. Other years we combined it with a vacation in the Florida Keys. There was always plenty to do in the water and on land. Sometimes it was theme parks, snorkeling or swimming with dolphins in Key Largo or the Miami Seaquarium.

Swimming with Flipper

Stacey often made a killer meal for the entire family on Thanksgiving Day. On most other evenings, nobody wanted to cook, so we propped up the local economy by eating out. We had a couple of great family dinners at the Aruba Beach Café and the Casablanca Café.

FAIRFAX COUNTRY CLUB

New Years and Valentine's Day (2000-2014)

For a decade, we often celebrated Valentine's Day and New Year's Eve at the Fairfax Country Club with our friends Mike and DeAnn Boehm, Tony and Glenna Hahn, and Mike and Mary Jenkins. They were always kind and thoughtful to include us in their plans. It was an evening where we could leave the stress of our daily lives behind, and act like the teenagers we all wanted to still be. After all, everyone is required to grow older in life, but we are not all required to grow up.

DeAnn & Mike Boehm, Kerry & Alice Kachejian, Tony & Glenna Hahn

ANNAPOLIS

Alice and I have often enjoyed visiting the city of Annapolis. At one point, we almost bought a condo there as a weekend retreat. We have dear friends, Dick and Georgie Franyo, that have invited us to numerous events that benefit the local community. When our children were little, Georgie was a neighbor. Her daughter, Christina Hancock, and Kara became best friends in first grade. Georgie opened her own Pilates studio in Old Town Alexandria, where Alice has been a long-time client. Dick was a former paperboy as well, and later went into investment banking. Since retiring, Dick built the widely-acclaimed Boatyard Bar & Grill. He serves on a number of boards, and both he and Georgie have been passionate about sponsoring fundraising events for the Annapolis Maritime Museum (Boatyard Beach Bash) and the Chesapeake Bay Foundation (Bands in the Sand). Annapolis is a better community for all of their contributions.

Dick & Georgie Franyo with Alice and Kerry

CHRISTMAS

Christmas in Pennsylvania (1993-2015)

While we spent most of our Thanksgivings in Florida with Alice's family, we usually spent Christmas at our home in Virginia. We often had Christmas Eve dinner at a local restaurant. One year, it was a festive Christmas Eve dinner at the Gaylord National Hotel on the Potomac River. After Christmas, we'd head north for a few days to visit my family in Pennsylvania and celebrate a second Christmas at Grandma's house in West Chester.

Rockin' the Boat

Our family decided to do something different for Christmas and New Year's at the end of 2009 and signed up for a Royal Caribbean Cruise. To start the trip, we flew to Fort Lauderdale and spent Christmas night at the Harbor Beach Marriott where we had an excellent dinner with Alice's family. The next day, we sailed on the Independence of the Seas with Sandy Bost, and her two daughters Erin and Paula. The ports of call were Labadee, Haiti, St. Thomas, San Juan, and St. Martin.

Kachejian crew—all aboard

We had some very rough waters during the cruise. The crew blamed it on distant storms, but I was a bit skeptical as the weather forecast did not report any major storms. The schedule for the port calls had to be changed. I was most interested to see Labadee, as Haiti was a country I had not been to. We pulled into the Haitian port and began to explore. The beach area was nice and had a long zip line that ran for hundreds of meters across the shoreline. The crew had brought lunch from the ship and was preparing to serve us on the beach. Then the ocean waves intensified, and our ship began to bounce against the pier. A massive mooring rope broke, and one of the metal ramps used to offload supplies was crushed. The captain sounded the alarm and asked all passengers to quickly get back on the ship as it would depart immediately. We were told the conditions were unsafe for the ship, and it could be damaged if we did not leave soon. We spent less than two hours on the island. As we approached the pier, we could hear creaking noises as the ship shifted and the metal loading ramps were stressed. As I stood in line to reboard, I joked that if the ship sank in the port, we could stay in Labadee and dive the wreck. There was some nervous laughter from other passengers. When everyone was onboard the ship, we quickly pulled out of port. We felt cheated by Mother Nature.

About a week later, a massive earthquake leveled Haiti. Tens of thousands of Haitians died, and hundreds of thousands were homeless. The port of Labadee survived the earthquake and was used to bring in relief supplies. Haitians with jobs at the harbor and the local merchants were among the few people in the country able to continue working. Alice speculated that the rough waves we experienced during the cruise were potentially caused by undersea tremors that preceded the big earthquake. I think she was spot on.

WHITETAIL—SKI TRIPS

Skiing at Whitetail

In January 2005, I took Kara on a father-daughter ski trip to Whitetail Resort. She took a few basic lessons and was excited on her first trip up the ski lift. Once at the top, she got nervous at the realization she needed to ski down the mountain, and it looked steep and dangerous. I should have never encouraged Kara to look down the Black Diamond Expert slope on her first trip to the top. She felt like she was standing on the edge of a cliff. I tried to convince her that the Blue slope on the right was a really easy run compared to what she had just seen on our left. After a lot of encouragement, we tackled the Blue slope together in little bite size chunks. We'd ski ten yards across the slope and stop. Then we'd let a dozen other skiers pass by. It helped Kara to see some of the talented skiers who were young children. We'd ski our next ten-yard dash and take another break. The first run down the hill took about an hour, but it was a major morale booster for her. We made another trip up the ski lift and came down with more confidence. We took a break and celebrated with some hot chocolate. We made several more runs on different slopes and had a lot of fun. When we arrived home that night, Kara told Kent and Katie all kinds of stories about her day. Her initial anxiety had been replaced with pride that she conquered the slope.

In January of 2008, we made another family trip to Whitetail for skiing, snowboarding, and tubing. We spent the weekend with another military family, Don and Pam Johantges along with their kids, Sidney, Kelly, and Adam.

Whitetail Trip

CHAPTER 53

JIM BUSH

Over the years, Alice and I spent many weekends at her parent's house near Mount Vernon, Virginia. Jim and Betty Bush were both part of America's "Greatest Generation," whose early life experiences had been shaped by both the Great Depression and World War II.

Jim did not boast. I learned about his achievements a little bit at a time over a fifteen-year period. I am grateful to have the opportunity to share some of his stories, so his grandchildren and others can know of his service and remember him for the great man he was.

Jim Bush was a patriot. He served his country for almost 60 years over the course of three wars. In WWII, he was a crew member on several B-29 bombers, flying 26 combat missions in the Pacific theater. He manned the guns in the turret on the top of the aircraft and engaged attacking Japanese fighters. While defending the aircraft and crew, he was credited with two and a half kills. Jim lost many friends in combat and in accidents.

After WWII, he worked his way through Georgetown University School of Foreign Service and then settled down to raise a family. He began a long and distinguished career in the Air Force and the Intelligence Community. He served at the National Security Agency (NSA), the Air Force Security Service, the Defense Intelligence Agency (DIA), the Office of the Secretary of Defense and as a senior staff representative to the House Permanent Select Committee on Intelligence (HPSCI). Later in life, Jim moved on to the defense industry where he continued to serve his country by working on national security and intelligence issues.

* * *

The B-29 Superfortress was the first heavy bomber mass produced by the United States. One of the largest aircraft operational during World War II, it featured state of the art technology and was the single most expensive weapons project undertaken by the United States in World War II. The program ultimately cost $3 billion dollars, versus $2 billion for the Manhattan Project that developed the nuclear bomb.

Jim was a crew member on several different aircraft, and each had a unique name and graphics painted on by the crew. His favorite plane was called *King Size*, which featured a busty young girl painted on the front. It also had seven camels and three bombs painted near the cockpit. Each camel represented a flight over "the hump," a mission flying over the Himalayan Mountains. Each bomb represented a bombing raid on Japan. The aircraft commander of *King Size* was Lt. Colonel Loberg.

King Size crew—Jim Bush front row 2nd from left (Nov 17, 1944)

Two other B-29s Jim crewed on were *Dream Girl* and *Rush Order*. Naturally, *Dream Girl* had a busty young lady painted on the aircraft. Rush Order got its name in the Boeing factory. Constant design changes and quality problems plagued the early B-29 airframes. General Hap Arnold urgently needed the aircraft for the war and toured the factory floor in Wichita, Kansas to resolve production problems. He walked up to one airframe and asked why it was taking the team so long to modify it. He then pointed to the aircraft and said, "Make this aircraft a rush order." So, its name was born.

Early in the war, the only way for the United States to bomb Japan with the big B-29 was to fly missions from a base in India, over the Himalayas, and land on an airfield in China. For every ten aircraft that made it to China, there was enough spare fuel and ordinance to refill one aircraft to make the second leg, a bombing mission to Japan. To conduct a 50-bomber raid on Japan required 500 B-29 trips over the Himalayan Mountains. Ironically, the airfields they landed on in China were built by the communist Chinese, who were also fighting the Japanese. War courts strange bedfellows.

Decades later, Jim was a government senior executive and made an official trip to communist China. After a meeting with the Chinese military, Jim broke out a WWII photo album of his B-29 missions in China. The jaws of the Chinese officers dropped, and the excitement level in the room immediately spiked. More Chinese officers were summoned to the conference room, and all wanted to see the album. Amazingly, several of the senior Chinese officers were laborers at the airfield during the war. They recognized the scenery and some of the Chinese in the photos. The Chinese officials were emotionally overcome, and tears streamed down their faces. The U.S.-Chinese meeting transformed from an official visit to a reunion of former veterans.

Jim Bush (right) in China in WWII

Jim's crew was well-trained and respected. In June of 1944, his crew was selected to be the lead aircraft on the first B-29 strategic bombing mission flown over Japan. The target was an industrial complex, the Imperial Iron and Steel Works at Yawata, Japan. Of the 75 B-29s that departed from airbases in China, 47 attacked the primary target. Two Superfortress bombers were shot down by Japanese fighters, and five more were lost in accidents. The raid was minimally effective against the Yawata industrial target, but it signaled to the Japanese the beginning of the end. The Yawata mission, however, was different from the famous B-25 mission launched from U.S. aircraft carriers and led by Lieutenant Colonel James "Jimmy" Doolittle in April of 1942. Months after the Yawata mission, the U.S.-based B-29s on the Mariana Islands, enabling the bombing missions to be launched much closer to Japan, resulting in much more effective raids. Hundreds of American bombers were now able to routinely strike the Japanese mainland, culminating in the B-29 *Enola Gay* dropping an atomic bomb on Hiroshima.

One of my favorite stories from Jim was the time he had to bail out of a B-29. The aircraft had completed a bombing mission, losing two engines and a third damaged, and it was losing altitude. The crippled B-29 made it back from Japanese-held territory and had just crossed into friendly British-held territory over Burma. There was no place to land, and the crew was forced to bail out. Jim landed in a rice paddy where he lost much of his equipment, including his wedding ring. The crew survived and managed to work their way back to their base in India. After returning to the United States, Betty immediately asked Jim where his wedding ring was. Jim explained how he lost it. Betty had little sympathy for him, and if she had her way, Jim would have gone straight back to that rice paddy to find that ring.

The B-29 was pressurized in the crew areas, enabling personnel to survive high-altitude missions over the Himalayas. The long flights could get boring, and there were no restrooms on board. The crew shared a coffee can as a urinal, and the smell was often foul. One of the crew members decided to develop a solution. He fabricated a more sophisticated urinal by drilling a hole in the skin of the aircraft and welding a metal tube through it. On the inside of the plane, he welded a funnel with a simple water shutoff valve. The idea was straightforward and efficient. A crew member could relieve himself in the funnel. Once the funnel was filled, he could open the flow valve and the pressured air in the cabin would immediately blow the urine out of the aircraft. There was a small risk that some poor villager, miles below the plane, might get hit with frozen urine. But war is Hell.

The first test flight of the new urinal was highly successful, and morale markedly improved. A training issue, however, soon became apparent. A coffee drinking co-pilot came out of the cockpit to give it a try. While he was taking a wizz, he opened the flow valve. The urine in the funnel was rapidly drawn from the tube. It did its job well—perhaps too well—but the vacuum-like device did not stop with emptying its contents. In that same instant, the co-pilot's noodle got forcefully sucked into the tube. Thankfully it was still attached to him. While the guy screamed in pain, another crew member had to help him get unplugged from the valve. The co-pilot wound up with a big hickey on his doodad. Needless to say, the crew had learned a valuable lesson: don't open the flow valve too early.

* * *

In the early 1960s, Jim served as an intelligence officer in Germany during the Cold War. He was often on duty at a signals intelligence center in Bremerhaven, Germany.

Jim was on duty, 1 May 1960, the night the American U-2 surveillance plane, piloted by Gary Powers, was shot down over the Soviet Union. Jim had to place the call to report the loss of the aircraft. The report was immediately elevated up the chain of command, and soon, he was explaining what happened to senior government officials in the White House. At each level, he was asked the same question, "Are you sure?" Each time he was questioned, Jim would authoritatively respond, "Yes." Gary Powers was captured by the Soviets and imprisoned for almost two years. Powers was later traded back to the United States during a famous spy swap in Berlin. This Cold War trade was recreated in the movie "Bridge of Spies". Prior to the shoot down, Jim had met Gary at an airbase in Pakistan.

Jim's assignments in Washington D.C. had him in frequent contact with senior leaders in the American government. He had a drawer full of personal thank you notes from people like Casper Weinbrenner (Secretary of Defense) and Norm Mineta (Congressman and Secretary of Transportation). When his daughter, Alice, was about 11 years old, she went to work with her dad to see his office on Capitol Hill. While they were on the elevator, the doors opened and in walked Henry Kissinger, the former National Security Advisor and Secretary of State. Henry recognized Jim and called him by his first name. That's when Alice realized that her dad was someone important.

In one assignment, Jim had to brief senior government officials about how they would be evacuated from Washington D.C. during a national crisis. Jim had to inform the Speaker of the House, "Tip" O'Neill, about the evacuation plan. The Speaker was a beer-loving politician and had little time for extra briefings. Tip kept postponing the meeting. Eventually, Jim put his foot down and got an appointment on the Speaker's calendar. Jim told O'Neill that he would be quietly evacuated from the capital in a nondescript truck. Tip immediately asked, "What kind of truck will it be?" Jim replied, "What do you prefer?" The Speaker was quite clear, "I want a beer truck." So, Jim reported back to the continuity of government planners that they needed to reserve a beer truck for Tip O'Neill.

During the Reagan years, Daniel Ortega was the leader of Nicaragua. His Sandinista government aligned with Cuba and the Soviet Union in support of the Marxist revolution in El Salvador. That made Ortega and the Sandinistas an enemy of the United States. At one point, Ortega was believed to be importing MiG fighters from the Soviet Union, an action which potentially altered the balance of power in Central America.

During this period, Jim was on an official visit to neighboring Honduras. He received a directive to fly from Honduras to Nicaragua and deliver a personal message to Ortega. Jim delayed his return trip to the U.S. and headed for the Nicaraguan capital of Managua. Upon arrival, the Nicaraguan officials blindfolded Jim and took him on a circuitous route so he could not identify the location of the meeting to which he was going. After a long drive, the vehicle arrived at the meeting site, and he was escorted into an underground bunker.

President Ortega was there, and they got down to business. Jim delivered a direct and forceful message to the Nicaraguan leader. It was a heated meeting and to cap it off, Jim told the leftist leader that the attempt to hide the location of the bunker was a waste of time. The United States already knew where Ortega's secret bunker was. Jim then walked over to a map on the wall and pointed to the location. The room immediately got quiet, confirming he was correct. The message was clear: You can't hide from the USA. We will hunt you down and spank you. With that, Jim concluded the meeting and was escorted back to Managua airport to get home in time for dinner with Betty, who was making her famous twice-baked potatoes. All in a day's work.

Jim had a chance to visit Moscow during the Cold War. The Soviets knew who he was and assigned a team to tail him during the trip. The tail was clumsy and obvious. Jim had a free day in the Soviet capital and decided to travel on the subway to see the artwork painted on the walls of many stations. The Moscow Metro was considered an underground art museum. At every train stop, Jim stepped off the car and looked around at the large murals. The Soviet tail also stepped off the car. Before the train pulled out, Jim stepped back onboard, and sure enough, the Soviet agent followed him. After seeing enough of the artwork, Jim left the Metro network to get some lunch. He found a restaurant and went inside. Jim was the only customer at the time, so he was immediately seated at a small table. A moment later, a second customer came in and was seated at a nearby table. It was the same Soviet tail that had followed him through the Metro. Jim stood up, walked over to the surprised agent, introduced himself and asked him: "You've been following me all day. Won't you please join me for lunch?" The agent was unsure what to do. Soviet spy school did not instruct him on how to handle a situation like this. Jim insisted on having his guest at the table. The agent was embarrassed and declined the offer. The next question Jim considered asking was, "So what do you do for a living?"

Jim told me about his visit to Mount Weather, an underground FEMA facility in the mountains west of Washington, D.C. He had toured the facility many years before, and the tour leader had recounted an interesting story. At some point, Mount Weather had a roomful of alcohol that had been confiscated during the Prohibition era. The booze was transferred to Mt. Weather for storage. Perhaps it was criminal evidence that needed to be preserved. If Congress ever needed to evacuate the Capitol, many of them planned to relocate at Mt. Weather where they could all get drunk. That was a good story, and if it isn't true, it ought to be.

Although Jim always worked hard, he never lost his sense of humor. He had a "WRGAS" stamp on his Pentagon desk which he used on irrelevant and extraneous documents and programs. The Under Secretary of Defense of Intelligence, Dr. Al Hall, once asked him what WRGAS meant. Jim replied, "Who Really Gives A S***." Dr. Hall told Jim he wanted his own WRGAS stamp.

When Jim finally left his work in the government, he joined industry. He was a Vice President at a series of companies that were continually being acquired. He started at Planning Research Corporation (PRC) which was owned by Emhart, and later acquired by Black & Decker, then Litton and eventually Northrup Grumman. Jim always thought it was interesting how he could change companies so often without moving his desk.

While serving as a defense industry vice president, Jim Bush often visited officials in Washington, D.C. This was during the Reagan presidency, and George Bush was the Vice President. America was doing well. Jim Bush was still serving his country from industry. Life was good. However, Jim broke a tooth one morning while traveling to a meeting on Capitol Hill. He called his secretary at PRC and asked her to schedule an emergency dental appointment somewhere nearby. She called a local dentist and told the office that she needed an immediate appointment for Mr. Bush to repair a broken tooth. The dentist office was unsure who this new patient was, so they asked, "Who is he?" The secretary replied, "Mr. Bush is our Vice President. He is on Capitol Hill this morning for a meeting. He broke a tooth and needs an emergency dental appointment within the hour. Can you help?" The dental office was startled and replied, "Yes. Absolutely."

After hanging up the phone, the dental office went into overdrive: Vice President Bush is coming to our office in an hour! We need to prepare now and clean this place up! The office canceled appointments for other customers to make room for this distinguished patient. Jim's secretary called the dentist office again and reported, "Mr. Bush has left Capitol Hill and will be at your office in a few minutes." The frenzy continued. Minutes later, Jim Bush pulled up in a taxi and walked into the dentist office. The red carpet was rolled out. Jim approached the reception desk, and the confused staff asked, "Who are you?" Jim replied, "I'm Jim Bush. I broke my tooth, and my secretary made an appointment here. Thanks for helping me out on such short notice." The silence that followed was deafening.

* * *

While Jim was running around keeping the world safe for democracy, his wife Betty Bush ran the home front. She enjoyed making hand stitched teddy bears, spending time with her two daughters Debbie and Alice, and caring for her "baby," a poodle named Pooker. Being raised in the Great Depression,

Betty appreciated the value of a dollar. She and Jim were financially sound, but she liked to shop in thrift stores, an old habit that was apparently hard to kick. Some of these stores were in high-crime areas. That did not deter Betty, so she often took Pooker shopping in her Honda Accord.

One day, seventy-plus-year-old Betty Bush was shopping at her favorite discount store. When finished, she noticed a suspicious man loitering in the parking lot nearby. Betty got into her car. The man opened the door, grabbed Betty and pulled her out and threw her to the ground. He jumped in the vehicle. The young punk was carjacking an old lady. The thug rapidly started to back up, and almost ran over Betty. Heads turned at the commotion. Betty was screaming, "My baby! My baby! He's got my baby!"

An off-duty police officer was at the scene and drew his pistol. He shot at the tires of the car, attempting to disable it without hitting the baby inside. The car recklessly sped away. The call went out to the police that a carjacking had just occurred, and a baby was taken. Fortunately, the carjacker only had traveled a few blocks before he hastily abandoned the car. The Honda was quickly recovered, but the police only found a poodle inside. Betty was badly shaken and bruised, but she promptly thanked the cops for saving "her baby."

Our family watched the carjacking news story unfold on TV. The news reported that the stolen "baby," a poodle named Pooker, had been recovered at the scene. As for the cowardly punk, he was never caught.

* * *

Although Jim worked extended hours on national security issues, he spent many hours as a dad at swim practice with his young daughter, Alice. All the kids on the swim team got excited when it was Mr. Bush's turn to drive the early morning carpool, as he would always have a box of donuts ready for the tired swimmers on the ride home.

As a grandfather, Jim was a big teddy bear. Every time his family came to visit, he would get out from behind his desk, hug the kids and sit with them on the sofa. The TV would then change from cable news to the Disney channel. Jim enjoyed watching the cartoons with his grandkids. When it was time to leave, we would drive off in our car, and he'd stand in the door and wave to us all until we were out of sight.

For all of Jim's talents, he was not mechanically inclined. For example, he found out the hard way you aren't supposed to flush a diaper down the toilet. Jim also had an impressive collection of tools that he never touched. These tools were reserved for his two sons-in-law: Arnie Bauman and me. We had exclusive use of the tools to work off Betty's "honey-do" list. Debbie (Bush) and Arnie would drive several times a year from Florida to Virginia to visit with Jim and Betty and work on that ever-growing "to-do" list. They would stay about five days and save a few days to explore the East Coast during the road trip, making it a working vacation. We are grateful for all the help they provided Jim and Betty over the years.

* * *

When Jim Bush was nearing his Pentagon retirement from the Office of the Secretary of Defense (OSD C3I), one of his good friends and colleagues was Jim Mayer. Mayer asked Jim Bush what kind of gift he wanted when he finally retired. Having spent his career in the intelligence field, Jim said he really would like to have the 7-foot-long panoramic photo of San Francisco that hung near their office. It was a one-of-a-kind high-resolution picture taken by an experimental aircraft camera while in flight. The military needed better cameras to plan amphibious landings, and this photo was a product of a prototype camera, that was never used operationally. But the photo had great sentimental value to Jim Bush. Jim Mayer arranged to have the picture presented to him at his retirement, to acknowledge his selfless service to the nation.

Jim Bush passed the 7-foot photo on to Alice and me many years later. When he died a month after the 9/11 attack, Jim Mayer continued to help the Bush family to understand their military benefits. When Jim Mayer passed, I attended his services. As I walked into the chapel, I was surprised to see a former business associate, Tony Tether, who was currently serving as the Director of DARPA. I asked Tony if he knew Jim Mayer, to which he replied, "Yes. Jim was my best friend. We worked together in the Pentagon." That surprised me because I thought Jim Bush and Jim Mayer had also been best friends from the Pentagon. Tony was clearly there with them. Tony gave a superlative eulogy at the memorial service, and we parted ways. A few years passed, and Alice was ready to part with the big San Francisco reconnaissance photo. I wanted to make sure it had a good home, so I thought about sending it to the Smithsonian Air and Space Museum. Then I recalled Tony had worked with my father-in-law at the Pentagon. I emailed Tony, and he told me the picture was his. He had given it to Jim Bush 40 years earlier. He was happy to take it back, so I delivered it to Tony's house. I was glad it found a good home.

* * *

In August of 1993, we learned that several old military aircraft, part of the Confederate Air Force, would visit nearby Manassas Airport. Among the aircraft was *FIFI,* the last flying B-29 Superfortress from WWII. We took Jim to the air show, and he showed us around the aircraft and the guns he had manned.

Jim Bush and Alice with FiFi

Jim had flown twenty-six missions before he returned stateside to be a trainer for new aircrews. He shot down two Japanese Zeros and was credited with half of another, that attacked his aircraft as they were on bombing missions over Japan. It was really special to reunite an old warrior with this historic aircraft.

I will always remember Jim Bush and his amazing stories. Jim now rests with Betty in Arlington Cemetery, overlooking the Pentagon and the Air Force Memorial where he served for so many years. We miss you, Pop Pop.

CHAPTER 54
DAVE & SANDY BOST

Alice and I met Dave and Sandy Bost in Cancun, Mexico in 1989. It was an inexpensive vacation, affordably priced to draw visitors back to the resort after a major hurricane. The hotels were cleaned up, but the palm trees had taken a beating. We hung out the entire week together, racing taxis through the streets of Cancun and enjoying the most popular restaurants in town. Since then, we shared many great times together and some exciting trips to Europe and the Caribbean.

Europe

In 1990, we took an extended trip to Europe. It started in London and then on to Germany, France, Switzerland, Italy, Liechtenstein, and Austria.

We rented a BMW 735, and each of us drove it on the autobahn at over 140 mph. I was surprised the car could carry four people with their luggage and still have such good performance. Germany had changed. The Soviet domination of Eastern Europe was collapsing. East Germans, Czechs and other citizens from former communist countries were now permitted to drive in Western Europe. The autobahn was more dangerous now, as it was cluttered with slow-moving East German Trabants. The communist car's top speed was about 70 mph. West Germans flying at 120 mph and East Germans moving at 60 mph on the same autobahn was a formula for disaster. Our trip tried to cover a lot of ground. One day, we had breakfast in Germany, lunch in France and dinner in Switzerland. That evening, we spent the night in a hotel overlooking Rhein Falls, the Niagara Falls of Europe, located near Schaffhausen, Switzerland.

We had a long drive to Italy and arrived at a beach resort the night the Italians won an important FIFA World Cup soccer match. When we arrived, we had no idea the World Cup was even being played, much less had been hosted in Italy. The Italians were up all night celebrating their recent victory, and we decided to join them. We had little sleep that night.

The next day, we spent time sunning on the Italian Riviera and later moved north through beautiful Lake Como, showcased by Robin Leach on his TV show "Lifestyles of the Rich and Famous." We took a small, scenic road through the northern Italian Alps. Some of the road tunnels on the mountains were only wide enough for a single car, and the guardrails were often nonexistent. If our car fell off the side of the cliff, we might die of old age before hitting bottom. We stopped at a mountaintop restaurant for dinner before approaching the border crossing with Switzerland. We had been forewarned that the Italian border checkpoint closed at 10:00 PM, so we got to the crossing a few minutes early. It was July and felt strange to be surrounded by snow. We got out of the car for a quick snowball fight. We were the last car to pass through the checkpoint and thought we were officially in Switzerland. Little did we know we were very wrong and just beginning a trip our wives later dubbed...

The Car Ride from Hell

We arrived at a Swiss border checkpoint a few kilometers later and were shocked to discover the Swiss guards had already closed the road and gone home for the night. We hit the horn, and no one replied. We got out of the car and yelled for help. Nothing. Perhaps yodeling would have been more effective. It was pitch-black and snowing at the top of the mountain pass. The temperature was dropping. We carefully turned around and made our way back to the Italian checkpoint. Same story. The Italians had now closed their border checkpoint with a heavy chain and also gone home. We were trapped at the top of the mountain between two countries. We had no bolt-cutters to get back into Italy or Switzerland. There was no way for us to bypass the road barriers as we were alongside a cliff. Dave and I tried to remain calm, but our troops began to panic. We hit the horn for several minutes and screamed from the top of the mountain. We were low on gas and did not want to spend the night in the car. I mentally assessed the situation. The ladies were definitely not going to be pleased. We had no bathrooms, no food or water, freezing temperatures, no communications, and no electricity to run a hair dryer. If we didn't get out of here, Dave and I were going to get killed by our spouses.

After about ten minutes of obnoxious horn blowing, an Italian border guard finally came back to the outpost and allowed us to re-enter Italy. He wasn't happy either. He was probably on his way to a World Cup party. We were momentarily relieved but now started a two-hour trip down the narrow mountain roads to the nearest all-night border crossing. Getting little sleep, the previous night from the World Cup celebration, we were now facing another all-night road trip that was not part of our vacation plan. I reminded everyone that the events of this night "would make a great story someday." That comment won me little sympathy. I knew I just needed to shut up and drive. [But now, years later this story is "in print."]

We finally entered Switzerland at about 1:00 AM and spent the next few hours driving up and down mountains and snaking around hundreds of switchback roads. The car was running on fumes. Fortunately, we found and all-night unmanned gas station. Unfortunately, it would only take one type of cash, Swiss Francs. We didn't have any, only some Italian lira, some German marks, and American dollars. We flagged down the only car we could see and pleaded with them to exchange currency. We paid double the official exchange rate just to get a little Swiss currency. Gas in Europe was expensive, so we only managed to get a partial tank of fuel. We had to make the gas last throughout the night drive, so Dave and I coasted down the mountain passes to save a few drops of fuel. At about 6:00 AM, we arrived at the West German border, tired, hungry and out of fuel again. The German border guard pointed to the nearest gas station, and we limped in on an empty tank. Two hours later, we were back in our condo in Bavaria. We slept for the next eight hours. During the following week, we took only day trips to local sites near Munich and Salzburg, Austria. The rest of the Europe trip was far more enjoyable.

The Lake Arrowhead Pig-napping

We often visited Dave and Sandy at their house on Lake Arrowhead near Waleska, Georgia. The Kachejian kids (Kent, Kara, and Katie) and the Bost kids (Erin and Paula) always had a great time together. Sandy and Dave had all the right amenities: a beautiful lake, a dock, a boat, a golf course and plenty of steaks and fishing. We agreed, why go anywhere else for a vacation?

Now the statute of limitations has long expired for this next story, so I can now publicly reveal the details of one of the great covert "rescue" missions ever attempted in the history of northern Georgia. Quite simply, we planned and executed the pig-napping of the century.

There was a lonely cast-iron pig that sat in a neighbor's yard across the inlet from Bost's house. Sandy thought the pig statue was ugly. While every pig had a right to be ugly, this one abused the privilege. That cold swine stared at Sandy every morning while she was drinking her coffee on the deck, and she wanted it gone. Sandy recruited Dave and the Kachejian's to help her with the devious plot. Being an animal lover, Dave wanted to find the pig a new home, somewhere out of view, so Sandy would never again be forced to behold the hideous beast. Dave and I quickly devised a plan to "rescue" the pig and deliver it to a nicer location, where a new homeowner would treat it with the dignity and respect that it deserved. The plan was finalized, and the pig-napping operation had begun. The mission was fueled by wine and beer.

After dusk that evening, Dave, Sandy, Kerry and Alice slipped down to the dock and slid into Dave's small—and stealthy—bass boat. We didn't want to turn on the motor, so we quietly paddled across the inlet to the far shore. We surveyed the property to make sure we were undetected. Then Dave and I got out of the boat and quietly approached the pig. We crouched as we moved and let the noise of the gusting wind mask the sound of our approaching footsteps. The pig remained silent, unaware what was about to befall him. We got up to the pig, gave him a couple of pats to keep him calm, and then tried to lift him. That cast-iron slab of bacon weighed over 200 pounds. On our third attempt, we finally lifted the ugly critter from its base and struggled to carry it back to the dock. We had barely managed to lower the pig into the bow of Dave's boat when we dropped it the last few inches. The stern of the boat violently lifted out of the water, almost launching Sandy and Alice into the lake.

We were now sweating and panting hard, but we did it. We had nabbed the pig. Dave and I jumped back in the boat. Captain Dave then eased us back from the dock. After we had paddled 100 meters away from the scene, Dave turned on the engines and gunned it. We were now off looking for new home for Mr. Pig.

After about ten minutes, Dave identified a suitable new owner. A neighbor he knew on another inlet that fortunately had a low dock so we could lift that 200-pound ham sandwich out of the boat. It was a real struggle to keep the boat steady, but we did it. And we left Porky Pig standing prominently on the new owner's dock to make them look like the guilty party.

There was only one thing left to do. We trolled back to Sandy and Dave's and broke out the beer. We swore an oath of secrecy that has been kept for 20 years. The full details were only revealed to Dave's closest friends at his memorial service. And now you know the rest of the story.

More of Dave

I could tell you a dozen other stories about our friend, Dave Bost. He was incredibly kind and generous. His company made after-market accessories for cars and trucks. When he learned my brother was a quadriplegic, Dave designed special handicapped decals for Kevin's wheelchair van. There was no charge, and the shipping was free.

Dave loved golf, and I was just learning. He gave me about 40 golf balls one day while I was playing the course at Lake Arrowhead. Every one of those balls went in the lake. Dave just shrugged while I built an artificial reef made of his golf balls.

Every 4th of July, Dave organized and often paid for the fireworks for the Lake Arrowhead community. He set up dozens of mortar tubes and hundreds of rockets. He used a floating dock to move the launch point to the middle of the lake. I was part of Dave's team and would launch the rockets while the neighbors watched on the shore. Near the end of the show, we had an accident, the premature detonation of a mortar. In layman's terms, the thing exploded on the dock, and I got hit with some plastic shrapnel and had some burns on the legs. No fear. Dave medicated me with plenty of cold beer.

We came back to visit for New Years in 2000. He and I spent several days rigging up the fireworks. I was able to show him some of the techniques I used in my Army explosives training. We set up a ring main and dual primed the fireworks. We had each circuit set up to fire with a simple light switch. When the new millennium arrived at the stroke of midnight, all the Bost and Kachejian kids got to stand on the deck and remotely launch scores of fireworks along the lake front. It was a great evening where a couple of new Dads were able to make some lasting memories for their young kids.

Memorial Service

I was able to visit Dave Bost a few days before he passed away in September 2009. His last words to me were, "I'll see you on the other side." And I replied, "Yes you will, my friend." And thank you, Lord, for giving us Dave.

Finally, I'd like to share with you a list of Dave's favorite things that were presented at his memorial service:

David's Favorite Things

His Family

God

Helping people

Being a volunteer fireman

Lake Arrowhead

Starr Vinyl

His friends

Entertaining

Fireworks

Rare steaks (cows still mooing)

Elvis

Fishing

Alex, Touie and sometimes Trey

ChaCha and Kat

Smart Drinks

Golfing

A challenge

Republicans

"Outstanding"

"Don't sweat the small stuff"

"It's another day in Paradise"

"Red, Blue, Yelloooo"

"You're the brightest star in my universe"

"We just want you to be happy"

Sandy, Erin and Paula

"Love you bigger"

Dave's Favorite Things

AFTERWORD

This book is about us: my family, friends, classmates, colleagues and associates. The hundreds of people I encountered and experiences we shared that shaped our lives. Seen through my eyes and told with my voice, I've described this rewarding journey that spanned across several generations and dozens of countries; from childhood to adulthood; through war and peace. I hope these stories brought many smiles to your face, and occasionally, tears to your eyes.

This metaphor seems fitting:

"The journey of life is like a man riding a bicycle. We know he got on the bicycle and started to move. We know that at some point he will stop and get off. We know that if he stops moving and does not get off, he will fall off." —William Golding

This book is my final newspaper, and it is now delivered. As I mark off its completion, it's time to pursue other things... there are a few more items on my bucket list. As the paperboy moves on and maybe even out of sight... don't worry... it doesn't mean his ride is over. It's merely a bend in the road.

Kerry Kachejian
June 2018

ABOUT THE AUTHOR

Kerry Kachejian began his career as a neighborhood paperboy in West Chester, Pennsylvania. His career took off in high school, as he cut lawns, worked in a deli, roofed houses, and cleaned up construction sites. He even made a fast ten bucks standing in a murder lineup. During this time, his family cared for his younger brother, who was tragically paralyzed in a bicycle accident.

Then came the American dream when he was offered an appointment to the U.S. Military Academy at West Point. He served the nation with distinction as a soldier, a defense industry executive, an award-winning author, and motivational speaker. He is a veteran of combat operations in Iraq and Afghanistan, as well as relief operations during Hurricane Katrina.

After studying Aerospace Engineering at West Point, Kachejian earned a Master's degree in Systems Engineering from Virginia Polytechnic Institute. He is also a Distinguished Graduate of the Industrial College of the Armed Forces, earning a Master's degree in National Resource Strategy. He is a Registered Professional Engineer.

Kachejian is Airborne and Ranger-qualified, and his military decorations and awards include the Legion of Merit, the Bronze Star Medal, and the Combat Action Badge. He was presented the Bronze de Fleury Medal by the Army Engineer Association and the Leadership Excellence Award presented by the Military Officers Association of America (MOAA). Kerry retired from the Army Reserve, holding the rank of Colonel. He has been featured in several media events, conferences and private engagements. His first book, *SUVs SUCK in Combat* received the Literacy Hero Award.

Kerry lived with his wife Alice and their three children near Springfield, Virginia for over thirty years. They recently moved to Delray Beach, Florida where he hopes to find a job delivering newspapers from a golf cart.

SUVs SUCK IN COMBAT

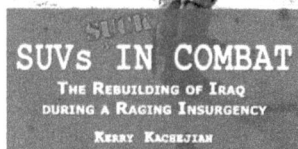

SUVs IN COMBAT
THE REBUILDING OF IRAQ
DURING A RAGING INSURGENCY
KERRY KACHEJIAN

It was an unbelievable mission - to rebuild Iraq while the U.S. military was fighting a raging insurgency. In 2004, the soldiers and civilians of the Gulf Region Division (GRD) answered the call to duty and began the largest and most complex reconstruction project ever undertaken by our nation. They made great personal sacrifices that few of their fellow Americans would dare endure.

This book tells the rest of the inspiring story, much of which was ignored by the mainstream media as "not newsworthy" or reduced to mere sound bites. In the face of imminent danger, the GRD team braved daily car bombs, rocket attacks, improvised explosive devices (IEDs) and kidnappings to rebuild thousands of projects throughout a chaotic war zone. These projects, spread throughout a hostile country, included schools, hospitals, police stations, oil production, electrical power and water treatment plants. Despite the odds, GRD was able to complete its critical strategic mission, and its members were awarded the Meritorious Unit Commendation. A few of the amazing stories include: - A massive car bomb on author's first day in Baghdad that leveled a nearby hotel. - High speed "Mad Max" drives through the streets of Baghdad in unarmored SUVs. - The dependence on security contractors who performed with great valor while protecting American civilians. - The perilous war waged on the reconstruction mission that was largely invisible to U.S. combat forces and the American public. - The accidental rescue of an American hostage. - Living and working in Saddam's great palaces. - A daring rescue mission in the Tigris River that ended in a tragic loss. - The parade of Congressional Delegations that diverted precious combat resources from the war effort. - The unbelievable (but true) story of how a Yahoo email message was used to send an urgent message to the author to "PLEASE SAVE US."

The lives of those who endured this mission have been forever changed.